II MACCABEES

VOLUME 41A

THE ANCHOR BIBLE is a fresh approach to the world's greatest classic. Its object is to make the Bible accessible to the modern reader; its method is to arrive at the meaning of biblical literature through exact translation and extended exposition, and to reconstruct the ancient setting of the biblical story, as well as the circumstances of its transcription and the characteristics of its transcribers.

THE ANCHOR BIBLE is a project of international and interfaith scope. Protestant, Catholic, and Jewish scholars from many countries contribute individual volumes. The project is not sponsored by any ecclesiastical organization and is not intended to reflect any particular theological doctrine. Prepared under our joint supervision, THE ANCHOR BIBLE is an effort to make available all the significant historical and linguistic knowledge which bears on the interpretation of the biblical record.

THE ANCHOR BIBLE is aimed at the general reader with no special formal training in biblical studies; yet, it is written with the most exacting standards of scholarship, reflecting the highest technical accomplishment.

This project marks the beginning of a new era of co-operation among scholars in biblical research, thus forming a common body of knowledge to be shared by all.

William Foxwell Albright
David Noel Freedman
GENERAL EDITORS

THE ANCHOR BIBLE

II MACCABEES

A New Translation
with
Introduction and Commentary
by

Jonathan A. Goldstein

DOUBLEDAY & COMPANY, INC.
GARDEN CITY, NEW YORK
1983

"Die Hellenistische Welt um 185 vor Chr." from GROSSER HISTOR-ISCHER WELTATLAS I edited by Herman Bengtson and Vladimir Milojcic, 5th edition. Reprinted by permission of Bayerischer Schulbuch Verlag.

CARTA'S ATLAS OF THE PERIOD OF THE SECOND TEMPLE, THE MISHNAH AND THE TALMUD by Michael Avi-Yonah. Copyright © Carta, Jerusalem 1966. Reprinted by permission of Carta Publishing Company, Ltd.

Qadmoniot V, 1972. Map from "Jerusalem Revealed" p. 43 reprinted by permission of the Israel Exploration Society.

Revue Biblique, XXXIII (1924), 381, Fig. 3 "Topographie des Campagnes Machabéennes" by F. M. Abel. Reprinted by permission of Librairie Lecoffre, France.

THE MACMILLAN BIBLE ATLAS by Yohanan Aharoni and Michael Avi-Yonah. Copyright © Carta, Jerusalem 1964, 1966, 1968. Redrawn with permission from Macmillan Publishing Company.

THE WESTMINSTER HISTORICAL ATLAS TO THE BIBLE, Revised Edition, edited by George Ernest Wright and Floyd Vivian Filson. Copyright 1956 by W. L. Jenkins. Redrawn with permission of the Westminster Press.

Coin pictures courtesy of Ya'akov Meshorer.

Library of Congress Cataloging in Publication Data

Bible. O.T. Apocrypha. Maccabees, 2nd.
II Maccabees.

(The Anchor Bible; v. 41A)
Bibliography: p. 129.
Includes indices.
1. Bible. O.T. Apocrypha. Maccabees, 2nd—
Commentaries. I. Goldstein, Jonathan A., 1929–
II. Title. III. Title: 2 Maccabees. IV. Series: Bible.
English. Anchor Bible. 1964. Anchor Bible; v. 41A.
BS192.2.A11964.G3 vol. 41A [BS1825.3] 220.7'7s
[229'.73]
ISBN 0-385-04864-5
Library of Congress Catalog Card Number 82–45200

In memory of my brother,
ALEXANDER M. GOLDSTEIN
(1935–1980)
and my teacher,
ELIAS J. BICKERMAN
(1897–1981)

THE APOCRYPHA

The term Apocrypha (or "Deuterocanonical Books" in Roman Catholic usage) is popularly understood to describe the fifteen books or parts of books from the pre-Christian period that Catholics accept as canonical Scripture but Protestants and Jews do not. This designation and definition are inaccurate on many counts. An apocryphon is literally a hidden writing, kept secret for the initiate and too exalted for the general public; virtually none of these books makes such a claim. Not only Roman Catholics but also Orthodox and Eastern Christians accept these books, wholly or partially, as canonical Scripture. Roman Catholics do not accept all of them as Scripture, for I and II Esdras and the Prayer of Manasseh are not included in the official Catholic canon drawn up at the Council of Trent. Many Protestant churches have no official decision declaring these books to be non-canonical; and, in fact, up to the last century they were included in most English Protestant Bibles. What is certain is that these books did not find their way into the final Jewish Palestinian canon of Scripture. Thus, despite their Jewish origins (parts of II Esdras are Christian and Latin in origin), they were preserved for the most part in Greek by Christians as a heritage from the Alexandrian Jewish community and their basic text is found in the codices of the Septuagint. However, recent discoveries, especially that of the Dead Sea scrolls, have brought to light the original Hebrew or Aramaic text of some of these books. Leaving aside the question of canonicity, Christians and Jews now unite in recognizing the importance of these books for tracing the history of Judaism and Jewish thought in the centuries between the last of the Hebrew Scriptures and the advent of Christianity.

PREFACE

Like my volume 41 in the Anchor Bible, this volume 41A contains chiefly my own efforts to solve the problems of the First and Second Books of Maccabees, though I am aware of, and try to acknowledge, my deep indebtedness to my predecessors. Where I believe my own views to be solidly based, I have presented my evidence for them and have tried to avoid presenting and refuting opposing views, in the belief that a commentary should not look like a debate. An important exception to this rule are the views of my late revered teacher, Elias J. Bickerman.

This and my earlier volume are among the thicker contributions to the Anchor Bible. They are so thick partly because I found myself making many discoveries that would not be believed if I did not present rather massive proof for them. Not everyone will want to read my volumes from cover to cover, but any literate person should be able to enjoy large sections of them.

First and Second Maccabees are classics and have always attracted big audiences. As reading matter they can stand on their own. Part I of my introduction to this volume gives sufficient background on Second Maccabees for the general reader. Parts II through V of the introduction and many sections of commentary are more technical. Some readers will choose to skip them; I hope others who are interested in the problems I try to solve will also find those more technical passages rewarding.

The reader may find that unfamiliar names and words make my book difficult. I hope that any such problems will be solvable through the use of a collegiate dictionary and the indices to this book.

As usual in the Anchor Bible, the translated text is divided into sections. In my commentary, a comment on an entire section is called an "introductory NOTE." Comments on passages are arranged in the order of the initial verses: a NOTE on 1:1–5 will appear before a NOTE on 1:2–5. Where two passages have the same initial verse, I comment on the longer one first: a NOTE on 1:1–7 will appear before a NOTE on 1:1–6.

The "sea of words" generated by my research turned the projected single volume on both books of Maccabees into two separate volumes, a fact which now gives me the opportunity to correct in the second volume errors I committed in the first. Of these, I should mention here the two worst.

There is the ten-day error that has affected my chronology in AB vol. 41, pp. 43, 165–67 and, to my knowledge, has not been noticed by anyone but me. I have corrected it in the present volume, pp. 117–19. And there is my unfortunate hypothesis that one of the sources of First and Second Maccabees was a work on the deaths of the persecutors that omitted to treat the Jews' repossession and cleansing of the temple. I called this hypothetical source *De Mortibus Persecutorum* (abbreviated: *DMP*). It is most unlikely to have existed as described. A pious Jew narrating the wondrous events of the time could hardly have omitted the repossession and cleansing of the temple even if he was concentrating on the deaths of the persecutors. And if such a work, a *"Hamlet* without the prince," had been written, it is hard to see how it could have survived and could have gone on attracting readers long enough to have been a source for First and Second Maccabees. The chronological difficulty that I tried to solve by the hypothesis of the source *DMP* is better solved by other means (see NOTE on II 14:1–4). I hereby disown most of Part V of my introduction to AB vol. 41. Only if points made there are endorsed or repeated here in AB vol. 41A do I still stand by them.

My repudiation of that section of AB vol. 41 leaves me with a task to perform. Nowadays a historian must always be concerned with the question of how much time elapsed between the events and the writing of the work that tells of them. If long years passed, the historian must try to ascertain how the author of that work knew about the events he narrates. As I show here in Part IV of my introduction, I am convinced that First Maccabees and the history of which the abridgment is preserved in Second Maccabees were written sixty years or more after the death of Judas Maccabaeus. Therefore, I must again play, in Part II of the introduction, the seductive, hazardous, and complicated game I played (and lost) in Part V of the introduction to AB vol. 41: I must try to reconstruct the sources that lay before both authors and, as far as possible, must try to show that the results are not mere products of my imagination. The procedures are somewhat difficult and the results inevitably lack complete certainty. Some readers may therefore prefer to skip over Part II of the introduction, as well as the many sections of commentary that deal with such source analysis.

In giving parts of the introductions to my two volumes the title "What Really Happened," I have no intention of claiming finality for my theories. Everything I present in my books is only what I *believe* to be the truth. The historians who wrote in First and Second Maccabees made mistakes. I try to correct those mistakes and to draw on reliable evidence from other sources, and I label the results of my efforts "What Really Happened."

In this volume II Esdras is the Greek translation of the Hebrew books of Ezra and Nehemiah, not the apocalyptic work called II Esdras in AB vol. 42.

The appendices were planned when there was to be but a single volume covering both First and Second Maccabees. Hence the first appendix in this volume bears the number VII, to follow Appendix VI of AB vol. 41.

I dedicate this volume to the memory of my brother, Alexander, and to the memory of my teacher, Elias J. Bickerman. My brother was a brilliant and talented rabbi who suffered from depressions that drove him to an untimely end. My teacher was a brilliant, creative, and generous scholar to whom I owe much in all my work. Our disagreements had no effect on his scholarly generosity. He welcomed refutations of his theories as much as he welcomed confirmations of them. I think he would have been pleased over my use of his own methods (of appreciating and analyzing ancient documents) to refute his theory that King Antiochus IV, in imposing a revised cult upon the Jews, was carrying out a reform requested by the Jews' high priest, Menelaus.

Other scholars have been generous to me as I wrote this book. I have enjoyed learned conversations with my colleague at the University of Iowa, George Nickelsburg. The following graciously answered my queries: L. Timothy Doty, Jonas Greenfield, Ya'akov Meshorer, Joachim Oelsner, Bezalel Porten, Martin Schwartz, the Abbé Jean Starcky, Michael Stone, C. B. F. Walker, and Herbert C. Youtie. Joseph Sievers kindly sent me a copy of his doctoral dissertation on the Hasmonaeans. The University of Iowa gave me excellent working conditions, and its department of history provided me with my helpful research assistants, James Skyrms, Warren Smith, Matthew Parsons, and Walter Bell. I am pleased to acknowledge here the help of my scholarly wife, Helen, and the encouragement I have received from my parents, Rabbi and Mrs. David A. Goldstein. My daughter, Risë, typed portions of the manuscript.

I wish also to thank the editors for their contributions. David Noel Freedman and David Graf made valuable suggestions, and Eve Roshevsky, Peter Schneider, and John Carter have done well in bringing this book at last before the eyes of its readers.

My lecture "Jewish Parties of the Time of the Hasmonaean Uprisings" has, unfortunately, not been published. It contained my argument for the date of the book of Jubilees, and I referred to it at AB vol. 41, p. 122, n. 110. My argument will appear instead in my article "The Date of the Book of Jubilees," to be published in *Proceedings of the American Academy for Jewish Research* 50 (1983).

Elias Bickerman changed the spelling of his name when he changed the language in which he was writing. In French he was Élie Bikerman; in German Elias Bickermann. In this volume I spell his name Elias Bickerman.

JONATHAN A. GOLDSTEIN

June 1982

CONTENTS

II MACCABEES

MAPS   507

APPENDICES

LIST OF MAPS

PRINCIPAL ABBREVIATIONS

A	*Codex Alexandrinus* (see Introduction, Part VII)
AB	Anchor Bible, 1964–
ABAW	*Abhandlungen der Bayerischen Akademie der Wissenschaften, Philosophisch-historische Abteilung*
AWW	Akademie der Wissenschaften in Wien, Philosophisch-historische Klasse
Abel	F.-M. Abel, *Les Livres des Maccabées**
Abel, *Géographie*	Idem, *Géographie de la Palestine**
Abel, *Grammaire*	Idem, *Grammaire du grec biblique**
AIPHOS	*Annuaire de l'Institut de philologie et d'histoire orientales et slaves*, Université libre de Bruxelles
ANET²	*Ancient Near Eastern Texts*, ed. by J. B. Pritchard, 2d ed. Princeton University Press, 1955
Arm	Armenian Version (see Introduction, Part VII)
BA	*Biblical Archaeologist*
BASOR	*Bulletin of the American Schools of Oriental Research*
BGU	*Ägyptische Urkunden aus den Staatlichen Museen zu Berlin: Griechische Urkunden*, vols. IV and VIII. Berlin: Weidmann, 1912, 1933
Bickerman, *Chronology*	Elias J. Bickerman, *Chronology of the Ancient World**
Bickerman, *Studies*	Idem, *Studies in Jewish and Christian History**
Bickerman, *Gott*	Idem, *Der Gott der Makkabäer**
Bickerman, *Institutions*	Idem, *Institutions des Séleucides**
Blass-Debrunner-Rehkopf, *Grammatik*	Friedrich Blass and Albert Debrunner, *Grammatik des neutestamentlichen Griechisch*, 14th ed., revised by Friedrich Rehkopf*
Bunge	Jochen G. Bunge, *Untersuchungen zum Zweiten Makkabäerbuch**
BZ	*Biblische Zeitschrift*
CHJ	*Cambridge History of Judaism*. Cambridge University Press, forthcoming
CIL	*Corpus Inscriptionum Latinarum*
CPJ	*Corpus Papyrorum Judaicarum**

* For further reference, see Selected Bibliography.

DAGR | Dictionnaire des antiquités grecques et romaines, eds. Ch. Daremberg and Edm. Saglio, 5 vols. in 10. Paris: Hachette, 1877–1919

Dan LXX | The old Greek version of Daniel

Dan Th. | The Greek version of Daniel ascribed to Theodotion

DJD | *Discoveries in the Judaean Desert.* Oxford: Clarendon Press, 1955–

Enc. Bib. | Encyclopaedia Biblica ($=$*Enṣiqlopediah miqra'it*). Jerusalem: Bialik Institute, 1955– (in Hebrew). References to columns

Enc. Jud. | Encyclopaedia Judaica. New York: Macmillan, 1972. References to columns

Ep. 0, Ep. 1, Ep. 2 | Epistle 0, Epistle 1, Epistle 2 (see pp. 2, 24)

Exler | Francis X. J. Exler, *The Form of the Ancient Greek Letter**

FGH | *Die Fragmente der griechischen Historiker,* ed. by F. Jacoby. Berlin: Weidmann; Leiden: Brill, 1923–

G | Chapter and verse numbers of the Greek text of the Bible which differ from the numbers in the Hebrew text are designated by "G"

Ginzberg, *Legends* | Louis Ginzberg, *The Legends of the Jews**

Greek-English Lexicon | Henry George Liddell and Robert Scott, *A Greek-English Lexicon,* 9th ed., revised by Henry Stuart Jones and Roderick McKenzie*

Grimm | Carl L. W. Grimm, *Das zweite, dritte, und vierte Buch der Maccabäer**

H | Chapter and verse numbers of the Hebrew text of the Bible which differ from the numbers in the Greek text are designated by "H"

Hanhart or Hanhart's edition | *Maccabaeorum liber II,* Septuaginta: Vetus Testamentum Graecum Auctoritate Societatis Litterarum Gottingensis, vol. IX, fasc. II. Göttingen: Vandenhoeck & Ruprecht, 1959, ed. Robert Hanhart

HTR | *Harvard Theological Review*

HUCA | *Hebrew Union College Annual*

I | First Maccabees

II | Second Maccabees

III | Third Maccabees

IV | Fourth Maccabees

IEJ | *Israel Exploration Journal*

J. *AJ* | Josephus, *Antiquities of the Jews*

J. *Ap.* | Josephus, *Against Apion*

J. *BJ* | Josephus, *Bellum Judaicum=The Jewish War*

J. *Vita* | Josephus, *Life of Josephus*

* For further reference, see Selected Bibliography.

JBL	*Journal of Biblical Literature*
JTS	*Journal of Theological Studies*
Kühner-Gerth, *Grammatik*	Raphael Kühner and Bernhard Gerth, *Ausführliche Grammatik der griechischen Sprache**
L, l, L'	Groups of "Lucianic" manuscripts (see Introduction, Part VII)
La	Latin Version (with manuscripts indicated by superscript capitals; see Introduction, Part VII)
LCL	Loeb Classical Library. Harvard University Press
M.	*Mishnah*
Mayser	Edwin Mayser, *Grammatik der griechischen Papyri aus der Ptolemäerzeit**
Megillat Ta'anit	Published in Hans Lichtenstein, "Die Fastenrolle," HUCA 8–9 (1931–32), 257–351; for a brief account of this list of commemorative days on which fasting is forbidden, see AB vol. 41, p. 53, n. 40
Migne	J.-P. Migne, *Patrologiae Cursus Completus Series Latina,* Paris, 1843–90, and *Series Graeco-Latina,* Paris, 1857–1934
Mørkholm	Otto Mørkholm, *Antiochus IV of Syria**
Nilsson, II	Martin P. Nilsson, *Geschichte der griechischen Religion,* vol. II, 2d ed.*
OCD²	Oxford Classical Dictionary*
OGIS	*Orientis Graeci Inscriptiones Selectae,* ed. by Wilhelm Dittenberger. Leipzig: Hirzel, 1903–5
Otto and Bengtson	Walter Otto and H. Bengtson, *Zur Geschichte des Niederganges des Ptolemäerreiches**
PAAJR	*Proceedings of the American Academy for Jewish Research*
Parker and Dubberstein	R. A. Parker and W. H. Dubberstein, *Babylonian Chronology**
Pass.Mac. W	See p. 128
PW	Pauly-Wissowa et al., eds., Realencyclopaedie der klassischen Altertumswissenschaft. References to columns; volumes in the second series are indicated by a Roman numeral followed by "A" (IA, IIA, etc.)
q	An important class of minuscule manuscripts (see Introduction, Part VII)
1QM	The War Scroll from Qumran. Published in Eleazar L. Sukenik, *The Dead Sea Scrolls of the Hebrew University* (Jerusalem: Magnes, 1955)

* For further reference, see Selected Bibliography.

1QpHab	The commentary on Habakkuk from Qumran. Published in *The Dead Sea Scrolls of St. Mark's Monastery,* ed. by M. Burrows, John C. Trever, and W. H. Brownlee (New Haven: American Schools of Oriental Research, 1950–51), vol. 1
1QS	The Manual of Discipline from Qumran. Published in Burrows et al., vol. II 2
RB	*Revue biblique*
REG	*Revue des études grecques*
REJ	*Revue des études juives*
RHR	*Revue de l'histoire des religions*
Roller	Otto Roller, *Das Formular der paulinischen Briefe**
Roscher	W. H. Roscher, ed. *Ausführliches Lexikon der griechischen und römischen Mythologie.* Leipzig: Teubner, 1897–1937
RSV	*Revised Standard Version*
Schol. Megillat Ta'anit	Old commentary on *Megillat Ta'anit,* published in Hans Lichtenstein, "Die Fastenrolle," HUCA 8–9 (1931–32), 323–51
Schunck, *Quellen*	Klaus-Dietrich Schunck, *Die Quellen des I. und II. Makkabäerbuches**
Schürer	Emil Schürer, *Geschichte des jüdischen Volkes im Zeitalter Jesu Christi**
Schürer (New English version)	Idem, *The History of the Jewish People in the Age of Jesus Christ**
Sel., Sel. Bab., Sel. Mac. (always preceded by a year number)	Of the Seleucid era, of the Babylonian Seleucid era, of the Macedonian Seleucid era (see p. 22; plain "Sel." is used only where there is some reason to leave ambiguous which Seleucid era is meant)
Studies Smith	*Christianity, Judaism, and Other Greco-Roman Cults: Studies for Morton Smith at Sixty,* ed. by Jacob Neusner. Leiden: Brill, 1975
Sy	Syriac Version (see Introduction, Part VII)
Syll.[3]	*Sylloge Inscriptionum Graecarum,* ed. by W. Dittenberger, 3d ed. Leipzig: Hirzel, 1905–24
TB	Babylonian Talmud
TDNT	*Theological Dictionary of the New Testament,* ed. by Gerhard Kittel*
Theodoretus	Quotations of Second Maccabees by Theodoretus (see p. 128)
To.	Tosefta
TP	Palestinian Talmud
V	*Codex Venetus* (see Introduction, Part VII)

* For further reference, see Selected Bibliography.

Welles, *Royal Correspondence*	C. Bradford Welles, *Royal Correspondence in the Hellenistic Period**
Will, *Histoire*	Édouard Will, *Histoire du monde hellénistique**
ZAW	*Zeitschrift für die alttestamentliche Wissenschaft*
ZDPV	*Zeitschrift des deutschen Palästina-Vereins*
Ziemann	Ferdinand Ziemann, *De epistularum Graecarum formulis sollemnibus quaestiones selectae.* Diss. Universitas Fridericiana Halensis. Halis Saxonum: Karras, 1910
ZNW	*Zeitschrift für die neutestamentliche Wissenschaft*

* For further reference, see Selected Bibliography.

INTRODUCTION

I. THE CONTENT AND CHARACTER
OF SECOND MACCABEES

The faithful Israelite living in Judaea under the rule of the Ptolemies and the Seleucids in the third and second centuries B.C.E. learned from childhood that the LORD's Chosen People had nothing to fear if they kept the LORD's commandments. Subjection to the great empires of Persia and the Hellenistic kings had brought stability and security over long periods, which in part compensated for galling exploitation and servitude and for episodes of devastating warfare. Then, under the Seleucid Antiochus IV from 167 to 164 B.C.E., obedience to the LORD's commandments became a crime punished with extreme severity. No harsher trial ever tested the monotheistic faith of the Jews.

The outcome was entirely unexpected: the desperate resistance of the Jews prevailed, and for a time the "yoke of foreign empires" was lifted from the Jews as they became independent under the Hasmonaean dynasty. After the centuries of heartbreaking delay, were the glorious predictions of the prophets of a mighty restored Israel being fulfilled? For the Jews, the events cried out for an interpretation in accordance with the teachings of the Torah and the Prophets. God's favor had departed from Israel in the dark days of the destruction of the two kingdoms. If now God's favor had fully returned after the harshest time of troubles, it was necessary for the people to know how and why; otherwise, they might again lose His favor.

The tradition of the Greek and Roman Christian churches has preserved two Jewish historical works which explain to the Chosen People the time of troubles and the victories which followed. Early in the Greek manuscript tradition these works received the titles First and Second Books of Maccabees. However, in the books themselves and in the earliest sources, "Maccabee" or "Maccabaeus" never occurs in the plural, appearing only as an additional name of the hero Judas. Clement of Alexandria and Origen, the earliest of the Church Fathers to mention the books by name, call them *Ta Makkabaïka,* "Maccabaean Histories," from which title persons who spoke loosely probably turned to call all the heroes in the stories "Maccabees." The first datable occurrence of such use of "Maccabees" for the heroes is in Tertullian *Adversus Judaeos* 4, of ca. 195 C.E. From then on, the Fathers speak of the "Books of Maccabees."[1]

These two books present sharply different accounts; indeed, we shall find that their authors were bitter opponents. The webs of doctrinal subtleties, of charge and countercharge, which characterize the polemics of monotheistic sects against the rivals they call "heretics"—these webs give rise to some of the most complicated puzzles in the history of literature. So it is with our two books. First Maccabees and the original of which Second Maccabees is an abridgment were written in close succession as propaganda after decades of controversy. The difficult task of interpreting such works has been made more difficult by the almost perverse skepticism of scholars toward them since the time of the Renaissance.[2] Propagandists can and do lie, but propagandistic historians lie only where it is to their advantage and only where there is small danger of being exposed. Since each of our two books presents one of two extreme opposing views, they can be made to act as a check one upon the other. Thus, one can sharply restrict the field for imaginative scholarly skepticism which would reject or radically alter their accounts.

First Maccabees is a history of the rise of the Hasmonaean dynasty, from the daring deeds of the zealous priest Mattathias to the reign of John Hyrcanus, high priest and prince of the Jews by dynastic heredity. It demonstrates that the Hasmonaean family was chosen by God to be the bringers of permanent victory to Israel and to rule the Chosen People as high priests and princes, at least until a true prophet should arise. We are justified in calling the author of First Maccabees the "Hasmonaean propagandist."

Here, our subject is the Second Book of Maccabees. The form of Second Maccabees is strange. The book begins with two letters. The first (II 1:1 to 1:10a . . . "in the 188th year") we shall call Epistle 1 (Ep. 1), and the second (II 1:10b, "The people . . ." to 2:18) we shall call Epistle 2 (Ep. 2). At 2:19 begins a history which the writer in his preface (2:19–32) says is an abridgment of the work of one Jason of Cyrene on Judas Maccabaeus and his brothers, the purification of the "greatest" of temples and the dedication of the altar, and the wars against Antiochus IV Epiphanes and Antiochus V Eupator, and the miraculous divine interventions and glorious victories which then occurred. This history continues until the end of the book at 15:39, where the writer says he has

---

[1] "Maccabaean Histories": Clement of Alexandria *Stromateis* i 21.123; v 14.97; Origen *Contra Celsum* viii 46, etc. See Abel, pp. viii–x. The loose usage may appear already at Hippolytus *De Antichristo* 49, where the manuscript tradition has two readings, *Makkabaiois* and *Makkabaïkois*.

First Maccabees goes far beyond the lifetime of Judas Maccabaeus and dwells upon the importance of his brothers, so that its original title could hardly have been "Maccabaean History"; indeed, we know it was not. See AB vol. 41, pp. 14–21.

[2] See AB vol. 41, p. 37, n. 2.

reached the end of his task, "since thereafter the city [Jerusalem] has been in the hands of the Hebrews." The abridger thus implies that the work of Jason of Cyrene extended further, since the task the abridger set himself was to abridge Jason's work. Had he covered Jason's narrative to the end, he would have concluded by writing, "Since Jason ended his work at this point, my work, too, is done."

We know of Jason of Cyrene and the history he wrote only from the abridgment. The abridger described his own methods and the scope of his own work in a brief preface (2:19–32). When properly understood, that preface tells us the abridger claims to have added nothing to the content of the book: he only abridged and restyled. Careful study of Second Maccabees suggests there is no reason to reject these claims of the abridger. He indeed abridged a previously existing work. The narrative reads mostly like a chain of isolated incidents, as if the abridger picked out high points and was not much concerned with continuity. Several passages have traits strongly suggesting they are abridgments.[3] Like the original as described in the preface, the abridged work has as the chief hero Judas Maccabaeus, focuses much attention on the temple, regards as among the chief villains the persecuting kings Antiochus IV and V, and makes the narrative teem with miracles, in sharp contrast to the history without miracles given in First Maccabees. Hence, we may speak of the content of the abridgment as indeed the work of Jason of Cyrene. Henceforth we shall call II 3 to 15 "the abridged history."

According to the abridger, the work of Jason was a voluminous one, in five books. A "book" (biblion) was originally a roll of papyrus, and lengthy works would be subdivided into books. The length of such books could vary, as one can see from the great variety in the length of the books of Josephus' War. If Jason's books were all as long as Josephus BJ ii, the five would amount to one good-sized modern volume. But ancient books were copied by hand on only one face of the papyrus or parchment in letters usually larger than our standard typefaces. Thus, even a moderately long work would be very unwieldy. Moreover, ancient readers read aloud, so that going through such a work would consume considerable time. Specialist readers might plow through the still longer works of Polybius and others, but the "general reader," whom the abridger contemplated as his audience, could easily have found Jason's mere five books forbidding.

The author of First Maccabees expended great effort to find material (I

---

[3] For a refutation of the view that the "abridger" wrote an original work and only pretended to be abridging the work of a fictitious Jason of Cyrene, see Robert Doran, *Temple Propaganda: The Purpose and Character of 2 Maccabees* (The Catholic Biblical Quarterly Monograph Series, 12; Washington, D.C.: Catholic Biblical Association of America, 1981), pp. 80–83. Passages which bear the marks of abridgment: see NOTES on 12:10–31, on 12:13, on 12:36, on 13:19, and on 13:22–26.

9:22) and added to the bare facts speeches, prayers, and propagandistic comments. Nevertheless, he dealt with the entire history of the Hellenistic reform, the atrocities of Antiochus IV, and the careers of Mattathias and Judas Maccabaeus in nine chapters. In factual background, Jason added to that material only the events of the high priesthood of Onias III in II 3. It might be hard to imagine how he could have stretched the narrative into five voluminous books. We certainly cannot reconstruct the original, but it was probably full of long and theatrical dialogue and speeches and prayers and preaching by the author.

Indeed, in ancient times both Jews and pagans before going into battle would offer up prayers, and the commander would deliver a speech encouraging his troops. After victories there would be rituals of thanksgiving to the deity or deities. The secular-minded Greek historian Thucydides hardly bothers to report such routine acts. In his narrative of Judas' career, the pious author of First Maccabees gives only a selection of them (prayers: 3:46–53, 4:30–33, 7:37–38, 40–42; speeches: 3:17–22, 58–60, 4:8–11, 17–18, 5:32; thanksgiving: 4:24, 5:24). One might have thought the abridger would be glad to omit such passages, but he preserves them at almost every opportunity (prayers: 8:2–4, 14–15, 10:16, 25–26, 11:6, 12:6, 15, 28, 36–37, 13:10–12, 14:15, 15:21–24; speeches and watchwords: 8:16–23, 11:7, 13:12, 14–15, 15:8–16; thanksgiving: 8:27, 29, 10:7, 38, 15:34). The unabridged work probably had still more.

The Hasmonaean propagandist treats the sufferings of the martyrs in only a few verses (I 1:57, 60–63, 2:29–38). The abridger gives them far more (II 6:10 – 7:42), yet even he describes their tortures with stark brevity and quotes at most a few words from a martyr. Jason may have given each a long conversation with the persecutor and may have added lengthy descriptions of the tortures and comments of his own such as we find in Fourth Maccabees.

In addition to the preface there are a few other passages which are certainly original with the abridger,[4] notably those expressed in the first person singular; even in them, the abridger's attitudes may have been identical to those of Jason. Where I have felt the necessity of admitting our ignorance as to who is responsible for the peculiarities of a passage, the abridger or Jason of Cyrene, I have used the expressions "the writer" or "our writer," reserving "our author" for the author of First Maccabees, as in AB vol. 41.

If Ep. 1 and Ep. 2 had been omitted, no one would have missed them. Indeed, both letters contradict the narrative of the abridged history.[5] Let us therefore examine first the character of the abridged history. There are

---

[4] 6:12–17, 10:9–10, 13:26, and 15:37–39; probably the other verses marking the end of a section also belong to the abridger: 3:40, 7:42, and 14:46(end).

[5] See p. 25.

many contrasts between Jason's work and First Maccabees. Jason takes great pains to illustrate the sanctity of the temple, a point taken for granted in First Maccabees. Though Jason has heroes other than Judas, Judas' brothers are not among them. Particularly prominent is the figure of the high priest Onias III, a man passed over in silence in First Maccabees. The abridged history, indeed, begins (II 3:1–40) with a bold assertion of all these points of contrast: because of the merit of the high priest Onias III in enforcing the provisions of the Torah, miraculous divine intervention prevented Heliodorus, the minister of the Seleucid king Seleucus IV, from seizing for the royal treasury the money deposited in the temple.

Well might Jason begin at this point, the first miracle attested for the second temple, a miracle which ushered in a period which passed belief both in its disasters and in its triumphs.[6] Wickedness among the Jews enters the narrative in the person of Onias' enemy, Simon of the priestly course Bilgah, administrator of the temple, who spitefully proposes to the king's officials that the money on deposit can be seized. Where in First Maccabees we find only a general mention of wicked men as the instigators of Hellenization in Jerusalem, Jason of Cyrene traces it first to the removal of the pious Onias III from the holy city. Onias went to Antioch to appeal to Seleucus IV to curb the machinations of his enemy Simon (4:1–6).

In the absence of the pious priest from Jerusalem, his wicked brother Jason (whom we shall call "Jason the Oniad") supplanted him as high priest by promising increased revenue to the new king, Antiochus IV (4:7). At the same time, the wicked Jason purchased from the willing king a new royal policy toward the Jews as well as important privileges for himself and his impious followers. No longer would royal policy bind the Jews to observe the commandments of the Torah. Jews could now introduce Greek political and cultural institutions and have the privileges of "Antiochene" citizenship.[7] Jason himself received the important prerogative of drawing up the list of those so privileged and proceeded to bring his fellow Jews over to the Greek way of life (4:7–12).

The result was that priests ignored the temple cult for the newfangled Greek pastimes, and their neglect of God's laws brought down upon them the just punishment that soon followed: the Greeks whom they aped became the instruments of retribution (4:13–17). The sins grew worse. Jason did not shrink from sending offerings to idols (4:18–20). Nevertheless, punishment was not immediate. After attending to dangers from the direction of Ptolemaic Egypt, Antiochus IV even paid a friendly visit to Jerusalem (4:21–22).

Jason's pontificate lasted three years. Thereupon, however, the still

---

[6] See AB vol. 41, pp. 12–13, 49.

[7] For the meaning of "Antiochene" citizenship, see NOTE on 4:9–15.

more wicked Menelaus, brother of the troublemaker Simon, supplanted the wicked Jason by offering Antiochus still higher revenue. Jason crossed the Jordan into exile in the Ammanitis. However, Menelaus could not raise the promised amount in taxes. In his peril, he stole from the temple to bribe royal officials. Onias III, ready to expose the thievery, took asylum at Daphne. By yet another bribe Menelaus induced a royal official to lure Onias from asylum and slay him. Antiochus IV, still no enemy of the Jews, had the murderer executed. Menelaus and his followers, however, continued to provoke the wrath of the righteous by plundering temple property. Rioting broke out in Jerusalem. The king summoned Menelaus to render account, but Menelaus again purchased safety by bribing an official, so that the Jewish elders protesting his depredations were themselves outrageously put to death (4:23–50). Wickedness of Jews was reaching its full measure.

Dire omens accompanied Antiochus' "second" expedition to Egypt. In the course of the campaign, a false rumor spread that Antiochus was dead, and Jason the Oniad returned from exile in a brutal but abortive attempt to seize power from Menelaus. Though Menelaus was driven to take refuge in the citadel, Jason was forced to withdraw and later came to a deserved miserable end (5:1–10).

Antiochus, however, inferred that the Jews were in revolt and brutally suppressed them as "rebels" and sacked the temple. Indeed, he had become the "rod of God's anger" against the wicked, but he arrogantly believed that God would not punish infractions against His temple after the sinners had been chastised (5:11–21).

The Jews had more punishment to suffer. First, they were harried by the king's officials. Then, a force under Apollonius the Mysarch perpetrated a massacre at the holy city. Judas Maccabaeus and a small group of companions were driven to flee Jerusalem and take refuge in the wilderness (5:21–27). There is no trace in the abridged history that Jason of Cyrene deigned to mention the zealous priest Mattathias, who is so prominent in First Maccabees[8] as the first heroic Hasmonaean.

The worst was yet to come. The king dispatched an Athenian, Geron, to force the Jews to violate the Torah. Jerusalem's temple was to be called the temple of Zeus Olympios; the Samaritan temple on Mount Gerizim was to be called the temple of Zeus Xenios. All Jewish observance was forbidden, on pain of death. Martyrdoms were many and Jason describes them vividly so as to display the steadfast piety of the victims and their faith in resurrection and in divine vindication (6:1 – 7:42).

From First Maccabees one can infer that but for the rise of Mattathias and his sons the deaths of the martyrs would have been in vain.[9] In contrast, Jason insists that their martyrdom was not in vain. It brought God

[8] Ch. 2.
[9] See AB vol. 41, pp. 4–7.

to have mercy on His people (II 7:37–38). Again and again Judas Maccabaeus and his men prayed for divine aid and received it, as could be seen from their ever-growing successes against the enemy. Throughout, Judas and his men scrupulously observed the commandments of the Torah, especially the commandment to rest on the Sabbath. The families of the martyrs received a share of the spoils, as if the martyrs had been partly responsible for the victories. By their success in vanquishing their wicked enemies, Judas and his men forced even the wicked general Nicanor to acknowledge God's power to protect His righteous people (8:1–36).[10]

In First Maccabees, between this expedition of Nicanor and the Feast of Dedication, Judas and his men defeat an expedition led by the regent Lysias; no expedition of Lysias occupies that position in Second Maccabees.[11] Up to this point, the mention of direct divine intervention against Antiochus IV and his subordinates is as absent from the abridged history as it is from First Maccabees. Miracles begin to appear in Second Maccabees with chs. 9 and 10. To complicate matters, in these chapters there is a severe dislocation in the narrative.[12] In its original order, the narrative proceeded with the account of how Judas and his men recovered Jerusalem and the temple, reestablished the sacrificial cult, celebrated the occasion after the manner of the festival of Tabernacles, and decreed that the eight-day festival in honor of the purification of the temple be made an annual observance (II 10:1–8). From now on, when I write of the abridged history, I mean the original abridgment, with 10:1–8 restored to its proper position, preceding 9:1–9.

First Maccabees and the abridged history disagree even on the name of the festival. At I 4:59 it is called "Days of the Dedication of the Altar"; at II 10:5 and 8 the name implied for it is "Days of the Purification of the Temple." After treating the festival, the abridged history turned to describe the miraculous and gruesome death of Antiochus IV. God himself brought the wicked king to perish in tardy repentance near Ecbatana (II 9). The events which occurred under the regime of the child Antiochus V and his chief minister Lysias follow. After the death of a minister who might have advocated a just policy toward the Jews, the Jews have to face wars against neighboring peoples stirred against them by hostile Seleucid officials. There is a miracle, as Judas, helped by supernatural beings, leads his men to victory, but members of his family, including his brother Simon, are somehow involved in a scandalous failure (10:9–38).

At this point, Jason of Cyrene places a first expedition of the regent Lysias, which Judas repulses at Beth-Zur. It is similar to the campaign of Lysias dated before the Feast of Dedication at I 4:28–35. However, unlike the report in First Maccabees, Judas here wins with the help of a

---

[10] On the "footnote" in 8:30–32, see NOTE ad loc.
[11] See pp. 55–63.
[12] See introductory NOTE on ch. 9.

supernatural cavalier, and his victory is followed by a formal peace between Lysias and Judas. The peace treaty ends the persecution and restores the temple to the Jews. As evidence for his account, Jason presents the official correspondence of Lysias, Antiochus V, and two Roman ambassadors (II 11).

According to Jason, the regime at Antioch was unable to make its officials and the gentile populations adjacent to Judaea observe the peace. Jews living in gentile areas suffered atrocities. Judas and his men avenged the dead and saved the living in a series of expeditions during which they scrupulously observed the Sabbaths and festivals. Whereas in First Maccabees (I 5:54) the author proudly notes at the close of Judas' victorious campaign the remarkable fact that not one man in the Jewish army was killed, Jason calls attention to the providential miracle in the course of the very next campaign: on the Jewish side only sinners fell. Jason lays great stress on the fact that Judas saw to it expiatory sacrifices were offered for the fallen sinners; thereby Jason deduces that heroic Judas, too, shared the belief in the resurrection (II 12).

Next we read of the expedition of Lysias and Antiochus V to suppress the rebellious Jews. Jason dates it in the year 149 of the Seleucid era (from September 22, 164, through October 9, 163 B.C.E.). For the first time in the abridged narrative, an absolute date appears, one which irreconcilably contradicts the chronology at I 6:20.[13] Jason reports that at the outset of the expedition Menelaus approached the chief minister and the king hoping to be confirmed as high priest, but instead God saw to it that the two viewed Menelaus as the cause of the troubles and had him executed at Beroea in a manner entirely befitting his sins (II 13:1–8).

The boy-king furiously sought to avenge his father's fate upon the Jews, but brave Judas and his brave men inflict a reverse upon the king's army near Modeïn, a site unmentioned at this point in First Maccabees. At first even treason in their own ranks does not break the brave resistance of the Jews at Beth-Zur, but those besieged there finally withdraw under a truce. Nevertheless, Judas defeats the Seleucid forces (no such victory is claimed in First Maccabees), and the king and his chief minister have to give up all thought of pursuing their campaign on receiving news of the revolt of Philip, a trusted minister at Antioch. Here, too, Jason contradicts First Maccabees, for there the enemy at Antioch is the rival guardian for Antiochus V whom Antiochus IV appointed on his deathbed (I 6:55–56). Though the text here describing how an honorable peace was then made bears the marks of drastic abridgment, it is clear that Jason's narrative, unlike First Maccabees, said nothing of Antiochus V's demolition of Jewish fortifications in violation of his own word. On the contrary,

---

[13] On the Seleucid era and its two forms, see p. 22. Absolute date: see NOTE on 13:1.

Jason tells us that Lysias even defended the peace with the Jews against the bitter objections of the citizens of Ptolemais (II 13:9–26).

However, Lysias and Antiochus were soon to fall. "Three years later," as Jason misleadingly says,[14] Demetrius I seized power and had the boy-king and his chief minister put to death. A certain wicked Alcimus, who had already been high priest, now sought confirmation in office from Demetrius. To secure the king's support, he denounced both Judas and the group of pious Jews called the "Asidaioi" as rebels and as disturbers of the peace of the kingdom. Alcimus complained that he had himself been driven from his high priestly office by their turbulence; Judas must be destroyed. With the concurrence of his advisers, Demetrius sent Nicanor to reinstate Alcimus, destroy Judas, and disperse Judas' followers. To cope with the Seleucid force, the Jews first prayed for divine aid, and Judas sent out a force under his brother Simon, who suffered a mild defeat. Jason here may tacitly suggest that only Judas himself was worthy of divine intervention. Indeed, rather than clash with Judas, Nicanor made peace with him and became his friend (II 14:1–25).

Much of this account is in sharp contrast with First Maccabees. There, Alcimus, spokesman of renegades, accuses not the Asidaioi but only Judas and his brothers. Asidaioi, but not Judas and his brothers, are so foolish as to trust Alcimus and the Seleucid agents (I 7:5–30).

For Jason, the period of mutual trust ends when Alcimus appeals to Demetrius and accuses Nicanor of treason for showing favor to Judas. Ordered by the king to take Judas prisoner, Nicanor, frightened by his precarious position, turns into an enemy of the Jews and their God. Unable to capture Judas, he threatens to destroy the temple if the Jews do not surrender the man. The Jews respond by turning to prayer; rather than submit to arrest by Nicanor's soldiers, Razis, a venerated Jewish elder, theatrically commits suicide, firm in his belief in the resurrection. Impious Nicanor even orders Jews to violate the Sabbath in pursuit of Judas (II 15:1–5).

Judas, however, bravely prepares for battle and rallies his men with biblical texts and with the report of his own miraculous dream: he saw the pious Onias III praying for the Jewish defenders, and with Onias appeared the prophet Jeremiah, who handed Judas a sacred golden sword with which to defeat the enemy. With prayer Judas and his men went into battle against Nicanor, and in a great manifestation of God's power slaughtered the vast enemy force and its leader, and fixed Nicanor's severed head and hand in sight of the temple he had threatened to destroy. The Jews decided to celebrate the date, 13 Adar, annually as the "Day of Nicanor" (15:6–36).

From then on, says the abridger, the Jews possessed Jerusalem. At this

---

14 See NOTE on 14:1–4.

point, therefore, he ends his work (15:37–39). Jason probably continued at least to the death of Judas in spring, 160 B.C.E., for he told "the story of Judas Maccabaeus and his brothers" (II 2:19) and knew of the treaty of 161 B.C.E. between Rome and the Jews (II 4:11).[15] In the abridger's view, the death of Judas and its immediate aftermath were unedifying. Still less would he have wished to tell of the rise to power of Judas' brothers and their descendants. The abridger was probably also aware of the artistic advantages of stopping where he did. Thereby his narrative came to fall into two parallel sections, each telling how an enemy threatened the Jews and the temple, how one or more Jews bravely suffered martyrdom, how the Jews finally triumphed whereas their enemy suffered a retributive death, and how the Jews established an annual commemorative festival. In each of the two parallel sections, the first celebration of the festival serves as the climax.

Two other contrasts between the narrative of the abridged history and that of First Maccabees are noteworthy. The military statistics given in the two works, on the size of armies and on the number slain in battle, never agree. Ancient authors had wide freedom to invent or alter such figures,[16] and we shall find reason to believe that here one of our two historians is deliberately contradicting the other. First Maccabees is remarkable for its geographical precision: sites of battles and important events are almost always named, and nowhere can the author be shown to have committed a geographical blunder. The abridged history, in contrast, is vague on matters of geography, and Jason of Cyrene demonstrably committed geographical blunders.[17]

Having examined the narrative of the abridged history, let us turn to investigate what the book teaches. Throughout his history, our writer insistently preaches on several themes. Among these are God's relationship to the Jews, the holiness of the temple of Jerusalem, the position of the Hasmonaean family and their pious opponents in God's scheme of history, the value of martyrdom, and the doctrine of resurrection.

On God's relationship to the Jews, the abridged history has a rather straightforward conception. Normally the Jews' protector, the LORD punishes them promptly and severely for sin, the promptness itself being a mark of mercy because it prevents the Chosen People from incurring still worse punishment by further sin. As soon as the punishment has reached sufficient measure and the Jews have repented, God turns merciful. Thereupon He again protects them, and if any pagans, used by Him as the rod of His anger, arrogantly go beyond their mandate and commit wanton cruelty against the Chosen People, the LORD punishes them. Any Jews

[15] See pp. 4–5 and NOTES on 4:11 and 15:37.
[16] See NOTE on 8:24.
[17] See NOTES on the following passages: 8:8–34, 10:14–15, 24–38, 12:17, 21, 15:7–30.

who suffered or perished undeservedly in the time of punishment will be resurrected to receive their recompense.[18]

Thus our writer's message to the Jews is one of hope, but also of stern admonition. Despite the promises of the prophets to the contrary,[19] even after the end of the Babylonian exile, God may punish His people if they sin, using cruel foreigners as the "rods of His anger." Violations of the explicit words of the Torah might be easy to define. But the high priest Jason and his followers probably argued that their Hellenizing program, including the gymnasium, was permitted by the Torah. Only the course of events proved how it provoked the wrath of God.[20] In the future, too, acts which might seem to be permitted by the Torah might prove to be equally offensive to God. Our writer could well be warning his contemporaries that their present practices might be so offensive to God. We shall have to consider what practices of his own time he could have had in mind.

More complex is the attitude in the abridged history toward the temple in Jerusalem. Its complexities have not been fully appreciated. The writer was an ardent monotheistic adherent of God's law as revealed in the Torah and confirmed in the books of Kings. One might expect him to hold that the second temple, built after the Babylonian exile to replace Solomon's, was again "the Place which the LORD has chosen," the sole temple in the world, in the sense that only there can sacrifices be offered to the one true God. Such, indeed, seems to be the view of the Hasmonaean propagandist,[21] but the writer of the abridged history disagrees!

Though he stresses that the temple is indeed "the Place," he respects the temple of the Samaritans and their holy mountain, Mount Gerizim.[22] In what seems to be carefully guarded language, he speaks of the temple as the "greatest" and "holiest" but not as the only one in the world. Elsewhere, his apparently guarded language asserts the truth, that the Place at Jerusalem was chosen in the past, but does not go on to assert that God's act of choice then is still fully valid in the present.[23]

The reason cannot be that our writer respects his pagan readers and admits that pagan shrines are temples, too. He never uses his words for

[18] Prompt punishment: 4:15–17, 6:12–17, 7:18, 32–33, 10:4; mercy upon repentance: 2:22, 6:16, 7:6, 29, 33, 37–38, 8:5, 27, 29; punishment of arrogant pagans: 7:16–19, 34–37, 8:34–36, 9:3–28, 15:28–35; resurrection: 7:9, 11, 14, 23, 29, 36, 12:43–45, 14:46.

[19] Isa 51:22, 52:1, 54:7–10; Jer 31:22–36; Nah 1:15 (2:1 H.), Lam 4:22, etc.

[20] See my article, "Jewish Acceptance and Rejection of Hellenism," *Jewish and Christian Self-Definition,* ed. by E. P. Sanders with A. I. Baumgarten and Alan Mendelson (Philadelphia: Fortress Press, 1981), II, 67–69, 75–81.

[21] What one might expect: Deut 12:2–14, etc.; II Kings 22:8, 15, 19, etc.; Hasmonaean propagandist's view: I 3:49–51 (see NOTES ad loc. in AB vol. 41), 7:37.

[22] "The Place": 3:2, 12, 18, 30, 38; 5:16, 17, 19, 20; 8:17. Samaritan temple: 5:23, 6:2; see NOTES ad loc. and Appendix VIII, NOTE on J. *AJ* xii 5.5.259, *founded . . . Garizein.*

[23] "Greatest" and "holiest": 2:19, 5:15, 14:13, 31; cf. 2:22, 3:12, 13:11. Guarded assertion on God's choice: see NOTE on 14:35, *chose . . . midst.*

"temple" (*hieron, naos*) of a pagan shrine. He calls a pagan shrine, rather, *temenos*[24] or uses a neuter noun or adjective derived from the name of the god to which it was sacred.[25] There is no exception to this rule in 14:33. There, the pagan Nicanor speaks and uses *hieron* as a pagan would. Thus, our writer recognizes only Israelite temples, and he recognizes more than one; of these, he insists that the one in Jerusalem is the greatest and holiest. Some of these equivocations are due to the fact that Jason of Cyrene drew on one source which believed in the sole legitimacy of Jerusalem and on another which did not.[26] But the writer's insistence on the superlative greatness and holiness of the temple in Jerusalem, even as he acknowledges the legitimacy of Mount Gerizim, is so strong that he must be writing against some point of view. Against whom is he writing, and why?

It is not difficult to reconstruct the background and to find in sources contemporary with the early Hasmonaeans or with our writer reflections of the opposition he faced. Words thought to be the inspired utterances of prophets informed the Chosen People that God had abandoned the first temple, depriving it of all holiness and leaving it to be destroyed.[27] As far as Jews knew, God had signified his acceptance of the Tabernacle in the wilderness and of the first temple in Jerusalem by sending miraculous fire down from heaven to devour the offerings on the altar.[28] Such fire never came down to signify the divine election of the second temple. Even before the persecution perpetrated by Antiochus IV, there were *Jews* who believed that the second temple was incompletely holy, if at all, and that sacrifices could be offered to the LORD at other Jewish shrines in places far removed from Jerusalem. If I am right in my interpretation of Ep. 1 (II 1:7), Jason the Oniad served as high priest of a Jewish temple in Transjordan after being deposed as high priest of the temple in Jerusalem.[29] Our writer seems to have been glad for every opportunity to condemn Jason the Oniad, yet the abridged history passes in silence over the Oniad's priestly service at a schismatic temple. In these facts we can find one more confirmation of the peculiarity of our writer's attitude toward the second temple, unless Jason of Cyrene knew nothing of the Transjordanian sanctuary.[30]

Surviving texts reveal other ways in which the sanctity of the second temple was questioned. According to the Testament of Moses,[31] valid sacrifices could not be offered there. The reason is not given. A likely

---

[24] 10:2; see NOTE ad loc.

[25] 12:26.

[26] See Introduction, Part II, sections 4–5, and introductory NOTE on ch. 3.

[27] Jer 7:3–15; Ezek 24:21; Lam 2:7, etc.

[28] Lev 9:24; II Chron 7:1–3; cf. Ezra 6:16–18.

[29] See NOTE on 1:7, *Jason . . . Kingdom.*

[30] Jason's ignorance is conceivable, though the authors and recipients of Epp. 0 and 1 must have known of the Transjordanian temple.

[31] 4:8.

guess is, because miraculous fire had not yet come down from heaven.[32] According to the book of Enoch, all offerings at the second temple were unclean (implying, even those under Onias III!), and the building was destined to be replaced by another from heaven.[33] Such were the beliefs of some Jewish sects even before the dreadful events of the 160's B.C.E.[34]

Then came the brutal sack of the temple by Antiochus IV (169 B.C.E.) and the still more shocking desecration (167 B.C.E.). Should these events not be taken as the final proof that the second temple of Jerusalem had not been chosen by God or, if chosen, had been abandoned?

Onias IV, the son of our writer's hero, Onias III, must have held that the second temple had not been chosen.[35] He also seems to have believed that a legitimate Jewish high priest could come only from his own Oniad line.[36] On the assumption that God had not yet fully chosen the second temple, the Oniad line could be regarded as the last surviving link to Israel's original cult institutions, other than the Torah. However, already one non-Oniad had been appointed high priest when Onias IV was but a child, the notorious Menelaus.[37] Then the Seleucid regime of Antiochus V deposed and executed Menelaus and passed over the eligible Onias IV, raising to the high priesthood yet another non-Oniad, Alcimus, and pious Jews accepted that appointment. Thereupon, Onias IV left Judaea and took service under Ptolemy VI Philometor, king of Egypt.[38] There, Onias acted upon his beliefs about the temple and the high priestly prerogatives of his family. Quoting Isa 19:19 as prophetic justification, he sought and received the permission of Ptolemy VI and established a Jewish temple at Leontopolis near Heliopolis in Egypt before the king's death in 145 B.C.E.[39] That temple was to survive for more than two centuries,[40] and even rabbinic texts grudgingly concede some legitimacy to vegetable sacrifices offered there.[41]

Onias IV was not the first to found a Jewish shrine for the offering of

[32] The guess had not occurred to me when I wrote my article "The Testament of Moses: Its Content, Its Origin, and Its Attestation in Josephus," *Studies on the Testament of Moses,* ed. by George W. E. Nickelsburg, Jr. (Septuagint and Cognate Studies, no. 4; Cambridge, Mass.: Society of Biblical Literature, 1973), pp. 44–52; see esp. pp. 48–50.

[33] Offerings unclean: 89:73; new temple from heaven: 90:28–29.

[34] The relevant part of the Testament of Moses dates from 166 or early 165 B.C.E.; see AB vol. 41, pp. 39–40. The relevant stratum of the book of Enoch was written near the end of the third century B.C.E., earlier than I suggested at AB vol. 41, pp. 40–42. See, for the present, Part V, nn. 16, 34.

[35] J. *AJ* xiii 3.1.62–68.

[36] See my article, "The Tales of the Tobiads," in *Studies Smith,* Part III, pp. 111–12.

[37] 4:23–26 with 3:4.

[38] J. *AJ* xii 9.7.383–88; II 13:3–8, 14:3.

[39] J. *AJ* xii 9.7.388, xiii 3.1–3.62–72; Hans Volkmann, "Ptolemaios 24," PW XXIII² (1959), 1717.

[40] J. *BJ* vii 10.2–4.421–36.

[41] *M. Menaḥot* 13:10, TB *Menaḥot* 109a–110a.

sacrifices in Egypt. By his time the much earlier temple at Elephantine[42] may have been forgotten,[43] but he himself in his petition to Ptolemy VI attests to the existence of others: "When I came . . . to Leontopolis in the nome of Heliopolis and to other places where our nation has settled, I found that most of them have temples [hiera] contrary to what is proper, and for this reason they are hostile toward one another, as is the case with the Egyptians because of the multitude of their temples [hierôn] and their divisions of opinion over religion."[44]

Now, let us return to ask, against whom is our writer arguing? He reports how supernatural apparitions protected the temple,[45] thus giving good proof God cares for it, that it is holy; but the apparitions still fall short of the divine sign which proved the election of the Tabernacle and of Solomon's temple. God did answer prayers offered at the temple,[46] but God can answer prayers from an unclean place.[47] Therefore, the efficacy of the prayers is no refutation of the teaching of the book of Enoch, that the offerings at the second temple were unclean. The Testament of Moses and the book of Enoch do not deny all holiness to the second temple and its site; nowhere do they grant that a legitimate Jewish temple can be built at another place on earth. Jason the Oniad served as high priest in Jerusalem; clearly he believed the second temple had some sanctity. Onias IV himself did not deny that the temple in Jerusalem was holy. Indeed, he sought to pattern his after the one in Jerusalem.[48] At most he asserted that the second temple was not the Chosen Place so as to exclude all others. The abridged history thus opposes all these authorities on some issues, but it is diametrically opposed to none of them, and its arguments cannot be said to be effective against any of them!

Rather, it would appear that our writer aimed his book at those many Jews for whom the facts of history seemed to prove that God had not accepted the second temple as holy. In their view, first came the atrocities of Antiochus IV to demonstrate God's rejection of the sanctuary. To be sure, Judas Maccabaeus had won victories and purified and protected the temple, but thereafter the sanctuary and the holy city fell under the power of the "wicked" Hasmonaean high priests and princes. Our writer insists that the miraculous thwarting of Heliodorus, the victories of Judas Maccabaeus, the purification of the temple, and the mere fact that Jews (even

---

[42] See Bezalel Porten, *Archives from Elephantine* (Berkeley and Los Angeles: University of California Press, 1968), pp. 105–22.

[43] But see *Aristeas to Philocrates* 13.

[44] J. *AJ* xiii 3.1.65–66; see also Morton Smith, *Palestinian Parties and Politics that Shaped the Old Testament* (Columbia University Press, 1971), pp. 90–93.

[45] 3:24–30, 10:29–30, 11:8–10, and perhaps 15:34.

[46] 10:25–30, 11:6–10, 14:34–36 with 15:20–34.

[47] See Josh 22:19; the Transjordanian Judge Jephthah certainly offered up an effective prayer (Judg 11:30–33).

[48] J. *AJ* xiii 3.1.67.

Hasmonaeans) thereafter controlled the holy city[49] are enough to prove that even in his own time the temple at Jerusalem was the holiest in the world.

The abridged history seems to fall into two parts, with the institution of the annual observance of the Days of Purification as the climax of the one, and the institution of the annual observance of the Day of Nicanor as the other. But the abridger's preface and epilogue and preaching ignore the commemorative festivals. Those festivals, too, only serve to illustrate the holiness of the temple.

In sum, our writer's message on the temple is again a stern one: the holiness of the temple is no guarantee that God will protect it. If the Jews sin, the anger of the LORD may strike the temple, too (II 6:18–20).[50]

The intense interest of both Jason and the abridger in Judas Maccabaeus and his family, the Hasmonaeans, is indicated at the very outset of the abridger's preface, where he summarizes the content of the unabridged work. There (II 2:19) the abridger mentions Judas and his brothers first and the temple only after them! Yet our writer's treatment of the Hasmonaean family is most peculiar and is in striking contrast to that in First Maccabees. Where First Maccabees was written to prove the legitimacy of the Hasmonaean dynasty of high priests and princes descended from the zealous priest Mattathias, our writer does not deign to mention Mattathias and pointedly makes every effort to show that Judas' brothers were at best ineffective and at worst tainted by treason and sin.[51] The author of First Maccabees repeatedly attempts to portray the feats of the Hasmonaean brothers as equaling those of the great heroes of scripture, of Joshua, the Judges, Jonathan, and David. The abridged history shows nothing of the kind, though Jason and the abridger admired Judas. Judas' acts may be presented as fulfillments of prophecy but never as equivalents of the great deeds of earlier heroes.

The Hasmonaean propagandist exposes what he views as the errors, the folly, and even the baseness and sinfulness of pious Jews who differed with the Hasmonaeans on whether it was permitted to resist the pagan king (I 2:7–8) and to wage defensive warfare on the Sabbath (I 2:29–41) and also on accepting Alcimus as high priest (I 7:5–18). The author of First Maccabees concedes that the pious martyrs were brave, but in his view their kind of courage brought only their own deaths (I 1:62–63). His silence on the doctrine of the resurrection of the dead at I 1:63 and in Mattathias' farewell address (I 2:49–68) is eloquent: he did not believe in resurrection. The Hasmonaean propagandist went out of his way

---

[49] 15:37.

[50] Cf. p. 13.

[51] On the refusal to mention Mattathias, see AB vol. 41, p. 79. Negative portrayal of Judas' brothers: 10:19–22, 12:36–40, 14:17; perhaps also 12:24, though Jason does not identify the dupes as members of the Hasmonaean family. Greek "Dositheos" and Hebrew "Jonathan" are synonyms ("gift of God").

to mention by name the group of pious Jews called "Asidaioi," who at one time joined forces with the Hasmonaeans (I 2:42) and yet at another broke with them, with disastrous results (I 7:11–18).

Our writer, in contrast, presents the pious, including the Asidaioi, as steadfast followers of Judas (II 14:6), and he implies that Judas himself agreed that even defensive warfare was forbidden on the Sabbath (II 15:1–5) and that the courage and suffering of the martyrs gained for the Jews God's invincible support (II 8:3, 28–30). He insists that Judas himself believed in the resurrection of the dead (II 12:43–45). We may thus infer that our writer opposes the doctrines of the Hasmonaeans quite as much as their dynastic pretensions.

In another respect our writer seems to agree with the Hasmonaean propagandist, but there, too, a significant difference can be found. Both present the pious Jews as unaggressive and law-abiding, and their enemies as aggressors and lawless disturbers of peace. There is a large measure of truth in their presentation of the facts. The beliefs of pious Jews forced them to be astonishingly loyal to their pagan rulers,[52] and the weakness of the nation long made aggressive policies impossible. All campaigns of Judas Maccabaeus could be portrayed as defensive. Nevertheless, the Torah commands Jews to attack idolatry in the Promised Land (Exod 23:23–24, 31–33, 34:12–16; Deut 12:2–3) and permits them to wage aggressive warfare (Deut 20). The later Hasmonaeans (John Hyrcanus I, Judas Aristobulus, and Alexander Jannaeus) aggressively wiped out idolatry in the Holy Land and made wide conquests, which included the cities of Scythopolis and Azotus. One is thus not surprised to find the Hasmonaean propagandist recording how Judas and Jonathan attacked Azotus and destroyed the works of idolatry there (I 5:68, 10:83–85, 11:4) though he does not report that Azotus ever attacked the Jews. In contrast, we find our writer passing in silence over Judas' attack on Azotus. He also stresses the peaceful relations between Scythopolis and the embattled pious Jews (II 12:30–31), whereas the rival historian says nothing of them. The Hasmonaean propagandist argues that Judas' siege of the Akra was a defensive response to the provocations of the garrison there (I 6:18–19), whereas our writer passes over the event in silence. All these contrasts suggest that our writer is opposing the aggressive policies of the later Hasmonaeans. It looks as if he wishes to deny their claim that their wars were but the completion of the work of the great Maccabaeus.

What can be inferred about Jason's purposes from our study of the teachings in the abridged history? His general warning to the Jews against sin might seem to be vague. One clear aim of his is to assert the holiness of the second temple against those who denied it. That is not his sole pur-

---

[52] See NOTE on 1:7, *Jason . . . Kingdom.*

pose, however. The Hasmonaeans, too, believed in the holiness of the second temple. Nevertheless, Jason seeks to discredit all Hasmonaeans except Judas, attacks doctrines known to have been held by the Hasmonaeans, and defends beliefs which they opposed. In Part III we shall find that Jason believed in the revelations in Dan 7–12, whereas the Hasmonaean propagandist exposed their falsity. Jason seems also to oppose the aggressive policies of the later Hasmonaeans. Indeed, those policies may be among the sins against which he felt he had to warn the Jews. In Part IV we shall argue that Jason wrote in the time of the later Hasmonaeans. Surely, then, one purpose of Jason was to refute Hasmonaean propaganda.

From the day that his father, Mattathias, rose in zeal to resist the persecution (I 2:15–26), Judas and his family were controversial. Wide groups among the pious opposed them. To meet that opposition, the Hasmonaeans must have developed their own propaganda long before the reign of John Hyrcanus I, the last period to be mentioned in First Maccabees. Thus, even if it is clear that Jason wrote to refute Hasmonaean propaganda, we have not yet shown that he wrote in reply to First Maccabees. At the end of Part IV, however, we shall be able to argue strongly for that conclusion.

Again unlike First Maccabees, the abridged history, written by a Jewish Greek, gladly notes that Jews can have beneficial covenants with Greeks, even when they are not military alliances, so long as there is no neglect of Jewish law. Such a beneficial covenant added to the merits of Onias III. Even outside Sparta and Rome righteous gentiles exist.

The combination of doctrines upheld in the abridged history cannot be made to fit the viewpoint of any Jewish group known to us.[53] This fact need not imply that the author was an isolated thinker in his time. Rather, it probably reflects our ignorance of the opinions which were circulating then among Jews.

Let us turn now to discuss the literary techniques used in the abridged history. The author and the translator of First Maccabees carried their rejection of Greek institutions so far that the translator refused to use the normal Greek language; the author took as his models the biblical historians, not Greek writers. Jason, who bore a Greek name and came from the Greek city of Cyrene, probably wrote his book in a Greek that was considered elegant at the time. Certainly the abridger wrote such Greek,

---

[53] Joseph Sievers has demonstrated this fact succinctly but in detail, for all groups except the Pharisees and the Asidaioi (*The Hasmoneans and Their Supporters from Mattathias to John Hyrcanus I* [Diss. Columbia University, 1981; Ann Arbor, Mich.: University Microfilms International, 1981], p. 11). The failure of our writer to uphold the exclusive legitimacy of the temple of Jerusalem would seem to exclude him from the Pharisees. As for the Asidaioi of I 2:41, 7:13, and II 14:6, we know little more of them than their name and hear nothing of them after the events treated in I 7 and II 14 (see NOTE on II 14:3–36).

with much alliteration and assonance and frequent plays on words. He also shows some avoidance of hiatus—that is, he avoids letting a word beginning with a vowel follow a word ending in one.[54] In his pursuit of brevity, the abridger has made superabundant use of participial constructions.[55]

Jason and the abridger seem to have followed the most popular stylistic and narrative patterns of Greek works of history. The accidents of text transmission have brought about the disappearance of most classical and Hellenistic Greek historical works, leaving us, besides Herodotus, only the austere Thucydides, Xenophon, and the censorious Polybius, who condemns the sensationalism of rival historians. Even the later compiler Diodorus Siculus is relatively austere. But Thucydides himself could produce sensational passages, and Polybius was guilty of the "sins" he condemned in others. If such tendencies could be found in the most serious of the Greek writers, all the more were they to be found in popular Greek history. The surviving fragments demonstrate that popular writers would play strongly upon the reader's emotions, with vivid portrayals of atroci-

---

[54] The abridger declares his intentions on style at 2:25 and 15:38–39 and at 2:31 says he aims to be brief. See also Jerome, *Prologus galeatus,* vol. XXVIII, cols. 593–604 Migne, quoted and translated at AB vol. 41, p. 16. On folio 13 verso of manuscript 542 appears a comment in Greek, comparing Second Maccabees to First Maccabees, as "displaying a character and peculiarity of style [*phraseôs idiôma*] and manner of composition [*lexeôn synthêkên*] tending more to the Greek."

"Second Maccabees was surely written in Greek, as is indicated by the vocabulary, which is quite different from that of the Septuagint translators. Apart from purely Greek expressions and terms which in themselves were foreign to Jewish thinking (e.g., *acropolis, ephêbos, paian, palaistra, petasos, triêrês*), conspicuous is the large number of words with prepositional prefixes and the considerable number of rare words or unusual word formations, which point to an author accustomed to the fine points of the Greek language" (Wolfgang Richnow, *Untersuchungen zu Sprache und Stil des zweiten Makkabäerbuches* [Diss. Georg-August-Universität zu Göttingen, 1966, unpublished], p. iv). Richnow's somewhat flawed dissertation is the most thorough study of the style of the abridged history known to me. Doran, *Temple Propaganda,* pp. 24–46, contains important observations on the syntax and style.

Some Greek authors were very consistent in avoiding hiatus (e.g., Isocrates and Demosthenes), and the rules they followed are well known. Others, however, allowed themselves many exceptions, and their rules concerning hiatus can be determined only by careful study. There may have been an evolution over time in the practices concerning hiatus. If we had more knowledge of Greek literature in the second and first centuries B.C.E., the abridger's practices might serve to give us his date. The mere fact that hiatus is far less common in the abridged history than in Thucydides (who is known not to have avoided it) suggests that the abridger had his own rule for avoiding it. His rule certainly allowed exceptions: he had no objection to hiatus after the word *kai* ("and") or after the *-ai* endings of the middle and passive voice; he frequently allows it after the *-ou* of the genitive case (Richnow, *Untersuchungen,* pp. 108–15; Richnow's survey of hiatus in Second Maccabees, however, is incomplete and contains minor errors; Doran, in *Temple Propaganda,* pp. 39–42, accepts Richnow's results and adds some good observations of his own).

[55] On the frequency of participles in the abridged history, see Ch. Mugler, "Remarques sur le second livre des Macchabées," *Revue d'histoire et de philosophie religieuses* 11 (1931), 419–23.

ties and heroism and with copious use of sensational language and rhetoric, especially when presenting the feelings of the characters.[56] In such theatrical histories, women often received great prominence. Some, but not all, such histories might pay great attention to visible and palpable interventions of the gods in history. The authors tend to express strong moral judgments and enjoy demonstrating that a malefactor received precise retribution, and they digress from their narratives to preach lessons to the reader.[57] The writer of a Greek popular history was free to show where his sympathies lay, to give exaggerated statistics, and to include minute descriptions of tortures and to compose sensational speeches of martyrs which no witness could have survived to report. Within the framework of the literary license allowed to such writers of history, it was still possible for them to give a faithful outline of the general course of events. Our study of Jason's methods will show him to have been in many ways a respectable historian even by modern standards.[58]

The abridged history contains echoes of Plato and Euripides and the orator Aeschines, and the writer uses metaphors derived from the terminology of the Greek theater.[59] Despite all these Greek elements, the abridged history is profoundly Jewish. Not only is it permeated with Jew-

[56] "Pathetic history," the term I used at AB vol. 41, p. 34 (cf. Bickerman, *Gott,* p. 147), is a modern expression, never used in antiquity. There is no good reason to assume that the patterns of sensationalism did not arise before the Hellenistic period. Rather, they seem to have been prevalent from the fifth century B.C.E. on. See F. W. Walbank, "Tragic History: A Reconsideration," *Bulletin of the Institute of Classical Studies of the University of London* 2 (1955), 4–14; "History and Tragedy," *Historia* 9 (1960), 216–34; Thomas W. Africa, *Phylarchus and the Spartan Revolution* ("University of California Publications in History," Vol. LXVIII; Berkeley and Los Angeles: University of California Press, 1961), 38–51; and especially Doran, *Temple Propaganda,* pp. 84–97.

[57] Women: Africa, *Phylarchus,* pp. 43–47. Phylarchus and Duris, two leading writers of "pathetic history," did not report divine interventions; see ibid., pp. 51–56. The *Suda* reports that Phylarchus wrote a work *On the Manifest Intervention of Zeus.* No fragments survive. It was not part of his historical narratives, and it may even have refuted another's assertion that such an intervention had taken place. Nevertheless, Greeks of the classical and Hellenistic ages were ready to see superhuman figures intervening in history (Herodotus i 87, vi 105, viii 36–39, 84; Dionysius of Halicarnassus vi 13; Pausanias i 13.8, 36.1, iv 32.4, viii 10.8–9, x 23.2; Plutarch *Themistocles* 15, *Lucullus* 10, *Aratus* 32; cf. Cicero *De natura deorum* ii 2.6–7). See Doran, *Temple Propaganda,* pp. 98–104; Pfister, "Epiphanie," PW, suppl. IV (1924), 293–94, 298–300.

On moral judgments as the function of history, see Diodorus i 2.2. Although precise retribution (as opposed to mere punishment) is found in the Hebrew Bible (I Kings 21:17–19, II Kings 9:30–37), it is far more characteristic of Greek narratives; see Doran, *Temple Propaganda,* pp. 94–95. On the Jewish and Greek models for the digressions to preach, see ibid., pp. 95–97.

[58] On Jason's methods, see Introduction, Part III; on other Greek popular historians, see Africa, *Phylarchus,* pp. 27–35, 38–51.

[59] Plato: see NOTE on 6:18–31 and NOTE on 7:22–29; Euripides: see NOTE on 4:1, *author . . . affair;* Aeschines: see NOTE on 15:38. For other poetic touches and allusions, see NOTES on 2:26, on 5:8, *fled . . . country,* and on 9:12, *Right . . . deity.*

ish religious doctrines; the writer on his own or by borrowing from his sources has made the narrative teem with scriptural allusions, almost as much as did the Hasmonaean propagandist.[60]

Strangely, in some aspects of chronology Jason, though he writes in Greek, emerges as "more Jewish" than the Hasmonaean propagandist, who wrote in Hebrew. Both give dates by the Seleucid era, but the Seleucid era had more than one form in the times of our authors and the events they narrated. The central government of the kingdom in its documents used the Macedonian form of the era, which numbered years beginning from autumn, 312 B.C.E. Jews of Judaea and Babylonians, in their local documents, used the Jewish and Babylonian forms, which numbered years beginning from the spring month of Nisan, 311 B.C.E. We do not know the exact calendar followed at this time by the Jews. It was not identical with the Babylonian calendar, and during the persecution it seems to have deviated from that calendar by two months. Normally, however, it deviated by no more than one month. Babylonian dated documents are abundant, and tables for converting their dates into Julian dates B.C.E. have been published. Hence, for the sake of convenience and simplicity, one can usually treat the Jewish form as identical to the Babylonian. Henceforth we need refer only to the Macedonian and Babylonian Seleucid eras (abbreviated as Sel. Mac. and Sel. Bab.).[61]

The Hasmonaean propagandist demonstrably used many dates on the Macedonian form as well as some dates on the Babylonian. A writer who gives dates on two distinct bases without ever calling attention to the distinction between them must be either indifferent to or ignorant of the distinction. Had the Hasmonaean propagandist been aware of the distinction, he would not have committed certain errors which we have exposed; clearly, then, he was ignorant of it.[62]

In Part III I shall present arguments to show that, unlike the dates in

---

[60] See the NOTES on the following passages: 3:30, 39, 5:17, 20, 21, thinking . . . soar, 6:30, ch. 7, 7:6, 9, resurrect . . . life, 14, 16–19, 17, 18, 22–29, 22–23, 23, 27, 28, 29, 33, 34, 36, 37–38, 8:3–4, 15, 16–23, 27, blessing . . . upon them, 30–32, 9:4–29, 4, 5–6, 7, 8, 9, 10, 11–12, 18, 10:10–38, 23, 24–28, 24, having assembled . . . marched, 26, 28, 29, 30–36, 30, 33–37, 34, 38, ch. 11, 11:8, 9, 10, 11–12, 13–38, 12:6, 22, 13:4, 17, 14:15, 35, 36, ch. 15, 15:2, 8, 12, 21, 22–24, 24, 27.

[61] On the forms of the Seleucid era, see AB vol. 41, pp. 21–24. On deviations of the Jewish form from the Babylonian, see also ibid., pp. 274–76. Tables: Richard A. Parker and Waldo H. Dubberstein, Babylonian Chronology (Brown University Press, 1956).

To convert Sel. Mac. dates to years B.C.E., subtract the number of the year from 313 if the date falls within or after the first lunar month after the autumnal equinox and before January 1; otherwise, subtract it from 312. To convert Sel. Bab. dates to years B.C.E., subtract the number of the year from 312 if the date falls within or after the first lunar month after the vernal equinox and before January 1; otherwise, subtract it from 311.

[62] Dates on both forms in First Maccabees: see Part II, section 3; errors in First Maccabees: see below, p. 58, and AB vol. 41, pp. 101, 315–19, 341–42, 343, 488. Josephus probably knew only of the Jewish or Babylonian Seleucid era and never suspected that another system could have been involved.

First Maccabees, those in the abridged history are consistently according to the Macedonian Seleucid era and that Jason was aware of the distinction. Here again is a contrast which can serve to discredit First Maccabees. Jason of Cyrene may even have denounced his rival's confusion; if so, the abridger omitted the passage.

The Macedonian Seleucid dates in First Maccabees outnumber the others to the extent that they supply the fundamental chronological framework of that work. We shall find in Part II, section 3, that the Hasmonaean propagandist drew those Macedonian Seleucid dates from a pagan source. Here, too, the procedure of Jason of Cyrene contrasts with that of his rival. Jason seems to have resolved to give his book the appearance of having a purely Jewish chronological framework. Where the author of First Maccabees repeatedly gives the dates of the accessions and deaths of the Seleucid kings, Jason gives dates only for events of *Jewish* history.[63]

A question immediately suggests itself: if Jason of Cyrene wished to present a fundamentally Jewish chronology, why did he not use the Jewish Seleucid era? There is more than one possible answer. First, he may have wished to use only the form of the era which was consistent with the documents in II 11; we shall see in Part III that those documents were vital for his chronology. Second, he surely was writing for an audience of Greek-speaking Jews, perhaps those of Antioch and the neighboring Greek cities of Syria, where the Macedonian Seleucid era was the sole form in use. Indeed, at two points the abridged history contains matter of interest to the Jewish community of Antioch: in 4:33–38 and in ch. 7, where the mother and her seven sons seem to come from Antioch.

What title Jason gave his work is hard to tell. The only clue is the description of the book's content at 2:19–22, which is much too long to be a title. The title may have been "The History of Judas Maccabaeus and

---

[63] On the chronological framework of First Maccabees, see Part II, n. 32. As for the abridged history, let us survey its chronology here. The thwarting of Heliodorus is dated in the high priesthood of Onias III (3:1). Not chronological indications but essential parts of the narrative are the following: the death of Seleucus IV and the accession of Antiochus IV (4:7); the quinquennial games at Tyre (a pagan ceremonial event; 4:18); the *Protoklisia* of Ptolemy Philometor (4:21). Where Jason gives intervals between events, they are always between events of Jewish history (4:23, 6:1, 10:3, 11:1, 14:1). At 5:1 the second departure against Egypt by Antiochus IV is a vitally important event in Jewish history because of its role in the prophecies of Daniel (Dan 11:30; see NOTE on 5:1). The death of Antiochus IV is dated at 9:1 only by its proximity to the purification of the temple (see pp. 58–59 and introductory NOTE on ch. 9). Even the dates of the official documents in 11:16–38 are surely taken from archives preserved by Jews and date events important for Jewish rather than Seleucid history. The date at 13:1 is one of Jewish history, probably deduced from Jewish evidence (see NOTE on 13:1). Obviously Jewish are the dates in 10:5, 12:32, and 15:36. At 14:4, Jason may have taken the precise Seleucid date of the accession of Demetrius I and, by adding the adverb *hôs* ("about"), turned it into the approximate date of the petition of Alcimus and his confirmation as high priest—a date of Jewish history.

His Brothers," but Jason's emphasis on the temple and his hostility to the brothers argues against it. On the other hand, the title of the abridgment may well have been "The Maccabaean History" (*Ta Makkabaïka*).[64]

Other aspects of the abridged history, including the dates at which Jason of Cyrene and the abridger wrote, require extended discussion. We shall treat them later. We turn now to Epp. 1 and 2. They, too, present complicated problems of interpretation, best left to the commentary, but something should be said about them here by way of introduction.

Ep. 1 is an authentic festal letter sent out by Jewish authorities in Jerusalem calling upon the troubled Jews of Egypt to repent of their sins and observe the "Days of Tabernacles in the Month of Kislev," the holiday commemorating the purification of the temple and the dedication of the altar by Judas Maccabaeus and his followers. The genre of the festal letter announcing a coming festival and often also calling for repentance can be traced back as far as II Chron 30:1–9 and is well attested in later antiquity among both Jews and Christians. Ep. 1 bears a date which can be shown to be equivalent to the year 124/3 B.C.E., and the content of the letter fixes its writing about November, 124 B.C.E. Within Ep. 1, at 1:7–8, an earlier authentic festal letter is quoted, which we may call Ep. 0. Ep. 0 was sent by the Jews of Jerusalem and Judaea to the Jews of Egypt in the reign of Demetrius II in 169 Sel. Bab., which can only be winter, 143/2.

The Jews of Egypt in 124 faced trouble, as Ptolemy VIII Euergetes II gained the upper hand in his dynastic war with his sister Cleopatra II, who had received Jewish support.[65] Moreover, the Jews of Jerusalem could accuse their brothers in Egypt of sin for continuing to tolerate and use, contrary to Deut 12:4–14, the Jewish temple of Onias IV at Leontopolis. Onias IV founded that temple before the death of Ptolemy VI (145 B.C.E.) and thus before the date of Ep. 0.[66] Ep. 0, calling upon Egyptian Jews to observe the commemorative festival of the temple of Jerusalem, can be shown to have been propaganda against the Oniad temple of Leontopolis, as much so as Ep. 1 with its allusion to the sin of the Egyptian Jews. Ep. 0 probably represents the earliest call from Jerusalem to Egyptian Jewry to observe the Days of Dedication.[67]

---

[64] Clement of Alexandria (*Stromateis* v 14.97) calls II Maccabees "the abridgment of the *Maccabaean History*" (*tên tôn Makkabaïkôn epitomên*), as if he knew that Jason's work bore the title *Maccabaean History*, but nothing else indicates that the unabridged work survived down to Clement's time. To write as he did, Clement need have known only the title used for II Maccabees in his own time and the fact that the book was an abridgment. See pp. 3–4.

[65] See NOTE on 1:1–5, *A good . . . time;* Elias Bickerman, *Studies in Jewish and Christian History,* II (Arbeiten zur Geschichte des antiken Judentums und des Urchristentums, Band IX; Leiden: Brill, 1980), 136–58; and my article in *Studies Smith,* Part III, pp. 113–16.

[66] See pp. 14–15.

[67] Allusion in Ep. 1 to sin: see NOTES on 1:7–8; Ep. 0 as earliest call: see NOTE on 1:7, *In the reign . . . 169.*

Unlike the abridged history, Ep. 1 is a translation from a Hebrew or Aramaic original[68] and can hardly have been an integral part of Jason's work or of the abridged history. Indeed, Ep. 1 contradicts the abridged history. Although both agree that the sin of Jason the Oniad brought the wrath of God down upon the Jews, in the abridged history the fatal sin of the Oniad was the establishment of a gymnasium and of other Greek-style practices at Jerusalem.[69] Epp. 0 and 1 say nothing whatever of the gymnasium and other Hellenistic patterns. The deadly sins of Jason the Oniad and his followers consist of his functioning at a schismatic temple in Transjordan and of his rebellion against the Seleucid empire and of the firing of the gateway to the temple and of the shedding of innocent blood (1:7–8). The abridged history, on the other hand, says nothing of the schismatic temple and fails to single out the others as deadly sins which brought God to punish the Jews. Indeed, we have found that the writers of the abridged history seem to regard Jewish temples outside Jerusalem as permitted.[70]

The senders of Ep. 1 say nothing of the victories of Judas Maccabaeus. Their silence implies that they did not believe that the victories were accompanied by miracles[71] and thus contradicts the abridged history. Also significant may be the fact that a resumption of the offering of incense is not mentioned in 1:8, in contrast to 10:3.[72]

Ep. 2 (II 1:10b–2:18) is written in idiomatic Hellenistic Greek.[73] Nevertheless, it cannot have been prefixed to the historical work by the author or by the abridger, for there are many contradictions between the two pieces of writing.[74] The account of the death of Antiochus IV at 1:13–16 contradicts the one at 9:1–28, both as to facts and as to chronology. The abridged history has its own peculiar attitude toward the temple at Jerusalem, asserting its superlative holiness but admitting the legitimacy of temples elsewhere. Ep. 2 strives to demonstrate that the temple at Jerusalem is the sole Chosen Place.[75] In the abridged history the writer undermines the Hasmonaean claims to royal and high priestly legitimacy. In Ep. 2 those aspirations are endorsed.[76] Ep. 2 can be shown to be another piece of anti-Oniad propaganda, forged (probably in Egypt) around November, 103 B.C.E., as a supplement to Ep. 1, in order to prove to the Jews of Egypt that God did indeed have His presence at Jerusalem and to call upon the Jews of Egypt, again sorely troubled, to observe the Days of

---

[68] See NOTE on 1:1–10a.
[69] 4:13–17.
[70] Pp. 13–17.
[71] See NOTE on 1:7–8.
[72] See NOTE on 1:8, *We brought . . . showbread.*
[73] But see p. 164.
[74] For proof of the rest of the statements in this paragraph see NOTE on 1:10b–2:18.
[75] 1:19–2:18.
[76] 2:17.

Dedication. Thus Ep. 2 again teaches the illegitimacy of the Oniad temple of Leontopolis.

There is a probable explanation for the presence of Epp. 1 and 2 at the head of Second Maccabees. It is that at some time after 78/7 B.C.E. someone wished to give the Jews of Egypt a scroll with narrative and festal letters for the Feast of Dedication analogous to the scroll of Esther for Purim and analogous to Third Maccabees for the Egyptian Jews' own festival of deliverance. By prefixing Epp. 1 and 2, which by then circulated together, to the abridged history, he accomplished his purpose.[77] Hence, Second Maccabees may be a liturgical text, even though Jason of Cyrene and his abridger had no intention of writing sacred scripture.

The contradictions between Ep. 1 and the abridged history are rather subtle and seem never to have been perceived until modern times. Even the contradictions between Ep. 2 and the abridged history on the death of Antiochus IV at first probably were unnoticed, but eventually they were felt to be intolerable and resulted in a drastic rearrangement of the narrative of the abridged history.[78]

Between 18 and 55 C.E. a Greek-speaking Jew, the author of Fourth Maccabees, took the abridged history as his source for a philosophical sermon.[79]

Josephus can be shown to have read the abridged history, but he was a descendant of the Hasmonaeans, and in almost every case he chose the version of the Hasmonaean propagandist in First Maccabees over the rival account, which he regarded as unreliable. The most important exception is Josephus' strong agreement with our writer on the high value of martyrdom, so that he echoes passages from II 6:18 – 7:42.[80]

---

[77] See p. 167 and AB vol. 41, pp. 551–57.

[78] See introductory NOTE on ch. 9.

[79] On the date, see Elias Bickerman, *Studies in Jewish and Christian History*, Part I (Arbeiten zur Geschichte des antiken Judentums und des Urchristentums, Band IX; Leiden: Brill, 1976), pp. 275–81. There is no reason to assume that the author of Fourth Maccabees had any other source for his narrative material. On the discrepancies between IV 3:19 – 4:4 and II 3, see introductory NOTE on II 3. The discrepancies between Fourth Maccabees and II 6:18 – 7:42 are all within the bounds of ancient literary license; see Moses Hadas, *The Third and Fourth Books of Maccabees* (New York: Harper, 1953), pp. 92–94 (first paragraph). On the discrepancy between the title in IV 4:2 and II 3:5, see Bickerman, *Studies*, Part I, pp. 278–80. The mention of Antiochus' march eastward at IV 18:5 need not have been derived from the unabridged work of Jason of Cyrene. Indeed, nothing else indicates that the author of Fourth Maccabees had more information than that in the abridged history. Jason of Cyrene and the abridger had good reason not to mention the king's march eastward at its proper place (see NOTE on II 9:1–3). A generation later, a reader of the abridged history would not have known of those constraints and, on reading II 6:18 – 9:1, could easily have inferred for himself that Antiochus marched eastward after the martyrdoms in II 6:18 – 7:42, for the king was not involved in the events of II 8. Correct accordingly AB vol. 41, pp. 56–57, n. 10.

[80] At AB vol. 41, p. 56, n. 10, I argued that Josephus might have known the unabridged work of Jason of Cyrene, but here in n. 79 I refuted most of the points I made there. The sole remaining hint that Josephus knew the unabridged work of

Greek-speaking Jews might consider Second Maccabees holy, but it could never be so for Jews whose language was Hebrew or Aramaic. The great wars of the Jews with Rome and the inroads of Christianity were to leave few Jews who could consider a Greek work as holy. Hence, although the theology of Second Maccabees was so acceptable to Jews that martyr tales in rabbinic literature are probably influenced by it, the book was preserved only by the Church. Already the author of Heb 11:35–36 alludes to the martyrdoms reported in II 6:18 – 7:42. Medieval Jews were glad to draw on Second Maccabees for inspiration when they rediscovered it in the possession of their Christian contemporaries.[81]

Jason of Cyrene are the documents of the Samaritans and Antiochus IV at *AJ* xii 5.5.258–64. But Josephus could have found the documents elsewhere. On the clues proving Josephus knew the abridged history, see AB vol. 41, pp. 55–61, and especially introductory NOTE on II 7; see also Appendix XI and NOTE on II 6:18–31 and on 5:14.

[81] On Heb 11:35–36, see AB vol. 36, pp. 203–4. Allusions to Second Maccabees in the Church Fathers and in early medieval Jewish works: AB vol. 41, pp. 26–27, n. 58. Martyr tales in rabbinic literature: TB *Giṭṭin* 57b, *Midrash Ekha Rabbah* 1:50 (to Lam 1:15). Other sources listed by Gerson D. Cohen, "The Story of Hannah and Her Seven Sons in Hebrew Literature," *Mordecai M. Kaplan Jubilee Volume* (New York: Jewish Theological Seminary of America, 1953), Hebrew section, pp. 109–10, n. 3. Cohen, pp. 109–22, gives a thorough treatment of these texts and a list of the medieval works based on them.

II. THE SOURCES OF FIRST MACCABEES AND THE ABRIDGED HISTORY

Our authors were competent historians, but as we shall see in Part IV, they wrote more than one generation after the events occurred. They had to draw on sources, whether written or oral. They were also literary artists and were not limited to cutting and pasting material given them by others. They could recast it and weave it into a harmonious whole.

Some of the sources which served our authors still survive, notably the documents they quote. But the surviving sources cover only part of the narratives of First Maccabees and the abridged history. To reconstruct the character of sources which no longer exist from the clues which survive is a hazardous task, full of guesswork. Nevertheless, an account written long after the events took place can be reliable only if there was reliable content in its sources. To assess the reliability of First Maccabees and the abridged history, we must accept the hazardous (and difficult) task of trying to track down their sources.

Both authors knew and reacted to Dan 7–12, which thus served them as a source. In Part III we shall consider the complicated problems involved.

Even surviving documents can lie or can have been forged. We begin our investigations, therefore, with the documents quoted in our books.

1. The Quoted Documents

Our authors show their interest in presenting a well-founded account in the way they quote official documents. Some of the documents are quoted in full, even when they do not entirely substantiate the authors' theories.[1] Such documents must be distinguished from the free compositions of our writers. The Greek and the Roman historians and those of the Bible all took the liberty of composing speeches, letters, or poems to fill out their narratives.[2] It might not be easy to distinguish such a composition from a

[1] See pp. 57–63, and NOTES on II 9:19–27 and AB vol. 41, pp. 357–58, 405, 501, 504–5.
[2] See Albin Lesky, *A History of Greek Literature* (New York: Crowell, 1966), pp. 325–26, 474, 476–77, 620, 624–25, 627, 768, 775; Günther O. Neuhaus, *Studien zu den poetischen Stücken im 1. Makkabäerbuch* (Forschung zur Bibel, Band XII;

real document. In fact, however, the documents of the Seleucid kings and chief ministers, of the Romans, and of the Spartans in their dealings with the Jews and with their commanders and high priests conform so well to the usages of the time and fit so badly the purposes of our authors that we have no trouble recognizing them as real sources,[3] not products of the historians' imaginations.

Quite different are the letters at I 5:10–15, 10:52–56, 70–73, and all the quoted speeches. All conform to the stylistic and rhetorical practices of our authors[4] and completely fit *their* purposes. There is no reason to assume that any of these pieces should have been preserved in Jewish archives. They are not real documents but literary compositions.

As for the documents which we have called real sources, at least one bears witness that it was kept on deposit at Jerusalem.[5] It would indeed be normal for archives of the Jewish nation, of the Council of Elders, of the kings, and of the high priests to have been kept at Jerusalem. Josephus bears witness to the existence of archives at Jerusalem, some of them kept by priests.[6] Hence, the documents attesting relations between the Seleucid, Roman, and Spartan governments and the Jews could well have been preserved in such archives.[7]

If the Hasmonaean propagandist took the documents from archives kept at Jerusalem, there is one strange fact. Official letters in the Hellenistic world were dated at the end.[8] The Hasmonaean propagandist was intensely interested in chronology, yet on no occasion was he able to give a date for an event in his narrative by copying it from an official letter. We may conclude that the archivists, in making file copies, did not copy the dates.

On the other hand, the documents at II 11:16–21, 27–33, and 34–38 all bear dates. The archivists who would have filed them worked in the time of the high priest Menelaus and could have followed different proce-

---

Würzburg: Echter Verlag, 1974), pp. 9–11; Otto Eissfeldt, *The Old Testament: An Introduction* (New York and Evanston: Harper & Row, 1965), pp. 12–18, 120–21.

[3] I 8:23–32, 10:18–20, 25–45, 11:30–37, 57, 12:6–18, 20–23, 13:36–40, 14:20–23, 24c–24k (=15:16–24), 15:2–9; II 9:19–29, 11:16–21, 22–26, 27–33, 34–38. See the NOTES on each piece and AB vol. 41, pp. 37–38.

[4] On how I 5:10–15, 10:52–56, 70–73 imitate biblical models in the manner of the rest of First Maccabees, see NOTES ad loc.

[5] I 14:49; cf. I 14:24k (=15:24).

[6] *BJ* ii 17.6.427, vi 6.3.354; *Ap.* i 7.31, 35; cf. *Vita* 1.6.

[7] Cf. Klaus-Dietrich Schunck, *Die Quellen des I. und II. Makkabäerbuches* (Diss. Greifswald; Halle [Saale]: Niemeyer, 1954), pp. 32–36, 87. The "Jews, the citizens," who were addressees of the letter at II 9:19–29, if it is authentic, may at the time have constituted the "nation," which could file its papers in the archives; or the letter may have been preserved among the documents of the high priest Menelaus, who probably presided over the community of Antiochenes at Jerusalem. See p. 85.

In refutation of the erroneous theory in AB vol. 41, p. 98 (last paragraph), see NOTE on II 11:13–38.

[8] See NOTE on 1:10a.

dures from their successors who filed the documents used by the Hasmonaean propagandist. As for the document at II 11:23–26, as a copy sent to the Jews of the king's letter to Lysias, it never bore a date. The letter at II 9:19–27 is undated, but by our reasoning it should have borne a date and should have been so filed in the archives because it is a royal letter directly to the Jewish Antiochenes, from the time of Menelaus. But if the copy in the archives bore the date, which was the time of the king's final illness (149 Sel. Mac.), Jason of Cyrene proved to his own satisfaction that the date was wrong and omitted it.[9]

2. The Poems in First Maccabees

Just as the song of Deborah (Judg 5) served the author of Judges as a source, so the Psalm of Alcimus lay before the Hasmonaean propagandist.[10] Other poems are embedded in his narrative.[11] Can any be contemporary with the events so as to have served that author as sources? All those poetic pieces fit the purposes of the Hasmonaean propagandist, and some could have been written only in his time.[12] All draw on biblical models in accordance with his principles of style.[13] Most add no new information to the narrative,[14] and those which do[15] give no more indication than the rest of being poems from the time of the events rather than cre-

[9] Dates omitted from copies sent to third parties: see NOTE on 11:23–26. Jason's proof of the date of the death of Antiochus IV: see pp. 57–63.

[10] I 7:16–17; see AB vol. 41, pp. 332–33.

[11] I 1:25–28, 36–40, 2:7–13, 49–68, 3:3–9, 45, 4:30–33, 9:21, 14:4–15. Neuhaus, *Studien*, is not a safe guide to the poems. Neuhaus, pp. 36–37, decides that other passages should be regarded as poems. Most, however, belong to the flow of the biblical style in the main narrative of the Hasmonaean propagandist: 2:44, 3:50–53 (essential for understanding the purpose of what is narrated in the prose of vs. 49), 4:38, 9:41. As for I 4:24, it follows the precedent of I Chron 16:34, II Chron 20:21, and reflects the Hasmonaean victory liturgy; see AB vol. 41, pp. 265, 286–87.

[12] Especially is this true of the blatant propaganda at I 2:49–68 (Hasmonaeans are to fight zealously for the Torah and are to aspire to the gifts of lordship, priesthood, judgeship, kingship, and prophecy; see AB vol. 41, pp. 7–8) and 14:4–15 (Simon's reign is past but was a golden age of peace and fulfillment of prophecy; see AB vol. 41, pp. 490–92).

[13] See AB vol. 41, NOTES ad loc.

[14] I 1:25–28, 2:7–13, and 3:45 have much the same emotional literary function as II 3:14(end)–21. In addition I 2:8 teaches the Hasmonaean lesson, that it was disgraceful not to resist the arrogant impious persecutor.

I 9:21 may be a quotation from a real dirge on Judas, but it is patterned on biblical stereotypes and adds no information.

Cf. Neuhaus, *Studien*, p. 217, paragraph headed "Typisierung."

[15] I 1:37–39 gives effects of the establishment of the Akra. One might argue that the verses contain only the author's inferences, some of them mistaken, but for all we know, they could equally well reflect information in a source.

I 3:5 and 3:8 tell how Judas acted early against Jewish sinners, daring even to enter the towns, a fact which may go beyond what is implied by Mattathias' accomplishments (2:44–48) and Judas' position as Mattathias' successor.

ations of the author. We may conclude, then, that the Hasmonaean propagandist composed them all[16] to rouse the readers' emotions over national disasters and triumphs and to preach the claims of Hasmonaean Simon and his descendants to princely and high priestly legitimacy.[17]

One must ask, why, then, did the Hasmonaean propagandist not write poetry on the first Hasmonaean high priest, Jonathan? A probable answer can be given. The vast majority of pious Jews agreed on the merits of Judas. Surely his achievements deserved a reward to him and to his family. Unlike Judas, Jonathan left descendants who might have pressed claims rivaling those of Simon's line.[18] Hence, our author, serving the interests of Simon's descendants, merely reports Jonathan's achievements but waxes eloquent and poetical over Judas and Simon.[19]

Except for the Psalm of Alcimus, the poems in First Maccabees are thus the same sort of thing as the speeches in classical and biblical works of history: they may reflect what was actually said, felt, and done; they may be drawn from sources; but they themselves are the product of the author's literary art.

Similar in purpose to the poems in First Maccabees are the numerous allusions to the language of biblical stories about hero-priests and hero-princes and kings in the narratives about Mattathias, Judas, and Simon (and only to hero-judges in the account of Jonathan). Indeed, the poems themselves are full of such allusions. The abridged history, too, contains many echoes of biblical passages, but none of hero stories. In First Maccabees, the allusions converge on the themes that Mattathias, Judas, and Simon are as deserving of the high priesthood as Phineas[20] and as deserving of judgely and princely power as Joshua,[21] Gideon,[22] Jephthah,[23] Jonathan (Saul's son),[24] Saul,[25] David,[26] and Solomon.[27] The allusions thus

---

[16] Correct accordingly AB vol. 41, p. 21. Cf. Neuhaus, *Studien*, pp. 104–10, 182–84, 215.

[17] Cf. Neuhaus, *Studien*, pp. 111–12, 220–23.

[18] I 13:16–19; J. *AJ* xiii 6.5.204, *Vita* 1.3.

[19] Cf. the improbable theory of Neuhaus, *Studien*, pp. 119–21, that the Hasmonaean propagandist shared the opinion of the Qumran sect, that Jonathan was a wicked priest!

[20] I 2:1, 15–26, 54; see AB vol. 41, pp. 6–7.

[21] Joshua is called a "Judge" at I 2:55 because Jonathan was equated with him! See AB vol. 41, pp. 240, 377, 381, 393, 395, 443. Echoes from the stories of Joshua in the narrative on Judas: see AB vol. 41, pp. 264, 265, 298. Jonathan equated with Joab: see ibid., p. 381.

[22] See ibid., p. 342.

[23] See ibid., pp. 295–96, 298. It is worth noticing that the Hasmonaean propagandist does not write strong echoes of Judg 11:14–24 at I 15:28–35. He did not want his reader to equate Simon with the unfortunate Jephthah!

[24] See AB vol. 41, pp. 247, 270, 421.

[25] See ibid., pp. 295, 342, 375. The author never suggests that Hasmonaeans could sin like Saul: though Saul failed to enforce the complete ban on the Amalekites, Judas wiped out the Baianites (I 5:5).

[26] See AB vol. 41, pp. 7, 235, 240–41, 242, 244, 246, 248, 251, 259, 260, 261, 263,

serve the purposes of the Hasmonaean propagandist, and they should not
be ascribed to an earlier source.

3. The Chronicle of the Seleucid Empire

Elias Bickerman discovered that in First Maccabees two different forms
of the Seleucid era are employed. Dates of royal Seleucid history are
reckoned according to the Macedonian Seleucid era (Sel. Mac.), which
ran from autumn 312 B.C.E. Dates of local Jewish history are reckoned
according to the Babylonian Seleucid era (Sel. Bab.), which ran from 1
Nisan (spring) 311 B.C.E. Bickerman correctly inferred that the author
drew on at least two sources: on a non-Jewish work dealing with Seleucid
history, which was dated according to the Macedonian Seleucid era, and
on Jewish records, works, or traditions, which were dated according to
the Babylonian Seleucid era.[28] However, for most of the dates in First
Maccabees it is impossible to prove that they are reckoned on one form of

---

264, 265, 266, 270, 284, 302, 321, 374, 522. There seem to be few if any echoes of
the stories of David in the narrative of the career of Simon (but cf. I 13:25 with II
Sam 21:12–14). The reason may well be that Simon in some respects outdid David.
When David was powerful enough to attack unconquered enclaves with Judaea, he
took the citadel of Jerusalem but not Gezer (see I Kings 9:16), whereas Simon, as
soon as he was free from Seleucid domination, took both. On taking the citadel,
David promoted the ambiguous Joab to be army commander, whereas Simon
promoted his virtuous son, John. At I 13:49–53 there are just enough hints of II
Sam 5:7, 9, and I Chron 11:4, 6–8, to make the well-informed audience of the Hasmonaean propagandist understand how Simon was superior. Again, Simon's vigorous
old age and charge to his sons to carry on his work (I 16:2–6) are in vivid contrast
to the conduct of the senile David (I Kings 1:1 – 2:10).

[27] Allusions to the stories of Solomon in the chapters on Simon: see AB vol. 41,
pp. 490, 491, 492. Like Solomon, Simon fortified Gazara (I Kings 9:15, 17; I
13:48). There may be an echo of I Kings 1:40 in I 14:11. The author's care, at I
14:14, to say that Simon "sought to fulfill the Torah" demonstrates Simon's superiority over the sinful Solomon (I Kings 11:1–11), just as I 14:4, 8–12, and Simon's
support of the poor in I 14:14 may be intended to contrast with the onerous taxes
and forced labor imposed by Solomon (I Kings 4:6–7, 5:2–3, 27–30, 9:15–22,
12:1–18). Simon's offer to pay 100 talents for the cities claimed by Antiochus VII
(I 15:28–35) contrasts with Solomon's cession of cities to King Hiram of Tyre for
120 talents (I Kings 9:10–14).

[28] Bickerman, "Makkabäerbücher," PW, XIV (1930), 781–84; Bickerman, Studies,
II, 142–44; Bickerman, Gott, pp. 155–57; AB vol. 41, pp. 21–24, 540–43. Cf.
Schunck, Quellen, pp. 16–19. At p. 19, n. 1, and pp. 28–31, Schunck wrongly argues
that the Jewish Seleucid era followed by the author of First Maccabees began 1
Nisan 312 B.C.E. He was driven to that conclusion especially because he regarded the
date at I 6:20 as correct. See, however, AB vol. 41, pp. 24, 315–18. On Schunck's
hypothesis, the Days of Dedication, as dated at I 4:52, would have occurred before
the writing of the letter at II 11:27–33; we have demonstrated the contrary (pp.
56–63).
We discussed the forms of the Seleucid era on p. 22.

the era rather than the other,[29] and some dated events can be viewed both as events of royal and as events of local Jewish history.[30]

Klaus-Dietrich Schunck discovered other evidence to confirm and improve Bickerman's theory and remove the ambiguities. Schunck observed that from a purely formal viewpoint the dates in First Maccabees fall into two groups:[31] dates of Seleucid history are so numerous as to form the chronological skeleton of the book and are given by year number alone.[32] With three exceptions,[33] dates of local Jewish history, if they have the year, also have the month and sometimes also the day. Only at I 1:29 does the Hasmonaean propagandist date a later event by a definite interval from a dated earlier one. The earlier date (at I 1:20) is clearly of a royal Seleucid event, and the interval can be shown to be derived from a source which used the Macedonian Seleucid era. The interval at I 4:28 lies between events in Judaea; we have argued that it is a piece of deliberate obscurity by the Hasmonaean propagandist to cover up embarrassing facts.[34] We can thus distinguish on an objective basis in First Maccabees between dates of royal Seleucid and dates of local Jewish history and can discern the styles of two different kinds of chronicles.[35]

Schunck went on to demonstrate that all the royal Seleucid dates are embedded in narratives of purely Seleucid history. Thus he was able to delineate a coherent and well-defined set of passages which the Hasmonaean propagandist must have derived from a history of the Seleucid empire. We shall call it the "Seleucid Chronicle." At least the following passages were drawn from it:[36] 1:1–10, 16–20, 29,[37] 3:27–37,[38]

---

[29] E.g., the date at I 6:20 is wrong and fits neither era (AB vol. 41, p. 315); the date at I 9:1 would be the same for either era.

[30] One could argue that I 1:54 dates both a royal act and an event in Judaea; see also AB vol. 41, p. 416, and Schunck, *Quellen*, pp. 19–20.

[31] Schunck, *Quellen*, pp. 20–24.

[32] I 1:7, 10, 20, 3:37, 6:16, 7:1, 10:1, 57, 67, 11:19, 13:41, 14:1, 15:10.

[33] I 2:70, 6:20, 13:41; the author probably derived all three dates by inference. See introductory NOTE on II 8 and AB vol. 41, pp. 315–18. The date at I 13:41 could have been inferred from the date in the document at I 14:27.

Strangely, at pp. 22–24, Schunck regards the date at I 13:41 as one of Seleucid history and does not count it as an exception; whereas, at p. 66, he assigns 13:41 to the author of First Maccabees.

Logically, there is only one way in which the date at I 13:41 could be a royal Seleucid date; if the Hasmonaean propagandist took it from the letter in I 13:36–40. But nowhere else was he able to get a date from a royal letter (see p. 29). See also AB vol. 41, p. 478. By the argument there, "Independence Day" for the Jews could have been 27 Iyyar, 170 Sel. Mac., identical to 27 Iyyar, 170 Sel. Bab. (mid-spring, 142 B.C.E.). But the more likely possibility for "Independence Day" is 3 Tishri, and 3 Tishri, 170 Sel. Mac. (Ocober 18, 143 B.C.E.) would be an impossible date because it came before the snowfall which balked Tryphon (I 13:22).

[34] On I 1:29, see NOTE on II 5:24–27. On I 4:28, see AB vol. 41, pp. 268–69.

[35] Schunck, *Quellen*, p. 31.

[36] Ibid., pp. 37(last paragraph)–43. Many more passages in I 9:32 – 16:18 probably drew on the Seleucid Chronicle. See Appendix X. The objections of Günther O. Neuhaus ("Quellen im 1. Makkabäerbuch?" *Journal for the Study of Judaism in the*

6:1–17,[39] 63(end), 7:1–4, 10:1–2, 48–58, 67–68, 11:1–3, 8–19, 38–40, 54–56, 13:31–32, 14:1–3, 15:10–14, 25, 37, 39(end). The Seleucid Chronicle was organized around the reigns of the legitimate kings of the Seleucid empire.[40] Drawing upon the Chronicle, the Hasmonaean propagandist was able to date acts of Antiochus IV in 143 (1:20) and in 147 (3:37) and probably also in 145 Sel. (1:29). The fact suggests that the Chronicle was an annalistic history, treating the kings' acts calendar year by calendar year. There is no way of determining who was its author.[41]

Did Jason of Cyrene use the same Seleucid Chonicle? Though the abridged history gives but few dates, we have argued that for much of his narrative Jason deliberately avoided doing so in order to protect the veracity of the book of Daniel from being challenged.[42] He also preferred to date only Jewish events,[43] few of which were to be found in the Seleucid Chronicle.[44] There are strong indications that Jason used the work. I have demonstrated that the date at II 14:4 must be reckoned on the Macedonian Seleucid era; Jason could well have derived it from the accession date of Demetrius I as given in the Seleucid Chronicle.[45] The account of the death of Seleucus IV at II 4:7 uses the very same euphemism which seems to have been used by the regime of Antiochus IV to refer to that event.[46] In addition, Jason may have found in the Seleucid Chronicle the details at II 4:21–22, 30–31, 5:1,[47] 9:1[48] and 29,[49] 10:11–13,

---

Persian, Hellenistic and Roman Period 5 [1974], 165–68) to Schunck's theory of the Seleucid Chronicle have no weight. There is no reason why a Greek historian of the Seleucid dynasty should follow the historical patterns of Jewish or Babylonian chroniclers; if the Hasmonaean propagandist gave the material he took from the Seleucid Chronicle an anti-Seleucid coloring, that is only to be expected.

[37] I 1:1–10 has been strongly recast from the Jewish point of view but still reflects Seleucid dynastic propaganda; see AB vol. 41, pp. 194–97, and Schunck, *Quellen,* p. 44. We have added I 1:29 (see n. 34), which was not listed by Schunck.

[38] The Hasmonaean propagandist has retouched the account in vss. 29 and 34–36; see AB vol. 41, pp. 251–52.

[39] Especially surprising in a Jewish source and natural for the pagan Seleucid Chronicle is I 6:11. On the other hand, Jewish legends must have contributed to the account at I 6:1–17 of the death of Antiochus IV, especially in vss. 1, 5–7, and the first half of vs. 8; see NOTE on II 9:1–3, NOTE on II 9:2; and AB vol. 41, pp. 307, 309–10. Also of Jewish origin is the king's speech in I 6:10–12.

[40] Further efforts to characterize the content and methods of the Seleucid Chronicle: Schunck, *Quellen,* pp. 46–49.

[41] Ibid., pp. 50–51.

[42] See pp. 63–69.

[43] See p. 23.

[44] Cf. Bickerman, *Gott,* pp. 165–66; Schunck, *Quellen,* pp. 84–87.

[45] See NOTE on 14:4, *he . . . 151.*

[46] See NOTE on II 4:7; the Athenian document, OGIS 248, was surely phrased to please Antiochus IV.

[47] But see NOTE ad loc.

[48] But see NOTE ON 9:1–3.

[49] But see NOTE ad loc.

13:24(end)–26, 14:1(end)–2, and perhaps also the details at II 4:38[50] and 8:10.[51]

We have deduced from II 4:7 that the Seleucid Chronicle treated the death of Seleucus IV. Another clue pointing to the same conclusion is the mention of Seleucus (IV) at I 7:1 as the father of Demetrius I, without any further explanation, as if the writer assumed his audience knew the earlier periods of Seleucid history. The Chronicle treated the reign of Antiochus VII at least as far as the death of Simon (January or February, 134 B.C.E.) and was used by the Hasmonaean propagandist and by Jason of Cyrene. We have no way of determining more narrowly when it was written.

4. The Memoirs of Onias IV

I have demonstrated elsewhere[52] how Josephus and Jason of Cyrene preserve material drawn from a propagandistic work written in Ptolemaic Egypt between 131 and 129 B.C.E. by the Jewish priest Onias IV (founder of the schismatic Jewish temple at Leontopolis in Egypt).[53] In

---

[50] The execution of Andronikos was an important event of the reign of Antiochus IV; see NOTE on 4:31–38.

[51] The king's thirst for money; see NOTE ad loc.

[52] See Jonathan A. Goldstein, "The Tales of the Tobiads," Studies Smith, Part III, pp. 85–123, and cf. AB vol. 41, pp. 57–59. I hold to my views notwithstanding the objections of Doran (Temple Propaganda, pp. 17–18). Doran has misstated my position. From evidence in Josephus, not from II 3:1, I concluded that Onias IV held his family was "the sole unbroken earthly link to the cult prescribed by God in the Torah" and that he believed the second temple at Jerusalem was not (or was not yet) the Place which the LORD chose as the exclusive site for His temple (Studies Smith, Part III, pp. 111–12). Doran was right, however, to point out the fallacy of my statement (ibid., p. 112), that II 3:1 "reflects a view . . . that the second temple is not, or is not yet, the place which the LORD hath chosen." I do not believe that Doran has refuted my demonstration that two sources lie behind the account of the thwarting of Heliodorus. One of those sources, Version B, assigns pivotal importance to Onias III, strangely mentions Hyrcanus the Tobiad, and has striking parallels in Third Maccabees. To my mind, these factors suffice to connect Version B with Onias IV; see introductory NOTE on II 3 and NOTES on the following passages: 3:1, 2, 24–39, 32–35. If Jason of Cyrene drew on the work of Onias IV for his account of the thwarting of Heliodorus, he could have drawn on it elsewhere, too.

Joseph Sievers (The Hasmoneans and Their Supporters from Mattathias to John Hyrcanus I [Diss. Columbia University, 1981; Ann Arbor, Mich.: University Microfilms International, 1981], p. 8, n. 251) finds that the unfavorable portrayal of Onias II at J. AJ xii 4.1–3.158–67 disproves my hypothesis on the authorship, date, and purpose of what I call the work of Onias IV. I disagree. I believe I established firmly the probabilities that Onias IV was the author and that he wrote from a pro-Ptolemaic point of view. If Onias II was disloyal to the Ptolemaic kingdom, Onias IV had to disown him, just as Jason of Cyrene, who believed that normally the Jerusalem temple and its priests were holy, had to disown the sinning priests, Jason, Menelaus, and Alcimus.

[53] See p. 15.

that work he treated his own career and his ancestors, especially his father, Onias III;[54] he touched upon their Tobiad kinsmen,[55] and upon the kings who ruled the Ptolemaic and Seleucid empires in the third and second centuries B.C.E. At least one scholar has noticed that a step is missing from my demonstration: I failed to show how the work by Onias IV might fit into the known Hellenistic and Jewish genres of writing.[56]

I cannot completely supply what is lacking. Unfortunately, what might have been the best parallels have not survived, and in their absence, one can only speculate. Nevertheless, the complete work of Onias IV may well have consisted of his *Memoirs* (*hypomnêmata*),[57] analogous to the lost *Memoirs* of Kings Herod I[58] and Ptolemy VIII[59] and of Aratos of Sikyon.[60] Of all three, the fragments are very scanty. Still, the *Memoirs* of Ptolemy VIII contained material on Ptolemy II,[61] and the *Memoirs* of Aratos probably contained a sketch of the history of the Achaean League in the period before his career.[62] The stories of the Tobiads Joseph and Hyrcanus and of the career, deposition, and death of Onias III similarly would be part of a sketch by Onias IV of the events which preceded his own career. As Aratos praised or blamed the Macedonian kings who affected the Achaean League,[63] so Onias IV praised Ptolemies and condemned Seleucids. As Aratus in his *Memoirs* defended himself against bitter criticism for having brought the Peloponnesus back under the yoke of the kings of Macedonia,[64] so Onias IV could have defended himself against criticism for his collaboration with the Ptolemies and for having founded a schismatic temple.

Characteristics of the work of Onias IV are great interest in Onias III, both in his lifetime and after his death, even to the point of exaggeration; friendliness to the Ptolemies and hostility to the Seleucids; sympathy for Ptolemy VI Philometor and intimate knowledge of his affairs; interest in the author's pro-Ptolemaic kinsman Hyrcanus the Tobiad, and, after Hyrcanus' death, in the further anti-Seleucid activities of his private armed force, the Tubiakenoi or Tubians; unfavorable portrayal of those who usurped the high priestly prerogatives of the Oniad line; and assertion of

[54] The man of II 3:1–35, 4:1–7, 33–38.
[55] See NOTE on 3:11.
[56] Arnaldo Momigliano, Review of *Studies Smith*, JTS 29 (1978), 216–17.
[57] See Erich Berneker, "Hypomnema," Der kleine Pauly, II (1967), 1282–83.
[58] J. *AJ* xv 6.1–3.164–74; FGH 236.
[59] FGH 234.
[60] FGH 231.
[61] In book iii; FGH 234, F 4 (=Athenaeus xiii 576e–f).
[62] See Jacoby, FGH, II D (Berlin: Weidmann, 1930), 654; cf. Polybius ii 40, where Polybius may imply that he takes his account of the early history of the league from Aratos' *Memoirs*.
[63] Plutarch *Aratus* 38.4, *Agis and Cleomenes* 37 (=*Cleomenes* 16). 3, Polybius ii 47.5 (=FGH 231, F 4).
[64] Plutarch *Aratus* 38.11; cf. *Agis and Cleomenes* 38 (=*Cleomenes* 16=FGH 231, F 4).

the doctrine that the second temple is not (or is not yet) "the Place which the LORD has chosen," so that Israelite temples elsewhere can have some legitimacy.[65] Probably derived, in whole or in part, from Onias IV are the following passages, as we show in our commentary: II 3:1-23, 26-28, 31-36,[66] 4:1-6, 23-50,[67] 5:5, 11-16, 23, 9:29, 12:17-18 (and perhaps 19-20), 35, 13:3-8, 15:11-16.[68]

Onias IV could view the Hasmonaeans only as usurpers. The Hasmonaean propagandist, relying on the Seleucid Chronicle and (as we shall see in the next section) on the Jewish common source of First and Second Maccabees, knew how tendentious and false were the *Memoirs,* at least in their treatments of the Hellenization and sack of Jerusalem and perhaps of other events, too. The Hasmonaean propagandist, however, may have drawn upon the *Memoirs* for later periods.[69]

5. The Jewish Common Source of First and Second Maccabees

We have shown that First Maccabees and the abridged history both drew on a Seleucid Chronicle. But the Seleucid Chronicle could supply only part of the two narratives; the details on internal Jewish matters could not have interested a historian of the Seleucid dynasty. Nor does it seem likely that Onias IV gave a detailed account of the glorious deeds of the Hasmonaean family. J. G. Bunge has taken the arguments of German predecessors and gone on to present an elaborate case to prove that a common Jewish source underlies the accounts of the career of Judas in First and Second Maccabees.[70] Most of his arguments for a common source are valid, but the characterizations of that source by Bunge and his predecessors are questionable, and their treatments are inaccessible to readers who do not know German. My own treatment in AB vol. 41[71] contains good points but is gravely impaired by its dependence on improbable hypotheses. Hence, there is good reason to lay before the reader yet another argument for a common Jewish source for the abridged history and for I 1:1 – 9:22. Let us henceforth call that hypothetical literary work the "Common Source."

[65] See NOTE on 1:7, *Jason . . . Kingdom,* and NOTE on 1:10b – 2:18.
[66] See introductory NOTE on II 3.
[67] See NOTE on 4:1-38 and NOTE on 4:23-50.
[68] See NOTE on 15:12-16.
[69] False treatments in the *Memoirs:* see my article in *Studies Smith,* Part III, pp. 121-23; possible use of the *Memoirs* for later periods by the Hasmonaean propagandist: see Appendix X.
[70] Jochen Gabriel Bunge, *Untersuchungen zum zweiten Makkabäerbuch* (Diss. Rheinische Friedrich-Wilhelms-Universität zu Bonn; Bonn: Rheinische Friedrich-Wilhelms-Universität, 1971), pp. 207-63; predecessors listed on p. 208, n. 2.
[71] Pp. 90-103.

Our sole evidence for the Common Source is in the astonishing extent of agreement and of verbal echoes discoverable in two such bitterly opposed histories. These agreements and echoes must be the foundation for our reconstruction of the Common Source; otherwise, we risk prejudging the nature of that work.[72] The agreements and echoes are between I 1:11 – 7:49 and II 4:7 – 15:36 and are treated in detail in the commentary.[73]

In no case do our two historians agree on the number of troops on either side in a battle, but that fact is no argument against the existence of the Common Source. Ancient authors were very free with such figures.[74] Jason may have deliberately made his numbers different from those in First Maccabees.

Our research reveals that the Common Source told of the establishment of a gymnasium and other Hellenistic institutions at Jerusalem by Jason the Oniad and held that God's resulting wrath brought war and persecution upon the Jews. The Source gave details of the sack of Jerusalem by Antiochus IV, the expedition of Apollonius the Mysarch, the imposed cult, and the sufferings of the martyrs, and went on to the great victories of Judas Maccabaeus.

We are entitled to use another guiding principle for reconstructing the content of the Common Source: the fact that both our authors found it inadequate for their purposes, so that each wrote his own work. We may expect that the Common Source did not concentrate single-mindedly on the greatness of the Hasmonaeans and did not work to prove their high priestly and princely legitimacy. We may also expect that the author of the Source was not intent on protecting the veracity of the prophecies in Daniel or on asserting the doctrine of the resurrection of the dead or on

[72] Thus Schunck (*Quellen*, pp. 52–74) believes that the Common Source was a biography of Judas (p. 68), characterized by an abundance of biblical allusions. Schunck took as his fundamental clue I 9:22. But the clue does not necessarily imply the conclusion. Philo wrote a *Life of Moses* on the basis of the last four books of the Pentateuch, but those books themselves are not a biography of Moses. See also pp. 31–32.

[73] For arguments demonstrating the existence of the Common Source, see the NOTES on the following passages: 4:1–38, 7–20, 5:1–23, 24–27, ch. 6, 6:10–31, ch. 7 (p. 300), ch. 8, 8:1, 2–7, 8–35, 9, 11–15, ch. 9, 9:1–3, 2 (*He had . . . the town*), 3 (*news . . . Nicanor*), 4–29, 10:1–2, 3, 4, 5, 6, 7, 8, 10–38, 15–23, 24–38, 24 (*a huge force . . .*), 11:1, 2–3, 5–6, 11–12, 13–38, 12:18–19, 20–25, 26–31, 32–45, 36, ch. 13, 13:1, 23, 14:3–36, 3–4, 3 (*Perceiving . . . secure*), 15:6–36, 22–24. The NOTE on ch. 3 and the NOTE on 3:24–39 prove the existence of the source of Version A, which the argument on pp. 39–40 shows to be identical with the Common Source (for we account for the absence of apparition stories from First Maccabees at p. 39). Other NOTES work from the assumption of the existence of the Common Source but do not demonstrate it, those on 4:11, 21–22, 5:27, 6:11, 18–31, 8:27, 10:1–8, 34–36, 12:1–9, 3–9, 10–31, 15, 29–31, 13:3–8, 24–26, 14:1–2, 17, 26–30, 37–46, 15:1–5, 12–16. At AB vol. 41, p. 100, I was wrong to state that vivid parallels to I 4:36–59 do not occur in the story of the Days of Purification at II 10:1–8.

[74] See NOTE on 8:24.

discrediting the Hasmonaeans. Indeed, we find, within the continuous series of events covered by both our writers, that one or the other deliberately omitted matter that probably stood in the Common Source. The Source told in detail of non-Hasmonaean martyrs[75] and war heroes[76] and touched on Hasmonaean blunders[77]—all matters omitted by the Hasmonaean propagandist.[78] The Source also told of the establishment of the Akra,[79] of Mattathias, of the Hasmonaean decision to wage defensive war on the Sabbath,[80] and of Simon's successful campaign in Galilee[81]—all matters omitted by Jason.

In the events narrated by both, the abridged history differs from First Maccabees in telling repeatedly of superhuman apparitions.[82] In view of what we know of the methods of Jason of Cyrene,[83] it is unlikely that he invented such reports. He must have found them in a source. Indeed, at least one of the apparitions is attested in a source contemporary with the events,[84] and so is the sword of II 15:15–16.[85] Since Jason drew on the Common Source for all the narrative in which the reports of apparitions are embedded, we may infer that the apparitions were mentioned already in the Common Source and that the beliefs of the Hasmonaean propagandist led him to exclude them as at best hallucinations.

Can we say of any matters which occurred before the Hellenizing reforms of Jason the Oniad and after the Day of Nicanor that they were treated in the Common Source? The allusion at II 4:11 renders it probable that the Common Source told of the treaty with the Romans, narrated at I 8:17–32 from a highly biased Hasmonaean point of view.[86] One might deduce from I 9:22 that the Source ended with the death of Judas.

The story of the thwarting of Heliodorus in II 3 draws on two sources, Version A and Version B. Version B came from the *Memoirs* of Onias IV.[87] Can we ascribe Version A to the Common Source? The kind of apparition mentioned in Version A occurred several times in the Source, and in the abridged history one apparition is presented in terms suggesting

[75] See NOTE on 6:10–31 and introductory NOTE on II 7 (pp. 299–300).
[76] See NOTE on 12:18–19 and NOTE on 12:32–45.
[77] See NOTE on 10:15–23 and NOTE on 12:20–25 and NOTE on 14:17.
[78] On other omissions of his, see NOTES on the following passages: 10:10–38 (the role of Seleucid officials), 12:3–9.
[79] I 1:33–38; see NOTE on II 5:24–27.
[80] See introductory NOTE on II 8.
[81] I 5:14–17, 20–23; see NOTE on II 12:10–31 and AB vol. 41, p. 85.
[82] 5:2–3, 10:29–30, 11:8–10; perhaps also 12:22 and 15:27; we shall also be able to assign 3:24–25, 29–30, to the Common Source (see pp. 39–40 and introductory NOTE on ch. 3).
[83] See Introduction, Part III.
[84] See introductory NOTE on ch. 11.
[85] See NOTE on 15:14–16.
[86] See AB vol. 41, pp. 357–60.
[87] See NOTE on 3:24–39 and introductory NOTE on ch. 3.

it was identical to the supernatural figure of Version A.[88] We may thus assume that Version A was drawn from the Common Source.

If First Maccabees is focused upon the Hasmonaeans, the abridged history, though it mentions other heroes, is focused upon Judas, Onias III, and the martyrs. The Common Source, in treating both Mattathias and non-Hasmonaean heroes, lacked the sharp focus of either work. If only for this reason, it is wrong to describe the Common Source as a "Biography of Judas."[89]

Rather, we should see how the Common Source, as reconstructed by us, fits into the tradition of Jewish historical writing. All the historical books of the Bible contain biographical material, sometimes covering a hero from birth to death. But in every case, the larger scheme of the work is not to narrate the life of a hero but to tell of an Age of Wonders when God was acting in history. Characteristically, a Jewish writer will show how the nation (or its ancestors) accumulated sin (or merit) and incurred punishment (or reward), often miraculously. When the writer records sin and punishment, he may go on to tell of repentance, divine forgiveness, and restoration of the repentant sinners.

We would do well to stress another point, since the contrary has been forcefully asserted.[90] Those Jewish writers of history who so stressed sin and merit as causal factors were not utterly blind to material causation. The authors of Kings and Chronicles abundantly attest the rebellions of kings Jehoiakim and Zedekiah against Babylon. Their narratives thus do not ascribe the Babylonian wars against the kingdom of Judah *solely* to violations of the Torah. Hence, if a passage such as II 5:11 gives Antiochus IV a rational motive for smiting the Jews (his belief that they were rebels), rather than leaving him as the blind "rod of God's anger,"

---

[88] See introductory NOTE on ch. 11.

[89] On Schunck's view, see n. 72. Bunge (*Untersuchungen*, p. 211, n. 13) may have had misgivings about calling the Common Source a "Biography of Judas." A complete biography would have begun with Judas' birth. No trace is left of such a story; though I 2:66 might have been drawn from a biography, the entire context is clearly a creation of the Hasmonaean propagandist. See n. 12. If the Common Source had been focused sharply on Judas, one might have called it a "biography" in the same sense that the memoirs of Nehemiah in the Bible are an autobiography: they trace the acts of the hero through a critical period.

[90] Bickerman (*Gott*, pp. 30–34) holds that "If a Jew wished to understand how the persecution resulted from the events of contemporary history, he had to make use of pagan sources." Without such aid, he thinks, neither the Hasmonaean propagandist nor Jason of Cyrene could have presented any other cause for the events than Jewish sin or gentile arrogance! His assertion is demonstrably false not only for the books of Kings and Chronicles but also for First and Second Maccabees, and it is false even for passages in those books which were not drawn from the Seleucid Chronicle. Bickerman's analysis of First Maccabees at *Gott*, pp. 30–32, neglects important facts. E.g., at I 6:55–61, the Jewish writer honestly admits that Antiochus V and Lysias were not defeated by the Jews and has them acting from rational motives in their withdrawal from Jerusalem; he also portrays them as *not* acting arrogantly against Jews who surrendered (I 6:49, 54).

there is no reason to hold that it does not belong to the Jewish Common Source.

The Common Source probably began, like the abridged history, with the thwarting of Heliodorus, the first miracle to occur in the time of the second temple, a miracle in response to the merit of the high priest or of the people. The Source traced an Age of Wonders (and Horrors) both inside and outside the Hasmonaean circle. It traced a record of sin, punishment, repentance, divine forgiveness, and restoration. If the wonders ceased, the author would bring his book to an end. We may assume that the Common Source ended with the death of Judas or perhaps with the wondrous death of Alcimus (I 9:54–56), for thereafter long years elapsed which contained nothing miraculous. It is thus best to regard the Common Source as yet another Jewish history of an Age of Wonders.

6. Chronological Sources for Events of Jewish History

We must now consider two difficult questions. What chronological scheme, if any, was used in the Common Source? And what sources or inferences served as the bases for the dates of purely Jewish events in First Maccabees and in the abridged history? Our reconstruction of the Common Source is necessarily hypothetical. The work itself is not available to be examined.

If the Common Source had contained a solid chronological skeleton, the author of First Maccabees would have had no need to go to the Seleucid Chronicle. Moreover, a sufficiently complete chronology in the Common Source would have served so well as a refutation of the prophecies of Daniel that it is hard to see how Jason of Cyrene would have drawn upon it. During the Age of Wonders, the puzzling prophecies of Daniel had been published and had played an important role.[91] A pious chronicler of that age could have been as reluctant as Jason of Cyrene was to give the sort of chronology that would make the puzzles conspicuous. The author of the Common Source may also have written so late that many of the dates had been forgotten. Indeed, the Hasmonaean propagandist and Jason, competent historians, used official documents and the Seleucid Chronicle to correct or supplement the account in the Common Source. Probably, then, both authors knew that the Source, though generally reliable, was written late enough to be lacking some details of chronology.

We cannot infer, from the silence at I 9:5–18, that the Common Source gave no date for the death of Judas. The Hasmonaean propagandist may have chosen to omit the exact dates of the deaths of his heroes, Judas,

---

[91] Jason of Cyrene believed devotedly in the prophecies of Dan 7–12; see Introduction, Part III. On those prophecies, see AB vol. 41, pp. 42–51.

Jonathan, and Simon.[92] Certainly, however, the Common Source gave no absolute dates for the sack of Jerusalem by Antiochus IV, for the expedition of the Mysarch,[93] for the king's decrees imposing changes on the Jews' religion,[94] and for the victory over Nicanor in the reign of Demetrius I.[95]

Of the two dates for Jewish events in the abridged history, the one at II 13:1 was probably inferred from mention of the sabbatical year in the Common Source,[96] and the one at II 14:4 from the Seleucid Chronicle.[97] The reference to the sabbatical year at I 6:49, 53, also came from the Common Source. The Hasmonaean propagandist probably derived by inference the dates at I 2:70, 6:20, and 13:41.[98]

Did the Common Source give any dates? The remaining possibilities evidenced by First Maccabees and the abridged history are few:

The year of the desecration of the temple altar by the Abomination of Desolation is given at I 1:54 and was known to Jason,[99] although there may have been controversy over whether the crucial act of desecration occurred on 15 or on 25 Kislev.[100] Thus, the date probably stood in the Common Source, and Jason may have omitted it because it was associated with the Abomination of Desolation, for him an enigmatic concept.[101] The date also was the point of departure for problematic prophecies in Daniel,[102] and Jason may have omitted it to avoid evoking challenges to the seer's veracity.

Similarly, it is probable that the Common Source gave the year of the Days of Dedication (=Days of Purification; I 4:52), and Jason's narrative implies a different date only because Jason found "documentary proof" that the date was wrong.[103] Jason gave a two-year interval between

[92] See AB vol. 41, p. 524.

[93] Sack: see NOTE on 5:1–23; expedition: see NOTE on 5:24–27.

[94] The Hasmonaean propagandist would have presented the date, if available, so as to expose the falsity of Dan 7:25: Judas defeated Nicanor, Gorgias, and Lysias and gained effective control over Judaea long before three and one half years elapsed. I shall show in my commentary on Daniel that in 7:25 the years are measured from the issuance of the king's decrees; correct accordingly AB vol. 41, p. 42.

[95] See NOTE on 15:6–36.

[96] See NOTE on 13:1.

[97] See NOTE on 14:4, he . . . 151.

[98] See n. 33.

[99] See pp. 57–63; the argument there supersedes AB vol. 41, p. 51, n. 35.

[100] In rabbinic literature, there are controversies over when an object like the meteorites of the Abomination of Desolation becomes an idol so as to be forbidden to Israelites (and a desecration to the temple altar). Does it do so immediately? Or only after it has been worshiped? See M. 'Abodah zarah 4:4; TB 'Abodah zarah 51b–52a; To. 'Abodah zarah 5(6):4.

I shall show in my commentary on Daniel that the seer at 8:14, 9:27, and 12:7, 11–12 measured from 25 Kislev; correct accordingly AB vol. 41, pp. 43, 224.

[101] See NOTE on 6:4–5.

[102] See nn. 94, 100.

[103] See Introduction, Part III, section 1.

the desecration and the purification of the temple,[104] an interval agreeing with no prophecy in Daniel. Clearly, for believers, the interval between the events, by itself, did not menace their faith. The author of the Common Source could thus have included the dates of both events and probably did so.

The date of Bacchides' arrival at Jerusalem (I 9:3) may have stood in the Common Source.[105] The author of the Source, himself a historian needing documents, may have had one giving the date of that event but none for the death of Judas.[106]

The date at I 9:54, too, may have stood in the Common Source, and the author may have chosen to give the date of Alcimus' sin against the temple court rather than that of the high priest's death, especially if the date of the desecration of the temple was in the Common Source but not that of the death of the desecrator, Antiochus IV.

The evidence thus shows that the dates at I 1:54 and 4:52 probably, and those at I 9:3 and 54 possibly, stood in the Common Source. Certainty is impossible. One can, however, demonstrate that the Hasmonaean propagandist could hardly have derived those dates either by inference from the ones given in the Seleucid Chronicle or by guesswork.[107]

---

[104] 10:3.

[105] The date at I 9:3 can hardly be Macedonian Seleucid, derived from the Seleucid Chronicle, as argued by Bunge (*Untersuchungen*, p. 373). As far as we know, the Seleucid Chronicle gave dates for royal accessions and deaths and royal expeditions, but not for campaigns by subordinates. If the Seleucid Chronicle had dated Bacchides' expedition, it would have done so by the time of its departure from Syria, not by that of its arrival at Jerusalem. In support of his thesis, Bunge (ibid.) urges that all important expeditions of the imperial army in First Maccabees have Macedonian Seleucid dates, citing 1:20, 3:37, 6:20, and 7:1. Of these, 6:20 does not contain a Macedonian Seleucid date but an error (see AB vol. 41, pp. 315–18), and 7:1 does not date the expedition of Nicanor.

[106] Panic provoked by Bacchides' arrival could have led to religious rituals (see p. 46) which might have been recorded in the temple archives.

[107] The Hasmonaean propagandist's procedure with the Seleucid Chronicle is clear: when he takes a date from there, he quotes an entire context, so that the date always applies to a royal Seleucid event, never to a local Jewish one. Between dated royal events, he puts those Jewish events which he thinks occurred in that interval. Most of these intervening Jewish events he leaves undated. If some few Jewish events bear dates in First Maccabees, there must be a special reason. The simplest explanation is that the Hasmonaean propagandist had Jewish sources for those dates. Let us consider them one by one.

The date of the desecration in 145 Sel. at I 1:54 stands between what is probably the royal Seleucid date 145 (at 1:29; see NOTE on II 5:24–27) and the royal date 147 Sel. (at 3:37). If the Hasmonaean propagandist (as well as Jason) had no dated Jewish sources, but only the Seleucid Chronicle and a Jewish story of the events in their sequence, by what criterion could he put the desecration in 145 rather than in 146 or even in 147 Sel.? Though the Seleucid Chronicle for 145 Sel., after telling of the Mysarch's expedition, may have spoken of the royal decrees (I 1:44–51), there was nothing to compel its author to treat the erection of the Abomination of Desolation in the Jews' temple. In any case, the desecration occurred in the Kislev after the expedition of the Mysarch and in the Seleucid Chronicle would have been recorded in 146 Sel. (Mac.). Even if the Hasmonaean propagandist had known that the three

We still must ask: What sources could have served the author of the Common Source and Jason and the Hasmonaean propagandist for purely Jewish events and their dates? Omitting the dates which we know our authors probably derived from the Seleucid Chronicle or by inference, as well as the one at I 14:27 (which is part of a document), we can list the following absolute dates, taking note of their patterns:

1:54 (imposition of the Abomination of Desolation on the temple

---

and one half years of Daniel ended with the beginning of the sabbatical year, the propagandist dated the sabbatical year in 150 Sel. (see AB vol. 41, pp. 315–18), and three and one half years before that would not be 145 Sel.

If I am wrong about the source of the date at I 1:29, and it, too, had somehow to be inferred by the Hasmonaean propagandist, the situation is still worse: by what criterion could he have excluded 144 Sel. as the year of the Mysarch's expedition and the desecration?

The date of the dedication in 148 Sel. at I 4:52 stands between the king's march eastward in 147 (at 3:37) and his death in 149 (at 6:16). By what criterion did the Hasmonaean propagandist put the dedication in 148 rather than in 147 or 149? One might suggest that he did so because the Seleucid Chronicle reported the lapse of a year mentioned at I 4:28. But the one-year lapse is probably the effort of the Hasmonaean propagandist to avoid reporting embarrassing facts (see AB vol. 41, p. 268). If he could have reported that the dedication occurred in 147 Sel., there would have been no embarrassing facts. Could he have used as chronological evidence the letter preserved at II 11:27–33? For him, with his ignorance of the Macedonian Seleucid era, that document would have dated the end of Lysias' expedition in Adar (the equivalent of Xanthicus), the twelfth month of the year, in 148 Sel.; since the dedication occurred later and in Kislev, the ninth month of the year, he would have had to put it in 149 Sel.!

The Hasmonaean propagandist's ignorance of the Macedonian Seleucid era gave him trouble in I 7–9. From the Seleucid Chronicle he learned that Demetrius I became king in 151 Sel. (Mac.), but he did not know that the date was still 150 Sel. Bab. (autumn 162 B.C.E.). Therefore, he was forced to imply that Nicanor, commander under Demetrius I, was defeated in 151 Sel. at the earliest, though the Day of Nicanor came in 150 Sel. Bab.; see AB vol. 41, pp. 341–42. The Hasmonaean propagandist was correct in narrating the Jewish embassy to Rome after the defeat of Nicanor (see ibid., p. 346), even though it was hard to squeeze it into the "few days" which seemed to remain in Judas' lifetime (see ibid., p. 343). The brevity of the interval was embarrassing and hard to believe. Only solid evidence could have forced it upon the Hasmonaean propagandist. The next date, the one at I 9:3, of Bacchides' arrival at Jerusalem, must have been firmly established, surely by being recorded in a source trusted by the propagandist.

The date at I 9:54 of Alcimus' decision in 153 Sel. to modify the temple court is close to no date from the Seleucid Chronicle. Before it stands the accession of Demetrius I in 151 (7:1) and after it the landing of the pretender Alexander Balas at Ptolemais in 160 Sel. (10:1). By what criterion could the Hasmonaean propagandist have assigned it to 153 Sel. unless he found the date in a trusted source?

Bunge (Untersuchungen, pp. 372–75, 383–84) argued that all Jewish year dates in I 1:1 – 9:22 were guesses or inferences from dates in the Seleucid Chronicle. At the beginning of this note we described what can be known of how the Hasmonaean propagandist used the Seleucid Chronicle. Bunge's theory is untenable, if only because he asserts, without good reason, that the Hasmonaean propagandist proceeded otherwise. In refutation of Bunge (Untersuchungen, pp. 375–78), see AB vol. 41, pp. 268–69, 273–81; his pp. 278–82 rest on chronological and exegetical errors; for the correct interpretations, see my NOTES on the passages cited by him.

altar): "On the fifteenth day of Kislev in the year 145" (day, month name, year).

4:52 (the Days of Dedication): "On . . . the twenty-fifth day of the ninth month [that is, the month of Kislev], in the year 148" (day, month number, month name, year).

9:3 (arrival of Bacchides at Jerusalem): "In the first month of the year 152" (month number, year).

9:54 (Alcimus' order to modify the inner court of the temple): "In the year 153, in the second month" (year, month number).

10:21 (Jonathan begins to serve as high priest): "In the seventh month of the year 160, on the festival of Tabernacles" (month number, year, festival [here equivalent to day]).

13:51 (Jews occupy the Akra): "On the twenty-third day of the second month, in the year 171" (day, month number, year).

16:14 (Simon and his sons come to Jericho): "In the year 177, in the eleventh month, which is the month of Shebat" (year, month number, month name).

Striking is the absence of uniformity, in contrast to the consistent formulation in the Seleucid Chronicle. One may infer that no single writer is responsible for all these dates, that the Hasmonaean propagandist has taken them from several sources.

The month and day dates of the Days of Purification (Ḥanukkah; I 4:52, 59; II 10:5) and of the Day of Nicanor (I 7:43, 49; II 15:35) were kept alive in the national memory by annual observance.[108] Our authors needed no written source for them, and perhaps even the related date at I 1:59 could have been drawn from oral tradition. Also preserved by annual observance were the day and month of the Jewish occupation of the Akra.[109]

There is one event in the abridged history which was not commemorated by an anniversary celebration and yet is dated within the Jewish year, though no year number is given: the return to Jerusalem of Judas and his men at Pentecost from Transjordan (II 12:31–32).

We should also examine the chronological indications in First Maccabees and the abridged history which are not absolute dates but intervals between two events. Of these, we have shown how our authors derived by inference or by preconception the ones at I 4:28,[110] 7:50;[111] II 10:3,[112] and 14:1.[113] I 1:29 probably represents a modification of what was in the Seleucid Chronicle.[114] The rest of the measured intervals are as follows:

108 Both are listed in *Megillat Ta'anit*.
109 It is listed in *Megillat Ta'anit*.
110 See AB vol. 41, pp. 268–69.
111 See AB vol. 41, NOTES on 7:43 and 50.
112 See pp. 57–63.
113 See NOTE on 14:1–4.
114 NOTE on 5:24–27.

II 4:23: "Three years had passed" (between the assumption of the priesthood by Jason the Oniad and Menelaus' mission as his ambassador to the king).

I 9:57: "The land of Judah was undisturbed for two years" (between the death of Alcimus and Bacchides' last effort to arrest Jonathan and his men).

We may add the note of near simultaneity between the purification of the temple and the death of Antiochus IV (II 9:1), probably drawn from the Common Source.[115]

This is an extremely peculiar collection of dated events. Those of I 9:54 and 10:21 involve both the high priest and the temple; those of I 1:54, 4:52; II 9:1, and 12:31–32[116] involve the temple; and those of I 16:14 and II 4:23 involve the high priest. Beginnings or ends of terms as high priest are found at I 9:54, 10:21, 16:14, and II 4:23. Other events can be brought into the same categories: the Akra of I 13:51 dominated the temple[117] and was captured by an army under the command of the high priest; the arrival of Bacchides at Jerusalem (I 9:3) must have frightened the people and the priests and probably occasioned the offering of special sacrifices and perhaps also a public fast.[118]

Josephus used a list of high priests which also gave the number of years each held office, running at least from Menelaus through the Hasmonaean Antigonus. Such a list, combined with the information in the document at I 14:27, could have yielded what we have in I 9:54, 10:21, 16:14, and (if it included Jason the Oniad) II 4:23.[119]

Should we look farther for possible chronological sources? The task can only be guesswork. As we shall see, the Common Source must have been written before 130 B.C.E.[120] Living memory could have provided its author with some of the dates. The importance of I 1:54 and 59 and 4:52 for the prophecies of Daniel[121] meant that some believers and some skeptics should have remembered the dates. The author of the Common Source himself might have remembered the month and year of the sin and death of Alcimus (I 9:54) if he viewed them as the last events of the Age of Wonders. Hasmonaean family tradition, if not living memory, might have provided the Hasmonaean propagandist with the two years of 9:57

---

[115] See pp. 57–59.
[116] See the parallel text, I 5:54.
[117] I 1:33–36, 4:41, 6:18, 14:36, and AB vol. 41, pp. 213–19.
[118] See I 3:42–54; II 10:25–26, 13:10–12, 14:15.
[119] See AB vol. 41, pp. 569–70; I demonstrate there that the list which lay before Josephus did not recognize Alexander Balas as a legitimate king able to appoint a high priest and reckoned Jonathan's high priesthood from his appointment by Demetrius II. But the Hasmonaean propagandist could have had a list drawn up according to Hasmonaean bias, recognizing Balas as legitimate.
[120] See below, section 7.
[121] See AB vol. 41, pp. 43–47, as corrected below, pp. 89–90, 92–94.

and with the date on Tabernacles in 10:21 and perhaps even with the year number there. He could have drawn the date at I 16:14 either from living memory or from the chronicle of the high priesthood of John Hyrcanus. On the other hand, it is harder to believe that living memory preserved what we have in I 9:3 and II 4:23.

Persian and Hellenistic kings are known to have kept running court journals in which, day by day (with accurate dates), the king's acts were recorded,[122] and conceivably the chronicle of the high priesthood of John Hyrcanus (mentioned at I 16:24) was such a court journal.[123] Could the high priests from Jason the Oniad down through Simon have kept dated journals so as to preserve all the dates we have concerning themselves and the temple?[124] A journal of the high priesthood of Jason the Oniad *may* have lain before the author of the Common Source so as to tell him of that Hellenizing priest's career and so as to give him the interval at II 4:23. Dates in the Common Source from the momentous decade of the pontificate of Menelaus were few, with none for the sack of Jerusalem by Antiochus IV or for the reception at Jerusalem of the decrees imposing religious changes. The fact suggests strongly that the author of the Common Source could draw on no such journal from Menelaus. The date at II 12:31–32 may have been transmitted by living memory. On the other hand, the dates at I 9:3 and 54 *might* have been drawn from a journal of the high priesthood of Alcimus.

Can the accounts of the careers of Jonathan and Simon in I 9:23 – 16:17 be based on high priestly journals?[125] That is most improbable, so few are the dates there, and so scarce is any information other than what could have been derived from the Seleucid Chronicle and from the quoted documents.[126]

---

[122] See Ulrich Wilcken, *"Hypomnêmatismoi," Philologus* 53 (1894), 110–20; Bickerman, "Testificatio Actorum," *Aegyptus* 13 (1933), 349–55; Guy T. Griffith, "Ephemerides," *OCD*², 386–87.

[123] Cf. Bickerman, *Gott,* p. 145. However, the chronicle of John's high priesthood need not have been a court journal. A literary author could have written the chronicle at the command of John (as Alexander the Great had Callisthenes write a history of his feats) or on his own initiative (as Ptolemy I wrote a history of Alexander; see Lionel Pearson, *The Lost Histories of Alexander the Great* [Philological Monographs Published by the American Philological Association, no. XX, 1960], pp. 22–49, 188–211). On the whole, I think a literary work is more likely than a court journal for the chronicle of John's high priesthood: if the Hasmonaean propagandist had had to refer his reader to a bulky court journal, with long sequences of boring routine entries, he would have gone on to write a readable literary history of John.

[124] Scholars have made the suggestion, especially for the high priesthoods of Jonathan and Simon; see Schunck, *Quellen,* p. 74, n. 2.

[125] See n. 124; Schunck (pp. 74–79) assumes that the answer to the question is "yes."

[126] See Appendix X.

7. When Was the Common Source Written?

The Common Source must have been written after the death of Judas Maccabaeus, at a time when it was no longer easy to determine the dates of the sack of Jerusalem by Antiochus IV, the expedition of the Mysarch, the publication of the decrees imposing changes on the Jews' religion, and the great victory at Adasa over Nicanor.[127] The author seems no longer to have been able to give a precise sequence for events of 164 and 163 B.C.E.[128] Nevertheless, he wrote when there was still accurate memory of the general course of events and of the names even of minor heroes and "persecutors."

If what I have called "story 3" of II 7 stood in the Common Source and was already then presented as an anti-Hasmonaean counterpart to the stories of Mattathias and his sons, the Common Source must have been written after Simon's death, which occurred in January or February of 134 B.C.E.[129] It could hardly have been written much later, and the accuracy of the content suggests an earlier date. The high priest Alcimus probably would have prevented publication of the Common Source in Judaea between the time of Judas' death and his own in the spring of 159 B.C.E. After the death of Alcimus, the Age of Wonders was clearly over. Long years followed, with no persecutions and no miraculous victories, and with no high priest in office to suppress an account which included heroic exploits of Hasmonaeans. With as yet no Hasmonaean rousing controversy by holding the high priestly office, most pious Jews would welcome the content of the Common Source. The survivors of the great events would want a record of them, as would the younger generation. Hence, the Common Source probably was written between May, 159, and October, 152 B.C.E.

Jonathan, as the first Hasmonaean high priest, already faced pious opposition.[130] The Common Source had no Hasmonaean bias. Could a nonpartisan pious Jew have written the Common Source in the high priesthood of Jonathan or Simon? We must concede that is a possible date for the writing, but less probable than the earlier period we have proposed. In any case, the Common Source was probably written between mid-159 and 132 B.C.E.

There is no real way to determine who was the author. A plausible guess is that he was Eupolemus the historian, who may well have been identical with Eupolemus the ambassador (I 8:17).[131]

127 The Common Source did not give the year of the victory; see n. 107.
128 See pp. 67–68.
129 See introductory NOTE on II 7.
130 See AB vol. 41, pp. 64–71.
131 Ibid., p. 359; Schunck, Quellen, pp. 72–74.

8. The Legendary Source

Historians in antiquity felt free to compose speeches and dialogue and frequently showed where their sympathies lay. We shall find when we study the historical methods of Jason of Cyrene that it is unlikely he went beyond those bounds. My study of his methods has convinced me that he never invented episodes or willfully distorted the order of events but always based his accounts on evidence.[132]

This inference of mine has driven me to postulate that Jason of Cyrene in II 13 also drew on what I call the "Legendary Source."[133] Rather than assume the existence of yet another source, others may prefer to abandon my theory on Jason's methods, but I consider it to be well established.

The Legendary Source need not be regarded as a mere device invented by me to solve the problems of II 13. Much of the material in II 6:18 – 7:41 is too anti-Hasmonaean to have stood in the Common Source[134] yet (if I am right) cannot be the invention of Jason. He could well have found it in the Legendary Source. There, too, he may have found the details of the "multiple deaths" of Antiochus IV (II 9:5–10).[135]

Clues for assigning material to the Legendary Source rather than to the Common Source would include demonstrable distortion of the real course of events to conform with the prophecies of Daniel and an anti-Hasmonaean tendency. The Legendary Source was written so late that few if any who lived through the events were alive to refute the chronological distortions, probably in the high priesthood of John Hyrcanus.

We could thus assign the following to the Legendary Source: much if not all of the story of Eleazar (II 6:18–31); one of the three stories which seem to underlie II 7:1–41;[136] and much if not all of II 9:3–9.

TABLE OF PROBABLE SOURCES
FOR EACH PASSAGE IN FIRST MACCABEES
AND IN THE ABRIDGED HISTORY

We may sum up our inferences as to the sources used by our writers in the following table. The arguments for assigning passages in the abridged history to the source or sources listed in the source column can be found in the commentary or in the section of Part II of the Introduction dealing

[132] See Introduction, Part III, section 1.
[133] See introductory NOTE on II 13.
[134] See NOTE on 6:18–31 and introductory NOTE on II 7.
[135] See NOTE on 9:4–29.
[136] See NOTE on 6:18–21 and introductory NOTE on II 7.

with the listed source. The poems in First Maccabees are treated in Part II, section 2. The arguments for the sources of I 9:23 – 16:24 are in Appendix X. References to arguments for the sources of I 1:1 – 9:22 are given in the endnotes.* The names of the sources have been abbreviated as follows:

CS – Common Source; Sel. Chr. – Seleucid Chronicle; LS – Legendary Source

Passage	Source
I 1:1–10	Sel. Chr.[137]
11–15	CS[138]
16–20	Sel. Chr.[139]
20–24	Sel. Chr. and CS[140]
25–28	Hasmonaean propagandist (poem)
29–40	CS[141]
29	Date inferred by Hasmonaean propagandist from Sel. Chr.[142]
36–40	Hasmonaean propagandist (poem) using facts from CS[143]
41–43	Sel. Chr. and CS[144]
44–64	CS[145]
2:1–5	CS or Hasmonaean family tradition[146]
6–14	Hasmonaean propagandist (poem) and transitional sentences
15–48	CS[147]
49–69	Hasmonaean propagandist (poem)
70	Inference from Hasmonaean family tradition[148]
3:1–26	CS[149]
27–37	Sel. Chr.[150]
38 – 4:29	CS[151]
3:45	Hasmonaean propagandist (poem)
4:30–33	Hasmonaean propagandist (prayer)[152]
34–61	CS[153]
5:1–60	CS[154]
61–64	Hasmonaean propagandist[155]
65–68	CS[156]
6:1–17	Sel. Chr. and CS[157]
18–63	CS[158]
63(end)	Sel. Chr.[159]
7:1–4	Sel. Chr.[160]
5–50	CS[161]
16–17	Psalm of Alcimus[162]
43, 49	Annual observance, if not CS
8:1–16	Hasmonaean propagandist[163]
17	CS[164]
18–20	Hasmonaean propagandist[165]
21–22	Inferred from document in vss. 23–32
23–32	Document
9:1–20	CS[166]
21	Hasmonaean propagandist (poem) or perhaps a surviving line from a real dirge for Judas
22	Hasmonaean propagandist
23–31	Family tradition
32	Sel. Chr. (?)
32–42	Family tradition

* The endnotes follow the table on pp. 53–54.

Passage	Source
I 9:43–49	Family tradition (and Sel. Chr.?)
44–46	Hasmonaean propagandist (speech)
47–53	Sel. Chr. (?)
54–57	CS? High priestly chronicle of Alcimus? Hasmonaean family tradition for the two years in vs. 57
57–72	Sel. Chr. (?)
73	Family tradition
10:1–6	Sel. Chr.
7–14	Living memory?
15–17	Inferred from vss. 18–20
18–20	Document
21	Inferred from vss. 18–20, except for date. Date remembered. Year perhaps calculated from a list of high priests
22–24	Inferred from documents in vss. 18–20 and 25–45
25–45	Document
46–47	Inferred from documents and stories which display loyalty to Alexander
48–58	Sel. Chr. (and Onias IV?)
59–66	Sel. Chr. and living memory and Onias IV
67–68	Sel. Chr.
69–89	Sel. Chr. (?)
11:1–19	Sel. Chr. (and Onias IV?)
20–27	Sel. Chr. (?)
27–29	Inferred from document in vss. 30–37
30–37	Document
38–40	Sel. Chr.
41–53	Sel. Chr. (?)
54–56	Sel. Chr.
57–59	Document
60–66	Sel. Chr. (?)
67–74	Living memory of Mattathias son of Absalom and/or Judas son of Chalphi, or their descendants
12:1–4	Inferred from document in vss. 6–18
5–23	Documents
24–48	Sel. Chr. (?)
49–53	Living memory
13:1–24	Living memory and Sel. Chr.
11	Living memory of Jonathan son of Absalom or his descendants
25–30	Hasmonaean propagandist's own observation of the cemetery
31–32	Sel. Chr.
33	Inferred from document (14:32–34)
34–35	Inferred from document in vss. 36–40
36–40	Document
41–42	Inferred from document (14:27)
43–48	Inferred from document (14:34); movable tower of vss. 43–44 from living memory
49–52	Inferred from document (14:34, 36–37); month and day of date in vs. 51 preserved by annual observance; year remembered or deduced from Sel. Chr.
53	Living memory (and Sel. Chr. or chronicle of John's high priesthood?)
14:1–3	Sel. Chr.
4–15	Document (14:27–49)
16–19	Inferred from documents at vss. 20–23, 24c–24k

Passage	Source
I 14:20–23	Document
24a–24b	Inferred from document at 24c–24k; Numenius' name remembered or derived from document in vss. 20–23
24c–24k	Document
25–26	Inferred from document in vss. 27–49
27–49	Document
15:1	Inferred from document in vss. 2–9
2–9	Document
10–14	Sel. Chr.
15–24=14:24b–24k	
25–37	Sel. Chr.
38–41	Sel. Chr. or living memory
16:1–10	Living memory (and Sel. Chr.?)
11–24	Chronicle of John's high priesthood and/or living memory
II 3:1–23	Onias IV and/or CS
24–25	CS
26–28	Onias IV
29–30	CS
31–36	Onias IV
37–39	Jason of Cyrene (?)
40	Jason of Cyrene or abridger
4:1–3	Onias IV and/or CS
4–6	Onias IV
7	CS and Sel. Chr.
8–22	CS[167]
23–50	Onias IV and/or CS[168]
30–31	Sel. Chr.
38	Sel. Chr.
5:1	Sel. Chr.
2–27	CS
5	Onias IV (?)
11–16	Onias IV (?)
6:1–9	CS
4	LS (?), Jason of Cyrene (?)[169]
10–11	CS
12–17	Abridger
18–31	LS (?)
7:1–41	CS, LS (?)
42	Abridger or Jason of Cyrene
8:1–29	CS
10	Inference of Jason of Cyrene[170]
30–36	CS (?)
9:1	CS and Sel. Chr.
2–3	CS
4–13	CS (and LS?)
14–18	Inferred from document in 9:19–27
19–27	Document
28	Abridger or Jason of Cyrene
29	Sel. Chr. and Onias IV
10:1–8	CS
9	Abridger or Jason of Cyrene
10–38	CS
11–13	Sel. Chr.
11:1–12	CS

Passage	Source
II 11:13–15	Inferred by Jason of Cyrene from the documents which follow
16–38	Documents
12:1–16	CS
17–18	Onias IV and CS
19–20	CS (and Onias IV?)
21–34	CS
35	Onias IV
36–43 (beginning)	CS
43 (end)–45	Inferred by Jason of Cyrene from vss. 40–43 (beginning)
13:1–2	CS
3–8	Onias IV
9–18	LS
19–21	CS (?)
22–23 (beginning)	LS
23 (end)–26	CS and/or Sel. Chr.
14:1–2	CS and/or Sel. Chr.
3–46	CS (date in 14:4 derived by inference from Sel. Chr.)
15:1–36	CS
11–16	Onias IV
35	Date preserved by annual observance
37–39	Abridger

137 Introduction, Part II, section 3.
138 NOTE on 4:7–20.
139 Introduction, Part II, section 3.
140 NOTE on 5:1–23.
141 NOTE on 5:24–27.
142 Ibid.
143 Introduction, Part II, n. 15.
144 The Seleucid Chronicle probably contained a description of the "Antiochene republic" of Antiochus IV. The Common Source recorded the establishment of the Antiochene community at Jerusalem and the disasters which followed. See NOTE on 4:1–38.
145 Introductory NOTE on II 6.
146 Introductory NOTE on II 8.
147 Vss. 15–28: introductory NOTE on II 8; vss. 29–38: NOTE on 6:11; vss. 39–48: introductory NOTE on II 8.
148 Introductory NOTE on II 8.
149 Ibid.; the Common Source was also the source for the poem in I 3:3–8. See NOTE on II 8:2–7.
150 Introduction, Part II, section 3.
151 See NOTES on the following passages: 8:9, 11:1, 2–3, 5–6.
152 Though the prayer is prose, it is the same sort of composition as the poems in First Maccabees.
153 See NOTES on the following passages: 11:11–12, 13–38, 10:1–2, 3, 4, 5, 6, 7, 8, and end of NOTE on 10:1–8.
154 See NOTES on the following passages: 10:10–38, 15–23, 24–38, 24, a huge force, 12:10–31, 18–19, 20–25, 27–31.
155 NOTE on 12:29–31.
156 NOTES on 12:32–45 and 36.
157 Introductory NOTE to ch. 9.
158 Introductory NOTE to ch. 13.
159 Introduction, Part II, section 3.
160 Ibid.

161 See Notes on the following passages: 14:3–31, 3–4, 3, *Perceiving . . . secure,* 15:6–36, 22–24.

162 AB vol. 41, pp. 332–33.

163 AB vol. 41, pp. 347–50.

164 Note on 4:11.

165 AB vol. 41, pp. 357–58.

166 Introduction, Part II, section 5. On the date in I 9:3, see also Introduction, Part II, section 6.

167 Vss. 21–22 may have been derived from a chronicle of the high priesthood of Jason the Oniad. Cf. p. 39.

168 The three-year interval in vs. 23 may have been derived from a chronicle of the high priesthood of Jason the Oniad (see p. 47).

169 See introductory Note on ch. 6 and Note on 6:4–5.

170 See Note on 8:10.

III. THE HISTORICAL METHODS OF JASON OF CYRENE

1. How He Proved His Assertions

In the abridged history we find unequivocal positions on important controversial points. The writer affirms, against the Hasmonaeans, that defensive warfare, too, is forbidden on the Sabbath;[1] that there will be a resurrection of the dead;[2] that the merit of the martyrs purchased the mercy of God and made possible the victory of the pious over the Seleucid empire;[3] and that Judas Maccabaeus himself agreed with all three of these points.[4] Jason held, probably against the Seleucid Chronicle, that on his deathbed Antiochus IV repented (too late!) of his acts of violence against the Jews and wished to make amends.[5] Against First Maccabees, Jason presented a different order of events and insisted that only two years elapsed between the desecration of the temple and its purification.[6] Especially striking is the manner in which the writer strives not only to assert but to prove his views.

It may have been easy for the writer to demonstrate that Judas opposed all warfare on the Sabbath, if stories in the Common Source hinted at the point. He would have only to cite them.[7] The resurrection of the dead was a matter of faith, indemonstrable by history, but Jason could allude to the inspired book of Daniel in which it was promised;[8] he could retell stories of the martyrs whose faith in the doctrine did not waver, even under terrible torture;[9] he could apply tortuous logic to a recorded act of Judas to demonstrate that Maccabaeus himself was a believer.[10]. To demonstrate the efficacy of the merit of the martyrs, he could draw on earlier sources

[1] See NOTE on 8:25–26.
[2] See AB vol. 41, p. 12, and II 7:9, 11, 14, 23, 29, 36, 12:43–45, 14:46.
[3] 7:38, 8:5, 27 (see NOTE ad loc.).
[4] See next paragraph.
[5] 9:13–17; on the probable content of the account of the king's death in the Seleucid Chronicle, see NOTE on 9:4–29.
[6] See pp. 56–63.
[7] See NOTE on 8:25–26.
[8] See NOTES on 7:9, *resurrect . . . life,* and on 7:14.
[9] Ch. 7; 14:41–46.
[10] See NOTE on 12:42–45.

to tell of grave crises followed by theatrical martyrdoms, followed in turn by great victories,[11] and again he could try to infer from recorded acts of Judas that Maccabaeus himself so believed.[12]

Most interesting are the last two points of controversy, for there Jason not only constructs a narrative, he presents the documents which for him prove his thesis. In both cases he misunderstands the documents.

The Seleucid Chronicle probably reported only that Antiochus IV died of an untimely disease, surrounded by his friends.[13] If so, the assertions of the Common Source and the Hasmonaean propagandist about the repentance and death of Antiochus IV were not enough for Jason, for they might reflect mere Jewish storytelling. Accordingly, he was glad to find a letter from the king himself "proving" the point.[14]

Most complicated of all is the case of the peculiar chronology in the abridged history. Restored to its original order and properly understood,[15] the abridged history emerges with a narrative sharply different from that in First Maccabees. Jason of Cyrene and his abridger told of the purification of the temple, *two* years after its desecration (10:3), then of the nearly simultaneous death of Antiochus IV (9:1), then of the troubles early in the reign of Antiochus V, culminating in the first expedition of Lysias against the Jews (10:10 – 11:38). The text is not only self-consistent, it contains evidence for its chronology in the documents quoted in chapter 11.[16]

We need not be surprised that Jason's rival, the author of First Maccabees, gave a sharply different order of events, one that was equally self-consistent: he told of the first expedition of Lysias as an event of the reign of Antiochus IV (I 4:26–35), then of the dedication of the new temple altar *three* years after the desecration (I 4:36–54), and, further on (I 6:1–16), of the death of Antiochus IV in 149 Sel. Mac. Had we no other evidence, it might have been difficult to choose between the two internally consistent accounts. The Hasmonaean propagandist seems to have derived his chronology by combining Jewish evidence, especially the Common Source, with the Seleucid Chronicle. One would like to know how Jason derived his.

---

[11] Ch. 6 followed by ch. 7 followed by ch. 8 and 10:1–8, 14:26–32 followed by 14:37–46 followed by ch. 15. Did Jason in his unabridged work narrate the death of Judas in battle without telling of any preceding martyrdoms? If so, he may have wished his reader to infer that one reason why Judas perished at that moment was for lack of being protected by the merit of martyrs. The point may have been an old one in anti-Hasmonaean polemics, and the mention at I 9:2 of the massacred Jews of Messaloth-in-Arbela (martyrs?) may have been intended as a rebuttal.

[12] See NOTE on 8:28.

[13] See NOTE on 9:4–29.

[14] See NOTES on 9:14–18.

[15] See introductory NOTE on ch. 9 and NOTE on 8:30–32 and NOTE on 9:3, *and of Timotheus and his men.*

[16] Although I treated in detail (at AB vol. 41, pp. 80–84) the peculiar order of events in these sections of Jason's narrative, my previous discussion needs revision.

There is no evidence against the assumptions that Jason consistently gave Macedonian Seleucid dates and understood the distinction between the two forms of the Seleucid era. On those assumptions, one discovers that Jason's interpretation of the documents quoted in II 11 is the foundation of his chronology. Pious Jews, as might be expected, preserved down to Jason's time the documents by which the royal government put an end to the persecution. As Jason presents them, the letters in 11:16–21 and 27–38 show that by 15 Xanthicus, 148 Sel. Mac. (March 12, 164 B.C.E.), negotiations were marking the end of Lysias' first expedition against the Jewish rebels. The undated letter of Antiochus V in 11:23–26 *seems* to have been written soon after Lysias' letter in 11:16–21 and at about the same time as the royal letter in 11:27–33. The undated letter mentions the death of Antiochus IV, and its content shows that it must have been written not long after that event.[17] Thus, Antiochus IV would have been dead before the end of March 164 B.C.E., at most a few months before. Thus far, the evidence would show only that Antiochus IV was dead before the end of Lysias' first expedition. Jason, however, believed that the Jews received the aid of a supernatural apparition against Lysias' army (II 11:8–10), and Dan 11:45 – 12:1 implies that such aid could come only after the death of the King of the North. Hence, Jason put the entire expedition in the reign of Antiochus V.

Now let us consider the matter of the interval between the desecration of the temple and the celebration of its purification and of the dedication of the new altar. It is noteworthy that Jason, after narrating the purification (II 10:1–8), turned immediately to tell of the end of Antiochus IV (II 9).[18]

The chronological sequence was not obvious: did the death of Antiochus IV follow the purification of the temple, and by an appreciable interval? Could Antiochus have heard of how the Jews recovered and restored the temple? The *news* of the king's death certainly reached Jerusalem weeks after the Feast of Dedication,[19] but Jews in Judaea who were contemporaries of the events may have believed that Antiochus IV died after having heard of the recovery and restoration, and that the knowledge contributed to the king's fatal melancholia. Indeed, religious-minded historians, both pagan and Jewish, tended to take it for granted that the temple robbery Antiochus IV repented on his deathbed or at least

---

[17] No evidence against the assumptions: see AB vol. 41, p. 544. Strictly speaking, the argument there does not prove the assumptions. Hence, we shall have to consider below what follows if the contrary is true.

On the problems of the month dates in the letters in ch. 11, see NOTES on the following passages: 11:21, 27–33, 38, *In the year 148, in* . . . ; see also concluding NOTE on 11:16–38. Implications of the content of the undated letter: see NOTE on 11:23–26.

[18] On the original order of the passages, see introductory NOTE on ch. 9.

[19] See AB vol. 41, Appendix III and p. 43.

died knowing that his schemes had failed.[20] In a common source for the abridged history and for First Maccabees, there was a report that just before his final illness the king had received some bad news from Judaea.[21]

The author of First Maccabees jumped to the conclusion that Antiochus IV died after hearing that the Jews had recovered and restored the temple.[22] The author of First Maccabees did not know that the dates he used were on two different bases. As usual, he took his date for the death of a king from his pagan source and found (I 6:16) that Antiochus IV died in 149 Sel. (*Mac.!*), but he understood the date as 149 Sel. Bab. Consequently, he thought it obvious that Antiochus lived to hear of the Jews' recovery and restoration of the temple, which fell in the ninth month of 148 Sel. Bab. (I 4:52).

Jason loudly contradicted his rival's miscalculation. Jason wrote, "It so happened that about this time Antiochus had made an unseemly retreat from the regions of Persis" (II 9:1). "About this time" might seem vague enough to allow Jason to agree with First Maccabees, but the imperfect tense of "it so happened" (*etynchanen*) strongly suggests that he believed the king's death (the immediate aftermath of the retreat) was nearly simultaneous with the celebration at Jerusalem. The news about the purification of the temple could not have reached Antiochus.[23] The latest event from Judaea known to the king before he died was Nicanor's defeat (II 9:3).[24]

Other things being equal, Jason would have been delighted with the poetic justice of having Antiochus die after hearing that the Jews had recovered and restored their temple. If Jason here departs from the natural tendency of pious authors, he must have had strong reason to do so. Some document or tradition in his possession must have informed him that the death of Antiochus IV and the Feast of Dedication occurred close together.[25] Whatever the source was, Jason may have followed it the more eagerly because it enabled him to contradict the account in First

---

[20] I 6:5–13; II 9:12–27; J. *AJ* xii 9.1.357–59; Jerome *Commentarii in Danielem* on 11:44–45; Polybius xxxi 9; on the exception to the tendency, see NOTE on 1:12–18.

[21] On the Common Source, see Introduction, Part II, section 5, and NOTE on 9:1–3.

[22] The death of Antiochus IV probably did follow the Feast of Purification. See AB vol. 41, pp. 43, 540, 545, 273–80, 307.

[23] Correct accordingly AB vol. 41, p. 83. The editor who transposed ch. 9 and 10:1–8 would have found a reference in 9:3 to the purification of the temple to be an obstacle to his project. We can imagine him deleting the reference, but it is much more likely that it would have deterred him from transposing the passages. Rather, since there was no such reference, he felt free to transpose.

[24] On the mention of Timotheus at 9:3, see NOTE ad loc.

[25] Indeed, whether one reckons on the basis of the Macedonian or of the Babylonian Seleucid era, the two events occurred in the same calendar year. The Days of Dedication (=Days of Purification) probably began October 16, 164 B.C.E., and the king's death was known at Babylon sometime between November 20 and December 18, 164. See AB vol. 41, pp. 273–80, and below, p. 60.

Maccabees. Perhaps Jason found a Seleucid source which recorded Aud-naios (=Kislev) as the month in which the king's death became known,[26] or perhaps his authority for the closeness in time of the two events was the Common Source; in the latter case, the Hasmonaean propagandist would seem to have deserted that good witness because of his own error, which we noted above: he interpreted his pagan source as contradicting the date given or implied for the king's death in the Common Source. On the death date of a king, it was only reasonable to follow the Seleucid Chronicle against a Jewish informant.

Now, how did Jason derive his two-year interval between the desecration and the purification of the temple? To get the date of the Days of Purification, he confidently accepted the report that they occurred at nearly the same time as the king's death, and from the documents in II 11 he inferred that the king died in 148 Sel. Mac. before the end of the month of Xanthicus. Annual observance preserved the memory of the month of the Days of Purification as Kislev. Xanthicus being equivalent to Adar, the third month after Kislev, Jason put the Days of Purification in Kislev, 148 Sel. Mac. He could have found another fact confirming this inference. Judas retook Jerusalem and purified the temple against the will of the Seleucid government; he must have done so before the arrival of the letter of Antiochus V which returned the temple to the Jews (II 11:23–26).

As for the date of the desecration, it does not appear in the abridged history. Jason may have omitted it to avoid rousing questions against the veracity of Daniel. Since he set the Days of Purification in Kislev, 148 Sel. Mac., his two-year interval implies that he put the desecration (cor-rectly!) in Kislev, 146 Sel. Mac. (=145 Sel. Bab.). Jews of Judaea were the ones most likely to preserve the date of the desecration, and they used the Babylonian form of the era.[27] Indeed, the Hasmonaean propagandist gives the date at I 1:54 in a form which is unambiguously in 145 Sel. Bab. That date probably stood in the Common Source and is decisively supported by a contemporary of the event, at Dan 8:13–14, 9:27, and 12:11–12.[28] Confident in his interpretation of the letters in II 11, Jason

[26] The possibility of such a Seleucid source is shown by the existence of the Babylonian clay tablet of n. 31. Error of the Hasmonaean propagandist: above, p. 58.

[27] Jason's omissions to protect Daniel: see AB vol. 41, p. 54. It is conceivable that the desecration was mentioned in the Seleucid Chronicle and that the Macedonian year number of its date could have been inferred from the annalistic structure of that work. In the case of a Jewish date, the Hasmonaean propagandist would natu-rally follow the "145" of the Common Source against the "146" of the pagan work. However, with each such apparent contradiction it becomes harder to believe that he could remain ignorant of the difference between the forms of the era and that he could go on trusting the Seleucid Chronicle (cf. pp. 22–23, 58).

[28] Form of date at I 1:54 is unambiguous: see Part II, section 3.

On Dan 8:13–14 and 12:11–12 as supporting the date, see AB vol. 41, pp. 43–44. In my commentary on Daniel I shall show Dan 9:27 means that within the last of

could reject the evidence of both the Common Source and the Seleucid Chronicle on the dates of the Days of Purification and the death of the king. But the date of the desecration, preserved by authorities from Judaea, was more firmly buttressed. On our assumption, that Jason knew of the difference between the two forms of the Seleucid era, he could have converted the "145 Sel. Bab." of the Jews of Judaea to "146 Sel. Mac."

What would follow if our assumptions are wrong and Jason was ignorant of the distinction between the two forms of the Seleucid era? Then he would have found that the desecration occurred in Kislev, 145 Sel., and the purification in Kislev, 148 Sel., three months before the letters of Xanthicus, 148 Sel. The interval between the desecration and the purification would then be three years, not the two of II 10:3. Moreover, as a consistent defender of the veracity of Daniel,[29] Jason would have jumped at the chance to record the three-year interval, because then between the desecration and the "vindication of the Holy" (conferred by the letter at II 11:23–26) three lunar years plus three lunar months would have elapsed, equal to the "two thousand three hundred mornings and evenings" of Dan 8:14.

We conclude that our assumptions, which were probable at the outset, are indeed true: Jason did know of the distinction between the forms of the Seleucid era. We also learn that Jason could have derived his chronology from his understanding of the documents in II 11. This possibility becomes a certainty when we note that Jason's chronology can be proved to be false. Although clues may be left in the remains from the past to prove historical truths, evidence which directly implies falsehoods is necessarily scarce.

Evidence available to us but not to Jason proves that he misread the letter at II 11:23–26 and thereby misdated the death of the king and the Days of Purification. Had he read the letter carefully, Jason might have avoided his error, but the points of difficulty there are fairly subtle and passed unnoticed.[30] The recently discovered evidence shows that news of the death of Antiochus IV reached Babylon in Kislev, 148 Sel. Bab.,[31] which is Kislev of 149 Sel. Mac. The undated letter in II 11:22–26, which mentions the king as dead, must be of 149 Sel. Mac. or later and cannot have followed close upon the one in II 11:16–21.[32] The death of

---

the seventy sabbatical weeks of years there will be a three-and-a-half-year period which will begin with the cessation of burnt offering and meal offering (i.e., with the desecration). Since the sabbatical week terminated with the end of the sabbatical year and the sabbatical year was 149 Sel. Mac., the desecration could be no later than 146 Sel. Mac.

[29] See below, section 2.

[30] See NOTE on 11:23–26 and NOTE on 11:23 and AB vol. 41, p. 81, n. 85.

[31] A. J. Sachs and D. J. Wiseman, "A Babylonian King List of the Hellenistic Period," *Iraq* 16 (1954), 204, 208–9.

[32] When 11:23–26 was written in the name of Antiochus V, had the boy become king because of the receipt of an *erroneous* report that his father was dead? If so,

the persecuting king and the purification of the temple came, not on or about the second anniversary of the desecration, but on or about the third. The expedition of Lysias, which ended in the negotiations of 148 Sel. Mac., must have preceded the death of Antiochus IV. Thus, on combining the evidence of the documents in II 11:16–38 with our knowledge of the true date of the death of Antiochus IV, we find the evidence proving the substantial correctness of the chronology presented in First Maccabees!

There can be no stronger proof of a litigant's case than one derived from documents collected and accepted as authentic by his opponent! We may thus accept the chronology of First Maccabees for the first expedition of Lysias, the duration of the desecration, the death of Antiochus IV, and the accession of Antiochus V. To doubt it, with no compelling cause, is skepticism for skepticism's sake.

We still must explain the strange fact of Jason's use of such evidence. Can he have been so mistaken? As an alternative, scholars have suggested that Jason is not responsible for the chronology of the abridged history and that the documents in II 11:16–38 have suffered from accidental corruption or from deliberate tampering by the abridger or a later redactor.[33]

11:23–26 could have been written in 148 Sel. Mac. and could even have been the "document copied below" mentioned at 11:17; see Bacchisio Motzo, *Saggi di storia e letteratura giudeo-ellenistica* (Contributi alla scienza dell'antichità pubblicati da G. De Sanctis e L. Pareti, vol. V [Firenze: Felice Le Monnier, 1925]), pp. 144–50. This hypothesis involves too many difficulties. It cannot save the chronology of the abridged history.

A contemporary of the events who lived through the reign of Antiochus V would have known that the supposed early accession was a mistake. Hellenistic writers did not pass over in silence false reports of the deaths of kings, especially when there were important consequences such as mistaken accessions. Cf. 5:5–16 and Livy xlii 16.7–9. The Babylonian king list (see previous note) now shows that for Babylonians Antiochus IV was the only king over the entire Seleucid empire from 143 Sel. Bab. until well into the second half of 148 Sel. Bab. (i.e., throughout 148 Sel. Mac.). If the false report had existed and had brought about a mistaken accession, how is it that neither the report nor the accession was recorded at Babylon? Moreover, pious Jews would have recorded, among the divine acts of retribution upon Antiochus IV, the fact that, while the tyrant still lived, his son usurped the throne. Even pious David had been so punished for his sin. We thus would learn that the author of Jason's source could not have been a contemporary of the events.

A noncontemporary can still produce a correct chronology. But we have to account for the preservation of the document in 11:23–26. If the supposed accession of Antiochus V in 148 Sel. Mac. was a mistake, either the father ratified his erring son's acts or he did not. If he had ratified them, the Jews would have recorded the fact. If he had not, the Jews would not have preserved a document recording the null and void concessions of a usurper. In 11:27–33 we do not have a document by which the father restricts the concessions of his erring son, for Antiochus IV would then have had to mention the usurpation.

[33] Schunck (*Quellen*, pp. 102–9) believes that in the original abridged history ch. 11 was placed in the reign of Antiochus IV. According to Schunck, a redactor understood from ch. 9 and from the spurious Ep. 2 (1:11–17) that Antiochus IV remained relentless toward the Jews until his final illness; therefore, the redactor was impelled to displace the story and documents of the amnesty into the reign of Antio-

If there has been tampering, the purpose cannot have been to vindicate the chronology of First Maccabees, for we were able to vindicate that chronology only by use of a date absent from Second Maccabees, and the abridged history is internally consistent. A tamperer wishing to vindicate First Maccabees would have changed the order of the events in the abridged history. It is hard to suggest any other motive for tampering that could have produced the extant narrative of the abridged history. Without compelling evidence, it is also wrong to suggest that the abridger distorted the text or added to it, contrary to his own declaration (II 2:28–31).[34] Our examination of the documents in the commentary will argue that there is no reason to suspect that they have been wrongly transmitted or that the year numbers in the dates have been corrupted. Scholars since 1927 have been almost unanimous in accepting the documents.[35]

When an ancient author appears to have misunderstood a document which he quotes in support of his thesis, there is all the more reason to trust the quoted text.[36] To assume that Jason could not have been mistaken requires us to alter the documents or to rearrange the self-consistent narrative in order to recover the "original text." When we moved II 10:1–8 to stand before ch. 9, there were strong clues for doing so in the text of Second Maccabees. The text itself contains no clues requiring us to alter documents of ch. 11 or to transpose narrative sections here. In this case, both procedures are violent steps, justifiable only if there is no alternative. There is no proof that Jason was so near the events in place and time that he could not have been mistaken. Rather, if the abridged history implies a false date for the death of a Seleucid king and contains a false chronology for the wondrous victories of Judas Maccabaeus, neither Jason nor any significant number of his readers was aware of the truth. A half century or more must have elapsed.

Jason does not say that the documents in ch. 11 are the evidence for his

---

chus V. But Schunck himself (p. 115) believes that the original abridged history told first the story of the amnesty and went on later with what is now ch. 9. If so, the abridged history, to portray Antiochus IV as relentless up to his final illness, would have had to make some brief remark to explain away the amnesty! Moreover, Schunck has no good explanation for the failure of the redactor to omit the thrice-given date, 148 Sel., or to change it to a date in the reign of Antiochus V. Schunck suggests that the redactor shrank from so altering the transmitted text. But the redactor, according to Schunck, had already transposed sections of the narrative! Schunck makes his position all the more untenable by suggesting (pp. 103–5) that the redactor, who shrank from altering dates, forged the letter at 11:22–26!

[34] Cf. R. Laqueur, "Griechische Urkunden in der jüdisch-hellenistischen Literatur," *Historische Zeitschrift* 136 (1927), 240–41.

[35] Decisive in winning general acceptance for the documents were Laqueur's arguments (*Historische Zeitschrift* 136 (1927), 229–40, par. 1); my commentary incorporates from his treatment what is still valid, making the necessary corrections. Near unanimity: see Christian Habicht, "Royal Documents in Maccabees II," *Harvard Studies in Classical Philology* 80 (1976), 12, and NOTE on 11:22–26 and NOTE on 11:34–38.

[36] Cf. AB vol. 41, pp. 38, 450–51, 501–4.

datings of the events. But he misreads the documents, and, so misread, they do imply his chronology. Again we note that although many clues may be left in the remains from the past to prove historical truths, evidence which directly implies falsehoods is necessarily scarce. Jason can hardly have had any other evidence for his chronology than his misreading of the documents.

Even many years after the events, an educated Jewish Greek should have been able, if he wished, to track down the true date of the death of Antiochus IV, which was available to the author of First Maccabees and to Polybius.[37] Clearly, Jason had no desire to search in non-Jewish sources for the date. Indeed, he probably rejected the correct date for the king's death, given in the Seleucid Chronicle. Should we not consider him a good historian if he preferred, over the say-so of other writers, a date he himself had derived from authentic documents?[38]

Jason's two years fit no interval in the prophecies of Daniel. That fact was not an insuperable difficulty for Jason. The seer of Daniel himself came to realize that events, including the dedication of the new temple altar, fit none of his prophecies, and for that reason he supplemented them with interpolations and fresh revelations.[39] Nowhere in the prophecies of Daniel is the interval between desecration and dedication specified; even Dan 9:27 says only that the interruption of regular sacrifices will begin a period of three and one half years which will end when "the decreed end is poured out on the desolator" or ". . . on desolation," whatever that may mean. Accordingly, Jason could accept the results of his own calculations, though he would have been happier had they fit accurately a prophecy of Daniel.

However, it must have taken Jason considerable labor and thought to find the documents which seemed to contradict the chronology which probably stood in the Common Source. He must not only have accepted the contradiction, he must have welcomed it. We cannot be certain why Jason was so pleased with the chronology he derived from the documents preserved by pious Jews. Nevertheless, the many instances we have found wherein Jason contradicts First Maccabees suggest that one strong motivation was to discredit the rival history.

2. How He Protected His Beliefs from Being Challenged

I have argued[40] that the author of First Maccabees, wherever possible, wrote to expose the falsity of Dan 7–11, whereas Jason of Cyrene, wher-

---

[37] I 6:16 (see also pp. 33–34); Polybius xxxi 9.
[38] Cf. Bickerman, *Gott*, pp. 149–50.
[39] See for the present AB vol. 41, pp. 42–44.
[40] AB vol. 41, pp. 44–54.

ever possible, wrote to defend the veracity of those chapters. In my earlier treatment I made mistakes and left many aspects of the topic untouched, so that more must now be said. Jason's commitment to Daniel is not immediately obvious, for he never mentions the seer by name. However, it is not difficult to demonstrate the fact from the way Jason treats the resurrection of the dead, a fundamental doctrine revealed at Dan 12:2. In First Maccabees there is a tacit but conspicuous denial of the tenet. Jason, in contrast, loudly asserts it, in language unmistakably reflecting Daniel.[41]

Jason knew enough of the facts of history to understand that some of them could be used to challenge the truth of Daniel, but he could not always meet his opponent's arguments head on. The facts sometimes all too obviously contradicted the seer's predictions. The seer had been so audacious as to predict a resurrection of the dead, to come shortly after the death of Antiochus IV (Dan 11:45 – 12:2)! Jason also had to hesitate because almost never could he be sure of the correct interpretation of Daniel. By Jason's time some of the predictions had to be taken as predictions of the ultimate future rather than as predictions for the reigns of Antiochus IV and Antiochus V. It was by no means clear which predictions had to be put off to the ultimate future. Jason's first task was to see to it that his own narrative should leave it possible that Daniel told the truth.[42]

Jason dealt with the difficulties of Dan 11:25–39 by making his narrative vague and by applying key words to show that the seer's prophecies were at least partly fulfilled. Thus, Jason spoke of the "second" expedition against Egypt of Antiochus IV in order to bear out the implication of Dan 11:25–30 that the king twice came to Jerusalem, each time after a campaign against Egypt.[43] We are about to examine instances of another method of Jason's: he would take facts which had been exploited in First Maccabees to expose the falsity of Daniel, and he would show that they had no bearing whatever on the topic, that Daniel must have meant something else.

Let us now consider the attacks in First Maccabees on Daniel's veracity with reference to events after Antiochus IV marched eastward. Dan 11:40 – 12:3 is a real prediction of the future which was never fulfilled; it is not a prophecy after the fact. The Final War, when the King of Assyria and Babylon shall overrun Judaea and Egypt, could be inferred from unfulfilled predictions of true prophets.[44] The meaning of Dan 11:41 is

---

[41] See n. 2.

[42] Hence, my suggestions in AB vol. 41, pp. 52(par. 4)–54(par. 2), are improbable. Jason would avoid basing his own chronology solely on any one interpretation of ambiguous passages in Dan 7–11 for fear of exposing his own narrative and Daniel's prophecies to challenge. Those suggestions in AB vol. 41 should be replaced by my arguments in the NOTE on II 13 and the NOTE on 13:1 and the NOTE on 13:3–8.

[43] See NOTE on 5:1.

[44] See Isa 19; Jer 43:8–13, 46:13–26, and perhaps 9:25; and Ezek 29–32. "They shall stumble much" (rbwt ykšlw) in Dan 11:41 may be derived from Jer 46:16.

difficult to establish. There is more than one possibility. Will Jews stumble? Or will the armies of the King of the South? Perhaps the seer drew on Jer 40:11, so that Edom, Moab, and Ammon are to be taken as the destinations of Jewish fugitives. Or perhaps, as Dan Th. 11:41 has it, Edom, Moab, and Ammon themselves will escape, as they escaped the campaigns of Nebuchadnezzar (Ezek 25:1–4; Jer 40:11). Certainly the King of the North is to win victories and capture gold and silver in Egypt, Libya, and Ethiopia, but reports from the east and the north will make him hasten in alarm and wrath to wipe out the Many, the pious Jews.[45] Then the King of the North will pitch his royal pavilion (*'pdnw*) between the seas[46] and the glorious holy mountain and will perish with no one to help him. At that point, in a time of unprecedented trouble, the angel Michael will rise to defend Israel, and the resurrection will occur. For the seer in Dan 11, the Abomination of Desolation was so important that he mentioned it repeatedly. Yet he did not predict there that the Abomination would be destroyed before the death of the King of the North.[47] An unbiased reader would draw the inference that it would be destroyed as part of the great redemption predicted in Dan 12.

The author of First Maccabees exposes every point at which these predictions proved false. Antiochus IV in his last campaign marched eastward, not toward Judaea or toward Egypt, Libya, and Ethiopia (I 3:31–37). Even in the east he failed to capture the treasures of gold and silver (I 6:1–4). The author of First Maccabees found no occasion to mention the fact that the armies of the king of Egypt did not stumble in the last months of Antiochus IV, but he showed how Jews, far from stumbling, won glorious victories (I 3:38 – 5:54, 5:63–68). The Abomination of Desolation was removed while Antiochus IV was still alive (I 4:43). Jews did not flee to refuges in Edom, Ammon, and Moab, but were escorted from Transjordan to safety in Judaea (I 5:9–54). Edom, Ammon, and Moab could not be said to have escaped Antiochus IV, since the king did not pursue them; and the three areas certainly did not escape punishment at the hands of the Jews (I 5:1–8, 65–68).[48] The Jews, not Antiochus, took rich spoils (I 4:23; 5:28, 51, 68; 6:6). The alarming messages came to the king from Judaea and Antioch, from the west, not from the east and north (I 6:5–7). Far from hastening in wrath to destroy the Jews, the king immediately fell into melancholia and repented. Far from having no one's help, he died surrounded by his friends, and he died in Persis, far from any pair of seas and from any holy mountain (I 6:8–16).

The Jews suffered a time that was unprecedentedly bad (or nearly so),

---

[45] See AB vol. 41, p. 46, n. 20.

[46] Cf. Joel 2:20.

[47] In my commentary on Daniel, I shall treat the ambiguous and possibly corrupt words of Dan 9:27.

[48] Yazer lay in Moab; see Isa 16:7–9 and Jer 48:31–32.

not in the immediate aftermath of the death of Antiochus IV but much later, after the death of Judas Maccabaeus (I 9:27). There was, indeed, a time of troubles (though one which was not unprecedented) around the time of the death of the King of the North, but in those troubles not the angel Michael but Judas Maccabaeus and his brothers were God's instruments in rescuing the Jews (I 5).[49] Daniel had spoken of the king's intent to doom to destruction[50] the pious (11:44). Ritual doom,[51] on the contrary, befell the Jews' enemies (I 5:5).

The failure of the resurrection to occur was too obvious to require comment. But events had happened which looked like miraculous limitations upon the power of the angel of death: not one man in Judas' army fell in combat (I 5:54), whereas the force of the arrogant and insubordinate commanders Joseph and Azariah had been slaughtered (I 5:55–62). The author of First Maccabees took care to narrate these wonders which Daniel had not foretold.

How did Jason respond to these challenges? The mere mention in First Maccabees of Antiochus' march eastward had been enough to belie Daniel's prediction of attacks by him on Judaea and Egypt. Accordingly, Jason avoids mentioning the march eastward. The abridged history has nothing about the march in its chronological place (in II 8) and at II 9:1 gives no explanation as to how the king happened to be campaigning in Persis just before his final illness. Were these details so unimportant that the abridger omitted them? Rather, it is likely that Jason himself chose to leave them out.

Nothing could be done about the failure in Dan 11 to foretell that the removal of the Abomination of Desolation would precede the death of the King of the North. One could, however, attempt to discredit the account given of the events in First Maccabees, and Jason seems to have done so.[52]

Where the author of First Maccabees took pains to say that the temple in Elymais which Antiochus failed to plunder was full of gold and silver (I 6:1–2), Jason (II 9:11) carefully said nothing of precious metals.

On the other hand, a few aspects of the last campaign of Antiochus IV could be made to fit the predictions of Daniel. In Jason's narrative the king, upon receiving the alarming reports from Judaea and Antioch, sets out in wrath and haste from Ecbatana to destroy the Jews (II 9:3–4). The king's route takes him from the east and north, for Jason found it possible to read Dan 11:44 as meaning "Reports shall make him hasten from the east and north. . . ." Jason viewed the strange word *'pdnw* ("his pavilion") in Dan 11:45 as a variant form of "Ecbatana," and he

---

[49] See especially the audacious description of Judas as noted in AB vol. 41, p. 304.
[50] Heb. *lhḥrym;* Dan Th. *anathematisai.*
[51] Again the verb is *anathematisai.*
[52] See pp. 56–63.

may have been aware of Ecbatana's location between two seas (the Caspian and the Persian Gulf).[53] If so, for him only "the glorious holy mountain" of Dan 11:45 remained unexplained. In Jason's account, the king dies in the midst of his army, but the stench of his body is such that no one can bear to be near him. Thus, as Antiochus IV dies, there is truly no one to help him (II 9:9–10, 18).[54]

Just as events of the end of the reign of Antiochus IV did not fit the predictions of Daniel, neither did the events of the reign of Antiochus V. But Antiochus V clearly was not the oppressor king described in Dan 11:28–45, so that there was no reason to expect fulfillment of Dan 11:40–42 in the reign of the boy king.

The seer of Daniel had used the words "King of the North" of all members of the Seleucid dynasty. Thus, the predicted wars and the resurrection could occur in the time of a much later royal oppressor. Whereas in First Maccabees the wars of Judas Maccabaeus against neighboring peoples are placed in the reign of Antiochus IV and thus belie Dan 11:40–42, in Jason's narrative they all come in the reign of Antiochus V and, thus presented, have nothing to do with Dan 11:40–42. Both authors may have been partly mistaken.

The cause of the sudden attacks upon Jews perpetrated by gentile peoples neighboring Judaea was, so far as we can tell, the fear among those peoples that the Jews, emboldened by their victory, would seek to fulfill the glorious predictions of Israelite empire uttered by the prophets. Those gentiles, living on land promised to Israel, believed preventive warfare was necessary and viewed the Jews living in their midst as a "fifth column."[55] Accordingly, the attacks must have begun very soon after the rededication of the temple. We have shown, however, that the rededication of the temple probably preceded the death of Antiochus IV,[56] so that at least some of the campaigns reported in I 5 may have been completed before the news of the king's death reached Jerusalem, and perhaps even before the king died. On the other hand, there seems to be no reason to doubt the report at II 12:32 that the campaigns were still going on after Pentecost, 163 B.C.E., in the reign of Antiochus V.

Bearing in mind what we already know of the methods of Jason and the Hasmonaean propagandist, we need only one more hypothesis to explain how the accounts of the events of 165 and 163 B.C.E. in the abridged history and First Maccabees could have arisen: the author of the Common Source himself did not write with chronological precision but organized the events topically rather than chronologically. If so, the Source presented, first, events in Judaea: the victories of Judas Maccabaeus (includ-

---

[53] See NOTE on 9:3, Ecbatana.
[54] See also NOTES on II 9.
[55] See AB vol. 41, p. 293.
[56] Ibid., pp. 43, 540, 545, 273–80, 307.

ing the repulse of Lysias) and the recovery of the temple and the fortification of Beth-Zur; next, the wars of Judas and his brothers on foreign soil
against hostile neighboring peoples; and, thereafter, the final mis-
adventures and death of Antiochus IV. There was probably only one indication of the chronological relationship of the three sets of events, the
remark that the death of Antiochus IV occurred about the same time as
the celebration of the purification of the temple.[57] The author of First
Maccabees would then appear to have taken the order of narration to be
the order of events. The report in the Common Source of a messenger
bringing to Antiochus bad news from Judaea is probably a fiction, reflecting what a pious Jew believed *must* have happened.[58] In his innocence,
the Hasmonaean propagandist deduced from the order of the narrative in
the Common Source that the messenger reported to Antiochus the Jews'
victories down through their repulse of Lysias as well as their purification
and fortification of the temple and their fortification of Beth-Zur (I
6:5–7). He may even have reflected intentionally the ambiguity of his
sources, for nowhere in I 5:1 – 6:17 does he say that any of the campaigns
against neighboring peoples either preceded or followed the death of Antiochus IV.

On the other hand, Jason proved to his own satisfaction that Antiochus
IV died in 148 Sel. Mac. at a time near that of the celebration of the
purification of the temple; he was sure that Lysias' expedition came after
the death of the persecutor king. Accordingly, he told of the expedition
only later, in II 11.[59] At II 9:3 the messenger to the doomed king probably reported only the defeat of the expedition of Nicanor and Gorgias.[60]
Jason thus refused to take the order of narration in the source to be the
order of the events. He had to decide where to put the wars of the Jews
with their hostile neighbors. By all accounts they began soon after the
purification of the temple, at a time close also to the death of Antiochus
IV. Jason believed traditions which asserted that in the campaign against
Timotheus of Ammon, as in resisting Lysias, the Jews received the aid of
miraculous apparitions.[61] He also believed the implication of Dan
11:45 – 12:1 that miraculous interventions could only follow the death of
the King of the North.[62] Hence, the campaign against Timotheus of
Ammon and all subsequent campaigns in the abridged history had to
come after the death of Antiochus IV. The chronology was all the more
attractive because it contradicted the one in First Maccabees.

Jason may have parried the challenges in First Maccabees to the verac-

---

[57] See pp. 58–60.
[58] See NOTE on 9:3, *news . . . Nicanor.*
[59] See pp. 57–58.
[60] See NOTE on 9:3, *and of Timotheus and his men.*
[61] See NOTE on 10:24–38 and p. 57.
[62] See NOTE on 8:16–23.

ity of Dan 11:41 in yet another way. Whereas in I 5 the wars are plainly against the ethnic groups, Edom, and Ammon and Moab, which are mentioned in Dan 11:41, Jason in II 10 and II 12 presents the hostile initiative as coming, not from those ethnic groups, but from Graeco-Macedonian commanders and their mercenary soldiers[63] and from ethnic groups not mentioned in Dan 11:41.

For Jason the passing of Antiochus IV brought no suspension of the power of death over the pious. Jason held that the prophecy of Dan 12:2 was for some time in the future. Jason did not mention the report (I 5:54) that not a man of Judas' army fell during the expedition to Gilead. In the abridged history, the only comparable report is the story of how God's providence saw to it that only sinners fell in combat (II 12:40). The restoration of the normal order of providence through the death of the wicked was noteworthy, but it was not a miracle on the scale of the resurrection of the dead.

Jason probably was unaware that Daniel first predicted that the great redemptive act of God would come at the beginning of the sabbatical year 164/3 B.C.E., then found that his prediction was proving false, and thereupon said it would come at the end of that year.[64] In any case, the author of First Maccabees took pains to broadcast that the sabbatical year was far from bringing salvation to the Jews (I 6:49, 53). Jason's failure in II 13 to mention the sabbatical year thus may reflect his intention to avoid reminding his reader of the challenges to the veracity of Daniel. When Jason tells of the deposition and execution of the high priest Menelaus, he puts the story in the opening stages of the expedition of Antiochus V and Lysias (II 13:3–8). In so doing, he may well be following his own interpretation of Dan 9:26–27.[65]

Our study shows that Jason, to protect his own cherished beliefs from challenge, would interpret events or pass them over in silence. More, we have found that Jason, to prove his own cherished beliefs and refute his opponents, would cite documents and narrate recorded historical facts. Often the facts and documents hardly lent themselves to his purposes; often he misunderstood them. If he had been inclined to forge documents and introduce fictitious events into his history, he surely could have presented a more effective case to us, who depend on him and on his rival for almost all our information. However, he would then have laid himself open to possible refutation by his contemporaries. These considerations combine to establish the presumption that Jason never went beyond the normal license allowed all ancient writers of history. He did compose speeches and dialogue and preach his own beliefs, but he never forged

---

[63] See NOTE on 10:10–38.
[64] See AB vol. 41, pp. 42–44.
[65] See NOTE on 13:3–8.

documents or fabricated events. We may assume that he always based his accounts on written or oral sources trusted by him. In ch. 13 there is, indeed, a very strange narrative, in which defeats are turned into victories, but I have found it possible to explain how the Legendary Source could have arisen to produce that strange account.[66]

[66] See introductory NOTE on ch. 13.

IV. WHEN WERE THE HISTORIES WRITTEN AND HOW ARE THEY INTERRELATED?

First Maccabees and Jason's historical work cannot have been written earlier than the later reign of John Hyrcanus, who ruled over Judaea from 134 to 104 B.C.E. Considerable time must have elapsed after 146 B.C.E. for the Hasmonaean propagandist to have committed the error at I 8:1, 9–10 of supposing that the war of the Achaean league with Rome (really of 146 B.C.E.) occurred in the lifetime of Judas Maccabaeus, who was killed in 160 B.C.E.[1] Similarly, time must have elapsed to allow Jason to commit his errors of geography, chronology, and fact.[2]

Jason probably drew on the *Memoirs* of Onias IV, written between 131 and 129 B.C.E., and the Hasmonaean propagandist may well have drawn on them, too.[3]

The Hasmonaean propagandist was ignorant of the difference between the Macedonian and Babylonian forms of the Seleucid era.[4] Under Seleucid rule, the Jews of Judaea must have received frequent written communications from the king and his officials, all dated by the Macedonian form. Even under John Hyrcanus I, Jews for a time were subject *de jure* and *de facto* to Antiochus VII.[5] If no one informed the Hasmonaean propagandist of the difference between the two forms of the era, we may infer that most of the Jews who were adults in 129 B.C.E., the year of the death of Antiochus VII, were no longer alive when the histories were written.

Neither First Maccabees nor the abridged history can have been written after the Roman conqueror Pompey captured Jerusalem in 63 B.C.E.[6] According to II 15:37, Jerusalem had been in Jewish hands from the death of Nicanor down to the time of writing. The Hasmonaean propagandist showers praise on Rome as a righteous republic and friend of the Hasmonaeans and the Jews,[7] with no suggestion that one day Rome will be an enemy. Jason, too, seems to have viewed Rome as a friendly power.

---

[1] See AB vol. 41, pp. 353–54.
[2] See pp. 19, 55–63 and NOTE on 6:4–5.
[3] See pp. 35–37 and Appendix X.
[4] See p. 22.
[5] J. *AJ* xiii 8.3–4.245–53.
[6] Schürer (New English edition), I, 238–40.
[7] I 8, 12:1–4, 14:24, 40, 15:15–24.

There is reason to believe that II 9:15 was written before the facts of
Sulla's siege of Athens (87–86 B.C.E.) became known in the eastern Mediterranean world and that II 12:29–31 was written to cast an implied
reproach upon the conquest of Scythopolis in the reign of John Hyrcanus
I (ca. 107 B.C.E.).[8] Thus, both our authors and the abridger wrote between the late reign of John Hyrcanus and 63 B.C.E.

It is indeed difficult to narrow the possibilities further, for the evidence
is ambiguous.[9] One might argue, from I 16:23–24, that when the Hasmonaean propagandist wrote, John Hyrcanus was still alive: "As for the
remainder of the history of John, his wars and his valorous deeds and his
wall building and his other accomplishments, all these are recorded in the
chronicle of his high priesthood, from the time he succeeded his father as
high priest." Had John been dead at the time of writing, should not the
end of vs. 24 have read, "from the time he succeeded his father as high
priest down to his own death"?[10] No. An author writing for an audience
who knew that John was dead could have written vs. 24 as we have it to
let the readers know that there was no gap between the events of the end
of First Maccabees and the beginning of the chronicle.

Indeed, it is perhaps more likely that I 16:23–24 was written after the
death of John. Similar references in the books of Kings always follow the
death of the king involved. True, our passage differs from the parallels in
Kings: John's death has not been reported. However, even in this aspect,
there is a parallel to our passage at Esther 10:2: there, the reader is referred to the royal annals for the further history of Ahasuerus and Mordecai, though the death of neither has been reported. But the book of
Esther contains clear hints to the audience that the time of Ahasuerus is
long past.[11] The author and the reader thus know that Ahasuerus and
Mordecai are long dead. Thus, in Esther, too, the reference to the chronicle presupposes that the prince in the story is dead. Should we not assume
the same concerning I 16:23–24?

On the other hand, I 16:23–24 is vague: the only specific act of John
mentioned is his building of the walls, as if that were the last of his feats
known to the author. But the patterns of the books of Kings and Chronicles may have dictated to the author that his only specific reference
should be to the walls. Generally in those books the formula referring the
reader to the earlier chronicles makes only vague references to wars and
is specific concerning only building projects. The only exceptions are the
conquests of Jeroboam II (II Kings 14:28), the sin of Manasseh (I Kings
21:17, II Chron 33:19), and the conspiracies of Zimri and Shallum (I

---

[8] Jason on Rome as a friendly power: 4:11, 11:34–38. On 9:15 and 12:29–31, see
NOTES ad loc., and cf. NOTE on 8:23, *division*.

[9] On the opportunities for confusion offered by the nicknames of the Hasmonaean
princes, see AB vol. 41, pp. 67–71.

[10] Cf. Bickerman, *Gott*, p. 145.

[11] See AB vol. 41, pp. 190–91.

Kings 16:20, II Kings 15:15). Even Jeroboam II was an inauspicious parallel for an author seeking to prove the legitimacy of the Hasmonaean dynasty.

John may well have built multiple walls late in his reign. We have no other sources whatever on his building of walls. It is possible that the author of First Maccabees viewed the building of plural walls as fulfillment of Amos 9:11 and Mic 7:11. The wall building there is to accompany great permanent victories of Israel (Amos 9:11–15; Mic 7:10–12, 14–20), including the conquest of Edom (Idumaea). To his contemporaries and immediate posterity, John could seem to have accomplished the beginning of such fulfillment. Especially if the chronicle of John's high priesthood made much of those prophecies, our author could have expressed himself as he does here.

Hence, I 16:23–24 is no proof that John is still alive. Furthermore, John Hyrcanus, in the later years of his reign, was a victorious prince, with good claims that God had granted him prophetic revelations.[12] Did such a prince need the arguments of First Maccabees to establish his legitimacy?[13] Could his claims have been discredited by the facts presented in the abridged history?[14] I think not. Moreover, in I 2:54, 57, the Hasmonaean propagandist portrays Mattathias as telling his descendants to aspire to be both high priests and kings.[15] John Hyrcanus never bore the royal title, though there are hints that he hoped his sons would be kings.[16] First Maccabees, however, reflects a controversy which such mere hopes could never have evoked.

The Hellenistic royal diadem was a white cloth band with decorated edges worn around the head. On the coins of the Seleucid kings, from Seleucus I on, it is shown knotted at the back of the head, with the two ends of the band hanging down over the neck.[17] The diadem was a pagan institution. No biblical king of Israel or Judah is said to have worn anything of the kind. John Hyrcanus' heir was Judas Aristobulus I, who took the title "king" and wore a diadem.[18] The Hasmonaean propagandist condemns the wearing of a diadem (I 8:14). Therefore, the wearing of a diadem was an issue in his time, but it could hardly have been one in the reign of John Hyrcanus. A book pushing the dynastic claims of the Hasmonaeans but condemning the diadem could not have been written under

---

[12] J. BJ i 2.7.68–69, AJ xiii 10.3.282, 7.299–300; To. Soṭah 13:5 and parallels.

[13] See AB vol. 41, pp. 72–78.

[14] See ibid., pp. 78–85.

[15] See ibid., pp. 7–8, 73, 240–41.

[16] See the section on John Hyrcanus I in my study, "The Hasmonaean Revolt and the Hasmonaean Dynasty" (Part II, Chapter 8, of The Cambridge History of Judaism, ed. by W. D. Davies and Louis Finkelstein [Cambridge: Cambridge University Press, forthcoming], vol. I).

[17] L. A. Moritz, OCD², s.v. "Diadem"; Percy Gardner, Catalogue of Greek Coins: The Seleucid Kings of Syria (Bologna: Arnaldo Forni, 1963), plate I, no. 6, plate III, nos. 2–4, etc.

[18] J. AJ xiii 11.1.301, BJ i 3.1.70.

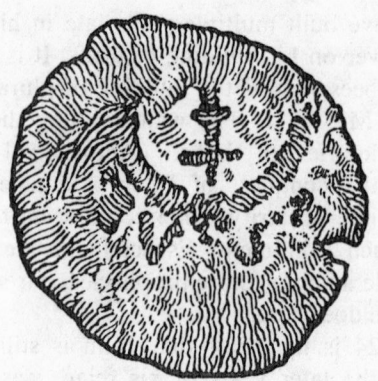

Figure 1

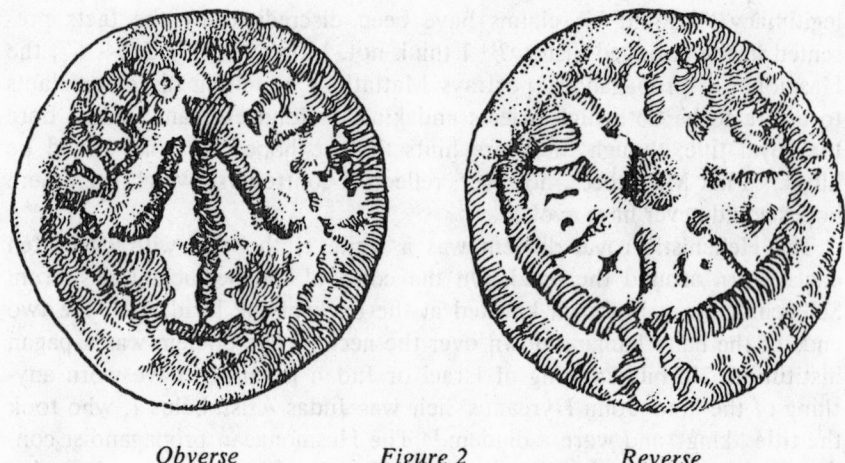

Obverse   *Figure 2*   *Reverse*

Aristobulus I (ruled 104–103 B.C.E.) or in the early years of Alexander Jannaeus (ruled 103–76 B.C.E.), for Jannaeus, too, at first bore the title "king"[19] and wore a diadem.[20]

However, Jannaeus' coins show that for a time he abandoned both the royal title and the diadem and hint that at a later period he resumed the royal title but refrained from wearing a diadem. The dating and interpretation of Jannaeus' coins is difficult and has provoked bitter controversy. Dr. Ya'akov Meshorer has shared with me his knowledge of the

[19] J. *AJ* xiii 21.1.320; *BJ* i 4.1.85.
[20] As is shown by his coins; see below, pp. 75–81.

numismatic facts,[21] but there are points in the argument that I am about to present on which he may not agree. I shall cite the types of the Hasmonaean and Herodian coins according to the numbers assigned to them in Meshorer's *Jewish Coins of the Second Temple Period.*[22]

Jannaeus may have been the first Hasmonaean to issue coins.[23] If so, the argument I am about to present could be made a little easier. There are Hasmonaean coins that bear Hebrew legends naming as high priest Yoḥanan (John) and Yehudah (Judas). Yoḥanan could be either Jannaeus' father, John Hyrcanus I, or Jannaeus' son, Hyrcanus II. Yehudah could be either Jannaeus' elder brother, Judas Aristobulus I, or Jannaeus' son, Aristobulus II. But even if some of the high priestly coins belong to Jannaeus' predecessors, Jannaeus still was the first Hasmonaean to issue royal coins, bearing his name with the title "king," in Greek, Hebrew, or Aramaic (*basileôs, hmlk, mlk'*).

It was the usual practice in the ancient world for a recently established minting authority to imitate the existing types that were current locally in order to secure greater confidence in the new coins.[24] Long generations elapsed between the last coins of the province of Judaea and the rise of the Hasmonaeans.[25] The kings of Israel and Judah had not issued coins. Hasmonaean chiefs of state, whether high priests or kings, in beginning to coin could follow as precedents only the coins of the pagan chiefs of state in their neighborhood. A Jewish high priest or king had to be careful not to violate the interpretations of Jewish law accepted by those Jewish groups upon which he depended for support. Pagan coins bore the head of a god or a king on the obverse side. Hasmonaean coins could not do so. If John Hyrcanus I indeed issued coins, he put on the obverse not a head but his own name and high priestly title in Hebrew, plus the formula *wḥbr hyhdm* (and the *ḥbr* of the Jews), the interpretation of which is a matter of controversy. These Hebrew words are enclosed within a knotted wreath

[21] In a letter of June 9, 1980. On the controversy, see Baruch Kanael, "Altjüdische Münzen," *Jahrbuch für Numismatik und Geldgeschichte* 17 (1967), 167–71.

[22] Translated from the Hebrew by I. H. Levine (Chicago: Argonaut, 1967). The book is marred by unfortunate slips and misprints. Meshorer has just finished a new work on Hasmonaean coins.

[23] So thinks Meshorer (*Jewish Coins*, pp. 41–58; "The Beginning of the Hasmonean Coinage," IEJ 24 [1974], 59–61), but many numismatists do not accept his view. In n. 29 I refute the argument brought against Meshorer by D. Barag and S. Kedar ("When Did the Hasmoneans Begin Minting Coins?" *Qadmoniot* 15 [1982], 29–32). I write these lines as I read the galley proofs and have not yet seen Barag and Kedar, "The Beginning of Hasmonean Coinage," *Israel Numismatic Journal* 4 (1980), 8–32. There is some cogency in the arguments of Uriel Rappaport that not Jannaeus but John Hyrcanus I was the first Hasmonaean to coin ("The Emergence of Hasmonean Coinage," *Association for Jewish Studies Review* 1 [1976], 171–86).

[24] Ibid., pp. 57–58, and Meshorer, "The Beginning of the Hasmonean Coinage," IEJ 24 (1974), 59–61.

[25] On the earlier coins of the province of Judaea, see Meshorer, *Jewish Coins*, pp. 35–40, and "A New Type of YHD Coin," IEJ 16 (1966), 217–19, and Arnold Spaer, "Some More 'Yehud' Coins," IEJ 27 (1977), 200–3.

of laurel leaves. This becomes the pattern for the obverse of the vast majority of Hasmonaean high priestly coins.[26]

Knotted wreaths surround the king's name and the rest of the designs on reverse types of the later Seleucid kings, beginning with Antiochus VI (145–142 B.C.E.), and are particularly prevalent on coins of Antiochus VII (139/8–129), VIII (121–96), and IX (115–95) and their successors. Knotted wreaths also surround the king's head on coins of Demetrius I (162–150) and II (145–140/39). The Hasmonaeans were not the only newly independent coining authority to copy the Seleucid knotted wreath. The name of the citizens of the newly autonomous Phoenician city of Tripolis appears within such a wreath on coins beginning in 112/1 B.C.E.[27] Despite the clumsiness of many of the engravers who worked for the Hasmonaeans, their coins show the knot in the wreath except when the dies ran off the metal blank.

Hasmonaean high priests could use the wreath without fear of evoking broad opposition; it was neither peculiarly royal nor peculiarly pagan.[28] Thus, the obverse type of the vast majority of Hasmonaean high priestly coins is hardly innovative.

The reverse side of the coins of Hasmonaean high priests (including Alexander Jannaeus) also becomes quite uniform, for the most part, and draws on an existing pattern: the symmetrical pair of cornucopias, the two horns being joined at the narrow end and diverging toward their broad end. Tied around the middle of each cornucopia is a ribbon, of which

[26] The Hasmonaean high priestly coins of which the obverses depart from this pattern are all very rare types bearing the name of Yoḥanan the high priest. Nos. 21, 21A, and 24 all bear on the obverse a palm branch around which is written the Hebrew legend (on no. 24 the legend is *yhwḥnn hkhn hgdl r'š hḥbr hyhdym*). No. 25 bears the same Hebrew legend as no. 24, written around a pair of cornucopias in parallel. If Yoḥanan of the palm branch coins is Jannaeus' son, Jannaeus originated the pattern. The pair of cornucopias in parallel occurs on the Seleucid coinage of Alexander II (128–123 B.C.E.) and Cleopatra Thea (125 B.C.E.); see Percy Gardner, *Catalogue of Greek Coins: The Seleucid Kings of Syria* (Bologna: Forni, 1963), pp. 82, 85, and plates XXII, 3, and XXIII, 1. The pair of cornucopias was surely as inoffensive as the symmetrical pair of cornucopias on most Hasmonaean high priestly reverse types. On the other side of no. 25 is a helmet, which has as its closest parallel one on a royal Seleucid coin minted at Ascalon (Uriel Rappaport, "Ascalon and the Coinage of Judaea," *La Parola del passato* 36 [fascicolo 201; 1981], 363).

The coins of Mattathias Antigonus that do not follow the pattern of the high priestly coins are, indeed, royal coins, for they present Antigonus in Greek as bearing the title "king."

I deliberately leave Hebrew *ḥbr* untranslated. It may refer to the Council of Elders or to the Sanhedrin. On the other hand, it may refer to the nation; see U. Rappaport, "On the Meaning of *Ḥeber ha-Yehudim*," *Studies in the History of the Jewish People and the Land of Israel* (Haifa: University of Haifa, 1974), III, 59–67 (in Hebrew). Or, indeed, it may refer to something else altogether.

[27] George Francis Hill, *Catalogue of the Greek Coins of Phoenicia* (Bologna: Forni, 1965), pp. 200–1 and plate XXVI, 2–4.

[28] Cf. Erwin R. Goodenough, *Jewish Symbols in the Greco-Roman Period* (13 vols.; New York: Pantheon Books, 1953–68), VII, pp. 148–53, 163–71.

the ends hang down. The one feature that may be original with the Hasmonaean high priests is the presence of a single poppy or pomegranate between the horns of the cornucopias. Pagan parallels have some other symbol between the horns. The ribbons hanging from the cornucopias are not to be taken as diadems symbolizing the royalty of the coining authority, as is clear from the fact that they appear on the republican coins of Greek cities. The pair of cornucopias, like the knotted wreath, evoked little or no opposition from pious Jews.[29] Again, despite the clumsiness of many of the engravers, one can see on the Hasmonaean high priestly coins the ends of the ribbons hanging down from the cornucopias.

Thus, the pattern of most Hasmonaean high priestly coins is truly innovative only in substituting the high priest's name and title for the usual head on the obverse. Alexander Jannaeus may have been the innovator even of this. But his royal coins certainly set new precedents, even when they drew on earlier patterns. Royal coins in the Hellenistic world usually showed the head of the king, wearing his diadem. If a Jew became a king in the Hellenistic age, how could he display his diadem on coins?

Of Jannaeus' royal coins, those that imitate Seleucid types most are nos. 5 and 5A. Both have on one side the anchor and on the other the lily,

[29] A Greek city issued such coins before the reign of John Hyrcanus I. See Barclay V. Head, *Catalogue of the Greek Coins of Ionia* (Bologna: Forni, 1964), p. 154 and plate XVII, 7 (of Lebedos in Asia Minor); the cornucopias on bronze coins of Philomelium in Phrygia may not be precisely symmetrical (see Barclay V. Head, *Catalogue of the Greek Coins of Phrygia* [Bologna: Forni, 1964], pp. 353–54 and plate XLI, 12); the coins of Ascalon with symmetrical paired cornucopias come from after Jannaeus' time (George Francis Hill, *Catalogue of the Greek Coins of Palestine* [Bologna: Forni, 1965], p. 111 and plate XII, 16–19).

A nearly symmetrical pair of cornucopias, with no symbol between them, occurs on one Seleucid coin of Alexander II (128–123); the narrow part of one horn crosses the narrow part of the other, and the two horns diverge toward their broad ends.

On the use of cornucopias by Jews, cf. Goodenough, *Jewish Symbols*, VIII, pp. 106–14.

D. Barag and S. Kedar (*Qadmoniot* 15 [1982], 29–32) insist that the coins of Yoḥanan the high priest are earlier than those of Alexander Jannaeus because the bunches of grapes dangling from the cornucopias are clear on coins of Yoḥanan but have become unintelligible dots on the coins of Jannaeus. To them the phenomenon is one of deteriorating craftsmanship. Their argument would be cogent only if the cornucopia with a dangling bunch of grapes could be shown to have been invented for the coins of the Hasmonaeans. In fact, the paired cornucopias on Seleucid coins (mentioned in this note and in n. 26) also have bunches of grapes dangling from them. From before 132 down to 110/9 b.c.e. the reverse of the coins of Judaea's neighbor, Ptolemais, shows a single cornucopia with dangling grapes and with a spike of grain projecting from its mouth, as on the best engraved of the Hasmonaean high priestly coins; see Leo Kadman, *The Coins of Akko Ptolemais* (Corpus Nummorum Palaestinensium, first series, vol. IV; Tel Aviv and Jerusalem: Schocken, 1961), pp. 44–45, 94–100, and plates II–III. Thus, a poor engraver under Alexander Jannaeus could have made botched representations of the established motif of dangling grapes, and a superior or more painstaking craftsman, under Jannaeus' son, Yoḥanan the high priest, could later have produced better ones.

which appeared on Seleucid coins known to have circulated in Jerusalem.[30]
On the reverse of no. 5A appears an anchor surrounded by a diadem
(the anchor is to be viewed with its hooks at the top, its shaft pointing
down). The knot at the bottom of the diadem and the hanging ends are
very clear. Similarly, on about half the examples of no. 5 the circle that
surrounds the anchor on the reverse shows traces of a knot at the bottom. Sometimes the traces are rudimentary, sometimes a bit clearer, and
sometimes they are as conspicuous as in no. 5A.[31] This use of a diadem
to surround the other symbols on the coin resembles the use of the wreath
by the Seleucids and by the Hasmonaean high priests, but to my knowledge it never appears on coins before those of Jannaeus. Around the
knotted diadem, both on no. 5 and on no. 5A, appear the Greek words
Basileôs Alexandrou ("of King Alexander").

On the obverse of no. 5A there is a parallel phenomenon. The circle
of dots surrounding the lily bud can be interpreted as a crown (or diadem?), for at the top of the circle appears a crescent-shaped ornament
(clasp?). Around the lily but inside the circle of dots are the Hebrew
words *yhwntn hmlk* ("King Jonathan"). Coin no. 6 also has the lily,
this time on the reverse within a plain circle of dots, with no words. The
innovative side of no. 6 is the obverse. It is purely Jewish, showing a
palm branch and, around it, the words *yhwntn hmlk;* surrounding the
words and the palm branch is a circle of dots with a rectangular ornament
(clasp?) at the top.[32] Like the surrounding knotted diadems, the circles
with ornamental clasps are, to my knowledge, absolute innovations.

On the very rare and poorly preserved lead coins (no. 7) there are
also traces that can be interpreted as the knot of a diadem. These coins
bear the Greek legend "of King Alexander."

Well-preserved examples of the beautiful "anchor-star" coins (no. 8)
on the reverse show the eight-pointed star surrounded by a clear, knotted

---

[30] There is a coin of Antiochus VII with a lily on the obverse and, on the reverse,
an anchor around which are written the king's name and title; the coin is said to
come from, or even to have been minted at, Jerusalem (Gardner, *Catalogue of
Greek Coins: The Seleucid Kings*, pp. xxxii, 75 and plate XX, 14). Uriel Rappaport
("Ascalon and the Coinage of Judaea," *La Parola del passato* 36 [fascicolo 201;
1981], 353–63) attributes the coin rather to the mint of Ascalon, but he, too, admits
that it circulated in Jerusalem.

The anchor also appeared on issues of Alexander II (128–123 B.C.E.); see Gardner,
Catalogue, p. 84 and plate XXII, 12, and Edward T. Newell, *The Seleucid Mint of
Antioch* (Chicago: Obol International, 1978), p. 86, no. 338. On other instances of
the lily, see Meshorer, IEJ 24 (1974), 59–61 and plate 9, and Spaer, IEJ 27 (1977),
200–1 and plate 25C.

[31] Clear knot on reverse of no. 5A: see Meshorer, *Jewish Coins*, plate II; traces
on no. 5: Meshorer assured me they do exist and sent me a drawing of an example;
clearer traces on no. 5: see Fig. 1, p. 74.

[32] The ornaments are not visible in the photographs printed in Meshorer, *Jewish
Coins*, plate II, but Meshorer sent me drawings of examples.

diadem.[33] There are many (later?) wretched versions of type 8 on which traces can be found of the knotted diadem. Coins of type 8 bear both the Hebrew and the Greek royal legends.

Late in the reign of Jannaeus come poorly engraved but dated anchor-star coins (no. 9), beginning perhaps with his twentieth year and certainly attested in his twenty-fifth (78 B.C.E.).[34] These coins bear the Aramaic legend *mlk' 'lksndrws* ("King Alexander"). Though the star and the anchor on the late dated coins are each surrounded by a circle, the circle has *no* trace of a knot so as to be interpreted as a diadem.

A numerous and varied group of Jannaeus' coins attests that for a protracted period he abandoned the royal title and the diadem. Nos. 12, 13, 14, 15, and 16 are all typical Hasmonaean high priestly coins, with an inscription within a knotted wreath on the obverse and a pair of cornucopias on the reverse. The inscription can be incomplete or illegible but never gives Jannaeus the royal title.

One might think that the coins calling Jannaeus "high priest" and those calling him "king" were contemporary, each type proclaiming one of his two titles. There is evidence to the contrary. Unaltered coins of types 5 and 5A are very rare. Ninety percent of such coins have been overstruck: on the obverse, with the inscription *yntn hkhn hgdl wḥbr hyhdym* surrounded by a wreath; and on the reverse, with the double cornucopias with a pomegranate between (nos. 17 and 17A).[35] The overstriking shows conclusively that the high priestly issues are later than the royal issues and that Jannaeus for a time abandoned the royal title. Only types 5 and 5A are known to have been overstruck.

One can question whether the absence of any trace of a knot on the circles surrounding the anchor and the star on the dated coins of type 9 is significant: could not a plain solid circle be interpreted as a diadem? It is true that plain solid circles surrounding the rest of the symbols on a face of a coin occur but rarely on issues of the mints of the Hellenistic period. But the ends of the diadems on the heads of the kings appear prominently on all pagan royal coins, and diadems appear clearly showing their ends on coins of the Jewish king Herod (nos. 41, 41A, 42). As far as I can judge from the published photographs, solid circles appear on coins (nos. 59B and 60) of Herod's son, the Ethnarch Archelaus (4 B.C.E.–6 C.E.). Josephus attests that Archelaus never used the royal title and never wore a diadem (*BJ* ii 1.1.2–3, 6.3.93, 7.3.111; *AJ* xvii 8.4.202, 11.4.317, 13.1–2.339–44). The engravers who worked for the

---

[33] See Fig. 2, p. 74.

[34] See J. Naveh, "Dated Coins of Alexander Janneus," IEJ 18 (1968), 20–25, and A. Kindler, "Addendum to the Dated Coins of Alexander Janneus," ibid., pp. 188–91. The coins bearing the date in the twentieth year are but few, and the date may be the error of the engraver, who did not leave enough room for the numeral signifying "fifth."

[35] Meshorer, *Jewish Coins*, p. 120.

Hasmonaeans were able to show the knot of the wreath and the ends of the ribbons hanging down from the cornucopias. Coins of Jannaeus display deliberate innovative royal symbolism, the clasped circle and the knotted diadem. Jannaeus' engravers conspicuously showed the knotted ends of the diadem on nos. 5, 5A, 6, 7, 8, 8A, and 8B and even on the wretched imitations of no. 8. According to report, examples of no. 9 bear dates from the twentieth and twenty-fifth years of Jannaeus. If "twentieth" is not an engraver's error, those coins were minted for at least five years; at the very least they were minted from more than one set of dies. Yet not one specimen of no. 9 bears traces of the knotted ends of a diadem. For all these reasons we may conclude that the solid circles on no. 9 are not diadems: the knotted ends have been omitted intentionally.[36]

The Hasmonaean propagandist strangely urges the royal claims of the Hasmonaeans but condemns the wearing of a diadem. We would want to explain that fact even if we did not have the evidence of the coins. Now the strange numismatic and literary phenomena help explain one another: at some time late in his reign Jannaeus indeed held the royal title while he abandoned the wearing of a diadem, following the course of which the Hasmonaean propagandist approved.

The literary and numismatic evidence concurs in suggesting that Jannaeus bore the royal title and wore the diadem from the very beginning of his rule. There may have been alternating periods of compromise and of royalist extremism in his reign. The early period, in which he had both the royal title and the diadem, probably lasted several years. At that time a believing Jew who took the title "king" was entitled to assume that the "messianic" prophecies of a glorious king after the Babylonian exile would be fulfilled in him. Political and religious opponents, however, might refuse to see in him the promised king, and all the more so if he failed to fulfill the prophecies. One defeat in battle would be enough to demonstrate to Jannaeus' opponents that he was not the promised king.[37] Even without a defeat, the diadem, of pagan origin, might arouse objections. Such opposition among the Jews seems to have led Jannaeus to yield and to abandon both the royal title and the diadem for a protracted period to judge by the abundance and numerous types of Jannaeus' coins which bear only the high priestly legend.

The royal anchor-star coins are also abundant and of numerous types, and no overstruck examples are known. One may guess that after years during which Jannaeus abandoned the royal title and the diadem, he resumed both in the middle of his reign. The dated coins of type 9 would

[36] The disappearance of the Hebrew word "king" (*mlk*) from the Hasmonaean coin legends may serve as further confirmation. See below, p. 81.
[37] See my sections on John Hyrcanus I and Alexander Jannaeus in *The Cambridge History of Judaism*, part II, ch. 8.

show that late in his reign Jannaeus again compromised to the extent of abandoning the diadem while remaining king. The compromise seems to have gone still further: Jannaeus and his successors seem henceforth to have refrained from styling themselves as "king" in Hebrew, since never again on a Hasmonaean coin does the royal title appear in Hebrew. On Jannaeus' late coins it appears in Aramaic and Greek and on those of Mattathias Antigonus (ruled 40–37 B.C.E.) only in Greek, as if henceforth the Hasmonaeans were muting their claims to be the fulfillers of "messianic" prophecies.[38]

On this evidence one might infer that the Hasmonaean propagandist wrote about 78 B.C.E., the time of the dated coins. But there are too many indications that he wrote earlier, especially the picture of Rome in I 8 as a harmonious and invincible republic. Rome was torn by internal struggles from 91 B.C.E. on, and long was unable to cope with such enemies as the Cilician pirates and King Mithradates of Pontus.[39] Hence, it is best to assume that the Hasmonaean propagandist wrote during the period of Jannaeus' high priestly coins and hardly later than 90 B.C.E. He advocated that Jannaeus resume the royal title which had been temporarily abandoned, but he opposed the wearing of the diadem, presumably because it was of pagan origin.

I have not repeated here my arguments from AB vol. 41, which were based upon rabbinic sources.[40] I still believe those arguments to be correct, but rabbinic sources contain so much confusion that each tradition has to be examined on its own merits, and I cannot demonstrate conclusively the reliability of the sources and the correctness of the interpretations underlying my earlier assertions. I also took it for granted that only a war between the Hasmonaean prince and the Pharisees could have been a serious enough challenge to provoke the writing of First Maccabees.[41] True as that may be, such confidence is unjustified when we know so little about the early history of the Pharisees and about the sectarian strife under John Hyrcanus I and his successors.

In AB vol. 41, I also argued that if First Maccabees or Jason's work had been published before 103 B.C.E., the author of Ep. 2 would not have written his erroneous account of the death of Antiochus IV.[42] But even if

---

[38] See, however, my discussion of the coin legends and the literary sources in my sections on Queen Salina Alexandra and King Hyrcanus II, ibid.

[39] See AB vol. 41, p. 63, and NOTE on 9:15 (provided Jason of Cyrene wrote after the Hasmonaean propagandist, as I believe he did).

[40] Pp. 67–71. Cf. Yehoshua Efron, "Šim'ōn ben Šeṭaḥ veYannay hammelekh," Sepher zikkaron li-Gedaliahu Alon (n.p.: Hakibbutz Hameuchad, 1970), pp. 69–109. I still believe that the earliest rabbinic traditions on King Yannay are factual and that the one at TB Qiddushin 66a can be defended against Efron's objections. Indeed, it may be superior to the parallel at J. AJ xiii 10.5–6.288–98.

[41] AB vol. 41, pp. 68–72.

[42] P. 62.

my date for Ep. 2 in 103 B.C.E. is correct,[43] the conclusion does not nec-essarily follow. Propagandists and their audiences do not always read his-tory books, and even if Jason's work and First Maccabees had not yet been published, certainly the Common Source already existed.[44]

Also in AB vol. 41, I presented arguments to show that the work of Jason of Cyrene was written after First Maccabees and that one of its principal aims was to refute Hasmonaean claims to royal and high priestly legitimacy.[45] It would be rash to claim that my arguments there provide conclusive proof, but I have found some further confirmation.[46] Let us now give a fresh statement of the main arguments.

Jason went to great effort to study and quote official documents, con-structing on their basis a chronology which could not have come from his traditional and literary sources. He was unaware that his chronology was false. But that chronology contradicts the account in First Maccabees.[47] Could Jason's chronological efforts have been directed against earlier Hasmonaean propaganda or some non-Hasmonaean work? Our study of the sources has established that earlier Jewish oral and written traditions had preserved some isolated dates but contained no detailed precise chronology. In order to construct one, the Hasmonaean propagandist had to make use of the Seleucid Chronicle, a source known also to Jason.[48] By itself, the chronological difference had no theological importance; Jason's own datings failed to fit the prophecies of Daniel.[49] It is hard to see any reason why Jason would have undertaken his chronological labors merely to refute the Seleucid Chronicle, a pagan book. But if thereby he could discredit First Maccabees, the propaganda of the hated Hasmonaeans, he was pursuing a goal worthy of his toil.

Jason probably had no such trouble in arriving at the other two year dates in the abridged history, but they, too, can be used to contradict and discredit First Maccabees, indeed on a point where the Hasmonaean propagandist drew a mistaken inference from the Seleucid Chronicle.[50] Can that be coincidence? The impression is further confirmed by the way in which the abridged history contradicts First Maccabees on seemingly insignificant matters of detail. On occasion, Jason went out of his way to be explicit on matters where the Hasmonaean propagandist erred.[51] These facts lead to the conclusion that Jason wrote in reply to First Maccabees.

[43] See NOTE on 1:10b – 2:18 and Appendix IX.

[44] See p. 48.

[45] Pp. 72–89.

[46] See NOTE on 6:10–31 (Jason can treat briefly material on which he agrees with First Maccabees) and NOTE on 14:1–4.

[47] Pp. 55–63.

[48] Part II, sections 3 and 6.

[49] See p. 63.

[50] See AB vol. 41, pp. 315–19, and NOTE on 13:1 and NOTE on 14:1–4.

[51] See p. 12 and AB vol. 41, pp. 84, 296–97, and NOTES on the following pas-sages: 8:30, 32, and 13:23.

The abridger knew the Purim story and may have drawn vocabulary from the Greek book of Esther, which was brought to Egypt in 78/7 B.C.E.[52]

To summarize: First Maccabees was written by 90 B.C.E.; Jason of Cyrene wrote his work by 86 B.C.E.; and the abridger produced his between 78/7 and 63 B.C.E.

[52] NOTE on 15:36.

V. WHAT REALLY HAPPENED:
THE CIVIC AND RELIGIOUS POLICIES OF
ANTIOCHUS IV

Some points in my account in Part VI of my Introduction to AB vol. 41 require modification. In addition, my critics have requested my reasons for rejecting the reconstructions of the course of events which Tcherikover and Bickerman have proposed. I shall provide those reasons here.

Strange indeed is the history of the interactions between Antiochus IV and the Jews. Any explanation of them must take account of the following strange facts:

1. Antiochus IV lent his support, in succession, to the high priests Jason and Menelaus. Jason, Menelaus, and their followers are often said to have been religious reformers. Nevertheless, there is no trace that the "reformers," in their period of power down to the expedition of the Mysarch early in 167, ever questioned the letter of the Torah. Indeed, there is positive evidence that even the most zealous pious Jews committed no physical act of resistance to the "reformers" until the time of the coup of Jason in 169 B.C.E.

2. Though we have good evidence concerning the existence of Jews in Judaea who rejected some or all of the commandments of the Torah, there is no trace that anyone there was devoted to the imposed cult before Antiochus IV decreed in 167 B.C.E. that the Jews had to observe it.

3. Until Mattathias' act of zeal in late 167 or early 166 B.C.E., Jews believed God forbade them to rebel against the king. Antiochus IV punished the Jews in four well-separated acts. If Jews would not rebel against the king, how did they come to be punished not once but four times?

4. There are many examples in history of a ruler forbidding some of his subjects to practice their own religion or imposing his own upon them. There are examples of a ruler imposing upon a whole ethnic or religious group subject to him the religious views of a part of that group. But Antiochus IV imposed upon all the Jews of Judaea and upon any others he deemed worthy of punishment a religion which was not his and had hitherto had no following whatever in Judaea.

We proceed, first, to establish these four facts, and, then, to try to solve the problems they pose.

1. The Conformity of the Hellenizers to the Torah

The Hellenizing program of the high priestly usurper Jason the Oniad was a response to the invitation of Antiochus IV to the subject populations of his empire that they should join his Antiochene republic and become Antiochene citizens. Thereby, they would acquire privileges, and the king might acquire for his own empire the sort of loyalty which had created the strength of the Roman republic.[1] Every Antiochene community probably had a gymnasium and an ephebic educational system through which boys would grow into future Antiochene citizens.[2] We do not know what was involved in the patriotic rituals of the Antiochenes of Jerusalem, but it appears that Jason and his followers could and did avoid idolatry and found it possible to argue that the Torah permitted their membership in the Antiochene republic.[3]

What happened when Jason was deposed and replaced by Menelaus? It is legitimate to infer that Menelaus, too, was a Hellenizer, even though the historian in Second Maccabees nowhere says so. The same historian refers to him solely by the Greek "Menelaus"; the priest's Hebrew name, "Onias," is preserved only by Josephus.[4] Had Menelaus, upon becoming high priest, abolished Jason's Hellenizing reforms, the authors of I 1:11–15, 64, and II 4:10–17 would never have been able to reason that those reforms were what roused the wrath of God and brought on the persecution. Some modern writers have tried to portray Menelaus as a more extreme Hellenizer than Jason.[5] Neither the writer in Second Maccabees nor any other surviving early source makes any such assertion.[6] Only Josephus' account[7] can be used to justify such portrayal, and that account is based either on Josephus' mistaken inferences or on the distortions of Onias IV.[8] Later in the course of his high priesthood, Menelaus may even have closed the gymnasium established by Jason![9] Menelaus' great sins were not extreme Hellenism but temple robbery, suborned murder, and violations of the laws of ritual purity.[10]

---

[1] See AB vol. 41, pp. 104–21.

[2] Ibid., p. 117.

[3] See NOTE on 4:19 and AB vol. 41, pp. 199–200, and my article, "Jewish Acceptance and Rejection of Hellenism," *Jewish and Christian Self-Definition*, ed. by E. P. Sanders, II, 67–69, 75–81.

[4] *AJ* xii 5.1.238, xx 10.3.235–36.

[5] E.g., Victor Tcherikover, *Hellenistic Civilization and the Jews* (Philadelphia: Jewish Publication Society, 1959), pp. 170–74.

[6] The evidence of Jubilees 23:16–24 contradicts the assertion. See below, p. 87.

[7] *AJ* xii 5.1.240–41, 9.7.384.

[8] See NOTE on 13:3–8 and my article in *Studies Smith*, Part III, pp. 121–22.

[9] See NOTE on 4:10–17.

[10] 4:32, 34, 39, 45, 47, 13:6, 8.

At first, therefore, under the high priests Jason and Menelaus, the Hellenizing program met no active resistance, a fact that the historians in First and Second Maccabees were later to deplore as a disastrous sin.[11] The fact is established not only by the accounts in First and Second Maccabees but by the implications of sources contemporary with the events. Most important of these sources is the book of Jubilees, but its importance has not been properly appreciated because its date has not hitherto been established. Now, however, one can show that a section of the book (23:11–31) was written between autumn, 169, and spring, 167 B.C.E.; the rest of the book may have been written during the same span of time and certainly was composed between Jason's reforms (of late 175 or early 174) and spring, 167 B.C.E.[12]

The preaching in the book of Jubilees demonstrably reflects Jason's reforms. The book stresses that Jews must not associate with gentiles.[13] The author perhaps goes out of his way to state that Greeks are just as bad as any other gentiles.[14] Although the participants in the gymnasium at Jerusalem did not exercise naked,[15] the possibility that they might do so seems to have evoked the stern warning at Jubilees 3:31. Thus the book contains examples of *verbal* opposition to Jason's program.[16]

The Testament of Moses speaks of dissension among the Jews and may allude to Jason's reforms,[17] but it says nothing of opposition to the reforms themselves. There is no allusion in Dan 7–12 either to Jason's reforms as an event or to opposition to them.[18] The pious did not take to *active* resistance against the Hellenizers until the high priesthood of Menelaus, and then they acted not against the Hellenizing program and the gymnasium but against other sins committed by the high priest and his associates, especially temple robbery. Even then, the resisters were unarmed, though they succeeded in routing the armed wicked and in killing their leader, the temple robber Lysimachus (II 4:32–42)! Armed resistance came still later. For this fact we have not only the implications of II

[11] I 1:11–15, 64, 2:49; II 4:10–17.

[12] See my article, "The Date of the Book of Jubilees," to be published in PAAJR.

[13] Jubilees 22:16–22.

[14] At Jubilees 37:10, the Ethiopic may mean that the "Kittim" were allies of Esau and his sons against Jacob and his. "Kittim" frequently means "Macedonians" or "Greeks" (AB vol. 41, pp. 191–92). However, the Ethiopic word in the context of Jubilees 37:10 may well mean "Hittites"; see Robert H. Charles, *The Book of Jubilees* (London: A. and C. Black, 1902), p. 216.

[15] See NOTE on 4:12.

[16] I shall demonstrate elsewhere that Enoch 90:6–9(first half) reflects events of the end of the third century B.C.E. Hence, the passage does not reflect events of the 170's and 160's B.C.E. Correct accordingly my article in *Jewish and Christian Self-Definition*, II, 81, and AB vol. 41, p. 41, n. 12.

[17] 5:1–6; see my article in *Jewish and Christian Self-Definition*, II, 81, and AB vol. 41, pp. 39–40.

[18] See *Jewish and Christian Self-Definition*, II, 81.

5:5–16 but also a witness datable between autumn, 169, and spring, 167 B.C.E.: Jubilees 23:16–24. The author there lists the transgressions which brought young pious Jews to fight their impious elders and then brought God to allow "the sinners, the gentiles" (i.e., Antiochus IV and his army) to sack Jerusalem and massacre her inhabitants. The transgressors are not said to be Hellenizers but embezzlers, robbers, and violators of the laws of ritual purity. These are the sins of Menelaus, not the Hellenizing policies of Jason the Oniad![19]

Indeed, down to that point, there had been good religious reasons for pious Jews to tolerate the Hellenizers. The Hellenizers had the support of the foreign king God had placed over the Jews. For centuries now, Jews had believed that God required them to obey such kings.[20] The Hellenizers could claim that the letter of the Torah permitted their practices.[21] Jason's reforms set aside only the interpretations of the Torah which barred close association with gentiles. Under Jason and even under Menelaus most Jews thought that the rest of the Torah was still being observed. Only at Enoch 89:73 do we find the complaint that even under the early post-exilic priests the laws of ritual purity were violated in the temple. From Jubilees 23:21 and Test Moses 5:3 we learn that the purity of the temple was violated during the high priesthood of Menelaus; perhaps, however, the writers refer only to the fact that Menelaus conducted Antiochus IV into the inner parts of the temple.[22]

Enoch, Jubilees, and the Testament of Moses are sectarian works, preserved only by a narrow tradition.[23] The sources preserved in the mainstream of tradition contradict them. Before spring, 167 B.C.E., there was only one gross violation of ritual law: Menelaus conducted the pagan king into the inner parts of the temple. From I 1:11–59 and II 6:1–2 we can infer that until the royal decrees of spring, 167, and perhaps until Kislev of that year, the laws of ritual purity continued to be observed, and the prescribed sacrifices continued to be offered. The contemporary witnesses of Dan 7–12 are absolutely silent on any earlier violations: the first interruption in the prescribed rituals came with the imposition of the Abomination of Desolation in Kislev, 167 B.C.E.

---

[19] 4:32–50, 5:5–7 (see NOTE on 5:5–16), 13:6, 8; cf. Test Moses 5:3–4 (Jason the Oniad certainly was of high priestly stock). At AB vol. 41, p. 122, I was wrong to say that the pious began to resist the Hellenizers as Hellenizers before Antiochus IV sacked Jerusalem in 169 B.C.E.

[20] See NOTE on 1:7, Jason . . . Kingdom.

[21] See AB vol. 41, pp. 199–200, and Jewish and Christian Self-Definition, II, 67–69.

[22] 13:8 may refer to the same fact. See my article, "The Date of the Book of Jubilees," to appear in PAAJR.

[23] Only the Ethiopian Church preserved Enoch and Jubilees, and the Testament of Moses survives through a single palimpsest.

2. Denial of the Authority of Commandments
by Jews in Judaea before 167 B.C.E.

On our topic there is one firsthand source, the book of Jubilees.[24] The author surely wrote against a broad spectrum of opponents, including the Hellenizers who observed the letter of the Torah but associated with Greeks, and also including rigorist Jews who would associate with no gentiles but rejected the sectarian solar calendar advocated in Jubilees.[25] He also argues against Jews who rejected the letter of one or more commandments. Thus from Jubilees 15:33–34 we learn that there were Jews who rejected the commandment to circumcise their sons. The author of Jubilees is concerned over the corporate guilt that such Jews would bring upon the entire community of Israel. Other pious Jews may simply have considered them complete apostates, outside the community, and many of the non-circumcisers may have agreed.[26] Many, if not all, of the non-circumcisers probably rejected the authority of the entire Torah.

Very interesting in Jubilees is the insistence, contrary to the implications of the stories in Genesis, that the patriarchs already observed the regulations later revealed to Moses. For an author writing to influence Jews who believed in the validity of the books of the Torah from Exodus through Deuteronomy, there was no need for so extreme a tactic. The insistence, indeed, demonstrates that the writer of Jubilees faced Jews who held that only the practices of the patriarchs of Genesis were binding, Jews who rejected the commandments in the later books of the Torah, revealed through Moses. Let us call such Jews "Patriarchalists." Patriarchalists still would have had to practice circumcision (Gen 17:10–14) and would have held to some observance of the Sabbath (Gen 2:2–3) and of the taboo against nudity (Gen 3:7, 21). They might have abstained from intermarriage, but they would have been as ready as Abraham for cordial relationships with non-Jews. The Patriarchalist point of view probably is quoted at I 1:11, as an argument to justify the reforms of the high priest Jason. Nevertheless, it is clear that Jason and Menelaus and the majority of their followers were not Patriarchalists. Even bitter pious foes of the two high priests do not say that under them the Torah of Moses ceased to be observed.[27]

Thus, the book of Jubilees reflects the existence of complete apostates,

---

[24] See p. 86.
[25] See my article cited in n. 22.
[26] See Gen 17:14.
[27] See pp. 85–87. Patriarchalists were important enough to provoke the vigorous reaction of the author of Jubilees. Nevertheless, apart from Jubilees and I 1:11, I know of no evidence that Patriarchalists existed in the second century B.C.E.

of non-circumcisers, of Patriarchalists, and of "Hellenizers" such as Jason
and his followers. The cult imposed upon the Jews by Antiochus IV in
167 B.C.E. involved the worship by Jews of multiple deities represented by
meteorite cult stones (*maṣṣēbōt*) and the sacrifice of pigs and eating of
pork.[28] A case that such was the original religion of Israel could have been
made from Genesis;[29] but, if it had been made in Judaea when the author
of Jubilees wrote, he would not have been silent. He would have
presented loud evidence to refute it.[30] Hence, we may be sure that when
the author of Jubilees wrote he had never heard of Jews arguing for such
a cult.

3. The Four Punitive Actions of Antiochus IV

From First Maccabees and from the abridged history we learn that Antiochus IV proceeded against the Jews in four actions well separated from
one another. These were (1) the king's sack of Jerusalem in 169 B.C.E.
and his appointment thereafter of officials to control the Jews and the Samaritans (I 1:20–24; II 5:11–23); (2) the expedition of Apollonius the
Mysarch, early in 167 B.C.E., which struck hard at Jerusalem and her people and fortified the Akra and established its garrison (I 1:29–40; II
5:24–26);[31] (3) the royal decrees of early spring, 167 B.C.E., prohibiting
obedience to the Torah and requiring observance of the imposed cult (I
1:44–53);[32] and (4) the forcible implementation of the decrees, first
with the erection of the Abomination of Desolation upon the temple altar
on 15 Kislev (December 6), 167 B.C.E., and thereafter with the continuing punishment of pious Jews who refused to conform (I 1:54–63; II
6–7, 10:5).

Action 4 is separated from action 3 not only by the narrative of I
1:44–53, 54–63. Action 3 is dated by the fact that it is the last event
known to the seer of Dan 7:25 ("He shall *think* to change the times and
the Law"). Mere *thinking* to change the "times" (the Sabbaths and festivals to be observed by Jews) and the Law is different from the forcible
implementation which constitutes action 4. As I shall show in my commentary on Daniel, the end of Dan 7:25 measures three and one half
years from action 3 to the beginning of the sabbatical year in Tishri, 164

[28] See AB vol. 41, pp. 141–58.
[29] See ibid., p. 262; eating of pork: Gen 9:2 and the absence of any later prohibition in Genesis; cf. Isa 65:4, 66:17.
[30] Cf. my article cited in n. 22.
[31] For the date, see my article, "The Apocryphal Book of Baruch," PAAJR 46–47
(1979–80), esp. pp. 179–85, and correct accordingly AB vol. 41, pp. 42, 163.
[32] On the failure of the abridged history to present action 3 as a distinct stage, see
introductory NOTE on II 6.

B.C.E.[33] Hence, action 3 occurred in Nisan, 167 B.C.E., about eight months before action 4.

Difficult though they are to interpret, the writings of the contemporary seers also confirm the historicity of all four actions.[34]

The four separate actions call for explanation. If the king had had a single motive (e.g., to civilize the Jews or to punish them for Jason's coup [5:5–11]), would he not have done so in one step? Even if God Himself had driven the unwitting king to be the rod of His anger, would He have impelled Antiochus IV to four actions, the last of which, far from inducing the Jews to repent, forced them to sin?[35]

To explain four such separate royal actions, the most natural assumption is that in each case Antiochus IV responded to a recent stimulus. Such a stimulus we would naturally expect to have been some provocation

[33] Correct accordingly AB vol. 41, p. 42. Normally, Tishri fell in September–October, but by 164 B.C.E. the Jewish calendar was to be defective; see AB vol. 41, pp. 274–80.

[34] Sack of 169: Dan 11:28, 9:26 (cf. 7:25, "He . . . shall wear out the saints of the Most High," and 8:13, "and the sanctuary . . . the victim of trampling"); Jubilees 23:22. See also Test Moses 6:1–9 as reconstructed by me in *Studies on the Testament of Moses*, ed. by George W. E. Nickelsburg, Jr. (Septuagint and Cognate Studies, no. 4 [Cambridge, Mass.: Society of Biblical Literature, 1973]), pp. 45–47.

The Mysarch's expedition: Dan 11:30(end), 39 (see pp. 92–94). See also Test Moses 6:9 as interpreted by me at *Studies on the Testament of Moses*, p. 47 (the verse is wrongly cited there as 6:8). Jubilees 23:22–23 might include the expedition of the Mysarch, but see n. 134.

Royal decrees: Dan 7:25, "He shall speak words concerning the Most High . . . and he shall think to change the times and the Law" (on *l^eṣad* as "concerning," see AB vol. 41, p. 140, n. 224); 11:36, "The king shall act arbitrarily and arrogantly lord it over every god. Concerning the God of gods he shall say things past belief."

Implementation: Dan 8:10–13, 24–25, 9:27, 11:31, 36(end)–38 ("Yet he shall prosper until the Wrath of God shall come to an end, for utter ruin shall have been accomplished. Though he shall pay no heed to the gods of his forefathers, and to the Delight of Women or any other deity he shall pay no heed, for he shall lord it over them all, yet he shall honor the god of strongholds on his altar base, and he shall honor a god whom his forefathers did not recognize, with gold and silver and precious stones and costly gifts"), 32–35; Test Moses 8:1–5; Enoch 90:11. On the god of strongholds, see n. 53 and pp. 106–10.

(The analysis and translation here of Dan 11:36–38 supersede those at AB vol. 41, pp. 45–46. Dan 11:30–39 should now be read in the order 30, 39, 36 [through *npl'wt*, "past belief"], 31, 36[end]–38, 32–35.)

Decrees mixed with implementation: Test Moses 8:1–5.

The massacres reflected at Enoch 90:8, for the writer of the original stratum, occurred at the end of the third century B.C.E., but the supplementer who added to Enoch 90 the victories of Judas Maccabaeus may have felt that those massacres included one or more of the actions of Antiochus IV. The reference to "kings who share in their guilt and punish them" at Test Moses 5:1 may include all four royal actions.

On Josephus' confused combination of all four actions together at *AJ* xii 5.4.248–56, see AB vol. 41, Appendix V.

[35] Surely pious Jews examined their deeds and sought to repent already after action 1. Repentance of Jews at the latest after action 2 is attested at Jubilees 23:24–26; cf. II 5:27. The existence of righteous and presumably repentant Jews after action 3 is attested at I 1:53.

by the Jews, whether real or imagined by the king. In seeking what such provocations could have been, we must bear important factors in mind. Pious Jews at first could not venture on direct rebellion against the foreign king God had placed over them; the first direct rebellion against Antiochus IV by Jews was Mattathias' act of zeal.[36] We can understand how the king mistook, as a most untimely rebellion against himself, Jason's coup and the armed opposition of the pious to Menelaus.[37] But nothing like a direct act of Jewish rebellion preceded actions 2, 3, and 4.[38]

What provocative acts could Antiochus have imagined the Jews to have committed? How often could the king have been mistaken about their intentions? We cannot expect our ancient Jewish sources to have preserved many clues for answering these questions. Jews at the time were so habituated to thinking in terms of sin and punishment that almost all our sources go no further to find the king's motive for acting as he did: he must in some way have been the rod of God's anger. Only for action 1 do we find Jason of Cyrene[39] and Josephus[40] giving a plausible human motivation, one confirmed by Jubilees 23:20 and by Epp. 0 and 1:[41] the king believed that the Jews had rebelled, though both troublemaking factions among the Jews seem to have thought otherwise of their actions.[42]

What happened between the sack and the Mysarch's expedition? Our only explicit information is at II 5:22-23: Jews and Samaritans had to suffer from the hostile actions of Philip and Andronikos, the officials the king had put in charge of them; and, worst of all, Jews had to suffer from the haughty overlordship of Menelaus.

To what Jewish actions were Philip and Menelaus responding? Again, they could not have been facing a rebellion against the king's rule. The belief that God would punish such rebellion surely still stood firm.[43] But let us consider how pious Jews, believing that Antiochus IV was the rod

---

[36] See NOTE on 1:7, *Jason . . . Kingdom*, and AB vol. 41, pp. 5, 229 (2:7-8), and 231-32 (NOTES on 2:7-8). The evidence presented there is confirmed by II 8:1-5 and by Dan 11:32-33. The word w'św ("and they shall take action") at Dan 11:32 might refer to pious armed resistance before the rise of the "little help," Mattathias. Even then, such resistance clearly came after action 4, which is reflected in Dan 11:31. Jason of Cyrene would gladly have told of pre-Hasmonaean armed resistance to confirm w'św at Dan 11:32 had he known of any. The senders of Epp. 0 and 1 probably would have mentioned any such rebellion alongside that of Jason (see NOTE on 1:7, *Jason . . . Kingdom*). No hint of Jewish rebellion is to be found in the Testament of Moses. On the horned lambs of Enoch 90:6-9(first half), see n. 16. The horned rams of later verses act with Judas Maccabaeus.

[37] See NOTE on 5:5-16.

[38] That consideration by itself suffices to render Tcherikover's theory untenable. See below, pp. 98-99.

[39] 5:5-7, 11.

[40] *AJ* xii 5.3.246-47, *BJ* i 1.1.31-32.

[41] Jubilees 23:20: see p. 87. Epp. 0 and 1: at II 1:7-8; see NOTES ad loc.

[42] See NOTE on 5:5-16.

[43] See n. 36. Confident of their own loyalty to the king, pious Jews at first had no fear of the expedition of the Mysarch (I 1:30; II 5:25-26).

of God's anger, would have reacted to the sack of 169 B.C.E. The Jews had experienced no such disaster since the fall of Jerusalem to Nebuchadnezzar in 586, over four centuries before. Some Jews must have reasoned: only a new sinful development among the Jews could have provoked this new manifestation of God's wrath. The Antiochene "reform movement" was a new development, and its compatibility with the Torah was questionable: the author of Jubilees denounced many aspects of that movement as hateful to God,[44] although he did not yet regard it as the pivotal sin which brought on the sack.[45]

Pious Jews who inferred that the Antiochene movement had brought down upon them the wrath of God would do everything in their power to "wipe out the evil from their midst,"[46] even while they maintained their own loyalty to the king. For such pious militants, events had proved that it was not enough to punish temple robbers such as Lysimachus (4:39–42); God obviously was angry at Jewish toleration of any Antiochene Jews. Acting on such inferences, pious Jews might indeed harass and kill Antiochene Jews as sinners and would then have provoked repressive responses by Philip and Menelaus.

But what of the Samaritans, who are also reported to have suffered punishment between action 1 and action 2 (5:23)? The Samaritans themselves probably were innocent of attacks of Antiochenes. There is no evidence of any Antiochenes from Shechem, and Antiochus IV did not sack the Samaritan temple on Mount Gerizim. But Jews, too, lived in Samaria,[47] and they may have followed the example of the Jews of Judaea in harassing Antiochenes. Andronikos, the royal officer, may have proceeded against the Samaritans only because he did not know how to distinguish them from Jews. Certainly the Samaritans later complained that Andronikos' successors made that mistake.[48]

Thus far we have only argued from probability to suggest that pious Jews tried to wipe out the Antiochenes and thus provoked the repressive acts of the royal officials. Clues in the sources can be used to confirm the hypothesis. Jubilees 23:23 may reflect not only the sack of 169 B.C.E. but also events between it and the expedition of the Mysarch. If so, the young militants in Jubilees 23:16–24 who take arms against Jewish sinners may include not only those who resisted Jason and Menelaus just before the sack but also those who tried to wipe out the evil of the Antiochenes in the months that followed.

Dan 11:30–39, if we could be sure how to interpret those verses, would provide important information on what happened after the sack of 169

---

[44] See p. 86.
[45] See p. 87.
[46] Cf. AB vol. 41, p. 122, where this factor driving pious Jews to violent action against Antiochenes is made to operate too early, before the sack of 169 B.C.E.
[47] See Appendix VIII, p. 527.
[48] J. *AJ* xii 5.5.260–61, quoted at the head of Appendix VIII.

B.C.E. The first clauses of Dan 11:30 are clear. They tell of the Roman ultimatum of 168 B.C.E. to Antiochus IV to withdraw from Egypt and of the king's compliance and its aftermath.[49] The middle and end of the verse are difficult. The words wšb wz'm 'l bryt qdš w'śh wšb ("and he shall return, and he shall be enraged against the Holy Covenant, and he shall act, and he shall return") would imply at first sight that the enraged king in person[50] on withdrawing from Egypt to the territory of his own kingdom[51] physically attacked the Jews before returning to Antioch. But our explicit sources exclude any physical attack by Antiochus IV on Jerusalem in 168, for they report no such action between the sack of 169 and the expedition of the Mysarch in 167. Our early sources, indeed, exclude any physical attack in Judaea by Antiochus IV in person after 169 B.C.E.[52]

Alternatively, if we take the first wšb ("and he shall return") in Dan 11:30 to mean a return of Antiochus IV all the way to Antioch, we can have the king be enraged there against the Jews and have him act against them by sending the expedition of the Mysarch; but then, what is the meaning of the second "and he shall return"? A further difficulty with this alternative interpretation is that Dan 11:39, far removed from Dan 11:30, is the only verse of the chapter that tells what the expedition of the Mysarch did. The first clause of Dan 11:39 as it stands, with its Masoretic vowels, makes no sense ("He shall do to the forts of strongholds with a foreign god"). The consonantal text (w'śh lmbṣry m'zym 'm 'lwh nkr) makes sense and can be rendered "He shall cause to become fortifiers [read mᵉbaṣṣᵉrēy] of strongholds[53] the people of a foreign god." "People" ('am) in such contexts means "soldiers."[54] Other considerations will lead me to prefer a somewhat different reconstruction of Dan 11:39,[55] but even at this point it is clear that fortification and soldiers who belong to a group foreign to pious Israelites are involved. The end of the verse, "making them rulers over the many and distributing land as wages," lets

---

[49] See AB vol. 23, pp. 297–98 (first par.).

[50] See AB vol. 41, p. 212, par. 5.

[51] Cf. the returns of kings in Dan 11:9, 13, 28.

[52] See AB vol. 41, p. 45.

[53] At AB vol. 41, p. 46, I accepted H. L. Ginsberg's ingenious hypothesis (*Studies in Daniel* [New York: Jewish Theological Seminary of America, 1948], pp. 42–43, 46–49), that "strongholds" (m'zym) is a mistaken translation into Hebrew of ḥsyn, the original author's Aramaic word for "the pious [plural]." The hypothesis cannot stand because the Hebrew of Dan 11 has both the singular "stronghold" (m'wz; vs. 31) and the plural "strongholds" (m'zym; vss. 38–39). If the translator saw the same ḥsyn before him in all three cases, how could he have misread it as ḥsn ("stronghold") in vs. 31 but as ḥsnyn ("strongholds") in vss. 38–39? By reading mᵉbaṣṣᵉrēy ("fortifiers") instead of mibṣᵉrēy ("fortresses"), we eliminate the tautology, so that Ginsberg's hypothesis is unnecessary for vss. 38–39. We shall find other reasons for preferring our own reading (pp. 106–12). At most, Ginsberg's hypothesis would be valid for m'wz in vs. 31 (but see p. 108).

[54] See AB vol. 23, p. 272.

[55] See pp. 106–7.

us know that the soldiers not only make fortifications but they also dominate the "Many" (i.e., pious Jews) and receive land in Judaea from the king as colonists.[56] We recognize the fortification of the Akra and the establishment of its garrison, actions accomplished by the expedition of the Mysarch.

Indeed, I have shown how Dan 11:30–39 came to be out of sequence and how the original order was 30, 39, 36(beginning), 31, 36(end)–38, 32–35.[57] I have further argued[58] that the words of Dan 11:30, wz'm 'l bryt qdš w'śh wšb ("and he shall be enraged against the Holy Covenant and shall act and return"), report that the king, on withdrawing from Egypt in 168 B.C.E., directed only verbal rage (wz'm) against the Jews and then merely passed by[59] Judaea and returned to his capital, Antioch.

The king would have had good reason then to curse the Jews, who in the previous year (when the Romans had been too busy in Macedonia to interfere with his operations in Egypt) had prevented him from completing his conquest of the Ptolemaic empire.[60] After so resounding a blow to his prestige as his forced withdrawal from Egypt in 168, Antiochus IV, a usurper,[61] also had good reason to hasten back to his capital and consolidate his position. It was no time to be diverted into taking vengeance upon the Jews.

The last words of Dan 11:30 are of great interest to us now: we learn from them that, on his return to Antioch, Antiochus IV gave a sympathetic hearing to "deserters of the Holy Covenant" (wšb wybn 'al 'zby bryt qdš). By that time, pious Jews, having experienced ample evidence of God's wrath, knew that the Hellenizers, whom they had left unopposed for years, were deserters of the Holy Covenant who had brought God's rage down upon the Chosen People. If Menelaus and his followers were not suffering from the attempts of pious Jews to "wipe them out," what else could have driven them to appeal to the king for help? If my reconstruction of the original order of Dan 11:30–39 is correct, the action of the king in response to the pleas of Menelaus and his followers was the expedition of the Mysarch.

The Akra and its garrison seem to have been established at least in part to protect native Jewish "sinners."[62] The fact would confirm our inference that the Mysarch came to avenge and protect the harassed Antiochenes of

---

[56] On the "Many" as pious Jews, see AB vol. 41, p. 46, n. 20. Military colonists held land as compensation for their service to the king; see Bezalel Bar-Kochva, The Seleucid Army (Cambridge Classical Studies; Cambridge University Press, 1976), pp. 21–39, 45–46, 57–58, 201.

[57] AB vol. 41, pp. 45–46 (as corrected here in n. 34).

[58] Ibid., pp. 212–13.

[59] See ibid., p. 213. Dan 7:25, "He shall speak words concerning the Most High," also reflects mere words of Antiochus IV.

[60] See NOTE on 5:5–16.

[61] See AB vol. 41, pp. 197–98, and NOTE on II 9:24–25.

[62] I 1:34, 4:2, and AB vol. 41, NOTE on 4:2, men of the Akra.

Jerusalem, not merely to gratify Antiochus IV in his hatred against the Jews.[63]

The king's decrees on the imposed cult and their implementation (actions 3 and 4) have been most puzzling to observers ancient and modern. We have documentary evidence that the actions were *punishment* for the "wickedness" of the Jews.[64] But from that point on, there are a host of difficulties.

The expedition of the Mysarch was completely successful in punishing pious Jews. At first it met no resistance whatever, and the garrison in the Akra long was able to crush pious militants.[65] Surely it was largely successful in protecting Jewish Antiochenes. Even if pious militants continued to harass Antiochenes, it is unlikely that such harassment by itself could have provoked Antiochus, within perhaps a few weeks and at most within three months, to take the unprecedented steps that constitute action 3. Yet it is hard to see what else Jews could have done within that brief period to incur yet another kind of punishment. Pious Jews still must have believed it was forbidden to rebel against the king. To take 5:27 as a hint that Jews rebelled against the royal government before action 3 is surely wrong.[66] There is still less reason to read any such thing into the corrupt and fragmentary Test Moses 7, which may well be a version (supplemented by a later seer) of what once covered the period.[67]

Furthermore, the chronology of actions 3 and 4 is very strange. The king issued his decrees in Nisan (April), 167 B.C.E.,[68] and pious Jews were immediately dismayed and intimidated by them.[69] They still believed their own God would punish them if they rebelled against the king. Antiochus IV had a loyal garrison in the citadel of Jerusalem. The Jews' high priest was the king's own appointee and was not famous for piety. By royal order, Jewish officials to conduct the imposed cult throughout Judaea had been appointed, and forsakers of the Torah had gathered around them and committed (unspecified) wicked acts.[70] Nevertheless,

63 See NOTE on II 5:23–24, *Disposed . . . slaves.*

64 J. *AJ* xii 5.5.260, 263, as translated and interpreted in Appendix VIII.

65 I 1:34–38, 2:7–8, as interpreted in AB vol. 41; I 2:31–38; II 5:22, 6:11 (it is legitimate to infer that Philip was in command of the Akra).

66 At II 5:27 we read of the departure of Judas Maccabaeus and a tiny group of supporters from Jerusalem in the immediate aftermath of the Mysarch's punitive attack on Jerusalem. Even if true (see NOTE ad loc.), this report cannot explain the punitive policy of Antiochus IV. Even according to the abridged history, Judas and his followers thereafter lived quietly in the wilderness, obeying the Torah at a time when it was still permitted by the king's own law to do so. On the horned lambs of Enoch 90:6–9(first half), see n. 16.

67 See n. 160.

68 See pp. 89–90.

69 I 1:52–53; Dan 7:21, 25 (see p. 90).

70 I 1:51–52. At AB vol. 41, p. 224, par. 2, I was wrong to include Geron the Athenian (of II 6:1) among the officers mentioned in I 1:51. If I 1:51–53 was written on the model of II Chron 19:4–20:31, as I suggested at AB vol. 41, p. 224, Antiochus' appointed officials, like Jehoshaphat's, were Jews. Gr. *episkopoi*, trans-

the decrees were not implemented until 15 Kislev (December 6). Despite the royal orders to offer sacrifices in every town (I 1:51), no sacrifices were offered before that date. Moreover, the actual implementers of the decrees were agents of the king who came directly from him and were distinct not only from the local Jewish officials and from the high priest but also from the garrison in the citadel.[71] Why was there no implementation for eight months? Why did the royal authorities in Judaea fail to put the decrees into effect, so that other agents finally had to come from the king to do so?

4. The Imposition by Antiochus IV upon the Jews of a Cult that Was Not His Own

Bickerman rightly pointed out the unique feature of what Antiochus IV did to the Jews. The religion of Antiochus IV was completely different both from the imposed cult and from the religion of the Jews upon whom he imposed the changes.[72] There are plenty of examples in which a ruling government forbids religious practices of a subject population whose religion it does not share. Antiochus IV watched the Romans extirpate the observances of the Bacchanalia from Italy.[73] Roman emperors were to forbid the practices of the Druids.[74] The emperor Hadrian was to ban circumcision and the teaching of the Torah by Jews.[75] The effort to wipe out heresy is a common phenomenon in the history of Christian states.

There are also examples wherein a government imposes its own religion upon its subjects. In the fourteenth century B.C.E., King Akhenaten (Amenhotep IV) of Egypt attempted to impose on his subjects his own

---

lating Heb. *peqīdīm*, can mean "officers" and does not have to be translated "officials to watch over." As Jehoshaphat appointed Jewish judges to administer justice, so Antiochus would have had Jewish officials appointed to carry out the observances of the imposed cult. See n. 120.

[71] At I 1:54 we are not told who carried out the king's will, but nothing indicates that the implementers were either Menelaus and his followers or the garrison in the citadel. At II 6:1 the king's only agent is "Geron the Athenian." At Dan 11:31 the implementers are "arms" (*zr'ym*) which arise directly from the king. Therefore they can be neither the "deserters of the Holy Covenant" (to whom the king gave a sympathetic hearing) nor the "fortifiers" of the citadel (who were already in Jerusalem); see pp. 93–95.

[72] *Gott*, pp. 117–20; *The God of the Maccabees* (Studies in Judaism in Late Antiquity, ed. by Jacob Neusner; Leiden: Brill, 1979), vol. 32, pp. xii–xiii; cf. AB vol. 41, pp. 139–58.

[73] AB vol. 41, pp. 125, 131–40, 158.

[74] Tcherikover, *Hellenistic Civilization*, p. 478, no. 40; Stuart Piggott, *The Druids* (New York and Washington: Praeger, 1968), pp. 127–30.

[75] Emil Schürer, *The History of the Jewish People in the Age of Jesus Christ* (New English version, rev. by Geza Vermes and Fergus Millar; Edinburgh: T. & T. Clark, 1973), vol. 1, pp. 534–57.

religious views, according to which only the sun disk Aten and the king himself were divine.[76] In Babylon in the sixth century B.C.E., King Nabonidus provoked the bitter opposition of his subjects when he sought to impose religious changes in accordance with his own view that the moon-god Sin was the greatest of the gods, rather than Marduk, the god of Babylon.[77] King Manasseh of Judah is reported to have slain many innocent persons[78] and also to have carried through religious changes regarded as sinful[79] by the author of the book of Kings. We may infer that at least some of the "innocent persons" were slain because they opposed those religious changes. Certainly King Josiah of Judah used force to impose upon all his subjects the acceptance of the commandments in the book of Deuteronomy.[80] After the Reformation, Protestant princes tried to impose Protestantism upon their Catholic subjects, and Catholic princes Catholicism upon their Protestant subjects.

Finally, there are examples of a ruler imposing upon a whole ethnic or religious group subject to him the religious views of a part of that group, even when the ruler himself does not adhere to their religion. When a ruler does so, we may always assume he acted in response to a request by holders of the views that their views be imposed. Artaxerxes I of Persia is reported to have imposed upon the Jews of a wide area of his realm the observance of the Torah as taught by Ezra.[81] In the eleventh and twelfth centuries C.E., Kings Alfonso VI, VII, and VIII of Castile in Spain gave Rabbanite Jews power to impose their will upon the Karaite Jews of the kingdom,[82] but the sources seem to indicate prohibition of Karaite teaching and practices rather than imposition upon the Karaites of Rabbanite observances.

It is hard, however, to find any parallel for the actions of Antiochus IV against the Jews by which the king, who was not a Jew, imposed practices which did *not* belong to his own religion upon the Jews of Judaea, practices which hitherto had had no following whatever there.

---

[76] There are controversies over the meaning of the scanty sources on Akhenaten's religious innovations. See Alan Gardiner, *Egypt of the Pharaohs* (Oxford: Clarendon Press, 1961), pp. 214–35; Cyril Aldred, *Akhenaten: Pharaoh of Egypt* (New York: McGraw-Hill, 1968), pp. 163–96, 213–60.

[77] See *Ancient Near Eastern Texts,* ed. by James B. Pritchard (2d ed.; Princeton: Princeton University Press, 1955), pp. 305–6, 308–16, and *The Ancient Near East: Supplementary Texts and Pictures,* ed. by Pritchard (Princeton: Princeton University Press, 1969), pp. 560–63. I hope to treat the case of Nabonidus in detail later.

[78] II Kings 21:16.

[79] II Kings 21:2–9.

[80] II Kings 22:8 – 23:25.

[81] Ezra 7:1–26; see also the Passover Papyrus, sent under Darius II of Persia, as restored by Bezalel Porten (*Archives from Elephantine* [Berkeley and Los Angeles: University of California Press, 1968], p. 129).

[82] Yitzhak Baer, *A History of the Jews in Christian Spain* (Philadelphia: Jewish Publication Society of America, 1961), I, 51, 65, 77, 95; Abraham ibn Daud, *Sefer Ha-Qabbalah (The Book of Tradition),* ed. and trans. by Gerson D. Cohen (London: Routledge & Kegan Paul, 1967), pp. 95–99.

We look in vain in the ancient sources for any appreciation of these difficulties. The authors of the surviving Jewish sources followed the beaten tracks of Jewish historical interpretation. The seer of Daniel either leaves the royal decrees unexplained (7:24–25, 9:27) or ascribes them to a human arrogance which the king directs against all gods (8:10–13, 11:31, 36–38). For the seers of Enoch 85–90 and the Testament of Moses, the royal decrees and the persecution do not require any royal motivation; they are merely one more step in a series of dreadful visitations to punish the Chosen People for sin. Even the perspective of later generations did not let Jewish observers penetrate the motives of the persecutor king. The Hasmonaean propagandist connected the decrees and the persecution with earlier impious projects of Antiochus IV,[83] but to explain why they came when they did could only point to the wrath of God (I 1:64). The statements of causal analysis in the abridged history contain nothing more than that explanation (II 4:15–17, 6:9[end], 12–16). Only as an afterthought does the royal arrogance enter (II 7:16, 19, 34, 36). Even if the king's actions were to be ascribed to insane arrogance, we would have to explain why he behaved thus at that particular time. His other policies during the period do not give the impression of impious insanity.

No more satisfactory are ancient non-Jewish observers. According to a Greek account,[84] Antiochus IV, after entering the Holy of Holies during his sack of Jerusalem in 169, wished to abolish the "misanthropic and lawless" customs of the Jews. The author would be putting the decrees two years too early, and we would still have to ask, "Why did the king act then, or even in 167?" The Jews had been following the Torah for centuries and had done so for years under Antiochus IV. Tacitus, too, says (*Histories* v 8) only that the king wished to "remove the superstition of the Jews and give them the Greek ways of life," and to "change the detestable nation for the better," but the imposed cult was not Greek, and Tacitus gives no reason why the king acted at that particular time.

5. How Can We Explain the Decrees on the Imposed Cult and the Strange Timing of Their Implementation?

Modern scholars have perceived some of these difficulties and have presented theories to solve them. Though the proposed solutions are untenable, they have some merit.

Tcherikover reconstructed what happened as follows:[85]

Antiochus IV punished the unruly pious Jews of Jerusalem and Judaea

[83] I 1:41–43; see AB vol. 41, pp. 119–20, 131, 221.
[84] Diodorus xxxiv–xxxv 1.3–4.
[85] Tcherikover, *Hellenistic Civilization*, pp. 189–200.

by revoking their privileges and subjecting them to a privileged colony of military settlers, the garrison in the Akra. That garrison consisted largely of Syrian pagans. As a matter of course, the Syrian colonists assumed they had the right to introduce their own religious rituals into the local temple. The idolatrous cults in the temple were merely those rites of the garrison.[86] On seeing the temple so violated, pious Jews rose in *religious* revolt, and Antiochus IV responded by prohibiting them from practicing their *religion*.

Tcherikover's theory is untenable and fails to solve the problems. There is reason to believe that the garrison in the Akra did not consist of Syrian pagans,[87] and when it was established it probably did not use the temple.[88] Jews certainly did not rebel against the king before Mattathias' act of zeal. The imposed cult was not a Syrian paganism but a heterodox Judaism, and Antiochus did not merely prohibit the Jews from observing their own religious rites, he imposed other rites upon them.[89] Tcherikover was unaware of the problems of timing and made no attempt to solve them.

Quite different is Bickerman's reconstruction of the events. In Bickerman's view, just as Ezra and his circle in the fifth century B.C.E. got power from Artaxerxes I of Persia to impose the Torah upon Jews, so Menelaus and his faction in the second century B.C.E. successfully sought decrees from Antiochus IV imposing upon the Jews of Judaea their own concept of what Judaism should be.[90] Bickerman's theory has the merit of rendering Antiochus' actions upon the Jews no longer unparalleled in human history. It also recognizes that the imposed cult was a heterodox Judaism.

[86] So reluctant is Tcherikover to use the testimony of the book of Daniel (*Hellenistic Civilization*, pp. 398–400) that he abstains from invoking the mention of the "God of strongholds" (*'lh m 'zym*) at Dan 11:38 as evidence for his theory.

[87] See pp. 106–12. The Seleucid kings at this time probably made no use whatever of Syrians in their military forces; see B. Bar-Kochva, "The Status and Origin of the Garrison at the Akra on the Eve of the Religious Persecutions," Zion 38 (1973), 43–47 (in Hebrew, with English summary, pp. i–ii).

[88] I 1:36–39; the seer at Dan 11:39 would not have passed over such a violation in silence.

[89] AB vol. 41, pp. 139–58, 261–62. I have shown (AB vol. 41, pp. 152, 155) how the worship of the consort and child of the LORD are attested as practices of heterodox Jews which were condemned by prophets.

[90] *Gott*, pp. 120–36; see also Appendix VIII, introductory NOTE to commentary on J. *AJ* xii 5.5.258–64. As reconstructed by Bickerman, the reform he ascribes to Menelaus contrasts strangely both with Ezra's reform and with the statements at I 1:44–51. According to Ezra 7:25–26, King Artaxerxes I of Persia empowered Ezra to impose the Torah not only upon the Jews of Judaea but upon all the Jews of the huge Transeuphrates province. Antiochus IV ruled over the entire Transeuphrates province, in which large numbers of Jews resided. The high priest had moral and religious authority, if not political authority, beyond Judaea (Deut 17:12; see AB vol. 41, pp. 431–32). If Menelaus and his group were fanatical enough to impose their reform on the Jews of Judaea, why did they not follow Ezra's example, of which they could read, and ask the king to impose the reform on all the Jews of the Transeuphrates province or of the entire kingdom? Indeed, according to I 1:44–51, the king did send letters to his entire kingdom announcing his decrees on the imposed cult!

Furthermore, it seems to be confirmed by the direct testimony of Josephus.[91] The words of the contemporary witness Daniel can be translated, "He shall give sympathetic attention to those who desert the Holy Covenant, and arms shall arise from him and desecrate the temple . . . and remove the continual offering and set up the Abomination from Desolation" (11:30–31).[92] What more direct testimony could one desire for the theory that Antiochus imposed the heterodox cult in response to requests from apostate Jews? Bickerman's theory was accepted by Hengel, who presented further argument in support.[93]

Nevertheless, we have argued to show how Dan 11:30–39 must be interpreted otherwise.[94] Josephus' statements can be shown to be untrustworthy.[95] And Bickerman's theory is untenable for other reasons. According to I 1:44, the customs of the imposed cult were foreign to the land of Judaea. The author of the book of Jubilees would have attacked the imposed cult in detail if it had been the ideology of a noticeable faction among the Jews when he wrote. The author of Jubilees 23:11–31, if confronted by so sinful a doctrine, would have singled it out for at least part of the blame which brought upon the Jews the cruel sack of 169 B.C.E. Thus, in 175 B.C.E. and even as late as the aftermath of the sack of 169 B.C.E., a pious writer in Judaea was still unaware of the ideology of the imposed cult.[96] We would have to assume that the ideology of the imposed cult sprang up like a mushroom and grew rapidly in the time between autumn, 169, and the publication of the king's decrees in April, 167.

We may grant, for the sake of argument, the possibility of that rapid growth, but there are further difficulties. Documentary evidence shows that actions 3 and 4 were *punishment,* contrary to Bickerman's theory. Documentary evidence also shows that far from being a fanatic who imposed a heterodox cult upon his fellow Jews, Menelaus himself was the one who at last successfully petitioned the royal government to desist from imposing it.[97] At II 4:16 we learn that the Antiochenes of Jerusalem, far from seeking the royal imposition of the cult, were its victims.

The chronology of the events is extremely awkward for Bickerman's interpretation. Menelaus before 169 B.C.E. had been in difficulties with the royal government and had faced riots against his high priestly administra-

---

[91] *AJ* xii 9.7.384; Bickerman, *Gott,* pp. 126–27.

[92] See Bickerman, *Gott,* pp. 126, 170–71.

[93] *Judaism and Hellenism* (Philadelphia: Fortress Press, 1974), pp. 283–303; see now, however, Klaus Bringmann's refutation of Bickerman and Hengel ("Die Verfolgung der jüdischen Religion durch Antiochos IV. Ein Konflikt zwischen Judentum und Hellenismus?" *Antike und Abendland* 26 [1980], 180–82).

[94] See n. 34 and pp. 92–94.

[95] See NOTE on 13:3–8.

[96] See pp. 86, 88–89.

[97] Actions 3 and 4 as punishment: see Appendix VIII, introductory NOTE; Menelaus' petition: 11:29, 32 (see NOTE on 11:27–33).

tion.[98] In 169 B.C.E. pious Jews had besieged him so that he had to be rescued by the royal army.[99] In 167 B.C.E., not long before the decrees imposing the cult, Menelaus had needed the further protection of the Mysarch's expedition and the establishment of the garrison in the Akra.[100] By that time Antiochus IV surely was aware that Menelaus, far from being a successful high priest, had been a drain on the royal resources. Even so, the king may have thought that the best way to discipline the unruly Jews was to show his own determination and keep Menelaus in power. To have deposed him would have been to have yielded to the pressure of the Jewish "rebels." It is hard, however, to see how Antiochus could have embarked on a risky policy at the request of so unsuccessful an official. In contrast, Nehemiah gave good service to Artaxerxes I (Neh 1:11 – 2:6), and so, probably did Ezra's circle. Onias IV, too, received the grant of his petition from Ptolemy VI in return for tangible good services.[101]

Still more puzzling, under Bickerman's interpretation, are the subsequent events, if my chronology is correct. Menelaus, who had sought the imposition of the cult, held power in Jerusalem as high priest and had the support of the garrison of the Akra. Nevertheless, the decrees published in April were not implemented until December!

Yet another difficulty for Bickerman's theory is the fact that only the unreliable conjecture of Josephus and the ambiguous words of Dan 11:30–31 can be made to support it. All other sources, both pagan[102] and Jewish, if they say anything about the origin of the imposed cult, ascribe it to the intentions of Antiochus IV himself, not to advice given to him by Jews.[103] The difficulty cannot be dismissed by the assertion that generally "the monarch alone was praised or blamed for his decision,"[104] whether it was his own idea or that of an adviser. The generalization is far from being true in literature.

The authors of the books of Samuel, Kings, and Chronicles show great

---

[98] 4:27–50.

[99] 5:5, 11; see NOTE on 5:5–16.

[100] See pp. 94–95.

[101] J. AJ xiii 3.1–2.62–71.

[102] Diodorus xxxiv–xxxv 1.3–4; Tacitus *Histories* v 8; Porphyry *De abstinentia ab esu animalium* iv 11, and FGH 260, F 51, 53–54.

[103] Cf. Isaak Heinemann, "Wer veranlasste den Glaubenszwang der Makkabäerzeit?" *Monatsschrift für Geschichte und Wissenschaft des Judentums* 82 (1938), 146–54. Heinemann did not know of the date and relevance of Test Moses 8 (see n. 34).

[104] So pleads Bickerman (*The God of the Maccabees*, p. xii). The very example which Bickerman cites there, the royal decree of 1492 expelling the Jews from Spain, helps to disprove his case. Jewish writers of the time took pains to ascribe its origin to evil counsel received by the monarchs (see below) rather than to King Ferdinand and Queen Isabella themselves. See Yosef H. Yerushalmi, *The Lisbon Massacre of 1506 and the Royal Image in the Shebet Yehudah* (Hebrew Union College Annual Supplements, no. 1; Cincinnati, 1976) and the review of it by Lionel Kochan, *Journal of Jewish Studies* 30 (1979), 103.

interest in the counselors of the kings, whether their advice was for good or for ill. Those writers held that God would favor the king only if he hearkened to the voice of the "righteous" counselors (usually prophets or priests) and rejected the advice of the "wicked." There was another tendency, shared by writers both Jewish and gentile. Though everyone knew that wicked kings could exist, the king (or emperor) was regarded as a normally beneficent figure in ancient and medieval thought, pagan, Jewish, and Christian.[105] If a monarch acted wickedly, writers would search the evidence to find who had been his evil counselor. Jewish authors proceeded in this manner not only with Jewish monarchs;[106] indeed, Jews regarded as normally benevolent even the Babylonian, Persian, and Hellenistic kings whom God had placed over them as punishment for their sins.[107] The evil acts of those kings, too, were usually found to come from the advice of evil counselors.[108] The figure of the potentate's evil counselor is surprisingly rare in the surviving Greek and Latin fiction, including epic and dramatic poetry as well as prose.[109] Nevertheless, pagan Greek and Roman historians and philosophers, too, were interested in the figure of the evil counselor.[110]

I have cited instances of the figure of the evil counselor in ancient literature outside First and Second Maccabees. One still might claim that the examples are rare enough to justify the generalization that usually the monarch alone was praised or blamed for his course of action. But First and Second Maccabees themselves are outstanding for the frequency with which such figures appear. The author of First Maccabees is hostile enough to Hellenistic kings to have ascribed all their "wicked" acts to

---

[105] See II Sam 8:15, 14:4–20; Isa 32:1; Roland de Vaux, *Ancient Israel: Its Life and Institutions* (New York: McGraw-Hill, 1961), pp. 110–13; Anneliese Mannzmann, *"Basileus,"* Der kleine Pauly, I (1964), 832–35; Otto Gierke, *Political Theories of the Middle Age*, trans. by Frederic William Maitland (Boston: Beacon, 1958), pp. 30–37.

[106] Evil counselors of Jewish kings: I Kings 12:1–16, 18:5–27; II Chron 22:3–5; J. *AJ* xiii 10.6.293–98, 11.1–2.303–10; TB *Qiddushin* 66a. One should include here the instances where the king's evil counselors were his wives; see I Kings 11:1–8; II Kings 8:18, and the general implication of the stories in I Kings 16:29 – 22:40; II Kings 9:30–37 (King Ahab, though sinful, repents; unrepentant Jezebel is the originator of his crimes). Cf. also II Sam 24:1; Amos 7:10–11.

[107] II Kings 25:27–30; II Chron 36:22–23; Ezra 1:1–8, 6:1–15, 7:1–28, 9:9; Neh 9:37; I Bar 1:11–12; II 3:1–3, 4:4–6. See NOTE on II 4:7–50.

[108] Haman in the book of Esther is not the only such evil counselor. See Ezra 4:4–24; Dan 6:4–24 (cf. Dan 3:8–12); Bel and the Snake 28–42; Philo *In Flaccum* 4:18–24, *Legatio ad Gaium* 26–29.166–78, 30.203–6. See also the instances in First and Second Maccabees, cited below, nn. 111, 112. A Jewish author in his narrative lets Ptolemy IV save face by falsely claiming to have been misled by evil counselors (III 6:23–26, 7:1–6). Jews also knew the story of how Nadan misled Esarhaddon (Ahikar 3:7 – 4:3).

[109] There is Paphlagon (Kleon) in Aristophanes' *Knights*.

[110] See Plato *Republic* viii 549d–550b, 564d–565f, *Epistle* 3.316d; Plutarch *Dion* 11–14, 25, 35–36; Herodotus vii 5–6, 9 (cf. 10–18); Diodorus xi 1.3; Polybius xxviii 21; Tacitus *Histories* i 6, *Annals* xiv 51.5–6, 57, xv 61.4, xvi 18.6–7.

their own innate wickedness. Nevertheless, he seizes every opportunity to expose to the reader those kings' priestly and non-priestly counselors from Judaea.[111] Jason of Cyrene regards Hellenistic kings as normally benevolent and parades the wickedness of the evil counselors, whether they be pagans, non-priestly Jews, or priests.[112] If a high priest had been responsible for the imposed cult, he would have been as infamous in Jewish history as King Manasseh of Judah.[113] The author of First Maccabees leaves the greatest sinners anonymous but wishes to discredit the immediate predecessors of the Hasmonaeans as high priests.[114] Is it conceivable that he could have been silent over such heinous high priestly sin? In the abridged history, we find specific condemnation of the sins of the high priests Jason[115] and Alcimus[116] and specific condemnation of Menelaus as cruel, as a temple robber, as a briber, and as a sinner against the ritual purity of the altar.[117] Is it conceivable that the writer in Second Maccabees could have been silent over a still more heinous high priestly sin?

My attempt in AB vol. 41[118] to solve the problems of the actions of Antiochus IV against the Judaism of the Torah involves, I think, fewer difficulties. There I argued that the imposed cult emanated from Antiochus IV himself. An admirer of the Romans, the king applied Roman methods wherever he could. He had observed how Roman authorities dealt with the Bacchanalia, a sect viewed by them as subversive. As seen by Antiochus IV, the Jews resembled that sect. Accordingly, he employed those Roman methods against the Jews. My solution agrees entirely with the sources in ascribing the measures to the king himself, acting without the prompting of Jewish counselors. Moreover, the timing is easily explainable. Menelaus, though no saint, knew how Jews would react to the imposition of idolatry upon them. Like Petronius, the governor for the Roman emperor Gaius Caligula,[119] Menelaus went through such perfunctory motions as appointing officials to administer the imposed cult[120] but otherwise dragged his feet as long as he could, just as later he was to peti-

---

[111] I 1:13, 6:21–27, 7:6–7, 25, 9:58–59, 10:61, 11:21, 25, 13:21, 16:18. It is noteworthy that even the author of First Maccabees allows Antiochus IV to claim that he had been benevolent (6:11).

[112] II 3:4–6, 10, 4:8–17, 24–25, 43–50, 10:12–13, 13:3, 14:3–11, 26.

[113] II Kings 21:1–17, 23:26, 24:3–4; Jer 15:4.

[114] See AB vol. 41, p. 67. By implication, the pious priests at I 4:42 discredit Menelaus (see NOTE on II 10:1–8). Alcimus is named and discredited at I 7:5–25, 9:54–56.

[115] 4:7–20, 5:6–10.

[116] 14:3–10, 26–27.

[117] 4:25, 32, 34, 39, 45, 47, 5:23, 13:6, 8.

[118] Pp. 125–60.

[119] Philo Legatio ad Gaium 31–34.207–60; J. AJ xviii 8.2–6.261–88.

[120] I 1:51; see pp. 100–1 and n. 70. In I 1:51 "he [Antiochus IV] appointed" surely means that the officers were appointed by the king's orders, not by the king himself. The logical person to be given the duty of appointing them would be Menelaus, a person whom the author of First Maccabees steadfastly refuses to mention (see AB vol. 41, p. 67).

tion for an end to its imposition.[121] Not surprisingly, the Jewish authors
who had good reason to loathe Menelaus give him no credit for so dragging his feet. By late 167, however, the failure to implement the decrees
came to the attention of the king. Still reluctant to depose the high priest
who had cost him so much effort to keep in office,[122] Antiochus now sent
his own agents to enforce compliance with the decrees.[123] As for the inaction of the garrison in the Akra before late 167 B.C.E., the king's decrees
on the imposed cult were not addressed to the garrison but were sent "to
Jerusalem and to the towns of Judah,"[124] presumably to the high priest
and to the various local community organs. Had Menelaus sought the aid
of the garrison, he could have had it, but he was dragging his feet.

My solution in AB vol. 41, however, is vulnerable to serious objections.
First, it seems to leave the actions of Antiochus IV unique in human history: the king imposed changes upon a religion which was not his own.
This objection is not necessarily fatal. Unique phenomena do happen in
history. In many ways, Antiochus IV was a unique Hellenistic king, not
least in his efforts to copy Roman methods even where those methods
were grotesquely inappropriate.[125] If Antiochus IV thought the Jews were
similiar to philosophers[126] or to the worshipers in the Bacchanalia, the assumption that he used Roman methods against the Jews, far from ascribing unique behavior to him, fits the known character of the king.

A very serious objection against my solution is the fact that a fundamental difference exists between the Roman suppression of the Bacchanalia on the one hand and actions 3 and 4 on the other: the Romans prohibited the present practices of the worshipers; they did not impose other
practices upon them. I tried to take account of this difficulty before,[127]
and something more can be said now.

The Romans, because they themselves were worshipers of mighty
Bacchus, felt secure in suppressing the Bacchanalia. Otherwise, they
might have been deterred by the lessons proclaimed by believers, and
upon the tragic stage, of how Dionysus-Bacchus punished those who in-
terfered with his worship.[128] In the Seleucid kingdom, the stories about
how dangerous it was to provoke the God of the Jews may have been
equally well known. Even if Antiochus IV did not believe those stories,

---

121 11:29–32.
122 See pp. 100–1.
123 See n. 71.
124 I 1:44.
125 See AB vol. 41, p. 104.
126 Ibid., pp. 126–28.
127 Ibid., pp. 139–42.
128 Euripides' *Bacchae* forcefully demonstrates those lessons. It was vastly popular
in the Graeco-Roman world. See *Euripide: Les Bacchantes,* ed. by Jeanne Roux
(Paris: "Les Belles Lettres," 1970–72), I, 71–76. For other texts, see Park McGinty,
"Dionysos's Revenge and the Validation of the Hellenic World View," HTR 71
(1978), 77–94.

large numbers of his subjects may have. Those subjects would think their king to be a doomed man if he roused the wrath of the God of the Jews.[129] Hence, the king would have had good reason to seek some "pristine" Jewish cult to replace the "degenerate" form which had driven the Jews to insubordination and outright rebellion. Scriptural texts could be used to prove the earlier existence of a Jewish religion which knew nothing of the revelations ascribed to Moses and the prophets,[130] and even to show that there had been Jews who held those revelations to be spurious or invalid.[131] If those revelations were invalid and if the king imposed that earlier religion upon the Jews, the powerful God would not be deprived of worshipers, and the king could appear to be safe from His wrath.

If the king was to perceive the similarities between Judaism and the Bacchanalia and formulate the imposed cult, he or his agents would have to have had considerable knowledge of Jewish literature and practices. The surviving sources suggest strongly that as a rule Hellenistic kings and gentile commoners paid little or no attention to such matters, even though Greek translations of the Jewish texts were available. Nevertheless, I have argued that Greek philosopher-"anthropologists" showed sufficient interest in the Jews to have served as the king's informants,[132] and I have suggested that a small community of heterodox Jews could so have served Antiochus.[133] When the author of Jubilees wrote, no such community existed in Judaea. There are, however, hints that the garrison of the Akra was just such a community of heterodox Jews.

Another factor encourages us to follow up those hints. Even when seen in the light of King Antiochus' infatuation with Roman methods, actions 3 and 4 remain strange. In searching for an explanation, one naturally asks, what new element entered the situation to evoke entirely new royal responses? The evidence suggests that there were no radical changes among the Jews of Judaea before 25 Kislev, 167 B.C.E.: they might try to wipe out Jewish sinners, but they continued to abstain from rebellion

[129] Greeks tended to compare or equate the God of the Jews with Dionysus; see AB vol. 41, p. 129.

[130] See AB vol. 41, pp. 148–51, 152, 155, 157, 262. Add the texts showing there were Jews who ate pork (Isa 65:4, 66:17). Isa 65:7 and the repeated references to the "high places" (*bāmōt*) in the books of Kings demonstrate that Jews sacrificed to their God elsewhere than in the Chosen Place.

[131] Esp. Jer 44:17–19.

[132] AB vol. 41, pp. 140–41; there I followed the dubious view that Strabo xvi 2.35–37 reproduces the views of Poseidonius. I also was wrong to interpret "tyranny" in that passage from Strabo as meaning Jewish intolerance of pagan practices on Jewish soil. In context it clearly refers to the aggressive policies of the Hasmonaeans. Strabo would still serve as evidence for Greek intellectuals' views of Judaism, and though his date is long after our period, the fragments of the early writers I cited there, of Theophrastus and Hecataeus, are sufficient to make the point.

[133] AB vol. 41, pp. 141–42. By "heterodox Jews" I mean only Jews who did not accept the full authority of the Torah. I do not mean to imply that there existed a single recognized orthodox Jewish creed at the time.

against the king. So far as we know, there were no radical changes then in the condition of the Seleucid empire outside Judaea. Thus, one is tempted to look at the one new element attested by the sources: the presence of the garrison in the Akra of Jerusalem.

I have called attention to the peculiar expressions used to designate the garrison. The men of the "sinful nation," the "people of a foreign god," are unlikely to have been gentiles and probably were heterodox Jews.[134] Contrary to my earlier assumption, they are also unlikely to have included the Antiochenes of Jerusalem.[135] Rather, they certainly were soldiers. They certainly established some sort of military colony at Jerusalem.[136] At Dan 11:39 they are called "fortifiers" of plural "strongholds."[137] In Judaea the garrison of the Akra is known to have fortified only one stronghold, the Akra itself.[138] We thus learn that the men of the garrison had previously built strongholds elsewhere in the Seleucid empire. For this reason we cannot retain our earlier translation of Dan 11:39: Antiochus did not cause the men of the garrison to become fortifiers; they already were fortifiers.

H. L. Ginsberg, following the hint of the Syriac version, has provided the key to a good solution. Ginsberg has argued that the wretched Hebrew

---

[134] See AB vol. 41, pp. 123–24. The document at I 14:36 distinguishes the men of the Akra from gentiles. Consequently, Jubilees 23:23–24 cannot include the establishment of the Akra. In Jubilees 24:28 (wrongly cited as Jubilees 24:8 at AB vol. 41, p. 124, n. 120), "the sinners, the gentiles" can hardly be heterodox Jews; they must be the real gentile soldiers of the Macedonian kings ("Kittim") who, beginning with Alexander's devastating siege of Gaza in 332 B.C.E., repeatedly turned Philistia into a battleground. Hence, "the sinners, the gentiles" of Jubilees 23:23–24 surely are complete gentiles.

[135] The author of First Maccabees does nothing to identify the garrison (I 1:34–37) with the Antiochenes (I 1:11–14). The Antiochenes arose "in Israel," in Judaea and Jerusalem (I 1:11); the garrison consisted of "foreigners" (I 1:38). The words at I 6:22–27 in my translation might seem to imply that the men of the Akra were Jews of Judaea, but in the Greek (and the underlying Hebrew) the quotation probably comes from the wicked Israelites of vs. 21. I 6:21–22 should then be translated, "Some of the men of the Akra slipped through the siege lines. Some wicked Israelites joined them and went to the king and said, 'How long . . .'" I 4:2 shows that men of the garrison were throughly familiar with the terrain of Judaea. At AB vol. 41, p. 264, I drew the inference that those men must have been native Jews. Renegade Jews could easily have joined the garrison once it had been established. Individuals from Judaea could also have had long careers in the royal army so as to be trusted enough to be included in the garrison to control turbulent Jerusalem. Furthermore, by the time of the events of I 3:42–4:25, the garrison had been in Judaea for over two years, so that the guides of I 4:2 need not have been natives of the country.

Similarly, Daniel does nothing to identify the Antiochenes ("deserters of the Holy Covenant"; 11:30) with the "fortifiers" in the Akra (11:39). Correct accordingly AB vol. 41, p. 124, and delete the first sentence of ibid., p. 220, NOTE on 1:37. Correct also ibid., pp. 219–20, NOTE on 1:34: the "breed of sinners" could indeed have been a *part* of the Mysarch's army.

[136] See AB vol. 41, pp. 109, 123–24, 220.

[137] See p. 93.

[138] I 1:33–38, 14:36.

of Dan 11 is a translation with numerous errors from an Aramaic original.[139] Where the Hebrew text has w'śh ("And he shall do" or "And he shall cause to become"), the Syriac version has wy'br ("And he shall pass" or "And he shall transfer"). In ancient Aramaic scripts r was frequently indistinguishable from d. The Hebrew w'śh could thus be the result of misreading wy'br ("And he shall transfer") as wy'bd ("And he shall do"). We could then translate Dan 11:39 as "And he shall transfer the fortifiers of strongholds,[140] the people of a foreign god, whom he recognizes and honors greatly,[141] and he shall place them in rule over the Many and shall parcel out land as wages."[142]

Fortunately, we possess some information on what the religion of heterodox Jewish soldiers might have been like and on how they could function in the Seleucid empire. Many soldiers were among the Jews who fled to Egypt after the murder of Gedaliah, taking Jeremiah the prophet with them. They settled together in Tahpanhes in the eastern Delta.[143] It is likely that those soldiers supported themselves by serving the king of Egypt as mercenaries and that many of those Jews who settled in Migdol, Noph (Memphis), and the land of Pathros (Upper Egypt)[144] also did so. In that case we could call those Jewish communities "military colonies." From Jeremiah 44 we learn that those communities worshiped the Queen of Heaven, in defiance of Deuteronomy and the words of Jeremiah.

We do not know the subsequent history of those Jews in Egypt who defied Jeremiah. There is no direct evidence that they became professional soldiers. But we have documents from the fifth and fourth centuries B.C.E. belonging to the military colony of Jews at Elephantine in southern Egypt. Those Jews either did not know Deuteronomy and the rest of the Torah or refused to recognize their authority, for they offered sacrifices at their own local temple and recognized plural deities, some of whom were female.[145] Members of any of the pious sects in Judaea in 167 B.C.E.

---

[139] *Studies in Daniel*, pp. 41–61. Cf. AB vol. 23, pp. 14–15.

[140] Taking the *l* of *lmbṣry* as the sign of the direct object (Stanislav Segert, *Altaramäische Grammatik* [Leipzig: VEB Verlag Enzyklopädie, 1975], pp. 350, 408). One might expect the destination of those transferred to be specified, but their destination becomes obvious farther on in the verse, where they are said to be placed in rule over the Many (i.e., over the pious Jews of Judaea and Jerusalem; see n. 56).

[141] The Hebrew text of the relative clause is vague and ungrammatical. The sense seems to be that the transferred persons are the people of the god whom Antiochus in Dan 11:38 is said to have recognized and honored. We have argued (pp. 92–94) that Dan 11:39 originally stood well before Dan 11:38. Perhaps the ungrammatical clause is an interpolation made when Dan 11:39 came to stand after Dan 11:38.

[142] See n. 56.

[143] Jer 41:16 – 43:7.

[144] Jer 44:1.

[145] Emil G. Kraeling, *The Brooklyn Museum Aramaic Papyri* (New Haven: Yale University Press, 1953), pp. 81–91. Porten, *Archives from Elephantine*, tries repeatedly to minimize the heterodoxy of the Elephantine Jews, but even he must concede there was some (pp. 154–58, 160–64, 171, 173–79). There are logical weaknesses in

would have regarded the Jews of Elephantine as heterodox. As for their own great masculine God, the Jews at Elephantine called Him "Yaho the God Who Is in Yeb the *Fortress*."[146] We may infer that after being transferred several times from one fortified military base to another, such Jews might have come to call their God "the God of strongholds" as at Dan 11:38 and might even have come to call His temple "the stronghold" as at Dan 11:31. They themselves might have been called the "fortifiers of strongholds" as at Dan 11:39.

When the Elephantine Jews suffered at the hands of their hostile Egyptian neighbors, they turned for help to the Jews of Judaea and to imperial authorities in Judaea, Samaria, and Egypt. To conciliate the Egyptians and win the support of the Jews of Judaea, the Elephantine Jews gave up offering animal sacrifices and made changes in their observance of the Passover.[147] We may infer that if the colonists had not had to appeal for help, they might have continued their previous practices undisturbed. Nothing indicates they yielded on any other points. They probably rebuilt their temple after its destruction.[148]

The Elephantine community thus can serve to show us that the religion of a Jewish military colony could have been polytheistic and not in conformity with the Torah. There is no need to assume that the garrison of the Akra was descended from the Jews of Elephantine.

The Seleucid empire is known to have made use of Jewish military colonies. Antiochus III, knowing the loyalty of Jewish soldiers, ordered his governor Zeuxis to "transfer" (*metagagein*) two thousand Jewish families from Mesopotamia and settle them in the troubled areas of Lydia and Phrygia, in the *"forts* and most strategic places" (*ta phrouria kai tous anankaiotatous topous*). He promised them that they could live by their own laws. Were those laws the Torah? Or were those Jews heterodox? Noteworthy is the fact that the natives of Phrygia used cult stones to represent the deities they worshiped.[149] The Seleucid empire had to cede Phrygia in 188 B.C.E. by the terms of the Peace of Apameia. Could the Seleucid kings have continued to maintain their Jewish military units after withdrawing them from Phrygia? Could Antiochus IV have finally trans-

---

his arguments. To prove that deities mentioned in the Elephantine papyri were Aramaean (Porten, pp. 164–73) is not yet to prove that they were not also Jewish for the Elephantine colonists. Polytheistic peoples can have gods in common. Porten begs the question when he asserts that 'Anathi, father of indubitably Jewish Jedaniah, bore a non-Jewish name (p. 149, n. 132) and also when he asserts the same of Bethelnathan, son of indubitably Jewish Jehonathan (ibid., n. 133). Observance of the Sabbath at Elephantine may have differed from the commandments in the Torah (Porten, pp. 126–27).

[146] Kraeling, *Aramaic Papyri*, p. 85. The Aramaic word is *byrt'*.
[147] Porten, *Archives from Elephantine*, pp. 128–33, 278–82, 284–93.
[148] Ibid., pp. 294–95; cf. J. *AJ* xiii 3.1.65–66.
[149] Transfer of Jews: J. *AJ* xii 3.4.149–50; for other glimpses of Seleucid use of Jewish soldiers, see NOTE on 8:20 and J. *AJ* xii 3.1.119. Stone worship in Phrygia: Wolfgang Fauth, "Kybele," Der kleine Pauly, III (1969), 383.

ferred such units to the Akra in Jerusalem? There is no solid evidence, but there is a hint. From 169 B.C.E. the commander for Antiochus IV at Jerusalem was Philip the *Phrygian,* and he became commander of the Akra when it was established.[150] This Philip could have been familiar with the Jewish soldiers who had been stationed in his homeland. Such a person could have suggested to Antiochus IV the transfer of units of those loyal but heterodox Jews to curb turbulent Jerusalem, or the king himself might have borne in mind who was his commander at Jerusalem and thus have turned to those Jews for the garrison of the Akra.

It would be rash to insist upon the hypothesis connecting the garrison of the Akra with the Jewish settlers in Phrygia, for it rests upon a mere hint. Nevertheless, it fits well with our more solidly based assertions that the garrison consisted of heterodox Jews who had previously *somewhere* built forts so as to be called "fortifiers of strongholds." Just as Antiochus III gave orders to transfer (*metagagein*) Babylonian Jews to Phrygia, so Antiochus IV transferred (*wy'br*) heterodox Jews to the Akra.

In Dan 11:22–24 the seer may have expressed his belief that Menelaus plotted to bring upon Jerusalem the garrison of "fortifiers."[151]

Having established the likelihood that the garrison of the Akra consisted of heterodox Jews transferred from outside Judaea, can we use the fact to solve the problem of explaining the imposed cult? The fact is certainly in harmony with the absence of any earlier trace of the imposed cult in Judaea.[152] One might be surprised by the extent of the heterodoxy of the men of the Akra, assuming that the imposed cult was indeed their religion: they would be Jews who did not recognize the authority of the Torah;[153] they worshiped multiple deities in the form of *maṣṣēbōt*;[154] they offered sacrifices, but not those prescribed by the Torah, and did so outside the temple in Jerusalem;[155] they offered up pigs and ate pork;[156] they did not practice circumcision;[157] they may have observed Sabbaths and festivals, but, if so, the Jews who followed the Torah viewed their manner of observance as violation of those holy days;[158] surely the calendar of the heterodox Jews differed from that used by any sect of Torah observers. However, ancient Jewish writers attacked many groups of Jewish "sinners." Those writings attest that almost every one of the traits we

---

150 II 5:22, 6:11 with I 1:33 and 2:31–38.
151 See NOTE on 5:23–24, *Disposed . . . slaves.*
152 See pp. 88–89.
153 Cf. I 1:56.
154 See AB vol. 41, pp. 142–57.
155 I 1:47, 54–55, 59, 2:15–25; II 6:7–8, 21, 7:42.
156 I 1:47–48, 62–63; II 7:1.
157 I 1:48, 60–61; II 6:10.
158 I 1:45; II 6:6, 11; J. *AJ* xii 5.5.259 (translated at the head of Appendix VIII) does not prove that the heterodox "fortifiers" in the Akra did nothing to observe the Sabbath. It only shows that Samaritans observed the day in much the same manner as pious Jews.

have ascribed to the men of the Akra belonged to one or another group of Jews.[159] The contemporary observer, the seer of Dan 11:38–39, calls the god of the imposed cult the "god of strongholds" and says that the men of the Akra, the "fortifiers of strongholds," are the people of that god.[160]

According to my theory in AB vol. 41, Antiochus IV himself jumped to the conclusion that the Jewish religion was analogous to the Bacchanalia, as an imported seditious degeneration from a pristine cult; and he, with the help of expert informants, determined what that original cult was.[161] The hypothesis is not impossible but involves some improbabilities. According to Livy, the Roman authorities justified their suppression of the rites of the Bacchanalia by claiming they were suppressing "foreign rites" (sacra externa),[162] even though they also banned the Bacchanalia in parts of Italy where the rites were undoubtedly indigenous.[163] "Foreign" to the Roman authorities thus would have meant "foreign to Rome." If Antiochus IV had been strict in drawing his analogies, how could he have been drawing at all on Roman methods when he punished the Jews by requiring them to observe the imposed cult? Both the religion of the Torah and the heterodox cult were foreign to the king!

There is another difficulty: my hypothesis in AB vol. 41 does not account well for the gap in time between the expedition of the Mysarch and the proclamation of the imposed cult. Antiochus IV was aware, from the beginning of his difficulties with the Jews, of how the Romans dealt with the Bacchanalia. Why did it take him so long to perceive that the Jews were a fit object for the same sort of procedure?

One can, however, imagine that the king indeed required time to determine his own policy toward the Jews and especially to secure the informa-

---

[159] See AB vol. 41, pp. 148–55; non-circumcision: Jubilees 15:33–34; sacrifice outside the temple and eating of pork: Isa 65:3–4.

[160] The very obscure and mostly illegible ch. 7 of the Testament of Moses may have suffered extensive rewriting in Herodian and post-Herodian times (see my article in Studies on the Testament of Moses, ed. by George W. E. Nickelsburg, Jr., pp. 45–47). In its original state, however, it may have referred to the garrison in the Akra as impious cruel gluttons possessing power over the pious. If so, it is interesting that 7:9 contains allusions to Dan 7:8 and to Isa 65:5, the verse which follows the one condemning eaters of pork (see n. 159). Among the unintelligible fragments at the end of the unique Latin manuscript which preserves Test of Moses 7 are the two letters su, which may have been part of the Latin word for "pig."

If the heterodoxy of the men of the Akra was so great, one might be surprised that the document at I 14:36 condemns them only for violating the laws of ritual purity. But even during the persecution, the garrison only carried out the king's orders. After the imposed cult ceased to be enforced, the kings wanted peace in Judaea and certainly did not want the garrison to provoke the pious by acts of murder and gross sacrilege. But so complicated were the Jewish laws of ritual purity that soldiers ignorant of them could violate them unintentionally by seemingly trivial acts. After so many years of antagonism, the soldiers of the garrison had a tendency to commit such violations deliberately.

[161] Pp. 125–59.

[162] xxxix 16.8–9.

[163] AB vol. 41, pp. 137, 158; Livy xxxix 13.8–9, 15.6–7, 17.6–7.

tion he needed for formulating the imposed cult. That factor might explain the delay. And since Antiochus IV is known to have tried to apply Roman methods even where they were grotesquely inapplicable,[164] the lack of strict parallelism is not necessarily fatal to my hypothesis. A revised hypothesis, however, accounts for the facts much better: information provided by the men of the Akra was the stimulus that provoked Antiochus IV to issue his proclamation on the imposed cult. The men of the Akra came on the scene to say that the religious practices of the unruly pious Jews were originally "foreign rites" and to say that their own practices were the original religion of Israel. Indeed, they may have been aware of how the Torah had been brought from Babylonia and imposed upon the Jews of Judaea by Ezra.[165] Habituated as Antiochus IV was to think of using Roman methods, he would not have noticed the lack of strict parallelism. On hearing that the rites of the followers of the Torah were *sacra externa,* the king could have proceeded directly to suppress those rites and impose the "native cult" of the heterodox garrison, even without the aid of a "brain trust" of philosopher-"anthropologists."

What of the strange timing of actions 3 and 4, with many months elapsing between them? The garrison of the Akra was in Jerusalem and long successfully intimidated pious Jews. Could they have refrained so long from aiding in the imposition of their own religion upon the followers of the Torah? They could. History contains examples wherein a religion split into irreconcilable sects, and yet members of one of those sects had no desire to impose their beliefs and practices on the other adherents of the religion. The members of such a sect were concerned, so to speak, solely with their own salvation, not with that of others. Some of those sects were Jewish.[166] The same may have been true, then, of the men of the Akra in 167 B.C.E.[167] They may have worshiped their God of Fortresses in the

---

[164] AB vol. 41, pp. 104–5.

[165] Ezra 7:1–26.

[166] The worshipers of the Queen of Heaven in Jeremiah 44 made no effort to impose their beliefs and practices on Jeremiah and Baruch. The Qumran sect withdrew as far as possible from association with those outside their community, whom they regarded as the wicked; they believed they should make no effort to impose their ways upon outsiders before the great war at the end of history (see Yigael Yadin, *The Message of the Scrolls* [New York: Simon and Schuster, 1957], pp. 114–31, 173–76). On the Druze sect of Islam, see M. G. S. Hodgson, "Durūz," Encyclopaedia of Islam, new edition, II (1965), 633a.

[167] From I 1:36–37 we need not infer that the garrison from the first intended to provoke the wrath of followers of the Torah. The mere fact that they did not follow the laws of the Torah on ritual purity meant that if any of them entered the temple he defiled it, no matter what his intent. Any armed police action of theirs in Jerusalem could shed "innocent" blood. From Kislev, 167, the garrison received and obeyed orders to enforce the imposed cult (I 2:31; II 6:11; cf. I 1:58 and 2:15, where one cannot be sure that the men of the Akra were involved). Still later, they faced the wrath of the resurgent militant pious Jews (I 4:41, 6:18–20, etc.; II 8:8, 15:31–32). From that time on, they had good reason to retaliate with provocative acts (I 6:18, 14:36).

Akra itself and may have been completely uninterested in the temple. Moreover, one can interpret Dan 11:23–24 to mean that the "fortifiers" in the Akra and Menelaus were allies,[168] and then we could easily imagine how the garrison acquiesced cooperatively while the high priest dragged his feet in complying with the royal decrees on the imposed cult.

If the reconstruction proposed here is correct, Antiochus IV imposed the cult on the Jews as punishment, thinking to follow the analogy of the Roman suppression of the Bacchanalia; the main core of the solution I gave in AB vol. 41 would then stand firm. But the imposed cult was the religion of the garrison of the Akra, as suggested by Tcherikover, and it was the religion of an existing heterodox Jewish sect, as suggested by Bickerman![169]

I hold to my views after reading the recently published tantalizing Greek inscription published by S. Applebaum ("A Fragment of a New Hellenistic Inscription from the Old City of Jerusalem," in *Judaism in the Second Temple Period: Abraham Schalit Memorial Volume,* ed. by A. Oppenheimer et al. [Jerusalem: Yad Izhak Ben-Zvi and Ministry of Defence, 1980], pp. 47–60 [in Hebrew, with English summary on p. iii]). The fragment, in lettering of the middle of the second century B.C.E., records that a Greek-speaking community swore an oath by the god Ares *Athlêtês* concerning something connected with an *akr-* (*akra?*). The swearers might be Greeks stationed in the Akra alongside my heterodox Jews; they might even be those heterodox Jews. On the other hand, the stone could have been brought to Jerusalem from elsewhere either in ancient or modern times. It could have come, for instance, from the Graeco-Macedonian colony of Samaria (see p. 534). In fact, the provenience of the fragment is too doubtful and the surviving portion too scanty to justify conclusions. Applebaum's attempt to reconstruct the full content is not convincing; his interpretation does not even pay attention to the tenses of the preserved verbs.

---

[168] See NOTE on 5:23–24, *Disposed . . . slaves.*
[169] I was aware earlier of some of these possibilities; see AB vol. 41, pp. 142 (n. 236), 159 (n. 336).

VI. WHAT REALLY HAPPENED: CHRONOLOGICAL TABLE

Though the authors of both books of Maccabees believed they were writing truth, both made mistakes, took literary license, and passed over embarrassing facts in silence. The reader of only a translation and commentary might find it hard to determine the outline of the true course of events. To reduce the difficulty, in AB vol. 41, Introduction, Part VII, I prepared a table. That table now needs to be corrected in several places, as is done in the following table. In the first column appears the approximate Julian date B.C.E. where it can be determined. In the second column appears a brief summary of the events so dated. In the third column appear the sources in our two books for the events. Only if our two books fail to give important information included in the summary is a reference given to a source outside them. Courses of events are listed in the order of the dates at which they began, with longer courses of events listed before shorter ones. Events which are given no dates probably occurred between the nearest dated events above and below them in the table. The endnotes* tell the reader where to find arguments for the dates and facts listed, except when such arguments are easy to find in my commentary to the sources.

Dates (B.C.E.)	Events	Sources
From 189 or 188 to 177	Antiochus (the future Antiochus IV) serves as hostage in Rome for the Seleucid empire, vanquished by Rome in 190.	I 1:10; Stephen V. Tracy, "Greek Inscriptions from the Athenian Agora: Fifth to Third Centuries B.C.," *Hesperia* 51 (1982), 61–62
July 187[1]	Seleucus IV reigns over the Seleucid empire and sends his son to take the place of Antiochus as hostage in Rome.	Appian *Syriakê* 45

* The endnotes follow the table on pp. 122–23.

Dates (B.C.E.)	Events	Sources
	The royal minister Heliodorus comes to confiscate money on deposit in the temple in Jerusalem but fails to do so. Some Jews believe God miraculously prevented him.	II 3:4 – 4:1; Dan 11:20
	The high priest Onias III, under political pressure from opponents, goes to Antioch to appeal to the king.	II 4:1–6
September 3, 175[1]	Seleucus IV dies or is murdered.[2]	II 4:7; Appian *Syriakê* 45
Later in 175[3]	Antiochus IV, brother of Seleucus IV, seizes power over Seleucid empire.	I 1:10; II 4:7
	In an effort to strengthen the Seleucid empire by copying institutions and ideas he had learned at Rome, Antiochus proclaims an Antiochene republic, analogous to the Roman republic, and invites individuals and communities subject to him to accept Antiochene citizenship.[4]	I 1:41–43; II 4:9
Later in 175 or early in 174[5]	Jason, brother of Onias III, purchases the favor of Antiochus by offering him increased revenue and by bidding high for the privilege of being the founder of the Antiochene community at Jerusalem. Antiochus appoints Jason high priest in place of Onias and allows Jason to found an Antiochene citizen-community at Jerusalem with gymnasium and ephebic institutions, exempt from Jewish law.[6]	I 1:11–15; II 4:7–20
Before Jason's replacement as high priest by Menelaus[7]	Young Ptolemy VI celebrates his *Protoklisia.* Apollonius son of Menestheus, representing Antiochus IV at the celebration, discovers that the Ptolemaic empire is plotting a war against the Seleucid realm. On receiving this information, Antiochus takes defensive measures in the direction of the Ptolemaic border. At the end of these maneuvers, he passes through Joppe and then goes to Jerusalem, where he gets a splendid reception from Jason and the Jerusalemites.	II 4:21–22
172, probably after September 20[8]	Menelaus offers Antiochus IV still more revenue and thus wins appointment as high priest in place of Jason. Jason takes refuge in the Ammanitis.	II 4:23–26
	Unable to produce the promised revenue, Menelaus in his trouble uses temple vessels to bribe a royal minister, Andronikos, while Antiochus IV is away from the capital. Onias III from the sacred place of asylum at Daphne reproaches Menelaus.	II 4:27–33
After 1 Tishri (September 28), 170[9]	Andronikos entices Onias to leave his place of asylum and kills him. On returning to the capital, Antiochus, indignant, executes Andronikos.	II 4:34–38

Dates (B.C.E.)	*Events*	*Sources*
	Depredations of temple property by Menelaus and his brother Lysimachus rouse the wrath of pious Jews. A bloody riot ensues. Members of the Jewish Council of Elders press charges against Menelaus, but again by bribing a royal official Menelaus escapes punishment.	II 4:39–50
November, 170–summer, 169	Antiochus IV vigorously repels Ptolemaic aggression, invades Egypt, and overruns all but Alexandria.	I 1:16–20; cf. II 5:51
Late summer or early autumn, 169[10]	Jason and his followers, upon a false rumor of Antiochus' death, try to capture Jerusalem. Pious Jews rise against both Jason and Menelaus. Antiochus regards all but Menelaus' faction as rebels, punishes the city, plunders the temple, and attempts to reestablish order, confirming Menelaus in power over the Jews.[11]	I 1:20–28; II 5:1–23; cf. II 1:7–8
July, 168[12]	Antiochus IV, almost successful in his second attempt to conquer Egypt, withdraws completely from the Ptolemaic empire upon receiving a Roman ultimatum. On his way back to Antioch, he utters threats against the turbulent Jews, and on his return he hears the complaints of Menelaus and the Antiochenes of Jerusalem, under attack by pious Jews.[13]	Dan 11:29–30
February or March, 167[14]	Antiochus IV, in response to complaints of Antiochenes of Jerusalem, sends a punitive expedition under Apollonius the Mysarch. Pious Jews of Jerusalem are massacred. Privileges of Jerusalem and Judaea are revoked and punitive taxes imposed. Troops fortify and help man Akra (the citadel) north of the temple to preserve order and protect the Antiochenes.	I 1:29–40; II 5:23–27
Nisan (between April 1 and April 29), 167[15]	Antiochus IV decrees that on penalty of death the turbulent Jews, including all those in Judaea, must cease observing the Torah and follow an imposed polytheistic cult, said to be a "purified Judaism," free of the tendencies which had turned the Jews into "rebels."	I 1:44–51
	Enforcement of the decrees is at first probably sporadic, as even Antiochene Jews fear to anger their God,[16] though some Jews obey the king. Royal officials begin to persecute pious Jews.	I 1:51–53
15 Kislev (December 6), 167	Antiochus IV takes drastic measures to enforce the imposed cult. "Abomination of Desolation," a framework containing three meteorites representing the three gods of the imposed cult, is placed upon the sacrificial altar of the temple.	I 1:54

Dates (B.C.E.)	Events	Sources
25 Kislev (December 16), 167	An Athenian expert helps direct the practices of the imposed cult. The practices in the temple include monthly sacrifices on the twenty-fifth[17] and violation of the laws of ritual purity. Outside the temple, too, force is exerted throughout Jerusalem and Judaea to compel Jews to violate the Torah. The Samaritans petition successfully to be exempted from the decrees,[18] but many pious Jews suffer martyrdom. Cities of the Antiochene republic rigorously compel their Jews to follow the imposed cult.[19]	I 1:54–64; II 6–7; J. *AJ* xii 5.5.257–64
Very late 167 or sometime in 166	Mattathias' zeal leads him to rebel against a king who forces Jews to violate the Torah. He and his family, the Hasmonaeans,[20] attract followers and wage guerrilla warfare against the royal government and against Jews who violated the Torah. Some Pietist Jews still believe that God forbids violent rebellion and trust, in vain, the prophecies that God will protect Sabbath observers. Believing that God forbade them to flee or defend themselves on the Sabbath, they are massacred by royal troops. Mattathias decided that God must have intended to permit Jews to *defend* themselves on the Sabbath. Many Pietists agree and join forces with the Hasmonaean party.	I 2:1–48; II 6:11
Between April 20, 166, and April 4, 165	Mattathias dies. Judas takes command.	I 2:70 – 3:2; cf. II 8:1–5
	Judas' force defeats expeditions of Apollonius and Seron.	I 3:10–24; cf. II 8:5–7
	Philip, royal commander at Jerusalem, unable to cope, appeals to the royal government for help.[21]	II 8:8; cf. I 3:25–26
165, probably between May 20 and June 18	Antiochus IV marches off with half the royal army to tax (and loot) the eastern regions claimed by the Seleucids. He appoints his little son Antiochus coregent king over the western part of the empire, with Lysias as his guardian and as chief minister over that same area. Lysias receives half the royal army, with the task of maintaining order in the western part of the empire.	I 3:27–37; FGH 260, F 32
	The governor of Coele-Syria and Phoenicia, Ptolemy son of Dorymenes,[22] responds to Philip's appeal by sending a strong force under Nicanor and Gorgias. From their base at Ammaus, Nicanor and Gorgias fail to crush Judas' band and instead are routed by them.	I 3:38 – 4:27; II 8:8–29, 34–36

Dates (B.C.E.)	*Events*	*Sources*
24 Ab on defective calendar (July 29), 165	Jews return to open observance of the Torah.	*Megillat Ta'anit* 24 Ab
Some months later, surely not long before March, 164[23]	Lysias himself undertakes to stop the Jewish rebels. After careful preparation, he approaches Judaea from the south and fights a bloody battle with Judas' army at Beth-Zur. Non-Hasmonaean pious Jews try to negotiate with Lysias in Judaea for an end to the persecution. Menelaus similarly appeals to the royal government at Antioch.	I 4:28–35; II 11:1–21, 29
	Roman ambassadors in a letter to the Jews offer to support the Jewish case before the coregent king, at Antioch.[24]	II 11:34–38
15 Xanthicus (March 12), 164	A letter in the name of the coregent offers Jews an end to the imposed cult, permission to observe the Torah, and amnesty, if they will cease fighting and return to their homes by 30 Xanthikos (March 27).	II 11:27–33
28 Adar (March 25), 164	The majority of Jews accept the coregent's offer by this date and observe it annually as the anniversary of the end of the persecution. The Hasmonaean party ignored the coregent's offer, to judge by the failure of our author to mention it.	*Megillat Ta'anit* 28 Adar; contrast I 4:35
March 25– October 13, 164	Pious Jews wait through the festivals of Tabernacles and the Eighth Day of Solemn Assembly for prophesied miracles to occur— in vain.[25]	
1 Tishri on defective calendar[26] (July 25), 164	Sabbatical year begins, according to the defective calendar. Pious Jews dare to deny the high priest Menelaus the right to control the temple.[27] Pious priests purify the temple and destroy the Abomination of Desolation.[26]	I 4:42–46; II 10:3; Dan 11:24(end)
Tishri- Marḥeshvan on defective calendar (between July 25 and September 18)[26]	Jews build and prepare a new sacrificial altar and temple vessels.	I 4:47–48; II 10:3
23 Marḥeshvan on defective calendar (September 14), 164[26]	Judas' men remove from the temple court the illicit lattice.	*Megillat Ta'anit* 23 Marḥeshvan

Dates (B.C.E.)	Events	Sources
27 Marḥeshvan on defective calendar (September 18), 164[26]	Jewish priests resume sacrifice of meal offerings in the temple, upon the new altar.	Ibid., 27 Marḥeshvan
3 Kislev on defective calendar (September 24), 164[26]	Jews destroy the idols which stood by private dwellings in Jerusalem.	Ibid., 3 Kislev
25 Kislev on defective calendar=25 Tishri on fully intercalated calendar (October 16), 164[26]	Judas, following biblical precedents, prolongs the doubtful festival of Tabernacles for a celebration of the dedication of the new sacrificial altar along with the new candelabrum, incense altar, and table. The dedication occurs on 25 Kislev, with the celebration continuing for a total of eight days.[26]	I 4:49–58; II 1:8–9, 10:3–7
Late 164 or 163	The Jews decide to make the eight-day celebration an annual observance, at first under the name "Festival of Tabernacles in the month of Kislev," later under the name "Days of Dedication."	I 4:59; II 10:8; cf. II 1:8–9, 2:16
November or early December, 164[28]	Antiochus IV dies in the course of his campaign in Iran. On his deathbed he appoints the courtier Philip to replace Lysias as guardian of his little son and heir, Antiochus.	I 6:1–16; cf. II 9
From soon after Feast of Dedication (perhaps before the death of Antiochus IV), 164, to sometime in April 163[29]	The Jews under the leadership of Judas and his brothers Simon and Jonathan win victories over hostile neighboring peoples and Seleucid officials. The insubordinate Jewish commanders, Joseph and Azariah suffer a bloody defeat at Jamnia.	I 5:1–62; II 10:14–38, 12:1–31
Late 164 or early 163	Judas sees to it that the temple mount and Beth-Zur are fortified.	I 4:60–61
Late 164 or early 163	News of Antiochus IV's death reaches Antioch. Lysias becomes chief power in the regime of little Antiochus V. Philip, Antiochus IV's choice to replace Lysias, fails to win control and flees to Ptolemaic Egypt.[30]	I 6:17; II 9:29, 10:11
February 8, 163	Jews at Jerusalem, 1,150 days after the desecration of 25 Kislev, 167, receive a copy of a letter from Antiochus V announcing the death of Antiochus IV and restoring the temple to the Jews and thus "vindicating the Holy."[31]	II 11:23–26; Dan 8:14
Probably early 163	Ptolemy Makron, a high courtier under Antiochus V, advocates a just policy toward the Jews but falls from favor and commits suicide.	II 10:12–13

Dates (B.C.E.)	*Events*	*Sources*
Just after Pentecost on the defective calendar (late April or May), 163[32]	Judas conducts successful campaign against Idumaea and Azotus.	I 5:65–68; II 12:32–45
Late spring, 163[33]	Judas assembles a Jewish army and besieges the Akra.	I 6:18–20
By June 28, 163[34]	Antiochus V and Lysias march on Judaea with a large force by way of Idumaea and besiege Beth-Zur. Judas lifts the siege of the Akra to go to relieve Beth-Zur, but at the battle of Beth-Zechariah the Jews are defeated, and Judas' brother Eleazar is killed. Jewish diehards, hoping for a miracle, are besieged in the temple. The Hasmonaean family probably hid in the mountains.	I 6:21–48; II 13:1–19
Some weeks after the battle of Beth-Zechariah	The Seleucid besiegers allow the Jews in Beth-Zur, hard-pressed by siege and by the food shortage of a sabbatical year, to make peace and withdraw. Beth-Zur is garrisoned by Seleucid troops.	I 6:49–50; II 13:20–22
	Jews besieged in the temple are similarly hard-pressed. The seer in Dan 12:7 predicts they will be crushed.[34]	I 6:48–54; cf. II 13:22
1 Tishri on the defective calendar (August 12), 163, 1,335 days after the desecration of 25 Kislev, 167[35]	The sabbatical year ends and the date goes by for the miraculous consummation of history predicted by the seer in Daniel.	Dan 12:12
Sometime in the course of the campaign of Antiochus V and Lysias[36]	Antiochus V deposes Menelaus from the high priesthood and sends him to Beroea in Syria for execution.[36]	II 13:3–8; J. *AJ* xii 9.7.383–85
After the deposition of Menelaus and no later than the peace of Antiochus V (January 5 or March 5, 162)	Antiochus V appoints the pious Alcimus as the new high priest, thus winning some pious Jews away from the rebellion. The neglected Oniad heir to the high priesthood then or soon after leaves Judaea for Ptolemaic Egypt, where some years later he establishes a Jewish temple at Leontopolis.	J. *AJ* xii 9.7.386–88; cf. II 14:3
28 Shebaṭ, 162 (January 5, if by the defective calendar, or March 5, if by	Lysias and Antiochus V withdraw with their army from Jerusalem in order to crush the rebel regime of the minister Philip at Antioch.[38] Antiochus V makes full peace with the Jews. The Hasmonaean party appears to	I 6:55–63; II 11:22–26, 13:23–26

Dates (B.C.E.)	Events	Sources
the fully intercalated calendar)[37]	have held aloof from the agreements. Before departing, Antiochus sees to the demolition of the wall around the temple mount.	
Early autumn, 162	Demetrius, son of Seleucus IV, having escaped from Rome where he had been serving as a hostage, lands at Tripolis and claims to be king. The troops at Antioch rally to Demetrius and kill Lysias and Antiochus V.	I 7:1–4; II 14:1–2
Shortly afterward	Demetrius I confirms Alcimus as high priest and in response to a petition presented by him sends Bacchides with an army to Judaea to stop the fighting among the Jews. (Alcimus has the support of many Pietists and of some Hellenizers, but the Hasmonaean party and others violently oppose him.) To restore order, Bacchides executes some troublemakers from both the pious and the apostate factions; he leaves Alcimus troops to protect him. The Hasmonaean party refuses to deal with Bacchides.	I 7:5–20; II 14:3–4
	Judas leads violent opposition in countryside of Judaea to Alcimus' regime. Alcimus appeals to Demetrius I for additional help. Demetrius sends an army under Nicanor.	I 7:21–26; II 14:5–14
	After an indecisive skirmish at Dessau, Nicanor for a while has friendly relations with Judas, but Alcimus protests to the king, and Nicanor is ordered to capture Judas. Frustrated by what he viewed as non-cooperation by pious Jews, Nicanor threatens to destroy the temple after his coming victory over Judas. Horrified, the Jews pray.	I 7:27–38; II 14:15–36
	Faced with the prospect of being arrested by Nicanor's troops, the pious elder of Jerusalem, Razis, gives an inspiring example of courage and faith through his theatrical suicide.	II 14:37–46
13 Adar (March 8), 161[39]	Judas' army routs Nicanor's force in the battle of Adasa. Villagers of Judaea join in destroying the fugitives. The severed head and right hand of Nicanor are exposed within sight of the temple.	I 7:39–49; II 15:6–36
From sometime after March 10 probably to sometime before November 11, 161[40]	The national organs of the Jews, with the agreement of the Hasmonaean party, send an embassy to Rome which succeeds in establishing friendly relations, making a treaty of alliance, and having Rome warn Demetrius I not to oppress the Jews.	I 8; II 4:11

Dates (B.C.E.)	Events	Sources
	Demetrius I sends a punitive expedition under Bacchides against the Jewish rebels. The troops massacre Jews at Messaloth-in-Arbela in Galilee.	I 9:1–2
Nisan (April 13–May 11), 160	Bacchides' army reaches Jerusalem.	I 9:3
Shortly thereafter	Bacchides crushingly defeats the demoralized and shrunken Hasmonaean force at Elasa. Judas, brave to the end, falls. The surviving Hasmonaeans probably agree to cease resisting in return for the rights to take up and bury the dead and to go home in peace.	I 9:4–21
October, 152, to early winter, 143	Jonathan is high priest of the Jews.	I 10:21 – 13:23
Late November or early December, 143	Jewish authorities of Jerusalem and Judaea send a letter to the Jews of Egypt asking them to observe the Days of Dedication.	II 1:1, 7–9
From before late 142 to ca. February, 134	Simon is high priest of the Jews.	I 14:35, 13:36, 16:11–22
February, 134, to 104	John Hyrcanus reigns as prince and high priest of the Jews.	I 16:23–24; J. AJ xx 10.3.240
November or early December, 124	Jewish authorities of Jerusalem and Judaea send a letter to the Jews of Egypt, implicitly condemning the Oniad temple of Leontopolis and asking those Jews to observe the Days of Dedication.	II 1:1–9
103 to 76	Alexander Jannaeus reigns as high priest and king of the Jews. For part of his reign he relinquishes the title "king."[41]	J. AJ xx 10.3–4.241–42 and coins
Probably November or early December, 103	An Egyptian Jew opposed to the Oniad temple at Leontopolis forges and publishes a letter from the Jews of Jerusalem and Judaea, from the Council of Elders, and from Judas. The letter demonstrates the sanctity of the Jerusalem temple and its priesthood and the legitimacy of the Hasmonaean dynasty.	II 1:10b – 2:18
In the reign of Alexander Jannaeus, while he renounced the title of king, and before 90[42]	First Maccabees is written and published as propaganda to justify the dynastic claims of Alexander Jannaeus.	

Dates (B.C.E.)	*Events*
Shortly thereafter[43]	Jason of Cyrene publishes his history as a refutation of the dynastic propaganda, while respecting Judas Maccabaeus.
By ca. 76[44]	The abridged history is published and Epistles 1 and 2 are attached to it.

[1] Parker and Dubberstein, *Babylonian Chronology,* p. 23.

[2] See NOTE on 4:7.

[3] See NOTE on 4:7–38.

[4] AB vol. 41, pp. 104–21.

[5] See NOTE on 4:7–38.

[6] See AB vol. 41, pp. 111–21.

[7] See NOTE on 4:7–38.

[8] Ibid.

[9] See NOTE on 4:34.

[10] See AB vol. 41, p. 207.

[11] See NOTE on 5:5–16.

[12] See Mørkholm, pp. 93–94.

[13] See pp. 91–94.

[14] See my article in PAAJR 46–47 (1979–80), esp. pp. 179–85.

[15] See pp. 89–90.

[16] See AB vol. 41, pp. 158–59.

[17] The first *act* of idolatry in the temple probably coincided with the first of these monthly sacrifices, on 25 Kislev (December 16), 167. See AB vol. 41, NOTE on 1:54–59.

[18] See Appendix VIII.

[19] See NOTE on 6:8–9.

[20] See AB vol. 41, pp. 17–19.

[21] There is a possibility that Philip's appeal came after the next event in our table, Antiochus IV's march eastward. The author of First Maccabees is probably mistaken in thinking that the financial strain of the Jewish revolt drove Antiochus to undertake the expedition (see NOTE on 8:8–35). Either order of events is compatible with 8:8–9, 9:1–2.

[22] See NOTE on 8:8–35.

[23] The chief minister would avoid a protracted campaign against stubborn rebels. He surely had political rivals who were dangerous to leave behind in Antioch. Hence the next event, the negotiated peace, probably came not long after Lysias marched on Judaea. In his second expedition (I 6:28–54; II 13:1–22), Lysias could more easily afford a prolonged campaign, for with Lysias was the little king, far from the clutches of his political rivals. Because we cannot identify the month named at II 11:21, we cannot date the negotiations more narrowly. See concluding NOTE on 11:16–38.

[24] On the date of the letter in II 11:34–38, see NOTE on 11:38, *In the year 148, in . . .*

[25] See AB vol. 41, pp. 273–78.

[26] Ibid., pp. 276–80.

[27] See NOTE on 10:1–8.

[28] See p. 60.

[29] See pp. 63–69.

[30] See NOTE on 9:29.

[31] See NOTE on 11:23–26.

[32] See AB vol. 41, p. 293.

[33] Ibid., p. 315, an my article in PAAJR 46–47 (1978–79), 180–87.

[34] See AB vol. 41, p. 43, but read there and on p. 315 "June 28" instead of "June 27."

[35] Ibid., pp. 43–44.

36 See Note on 13:3–8 and, on the chronology of Menelaus' high priesthood, Note on 4:7–38.

37 See Note on 13:25–26.

38 Not the same man as the guardian appointed by Antiochus IV (I 6:14–15); see Note on 9:29.

39 See AB vol. 41, pp. 341–42.

40 Ibid., pp. 358–59.

41 See pp. 74–81.

42 See Introduction, Part IV.

43 Ibid., and p. 17, and AB vol. 41, pp. 78–89.

44 See AB vol. 41, pp. 551–57.

VII. THE WITNESSES TO THE TEXT

My translation of Second Maccabees is based on the edition of Hanhart.[1] All departures from the text of that edition are explained in the commentary. The editor in his introduction gives a good summary of the problems[2] and of the symbols used to display the witnesses to the text. Since in the commentary I frequently discuss those problems and use those symbols, I must give a brief explanation here.

In the ancient world, where printing was unknown, every published book was copied by hand from an earlier copy. Even a good scribe made errors, and with multiple copying they became more abundant than modern typographical errors. Readers and publishers who cared would make the scribes or special correctors check a new copy against the earlier copy.

There were other threats to a correct transmission of our book, sometimes more dangerous than mere scribal blunders. Words as time went on changed in meaning, and the old shape of human institutions came to be forgotten. Thus, parts of the story became unintelligible to the scribes. Instead of faithfully copying what lay in front of him, a scribe who fancied himself intelligent might make lesser or greater changes in a misguided effort to make his text more intelligible.

The thrilling books of Maccabees were popular. From an early date there were many copies in circulation, widely varying in their readings. Pious and conscientious collectors often would have their own copies corrected on the basis of more than one earlier specimen. In the process errors might be eliminated, but errors and misguided changes might also be added from manuscript to manuscript. Thus the lines of the transmission of the text become very complicated.

Even the author and his secretary could miswrite. Though there are many exceptions to the rule, in general the earlier the witness to the text,

---

[1] *Maccabaeorum liber II*, Septuaginta: Vetus Testamentum Graecum Auctoritate Societatis Litterarum Gottingensis, vol. IX, fasc. II (Göttingen: Vandenhoeck & Ruprecht, 1959), ed. by Robert Hanhart, henceforth called "Hanhart's edition."

[2] See also Robert Hanhart, "Zum Text des 2. und 3. Makkabäerbuches. Probleme der Überlieferung, der Auslegung und der Ausgabe" (*Nachrichten der Akademie der Wissenschaften in Göttingen, Philologisch-historische Klasse,* 1961), pp. 427–87; Vernerus Kappler, *De memoria alterius libri Maccabaeorum,* Diss. Academia Georgia Augusta (Göttingen: Dieterich, 1929), and *Les Anciennes Traductions latines des Machabées,* Anecdota Maredsolana, vol. IV (Abbaye de Maredsous, 1932), ed. by Donatien de Bruyne, Introduction.

the free from errors it is likely to be. Josephus used our book in the late first century C.E., long before our oldest surviving manuscripts were written. However, his allusions to Second Maccabees are few and brief and of no help in reconstructing the original text.

There are a few quotations from our book in the works of Christian authors who wrote before the copying of our earliest surviving manuscripts. The quotations serve only to prove that the principal types of texts known from the manuscripts were known already to early Christian writers.[3]

The most important witnesses to the text are therefore the manuscripts of the Greek and the manuscripts of the early translations of the Greek into Latin, Syriac, and Armenian.

Down through the first half of the ninth century C.E., Greek literary manuscripts were written in the uncial script, a style resembling large capital letters. In the ninth century a new style of writing, the minuscule, emerges, using smaller and more varied letter forms. In the course of the tenth century the minuscule becomes and thereafter remains the prevalent style for literary manuscripts. The custom now is to designate uncials by letters of the alphabet and minuscules by Arabic numerals. An important group of minuscules may also be designated by a letter of the alphabet.

The uncials of our book have no monopoly on the good or interesting readings. A special problem for our book (as for others in the Bible) is posed by the Lucianic recension, represented imperfectly but in its purest surviving form by the group of minuscules L (64 236 381 534 728) and still more imperfectly by the group l (19 62 93 542). Lucian, who was martyred in 311 or 312 C.E.,[4] had access to a rather good text of our books, in First Maccabees one very close to the text which lay before Josephus. But Lucian was that dangerous kind of text transmitter who did not merely copy what he read but used his intelligence wrongly to "improve" on material he thought unintelligible or infelicitously expressed. A reader of a Lucianic text without some other aid has no way of telling what is a valuable old reading and what is a mere guess of Lucian's.[5]

Even the oldest Greek uncial of our book is young enough to have been influenced by Lucian's work, although there is no proof that it actually was. Even the oldest uncial is so far removed from the time of the author that it is naturally full of scribal errors.

The following are the uncials:

A. The fifth-century *Codex Alexandrinus* of the Greek Bible, now in the British Museum.

V. The eighth-century *Codex Venetus* of the Greek Old Testament.

---

[3] See Hanhart's edition, pp. 11, 38, 44; de Bruyne, in *Les Anciennes Traductions latines*, pp. xlix–lvii.
[4] See Sidney Jellicoe, *The Septuagint and Modern Study* (Oxford: Clarendon Press, 1968), pp. 157–58.
[5] See Kappler, *De memoria*, pp. 33–54; Hanhart's edition, pp. 18–23; and cf. Jellicoe, *The Septuagint*, pp. 158–60, 168–71.

Though some scholars believe it shows Lucianic influence,[6] Kappler[7] and especially Hanhart[8] value it as an independent witness to the text of our book.

q. This symbol designates the one other important group of minuscules (29 71 74 98 107 120 130 243 370 731). Its origin is unknown, but it is free from Lucianic influence and may on occasion be the lone preserver of the correct text.

There are several ancient translations made from the Greek. Of these the Latin (La) is most important. All indications are that First and Second Maccabees were translated together from Greek into Latin. This old Latin translation is preserved in a series of manuscripts progressively conforming more and more to Lucianic and other extant Greek texts.[9] The best of the Latin manuscripts are La^L, La^X,[10] and the so-called Vulgate, La^V, which originally had nothing to do with Jerome's Vulgate Latin translation of the Hebrew Bible.[11] The best Latin manuscripts show an interesting independence of our Greek witnesses.[12] Indeed, the original of the old Latin translation can be shown to have been written between the middle of the first century C.E.[13] and the beginning of the third century C.E.[14] The Christian Father Cyprian, who wrote between 246 and 258 C.E., quotes from a version of the Latin translation quite close to our best Latin manuscripts.[15] There is also evidence that the Latin translators of First

---

[6] See Jellicoe, The Septuagint, p. 167.

[7] In Maccabaeorum liber I, Septuaginta: Vetus Testamentum Graecum Auctoritate Societatis Litterarum Gottingensis, vol. IX, fasc. I (Göttingen: Vandenhoeck & Ruprecht, 1936), ed. by Werner Kappler, p. 30.

[8] Hanhart's edition, pp. 16–17.

[9] De Bruyne, in Les Anciennes Traductions latines, studied the entire series.

[10] La^X has much less value in Second Maccabees than in First (de Bruyne, in Les Anciennes Traductions latines, p. xxv).

[11] La^V was in existence before Jerome did the Vulgate (see Bickerman, Studies, II, 178, n. 17).

[12] See de Bruyne, in Les Anciennes Traductions latines, pp. xii–li.

[13] See NOTE on 6:28.

[14] At I 3:55 the Latin renders "commanders of thousands" by tribunos and "commanders of fifties" by evocatos. Tribunes regularly commanded units of one thousand only before the time of the emperor Gallienus (253–268 C.E.); see Lengle, "Tribunus 5," PW, VI^2 (1937), 2437–38. In Latin one would expect to find "commander of fifty" rendered as "centurion." Evocati were soldiers invited to stay in the army after having served out the term of their enlistment. Although evocati were serving as centurions in the reign of Augustus, only later in the first century C.E. did such appointments become so common that a Latin writer could have used evocati instead of centuriones. On the other hand, at the beginning of the third century C.E. evocati could be promoted to still higher office and from then on were no longer a main source for the centurions of the Roman army. See Alfred von Domaszewski, Die Rangordnung des römischen Heeres (2d ed., rev. by Brian Dobson; "Landschaftsverband Rheinland rheinisches Landesmuseum Bonn und Verein von Altertumsfreunden im Rheinlande: Beihefte der Bonner Jahrbücher," Band 14; Köln und Graz: Böhlau Verlag, 1967), pp. ix, lx, 21, 78, 83, and Marcel Durry, Les Cohortes prétoriennes (Paris: É. de Boccard, 1928), pp. 120–21.

[15] See de Bruyne, in Les Anciennes Traductions latines, pp. l–li.

Maccabees may have consulted the Hebrew text and thus could have been Jews.[16] Even the best of the Latin manuscripts contains many scribal errors and mistakes in translation. Nevertheless, the Latin translation existed before the work of Lucian. It may be impossible to prove that the best Latin manuscripts are utterly free from Lucianic influence. Nevertheless, a case of agreement between *L* or *l* or both and the best Latin manuscripts often proves to give the most likely original meaning intended by our author, so often as to suggest that La[L] is indeed practically free from Lucianic influence and can serve as a key for discerning between the good readings of the text which lay before Lucian and Lucian's misguided "improvements."[17]

The Syriac version (Sy) is represented by de Lagarde's edition (SyI),[18] by Ceriani's photographic reproduction of a manuscript (SyII)[19] not used by de Lagarde, and by the text of the London polyglot Bible of 1657.[20] For Second Maccabees, its chief value lies in showing how an ancient reader understood the Greek.

The Armenian (Arm) has been insufficiently studied by scholars writing in languages accessible to me. Michael Stone tells me that some modern studies of it have been published in Armenian and that Hanhart's frequent citations of the Armenian version should not be taken as evidence that Hanhart studied it closely. According to report,[21] the Armenian version is very free but is usually close to the Latin and has value chiefly in confirming La, and particularly in cases where the best Latin manuscripts agree with the Lucianic recension.

With so complicated a situation, the historian and the textual editor cannot lay down rules to be followed mechanically. He must weigh the evidence of the witnesses according to the above principles and then consider historical probability, always bearing in mind that only our ignorance leads us to consider many possibilities as improbable.

Signs and Abbreviations Used in Giving the Witnesses to the Text of Second Maccabees

Uncials:

A V

V[c]: Reading of a corrector of V

---

16 See AB vol. 41, NOTE on I 11:39.

17 See Hanhart's edition, pp. 27–29.

18 *Libri Veteris Testamenti Apocryphi Syriace,* ed. by Paul A. de Lagarde (Lipsiae: Brockhaus, 1861).

19 *Translatio Pescitto Veteris Testamenti,* ed. by A. M. Ceriani, 2 vols. (Mediolani: Pogliani, 1876–83).

20 *Biblia sacra polyglotta,* ed. by Brian Walton, 6 vols. (London, 1655–57).

21 Hanhart's edition, p. 39.

Minuscules:

19 29 46 52 55 56 58
62 64 68 71 74 93 98
106 107 120 130 236 243
311 347 370 379 381 534
542 671 728 731 771

Groups of minuscules:

q: 29 71 74 98 107 120 130 243 370 731
L: 64 236 381 534 728
l: 19 62 93 542
$L'=L+l$

Combination:

$A'=A+106$

Ancient translations:

La: Old Latin, with the letters used by de Bruyne to designate the manuscripts written as superscripts to the right (La^L, La^X, etc.)

Sy: Syriac

SyI: Syriac text in *Libri Veteris Testamenti Apocryphi Syriace,* ed. by Paul Anton de Lagarde

SyII: Syriac text in *Translatio Syra Pescitto Veteris Testamenti,* ed. by A. M. Ceriani

SyIII: Syriac text in *Biblia sacra polyglotta,* ed. by Brian Walton

Arm: Armenian, as reported in Hanhart's edition of the Greek text

Quotations in early Christian authors:

Augustine, Cyprian, Lucifer, Theodoretus: Quotations of Second Maccabees in works of these authors as reported in Hanhart's edition

Pass.Mac.: Reading of the medieval *Passion of the Seven Maccabaean Martyrs* as reported in Hanhart's edition (may be followed by a letter indicating which manuscript)

Dashes are used between the symbols of witnesses to indicate that they belong to the same group.

L^{-64} or q^{-29}, etc.: The entire group L except for 64, or the entire group q except for 29, etc.

( ): Parentheses surround a witness which possibly but not certainly supports the reading under discussion.

SELECTED BIBLIOGRAPHY

No attempt has been made to present a comprehensive bibliography. The following is a selected list of works frequently cited or used by the author.

A. THE GREEK TEXT AND THE ANCIENT VERSIONS OF SECOND MACCABEES

See NOTES to Introduction, Part VII.

B. COMMENTARIES AND TRANSLATIONS

Abel, F.-M. *Les Livres des Maccabées*. Paris: Gabalda, 1949.

————, and Jean Starcky. *Les Livres des Maccabées* Paris. Éditions du Cerf, 1961.

Grimm, Carl L. W. *Das zweite, dritte, und vierte Buch der Maccabäer*, vierte Lieferung of *Kurzgefasstes exegetisches Handbuch zu den Apokryphen des Alten Testaments*, ed. by O. F. Fritsche. Leipzig: S. Hirzel, 1857.

Habicht, Christian. *2. Makkabäerbuch*, Band I, Lieferung 3 of *Jüdische Schriften aus hellenistisch-römischer Zeit*, ed. by Werner Georg Kümmel. Gütersloh: Mohn, 1976, pp. 167–285.

Kahana, Abraham. *Ha-sefarim ha-ḥitzonim*, vol. II. Tel Aviv: Hozaath M'qoroth, 1936–37, pp. 72–231.

C. OTHER WORKS

Abel, F.-M. *Géographie de la Palestine*. Paris: Gabalda, 1933–38.

————. *Grammaire du grec biblique*. Paris: Gabalda, 1927.

Alon, Gedalyahu. *Jews, Judaism and the Classical World*. Jerusalem: Magnes, 1977.

Avi-Yonah, Michael. *The Holy Land*. Grand Rapids, Mich.: Baker Book House, 1966.

Baer, Seligman (Yitzḥaq), ed. *Seder 'Abodat Yiśra'el*. Rödelheim, 5628 = 1867–68; reprinted, Palestine: Schocken, 5697 = 1936–37.

Bar-Kochva, Bezalel. *The Seleucid Army*. Cambridge Classical Studies. Cambridge University Press, 1976.

Bauer, Walter. *Griechisch-deutsches Wörterbuch zu den Schriften des Neuen Testaments und der übrigen urchristlichen Literatur*. 5th ed. Berlin: Töpelmann, 1958.

Bengtson, Hermann. *Die Strategie in der hellenistischen Zeit*. München: Beck, 1937–52.

Bickerman, Elias J. *Chronology of the Ancient World*. Cornell University Press, 1968.

————. *The God of the Maccabees*. Studies in Judaism in Late Antiquity, ed. by Jacob Neusner, vol. XXXII. Leiden: Brill, 1979 (a somewhat defective translation by Horst Moehring of *Der Gott der Makkabäer*).

————. *Der Gott der Makkabäer*. Berlin: Schocken, 1937.

————. *Institutions des Séleucides*. Paris: Geuthner, 1938.

————. "Makkabäerbücher," PW, XIV (1930), 779–800.

————. *Studies in Jewish and Christian History*, Parts I and II. Arbeiten zur Geschichte des antiken Judentums und des Urchristentums, Band IX. Leiden: Brill, 1976–80.

Blass, Friedrich, and Albert Debrunner. *Grammatik des neutestamentlichen Griechisch*. 14th ed., rev. by Friedrich Rehkopf. Göttingen: Vandenhoeck & Ruprecht, 1976.

Bunge, Jochen G. *Untersuchungen zum zweiten Makkabäerbuch*. Diss. Rheinische Friedrich-Wilhelms-Universität zu Bonn. Bonn: Rheinische Friedrich-Wilhelms-Universität, 1971.

Cohen, Gerson D. "The Story of Hannah and Her Seven Sons in Hebrew Literature," *Mordecai M. Kaplan Jubilee Volume*. New York: Jewish Theological Seminary of America, 1953. Hebrew section, pp. 109–22.

Collomp, Paul. *Recherches sur la chancellerie et la diplomatique des Lagides*. Paris: "Les Belles Lettres," 1926.

Corpus Papyrorum Judaicarum. Eds. Victor A. Tcherikover and Alexander Fuks. Harvard University Press, 1957–64.

Cross, Frank Moore. *The Ancient Library of Qumran*. Garden City, N.Y.: Doubleday, 1961.

Daniel, Suzanne. *Recherches sur le vocabulaire du culte dans le Septante*. Paris: Klincksieck, 1966.

Deissmann, Adolf. *Light from the Ancient East*. New York: George H. Doran, 1927.

Delorme, Jean. *Gymnasion*. Paris: É. de Boccard, 1960.

Dictionnaire de la Bible. Ed. by F. Vigouroux et al. Paris: Letouzey, 1912–.

Doran, Robert. *Temple Propaganda: The Purpose and Character of 2 Maccabees*. The Catholic Biblical Quarterly Monograph Series, 12. Washington, D.C.: Catholic Biblical Association of America, 1981.

Elbogen, Ismar. *Der jüdische Gottesdienst*. 3d revised ed. Frankfurt am Main: J. Kauffmann, 1931.

Exler, Francis X. J. *The Form of the Ancient Greek Letter*. Diss. Catholic University. Washington, D.C., 1923.

Fitzmyer, Joseph. "Some Notes on Aramaic Epistolography," JBL 93 (1974), 201–25.

Ginsberg, H. Louis. *Studies in Daniel*. New York: Jewish Theological Seminary of America, 1948.

Ginzberg, Louis. *The Legends of the Jews*. Philadelphia: Jewish Publication Society of America, 1909–38.

Goldstein, Jonathan A. "The Apocryphal Book of I Baruch," PAAJR 46–47 (1979–80), 179–99.

————. "The Date of the Book of Jubilees," PAAJR, in press.

————. "The Hasmonaean Revolt and the Hasmonaean Dynasty," ch. 8 of vol. I, part II, of *The Cambridge History of Judaism,* ed. by W. D. Davies and Louis Finkelstein. Cambridge University Press, forthcoming.

————. "Jewish Acceptance and Rejection of Hellenism," in *Jewish and Christian Self-Definition,* vol. II, ed. by E. P. Sanders with A. I. Baumgarten and Alan Mendelson. Philadelphia: Fortress Press, 1981, pp. 64–87, 318–26.

————. "The Tales of the Tobiads," *Studies Smith,* Part III, pp. 85–123.

————. "The Testament of Moses: Its Content, Its Origin, and Its Attestation in Josephus," *Studies on the Testament of Moses,* ed. by George W. E. Nickelsburg, Jr. Septuagint and Cognate Studies, no. 4. Cambridge, Mass.: Society of Biblical Literature, 1973, pp. 44–52.

A Greek-English Lexicon. Compiled by Henry George Liddell and Robert Scott. 9th ed., revised and augmented by Henry Stuart Jones and Roderick McKenzie. Oxford: Clarendon Press, 1940.

Gutman, Yehoshua. "The Story of the Mother and Her Seven Sons in the *Agadah* and in I and II Maccabees," *Sepher Yoḥanan Levi,* ed. by M. Schwabe and J. Gutman. Jerusalem: Magnes Press, 5709=1949, pp. 25–37 (in Hebrew).

Habicht, Christian. "Royal Documents in Maccabees II," *Harvard Studies in Classical Philology* 80 (1976), 1–18.

Hadas, Moses. *The Third and Fourth Books of Maccabees.* New York: Harper, 1953.

Hanhart, Robert. "Zum Text des 2. und 3. Makkabäerbuches," *Nachrichten der Akademie der Wissenschaften in Göttingen, Philologisch-historische Klasse,* 1961, pp. 427–87.

Hatch, Edwin, and Henry A. Redpath. *A Concordance to the Septuagint and the Other Greek Versions of the Old Testament (Including the Apocryphal Books).* Graz: Akademische Druck- u. Verlagsanstalt, 1954.

Heinemann, Isaak. "Wer veranlasste den Glaubenszwang der Makkabäerzeit?" *Monatsschrift für Geschichte und Wissenschaft des Judentums* 82 (1938), 145–72.

Heinemann, Joseph. *Prayer in the Period of the Tanna'im and the Amora'im.* Jerusalem: Magnes Press, 1964 (in Hebrew).

Hengel, Martin. *Judaism and Hellenism.* Philadelphia: Fortress Press, 1974.

Holleaux, Maurice. *Études d'épigraphie et d'histoire grecques,* vols. II–III. Paris: É. de Boccard, 1938–42.

Josephus. *Flavii Iosephi Opera.* Ed. by Benedictus Niese. Berlin: Weidmann, 1887–95.

————. *Josephus,* vols. I–IX. Edited with an English translation by H. St. John Thackeray, Ralph Marcus, Allen Wikgren, and Louis H. Feldman. The Loeb Classical Library. Harvard University Press, 1926–65.

Kappler, Werner. *De memoria alterius libri Maccabaeorum.* Diss. Academia Georgia Augusta. Göttingen: Dieterich, 1929.

Kellermann, Ulrich. *Auferstanden in den Himmel.* Stuttgarter Bibelstudien, 95. Stuttgart: Verlag Katholisches Bibelwerk, 1979.

Der kleine Pauly. Ed. by Konrat Ziegler and Walther Sontheimer. Stuttgart: Druckenmüller, 1964–75.

Kolbe, Walther. *Beiträge zur syrischen und jüdischen Geschichte.* Beiträge zur Wissenschaft vom Alten Testament, ed. by Rudolf Kittel, N.S., vol. X. Stuttgart: W. Kohlhammer, 1926.

Kühner, Raphael, and Bernhard Gerth. *Ausführliche Grammatik der griechischen Sprache.* Hannover and Leipzig: Hahn, 1898–1900.

Laqueur, R. "Griechische Urkunden in der jüdisch-hellenistischen Literatur," *Historische Zeitschrift* 136 (1927), 229–52.

Launey, Marcel. *Recherches sur les armées hellénistiques.* Paris: É. de Boccard, 1950.

Lichtenstein, Hans. "Die Fastenrolle," HUCA 8–9 (1931–32), 257–351.

Lieberman, Saul. *Hellenism in Jewish Palestine.* New York: Jewish Theological Seminary of America, 1950.

————. "On Persecution of the Jewish Religion," *Salo Wittmeyer Baron Jubilee Volume on the Occasion of His Eightieth Birthday,* ed. by Saul Lieberman. Jerusalem: American Academy for Jewish Research; New York: Columbia University Press [distrib.], 1974. Hebrew section, pp. 213–45.

————. *Tosefta Ki-fshuṭah.* New York: Jewish Theological Seminary of America, 1955–.

Marcus, Ralph. See Josephus.

Marrou, Henri I. *A History of Education in Antiquity.* New York: New American Library, 1964.

May, Gerhard. *Schöpfung aus dem Nichts: Die Entstehung der Lehre von der Creatio ex nihilo.* Arbeiten zur Kirchengeschichte, no. 48. Berlin and New York: de Gruyter, 1978.

Mayser, Edwin. *Grammatik der griechischen Papyri aus der Ptolemäerzeit.* Berlin and Leipzig: de Gruyter, 1938–70.

Meshorer, Ya‘akov. *Jewish Coins of the Second Temple Period.* Chicago: Argonaut, 1967.

Moreau, J., ed. *Lactance: De la mort des persécuteurs.* 2 vols. Sources chrétiennes, no. 39. Paris: Éditions du Cerf, 1954.

Mørkholm, Otto. *Antiochus IV of Syria.* Classica et Mediaevalia, Dissertationes, VIII. København: Gyldendalske Boghandel, 1966.

Motzo, Bacchisio Raimundo. *Saggi di storia e letteratura.* Contributi alla scienza dell'antichità pubblicati da G. De Sanctis e L. Pareti, vol. V. Firenze: Felice Le Monnier, 1925.

Neuhaus, Günther O. *Studien zu den poetischen Stücken im 1. Makkabäerbuch.* Forschung zur Bibel, Band XII. Würzburg: Echter Verlag, 1974.

Nickelsburg, George W. E., Jr. *Resurrection, Immortality, and Eternal Life in Intertestamental Judaism.* Harvard Theological Studies, XXVI. Harvard University Press, 1972.

————, ed. *Studies on the Testament of Moses.* Septuagint and Cognate Studies, no. 4. Cambridge, Mass.: Society of Biblical Literature, 1973.

Niese, Benedictus. *Kritik der beiden Makkabäerbücher.* Berlin: Weidmann, 1900 (=*Hermes* 35 [1900], 268–307, 453–527).

Nilsson, Martin P. *Geschichte der griechischen Religion,* vol. I, 3d ed. München: Beck, 1967.

————. *Geschichte der griechischen Religion,* vol. II, 2d ed. München: Beck, 1961.

————. *Die hellenistische Schule.* München: Beck, 1955.

Otto, Walter, and Hermann Bengtson. *Zur Geschichte des Niederganges des Ptolemäerreiches.* ABAW, N.S., Heft XVII. München: Beck, 1938.

Oxford Classical Dictionary. Eds. N. G. L. Hammond and H. H. Scullard. 2d ed. Oxford: Clarendon Press, 1970.

Parker, R. A., and W. H. Dubberstein. *Babylonian Chronology, 626 B.C.–A.D. 75.* Brown University Press, 1956.

Porten, Bezalel. *Archives from Elephantine.* University of California Press, 1968.

Preisigke, Friedrich. *Wörterbuch der griechischen Papyrusurkunden.* Berlin: Selbstverlag der Erben, 1925–31.

Rahlfs. See *Septuaginta.*

Richnow, Wolfgang. *Untersuchungen zu Sprache und Stil des zweiten Makkabäerbuches.* Diss. Georg-August-Universität zu Göttingen: unpublished, 1966.

Roller, Otto. *Das Formular der paulinischen Briefe: Ein Beitrag zur Lehre vom antiken Briefe.* Stuttgart: Kohlhammer, 1933.

Rostovtzeff, Michael. *The Social and Economic History of the Hellenistic World,* 2d ed. Oxford: Clarendon Press, 1953.

Sachs, A. J., and D. J. Wiseman. "A Babylonian King List of the Hellenistic Period," *Iraq* 16 (1954), 202–12.

Samuel, Alan E. *Greek and Roman Chronology.* München: Beck, 1972.

Schatkin, Margaret. "The Maccabean Martyrs," *Vigiliae Christianae* 28 (1974), 97–113.

Schmuttermayr, Georg. " 'Schöpfung aus dem Nichts' in 2 Makk. 7, 28?" BZ, neue Folge, 17 (1973), 203–22.

Schürer, Emil. *Geschichte des jüdischen Volkes im Zeitalter Jesu Christi.* 4th ed. Leipzig: Hinrichs, 1901–11.

————. *The History of the Jewish People in the Age of Jesus Christ.* New English version, revised and edited by Geza Vermes and Fergus Millar. Edinburgh: T. & T. Clark, 1973–.

Schunck, Klaus-Dietrich. *Die Quellen des I. und II. Makkabäerbuches.* Diss. Greifswald. Halle (Saale): Niemeyer, 1954.

Septuaginta. 2 vols., ed. by Alfred Rahlfs. Stuttgart: Privilegierte Württembergische Bibelanstalt, n.d.

Sievers, Joseph. *The Hasmoneans and Their Supporters from Mattathias to John Hyrcanus I.* Diss. Columbia University. Ann Arbor, Mich.: University Microfilms International, 1981 (order no. 8125394).

Stern, Menahem. "The Death of Onias III," *Zion* 25 (1960), 1–16 (in Hebrew with English summary).

————. *The Documents on the History of the Hasmonaean Revolt.* Tel Aviv: Hakibbutz Hameuchad, 1965 (in Hebrew).

Surkau, Hans-Werner. *Martyrien in jüdischer und frühchristlicher Zeit.* Göttingen: Vandenhoeck & Ruprecht, 1938.

Talmudic Encyclopedia (=*Enṣiqlopediah talmudit*). Jerusalem: Mosad Ha-Rav Kook, 5705[1945] (in Hebrew).

Tcherikover, Victor A. *Hellenistic Civilization and the Jews*. Philadelphia: Jewish Publication Society, 1959.

Theological Dictionary of the New Testament, ed. by Gerhard Kittel. Grand Rapids and London: Eerdmans, 1964–74.

Vaux, Roland de. *Ancient Israel: Its Life and Institutions*, trans. by John McHugh. New York: McGraw-Hill, 1961.

Wacholder, Ben Zion. The Letter from Judah Maccabee to Aristobulus: Is 2 Maccabees 1:10b–2:18 Authentic?" HUCA 49 (1978), 89–133.

Welles, C. Bradford. *Royal Correspondence in the Hellenistic Period*. Yale University Press, 1934.

Will, Édouard. *Histoire du monde hellénistique*. Nancy: Faculté des lettres et des sciences humaines, 1966–67.

Yosēfōn. Sefer Yosefon le-Yosef ben Gorion ha-Kohen. Jerusalem: Hominer, 5716[1955–56].

TRANSLATION
and
NOTES

1:1 – 2:18, introductory NOTE. On how the two letters, Ep. 1
(1:1–10a) and Ep. 2 (1:10b – 2:18), came to stand at the head
of Second Maccabees, see Introduction, p. 26.

I. EPISTLE 1: A CALL TO THE JEWS OF EGYPT TO REPENT AND OBSERVE THE FESTIVAL OF TABERNACLES IN THE MONTH OF KISLEV
(1:1–10a)

1 ¹ To our brothers the Jews of Egypt, greeting, your brothers the Jews in Jerusalem and in the land of Judah. A good peace ² may God make for you, and may He be good to you, and may He remember His covenant with His faithful servants Abraham, Isaac, and Jacob. ³ May He give you all a heart to revere Him and to do His will wholeheartedly and with a willing spirit. ⁴ May He open your heart to His Torah and to His commandments. (And may He make peace.)ᵃ ⁵ May He listen to your prayers and forgive you and not abandon you in an evil time. ⁶ And now, here we continually offer prayers for you.

⁷ In the reign of Demetrius in the year 169 we Jews wrote you, "In the affliction and in the distress which came upon us in the years from the time that Jason and his followers rebelled against the Holy Land and the Kingdom ⁸ and set fire to the temple gateway and shed innocent blood, we prayed to the LORD, and He hearkened to us. We brought animal sacrifices and fine flour, and we kindled the lamps and laid out the showbread." ⁹ And now we ask you to celebrate the Days of Tabernacles in the Month of Kislev.

10a In the year 188.

ᵃ On the words in parentheses, see NOTE on 1:1–5.

NOTES

1:1–10a (Ep. 1). Elias Bickerman ("Ein jüdischer Festbrief vom Jahre 124 v. Chr.," ZNW 32 [1933], 233–54=*Studies*, II, 136–58) first unlocked the secrets of this remarkable authentic document, which had puzzled readers ancient and modern. Many modern scholars had considered it to be a forgery. On the authenticity, see NOTE on vs. 7.

The letter is a well-ordered unit. In vss. 2–6 the senders comfort the Jews of Egypt in their time of trouble and tactfully call upon them to repent of their sin (of having a schismatic temple at Leontopolis; see Introduction, p. 24), for then God will hear their prayers and cease to punish them.

This preaching by itself might have fallen on deaf ears. The cardinal point of the ideology of those Jews in Egypt who had built the schismatic temple was that God once had chosen the temple at Jerusalem but had later rejected it, by letting it be destroyed in 586 B.C.E., and had never yet signified by any miraculous sign that He had again chosen the place so as to constitute it the sole legitimate place at which to offer sacrifices to the LORD (see Deut 12:2, 4–18, 26–29; cf. II Chron 7:1–2 with Ezra 6:16–18). Hence, the Jews of Jerusalem and Judah in vss. 7–8 strengthen the point of vss. 2–6: there is a proof of the LORD's renewed choice of Jerusalem in the recent example of their own time of trouble. In that terrible visitation even a part of the temple at Jerusalem was burned, all in punishment of heinous sin. Nevertheless, prayer at Jerusalem and in Judaea sufficed to gain God's pardon.

The Jews of Egypt in 124 B.C.E. knew the story of the persecution of the Jews by Antiochus IV and its wondrous end in the full restoration of the temple cult. There was no need to give them any more details than are found in vss. 7–8. Hence the senders could pass immediately to vs. 9, where they call upon the Jews of Egypt to observe the festival commemorating the restoration of the cult at the temple of Jerusalem, for in so doing the Jews of Egypt will be recognizing that God Himself has chosen the temple at Jerusalem and will win God's forgiveness (see I Kings 8:46–50). The transitions from vss. 2–6 to vss. 7–8 to vs. 9 are abrupt to us, but not to Jews of Egypt and Judaea in 124 B.C.E. One other thread ties vss. 2–6 to vss. 7–9: in vss. 2–6 the schismatic temple was founded by an *Oniad* priest; in vss. 7–9 the sin of rebellion is the sin of Jason the *Oniad*. Since the Oniads probably still enjoyed high prestige among the Jews of Egypt, the authors of the letter show their skill by avoiding open accusation of living Oniads.

Ep. 1 is an example of a festal letter, in which a Jewish (or Christian) authority calls upon the faithful to observe a coming festival or to take note of an adjustment in the calendar which will affect the date of a coming festival. (The Jewish calendar was lunar and required frequent adjustment to keep it in step with the seasons.) There are allusions to such letters at II Chron 30:1–9 and in Esther 9:20–32 (see AB vol. 41, Appendix IV). One might include as an example the Passover papyrus from Elephantine (ANET, p. 491). Later Jewish festal letters (in Aramaic) are quoted at To. *Sanhedrin* 2:5–6 and TB *Sanhedrin* 11a–b. Like our letter, Hezekiah's message at II Chron 30:1–9 joined a call for repentance to a call to observe a festival. Like our letter, those alluded to in Esther 9:20–32 called upon the Jews to observe a festival established to commemorate a recent event.

Ep. 1 survives in Greek, but whoever wrote the Greek either translated a Hebrew (less likely, an Aramaic) document or thought in Hebrew or Aramaic. The letter is written in almost complete accordance with the rules of Hebrew and Aramaic epistolary style, which were quite different from their Greek counterparts. On the rules of Aramaic epistolary style, see Joseph Fitzmyer "Some Notes on Aramaic Epistolography," JBL 93 (1974), 201–25; on those of Greek, see Francis X. J. Exler, *The Form of the Ancient Greek Letter* (Diss., Catholic University; Washington, D.C., 1923), and Ferdinand Ziemann, *De epistularum Graecarum formulis sollemnibus quaestiones selectae* (Diss., Halle; Halle: Karras, 1910). By the time of our letter, the Jews of Egypt had ceased to use Hebrew and Aramaic in their own documents (CPJ I, pp. 30–31, 44) but festal letters still may have gone out to them in a Semitic language.

The Greek writer, however, was not unskillful. He wished to preserve the flavor of a Semitic letter, but he was able to use idiomatic Greek. See NOTE on vss. 1–5(beginning), on vs. 5, and on vs. 9.

The letter bears witness to political realities we would not otherwise suspect. Both Ep. 1 and Ep. 0 (the letter quoted in vss. 7–8) came from a collective group of Jews and lack any reference to the powerful reigning Hasmonaean high priests, Jonathan (152–143 B.C.E.) and John Hyrcanus (134–104), even though both letters called for the observance of a festival made possible by Hasmonaean victories. There is no mention even of the Council of Elders (cf. I 12:6 and II 1:10). Perhaps even in the days of Jonathan and John Hyrcanus, the high priest and Council of Elders had no role in decisions on the calendar and the dates of the festivals, which rather were to be made by ordinary Israelites. See To. *Sanhedrin* 2:15; Esther 9:20–31; TP *Rosh hashanah* 1:3, p. 57b; *M. Rosh hashanah* 2:7; Bickerman, *Studies*, II, 147–48. The letters certainly reveal the limits of the powers of the high priests Jonathan and John: the commemorative festival receives the neutral name "Days of Tabernacles in the Month of Kislev," not the name favored by the Hasmonaeans, "Days of Dedication" (see AB vol. 41, NOTE on 4:36–54). The people decreed for Simon and his descendants the privilege that all official documents of the nation should go out in their name and be dated in their name (I 13:42, 14:43–44). However, John in this part of his reign is known to have forgone many of his dynastic prerogatives; see CHJ, I, part II, ch. 8.

1–5. Ep. 1 in outline appears to be a skillfully constructed letter, yet its wording, especially in vss. 1–2, has seemed strange and even clumsy to readers ancient and modern. My translation of vss. 1 and 2 follows literally the wording of the manuscripts of the class q, with one exception: English usage forbids the completely literal "Good peace and good may God make for you." With the reading of q, almost everything conforms to the rules of Aramaic style: vs. 1 contains the standard salutation of a Jewish festal letter ("To B

. . . : peace"), beginning with the name of the addressees. The senders call the recipients "brothers" and call themselves "your brothers." The Semitic salutation formula, "peace" (šālōm, šᵉlām), has been properly translated by the Greek as *chairein* ("greeting"), as at I Esdras 6:8 and I 12:20; the sole departure from Hebrew and Aramaic word order is the placing (for the sake of easier Greek) of "greeting" immediately after the receivers' names. Moreover, no "and" introduces the prayer for the welfare of the recipients which follows (see the examples from the second millennium B.C.E. on, collected by Fitzmyer, JBL 93 [1974], 214–15, and S. Loewenstamm, *"Mktb,"* Enc. Bib. 4 [1962], 968–74 [in Hebrew]). The prayer begins with an allusion to God's promise at Jer 33(Greek Jer 40):9, of ". . . all the good and all the peace which I shall make for them."

This smooth text, found only in q, is probably the original reading, not a learned correction, for it is easy to explain how it was turned into the reading of the other witnesses. Most Greek scribes did not fully understand the patterns used in Hebrew and Aramaic letters, even though they knew some of the peculiarities. Greek scribes had similar troubles at I 12:20 (see AB vol. 41, ad loc.). Here at II 1:1–2, the Greek scribes knew that one could render the Hebrew and Aramaic salutation formula, "peace," either idiomatically by *chairein* ("greeting"), as at I Esdras 6:8, or literally by *eirênê* ("peace"), as at II Esdras 5:7. They also knew that the elegant Greek way to render Hebrew *hṭyb* ("do good to") was by a simple Greek verb (*agathopoiein, agathynein*). When they found the word "peace" after the name of the senders, they assumed it was part of the salutation formula, and when they found the expression "may he do good" (*agatha poiêsai*), they thought it represented the Hebrew verb *hṭyb* and turned it into *agathopoiêsai*, missing the allusion to Jer 33(Greek Jer 40):9, where the Hebrew is *ṭwbh . . . "š*.

In English translation the resulting text may look unobjectionable: "To our brothers the Jews of Egypt, greeting, your brothers the Jews in Jerusalem and in the land of Judah: good peace! And may God be good to you . . ." In fact, it is a monstrosity. The salutation is neither Greek ("A to B, greeting," in that order) nor Semitic ("to B, A: peace"). Furthermore, when *eirênê* represents the Hebrew and Aramaic salutation formula "peace," it stands in the nominative case, as at II Esdras 5:7 (at II Esdras 4:17 the Greek gives an *indirect* quotation, in which the word *šᵉlām* is the direct object of "send"). Here in all witnesses to the text *eirênê* stands in the accusative case, and in most witnesses to the text the only verb of which "peace" could be the direct object has been turned into the intransitive *agathopoiêsai*. The "and" which once connected "peace" and "good" now stands, in most witnesses to the text, at the head of the prayer, contrary to Semitic usage. Such prayers for the welfare of the recipients begin to appear in Greek letters from the first century C.E., long after the period of our document (Ziemann, pp. 317–25), and then they *replace* the formula of salutation instead of appearing with it. Only a very careful Greek stylist would find the accusative case of *eirênê* strange, especially in a translated foreign idiom. Only a very careful Bible reader would question the extra "and," for biblical prose teems with the word. Scribes responsible for three Latin manuscripts (La^BMP) did feel the difficulty and suppressed the "and" and kept the verb "make." The scribes underlying La^{BMP} throughout display a tendency to revise the old Latin version by reading from Greek manuscripts which could well have included manuscripts of the class q.

The reading of q does have one strange feature: it contains the prayer for peace twice (in vss. 1–2 and in vs. 4). The prayer for peace appears in vs. 4 in all witnesses to the text, and in all it is out of place: peace is God's precious gift, given in answer to the prayers of the righteous or granted to forgiven repentant sinners. The senders are righteous; their prayer for the peace of the recipients can appear in vss. 1–2. But vs. 3 and the first words of vs. 4 imply that the Jews of Egypt are sinners who have not yet repented and have not yet been forgiven. In vs. 5 the prayers of the sinners are as yet unheard. Only after the mention of the possibility of God's forgiveness in vs. 5 is there room for a prayer for peace in vss. 3–5. Moreover, the prayer for peace in vs. 4 is strangely phrased: the word "you" is omitted (it has been inserted in the Lucianic recension). These clues suggest that the prayer for peace in vs. 4 arose from a very early marginal note to vs. 1. The note, "May he make peace" (*eirênên poiêsai*), told the reader that "peace" in vs. 1 was the direct object of "make." Written vertically in the margin, it extended from vs. 1 to vs. 4. An early scribe assumed that the marginal note recorded words accidentally omitted from the text. There was no sign the "missing words" belonged in vss. 1–2, so the scribe inserted them at vs. 4, where they are grammatical though illogical.

1. The discussion of Greek translations of the Hebrew word *šālōm*, referred to at AB vol. 41, p. 367, is now in the NOTE on vss. 1–5.

the Jews . . . Judah. Already at this time, Jerusalem has a status separate from and probably superior to the rest of Judaea (cf. Elias Bickerman, *Studies in Jewish and Christian History,* I [Arbeiten zur Geschichte des antiken Judentums und des Urchristentums, Band IX; Leiden: Brill, 1976], 240). On the other hand, the Jews write of themselves as an unprivileged group, for they do not call themselves a "nation" (*ethnos* or *dêmos*); cf. 11:34, and see Bickerman, *Studies,* I, 239–40, and AB vol. 41, pp. 194–96, 368.

1–5. A good . . . time. Our verses draw upon Jer 32(Greek Jer 39):39, Jer 33(Greek Jer 40):8–9; Lev 26:42; Deut 4:29–31; I Kings 8:30, 34, 36, 39, 49–50 (and the parallel verses in II Chron 6), and I Chron 28:9. All these texts deal with sin, punishment, and repentance. Here vss. 3–5, without saying so directly, imply that the Jews of Egypt have not been wholeheartedly serving the LORD and need forgiveness. The senders, unlike Job's friends, do not merely draw their inference from the fact of the evil time which has come upon the Jews of Egypt. In writing the letter they have chosen words which allude to a particular sin, the maintenance of the schismatic Oniad temple at Leontopolis, inasmuch as the passages in Kings and Chronicles all come from contexts which state that the temple at Jerusalem is "the place which the LORD hath chosen" to be the sole legitimate place for the offering of sacrifices (see Deut 12:2, 4–18, 26–29). To have quoted words from Deuteronomy would not have served the senders' purpose of condemning the schismatic temple, because in Deuteronomy the chosen place is not identified as Jerusalem. Lev 26:42 and Deut 4:29–31, as well as I Kings 8:49–50 (read with I Kings

8:48), speak of the sin and repentance of Jews like the Jews of Egypt, in exile from their homeland.

Vss. 1–2 wish the Egyptian Jews a *good* peace, as if they now lived under a bad peace, and vs. 5 suggests that the Egyptian Jews are living in a bad time. The implications fit the historical situation of the Jews of Egypt in late autumn, 124 B.C.E. By that time, Ptolemy VIII Euergetes II and his sister Cleopatra II agreed to end their bitter civil war. See Volkmann, "Ptolemaios 27," PW, XXIII² (1959), 1729–33; Will, *Histoire,* II, 365. Ptolemy's side had had by far the better of it, but the Jews under Oniad leadership (see Introduction, Part I, n. 64) had backed Cleopatra. Thus the peace could look so bad to them that the senders of the letter would be impelled to wish them a *good* peace. The senders may also have been thinking of Jer 8:15 and 14:19 and Isa 45:7.

1–2. *A good peace . . . to you.* The context of sin, captivity, forgiveness, and redemption at Jer 33(Greek Jer 40):7–9 is sufficient to explain why the senders drew on Jer 33:9 here. Did they also intend to allude to the Davidic king mentioned at Jer 33:15 and 17 and the entire "messianic" prophecy of Jer 33:2–26? Does "good peace" mean the final, messianic peace? Perhaps, but nowhere else in the literature of the early Hasmonaean period is there such an allusion to the hope in a Davidic messiah.

2. *may He remember . . . Jacob.* The Greek is ungrammatical. "Abraham," "Isaac," and "Jacob" are in the accusative case, as they should be after the preposition *pros,* but the appositive "servants" is in the genitive. The error probably reflects the Greek writer's familiarity with the Bible: he began by thinking of Exod 2:24, where the names of the Patriarchs are in the accusative with *pros,* but when he finished he was thinking of Lev 26:42, where the names are in the genitive case. Probably the senders intended to allude only to Lev 26:42, a context of repentance in exile. Exod 2:24 has nothing to do with sin and repentance, though it does deal with suffering Jews in Egypt.

3–4. *May He give . . . commandments.* This is the earliest known text of a prayer which is still used in the Jewish liturgy as part of the *Qᵉduššāh dᵉsidrā* (on the *Qᵉduššāh dᵉsidrā,* see Ismar Elbogen, *Der jüdische Gottesdienst* [3d rev. ed.; Frankfurt am Main: J. Kauffmann, 1931], p. 79). No single manuscript of the Jewish prayer book has a text identical to the one here, but in the various manuscripts word for word equivalents for each phrase can be found. See *Seder 'Abodat Yiśra'el,* ed. by Yitzḥaq Baer (Rödelheim, 5628; reprinted in Palestine by Schocken, 5697), p. 128.

Such prayers on behalf of a Jewish community imply, tactfully, that it has been less than perfect in obeying God and his commandments.

3. *May . . . revere Him.* The words echo Deut 5:26 (29G.) and Jer 32(Greek Jer 39):39. The pious senders believed that man had the ability and the duty to obey God, but from verses like Jer 32:39 they were convinced that God could help the obdurate to obey.

to do . . . spirit. The words echo I Chron 28:7 and 9, from a context in which David charges Solomon to build the temple. I am not sure why the Greek text, where I have translated "whole[heartedly]," has "great" (*megalêi;* Heb. *gādōl*) rather than the idiomatic "full," "whole" (*plêrei;* Heb. *mālē'*). The writer was a good Hebraist, but perhaps Hebrew was not his vernacular, and in quoting I Chron 29:9 from memory he may have strayed from good Hebrew idiom.

4. "To open the heart" would seem to be an idiom transferred to the heart from the eyes (cf. Ps 119:18) and the ears, but it may have been derived from Hos 13:6–8 by rendering in 13:8, "I shall tear open the closure of their hearts." The idiom appears in the New Testament (Acts 16:14) and in rabbinic Jewish prayers (TB *Berakot* 17a and the *Q*ᵉ*duššāh* *d*ᵉ*sidrā*). On the words in parentheses, see first NOTE on vss. 1–5.

5. The language is derived from I Kings 8:30, 34, 36, 39, 49–50 or from the parallel verses in II Chron 6. The Greek writer here renders Heb. *slḥ* ("forgive") by *katallagênai* ("be reconciled"), rather than by *hileôs einai* ("be merciful"), the stereotyped equivalent used in the biblical Greek written in Egypt. Like other Jewish writers in Egypt, however, our writer seems to avoid *syngnônai,* the usual Greek word for "forgive."

"Abandon you in an evil time" may simply reflect the situation of the Egyptian Jews; it may also be another echo of verses which the senders had in mind throughout the letter (I Chron 28:9; Deut 4:31). Cf. also Jer 2:27.

6. The prayer after the formula of salutation was a piece of conventional politeness, even though it was written especially for the situation facing the Egyptian Jews. After such courtesies the writer of a Hebrew or Aramaic letter would mark the transition to the informative part of the letter by using the formula "and now" (*w*ᶜ*th, wk*ᶜ*nt*). The ancient versions are correct in rendering Gr. *hôde* in our verse as "here" rather than "thus"; "here" is the meaning the word always has in Greek translations from the Hebrew Bible. Moreover, the senders have alluded to verses from Solomon's prayer concerning the temple of Jerusalem and the land of Judah that prayers there be particularly efficacious (I Kings 8:30–52, esp. 46–50). The receivers will now understand that prayers for them are being uttered where scripture says that prayer is most efficacious. A rebuke may also be implied: despite the continual prayers at Jerusalem, the Egyptian Jews are still in trouble because of their own sin (cf. Jer 11:14).

The letter of Jonathan and the Jews to their "brothers" the Spartans likewise conveys the news that the Jews of Judaea are continually praying for the welfare of the recipients (I 12:11).

7–8. The Jews of Jerusalem and Judah in referring to the troubles of 169–164 B.C.E do not mention the name of Antiochus IV. The senders would have viewed him as only the "rod of God's anger" (cf. Isa 10:5). The troubles came as a result of the heinous sins of Jason the Oniad. If the Oniad schismatic temple had not been their target, would the senders have blamed all on Jason? Perhaps.

The strongest proof that God had again chosen the temple in Jerusalem would have been a miracle there. A letter attacking the Oniad temple in Egypt might avoid alluding to the miraculous foiling of Heliodorus, in which Onias III had an important role (3:4–35). Supporters of the Hasmonaeans might have viewed their victories as miraculous, but the senders here do not even allude to the successes of Judas Maccabaeus in battle. Ep. 1 conforms to the views of those many Jews who (unlike Jason of Cyrene) still did not believe that they were living in a new age of miracles. Rather, the senders claim that the sins of Jason, as heinous as those of the worst kings of Israel and Judah (see below), should have caused the permanent destruction of the temple at Jerusalem and the permanent cessation of worship there. If prayers in Jerusalem and Judaea for the resumption of the daily offering at Jerusalem were nevertheless fulfilled, God must have again chosen the temple there.

Before Bickerman discovered (ZNW 32 [1933], 237–39=*Studies*, II, 140–42) that the passage "In the affliction . . . the showbread" should be enclosed in quotation marks, this part of the letter was unintelligible to modern scholars (but see R. Leszynsky, "Das Laubhüttenfest Chanukka," *Monatsschrift für Geschichte und Wissenschaft des Judentums* 55 [1911], 417), and ancient and medieval scribes showed their own perplexity in misguided attempts to alter the text. Well might such readers be perplexed! Quotation marks are a modern invention, and in a letter the word in the perfect tense which I have translated "we wrote" could be mistaken for an "epistolary perfect" and translated as present (see Mayser, II¹, 183). Thus, an unwary reader could render our verse "In the reign of Demetrius in the year 169 we Jews write you in the affliction . . ." Then the date in vs. 7 would contradict the date in vs. 10; and vss. 7–8 would present a weird view of history: that the troubles caused by Jason's sin were continuing in 169 Sel. (144 B.C.E. at the earliest). Worse, vss. 7–8 would tell the Egyptian Jews that despite prayer and sacrifice the Jews of Jerusalem and Judaea were still in trouble. Surely that information would not motivate the Jews of Egypt to observe the festival commemorating the restoration of the temple in Jerusalem! Ancient writers had ways of explicitly indicating a quotation, like the English conjunction "that" or formula "and I quote." But often ancient writers would fail to take advantage of such devices, and without warning after a verb of speaking, writing, sending, etc., they would give a quotation. See Ezra 4:17; Neh 6:6; Dan Th. 6:26; Dan LXX 4:34b; Acts 15:22; Bickerman (*Studies*, II, 141) cites parallels in Greek papyri. We shall call the quoted letter of 169 Sel. "Ep. 0."

Hebrew syntax uses *w-* ("and") to connect many sorts of grammatical constructions in situations where "and" is not used in English. A literal translation of Ep. 0 might seem very ambiguous. In the literal translation which follows, an "and" in parentheses represents a Hebrew *w-* which might or might not be omitted in a good English translation. In brackets I have called attention to other ambiguities: "In the . . . distress which came upon us . . . from the time that there rebelled Jason and his followers from the Holy Land and the Kingdom [is the rebellion said to be "from the Holy Land and the Kingdom," or are the followers?], (and) they [who?] set fire to the temple gate, and they [who?] shed innocent blood, (and) we brought . . . sacrifices . . . , and we kindled the lamps, and we laid out the showbread." How far does the temporal clause (introduced by "from the time that") extend?

To produce an unambiguous translation, one has to consider the patterns of biblical allusions in the letter, for our historical information is too scanty to decide the issue: both Jason's force and the Seleucid army "shed innocent blood" (5:6, 12–14); Callisthenes, who burned the gate(s) (8:33), is nowhere identified as a follower of Jason. "In the affliction and in the distress" might come from the generalizing context describing punishments, Deut 28:53, 55, 57, to which, however, there is no further allusion in the letter. Hence our phrase probably comes from the other possibility, the specific context of sin and punishment, at Jer 19:9. At Jer 19:4 the sins of Jews which incurred the punishment of Judah and Jerusalem are identified. Included are the acts of leaders of Judah, who "deserted" God and "rendered foreign" the Chosen Place and "shed innocent blood"; all three sins were committed by the Jews of the party of Jason the Oniad (the priests among them deserted the temple, II 4:14; and see also 4:9–16, 5:6). Our letter goes on in vs. 8 to mention the shedding of innocent blood. Hence, we may conclude that the subject of the verbs "set fire" and "shed" remains "Jason and his followers." The temporal clause refers to the sinners who caused the distress, and the main clause begins with the verbs which are in the first person, telling of the propitiatory acts of the righteous senders.

Jason had been high priest, head of the nation, and at the time of his rebellion was pressing his claim that he was still the legitimate high priest (II 4:23–26, 5:5–7). At the time of Jer 19:4 the heads of the nation, where deadly sins brought on the disaster, were the kings. The books of Kings, Chronicles, Jeremiah, and Ezekiel leave no doubt as to what were the deadliest sins of the kings. The archsinner among the kings of Israel was Jeroboam I (II Kings 17:21–23). Jeroboam I "rebelled" (Heb. root: *mrd*) against his lord and king (II Chron 13:6) and opened schismatic temples (I Kings 12:27–33); for confirmation that the senders had II Chron 13:4–11 in mind, see NOTE on vs. 8, *We brought . . . showbread*. As for the kings of Judah, the immediate cause of the final catastrophe of Judah and Jerusalem was the "rebellion" (*mrd*) of Zedekiah against the Babylonian king he had sworn to obey (II Kings 24:20; II Chron 36:13–19; Jer 52:3; Ezek 17:15). Just so, in our letter the dreadful troubles came after Jason's "rebellion" against the kingdom of which he had sworn to be a loyal subject. The sole official name of the Seleucid empire was "the Kingdom"; see Bickerman, *Institutions*, p. 3. On differences in vs. 7 from its biblical models, see NOTE on vs. 7, *Jason . . . Kingdom*. On the oath of the high priest and perhaps of all Jews to obey the pagan king, see J. *AJ* xi 8.3.318, xii 1.1.8, and 3.4.150.

Here, Hebrew "rebel against" is translated by Gr. *apostēnai apo*, as at II Chron 13:6 and Ezek 17:15 and at Jer 52:3 in Symmachus and the Syrohexaplar version (*mn mlk'*). Having recognized the biblical echoes in our passage, we no longer need hesitate over "there rebelled Jason and his followers from the Holy Land and the Kingdom." The "from" phrase modifies "rebelled," not "followers."

Other biblical texts look farther back in history for the king whose deadly sins brought about the destruction in 586 B.C.E. They place the blame on Manasseh, King of Judah (II Kings 21:10–17, 24:3–4; Jer 15:4). Manasseh violated the sacred structure of the temple by placing pagan altars and an asherah there (II Kings 21:5, 7) and also shed much innocent blood (ibid., vs. 16, 24:4); just so, Jason and his followers violated the temple by burning its gateway and shed innocent blood (5:5–10, 8:33). Thus our letter portrays Jason's sins as being as heinous as those of the worst kings of Israel and Judah.

7. *In the reign . . . 169*. Which form of the Seleucid era has been used here? If the date is on the Macedonian form, the year 169 Sel. ran from October 10,

144, to September 28, 143 B.C.E.; if the date is on the Babylonian form, the year ran from April 5, 143, to March 25, 142 B.C.E.

Even though ancient communications were slow, a festal letter to Egypt would not be sent far in advance of the date it proclaimed, for then the proclamation might be forgotten. The festal messages reflected in the *Mishnah* (*Rosh ha-shanah* 1:3–4) had a special urgency, for they conveyed to the pious the date of the beginning of the new month as fixed by observation by the authorities in Palestine. Couriers on those religiously important missions could make good time; in the third and fourth centuries C.E., couriers bringing the date of the first of Tishri (Rosh ha-shanah) crossed the Syrian desert between Tiberias and Pumbedita on the Euphrates in seven days or fewer (TB *Rosh ha-shanah* 20b–21a; Jacob Obermeyer, *Die Landschaft Babylonien* [Frankfurt am Main: I. Kauffmann, 1929], pp. 41–45, and cf. pp. 48–49). Couriers should also have made good time on the well-traveled route from Jerusalem to Alexandria in the second century B.C.E. (Bickerman, *Studies*, II, 146). Ep. 0 and Ep. 1 did not deliver news as urgent as the date of the beginning of the month. Nevertheless, to suggest that the letter was sent out even six weeks before 25 Kislev is probably to overestimate the lead time. Ep. 0 and Ep. 1, at the very earliest, went out in mid-autumn.

Law required that the name of the reigning king appear in the date of all documents. A change in the name of the king in two successive documents means either that the earlier king has died or that there has been a rebellion. See AB vol. 41, NOTE on 13:41. Ep. 0 named the king as Demetrius (II), not as Antiochus VI. Jonathan and the Jews were faithful subjects of the little king Antiochus VI from late summer, 145 B.C.E. (I 11:54 – 12:53; for the date, see AB vol. 41, NOTE on 11:54); and even after Jonathan fell prisoner to Tryphon (the treacherous minister of Antiochus VI), the Jews under Jonathan's brother Simon still recognized the regime and surrendered hostages to Tryphon (I 13:1–19). The author of First Maccabees does not wish to tell his readers when the Jews jumped to recognize Demetrius as king, for he stresses the fealty of the Jews to Antiochus VI. Nevertheless, material in First Maccabees implies that the Jews changed allegiance before the death of the helpless little king, surely in anger over Tryphon's acts; see AB vol. 41, NOTE on 13:34–42. The Jews could have done so at any time after Tryphon refused to release Jonathan and fulfill his side of the bargain through which he had received the hostages (I 13:14–19).

The subsequent narrative of First Maccabees shows that the Jews changed sides less than a year before the death of Antiochus VI. It runs as follows. Not long after Tryphon refused to release Jonathan, he marched on Jerusalem from the south, intending to relieve the besieged garrison of the citadel (the Akra), but was balked by a sudden snowstorm, an extremely rare event south of Jerusalem. Hence, we know that the events occurred during the winter. Tryphon next marched through Transjordan, where he killed Jonathan; and then he returned to Antioch, where not much later he had Antiochus VI killed and usurped the throne himself (I 13:20–24, 31–32).

The dated coins issued at Antioch show that the last year of the reign of Antiochus VI was 170 Sel. Mac. (Sept. 29, 143–Oct. 17, 142 B.C.E.; on the coins of Antiochus VI dated in 171 Sel. Mac., see AB vol. 41, NOTE on 13:41).

These coins of 170 Sel. Mac. are abundant and of many types, so that Antiochus VI cannot have perished early in that Seleucid year; his death must be placed in 142 B.C.E. If so, Tryphon's expedition against Jerusalem and the snowfall came at the earliest in autumn, 143 B.C.E. If Ep. 0 had been dated 169 Sel. Mac., as a festal letter announcing a festival in Kislev, it would have had to be sent in autumn of 144 B.C.E., a year before the events which induced the Jews to jump from Antiochus VI to Demetrius II. Hence the Jewish authorities who sent Ep. 0 and Ep. 1 used the Babylonian form of the Seleucid era, and the two letters are of November or early December, 143 and 124 B.C.E.

The date of Ep. 0 reflects a very transitory situation. By 3 Tishri, 170 Sel. Bab. (142 B.C.E.), the Jews were no longer dating by Seleucid Demetrius but by an era of their own independence (I 13:34–42, 14:27, 38–40; see AB vol. 41, NOTES on 13:41–42). It is hard to believe that a forger of a letter purporting to be written in 124 B.C.E. would pretend to quote an imaginary letter written during the brief period of 143/2 in which the Jews recognized Demetrius II as their king. Indeed, a forger would hardly have thought of quoting a letter of 143, but would probably have imagined a message from the time of Judas Maccabaeus, like Ep. 2. Hence, both Ep. 0 and Ep. 1 are authentic (cf. Bickerman, *Studies*, II, 144).

In fact, 143 B.C.E. was probably the earliest opportune moment for calling upon Jews of Egypt to observe the Feast of Dedication. In 164 B.C.E. the first observance of the festival appears to have been a spur-of-the-moment decision, allowing no time for a festal letter to Egypt; see AB vol. 41, NOTE on 4:36–54. By summer, 163 B.C.E., Judas' army had been defeated and partly dispersed, and a shrunken Jewish force was under siege in the temple (ibid., pp. 43–44, 47–48, 315, 322–24). The siege lasted until January or March, 162 (see ibid., p. 325), so that no festal letter could go out in November or December of 163. Before the end of the siege, or upon it, Alcimus became high priest, and as long as Seleucid force kept him in power, this pious Jew and loyal Seleucid subject probably opposed the observance of the festival which commemorated successful rebellion. During the brief interval between the defeat of Nicanor (in March, 161) and the final defeat of Judas Maccabaeus (in spring, 160) the Jews of Jerusalem and Judah could have sent a letter asking the Jews of Egypt to observe the Feast of Dedication, but there is no trace of such a letter.

In the course of the 150's Onias IV gained the favor of Ptolemy VI and became a leading figure among the Jews of Egypt and began to think of establishing his schismatic temple. As long as Egyptian Jewry and Onias IV prospered under Ptolemy VI, Egyptian Jewry was an unpromising audience for an appeal to observe the Feast of the Dedication of the temple where no one at all was high priest, or a usurping upstart was. With the rise of Jonathan to the high priesthood in autumn, 152 (I 10:21), the Jews of Jerusalem and Judah can become eager proponents of the Feast of Dedication. After the death of Ptolemy VI, the Oniads and the Jews backed the cause of his sister-widow, Cleopatra II, against her brother, Ptolemy VIII Euergetes II. Though Cleopatra's side had the worst of it in 145, her Jewish commanders Onias and Dositheos negotiated a peace settlement by spring, 144 (J. *Ap.* ii 5.49–50; Volkmann, "Ptolemaios 27," PW, XXIII, 1726), and at first may well have retained considerable power in the "coalition" regime of Cleopatra II and Ptolemy VIII (the events of J. *Ap.* ii 5.53–55 perhaps occurred in and after 131 B.C.E.; see my article in *Studies Smith,* Part III, p. 114, n. 104). The position of Cleopatra II, however, deteriorated so that by spring, 142, Ptolemy was able to humiliate her by marrying her daughter, Cleopatra III (Volkmann, PW, XXIII, 1727–28). The deteriorating position of the patroness of the Oniads was probably known in Jerusalem and Judaea and gave the anti-Oniads and the proponents of the Feast of Dedication their first real opportunity to send propaganda to Egypt.

distress. All Greek witnesses to the text have the enigmatic word *akmê* ("point," "edge," "culminating point," "ripe time," "prime," "vigor"), which makes a poor companion for "affliction." The reading must be very old but can hardly be correct. Ancient readers tried to improve upon it. The word is omitted in La^X. The Syriac translator and the scribe reflected in La^BM probably had *akmê* in their Greek texts but saw what was required, a word like "distress" or "persecution." In Hebrew, nouns derived from the root "afflict" (*ṣrr;* Gr. noun: *thlipsis*) frequently are used in parallel with nouns from the root "distress" (*ṣwq;* Gr. noun: *ananke*). See Deut 28:53, 55, 57; Isa 8:22, 30:6; Jer 19:9; Zeph 1:15; Pss 25:17, 107:6, 13, 19, 28, 119:143; Prov 1:27; Job 15:24. Hence one would expect *ananke* here, and a later Greek scribe (of ms. 58) did write *ananke* for *akmê*. A Gr. *nu* from the fourth century B.C.E. to the first century C.E. looked much like our capital "N," but often had its right vertical line curved inward. If the curve was deep enough, the *nu* could easily have been mistaken for a *kappa,* and if the letters which followed were not too clearly written, the next scribe would readily have jumped to the conclusion that *akmê* lay before him.

which came upon us. Cf. Ezra 9:13; Neh 9:33.

Jason . . . Kingdom. The biblical models for our verse lack "Holy Land" and instead of "Kingdom" have "king." These differences probably reflect the historical facts confronting the senders. The senders could condemn an Oniad, Jason, for heinous sin in and around Judaea. On being supplanted as high priest by Menelaus, Jason had gone to the Ammanitis (4:26), surely to the stronghold of his second cousin, Hyrcanus the Tobiad; see my article, "The Tales of the Tobiads," in *Studies Smith,* Part III, pp. 90–92. Hyrcanus built there, at the site now called 'Arāq el-Emīr, a fortified structure; see Paul Lapp, "The Second and Third Campaigns at 'Arâq el-Emîr," BASOR 171 (October, 1963), 24–26, 38–39, and correct accordingly my remarks in *Studies Smith,* Part III, p. 110, n. 89. Lapp argued that Hyrcanus' impressive structure, now called Qaṣr el-'Abd, was a temple, and Lapp also noticed its similarity as a historical phenomenon to the temple in Egypt founded by Onias IV (BASOR 171, 27–31; cf. Martin Hengel, *Judaism and Hellenism,* I, 273–74, and II, 180–82, nn. 93–113, and see introductory NOTE on II 1:10b–2:18). *If* Lapp is right, that there was a schismatic temple at 'Arāq el-Emīr, we can suggest a plausible meaning for Jason's "rebellion against the Holy Land."

One would naturally ask at least two questions: why did Hyrcanus build a temple? If Jewish sacrifices were offered there, who acted as priests? We have no information. However, the ideology of Jason's nephew, Onias IV, can be reconstructed from Onias' writings: the temple of Jerusalem is no longer, or is not yet, the "place which the LORD hath chosen," and hence Jewish temples can exist anywhere. If Jason held the same point of view, he would have been ready to maintain a "schismatic" cult at the temple built by Hyrcanus. Even in Jerusalem, opponents of the upstart Menelaus could have thought God's favor rested on the Transjordanian temple where a legitimate member of the high priestly line ministered.

The senders of our letter, however, were firm partisans of Jerusalem as God's elected place. To them there could be no doubt that Jason's schism was sinful. They had only to point to Josh 22:9–29. The narrative there implies that to have an altar for sacrifice in Transjordan is an act of *rebellion* (*mrd*) against the LORD. Hence, one would expect to have in our verse an accusation that Jason rebelled against the LORD. However, the senders had to argue from premises acceptable to their opponents. The Egyptian Jews could reply, with the Oniads, that in Josh 22 Transjordan was "unclean" (vs. 19) and the altar there unfit for sacrifice only because God had chosen Shiloh (Josh 22:29, 18:1; Jer 7:12), but now God has rejected both Shiloh and Jerusalem. The senders therefore do not make the fruitless charge of rebellion against God. Jason did not intend to rebel against God, but he certainly rebelled against the sanctity of the Holy Land. According to Zech 2:16, the land of Judaea became holy as soon as God allowed the exiled Jews to return and take possession of it. The same verse predicted that God would again choose Jerusalem. Onias IV and his followers might hold that the predicted divine election of Jerusalem still lay in the future, but they could not deny the truth of Zechariah's words and may well have held that Judaea was even now the Holy Land; see John J. Collins, *The Sibylline Oracles of Egyptian Judaism* (Diss. Harvard; Missoula, Mont.: Society of Biblical Literature, 1972), pp. 44–53. Hence, the senders could portray as rebellion against the Holy Land Jason's withdrawal across the Jordan to minister at a schismatic temple. In so doing they strained the Hebrew language, for nowhere else in Hebrew do we hear of rebellion against a land.

The silence of the abridged history in II 4:26 and 5:3–10, concerning service by Jason as priest of a schismatic temple, is no obstacle to our theory. For the writer, such service by Jason was no sin (see Introduction, pp. 13–17). Jason's coup, an attempt to seize control of the temple of Jerusalem, itself shows that Jason agreed with our writer in holding that temple to be greater than any other.

However, we began developing our theory with the proviso "*If* Lapp is right." Recent excavations suggest but do not yet prove that Lapp was wrong to identify Qaṣr el-ʿAbd as a temple (Ernest Will, "L'Édifice dit Qaṣr al ʿAbd à ʿAraq al Amir [Jordanie]," *Comptes rendus de l'Académie des inscriptions et belles-lettres*, 1977, p. 80; idem, "Recherches au Qasr el ʿAbd à ʿIraq al Amir," *Annual of the Department of Antiquities of Jordan* 23 [1979], 139–49). As Will points out (ibid., p. 147), Josephus (*AJ* xii 4.11.230) called it a "castle" (*baris*). Nevertheless, our theory does not necessarily fall if Lapp is wrong. The words of our passage and the allusions behind them would fit our theory just as well if Jason served at a temple in Transjordan of which no traces have been found.

Other peculiarities of the vocabulary used by pious Jews in the second century B.C.E. fit well with our analysis of our passage. If the senders of Epp. 0

and 1 called their country the "Holy Land," in contrast to Transjordan and other areas, they probably called themselves the "Holy People" (Isa 62:12), especially when contrasting themselves with "impious Hellenizers" like Jason and Menelaus. We find such vocabulary being used at 15:24 and at III 2:6 and at Dan 12:7; see also Dan 7:18, 21, 25, 27, and 8:24. The seer in Dan 9:26 speaks of Jason's supporters not even as sinful Jews but as "Jason's People." The passage is to be rendered as follows: "An anointed [priest; i.e., Onias III] shall be cut off [see II 4:33–34] . . . and the People of the successor prelate [i.e., Jason, who succeeded Onias III] shall destroy the city and the sanctuary"; see vs. 8 and 5:6–10.

As for the mention in our verse of "kingdom" rather than "king," Jason and Onias IV were both partisans of the Ptolemaic kingdom against the rival Seleucid empire and would not have denied rebelling against the Seleucids. Jason, indeed, appears to have adhered to the Jewish belief that God requires obedience to the reigning king. He rebelled only on receiving a false report that Antiochus IV was dead. At that moment Jason may have thought God was fulfilling Dan 2:44. In any case, Antiochus IV was a usurper, and it was unclear who would be his successor. Hence, for Jason and his supporters the rebellion was different from Zedekiah's: it was rebellion not against a king but against a kingdom destined to fall. The senders here concede to the Oniads and the Egyptian Jews the distinction between Jason and Zedekiah. Though Jason's sin was not identical to Zedekiah's, its gravity could be judged by its consequences, the dreadful events in Judaea from Antiochus' sack of Jerusalem in 169 until the victories of Judas Maccabaeus.

In conceding the distinction between "king" and "kingdom," the senders lost little. Both they and the recipients probably believed in a scheme of the history of the period of the Jews' subjugation. We find versions of this scheme preserved in Dan 2 and Dan 7: the Jews owe complete allegiance not merely to the individual king placed over them by God but also to each "kingdom" in the limited series of kingdoms destined to rule over large sections of the earth (including Judaea) until God sets up an everlasting kingdom for his righteous Chosen People. God's everlasting kingdom had not yet come, so obviously Jason was a sinful rebel.

Readers of I 1:11–15, 64 and II 4:7–17 might well be surprised to find nothing said here of Jason's deadly sin of Hellenizing. Had pious Jews in Jerusalem in 143 B.C.E. ceased to think of it as a deadly sin? At least in part, the senders here are being tactful with the receivers: many and perhaps most pious Jews in Egypt were Hellenized and associated freely with Greeks; cf. To. 'Abodah zarah 4(5):6=TB 'Abodah zarah 8a bottom. When the main issue was the schismatic temple, it would have been foolish to antagonize the recipients by preaching against Hellenism.

In fact, however, our document probably shows that as late as 124 B.C.E. (the date of Ep. 1) there were Jews who disagreed with the authors of First Maccabees and the abridged history and held that the Hellenism of Jason the Oniad and the Antiochenes was *not* the deadly sin which brought on the persecution. See my article in Jewish and Christian Self-Definition, II, esp. pp. 81–82.

The character of Jewish history from 586 B.C.E. to the Hasmonaean uprising cannot be understood without appreciating the impact of the destruction of the kingdom of Judah and of the teachings of the prophets vindicated by that disaster (Jer 21, 24:1–25:29, 27:1–29:19, 30:1–17, 32:1–5, 38:17–23, 52:1–27; Ezek 17; and cf. II Kings 24:18–25:21; II Chron 36:13–19). The event and the prophecies taught the Jews to avoid, at all costs, rebellion against the kings whom "the LORD had placed over them" (cf. Neh 9:36–37), for God would punish such rebellion with the calamities which struck Zedekiah's kingdom. The fact that the Jews learned their lesson explains their astonishing loyalty as mercenary soldiers. See Porten, *Archives from Elephantine;* J. *AJ* xi 8.3.316–19, 4.326–5.339; *Aristeas to Philocrates* 36–37=J. *AJ* xii 1.5.45–47; J. *AJ* xii 3.1.119, 4.147–53; *Ap.* ii 4.44; Marcel Launey, *Recherches sur les armées hellénistiques* (Paris: É. de Boccard, 1950), pp. 541–46, 551–52; Hengel, *Judaism and Hellenism,* pp. 15–18; Lucio Troiani, "Giuseppe, *Antichità giudaiche* XII, 150," *Athenaeum,* n.s., 58 (1980), 465–66 (where the correct rendering of the passage is the one in the middle of the first paragraph of p. 466). Cf. II 8:20.

Hence also comes the loyalty of Jews to capricious and even wicked sovereigns (Dan 1–6) and even to kings whose defeat was imminent (J. *AJ* xi 8.3.318); I shall show in my commentary on Daniel that Dan 11:14 reflects similar loyalty by the mass of Jews to Ptolemy V in ca. 202 B.C.E. Jews avoided rebellion even against a tyrannical foreign ruler; see Philo *De providentia apud* Eusebius *Praeparatio evangelica* viii. 14. 37–41, pp. 393c–94b, and the oath of the Essenes at J. *BJ* ii 8.7.140.

The Jews' fealty could be shaken only under two sets of circumstances. First, if pagan rivals disputed the right to imperial rule over Judaea, the Jews, deprived of divine revelation (see AB vol. 41, Introduction, pp. 12–13), were in a difficult position, for they had to choose between the rivals. It was probably the high priest Simon II who led the Jews through the difficult transition from Ptolemaic to Seleucid rule at the end of the third century B.C.E. If so, his feat won the loud praises of Ben Sira (Sir 50:1–24, and cf. Sir 10:4–5, 8). Second, Jews might rebel if the signs of the times indicated that their sentence of servitude had been fully served. The internecine struggles in the Persian empire at the beginnings of the reigns of Darius I and Artaxerxes III Ochus and the troubles at the beginning of the reign of Ptolemy V appear to have been read as such signs by some Jews, but the great mass of the Jewish nation remained loyal. I shall deal with these topics in my book *When Chosen Peoples Fall to Foreign Domination.*

Dreadful was the predicament of the Jews when Antiochus IV ordered them to violate the Torah. Their God would punish them disastrously whether they obeyed or rebelled! In the first years of the persecution there were no signs God was beginning to make the strong king's empire collapse.

A Machiavellian materialist would say that a people quiescent under foreign domination has no history. Pious Jews wrote their own history only when they saw God acting in it. In the long centuries of subjugation, they believed that God had sentenced them to suffer the absence of both miracles and prophecy until the time of redemption (see AB vol. 41, pp. 12–13). Hence, so far as we know, Jews wrote no contemporary history between the age of Nehemiah and the success of the Hasmonaean revolt.

8. *set.* . . . *gateway.* The Greek word *pylôn* means not a simple gate but a monumental gateway. Cf. 8:33, and see NOTE on 5:5–16(end).

we prayed . . . *to us.* Probably another echo of Solomon's prayer (I Kings 8:33–34), as in vss. 5. The Greek has "we were heard" instead of "he hearkened to us"; cf. Hebrew and Greek at Prov 21:13 and Dan LXX 10:12.

We brought . . . *showbread.* Cf. I 4:50–53. In contrast to the schismatic Jason (see 5:7–10), the righteous partisans of the temple of Jerusalem on being forgiven by God were able to resume the temple offerings and thus won yet more divine favor, just as the righteous kingdom of Judah enjoyed divine favor against the schismatic Jeroboam I; see NOTE on vss. 7–8. Our verse probably echoes II Chron 13:11.

The writer here alludes to the offering of the *Tamid,* the continual daily sacrifice (cf. II Chron 13:11), which consisted both of animal burnt offerings and of vegetable oblations (Exod 29:38–42; Num 28:3–8; *M. Tamid*). The Greek here for "burnt offering" (*'wlh*) uses the vague word *thysia* ("sacrifice"), and for "oblation" (*mnḥh*) uses "fine flour," but this is a usual practice in biblical Greek. See the Greek at Exod 29:40–42, where directions are given for the continual offerings (Exod 29:38–42) in the larger context of the dedication of the altar (Exod 29:36–43), and see Suzanne Daniel, *Recherches sur le vocabulaire du culte dans la Septante* (Paris: Klincksieck, 1966), pp. 204–22, 242, 256–58.

The kindling of the lamps (Exod 27:20–21; Lev 24:2–3) and the arraying of the showbread (Exod 25:30; Lev 24:5–9) were also continual rites, mentioned at II Chron 13:11, though the showbread was changed each Sabbath, not daily (Lev 24:8).

Conspicuous by its absence here is mention of the daily offering of incense (Exod 30:7–8), in contrast to II Chron 13:11 and I 4:50 and II 10:3. Antiochus IV did carry off the altar of incense in 169 B.C.E. (I 1:21), but did that act prevent the offering of incense? See AB vol. 41, p. 547, n. 1, and below, NOTE on II 2:5. It is possible that Antiochus IV continued to allow incense to be offered; see AB vol. 41, NOTE on I 1:45, and below, NOTE on II 10:3, *offered* . . . *lights.*

Also conspicuously absent are references to the desecration of the temple and the altar by Seleucid force and to the purification of the temple and the building of a new altar after the victory of the pious. It is unlikely that the facts were omitted merely because Ep. 1 gives an abridged quotation of Ep. 0. Rather, to have mentioned the purification would have implied the previous desecration, and the fact of desecration could have been used by partisans of the Oniads to argue that God still rejected Jerusalem. On the embarrassing lack of miraculous fire from heaven at the dedication of the new altar, see NOTE on 1:18. It was better to pass over the awkward points in silence.

The sequence of events here, with the offering of the continual daily sacrifice mentioned before the other ritual acts, contrasts with that at I 4:50–53. The difference is probably significant. The author of First Maccabees is ready to portray Judas and his men as following the dedicatory procedures of Moses and Solomon, whereas the pious senders of our letter and the writer at II 10:1–4 seem to have regarded such conduct as presumptuous and as unworthy of Judas. See AB vol. 41, pp. 280–81. Cf. also *M. Menaḥot* 4:4. On the other hand, I 4:50–52 and II 10:3 agree in ordering the ritual group, incense-lamps-showbread, and (except for omitting incense) so does our verse. Does that order reflect the practice of the authors' times? The indications in the Torah as to the sequence differ from that order and are inconsistent with one another and with II Chron 13:11 (Exod 30:6–8, 40:22–29; Lev 24:1–8). Rabbinic authorities disagreed on the sequence of lighting the lamps and offering the incense (TB *Yoma* 14b, 33a–b). According to *M. Menaḥot* 4:4, showbread to dedicate a new table had to be offered on the Sabbath (but see *M. Menaḥot* 11:8). Rabbinic sources do not tell us where the putting forth of the showbread came in the schedule of events on the Sabbath, which did include the kindling of the lamps and the offering of incense. One may infer, however, that under rabbinic law the laying out of the showbread came last in the sequence, as here, on the principle that daily rituals take precedence over those which are less frequent (TB *Pesaḥim* 114a).

9. "And now" is the standard formula in Aramaic and Hebrew letters to mark transitions. See NOTE on vs. 6. I translate by "we ask you" the Greek writer's *hina* with a subjunctive verb, a good idiom in Hellenistic Greek, unparalleled in Hebrew and Aramaic; see the *Greek-English Lexicon*, s.v. *hina*, B, II, 2b, and Abel, *Grammaire*, p. 272.

The holy days of Tabernacles in the seventh month (Tishri), ordained in the Torah, are called "Festival" or "Feast" (*ḥag, heortê*). Classical Hebrew texts never use the word "Festival" of later commemorative days such as Purim and Ḥanukkah, which are simply called "days" (Esther 9:21–22, 26–28, 31; I 4:59, 7:48–49; II 10:6–8; *Megillat Ta'anit*, etc.). To be accurate, one would have to call Ḥanukkah not "Feast of Dedication" but "Days of Dedication." On the connection of Ḥanukkah with Tabernacles, see AB vol. 41, pp. 273–80.

One might have expected our verse to specify how the Days of Tabernacles in the Month of Kislev are to be observed. Can our letter be incomplete, the specific instructions having been lost in the course of transmission? It is better to assume that the senders took for granted that the receivers would know how to observe the days. We may assume that Ep. 0 had given detailed instructions to the Jews of Egypt, that the name "Days of Tabernacles" was suggestive enough, and that the current observances in Judaea had become widely known in Egypt by the time Ep. 1 was sent.

Although polite "farewell" formulas appear at the end of ancient Greek (Ziemann, pp. 334–35) and Aramaic and Hebrew (Fitzmyer, JBL 93 [1974], 217) letters, their absence was common, too (see Welles, *Royal Correspondence*, nos. 19, 36, 44, 70, and Fitzmyer, JBL 93 [1974], 217).

10a. The date is surely meant to be the date of the letter, not the date of the festival, which was obvious to the recipients. Both in Greek and in Aramaic letters the date, if given, customarily appears at the end; see Exler, p. 99, and Fitzmyer, JBL 93 (1974), 217–18.

II. EPISTLE 2: A FORGED LETTER
TO THE EGYPTIAN JEWS
PURPORTING TO HAVE BEEN
WRITTEN IN 164 B.C.E.
(1:10b–2:18)

1 10b The people in Jerusalem and in Judaea and the Council of Elders and Judas to Aristobulus, tutor of King Ptolemy and member of the stock of the anointed priests, and to the Jews in Egypt, greeting and wishes for health.

11 Having been saved by God from great perils, we thank Him greatly as befits men who war against a king, 12 for God Himself cast away those who made war on the Holy City. 13 Indeed, when the commander and the apparently irresistible army accompanying him came to Persis, they were massacred in the temple of Nanaia through the trickery of Nanaia's priests.

14 Antiochus came with his Friends to the shrine intending to marry the goddess and thereby acquire the money in her rich treasury as dowry. 15 The priests of Nanaia's temple set the money before him, and Antiochus came with a few of his men into the precinct of the shrine. As soon as Antiochus had entered, the priests locked the temple. 16 Opening the secret trap door in the coffered ceiling, they rained stones down upon the thunderstruck commander. After dismembering and beheading the corpses they threw them out to the men outside. 17 In every way blessed is our God, Who delivered over the evildoers!

18 Inasmuch as we are about to celebrate, on the twenty-fifth of Kislev, the Purification of the Temple, we thought we ought to let you know, so that you, too, might celebrate it as Days of Tabernacles and Days of the Fire, as when Nehemiah, the builder of the temple and the altar, brought sacrifices.

19 When our forefathers were being carried off to Persia, the pious priests of that time secretly took some fire from the altar and hid it in a pit which was like a dry well and shut it up securely so that the

place remained unknown to all. 20 Many years went by, and then, in God's own time, Nehemiah received his commission from the king of Persia and sent the descendants of the priests who had hidden the fire to recover it.

21 When they reported that . . . they had found no fire but a viscous liquid,[b] Nehemiah ordered them to draw it up and bring it to him. After the sacrificial offerings had been placed upon the altar, Nehemiah ordered the priests to sprinkle the liquid over the firewood and over the offerings laid upon it. 22 When that had been done, after a while the sun, which had been covered by clouds, began to shine, and a great fire blazed up, to the astonishment of all.

23 As the sacrifice was being consumed, the priests and the whole assemblage uttered a prayer, in which Jonathan led and the rest, following Nehemiah, responded. 24 The prayer was as follows: "LORD, LORD, God, creator of all, awesome and powerful and just and merciful, our sole good king, 25 our sole provider, the sole just One Who is almighty and eternal, the preserver of Israel from every evil, the One Who chose and sanctified the patriarchs! 26 Accept our sacrifice for the sake of all Your people Israel, and guard Your portion and make it holy. 27 Gather together our dispersion. Free those who are enslaved among the nations. Look upon those who have been despised and abominated, and let the nations know that You are our God. 28 Put to torment the oppressors and the arrogant perpetrators of outrage. 29 Plant Your people in Your holy Place, as Moses said." 30 The priests went on singing hymns to the accompaniment of lyres. 31 When the sacrificial offerings had been consumed, Nehemiah ordered that they pour the remaining liquid, too, . . . large boulders.[c] 32 As soon as the command was carried out, a flame blazed up, and when the fire on the altar lit up in turn, . . . was consumed.

33 The news of the phenomenon spread. The king of the Persians received the report that the liquid had been found in the place where the priests being led into exile had hidden the fire and that by means of it Nehemiah and his followers had burned the sacrificial offerings. 34 After verifying the phenomenon, the king had the place fenced in and declared it holy. 35 The king took large sums of money and distributed them to Nehemiah and his followers. 36 Nehemiah and his followers called the liquid "nephthar," which means "purification," but it is commonly called "nephthai."

b On the omitted words, see NOTE on vs. 21.
c On the omitted words, see NOTE on 1:31–32.

2 ¹ In our documents we find that it was Jeremiah the prophet who commanded those who were being led into exile to take some of the fire, as we have just told you. ² They also show that the prophet gave the Torah to those who were being led into exile and admonished them not to forget the Lord's commandments and not to let their minds be led astray when they saw gold and silver images and the ornaments upon them. ³ With other words to the same effect, he exhorted them not to let the Torah depart from their hearts. ⁴ The text also said that the prophet, on receiving a divine revelation, ordered that the tabernacle and the ark should go with him. It went on to say that Jeremiah went out to the mountain which Moses ascended to see the heritage promised by God. ⁵ There, Jeremiah found a cave chamber and brought into it the tabernacle and the ark and the incense altar and blocked up the entrance. ⁶ Some of those who had come along went back to mark the path, but they could not find it. ⁷ When Jeremiah found out, he rebuked them, saying, "The place will remain unknown until God gathers His people together in the Age of Mercy. ⁸ At that time the Lord will bring these things to light again, and the glory of the Lord and the cloud will be seen, as they were over Moses and as Solomon, too, requested, in order that the Place should be greatly sanctified."

⁹ We are also told that Solomon in his wisdom offered a sacrifice in honor of the dedication and completion of the temple. ¹⁰ Just as Moses prayed to the Lord and fire came down from heaven and devoured the sacrifices, so Solomon prayed, and fire came down and consumed the burnt offerings.ᵈ . . . ¹¹ (And Moses said, "On account of . . . the sin offering . . . was consumed.") ¹² . . . So, too, Solomon celebrated the eight days.ᵈ ¹³ The same account is given also in the records and the memoirs of the time of Nehemiah, and also that Nehemiah founded a library and collected the books about the kings and those of prophets and the books of David and the letters of Persian kings on dedicatory gifts to the temple. ¹⁴ In the same manner, Judas reassembled for us the books scattered in the course of the recent war, and we have them. ¹⁵ If you have need of them, send messengers to fetch them.

¹⁶ As we said, we write you inasmuch as we are about to celebrate the Purification. Please celebrate the days. ¹⁷ God, Who saved His entire people and restored the heritage to us all . . . also . . . . the kingdom and the priesthood and the sanctification, ¹⁸ as He promised in

ᵈ⁻ᵈ On the gaps in the translation, see NOTE on 2:9–12.

the Torah. For we hope in God, that He will speedily have mercy upon us and gather us together from the lands under the heavens to His holy Place, for He has indeed delivered us from great evils and has purified His Place.

NOTES

1:10b – 2:18 (Ep. 2). The text of Ep. 2 is difficult and seems to contain gaps and corruptions. The preserver of the text may have been able to find only a tattered copy of the old propaganda piece, or perhaps here again we have an example of how material at the head of a scroll could suffer damage; see AB vol. 41, NOTE on 1:1, *smote . . . place.*

Ep. 2 cannot be what it claims to be: a letter of the Jews in Jerusalem and Judaea, the Council of Elders, and Judas (Maccabaeus), sent to the Jews of Egypt (vs. 10) after the death of Antiochus IV (vss. 13–16) and before 25 Kislev, asking the Jews of Egypt to celebrate simultaneously the festival of the Purification of the Temple (vs. 8). The strange account of the death of Antiochus is not an obstacle to the authenticity of Ep. 2. The first reports of the king's death to reach Jerusalem could well have been distorted by rumor, especially with the precedent of the death of Antiochus III (Diodorus xxviii. 3, xxix. 15; Justin xxxii. 2. 1–2). The decisive point is chronological. Antiochus IV died in the vicinity of Isfahan in 164/3 B.C.E. (AB vol. 41, pp. 307–9). His death became known at Babylon in the ninth month of the Babylonian year (British Museum Cuneiform Tablet BM 35603, published in A. J. Sachs and D. J. Wiseman, "A Babylonian King List of the Hellenistic Period," *Iraq* 16 [1954], 204, 208–9), or between November 20 and December 18, 164. Necessarily his death became known at Jerusalem later than at Babylon. Indeed, there is evidence that the regime of Lysias at Antioch suppressed the news for weeks; see AB vol. 41, p. 43. Even discounting that evidence, the news must have taken some ten days to travel from Babylon to Jerusalem, for under favorable conditions couriers over the shorter distance from Tiberias to Pumbedita took one week (see NOTE on 1:7, *In the reign*). In 164 conditions cannot have been favorable: the king's campaigns must have disturbed Babylonia and the eastern provinces; his absence and now his death may have laid the roads open to bandits; and Judaea was torn by war. The Jews of Egypt might have had frequent correspondence with the Jews of Judaea, but it could not proceed rapidly. Relations between the Seleucid empire and Egypt were bad in 164 B.C.E. (see NOTES on 5:1 and 9:24–25). Jewish couriers surely could not then cross Idumaea (II 12:32–37; I 5:58–66), nor had they access to any of the seaports. Certainly Joppe (12:3–7), Jamnia (12:8–9), Azotus (I 5:68), and Ptolemais (II 6:8) were hostile. Thus, there could have been no rapid postal service between Jerusalem and Alexandria. The speed of an ordinary courier was some sixty kilometers (thirty-seven and a half miles) per day (Reincke, "Nachrichtenwesen," PW, XVI^2 [1935],

1537–41). Between Jerusalem and Alexandria there were more than 350 miles, to be traversed under difficult circumstances. To reach its destination in time, Ep. 2 would have had to leave Jerusalem more than two weeks in advance. Even then, the senders surely would have known of the strong possibility that their message would arrive late and should have taken note of it in Ep. 2. Hence, if the ninth month at Babylon coincided with the ninth Babylonian month (Kislev) on the calendar used at Jerusalem, there was certainly no time to send Ep. 2 as a festal letter to Egypt.

On the local Jewish calendar at Jerusalem, the ninth month need not have coincided with the ninth month at Babylon (see AB vol. 41, p. 23). In fact, there is evidence to show that the ninth month fell earlier at Jerusalem than it did at Babylon, because the Babylonian calendar had had an intercalary month in 166 (Parker and Dubberstein, p. 41) and the Jews had been unable to intercalate their calendar since 167 (see AB vol. 41, introductory NOTE on I 4:36–54). According to I 6:8–17, the king's death came well after the Feast of Dedication, which occurred at the end of the ninth month. According to II 9:1, the two events were nearly simultaneous; see pp. 57–59. Surely, then, the news of the king's death could not have reached Jerusalem in time to be included in a festal letter like Ep. 2. See also fourth paragraph of NOTE on 1:18.

One cannot save the authenticity of Ep. 2 by viewing it rather as an invitation to celebrate the first anniversary of Judas' dedication, though the past tense of "he has purified" (aorist: *ekatherisen*) at II 2:18 might so indicate (cf. Kolbe, *Beiträge*, pp. 116–17). Long before Kislev of 163 the Seleucids were besieging Judas' men in Jerusalem (see AB vol. 41, pp. 43–44, and NOTE on 6:20). The siege was long. It ended shortly before 28 Shebaṭ (March 5), 162 (*Megillat Ta'anit* 28 Shebaṭ; AB vol. 41, p. 325), long after the Feast of Dedication. Even if Judas himself was not among the besieged (see AB vol. 41, pp. 322–23), no letter like Ep. 2 could have been sent from Jerusalem during the siege.

Nor could such a letter have been sent between the end of the siege in 163 B.C.E. and the death of Judas Maccabeus in 160. At that time at least the deliverance of the Jews from the siege and perhaps also the victory over Nicanor (I 7:39–49; II 15:25–33) were fresh in memory, and one would expect mention of them in the letter (especially since the events were vivid proof of God's election of the second temple as His Chosen Place; see below). These later incidents occurred under Antiochus V and Demetrius I, so that the word "king" in II 1:11 would have been plural. Truer reports of the death of Antiochus IV would have been fresh in memory and, even if encrusted in rumor and legend, would have been more like I 6:1–17 and II 9 than what we have here in II 1:13–17.

Finally, if Ep. 2 had truly been a public letter that reached Egypt before Ep. 1, Ep. 1 would have alluded to it, not to the obscure Ep. 0 (see NOTE on vss. 7–8).

One may plead that Aristobulus, to whom Ep. 2 is addressed, for some reason refrained from publishing it in 164, but there is no visible reason why Jews living under Ptolemy VI in 164 should not celebrate a Seleucid defeat, so why would Aristobulus have held the letter back from circulation?

Moreover, Ep. 2 tells the Jews of Egypt how to pray and seems to offer them consolation (see 1:26–28 and NOTES on 1:23–29, 1:27, and 2:17–18). If so, Ep. 2 implies that the addressees, the Jews of Egypt, were in distress in 164 B.C.E. There is no evidence whatever that the Jews under Ptolemaic rule were menaced in late 164 and early 163 B.C.E. If our evidence were more complete, these facts, too, would make it impossible that Ep. 2 is authentic. However, the hints in 1:26–28 and 2:18, that the Jews of Egypt are in trouble, are vague, and the struggles then between Ptolemy VI and his younger brother (the future Ptolemy VIII) could have made all Ptolemaic subjects fear the future (see Hans Volkmann, "Ptolemaios 24," PW, XXIII² [1959], 1723–24).

There are unmistakable signs that Ep. 2 is later than Ep. 1. Wherever Ep. 1 is cryptic, Ep. 2 explains matters for a later generation. Jason the Oniad, still notorious in 143, by the time of the pro-Hasmonaean propaganda in Josephus was a mere name unconnected with the wicked apostates. Even in 124 few Egyptian Jews reading Ep. 1 could fully have understood the reference to him in the letter of 143. Hence, the description of the persecution in Ep. 0, as "the events beginning with Jason's rebellion," was paradoxical. The chief villain to posterity was Antiochus IV, not the Jewish sinners against whom he was "the rod of God's wrath." Accordingly, the author of Ep. 2 presents Antiochus IV as the villain and does not mention Jason the Oniad.

The author of Ep. 1 was content with quoting Ep. 0, which strangely omits all mention of dedication or rededication, as if the festival commemorated a mere resumption of interrupted ritual rather than the dedication of a new altar to replace one defiled or the rededication of a desecrated sanctuary. Ep. 0 here may well be deliberately avoiding mention of embarrassing facts; see AB vol. 41, NOTE on 4:36–54. However, the audience of Ep. 2 was accustomed to the Feast of Purification and Dedication, to the Feast of Lights. To them the reference to the "Days of Tabernacles in the month of Kislev" was not only obscure, it was incomprehensible. Accordingly, Ep. 2 carefully explains and connects all these appellations ("purification": 1:18, 36, and 2:16; "dedication": 2:9, and cf. "be sanctified" at 2:8; "lights" connected with dedication: 1:18–36; "Tabernacles" connected with dedication: 2:9–12, and see commentary ad loc.).

Ep. 1 only names the festive days and tells nothing of how to observe them, probably because the senders did not need to provide the information (see NOTE on 1:9). Ep. 2 says the days are to be observed as "Days of Tabernacles" (1:18) for eight days (see NOTE on 2:9–12), provides a prayer to be recited (1:24–29), and suggests that a petroleum fire be lighted (see NOTE on 1:36). Ep. 1 comes from an anonymous group (see NOTE on 1:1–10[end]). Ep. 2 comes from the official organs of the Jews in Jerusalem and from the hero Judas.

Epp. 0, 1, and 2 all have in common the fact that they devote a surprisingly small part of their content to the festival they are supposed to announce. Of the nine and one half verses of Ep. 1, only 1:8(end)–9 treat it, and nothing is said to describe the victory of the pious. Of the thirty-five verses of Ep. 2, only 1:18 and 2:16 deal directly with the festival, to which we may add 1:23–30 (a prayer to be used) and 2:9–12 (eight days of observances). Again, nothing is said to describe the victory of the pious. Of the two quoted verses of Ep. 0, only 1:8(end) treats the festival. For all three letters, indeed, the festival was not the principal focus of interest. All three can be shown to be anti-Oniad propaganda. Ep. 0 makes the Oniad, Jason, the cause of all the disasters. Ep. 1 condemns the Oniad temple. Ep. 2 is pointedly addressed to a member of the "stock of the anointed priests," i.e., of the Zadokite-Oniad line. To see further how Ep. 2 fits into this sequence, we must consider its probable background in religious and political struggle. Ep. 2, despite its chaotic appearance, is a reasoned attack upon challenges to the holiness of the second temple prevalent at the time; see NOTE on 1:1–10 and on 1:7, *Jason . . . Kingdom,* and AB vol. 41, pp. 40, 58, and Cross, *Ancient Library,* pp. 101–2. Even loyal adherents of the holiness of the second temple recognized that it lacked important attributes of the first temple. Rabbinic lists of items missing from the second temple include all but one of those mentioned here in Ep. 2 (the altar of incense); see AB vol. 41, Appendix III, n. 1.

Onias IV and the partisans of the temple of Leontopolis surely did more than quote Isa 19:18–19 (see J. *AJ* xiii 3.1.64, 68; 2.71). They must have claimed that insecure Judaea and the contemporary temple of Jerusalem, lacking the sacred attributes, were no longer "the rest and the inheritance" or "the place which the LORD will choose," and, hence, that the Oniad temple of Leontopolis was at least equally legitimate; see Deut 12:8–14; Jer 7:3–15; Ezek 24:21; Lam 2:7; and cf. *M. Zebaḥim* 14:4–8 and J. *AJ* xiii 3.1.65–66. Indeed, they surely claimed their temple was more legitimate, since it was the seat of the legitimate high priestly line.

The point of the legends of the miraculous fire in the time of Nehemiah (1:19–36) and of the hiding of the tabernacle, ark, and incense altar (2:4–8) is to show from authoritative tradition that the second temple, whatever its deficiencies, still is chosen and favored by God, Who in His own time will restore what is lacking.

The author of Ep. 2 is neither modest nor cautious in countering the claims of the Oniads. He boldly asserts (2:17) that by the time of the purification of the temple in 164 God had already restored to Israel the "heritage" (*klêronomian, nḥlh*) of the Promised Land (cf. 2:4), so as to make the centralization of sacrificial worship at one sole sanctuary again obligatory (Deut 12:9–14). In 164 B.C.E. the assertion was true neither *de facto* nor *de jure.* Seleucid forces still held the Akra and much of Judaea and most of Samaria; Idumaeans held much of Judaea. The Seleucid empire long continued to exert its sovereignty over Judaea. Most Jews believed that God's sentence of servitude to foreign rulers was still in force, though fulfillment of the prophecies of Daniel and Enoch might be imminent.

The rest of 2:17 is difficult, probably because the text is defective; see ad loc., and correct accordingly AB vol. 41, p. 547. If our conjectural reconstruction of 2:17 is correct, the verse went on to predict that soon after the first Feast of Dedication God would restore to Israel "the kingdom, the priesthood, and the sanctification." Judas Maccabaeus and his contemporaries could indeed have been mistaken about the near future. But we know something about their aspirations. The author of First Maccabees is an ardent partisan of the Hasmonaean dynasty of high priests who were also princes and, eventually, kings. Yet even he, in telling of Judas' career, says nothing of aspirations of the nation for their own prince; aspirations for a king are all the more unlikely.

The high priest in 164 was still Menelaus. Judas' victorious band appears to have denied him any authority and to have excluded him from the temple (II 10:1; I 4:42; see NOTE on II 10:1–8), but Judas himself is not reported in early sources to have aspired to the high priesthood (on Josephus' error, see AB vol. 41, NOTE on I 8:17–20). Nor did the pious majority seek to choose their own priest after the removal of Menelaus; they meekly accepted Alcimus (I 7:8–16). "Sanctification" probably has two meanings here. It means making the land, the city, and the people holy so as to be immune from invasion. See AB vol. 41, NOTE on I 10:31, and Jer 2:3, 31:37–39; Joel 4:17; Obad 17. Such a hope could well be uttered by pious Jews at war, especially by believers in the prophecies of Daniel and Enoch. "Sanctification" also means performance of God's commandments and separation from the idolatrous and immoral influences of foreign peoples. See Lev 20, esp. vss. 7–8, 22–23, 26, and *Sifra Qedoshim*, ch. 9, par. 2, p. 91d Weiss. With their victory, the pious Jews of Judaea could indeed hope to perform God's commandments and cut themselves off from all pagan influences. But aspirations toward all three (kingdom, priesthood, and sanctification) suggest the reigns of the great Hasmonaeans Simon, John Hyrcanus, and Alexander Jannaeus. Simon and John Hyrcanus in the last years of their reigns came close to achieving all three, but their princely title never became kingly. Alexander Jannaeus was king and high priest at the beginning of his reign. By that time Hasmonaean conquests were so extensive that partisans of the dynasty could have claimed the Jews had recovered the "heritage." There can be no doubt of Jannaeus' aspirations: throughout his twenty-seven years at the head of the nation, he sought, without complete success, to fulfill the prophecies of a great and inviolable Israel. See CHJ, I, part II, ch. 8.

All these aspirations ran counter to Oniad hopes. The Oniad high priests had become chiefs of the nation because there were no kings. Though pious Jews were freed in 163 or 162 B.C.E. from the impious Menelaus, their high priests were to be Alcimus and Hasmonaeans, not Oniads. Oniad commanders and their followers fought in the armies by which Ptolemaic rulers sought to reconquer *for themselves* the lost territories in Syria and Palestine. Oniads were content to observe the Torah even while living under pagan rule side by side with pagans. See my article in *Studies Smith*, Part III, pp. 104–11, and J. *AJ* xiii 13.1–2.348–55.

Again stressing an anti-Oniad point, the writer at 2:18 twice calls the temple at Jerusalem "the Place" (cf. Deut 12:11, etc.).

Royal aspirations, as far as we know, were first avowed among Jews in the reigns of Aristobulus I (104–103) and Alexander Jannaeus (103–76). Other clues help us date our document. We have seen how Ep. 2 seems to hold forth the hope of divine aid to the distressed Jews of Egypt, as Ep. 1 had done in 124 B.C.E. (see NOTE on 1:1–5, *A good . . . time*). Jews had reason to fear the wrath of Ptolemy VIII Euergetes II in 124, but there were few opportunities after 124 for a propagandist to fabricate an anti-Oniad letter to console a menaced Egyptian Jewry. Instead of taking revenge, Euergetes II quieted the country with sweeping amnesties, and there was peace until his death in 116.

For a brief period after his death, the aged pro-Jewish Cleopatra II held considerable power (Otto and Bengtson, pp. 112–36). Even her sudden death between December, 116, and March, 115, brought no danger to the Jews. Cleopatra III, the widow of Euergetes II and daughter of Cleopatra II, at first dominated the government. She took over the cult names, Philometor Soteira, of the mother she hated, using this peculiar means to inflict *damnatio memoriae* upon Cleopatra II (Otto and Bengtson, pp. 136–44). Cleopatra III hated her own son, Ptolemy IX, with whom she shared the throne. Ptolemy IX may well have been hostile to the Jews from the beginning of his reign (cf. J. *AJ* xiii 10.2.278 and Otto and Bengtson, pp. 166–67). In any case, Cleopatra III soon displayed the pro-Jewish policy and firm alliance with the Oniads that Ptolemy VI Philometor and Cleopatra II held. Cleopatra III's trusted commanders were Chelkias and Ananias, sons of Onias IV (J. *AJ* xiii 10.4.285), and thereafter the Jews were secure as long as Cleopatra III was the dominant figure. Egyptian Jews knew only too well the hatred toward them in past years on the part of supporters of Euergetes II. They may have known already of the hostility toward them of the coregent Ptolemy IX. During this period Egyptian Jews could hardly have listened to Jewish propaganda attacking their Oniad protectors; still less would they have preserved it.

However, in 103/2 a grave menace came upon the Jews of Egypt from which the Oniads appeared powerless to save them. Cleopatra III had been holding her own in her war with Ptolemy IX, until the king in 103 landed in Coele-Syria and threatened to overrun Judaea and invade Egypt (J. *AJ* xiii 12.2.328–13.1.348). Worse yet, Ptolemy X, Cleopatra's new coregent, to whom she had entrusted part of the conduct of the war, broke with her for a short time in 103/2 (J. *AJ* xiii 13.1.350; Justin xxxix 4.3; J. Cohen, "Ad Justini XXXIX, 4," *Mnemosyne,* 3d series, 10 [1941–42], 229–30). At this point Ptolemy IX actually invaded Egypt, surely much to the consternation of the Egyptian Jews. The Oniad commanders were far away in Coele-Syria. One of them, Chelkias, had been killed while pursuing Ptolemy IX (J. *AJ* xiii 13.1–2.351–52). However, the threat quickly dissipated. There was a reconciliation between Ptolemy X and Cleopatra (Justin xxxix 4.4–5; Cohen, *Mnemosyne,* 3d series, 10 [1941–42], 229–30), and Ptolemy IX's attempt was repulsed (J. *AJ* xiii 13.2.352; Hans Volkmann, "Ptolemaios 31," PW, XXIII[2] [1959], 1745; Otto and Bengtson, pp. 190–91). Winter had barely begun, for Josephus (*AJ* xiii 13.2.352) reports that Ptolemy IX, on withdrawing, spent the winter at Gaza. For the evidence of papyri and inscriptions on the chronology, see E. Van 't Dack, "Le Conflit judéo-syro-égyptienne de 103/2 av. J.-C.," *Proceedings of the Sixteenth International Congress of Papyrology* (American Studies in Papyrology, vol. 23; Chico, Cal.: Scholars Press, 1981), pp. 303–12. Only during the dark days of Ptolemy IX's invasion of Egypt in 103/2, when the Oniads appeared powerless to help, could there have been a ready audience among Egyptian Jews for anti-Oniad propaganda stressing the sole legitimacy of the temple of Jerusalem and calling for the observance of the Hasmonaean and Jerusalemite Feast of Dedication.

No such propaganda could have been written later, for in 102, Ananias, the ranking Oniad, in effect gave up his claim to the high priesthood by supporting and preserving the Hasmonaean Alexander Jannaeus' claim to the kingdom of Judaea (J. *AJ* xiii 13.2.353–55; cf. xiv 6.2.99 and 8.1.131 and *BJ* i 8.7.175 and 9.4.190). Thereafter there is no trace of any attempt to assert for the temple of Leontopolis sanctity rivaling that of the temple of Jerusalem. So faithful were the Jews of Egypt to the temple of Jerusalem that even rabbinic texts could concede a limited legitimacy to the temple of Leontopolis (*M. Menaḥot* 13:10; TB *Menaḥot* 109a–10a; see Schürer, III, 146–48).

One strange aspect of Ep. 2 becomes explainable if it was written during the crisis of 103/2 B.C.E. One would expect Judas Maccabaeus and his contemporaries to dwell upon their glorious victories, won through the help of God. Instead, the letter barely alludes to them at 1:11–12 and 2:18. In 103/2, when both the Oniads and Hasmonaean Alexander Jannaeus were hard pressed, to call attention to the victories of Judas Maccabaeus would suggest that, though God was with Judas, He had turned against Jannaeus and the defenders of Jerusalem.

It was precisely in the period around 103/2 that we find extraordinary interest in the religious use of fire in Ptolemaic Egypt. See Otto and Bengtson, pp. 154–55; Louis Robert, *Études anatoliennes* (Paris: É. de Boccard, 1937), p. 33, n. 1.

Ben Zion Wacholder argues that, if not authentic, Ep. 2 "constitutes a unique type of Jewish Hellenistic forgery" ("The Letter from Judah Maccabee to Aristobulus: Is 2 Maccabees 1:10b–2:18 Authentic?" HUCA 49 [1978], 128–29). According to him, such forgeries all have one common characteristic: they purport to be by pagans praising Jews or aspects of Judaism. Even if Wacholder were correct about the uniqueness, the argument would say little for the authenticity of Ep. 2, in view of the small proportion of ancient literature and documents which has survived. In fact, the apocryphal book of I Baruch is an excellent, near-contemporary parallel; see my article in PAAJR 46–47 (1979–80), 179–99. One might also cite the Epistle of Jeremiah; see AB vol. 44, pp. 317–29. True, both works were originally not written in Greek, but Ep. 2 may have had a Hebrew original (see p. 164). Even if Ep. 2 was originally written in Greek, so was the book of Wisdom, which purports to be the work of King Solomon and was written for a Jewish audience, though it pretends to be addressed to the kings of the earth; see AB vol. 43, pp. 3–9, 63–64.

Who was the forger of Ep. 2? Clearly he was a person who favored the exclusive legitimacy of the temple of Jerusalem and the dynastic claims of the Hasmonaeans. Whereas the name of John Hyrcanus is conspicuously absent from Ep. 1 (see end of NOTE on 1:1–10a), the name of Hasmonaean Judas (Maccabaeus) appears after those of the national organs as a sender of Ep. 2, though even the author of First Maccabees did not claim that Judas was either high priest or *de jure* chief of state (see AB vol. 41, pp. 357–58). On the other hand, several things suggest that the author was only sympathetic to the Hasmonaeans, not a member of the Hasmonaean party. In Ep. 2 (1:18, 2:16) the festival receives the name "Days of Purification," not the Hasmonaean title, "Days of Dedication," though one might explain the fact by suggesting that the non-Hasmonaean name was the one then current in Egypt. But Ep. 2 has a non-Hasmonaean (if not an anti-Hasmonaean) flavor in saying nothing of Judas' brothers and in ascribing victory only to God, not to the Hasmonaeans. Do these traits reflect only the author's conventional piety and his attempt to mimic the conditions of 164 B.C.E., when the brothers were still not prominent?

The facts thus suggest that an opponent of the Oniads who was sympathetic to the Hasmonaeans wrote Ep. 2 in the dark days of November or early December, 103.

Where was the letter written? There is some evidence that Ep. 2 is a translation from a Hebrew original. See NOTES on 1:12, 18, and 36. First Esdras, the Greek Esther, and even Josephus' *Antiquities* demonstrate how Hebrew could be rendered into idiomatic literary Greek. A writer of Hebrew would be more likely to be found in Judaea, but we cannot exclude the possibility that one existed in Egypt. On the other hand, the conditions of the crisis of late 103 B.C.E. could well have made it difficult to send the letter from Judaea to Egypt. We may guess, then, that the author wrote in Egypt. Perhaps he was a descendant of Aristobulus, the addressee (see NOTE on 1:10b, *Aristobulus . . . priests*).

My late teacher, Elias Bickerman, sharply disagreed with my dating of Ep. 2 in 103/2 B.C.E. (for the present, see his remarks at *Studies*, II, 136–37). Out of respect for him I depart from my policy of not turning my commentary into a debate. I shall consider his arguments, as I understand them, and attempt to answer them.

The usages of politeness tend to change with the passing of time. A very useful way to date letters from a bygone age is to consider their salutations or greeting formulas. Ancient forgers of letters purporting to come from an earlier time show no concern to use the earlier greeting formulas; they used the formulas of their own time. Ancient writers of history who incorporated authentic early letters into their own works would frequently restyle them, again substituting the greeting formulas of their own time. See Bickerman, *Studies*, I, 117, and II, 33–37.

Bickerman did not accept my arguments that Ep. 2 was written originally in Hebrew. For him, Ep. 2 is in idiomatic Greek. Accordingly, one would expect the forger to use a normal Greek greeting formula. However, at 1:10b appears the peculiar greeting formula *chairein kai hygiainein*. Though I have translated it "greeting and wishes for health," literally it consists of two infinitives, "to have joy and to be healthy," conveying the wishes of the sender for the benefit of the recipient. The formula is attested already in the first half of the fourth century B.C.E. in an Athenian letter inscribed on lead (see Wilhelm Crönert, "Die beiden ältesten griechischen Briefe," *Rheinisches Museum* 65 [1910], 157; Jeanne and Louis Robert, "Bulletin épigraphique," REG 57 [1944], 208). If the formula is to serve to date the forgery of Ep. 2, it must have been rare or absent from the forger's environment (Egypt?) in other periods but common in his own time.

Ancient letters on papyrus from Egypt survive only by chance, and it is difficult to draw inferences from their statistics. With the help of a letter of October 12, 1978, from Professor Herbert C. Youtie, I have searched the published papyri. Since papyrology is a specialized subject, I shall give references in the abbreviated form used by papyrologists. Expansions of the abbreviations and complete bibliographical references can be found in John F. Oates et al., "Checklist of Editions of Greek Papyri and Ostraca," *Bulletin of the American Society of Papyrologists* 11 (1974), 3–26. I have found only ten examples containing the precise same greeting, datable between the mid-60's B.C.E. and 42

C.E.: BGU IV 1209, VIII 1873, 1880; P. Oxy. XXXVIII 2835, XLI 2979; P. Princeton III 161; PSI XIV 1404; SB V 7530, VI 9532, X 10240. One should, however, add the instances of greeting formulas where adverbial modifiers have been attached to one or both infinitives. Then the number of instances rises to 41, datable between the mid-60's B.C.E. and 99 C.E. (It would be tedious to list them all here; most can be found in Exler, pp. 32–33, and Youtie, "P. Mich. VIII 464: the Prescript," *Zeitschrift für Papyrologie und Epigraphik* 34 [1979], 86.) The prayer formulas from the third century quoted by Exler, p. 33, are different and should not be included.

Thus, no examples of the greeting formula used in Ep. 2 have been found in Egyptian papyri before the 60's B.C.E., but a fair number have been found between the 60's B.C.E. and 99 C.E. If we had only the evidence of the papyri, we would follow Bickerman's method and date Ep. 2 no earlier than 67 B.C.E. and no later than the closing of the Oniad temple in 73 C.E., by which time the temple in Jerusalem had been destroyed. However, study of the content of Ep. 2 makes any dating within those years unlikely. See Appendix X.

It would be rash to assume that, in Appendix X, I have proved it *impossible* that Ep. 2 could have been written between 67 B.C.E. and 73 C.E. Many strange things have happened in history. Nevertheless, at present I cannot see how a letter with the content of Ep. 2 could have been written during the period.

Another fact impedes mechanical application of the evidence of the greeting formulas in the papyri to date Ep. 2. The formula in Ep. 2 would be neither unprecedented nor unique in the second century B.C.E. In fact, it is attested earlier in the Athenian letter on lead and appears also at the head of a royal Seleucid letter written late in 164 (II 9:19–27). Special circumstances probably explain the use of the formula there; see NOTE on 9:19.

The forger of Ep. 2 may have thought that *chairein kai hygiainein* would suggest more strongly to his readers that Judas and his contemporaries wrote the letter. The writer of Ep. 2 consistently tries to outdo Ep. 1 (see above, p. 159). If the forger put into Ep. 2 a formula he thought to be more dignified and traditional for a festal letter than the simple *chairein* of Ep. 1, he would only have been true to his nature.

What other Jewish festal letters the fabricator may have seen, we cannot know. However, the Hebrew book of Esther was probably extant by 103/2, and the fabricator may well have read it; see NOTE on 1:18 and Bickerman, *Studies*, I, 234–39. Even if the fabricator had not read the Hebrew book of Esther, and even if the final author of the Hebrew book of Esther wrote a bit after 103/2 B.C.E. (as is possible), that author, too, wished to create an impression of authenticity and drew on known formulas of politeness. We should therefore note that the greeting formula quoted at Esther 9:30 from the letter of Mordecai and Esther is not the usual *šālōm* ("peace") but *šālōm weʾĕmet* ("peace and truth"), a formula which looks as strange as the one at the head of Ep. 2.

The combination "peace and truth" does occur elsewhere in good biblical Hebrew (II Kings 20:9=Isa 39:8; Jer 14:13; cf. Zech 8:19), but not in a greeting formula. Clearly, to the audience of the Hebrew Esther, the addition of "truth" to the common greeting "peace" was not jarring. Thus that audience probably knew of the use of such formulas in messages like the one reported at

Esther 9:30–31. If the Jews of Egypt by 103/2 had received similar messages, they, too, could have known of such formulas. Indeed, the *šālōm we'ĕmet* of Esther 9:30 may even have been the Hebrew equivalent of an Aramaic greeting formula prevalent in the Persian empire, *šlm wšrrt hwšrt lk* ("peace and health I have sent you"), a formula known to have been used also by Jews. See Fitzmyer, *JBL* 93 (1974), 215, and "The Padua Aramaic Papyrus Letters," *Journal of Near Eastern Studies* 21 (1962), 16, 18. For *šrrt* as "health," see the root *šrr* in the Syriac dictionaries. The Hebrew and Aramaic root *šrr*, like the root *'mn*, means "be firm," so that *šrrt*, like *'m(n)t*, could also mean "truth." Thus the Hebrew equivalent of *šlm wšrrt* could have been *šālōm we'ĕmet*, at the same time as the Greek equivalent of *šlm wšrrt* could have been *chairein kai hygiainein*. The unintelligible corrupt text at Greek Esther 9:30 may contain confirmations of this hypothesis. The Hebrew text which lay before Lysimachus, the Greek translator, may already have been corrupt. Nevertheless, "health" (*hygieias*) appears in Greek Esther 9:30, where it may reflect Heb. *'mt* (if so, correct accordingly AB vol. 41, p. 554). Thus the author of Ep. 2 may deliberately have used a greeting formula he knew to have been earlier in vogue. He may even have taken it from the reported letter of Mordecai and Esther. Bickerman does not grant that the expression "words of peace and truth" (*dibrēy šālōm we'ĕmet*) at Esther 9:30 reports the content of a greeting formula, but see AB vol. 41, p. 552, and I 1:30, 5:25, 48, 7:10, 15, 27, 10:3. Bickerman finds my suggestions of the equivalence of the Aramaic, Hebrew, and Greek formulas farfetched. The fact remains that neither he nor I can be sure what greeting formulas in Jewish festal letters purporting to come from Judas Maccabaeus would seem authentic to Egyptian Jews of the late second and first centuries B.C.E. For the present, one cannot be certain, but there is a good case for dating Ep. 2 in 103/2 B.C.E.

The author of Ep. 2 knew that the prophet Jeremiah was much respected in Egypt, where his prophetic career ended; cf. Philo *De cherubim* 49, and see the references cited by M. Stern, "The Death of Onias III," *Zion* 25 (1960), 7, n. 40. The author of Ep. 2 alludes to the Epistle of Jeremiah at 2:2, surely because the Epistle was popular among Egyptian Jews. The literate Jewish community of Egypt followed with respectful reverence the publication of texts from the authoritative collections at Jerusalem (2:14; cf. Bickerman, *Studies*, I, 225–45). There is evidence to suggest that the author of Ep. 2 made use of an already existing story of Jeremiah and the sacred furniture.

On the other hand, there is no evidence that the story of Nehemiah and the sacred fire existed before the author of Ep. 2 used it. For some reason he separated the story from the traditions about Jeremiah and only after telling it did he say that it was Jeremiah who told the priests to hide the fire. It looks as if the author tied the story of Nehemiah to the traditions about Jeremiah in order to enhance its credibility in the eyes of his audience. The story serves the author's purpose. He says that the source material is preserved in the library established by Judas Maccabaeus (2:14), but any such material could have perished by 103/2 B.C.E. It could have perished in a fire, or it could have been deliberately destroyed by the "impious" high priests Menelaus and Alcimus, etc. Thus, the author could have fabricated the material himself without fear of being exposed.

Though the text of Ep. 2 is difficult in places, we shall find that it can be read as a coherent piece of propaganda. Hence, there is no reason to assume that it has suffered interpolation (cf. Bunge, pp. 46–63, 95–143).

The practice of Hellenistic scribes was to place at the end of a document earlier documents which were evidence or provided motivation; see Bickerman, *Studies,* II, 108–11. Having fabricated Ep. 2 to have an earlier date than Ep. 1, the author of Ep. 2 may well have appended it to a copy of Ep. 1 and published them together. In any case, the content of both letters was timely, teaching that God would always defend and avenge Jews who kept the Torah and were loyal to the temple of Jerusalem. Readers of Ep. 2 would know that recently the Oniads themselves, despite their sin, had rescued the righteous Jews of Judaea from the atrocities perpetrated by Ptolemy IX (J. *AJ* xii 12.4.336–13.1.351). In so doing Chelkias had lost his life, perhaps because of his sin of pressing the claims of the temple of Leontopolis. By observing the Feast of Dedication and by due reverence to the temple of Jerusalem, the Jews of Egypt, too, along with the surviving Oniads, could hope for deliverance from peril. It may have been Ep. 2 and the reaction it aroused in the Jewish community of Egypt that drove Ananias to give up a possible Oniad restoration to Jerusalem and instead to support the claims of Alexander Jannaeus. From this point on, if not before, Jannaeus, supported by the adherents of the line of Onias and Zadok (=Ṣaddūq), could be called a "Sadducee"; see AB vol. 41, pp. 68–71.

10b. At AB vol. 41, p. 62, n. 3, and p. 552, I refer the reader to this NOTE. I was thinking, however, of the discussion of the greeting formula (pp. 165–66).

See NOTE on vs. 1, *the Jews . . . Judah.* The indications in our verse as to the status of the Jews on the eve of the Festival of Purification are noteworthy. On the one hand, by failing to use the national designation, "Jews," the author may give the Jews a still more modest status than they have in Ep. 1. Nevertheless, he presents them as having the privilege of possessing a Council of Elders. The author may have compromised between the formulas in vs. 1 and those in the letter at 11:27.

The author has not violated etiquette by naming the Council of Elders after the people. Both orders are found in authentic documents (people-Council: J. *AJ* xii 3.3.138; I 14:28; Council-people: II 11:27; I 12:6, 14:20). This is the latest datable reference to the Council of Elders under the Greek name *Gerousia,* for the mention of the "Gerousia of the children of Israel" at Acts 5:21 is part of the imitation of Exod 4:29–30 which runs through the passage, as is clear from the echoes of Exod 4:29–30 in Acts 5:12 and 14. Cf. also Greek Deut 5:23(20 H), and see AB vol. 41, NOTES on 8:15 and 12:6. We have no information to tell us whether the *Gerousia* was the same as the *Synhedrion* (=Sanhedrin).

Like the author of First Maccabees, the author of Ep. 2 knew that Judas might be a hero but held no high priestly or princely rank; see AB vol. 41, NOTE on 8:17–20. Hence the author here had good reason to place Judas' name last. Little did he know that he might have done still better to omit Judas' name altogether, as it was omitted from the Roman document at I

8:23–32 and from the documents at II 11:16–38, and as John Hyrcanus' name was omitted from Ep. 1.

Aristobulus . . . priests. The addressee is the Jewish philosopher who dedicated a book on the Torah to Ptolemy (VI Philometor) in which he followed the common literary practice of addressing the king by name. The book is now lost, except for quotations by Christian authors. Clement of Alexandria (*Stromateis*, ed. by O. Stählin and L. Früchtel [Berlin: Akademie-Verlag, 1960–70], v 97.7) so identified the Aristobulus here and the Ptolemy under whom he wrote. The reference here, in a forged letter of 103/2, is the earliest surviving testimony to Aristobulus and his book. All other sources on Aristobulus suggest that he was known to posterity solely through his book. In his book Aristobulus answered the questions of his king about the Torah. In other ancient books a "philosopher" could be portrayed as still more formally a tutor who taught his own lore to a monarch; see Richard Reitzenstein, *Die hellenistischen Mysterienreligionen* (Leipzig and Berlin: Teubner, 1927), p. 129. "Tutor" (*didaskalos*) was an official court title under the Ptolemies; see W. Peremans and E. Van 't Dack, *Prosopographia Ptolemaica, VI* ("Studia Hellenistica," 17; Louvain: Publications universitaires de Louvain, 1968), nos. 14647, 14652–53, 16510, 16512, 16966. The author of Ep. 2 probably inferred that Aristobulus merited the title "tutor of King Ptolemy" from the fact that the book was dedicated to the king and addressed to him. Only here, however, do we learn that Aristobulus was descended from the high priestly line. The attributed descent can hardly be the author's fabrication, for as a propagandist he could not afford to risk exposure by Oniads familiar with their own genealogy. In Egypt in 103/2 facts about Aristobulus could still easily have been in living memory. It is also possible that Aristobulus alluded to his descent in his book. On the problems connected with Aristobulus and his work, see Nikolaus Walter, *Der Thoraausleger Aristobulos* ("Texte und Untersuchungen zur Geschichte der altchristlichen Literatur," vol. 86; Berlin: Akademie Verlag, 1964), esp. pp. 13–26, 35–40.

As a descendant of the Zadokite-Oniad priestly line, Aristobulus was indeed an appropriate addressee for such a letter. He bore a Greek name, but so did many Jews in Egypt in his time (see Tcherikover in CPJ, I, 27–28), and so did the pious Judaean Antigonus of Socho (*M. Abot* 1:3) to say nothing of Jason the Oniad and Menelaus, who both served as high priests in Judaea. Aristobulus in his use of Greek and of Greek ideas appears to have been a conservative or moderate among Hellenizers, and his pious philosophical exposition of the Torah may have been an attack on the more extreme Hellenizing policies of his kinsman Jason. As the interpreter in Greek of the Jewish religious calendar (Anatolius *apud* Eusebius *Historia ecclesiastica* vii. 32. 17–18), he would be a logical recipient of a letter establishing a new festival. Furthermore, a surviving fragment of Aristobulus' book (*apud* Eusebius *Praeparatio evangelica* viii 10.12–17) shows how interested he was in divine manifestations of fire such as those described in II 1:19–34, 2:10–11. Cf. Ben Zion Wacholder, HUCA 49 (1978), 116–19.

The author or publisher of Ep. 2 may well have been a descendant of Aristobulus. Such a person could circulate the letter without being suspected of forgery. In any case, by late 103 so much time had elapsed that the addressee and his contemporaries were dead and few if any were left in Egypt to take exception to the blatant errors concerning events of sixty years before. For the use of "anointed" as indicating the high priest, see Exod 29:7; Lev 4:3, 5, 16, 6:15, 8:12, and 21:10, 12; Dan 9:26.

11. The verse has baffled interpreters ancient and modern. Abel, following C. Bruston, "Trois lettres des juifs de Palestine (2 Makkab. I–II, 18)," ZAW 10 (1890), 115, emended the text to read ". . . we thank Him greatly as the One Who warred against the king." The emendation is not supported by any witness to the text, would make vs. 12 repetitious, and is unnecessary. Jews well understood the hazards of resisting the kings God had placed over them (see NOTE on 1:7, Jason . . . Kingdom), and non-Jews, too, knew how dangerous it was for subjects to offer battle to their king (see Bickerman, Institutions, p. 17).

The Greek construction, hôs an with the participle, gives the reason for the action or event being discussed; see Arno Mauersberger, Polybios-Lexikon, vol. 1 (Berlin: Akademie Verlag, 1968), col. 87.

The author used the present participle "who war against," either because he wished to state a generalization or because he thought to reflect the reality of 164 B.C.E. If he believed that even after the death of Antiochus IV the Jews were still at war with the new king and heir, he was ignoring the peace of Menelaus (see NOTE on 11:27–33).

I have translated vs. 11 as if the author omitted the definite article before "king" because he was stating a generalization. However, the omission of the article may reflect the customary practice of omitting it when one referred to the Persian king, for the Seleucids were considered to be successors of the Persian kings.

12–18. Here alone in the ancient sources the death of Antiochus IV precedes the purification of the temple (see p. 58, n. 20). However, the account here agrees with 9:1 in implying that the king's death occurred very close to the purification of the temple. The tradition reflected at 9:1, on the other hand, left it uncertain whether the king's death preceded or followed the purification. That same equivocal tradition may have lain before the author of our letter. In that case, the author could have been so eager to have Judas report the great retributive act of God that he jumped to the conclusion that the king's death preceded the purification.

12–17. Our verses are introduced by the Greek particle gar ("for," as a coordinating conjunction), and must explain vs. 11: how is it that the senders, who war against a king, owe great thanks to God? Again, vs. 13 is introduced by gar and must explain vs. 12, and the case is the same with vs. 14. There can thus be no ambiguity in "those who made war" in vs. 12 or "the commander" in vs. 13. The enemy in the singular must be Antiochus IV, and the enemy in the plural must be Antiochus IV and his forces.

12. cast away. The Greek verb is used of things cast up onto shore by the sea.

made war . . . City. The Greek (parataxamenous en . . .) might be translated, more literally, as "made war in the Holy City." Either rendering would fit the facts of 5:11–26. However, in translations from the Hebrew, the Greek here, as typical translation Greek, would render the Hebrew nilḥam be- ("make war on"; Judg 8:1, 9:45, 11:9, 12, 27, 12:1, 3; Zech 14:3, 14). Even the fabricator of Ep. 2 probably knew that Antiochus' sin was not merely the few days of combat in Jerusalem but his years of hostile policy against the Holy City. Such a lapse from the generally idiomatic Greek of Ep. 2 suggests that the Greek is a translation from a Hebrew original.

13. *the commander . . . army.* Why is Antiochus here and in vs. 16 called "commander" (*hêgemôn*) rather than "king"? One may guess that before the author of Ep. 2 lay the same text of Isa 10:8 as lay before the Greek translator, who rendered the verse, "And if they say to him, 'You alone are commander'" (*kai ean eipôsin autôi Sy monos ei archôn*). Where the translator of Isa 10:8 used *archôn,* the Greek writer here could use the synonymous *hêgemôn.* Isa 10:5–19 condemns the king of Assyria for boasting of his invincible forces, and the mention here of the "apparently irresistible army" would confirm our guess that the author drew on Isa 10:8 to write of the latter-day tyrant of Syria (=Assyria; see AB vol. 41, NOTE on 1:21, *Arrogantly*).

Jews writing in the late second century referred to any part of the territory then controlled by the Parthian empire as "Persis." See Map 2 and NOTE on 9:1, *of Persis,* and AB vol. 41, NOTE on 3:31, and cf. vs. 19.

the temple of Nanaia. The temple was in Elymais (biblical Elam). Nanaia was a goddess of Mesopotamian origin. The Greeks identified her with Aphrodite and Artemis. See Map 2 and AB vol. 41, NOTES on 6:1–2.

14. "Friend" was a title borne by important royal officials; see AB vol. 41, second NOTE on 2:18. The marriage of the reigning king to a goddess was a rite with a long history in Mesopotamia and adjoining regions. See Samuel N. Kramer, *The Sacred Marriage Rite* (Bloomington: Indiana University Press, 1969). Antiochus IV is reported so to have married Atargatis of Hierapolis-Bambyke in Syria and to have taken the temple treasures as dowry (Granius Licinianus xxviii, p. 5. 3 Flemisch; Mørkholm, p. 132).

15. *shrine.* The word *temenos,* in pagan Greek, means "precinct," the enclosed holy area around a temple, but here the word is used, as often in Jewish Greek, to mean an illicit or pagan shrine. See AB vol. 41, NOTE on 1:47, *to build . . . shrines.*

16. For the true facts of the last campaign and death of Antiochus IV, see NOTES on ch. 9, and AB vol. 41, NOTES on 6:1–16. The author of Ep. 2 probably is influenced by folk memories of the death of Antiochus III, who with his whole army fell in battle against natives who were resisting his intention to rob the temple of Bel in Elymais (Diodorus xxviii. 3, xxix. 15; Justin xxxii. 2. 1–2). Here not armed natives but a handful of priests destroy the royal "commander" (see first NOTE on vs. 13); cf. the story of Judith. Surely God's hand was acting against Antiochus IV!

I have turned into idiomatic English a Greek passage which literally means "by hurling stones they struck down the commander [as] with thunderbolts." Though the author did not bother to mention the slaying of the king's Friends, he took it for granted the readers would understand: the severed heads are plural. Similarly, the author did not bother to describe in detail the fate of the king's army, mentioned in vs. 13. In the author's time it was well known how the armies of Antiochus III and Antiochus VII (Diodorus xxxiv–xxxv. 17. 1; Justin xxxix. 1. 1) perished when their kings fell. He did not know that the army of Antiochus IV survived their king!

The expression for "dismember" (*melê poiein*) occurs only here. Although scholars have pointed to a possible parallel at Dan 2:5 and 3:29, the Greek versions of Daniel render the passages differently. Hence one cannot be sure that the expression here is translation Greek rather than idiomatic Greek.

17. The narrator himself supplies the exclamation of thanksgiving to God; cf. Gen 24:27; II Sam 18:28; I Kings 8:15; Ezra 7:27; and see NOTE on 3:30.

"Delivered over" (*paredôke*) is the reading of the Lucianic recension, here supported by the Latin, Armenian, and Syriac, and therefore likely to be correct. A Hebrew original would have had *hsgyr* (cf. Deut 32:30 and *sgr* at II Sam 18:28). I can find no parallel for "gave [*sc.* to death?]" (*edôke*), the reading of other witnesses to the text.

18. Greek *agein* in contexts like ours and 2:16, and like vs. 9, means "celebrate"; in idiomatic Greek, it is the counterpart of Hebrew *'śh*. See I Esdras 1:1 with II Chron 35:1; I Esdras 5:51 with Ezra 3:4, etc.; Greek and Hebrew Esther 9:17–22, etc.; *Greek-English Lexicon,* s.v. *agô,* IV; Walter Bauer, *Wörterbuch zum Neuen Testament* (5th ed.; Berlin: Alfred Töpelmann, 1958), s.v. *agô,* 4. Frequently it is followed by the proper name of a festival, as in vs. 9. Here, too, "Purification" is a proper name of a festival, to be capitalized, as one can see from the way it is compared to the Days of Tabernacles at the end of our verse.

The writer calls upon the Egyptian Jews to join in the festive observances *in honor of* the purification of the temple; cf. the expressions on the observance of festivities in honor of dedication at Hebrew II Chron 7:9 and Neh 12:27. The Egyptian Jews could hardly join in the acts of purification at Jerusalem themselves. Indeed, the author seems to have thought of those acts as being complete at the time the letter was sent, for in 2:18 he speaks of the purification as an accomplished fact.

When Ep. 2 was fabricated, many Jews still refused to grant that Judas Maccabaeus and his followers had brought about a "dedication" (*ḥănukkāh*) of a new altar. A real "dedication" would have been accompanied by fire from heaven. Most Jews, however, granted that the temple had been purified. Hence, like Jason of Cyrene (10:5), the author of Ep. 2 speaks here, not of the Feast of Dedication, but rather of the Feast of Purification. See AB vol. 41, NOTE on 4:36–54.

If our reconstruction of the events (ibid.) is correct, only after the failure of miraculous fire to appear on 25 Kislev, 164 B.C.E., could there be an issue of whether to call the festival "Dedication" or only "Purification." Hence, we learn that Ep. 2 is probably anachronistic and therefore spurious. See also end of NOTE on 2:9–12.

The end of our verse reads like an expansion of 1:9, but its peculiar syntax puzzled both ancient scribes and modern readers. My translation is intelligible only because I have added the word "it," both occurrences of the word "as," and both occurrences of "days." I shall show that the additions are legitimate. Indeed, some of them also appear in ancient witnesses to the text. But the difficult reading of A', V, and some minuscules, without the additions, is probably closest to the original. In Greek after the word "celebrate" (*agête*) one would expect, as the direct object, a word in the accusative case, but "Tabernacles" and "the fire" are both in the genitive case. A reader might think that

"Tabernacles" is accusative plural since it appears without the article (but cf. I 10:21 and Greek Deut 31:10), but the Greek word (*skênopêgia*) in all other known texts appears in the singular; besides the instances in the Bible and in Josephus, there is the inscription from Libya (Jeanne and Georges Roux, "Un décret des Juifs de Béréniké," *Revue des études grecques* 62 [1949], 283, Inscription I, lines 1–2). La^{LXVP} all render the word as genitive.

To my knowledge there is only one parallel for the syntax here. It occurs in another passage purporting to come from a Jewish festal letter, Esther 9:19. Here is a literal translation of that verse; I italicize the nouns there which are analogous to "Tabernacles" and "fire" here: "Therefore the Jews . . . who dwell in unwalled towns celebrate the fourteenth day of Adar *joy, drinking, festivity*, and the *giving* of gifts to one another." Hebrew does not have the Greek case system; however, a glance at Esther 9:22 will show that the Hebrew of Esther 9:19 is elliptic, that "as a day of" is to be understood after "Adar," and that in Greek the italicized nouns would be in the genitive case. This parallel is the basis for my additions. Indeed, from II 2:16 it is clear that the author of Ep. 2 understood that "days" was to be supplied here as the accusative noun on which the genitives depend. The Hebrew Esther may well have been known in Egypt by 103/2 B.C.E., though the Greek Esther was not to be published until 78/7; see Bickerman, *Studies*, I, 231–45. Thus, the author of Ep. 2 could have been imitating Esther 9:19; see above, first NOTE on 1:10. The Hebrew Esther is written by a good stylist. His idiom must have been good in its time. Thus, even if the author of Ep. 2 was not imitating Esther 9:19, his elliptic prose here was good Hebrew idiom, but it makes very difficult Greek (cf. Kappler, *De memoria alterius libri Maccabaeorum* [Diss. Academia Georgia Augusta; Göttingen: Dieterich, 1929], pp. 64–65). The writer of the Greek Esther was careful not to translate 9:19 literally. Here is a very strong indication that Ep. 2 was originally written in Hebrew.

Just as at Esther 9:19 the author felt free to write elliptically because of the occurrence of "day" earlier in the verse, so the author of Ep. 2 may have relied on the "day" implicit in the expression "the twenty-fifth." However, the Greek text here is probably corrupt. To judge by Esther 9:17–19, 22, the word "it" has fallen out. "It" (*auton*) could easily have been lost from the apparently repetitious Greek (*hina kai autoi auton agête*). Indeed, the Syriac has "it," probably not because the intact text lay before the translator but because the translator restored it for good syntax. Cf. Hanhart's introduction to his edition, p. 30.

The twenty-fifth of Kislev was indeed celebrated as a Day of Tabernacles; see 10:6–7 and AB vol. 41, NOTE on 4:36–54.

Nowhere else is a Jewish Day of the Fire known. Ben Zion Wacholder ("The Letter from Judah Maccabee to Aristobulus," HUCA 49 [1978], pp. 112–15) tries to produce an attestation for such a festival by asserting that the Days of the Establishment of the Continual Offering (1–8 Nisan, according to *Megillat Ta'anit* 1–8 Nisan) commemorated the reinstitution of Continual Offerings after the Babylonian exile. But Ezra 3:1–6 makes it clear that after the exile the Continual Offerings were reinstituted in *Tishri*, in the seventh month.

Josephus, however, knew the Days of Dedication as the "[Days of] Lights"

(*Phôta*), and in Egypt fire must have been associated with the festival. The author of Ep. 2 here wishes to explain the association and at the same time to counter the argument of the supporters of the schismatic temple, that God had never signified His renewed choice of Jerusalem by sending down miraculous fire. If there had been such a miracle, surely Jews would have preserved and published records of it. Hence, the author of Ep. 2 does not dare to bring the missing miracle into Ezra 3:1–6 and 6:15–18. Instead he tells a story of how Nehemiah's dedication of the temple and its altar was accompanied by remarkable events which fell short of being memorable miracles.

A remarkable event probably would not have been enough to silence disbelievers in the validity of the second temple and the sacrificial worship there. Could the altar fire at God's Chosen Place be validly lit in any other way than by God? The miraculous deaths of Nadab and Abihu would suggest that the answer was "No." They had been slain for bringing "strange fire" before the LORD, and the context (Lev 9:24 – 10:2) suggests that "strange fire" was fire other than that sent by the LORD. Hence, the story here shows that the fire in the second temple was no strange fire but a continuation of the miraculous fire of the first temple. The problem would not have existed under the rabbinic interpretation of Lev 1:7, that an ordinary flame might be used to ignite the fire on the altar (TB *Yoma* 21b; the rabbis had to find other reasons why Nadab and Abihu perished [Ginzberg, *Legends*, III, 187–89, and the commentary *Kᵉlī yāqār* to Lev 10:1]).

I have inserted the word "as" to make "as when," though the word "as" is absent from all witnesses to the text. There can be no doubt that the Greek text from the first had only "when" (*hote*), a difficult reading which the Latin and the Syriac translators found untranslatable and therefore resorted to various paraphrases. Certainty is impossible, but one may guess that here a Greek translator misunderstood a Hebrew original. In Hebrew, *k'šr* can mean "as" (Gen 7:9, 16, 8:21, etc.), "when" (Gen 12:11, 18:33, etc.), and "as when" (Deut 22:26 [Greek: *hôs ei*]; Judg 16:22 [A: *hênika;* B: *kathôs*]; I Sam 6:6 [*hôs . . . hote*]; Isa 29:8 [*hôs . . . hon tropon*]). In biblical Greek, *k'šr*, meaning "when," is rarely rendered by *hote* (Ezek 37:18); it is usually rendered by other Greek words (*hênika:* Gen 12:11, 24:22, 52, 32:3, etc.; *epei:* Josh 4:1). But *hote* is a common word for "when" in the Greek Bible, and the writer in Ep. 2 in any case is clearly not bound by the stereotypes of biblical Greek.

My translation follows the reading of the very best witnesses to the text, AVLaᴸˣ (*ho oikodomēsas, qui aedificavit*). The other witnesses lack *ho*. It is hard to see how a later scribe would have inserted the word and easy to see how *ho* (written *O*) could have been lost before the *O* of *oikodomēsas*. The absence of *ho* does create difficulties, noticed by the later witnesses (Laᴮᴹ). Without *ho* the passage must be translated "as when Nehemiah on completing the construction of the temple and the altar brought sacrifices." No text says that Nehemiah or anyone else celebrated simultaneously the completions of the temple and of the altar! Indeed, both Ezra 3:1–13 and I Esdras 5:47–52 state unambiguously that when the altar was dedicated with sacrifices even the foundations of the temple had not yet been laid. (See, however, the version of I Esdras 5:52 at J. *AJ* xi 4.1.78; there is no reason to think that Josephus' text lay before the audience of Ep. 2.) The reading here of AVLa^LX identifies which Nehemiah is meant. There was good reason to do so. In the texts accessible to the author and to us, the builder of the altar and the second temple bears the name "Zerubbabel" not "Nehemiah" (Ezra 2:1–2, 3:1–13, 6:14–17; I Esdras 5:8 and 47–65, 7:4–7; Zech 4:8). Our passage is the oldest text reflecting the identification of Nehemiah with Zerubbabel. Jews could not understand how a member of the Davidic dynasty could bear only the Babylonian name "Zerubbabel." What, then, was his Hebrew name? The vagueness of the chronological data in the Bible allowed the proposition that his Hebrew name was "Nehemiah." See TB *Sanhedrin* 38a. Our passage thus introduces "Zerubbabel" under his supposed Hebrew name. Another reason for identifying which Nehemiah was meant was the existence of a contemporary of Zerubbabel by that name (Ezra 2:2; Neh 7:7).

Another reason leading to the identification of Zerubbabel with Nehemiah was the existence of I Esdras. This is not the place for a complete discussion of how I Esdras came to exist as another version of the stories of the return from the exile and the mission of Ezra, but something can be said.

The chronologies of the books of Ezra and Nehemiah and of I Esdras are difficult because the composers were propagandists who constructed their books from genuine documents of the Jews and of the Persian kings Cyrus (reigned over the Jews 539–530), Darius I (522–486), Artaxerxes I (465/4–425), and perhaps also Xerxes I (486–465/4; see Ezra 4:6). Ancient documents did not give the identifying numeral of a Persian king, so that later readers could not be sure which of the three kings Darius or the three kings Artaxerxes was meant. The Hebrew books of Ezra and Nehemiah, however, may have been written with good chronological knowledge. Their only difficult portion is Ezra 4:6–24. The passage is probably a digression to confirm the charges made in 4:4, that the "people of the land," namely Samaritans, were to blame for obstructing building projects in Jerusalem. According to the composer, not only did they do so in the reign of Cyrus, they also did so in the reign of Xerxes I (4:6), and *documents* prove they did so in the reign of Artaxerxes I (4:7–23). The composer shows that his digression is finished and that he is returning to his chronologically ordered narrative by repeating 4:5 in 4:24. Thereafter the narrative proceeds normally, with Ezra 5–6 in the reign of Darius I, and Ezra 7–10 and all of Nehemiah in the reign of Artaxerxes I.

If this interpretation is correct, the Hebrew Ezra shows the puzzlement of readers who did not understand the nature of the composer's digression, for then Artaxerxes' name at 6:14 would seem to be an insertion made by an uncomprehending hand. Readers repelled by the way in which Ezra 4:6–24 seemed to leave the narrative incoherent might reject the entire work. The composer of I Esdras perceived the difficulty of Ezra 4:6–24 and solved it in his own way. He accepted Ezra 1:1–11, leaving those verses in the reign of Cyrus (I Esdras 2:1–15). He then (I Esdras 2:16–30) took the interruption of building projects in Jerusalem as coming in the reign of Artaxerxes I, in accordance with the documents at Ezra 4:7–23. He omitted the obscure Ezra 4:6. This first Artaxerxes, however, the composer left with a very brief reign, for the entire interruption lasted but two years (I Esdras 5:70), though it ran through part of the reign of Cyrus and all of the reign of Artaxerxes into the second year of Darius, as if Cyrus' successor had been an Artaxerxes and as if there had been no Cambyses. Clearly the author of I Esdras lived so late he had no knowledge of the true chronology of the Persian kings, and neither had his audience.

Zerubbabel was known to have completed building projects at Jerusalem. Hence, at I Esdras 3:1 – 5:6 the composer tells us how Zerubbabel managed to end the interruption. The composer could move the material at Ezra 2:1 – 4:5 and 4:24 down into the reign of Darius (I Esdras 5:7–71) by presenting Zerubbabel and his followers as carrying out in the reign of Darius the still unfulfilled commands of Cyrus. Even Ezra 4:24 could be moved into the reign of Darius, for the composer of I Esdras 5:70–71 presents the verse in a quotation from Zerubbabel in which the Jewish prince gives his reasons from history for rebuffing the Samaritans. Otherwise, from 6:1 on, I Esdras runs parallel to Ezra-Nehemiah, with one noteworthy exception: the figure of Nehemiah has been eliminated from I Esdras.

Apparently, the composer of I Esdras could not accept some of the beliefs of the composer of Ezra and Nehemiah. We may guess that the author of I Esdras did not like the personality of Nehemiah and eliminated him from his narrative. The Nehemiah at I Esdras 5:8 is the contemporary of Zerubbabel (Ezra 2:2, Neh 7:7), not the hero of the book of Nehemiah. Otherwise, in I Esdras "Nehemiah" occurs only at 5:40, clearly a harmonizing interpolation, for it makes the subject of the sentence compound though the verb is singular, and the name "Nehemiah" is absent from the parallel passages, Ezra 2:63 and Neh 7:65.

It was Nehemiah who brought an end to the prohibition on building projects at Jerusalem, issued under Artaxerxes I. The author of I Esdras knew the document prohibiting construction. In order to displace Nehemiah as the hero who ended the prohibition, he introduced the fantastic story of Zerubbabel (I Esdras 3:1–63).

Why should a Jewish writer, who admired Ezra, abhor Nehemiah to the point of eliminating him from history? We may make a plausible guess: Nehemiah was a bitter enemy of Tobiah (a Tobiad) and of Tobiah's Zadokite priestly friends, who were ancestors of the Oniads (Neh 6:12–19; 13:4–8, 28). May not I Esdras be another piece of Oniad propaganda, an early one since the author of Ep. 2 seems to take for granted its veracity?

Ben Sira identifies Nehemiah as the glorious builder in a context which would permit a biased reader to identify Nehemiah with Zerubbabel (Sir 49:11–13). By 103 B.C.E. the Greek version of Ben Sira's book was circulating in Egypt (Sir Prologue 25), so that the author of Ep. 2, without reading the book of Nehemiah, could know of the great builder. On reading in I Esdras 3:47 that Zerubbabel was the one who got permission to build Jerusalem, the author of Ep. 2 and Egyptian Jews would readily jump to the conclusion that "Zerubbabel" was another name for Nehemiah. Thus, contrary to the intentions of the composer of I Esdras, Nehemiah's name could have been brought back into Jewish history, and Nehemiah could emerge possessing not only his own achievements but Zerubbabel's as well! The same cause may have led to the acceptance of the chapters of our book of Nehemiah (in Hebrew and in Greek, Ezra and Nehemiah constitute one book). The author and his audience know of "Nehemiah's memoirs" (2:13), and though it is possible that the memoirs still circulated independently of our book of Nehemiah, it is not likely. Meanwhile, Ezra 1–10 may well have been rejected for their incoherence and for contradicting I Esdras. Ep. 2, indeed, contains many apparent echoes of the book of Nehemiah. See NOTES on vss. 20, 23, 24, 25.

Since "Zerubbabel-Nehemiah" dedicated the altar and temple with sacrifices on the festival of Tabernacles (I Esdras 5:46–50), the "as when" clause explains both "of Tabernacles" and "of the fire."

19–36. The author wishes to demonstrate the divine origin of the altar fire of the second temple by telling of a wonder which nevertheless was not quite a miracle; see NOTE on 1:18. The ancients knew of the petroleum (naphtha) in Mesopotamia (Strabo xvi. 1. 15, C743; Robert J. Forbes, *Studies in Ancient Technology* [Leiden: Brill, 1955], I, 1–120). They also knew of the Persians' reverence for fire, and probably also of their preservation and transport of sacred fire and maintenance of fires fed by petroleum; see Jacques Duchesne-Guillemin, *Symbols and Values in Zoroastrianism* (New York: Harper and Row, 1966), pp. 65–74. Hence, the author can speak of the preservation of the altar fire in the form of viscous petroleum and of the Persian king's consecration of the "oil well" as the source of the holy fire. Did the author mean to suggest that all oil wells in Mesopotamia and all Persian fire temples were relics of the hiding of the altar fire? On fire temples see Mary Boyce, "On the Zoroastrian Temple Cult of Fire," *Journal of the American Oriental Society* 95 (1975), 454–65; Klaus Schippmann, *Die iranischen Feuerheiligtümer* ("Religionsgeschichtliche Versuche und Vorarbeiten," vol. 31; Berlin: Walter de Gruyter, 1971).

The author avoids saying where the fire was hidden. He says, however, that it was hidden when the Jews "were being carried off" (imperfect tense, vs. 19) or "had been led" (aorist participle, vs. 33) into exile, and that it was found just after Nehemiah received his commission, and that a Persian shrine to sacred fire marked the spot. Thus he hints that the fire was hidden in Mesopotamia.

For parallels to the story of the preservation and recovery of the sacred fire, see NOTE on 2:2–8.

There are legends connecting Jeremiah with the Persian prophet Zarathushtra, who held fire to be holy; see Joseph Bidez and Franz Cumont, *Les Mages hellénisés* (Paris: "Les Belles Lettres," 1938), I, 49–50.

19. On the author's use of "Persia" for "Babylonia," see the first NOTE on 1:13. In "the pious priests of that time" is there a contrast only with the wicked priests of that time, or also with the sinning Oniads of the author's time?

in a pit . . . dry. I translate a Greek text reconstructed from La^{LXVP}, *en koilômati taxin phreatos echonti anydrou.* There is a common Greek construction *taxin tinos echôn,* "having the character of," in which the participle (*echôn*) agrees grammatically with the object being described (here, the pit). In its regular use, the construction compares the object being described with another object (here, a well), and any adjective agrees with the latter object. See Adolf Wilhelm, "Zu einigen Stellen der Bücher der Makkabäer," *Akademie der Wissenschaften in Wien, Philosophisch-historische Klasse: Anzeiger* 74

(1937), 16–17. The reconstructed version fits the rule. The scribes of the Greek manuscripts, however, were led by a series of corruptions away from the construction which otherwise they would have recognized. The earliest stages of corruption are visible in A. A scribe, after writing the masculine plural nominative participle *labontes* ("took," in our translation) expected the next participle to be masculine plural nominative and wrote *echontes* instead of *echonti*. It was difficult to make sense of the result, but by the small change of reading *anydron* for *anydrou*, one gets the text of A, in which our passage can be forced to mean ". . . hid it in a pit, keeping the condition dry." So harsh is the Greek that later scribes could not accept it, and by a small change they turned *echontes* into *echontos* (q, *L'*) and *L'* turned *anydron* back into *anydrou*. The result is strange Greek, but grammatical, and might be translated ". . . hid it in a pit, a well which happened to be dry." For the use of the genitive instead of an appositive, see Raphael Kühner and Bernhard Gerth, *Ausführliche Grammatik der griechischen Sprache: Satzlehre* (4th ed.; Leverkusen: Gottschalk, 1955), I, 264–65.

shut it up securely. For this meaning of *(kat)asphalizesthai*, cf. Matt 27:64–66 and III 4:9, and see Wilhelm, "Zu einigen Stellen," pp. 17–19.

20. The author takes it for granted that his audience knows the story of Nehemiah's commission from the Persian king. Did he avoid specifying the number of years because he knew how difficult it was to fit into history Jeremiah's seventy years (Jer 25:11–12, 29:10; Dan 9:2) and the figures of the apocalyptic seers?

21–32. The author wishes his readers to think that the wonderful event at the temple of Jerusalem was similar to Elijah's miracle at Mount Carmel (I Kings 18:30–39). Cf. vss. 21–22 with I Kings 18:33–38, and vs. 25(end) and vs. 27(end) with I Kings 18:36.

21. The Greek text (*hôs diesaphêsan hêmîn mê heurêkenai pyr*) is literally "When they reported to us not to have found fire." The author certainly did not imagine the senders as contemporaries of Nehemiah! Probably the text is slightly corrupt; the Lucianic recension omits *hêmîn* ("to us"). But how did the word get into the text? Bernhard Risberg ("Konjekturer till några ställen i de apokryfiska böckerna," *Eranos* 15 [1915], 33–35) suggested that *hêmîn* is a corruption of *ê mên* ("verily"). Less likely, a direct quotation may have originally stood here "We did not find fire" (*hêmîn ou heurêtai pyr*), as in 1:7–8. If so, a scribe expecting an indirect, not a direct, quotation changed the verb to the infinitive and the negative *ou* to *mê*. The author in giving a direct quotation here may have been making an elegant allusion to Gen 26:32.

The viscous liquid was petroleum; see NOTE on 1:36.

23–29. The author gives the words of the prayer because he wishes the Jews of Egypt to use them in observing the Feast of Purification. The prayer does fit the situation facing Egyptian Jews, and the reference to God's "holy Place" in vs. 29 certainly makes an anti-Oniad point. One can see anti-Oniad propaganda also in the assumption that prayer offered in Jerusalem should be efficacious for all Israel and in the hostility to all gentiles who rule Jews. The Oniads long preached that Jews should be loyal to their Ptolemaic benefactors. See Introduction, Part II, section 4.

23. The prayer was recited "verse by verse," Jonathan reciting a passage,

Nehemiah repeating it after him, and the whole assembly repeating it after (or perhaps along with) Nehemiah.

Who is "Jonathan"? He is not identified as high priest, nor would any high priest Jonathan fit the time either of Zerubbabel or Nehemiah. But in any case the high priest did not lead antiphonal singing. That was a function for the temple singers.

The author of Ep. 2 may have had in mind Mattaniah son of Zabdi son of Asaph "who was the leader to begin the thanksgiving in prayer" (Neh 11:17). Mattaniah is also mentioned as a Levite among the first exiles to return to Jerusalem, at I Chron 9:15. One may infer, without reading the book of Nehemiah, that he was a temple singer, for he was descended from the great psalmist Asaph. And at I Esdras 5:57–58 we learn that the descendants of Asaph sang at the festivities upon the completion of Zerubbabel's temple. The author may have made a mistake here in substituting for "Mattaniah" ("gift of the LORD") the synonymous name "Jonathan" ("the LORD gave"). On the other hand, the author may have been correct. There is evidence that Jews would tolerate etymological transpositions of personal names, so that "Mattaniah" and "Jonathan" would name the same person. Consider the names used to refer to the high priests called "Onias" in Greek. The Greek transcription "Onias" reflects an original "Ḥonyā." In rabbinic texts the Oniad temple at Leontopolis is always called "the house of Ḥonyō." However, in the Hebrew of Sir 50:1, Onias, father of the great Simeon, is Yōḥānān (=John; Greek mss. B and S read *Ioniou*). At TP *Yoma* 6:3, p. 43c–d, the son of Simeon the Just is Nᵉḥunyōn, and at *Sifra Emor,* sec. 1, par. 14, p. 94a Weiss, a person is called both "Nᵉḥunyā" and "Ḥonyā." One may also cite the transposition of the names of Jehoiachin (II Kings 24:6, etc.)=Jeconiah (Jer 24:1, etc.)=Coniah (Jer 22:24, etc.).

24–25. Cf. the content of our verses with the first two sections of the *'Amidah,* the obligatory cycle of Jewish prayer: ". . . LORD, our God and God of our fathers, the great, powerful, and awesome God . . . creator of all, who remembers the merits of the patriarchs and will bring a redeemer to their descendants, king who helps and saves. . . . He who provides for the living . . . and sets free the imprisoned." The formulas may have been in use already in daily rituals at Jerusalem. See E. J. Bickerman, "The Civic Prayer for Jerusalem," *Harvard Theological Review* 55 (1962), 163–85, and Joseph Heinemann, *Prayer in the Period of the Tanna'im and the Amora'im* (Jerusalem: Magnes Press, 1964), pp. 138–57 (in Hebrew, with English summary at pp. x–xii).

On the use of such formulas as "our sole . . ." in early Christian sources, especially in Jewish sources adapted for Christian use, see Erik Peterson, *Heis Theos* (Göttingen: Vandenhoeck & Ruprecht, 1926), pp. 139, 196, 281, 300–1, 310.

24. *LORD, LORD.* Jews learned from the Torah that Moses' formula of prayer and praise, which began by repeating God's name, "LORD, LORD" (Exod 34:6–7), was particularly efficacious. It helped secure forgiveness for that worst of sins, the golden calf (cf. Matt 7:21–22 and Luke 6:46). Hence we find the formula at Greek Esther 4:17b; Jubilees 14:2 and 8; and III 2:2. It is used repeatedly in the Jewish liturgy for the Day of Atonement.

creator of all. Jer 10:16, 51:19; cf. Isa 45:9

awesome and powerful and just and merciful. All four attributes are found in Nehemiah's prayer for the forgiveness of sin (Neh 9:31–33). See also Deut 10:17 and Jer 32:18.

our . . . king. Literally, "our sole king and good," but my translation gives better idiom in Hebrew, Greek, and English and also leaves the worshipers still recognizing that the kings placed over them by God, though evil, are still sovereign; see NOTE on 1:7, *Jason . . . Kingdom.*

25. *our sole provider.* Jews have learned the lesson of Hosea's reproof (Hos 2:23). Cf. Pss 136:25, 145:15.

the sole just . . . eternal. Lit. "the sole just and almighty and eternal." The literal rendering is redundant, for "just" has already been mentioned; Greek idiom allows my translation. God's uniqueness, omnipotence, eternity, and justice are mentioned in the prayer at Neh 9:5–8.

preserver . . . evil. Cf. Gen 48:16.

the One . . . patriarchs. Cf. Isa 14:7, 41:8, 44:1–2; Neh 9:7. The "sanctification" may reflect both God's protection of the patriarchs from harm and his separation of them from foreign influences and idolatry; see NOTE on 1:10 – 2:18. Nowhere in the Hebrew Bible are the patriarchs said to have been "sanctified." Rather, in the Torah and in Jeremiah the people of Israel are said to have been sanctified, and Ezekiel predicts the people will be sanctified again (Exod 31:13; Lev 20:8, 22:32; Jer 2:3; Ezek 20:12, 37:28). Nor are the patriarchs alone said to have been "chosen"; Isa 14:1, 41:8, and 44:1–2 surely speak of the people of Israel. Jewish prayers now repeatedly address God as the One "Who has chosen *us* and sanctified *us* through His commandments." Evidently, the author of the letter portrays the senders as believing that Nehemiah and they themselves still lived in the Age of Wrath, when Isa 14:1 and Ezek 37 had not yet been fulfilled. The composers of the Jewish prayers now in use also believed that the prophecies of Isaiah and Ezekiel had not been fulfilled; even before fulfillment of the prophecies Israel stands chosen and sanctified through God's commandments.

26. Nehemiah's generation (and, by implication, the senders of Ep. 2) are portrayed as hoping that their achievements, now followed by their sacrifice and prayer, will bring an end to the Age of Wrath. Israel throughout, even in the Age of Wrath, remains "God's portion" (Deut 32:9) and will again be sanctified (see NOTE to vs. 25).

27–28. The author probably has Isa 49:25–26 in mind.

27. The prayer asks for the fulfillment of Deut 30:4 and of Isa 49:6–7; the people are still enslaved (as threatened at Deut 28:68) and despised (as threatened at Deut 28:37). All three descriptions of the nation (enslaved, despised, abominated) occur at Isa 49:7. Aquila, Symmachus, and Theodotion in translating Isa 49:7 use the same Greek words as appear here.

Look upon. I.e., look with favor upon (*epide*); cf. Exod 2:25 and II 8:2.

and let . . . God. Cf. Isa 49:25–26, 37:20.

28. Here, too, the author probably looks to Isa 49:25–26; cf. also Isa 29:5; Jer 50:33ff.

29. See Exod 15:17.

30. *went on . . . lyres.* The Greek verb *epepsallon* (Hebrew root: *zmr*) may

mean simply "sang." The author may have based our verse on I Esdras 5:57–58 (Ezra 3:12).

31–32. The Greek is ungrammatical and difficult to understand. A literal translation would be "As the sacrificial offerings were consumed, Nehemiah ordered to pour the remaining liquid, too, larger stones. As soon as this was done, a flame blazed up, and when the fire on the altar lit up in turn, it was consumed." What is the connection of the "larger stones" with the rest of the first sentence? What are they larger than? What is the antecedent of "it" in the second sentence? Grammatically and logically the antecedent cannot be the fire on the altar. There may be a further difficulty. In vss. 33 (see NOTE ad loc.) and 36, the author implies that Nehemiah used the liquid for some act of purification. Should there not be some reference to purification in vss. 31–32? Perhaps. But it is also possible that the author was constrained by his convictions to speak of "purification" instead of "dedication"; see NOTE on 1:18(beginning).

To return to the other problems of vss. 31–32: Greek sometimes uses the comparative adjective in the sense of "very . . ."; see Kühner-Gerth, *Grammatik*, II, 305–7. "Larger stones" could be "very large stones," and hence comes my translation, "large boulders." To make good sense of vs. 31 one need only assume that the word *epi* ("upon") has been lost before "large boulders." However, we must also take note of the author's effort to have the wonder in the time of Nehemiah come close to Elijah's miracle at Mount Carmel. The miraculous flames in the time of Elijah devoured the stones of the altar (I Kings 18:38). It would have been a bad omen indeed if the new altar of Zerubbabel-Nehemiah had been destroyed by the rediscovered fire. On the other hand, the event would be all the more wondrous if the flames devoured stones even larger than the stones of the altar. In the Greek of the second sentence "it was consumed" is one word, *edapanêthê*. "It" has been added in my translation above because English grammar requires the word. Apparently the subject of "was consumed" has been lost. It would be very easy to restore as the subject "the remaining liquid" or "the stones and the remaining liquid." For the use of a singular verb with such a compound subject, see Kühner-Gerth, *Grammatik*, I, 77–81. If so, in telling the story in this manner, the author of Ep. 2 achieved his desired close approach to Elijah's miracle: fire wondrously blazes up on the altar and consumes the remaining petroleum at the same time as a petroleum fire nearby consumes large stones.

33. *had burned*. The learned writer of the Greek took advantage of the ambiguity of the verb *hagnizein*, which can mean both "purify" and "burn [as an offering]." See A. C. Pearson, *The Fragments of Sophocles* (Cambridge: Cambridge University Press, 1917), I, 74.

34. The Greek is elliptic but correct. I have supplied the noun "place" from vs. 33; some ancient scribes and translators did the same.

35. Here the correct reading has been preserved only by one witness to the text, A. The elegant writer of the Greek used here the demonstrative pronoun *hois* after *kai*. See the *Greek-English Lexicon* s.v. *hos*, A, II, (p. 1259a), and Kühner-Gerth, *Grammatik*, II, 228. In my translation, I have substituted the antecedent "Nehemiah and his followers" for the pronoun. The scribe(s) who gave rise to all other witnesses to the text did not recognize the dative demon-

strative *hois,* which is otherwise unknown in biblical Greek. They added a word which could take a dative to produce "The king took large sums of money and distributed them to those whom he favored." The resultant text is unsatisfactory, for it leaves obscure who they are whom the king favored. The Persian kings were well known for giving generous gifts at every opportunity (Thucydides ii 97.4; Xenophon *Cyropaedia* viii 2.7).

36. According to the author, at least the common ancient name for petroleum, "napht(h)a" is Hebrew in origin and arose from Nehemiah's wondrous event; perhaps he also intended to claim that here was the first discovery of petroleum. Both assertions are false. Petroleum was known to the Sumerians, Babylonians, and Egyptians by 2000 B.C.E., and the word comes from the Akkadian *naptu.* See R. J. Forbes, *Studies in Ancient Technology,* I, 7–17, 84. In Hebrew the word became *nēpht;* in Aramaic, *nephtā* or *naphtā.* Greeks probably learned of petroleum from Aramaic-speaking Syrians. In Greek there is a strong tendency not to tolerate an unaspirated consonant next to an aspirated one; see Herbert W. Smyth, *Greek Grammar* (Cambridge, Mass.: Harvard University Press, 1956), pp. 25–26. Thus, Greeks would turn *naphtā* into *napta* or *naphtha* even though otherwise *t* is regularly represented by *t,* not by *th.* Hence comes the uncertainty of the aspiration in the various Latin versions. The author gives *nephthai* as the commonly used form of the noun, and the final *i* or *e* sound is abundantly attested in the witnesses to the text. I do not know why the *i* sound has been added. Perhaps the author thought it would represent a well-known sound shift away from his imagined Hebrew original *nephthar.* Loss of final *r* in vulgar pronunciation of Hebrew and Aramaic was common; see AB vol. 41, pp. 16–17, n. 28. A sound shift from *-ar* to *-aei* in Greek transcriptions from Aramaic is attested in the manuscript of Hesychius' *Lexicon* 972, s.v. *adaei,* where *Adaei* is given as the name of the Babylonian month Adar.

The author knew enough Hebrew to strain the Hebrew language in his effort to give a Hebrew origin for *nephtā;* he viewed *nephtā* as a corruption of the Hebrew *nephtār* (*niphtār* in Masoretic Hebrew). Literally, the word means "released," "declared free of obligation." Only by a forced extension can the word be made to mean "purified," and by still more violence, "purification." The author, however, was determined to find in Nehemiah's rites precedents for the Feast of Purification.

2:1. The author tries to disarm skeptics by asserting the connection of the story of the wondrous fire with Jeremiah and with texts about Jeremiah which were already known (see NOTE on vss. 2–8). I have translated Greek *apographais* here as "texts." Usually *apographê* means "list," but at Dan LXX 10:21 it is used of an important heavenly document. Vss. 2–3 let us know that one of the "texts" was the apocryphal Epistle of Jeremiah, and in vs. 4 one of the "texts" is called a *graphê,* a word which can mean "scripture," and I have not hesitated to translate it, too, as "text."

In Hebrew and Aramaic and biblical Greek "find" was the usual word for ascertaining a fact from documents (Ezra and II Esdras 4:15, 19, and 6:2; I Esdras 2:17, 21, and 6:22; Neh 13:1; II Esdras 23:1; Esther 6:2; Dan 12:1). In citing readings found in manuscripts of classical texts, ancient Homeric and rabbinic scholars used the expression "we find written . . ." See Saul Lieberman, *Hellenism in Jewish Palestine* (New York: Jewish Theological Seminary of America, 1950), pp. 21–22, esp. n. 11. In many of these instances, the verb "find" is impersonal ("it is found that . . .") or appears with the "editorial we" ("we find that"). Ancient scribes and modern readers, expecting an impersonal verb or an "editorial we" were puzzled by the Greek of our verse, where "Jeremiah" is the grammatical subject of "is found." They wrongly tried to improve the text. In elegant Greek there was a strong tendency to use personal rather than impersonal constructions ("Jeremiah is found that . . ." rather than "it is found that Jeremiah . . ."); see Kühner-Gerth, *Grammatik*, II, 367, and Abel, *Grammaire*, pp. 278 and 363. In translating I have substituted "we find that Jeremiah . . ." only for the sake of good English idiom.

who . . . exile. My translation is based on the reading *metagomenous*, preserved in VLa^{VBM} and many minuscules. Other sources have *metagenomenous* or *metaginomenous*, a word which might mean "posterity," as if Jeremiah's command was for the priests' descendants and not for the priests themselves. Probably an early scribe absentmindedly added the letters *en* or *in*, and later scribes without hesitation guessed that the false reading before them meant "posterity," but in fact the word is almost unknown elsewhere and never occurs with that meaning. Furthermore, Jeremiah's commands were surely to the living, not to the unborn.

2–8. Our vss. 2–3 show that the apocryphal Epistle of Jeremiah was already known in Egypt. As my teacher, Elias Bickerman, noted in an unpublished work, the apocryphal epistle must be a product of the Hellenistic age: it gives Nebuchadnezzar the Hellenistic title "King of the Babylonians" instead of his real title, "King of Babylon," and such pseudonymous compositions were virtually unknown earlier in the ancient Near East but were fabricated in great numbers in the Hellenistic period.

A legend that Jeremiah kept the ark from being carried off to Babylon was known to Alexander Polyhistor (first century B.C.E.), who probably derived it from the work *On the Kings in Judaea* by Eupolemus. See FGH 723, F 1–5, especially F 5 (Eusebius *Praeparatio evangelica* ix 39). The author Eupolemus may well be the Jewish diplomat who went to Rome in 161 B.C.E. (4:11; see AB vol. 41, NOTE on I 8:17–18). Such a person could have been a vigorous partisan of the holiness of Jerusalem so as to collect and publish or fabricate legends explaining why sacred Jerusalem nevertheless lacked the sacred furniture, and the author of Ep. 2 could have read the work and then, in vs. 4, could have called it "the text"; see Ben Zion Wacholder, HUCA (1978), 122–24 (first par.). According to the fragment of Eupolemus, Jeremiah kept only the ark and the tablets when Nebuchadnezzar had the temple plundered, so that if Eupolemus was the source for the author of Ep. 2, the author has further embroidered upon the tale; cf. Christian Wolff, *Jeremia im Frühjudentum und Urchristentum* ("Texte und Untersuchungen zur Geschichte der altchristlichen Literatur," Band 118; Berlin: Akademie-Verlag, 1976), pp. 16–17, 20–26, 62–63.

Stories of the preservation of sacred objects by leaders of defeated and exiled nations, with a view toward a glorious future, are common. Virgil's Aeneas so preserves the "defeated Penates" (*Aeneid* i. 6, 68). Nevertheless, here among the Jews in the Hellenistic period we find a legend of the *burial* of sacred ob-

jects, including a box (the ark), a legend vividly paralleled by Samaritan beliefs (J. *AJ* xviii 4.1.85–87; Adalbert Merx, *Der Messias oder Ta'eb der
Samaritaner* ["Beihefte zur ZAW," 17; Giessen: Töpelmann, 1909], pp. 28,
30, 39–40, 45–46). Before the time of Eupolemus, the Greek poet Rhianos of
Crete wrote an epic of the fall and rebirth of Greek Messenia, of which a summary survives in Pausanias (see Pausanias iv. 6. 1–3). Rhianos was a contemporary of Eratosthenes (ca. 275–194 B.C.E.). In the epic Rhianos described
(Pausanias iv. 20. 3–4, 26. 4–8, 27. 5) how the hero, Aristomenes, in accordance with prophecy, hid away the text of the sacred Messenian mysteries so
that they would survive the imminent fall of Messenia and guarantee her future rebirth and how after generations the bronze "urn" (*hydria*) containing
the sacred text was dug up. The mysteries became central rites in the worship
of the restored Messenia. The "urn" was kept as a sacred object (Pausanias iv.
33. 5), and in an inscription of 92 B.C.E. probably the same container is called
not "urn" but "box" (*kamptra; Syll.*[3] 736, line 11). Eupolemus may have
fabricated our story of Jeremiah after the model of Rhianos' epic. See, however, Yehoshua Gutman, "Philo the Epic Poet," *Scripta Hierosolymitana* 1
(1954), 60–63.

Jewish writers did not need the stimulus of Rhianos. The biblical accounts of
the ark themselves left room for speculation, for the sacred furniture men-
tioned here is said at I Kings 8:4 to have been brought to the temple by
Solomon, yet it is not listed among the articles carried off by the Babylonians.
On Jewish speculations and for a suggestion on the real fate of the ark, see M.
Haran, "The Disappearance of the Ark," IEJ 13 (1963), 46–58.

Vss. 4–8 may well have been the source for the author of the *Lives of the
Prophets* (*Jeremiah* 9–15, published in Charles C. Torrey, *The Lives of the
Prophets* [Journal of Biblical Literature Monograph Series; Philadelphia: Soci-
ety of Biblical Literature and Exegesis, 1946], I, 22, 36).

On use of the traditions reflected here in Jewish literature written after the
second destruction in 70 C.E., see George Nickelsburg, "Narrative Traditions in
the Paralipomena of Jeremiah and 2 Baruch," *Catholic Biblical Quarterly* 35
(1973), 60–68.

2. Many witnesses to the text have the same error here as in vs. 1 (*meta-
genomenois* instead of *metagomenois*).

Nowhere else is Jeremiah said to have given the Torah (Greek: *ton nomon*)
to the exiles. One might instead translate *ton nomon* as "the law [against
idolatry]," but I think that either the author of Ep. 2 jumped to his own conclusion that Jeremiah gave them a copy of the Torah or else he found the information in a source, perhaps Eupolemus' work.

The prophet's admonition is a summary of the entire content of the
apocryphal Epistle of Jeremiah.

3. The precise content of the verse is found neither in Jeremiah nor in the
apocryphal epistle (but cf. Jer 31:32). Again the author of Ep. 2 may have
jumped to a conclusion (cf. Deut 4:9, 6:6–7) or have found his information in
Eupolemus.

4. Here at last the author of Ep. 2 seems to feel himself on sure ground.
Confidently he says that the story of the hiding of the sacred furniture is in a
"text" or "scripture" (*graphê*). Somewhat strangely, the author writes in the

past tense, "The text also said," as if he no longer could easily go and consult it.

Both in Greek and in English it is strange to find "the tabernacle and the ark" as subjects of "should go." Perhaps the word *labontas* has fallen out. If so, the translation would be "ordered persons to take the tabernacle and the ark and go with him." Cf. vs. 6.

The author of the legend wishes to leave the sacred furniture in a place that can be discovered only if God so wills (vs. 7). To put the articles in Moses' grave (see Deut 34:1–6) would render them unclean, but the same mysterious mountain might be expected to have other undiscovered hiding places.

5. The incense altar was not mentioned before, but it was a part of the furniture of the tabernacle. However, it is still strange to find it mentioned here. Jeremiah could not have hidden away the *complete* incense altar if its gold had been carried off to Babylon (see Exod 30:3; II Kings 25:15; Jer 52:19). There was an incense altar in the second temple (I 1:21, 4:49–50; II 10:3; J. *BJ* v 5.5.217–18). No other Jewish text says that the second temple was incomplete because it lacked the original incense altar. And why should the incense altar be singled out here? One can explain the omission here of the candelabrum: it was entirely of gold and had been carried off by the conquerors. But the table for the showbread, like the incense altar, was only partly of gold (Exod 25:25–28), and at Ezra 1:7–11 there is no record that it was brought back for the second temple. However, the author of Ep. 2 must be responsible for mentioning the incense altar here. No scribe could have had a reason for adding it! See also AB vol. 41, Appendix III, n. 1.

6. *those . . . along.* See NOTE on vs. 5.

7. *until . . . Mercy.* Cf. Deut 30:3–4; Isa 54:7–10. I have taken the liberty of restyling the Greek, which literally has "until God assembles the regathering of the people and mercy comes to be."

8. See Isa 40:5; Exod 40:34; Lev 9:23; I Kings 8:11, 9:3; II Chron 5:14, 7:2, 12, 16. Such wonders had never appeared in the second temple. The author, who believes that nevertheless the second temple was already sanctified, asserts that those miracles would make it "greatly sanctified."

9–12. The text is clearly defective. It is hard to see the connection between vs. 11 and vss. 10 and 12. Vs. 11 quotes Moses, but nowhere in the Torah is the quoted sentence to be found. The quoted sentence itself is enigmatic. Literally, the Greek has "On account of not having been eaten the sin offering was consumed" (*Dia to mê bebrôsthai to peri tês hamartias anêlôthê*). Vs. 11 appears to be referring to the problem of the sin offering at Lev 10:16–20, but in its present form the quoted sentence makes no sense when applied to that passage. At Lev 10:16–20 Aaron and his surviving sons did not eat the meat of the sin offering but let it be burned, and Moses *objected* to the fact, and accepted Aaron's explanation that as a mourner he could not eat the meat. Vs. 12 begins with the Greek word *hôsautôs* ("in the same manner," "so"). Logically, an act comparable to Solomon's eight-day celebration should precede.

The history of the time and even the text in its present defective state offer clues to what the intact original must have been. The naming of the Feast of Purification as the "Days of Tabernacles in the Month of Kislev" was puzzling, and so was the eight-day duration of the celebration. The author of *Schol.*

Megillat Ta'anit 25 Kislev also found the eight days difficult. The author here tries to solve the problems. Wise Solomon by inference copied Moses' procedure when he dedicated his temple and its altar and was granted the same kind of miraculous response that Moses received. Surely the lost words between the end of vs. 10 and the beginning of vs. 12 contained a reference to how Moses dedicated the Tabernacle and its altar by eight days of rites.

If so, we can now suggest what was the original reading of vs. 11 and show how it fitted into the author's demonstration that rites of dedication and purification should last for eight days. The only direct statement by Moses in Lev 10:16–20 is "For what reason did you not eat the sin offering in a holy place?" (Gr. *Dia ti ouk ephagete to peri tês hamartias en topôi hagiôi?*). By only small alterations in the existing text of vs. 11 we obtain "For what reason did you not eat the sin offering but it was consumed [by fire]?" (Gr. *Dia ti mê bebrôsthe to peri tês hamartias alla anêlôthê?*). From *ti* to *to* is a small step. In Hellenistic Greek *-sthe* and *-sthai* were pronounced alike, and *ALLA* before *AN* and coming shortly after *AM* looked confusingly repetitious and could have been lost by haplography. For *mê* as the negative in a question, see Friedrich Blass and Albert Debrunner, *Grammatik des neutestamentlichen Griechisch* (14th ed., revised by Friedrich Rehkopf; Göttingen: Vandenhoeck & Ruprecht, 1976), section 427.2.

The proposed restoration has the merit of making good sense in the context. We have deduced that before vs. 12 in the original text stood a confident assertion that Moses' dedication of the Tabernacle was an eight-day rite. Yet despite Lev 9:1, later Jewish texts prefer to regard events of Lev 9:1–10:20 as part of a rite separate from the *seven*-day consecration of the Tabernacle and the priests. See *Schol. Megillat Ta'anit* 25 Kislev and cf. Exod 29:30, 35, 37; Lev 8:33, 35. Rabbinic authorities seem to have taken the rites of Lev 9–10 as part of the twelve-day rites of dedication mentioned at Num 7; see Ginzberg, *Legends*, III, 181. Hence, one who wished to use Moses' dedication of the Tabernacle as a precedent for an eight-day rite had to prove that the eighth day mentioned at Lev 9:1 belonged with the seven days mentioned in Exod 29 and Lev 8.

The account at Lev 10:16–20 is difficult. Why did the pious Aaron have the meat of the goat of the sin offering burned? And why was Moses, though at first angry, pleased by Aaron's reply? The later Jewish authorities have their own explanation (see Rashi and *Sifra* ad loc. and Ginzberg, *Legends*, VI, 75, n. 387). The author of Ep. 2 seems to have interpreted the texts differently and to have taken Exod 29:33–37 (cf. Lev 8:31–35) to mean that, for the duration of the ceremonies consecrating the priests and the altar, the priests *must* eat a portion of each of "those things with which atonement was made," i.e., of each sin offering, and that the remainder of each sin offering still uneaten by the next dawn must be burned. So interpreted, Exod 29:33 makes the sin offerings of the dedication ceremonies unique among those mentioned in the Torah, since Exod 29:33 is the only text in the Torah which explicitly requires a priest to eat the meat of a sin offering (this is not the place to discuss the rabbinic texts which *deduce* that no sin offering confers atonement unless a priest eats of it). Hence, if Moses had reason to believe that Aaron and his surviving sons were all obligated to eat a portion of the sin offering brought on the eighth day, clearly the eighth day belonged with the first seven days of dedication.

Pious Jews knew their Torah. Hence, the author of Ep. 2 would have been able to express himself briefly as follows: "Moses' dedication ceremonies, too, lasted for eight days. The eighth day is to be reckoned with the first seven as a day when the special rule on sin offerings applied, as we learn from Moses' question, 'Why was the sin offering burned and not eaten?' Just as Moses' dedication ceremonies lasted for eight days, so Solomon . . . [as in vs. 12]."

No extant source says explicitly that Solomon's dedication ceremonies lasted for eight days. The author has argued from his own beliefs: if Solomon's dedication ceremonies coincided with Tabernacles, they must also have included the Eighth Day of Solemn Assembly (see II Chron 7:9). If Solomon was wise, his wisdom would have led him to copy Moses. In fact, Judas Maccabaeus and his contemporaries did have such difficulties with the biblical texts and precedents and used similar reasoning to solve them. See AB vol. 41, NOTE on 4:36–54.

The author's own analogies run counter to his reluctance to speak of a "dedication" in the time of Judas Maccabaeus. He does not adduce Hezekiah's eight days of *purification* (II Chron 28:22 – 30:27), but argues from the *dedications* by Moses and Solomon!

9. *We are also told.* Lit. "It is made clear." The sources are the stories of Solomon in I Kings 3:5–15, 8, and II Chron 1:7–12, 5–7.

10–11. At AB vol. 41, p. 278, I refer the reader to a NOTE here, but that discussion now stands in the NOTE on vss. 9–12.

10. See Lev 9:23–24 and II Chron 7:1.

13. The author probably alludes to I Esdras 5:46–50 or Ezra 3:1–4, which can be read as confirming that "Zerubbabel-Nehemiah" (see NOTE on 1:18) and his contemporaries celebrated the dedication of the altar on the eight-day festival of Tabernacles. However, the author's language implies more: that there is evidence for his other assertions in the archives kept at Jerusalem. He appeals to the great names of Nehemiah and Judas. He has expressed himself badly for impressing us, though he may have impressed the Jews of Egypt then. He speaks of the *anagraphai* of the time of Nehemiah. *Anagraphai* were official records, kept by priests or in archives (see J. *Ap.* i 2.9, 11; 4.20–21, 5.23, 6.28–29, 7.36). Such were the chronological lists of the Egyptian kings (see Werner Jaeger, *Diokles von Karystos* [Berlin: Walter de Gruyter, 1938], pp. 126–32), kept by the Egyptian priests, and reports of pagan miracles (see, e.g., the Chronicle of Lindos, summarized in English at Andrew R. Burn, *Persia and the Greeks* [New York: St. Martin's, 1962], pp. 210–11; cf. Peterson, *Heis Theos* [Göttingen: Vandenhoeck & Ruprecht, 1926], pp. 216–20). Such records from the times of Moses and Solomon did not exist in the time of Nehemiah, and Nehemiah's memoirs could hardly have mentioned Moses' and Solomon's dedications. What we have of the memoirs says nothing of his building of a temple or of the wondrous fire or of a library. See also end of NOTE on 1:10b – 2:18 (on the purpose served by the mention here of the collection of books by Nehemiah and Judas).

Nehemiah could have collected a library containing the books of Kings and the books of the Prophets and even some of the Psalms and the letters of (pagan) kings conferring pious gifts on the LORD's temple. But the author's conception of the library probably included the books of Chronicles and Ezra and Nehemiah as we have them, drawn up after Nehemiah's time, for they are about the kings and contain Nehemiah's memoirs and letters of the pagan kings; see AB vol. 12, pp. xviii, xxx–xlv, lxxxvii–lxxxix, and vol. 14, pp. xlviii–l, and lxviii(second par.)–lxx. The author's Psalter, too, probably included material written after the time of Nehemiah; see AB vol. 41, NOTE on 7:16–17.

14–15. The author's assertion about Judas' collection may well be true, but see introductory NOTE.

14. *scattered.* I have guessed at the meaning of the word here from the context. In Greek papyri of the third and second centuries B.C.E. in connection with money it means "lost." At J. *AJ* xii 2.4.36=Aristeas to Philocrates 29 it seems to mean "damaged, in bad condition."

we have them. That is to say, "Copies are extant in our possession," in case the recipients wished to verify the quoted texts. See Bickerman, *Studies*, I, 238.

16. The author has taken his readers far away from his original request that they observe the commemorative days. To remind them, he repeats it, and the Greek, as is proper, signals the resumption of the original topic by using the particle *oun*. Cf. the procedure of the composer of Ezra 4 as explained in NOTE on 1:18.

17–18. The letter reiterates here the reference in 1:11, to God's having saved the Jews of Judaea, and then closes with a pious hope that has the character of a prayer: a result of the observance of the Days of Purification may be that God will fulfill his promises, including the ingathering of the dispersed exiles. The fulfillment would save the Jews of Egypt from their present difficulties!

The text, however, is difficult. As the particle *gar* ("for," as a coordinating conjunction) shows, a new clause begins with "We hope." As the Greek text stands, the rest of vss. 17–18 ("God . . . Torah") is left without a verb. Greek often omits the present tense of the verb "to be," and therefore one might translate the passage "It is God who has saved his entire people and restored the heritage to us all and the kingdom and the priesthood and the sanctification, as he promised in the Torah." After that declaration, however, the "for" of the next clause would follow strangely: how could the *present* pious hopes of the Jews of Judaea explain God's *past* accomplishments? The declaration would also be false: God had restored only a part of the "heritage," none of the "kingdom," and little if anything of the "sanctification," and impious Menelaus was still high priest. See introductory NOTE. It is also strange that "to us all" occurs in the Greek *after* "the heritage," rather than before or after the whole series of God's restored gifts to Israel. Hence, I think that the word *apodôsei* ("will restore") has fallen out, and the original text was to be translated "God, Who saved His entire people and restored the heritage to us all will also restore the kingdom and the priesthood and the sanctification."

17. *Who saved . . . us all.* See Zech 8:7 and 12 in a context of the regathering of dispersed Israel from the east and the west (Egypt!) to a secure Jerusalem. Cf. also Isa 49:7–8. The author, in using the word "entire," might have in mind the remote past, but the reference to "restoration" and also the end of vs. 18 show that he is thinking primarily of recent events.

The "heritage" is surely the land as in Isa 49:8 and Jer 3:19 and 12:15 (cf. Zech 8:12 and Lam 5:2) and I 15:33–34. Though it is not inconceivable that some of Judas' contemporaries felt that the heritage had been restored with the withdrawal of Lysias and the end of the persecution, Jews and gentiles who were acquainted with the promises of the Torah and the Prophets knew otherwise; see AB vol. 41, introductory NOTE on ch. 5.

the kingdom . . . Torah. The author alludes to Exod 19:6. The author sees the righteous senders as confident that they have obeyed God (see Exod 19:5), and therefore they can expect fulfillment of the promise of Exod 19:6. Though the words of Exod 19:6 would appear to mean "a kingdom of priests," the Septuagint renders them as a "royal priesthood" or a "kingdom, priesthood" (basileion hierateuma; Symmachus and Theodotion render it basileia hiereis). The Greek uses basileion to mean "kingdom" at Dan LXX 7:22 and in the Alexandrinus at III Reigns 3:1 (I Kings 5:1), 14:8; IV Reigns 15:19. Cf. also Jubilees 16:18, and Robert H. Charles, The Book of Jubilees (London: A. and C. Black, 1902), p. 116.

The allusion to Exod 19:6 should be enough to show that hagiasmon here means "sanctification," not "temple." Indeed, the word renders Heb. miqdāš ("temple") only in the Greek versions of Ezekiel.

18. He will . . . evils. The author alludes to Deut 30:3–5, 31:17, and 21.

has indeed . . . Place. On the tense of "has purified," see NOTE on 1:18. Even so, the author's statement is puzzling. Nowhere has he told how God purified the temple. Indeed, the absence of miraculous divine intervention is probably the cause which drove the author to speak of purification rather than dedication (see NOTE on 1:18). Surely the author knew that not God, not even a wondrous petroleum fire, but pious priests purified the temple! I think here the author, like Jason of Cyrene at 4:7, hints that the "deliverance from great evils" is God's miracle which made possible the purification of the temple. There is probably also a polemic point in the author's climactic insistence, at the very end, that the temple is now ritually clean. Oniads would be unlikely to hold that the temple in which Onias III had been high priest was intrinsically unclean, but other Jewish sects did not stop with saying that the temple at Jerusalem lacked important sacred attributes; some held it to be totally unfit or unclean. See Test Moses 4:8; Enoch 89:73; Cross, Ancient Library, p. 101, and my article in Studies on the Testament of Moses, ed. by George W. E. Nickelsburg, Jr. (Septuagint and Cognate Studies, no. 4; Cambridge, Mass.: Society of Biblical Literature, 1973), pp. 48–50.

III. THE ABRIDGER'S PREFACE
(2:19–32)

2 19 Jason of Cyrene narrated the history of Judas Maccabaeus and his brothers, of the purification of the greatest of temples and the dedication of the altar, 20 and also of the wars against Antiochus Epiphanes and his son Eupator, 21 and of the manifest interventions from heaven in favor of those who vied with one another in fighting manfully for Judaism: few though they were, they took the spoils of the entire country and drove out the barbarian hordes 22 and recovered the world-renowned temple and freed the city and reestablished the laws which were on the point of being abolished. All this they accomplished because the LORD in the fullness of His grace became merciful to them. 23 What Jason of Cyrene told in five books, we shall attempt to abridge into a single volume. 24 His work is a sea of words, and the sheer mass of the material is formidable to anyone who wishes to plunge into the historical narrative. Perceiving these obstacles, 25 we have set ourselves the goals of providing entertainment for lovers of literature, a clear and memorable style for pursuers of wisdom, and edification for all who look into this book.

26 We ourselves hesitated to undertake the abridgment. Indeed, it exacts a price of sweat and sleepless nights. 27 The man who prepares a banquet and seeks to benefit his fellow man has no light task; just so, I have cheerfully accepted the pain for the sake of performing a public service. 28 We shall leave the exact and detailed narrative to the author of the unabridged work and proceed in our labors along the lines of an abridgment. 29 My relationship to the original author, I think, is like that between a builder and a painter. The architect of a new house has to think of the entire structure, whereas he who undertakes to draw a house in encaustic or paint has to consider the rules of perspective. Just so, 30 to go into a topic and explore its ramifications and inquire closely into details befits the original author of our history, 31 but a summarizer must be allowed to strive for brevity of expression and excuse himself from exhaustive treatment of the

facts. [32] Having added this much explanation to our statement of purpose, let us begin our narrative at this point, for it is silly to let the preface of our history grow long while abridging the history itself.

NOTES

2:19–27. The prefaces of ancient works were advertisements to attract the reader. The abridger here in vss. 19–23 does not give a systematic summary of his work or of the original on which it was based but touches on those features which he thinks will attract and hold the reader's attention; cf. Thucydides i 23.1–3, Tacitus *Histories* i 2–3, and Lucian *How to Write History* 53.

The abridger could have no reason to lie about the content of the work of Jason of Cyrene, copies of which must have been available in his time. The preface implies that the work before us is a faithful abridgment: the abridger has cut and restyled but has added nothing; see NOTE on 15:39, *so . . . history*. Skeptics may suspect that he has not been true to his declared principles. Since we cannot check the abridged history against the original work, all we can do is to check it against the description in vss. 19–23. With explainable exceptions, everything in the abridged history conforms to the description here (see NOTE on vs. 20), and everything in the description here can be found in the abridged history (see NOTE on vs. 19). There is no other information on Jason of Cyrene.

Apart from sketching the content of his book, a Greek historian in his preface tended to touch upon stereotyped topics. Such topics here are the great mass of raw material which the author has digested and rearranged (cf. Diodorus i 3.3–4 and 8) through hard labor (cf. Thucydides i 20.3, 22.3; Diodorus i 4.1; J. *BJ* i 1.5.16) for the benefit of the reader, so that the reader should be able easily to commit the contents to memory (cf. Diodorus xvi 1.1, xvii 1.2) and derive from them both edification (cf. Thucydides i 22.4; Diodorus i 1.1–3.5) and pleasure. Writers more austere than our abridger took pains to subordinate entertainment (*psychagôgia*) or pleasure (*to terpnon*) to edification (*ôpheleia, to chrêsimon*); see Lucian *How to Write History* 9, 13, and Dionysius of Halicarnassus *Letter to Pompeius Geminus* 6.

19. Our verse at its beginning contains the Greek particle *de,* as if Ep. 2 were organically linked to the abridged history. Since Ep. 2 contradicts the abridged history, we must suppose that the particle *de* was added when Epp. 1 and 2 were attached to the abridgment. Though Jason of Cyrene and the abridger were hostile to the Hasmonaean dynasty, they could not avoid giving prominence to the great Judas and his brothers. The reading public wanted to hear the stories of the heroes, and to attract the attention of that public the abridger mentions them even ahead of the temple. Jason and the abridger, indeed, were intent on refuting the history of Judas and his brothers published in First Maccabees and that fact may explain why they are mentioned at the very outset.

The brothers play only minor roles in the abridged history. An anti-Has-monaean propagandist could well have extended his book past the death of Judas into the career of Jonathan and beyond. The abridger certainly stopped before reaching the end of the original history (see pp. 5, 12). Unfortu-nately, there is no evidence to tell us whether the mention of the brothers here is a hint that Jason's narrative went beyond Judas' death. On the name "Mac-cabaeus," see AB vol. 41, NOTE on 2:4.

Though our writer has non-Hasmonaean heroes of his own (Onias III, Eleazar, the martyred mother and seven sons, Razis), they were so little known to his readers that it was useless to mention them in the preface.

Herod's magnificent temple still lay in the future. Hence "greatest" here reflects the writer's belief in the importance of the temple of Jerusalem. He contrasts it not only with pagan temples but with that of the Samaritans (cf. 6:2) and probably also with that of the Oniads and with those of any other schismatics who may have existed. See also pp. 13–16.

The word "dedication" (*enkainismos*) carried connotations which appear to have been matters of contention between Jewish sects; see end of introductory NOTE to 1:1–10a and NOTE to 1:18. The abridger here does not hesitate to speak of "dedication." It would thus appear that for him the word was not an issue and also that he failed to notice how carefully Jason of Cyrene avoided it and related words at 10:1–8 (see NOTE ad loc.).

20. One can understand the omission here of the name of Seleucus IV. The mission of Heliodorus (3:7–35) was wicked, but it was not an act of war. More puzzling is the omission of the name of Demetrius I. Nicanor fought bat-tles against the Jews and committed other acts of war (14:16–17, 29–46, 15:1–30) as Demetrius' commander, and Jason of Cyrene told of the war. Even the abridger gives as much importance to the Day of Nicanor, commem-orating the victory over Demetrius' commander, as to the Feast of Dedication! Hence, it is difficult, though not impossible, to suggest that the abridger's assessment of Demetrius I differed from Jason's.

Perhaps the abridger has singled out Antiochus IV and his son because of their cosmic importance as rods of God's anger whose excesses and whose fall ushered in the great new age of miracles. Antiochus IV is certainly so viewed in Dan 7–11. The pious must have been puzzled by the failure of the course of history to fulfill Dan 11:40–12:3. The seer in Dan 11 spoke only of anonymous Kings of the North and South and did not always differentiate fa-ther from son (in vs. 9, the King of the South is Ptolemy III; in vs. 11, Ptolemy IV; in vs. 14, Ptolemy V). When Lysias and Antiochus V besieged the temple the pious could view the event as a continuation of the troubles de-scribed in Dan 11:33–36 (though not of those in Dan 11:37–39). Cf. J. *BJ* i 1.4.40 and II 10:10–13. Believers must have held that the fulfillment of the rest of Daniel's prophecies had been postponed for some unknown reason. Demetrius' acts belonged to the period of the postponement and were not part of the cosmic scheme revealed in Daniel. The abridger could have held that Demetrius was not a persecutor. Demetrius wrongfully backed Alcimus (14:11–13, 27), but did nothing against Jewish religion. Alcimus, indeed, but for his sins would have been a legitimate high priest (14:3), and Demetrius' mistake was thus less heinous. Demetrius, at Alcimus' instigation, exerted pressure on Nicanor, but Nicanor's threats against the temple and his blasphemies were his own. Demetrius was not responsible for them.

Demetrius' acts were, however, part of the cosmic scheme revealed in Enoch 90:6–16, and Jason of Cyrene probably accepted that scheme; see AB vol. 41, pp. 96–97 (through line 2). Hence, we would have to infer that the abridger here, too, differed with Jason: he rejected or did not know the prophecies of Enoch.

21. A "manifest intervention" (*epiphaneia*) was a tangible event in which a supernatural being or force was perceived to act; see Martin P. Nilsson, *Geschichte der griechischen Religion,* Vol. II (2d ed.; München: Beck, 1961), pp. 225–27, and W. Kendrick Pritchett, *The Greek State at War, Part III: Religion* (Berkeley, Los Angeles, and London: University of California Press, 1979), pp. 6–7, 11–46. Jason of Cyrene reports such interventions at 3:24–25, 10:29–30, 11:8, 12:22, 15:27; cf. 5:2–4 and 14:15. The word is used of a less tangible apparition at 5:4.

Pious Jews were delighted to report how their guerrilla warriors throughout Judaea looted the property of wicked Jews and their pagan protectors!

"Barbarian" was the word Greeks used of all non-Greeks. Here a Jewish Greek uses "barbarian" of the *Greek-speaking* enemy. His choice of words becomes slightly less surprising when one realizes that an important connotation of the Greek word *barbaros* is "speaker of a foreign language," as in the Greek translation of Ps 114:1. To Jews of Judaea, the Seleucid troops were speakers of a foreign language. On the other hand, our writer uses *barbaros* to mean "savage" at 4:25, 5:22, 10:4, and 15:2.

Our verse contains the earliest known occurrence of the Greek word *Ioudaïsmos* ("Judaism"). The writer probably chose deliberately to use a word of this form in the same context as "barbarian," for he thus induced his literate Greek audience to remember the struggle of the loyal Hellenes against the "barbarian" Persians and against the "Medism" of Greek collaborators with the Persian empire; see NOTE on 4:13.

22. Schismatic Jewish temples were not world-renowned; only the temple at Jerusalem was. Jason reports the *de facto* recovery of the temple at 10:1, and at 11:25 quotes the royal document which restored it to the Jews *de jure.*

Not all Jews held that Jerusalem was free from the time of the victory over Nicanor down to the time of the abridger and beyond; see NOTE on 15:37.

To the pious, the decrees of Antiochus IV amounted to the abolition of the Torah. Jason and the abridger in some respects share the opinion of the author of Ep. 1: the persecution was a punishment for heinous sins, but the suffering and prayers of the pious won God's mercy (4:16–17, 6:12–16, 7:32–33, and 37–38, 8:27–29).

23. See Introduction, p. 5.

24. *sea of words.* The Greek has "flowing mass of numbers" (*chyma . . . arithmôn*). A "number" was a unit of about sixteen syllables of writing, the standard measure of length in Greek books, of which the earliest were the poems of Homer, written in verses of about sixteen syllables.

plunge into. La[P] so renders the Gr. *eiskykleisthai;* it is at least a good guess from the context.

25. *lovers of literature.* Lit. "those who wish to read."

clear . . . wisdom. I have given the Greek active verb *philophronein* the meaning "pursue wisdom" (*phronêsis*) on the analogy of the Greek verb *philosophein*. Elsewhere *philophronein* occurs only in the middle voice (see the *Greek-English Lexicon*, s.v.) and is derived not from *phronêsis* but from *philophrôn* ("friendly"), and the participle here, though active, might mean "friends" or "sympathizers." The context suggests that the verb here describes not sympathizers but persons especially interested in remembering what they read. If my guess on the meaning of *philophronein* is correct, a literal translation of our passage would be "ease in committing facts to memory for pursuers of wisdom."

edification. So I have translated Gr. *ôpheleian* ("help," "advantage"). Cf. the wordy preface of Diodorus Siculus (i 1.1–3.5).

26. The abridger may have known the poems of Callimachus, who lived in Alexandria in the third century B.C.E. In *Epigram* 29 Callimachus says that the task of abridging causes sleepless nights.

27. As the abridger implies, in the Hellenistic age a banquet (*symposion*) was an ambitious undertaking, involving elaborate food, drink, and entertainment; cf. Sir 32(35):1, and see Michael Coffey, "Symposium," OCD², p. 1028.

performing a public service. I translate here the reading of *L' La⁻ᵛ* (*tên tôn pollôn euchrêstian*). Other witnesses have *tên tôn pollôn eucharistian*, which might be translated "winning public gratitude."

29–30. The original author is like a builder, who works in three dimensions; the abridger is like a painter, who works in only two. Cf. Plutarch *Alexander* 1.

Greek epideictic orators spoke in praise or blame of some person or group, frequently on the occasion of a funeral or festival. The Greek historian Timaeus (*apud* Polybius xii 28a.1) similarly contrasted history, a "three-dimensional art," with "two-dimensional" epideictic oratory, saying that the difference between the two is as great as that between real buildings and the views and compositions in painted stage scenery.

29. *encaustic.* A Greek technique of painting which used hot colored wax (T. B. L. Webster, "Encaustic," OCD², p. 383).

perspective. I have guessed from the context that this is the meaning of the vague word *diakosmêsin* ("arrangement").

31. *summarizer.* Literally, the Greek has the vague "paraphraser" (*tôi tên metaphrasin poioumenôi*). To the abridger, we may infer, a paraphrase was always shorter than the original.

facts. I use the word here as a synonym of "history" in order to render the Greek noun *pragmateia*, which often means simply "history" in Polybius.

32. *statement of purpose.* Lit. "the things said first" (*tois proeirêmenois*). The abridger did begin by stating his purpose.

IV. THE MIRACULOUS THWARTING
OF HELIODORUS
(3:1-40)

3 ¹ Under the high priest Onias the inhabitants of the holy city enjoyed undisturbed peace, and there was the strictest observance of the laws, because of his piety and hatred of wickedness. ² It also frequently happened that even the kings honored the Place and contributed to the glory of the temple with the most sumptuous gifts. ³ In fact, Seleucus, king of Asia, provided for all the expenses of the sacrificial cult out of his own revenues. ⁴ There was a certain Simon from the clan of Bilgah who held the post of chief administrator of the temple. This Simon had a dispute with the high priest over the city office of market controller. ⁵ Unable to prevail over Onias, he went to Apollonius son of Tharseas, who was governor of Coele-Syria and Phoenicia at that time, ⁶ and divulged the information that the treasury at Jerusalem was full of untold sums of money, such that their total was incalculable. These funds, he said, had not been brought as offerings to the account for sacrifices; rather, it was possible for them all to fall under the provisions of the king's right to confiscate. ⁷ In conversation with the king, Apollonius reported the disclosures concerning the money. The king summoned Heliodorus, the chief minister, and sent him with orders to collect the aforesaid money.

⁸ Heliodorus set out at once, on the pretext that he was making a tour of inspection of the cities of Coele-Syria and Phoenicia, but in fact he meant to carry out the king's intention. ⁹ On his arrival at Jerusalem he was greeted warmly by the high priest and the city. He then told them of what had been divulged and revealed the purpose of his coming. When he asked whether the money really was as described, ¹⁰ the high priest declared that, contrary to the false report of the impious Simon, it consisted partly of deposits of widows and orphans ¹¹ and partly of deposits of Hyrcanus the Tobiad, a man of very high position, and that the total amounted to four hundred talents of silver and two hundred of gold. ¹² The depositors had put

their trust in the sanctity of the place and in the dignity and inviolability of the temple venerated throughout the whole world; to violate their trust, he said, was inconceivable. 13 Heliodorus, acting under the king's orders, replied that he had no choice but to confiscate the money for the royal treasury. 14 On the day he had set, he made his entrance, intending to carry out his inspection of the funds. Great was the anguish throughout the city. 15 The priests in their priestly vestments cast themselves before the altar and prayed heavenward to the Establisher of the laws of deposits to keep them safe for the depositors. 16 The appearance of the high priest was enough to break one's heart, for his expression and his altered color displayed his mental anguish. 17 The man was, so to speak, immersed in fear and trembling, so that the onlookers saw clearly the pain in his heart. 18 People were dashing in droves from their houses to join in mass supplication against the threatened dishonor to the Place. 19 The women, girt with sackcloth under their breasts, thronged the streets. Some of the maidens who were kept in seclusion rushed to the gateways, others to the parapets, and some peered out through the windows; 20 they all were stretching forth their hands to heaven in prayers of entreaty. 21 It was a pitiful sight, with people of all classes joining in prostrating themselves, and the high priest in great anguish over what seemed about to happen. 22 While the people prayed to the almighty LORD to keep the deposits safe and secure for the depositors, 23 Heliodorus undertook to carry out the king's decree.

24 He was already there at the treasury with his bodyguards when the Master of the spirits and of every power miraculously intervened, so that all who had the audacity to accompany Heliodorus in their terror over the power of God completely lost their strength and courage. 25 For they saw a horse, splendidly caparisoned, bearing an awesome rider. Charging like a flood, the horse struck at Heliodorus with his forehoofs. They saw that the rider wore a golden suit of armor. 26 Two other young men appeared to Heliodorus. They were of remarkable strength and surpassing beauty, clad in magnificent raiment. They stood by on either side and whipped him unremittingly, laying blow upon blow upon him. 27 Suddenly, Heliodorus fell to the ground and was immersed in deep darkness. His attendants hastily snatched him up and placed him in a litter. 28 The man had just now entered the aforementioned treasury with a large entourage and a full bodyguard; they proceeded to carry him out as one who had found that arms were of no help to him and who manifestly had learned the power of God! 29 Heliodorus, through divine action, lay

prostrate, speechless, and deprived of all hope and help. 30 The Jews, however, blessed the LORD Who had glorified His Place by a miracle; and the temple, which shortly before had been full of fear and trepidation was filled with joy and gladness over the manifest intervention of the almighty LORD. 31 Some of Heliodorus' friends made haste to ask Onias to pray to the Highest and grant Heliodorus his life, for he was altogether on the point of breathing his last. 32 The high priest, indeed, was apprehensive lest the king come to the conclusion that Heliodorus had been the victim of foul play perpetrated by the Jews. Hence, he offered up a sacrifice for the man's recovery. 33 As the high priest was performing the rites of atonement, the same young men, dressed in the same garments, reappeared to Heliodorus. Standing over him, they said, "Be very grateful to Onias the high priest, because for his sake the LORD has granted you your life. 34 As for you, now that you have been scourged by an act from heaven, proclaim the majestic power of God to all." Having spoken, they disappeared.

35 Thereupon, Heliodorus offered up a sacrifice to the LORD and made the most lavish of vows to the One Who had preserved his life and, after greeting Onias, marched back with his army to the king. 36 He bore witness to all concerning the acts of the supreme God which he had seen with his own eyes. 37 When the king asked Heliodorus what now was the right sort of man to send to Jerusalem, he replied, 38 "If you have an enemy or a plotter against your kingdom, send him there. He will come back to you scourged, if he survives at all, because a divine power truly surrounds the place. 39 Indeed, He Who dwells on high watches over that place and defends it and smites and destroys those who come to do it injury." 40 Such was the outcome of the affair of Heliodorus and the preservation of the treasury.

NOTES

Ch. 3. For the reason why Jason of Cyrene chose to begin his history with the miraculous thwarting of Heliodorus, see p. 7 and AB vol. 41, p. 49.

It is almost certain that the seer who wrote Dan 11 viewed the thwarting of Heliodorus as a miracle; correct accordingly AB vol. 41, p. 49. The seer certainly saw the event as among the most significant in the reign of Seleucus IV and used it to identify him at Dan 11:20, even though the identity of the kings in Dan 11:11–21 is not a matter of doubt for anyone who knows the history of the Seleucid dynasty. In Dan 11:20, Seleucus IV is called "he who shall cause to come one who shall attempt to exact tribute from the Glory of the Kingdom." "He who shall cause to come one who shall attempt to exact tribute" (*m'byr nwgś*) is an allusion to Zech 9:8, where God promises to "encamp at My house as a guard . . . so that no exactor of tribute shall again come against them" (*wl' y'br 'lyhm 'wd ngś*).

"The Glory of the Kingdom" is an epithet for the temple. At Ps 96:7–9 the nations are told to come to God's courts and bow to the LORD in the "Holy Glory" (*hdrt qdš*). As God's courts are His temple, so is the "Holy Glory," and Ps 96:10 celebrates the LORD as king, so that "Holy Glory" and "Glory of the Kingdom" can be synonyms. See also Ps 29:1, 2, 10, where heavenly beings (surely in heaven) are told to praise the LORD, and the worshipers in the "Holy Glory" (*hdrt qdš*) are told to bow to Him, and God is said to be king. The meaning "the temple" for "Glory of His kingdom" (*hdr mlkwtw*) at Ps 145:12 fits the context beautifully. "The temple" may also be the meaning of "My glory [*hdry*] which I bestowed upon you" at Ezek 16:13–14, for the passage has God addressing Jerusalem. Cf. also II Chron 20:21.

By alluding to Zech 9:8, the seer in Dan 11:20 conveyed his belief that when Heliodorus failed to collect the money on deposit in the temple, it was God who prevented him, in fulfillment of the promise made through Zechariah.

Our passage and Dan 11:20 are the sole sources for the thwarting of Heliodorus. Josephus treasured reports of the miracles of his God, but as a proud descendant of the Hasmonaeans, he despised what he viewed as the grandiose false propaganda of the rival Oniad line of high priests. As for the implications of the allusion at Dan 11:20 to Zech 9:8, Josephus could easily have failed to notice the allusion; if he noticed it, his prejudices led him to reject its implications. See my article in *Studies Smith,* Part III, pp. 85, 116–19.

The testimony of the seer of Dan 11:20, who surely lived through the reign of Seleucus IV, guarantees that there is a kernel of truth in our chapter: Seleucus IV indeed sent someone to collect money at Jerusalem, but that person failed to collect it. Before we try to determine what really happened, we must consider the complicated narrative traditions reflected by the story here.

For our chapter, Jason of Cyrene drew on two sources with widely differing beliefs. One was the *Memoirs* of Onias IV; the other probably was the Common Source. See pp. 39–40.

Vss. 1 and 11 show characteristic traits of Onias IV, and so, probably, does vs. 2; see NOTES ad loc. Onias IV must therefore have told the entire story of his father's encounter with Heliodorus, and the substance of vss. 3–10 and 12–14, 23, must have stood in his account. The essential content even of vss. 15–22 also goes back to Onias IV, as is indicated by the fact that the verses are imitated in III 1:16 – 2:20. Naturally, the Common Source must have had a parallel narrative of the events of vss. 1–23 leading up to the divine intervention.

(I shall argue elsewhere that Third Maccabees was written sometime after the *Memoirs* of Onias IV, as counter-propaganda. The book demonstrates that not only Ptolemy VIII Euergetes II had put Jews in jeopardy; earlier, Ptolemy

IV Philopator had had criminal intentions against his Jewish subjects, and only divine intervention had saved them. Onias IV, on the other hand, had tried to show that Ptolemy VIII was only a temporary aberration and that Jews should put their trust in the Ptolemies.)

The references to "the Place" (*ton topon*) here in vss. 2, 12, and 18 are out of character for Onias IV, though in character for the Common Source, for Jason of Cyrene, and for the author of III 2:1–10. Jason may have put the references into the narrative he derived from Onias, or he could have drawn them from the parallel in the Common Source. Similarly, the author of III 2:1–10, 14, writing to refute the *Memoirs* of Onias IV, could have himself introduced references to "the Place" into his counterpart of Onias' narrative.

The story in vss. 24–36 is a compound of two versions, Version A (vss. 24–25, 29–30) and Version B (vss. 26–28, 31–36); see NOTE on vss. 24–39. Version A asserts the sanctity of the second temple and cannot belong to the *Memoirs* of Onias IV; it probably comes from the Common Source. Therefore, Version B comes from the *Memoirs*.

On vss. 37–39, see NOTE on vss. 24–39.

The story here, as it stands and in both of its earlier versions, is an example of a prevalent narrative pattern found in the ancient Near East and Greece, of how a god defended his temple from desecrators or robbers. See Niels Stokholm, "Zur Überlieferung von Heliodor, Kuturnaḫḫunte und anderen missglückten Tempelräubern," *Studia Theologica* 22 (1968), 1–22. A Babylonian clay tablet (perhaps of the second half of the sixth century B.C.E.) tells how Enlil and the other gods sent a *šēdu*-demon against Kuturnaḫḫunte, King of Elam, and his *nisakku*-official to prevent them from taking a diadem from the Ekur temple at Nippur (see Stokholm, "Überlieferung," pp. 8–18, and for the date of the tablet, A. H. Sayce, "The Chedorlaomer Tablets," *Proceedings of the Society of Biblical Archaeology* 28 [1906], 194, and 29 [1907], 13–14). A *šēdu* could have the form of a man-headed winged bull and thus would be a good parallel for the awesome rider and horse of Version A. Herodotus (viii 35–39) tells how the gods preserved the sacred treasures of Delphi from being despoiled by the army of Xerxes in 480 B.C.E. According to one account (Herodotus viii 37), thunderbolts from heaven struck the invaders, and two peaks broke off from Mount Parnassus and rolled down upon them. According to another (Herodotus viii 38–39), the Persian army was pursued by two superhuman figures armed as heavy infantrymen, parallel to the two young men of Version B. The evidence assembled by Stokholm makes it clear that whenever a king or his agent unexpectedly failed to despoil or desecrate a temple, Greeks and members of the ancient Near Eastern peoples would tend to follow the age-old pattern in telling of the event.

Now we can turn to ask, what really happened to prevent Heliodorus from seizing the money on deposit at the temple? No one can prove that superhuman beings did not intervene. Nevertheless, details of Version A contradict details of Version B (see NOTE on vss. 24–39), and we know such tales were stereotypes in the ancient Near East and Greece; these two facts strongly suggest that nothing supernatural occurred.

Version B, in which only Heliodorus saw his assailants, would be compatible with his having suffered an epileptic fit. Even if Heliodorus had been known to have been epileptic, ancient observers would have regarded the event as a divine intervention because of the timing of the attack and because all epileptic fits were commonly viewed as supernatural interventions by demons or deities; see Eric R. Dodds, *The Greeks and the Irrational* (Berkeley, Los Angeles, and London: University of California Press, 1951), pp. 66–68, 77, 83–85 (nn. 10, 11, and 20; with n. 20, cf. TB *Shabbat* 61a, 67a, and *Leviticus Rabbah* 26:5). My friends who are psychiatrists and psychologists tell me that it is unlikely hallucinations otherwise produced either Version A or Version B, for nothing suggests that Heliodorus and his men were mentally ill, drunk, or drugged.

According to Version A, all those present at the temple treasury saw the awesome rider and horse. Should we ascribe the supernatural detail simply to storytellers who followed the old pattern? There is another possibility. Heliodorus may have been of non-Greek, Syrian extraction (see NOTE on vs. 7, *Heliodorus . . . minister*); even if he was a Greek he would have been familiar with the old story pattern. Not long before, in 187 B.C.E., King Antiochus III had perished in an attempt to despoil a temple (see NOTE on 1:16). Heliodorus and his men may have been afraid of divine wrath and may have colluded with Onias III to produce Version A as their excuse for not obeying the king's order to collect the money. Rationalizing storytellers who found the awesome horse and rider hard to believe could then have produced Version B.

The author of IV 3:19 – 4:4 had as his source our chapter, but he wrote from memory, unable or unwilling to verify his own version; cf. the procedure of Josephus as described at AB vol. 41, pp. 60–61. Thus, the author of IV 3:19 – 4:4 has given the wrong cult epithet to Seleucus IV, has confused Heliodorus with Apollonius, and the single horseman of vss. 24–25 with the multiple whip bearers of vss. 26 and 33–34, and has made Apollonius himself beg for intercession.

Onias IV was well acquainted with the official terminology used in the Hellenistic kingdoms, and so was Jason of Cyrene. Our chapter is full of such terminology; see Bickerman, *Studies*, II, 161–71, nn. 16, 23, 26, 29, 37, 53–56, 86, 87. Bickerman's article on our chapter (ibid., pp. 159–91) opened the way to solving most of the problems but now requires many corrections.

Some Jews saw in the repulse of Lysias' first campaign (ch. 11) a repetition of the miraculous thwarting of Heliodorus. See introductory NOTE on ch. 11.

1. This Onias, who served under Seleucus IV (vs. 3), is the third high priest by that name in Josephus' list (*AJ* xii 4.1.156–57, 10.223–25; cf. xx 10.3.236). The author here implies that Onias punished severely all violators of the Torah. In Josephus' account, Onias III is a mere name, for Josephus wished to portray the later Oniads as insignificant or wicked; see Appendix XI. On allusions to Onias III in the contemporary apocalypses, see NOTE on 4:34.

We may be sure that Jason of Cyrene drew our verse from the *Memoirs* of Onias IV. Though our writer believes passionately in the sanctity of the temple in Jerusalem, he begins his narrative with the strange assertion that only Onias' piety (not divine providence!) gave the holy city the blessings of peace, an idea natural for the pen of the righteous priest's son.

undisturbed peace. Josephus challenged the claim; see my article in *Studies Smith*, Part III, pp. 86, 121.

2–3. The kings who ruled Judaea during the high priesthood of Onias III were the Seleucids Seleucus IV (187–175) and Antiochus IV; see also AB vol. 41, NOTES on 8:4 and 14:13. The generosity of the dynasty to the temple went back to the conquest of Jerusalem from the Ptolemies in 200 by Antiochus III, long before Onias III became high priest. Out of gratitude for Jewish cooperation, Antiochus III conferred great privileges on Jerusalem and Judaea (J. *AJ* xii 3.3–4.133–46; see Bickerman, *Studies*, II, 44–85).

The sacrificial cult at the temple of Jerusalem required large quantities of unblemished animals, grain, oil, and incense and was therefore expensive. The continued generosity of the king in the high priesthood of Onias III was remarkable, because the Seleucid empire came under severe financial strain when the Romans defeated it and in 188 imposed peace terms which deprived it of rich provinces and included payment in installments of a heavy indemnity. See AB vol. 41, NOTES on 8:7–8. To get money the kings were reduced to robbing temples; Antiochus III was killed attempting to rob one in 187 (Diodorus xxviii. 3, xxix. 15; Justin xxxii. 2. 1–2).

On the other hand, Hellenistic kings were pleased to increase their popularity by showing generosity to temples both Greek and non-Greek whenever their resources permitted (Bickerman, *Institutions,* pp. 123–24).

2. In the abridged history the expression "it happened that . . ." (*synebaine* or *synebê,* governing an accusative and an infinitive) seems to imply that what happened was something contrary to normal expectations (4:30, 5:2 and 18, 9:2 and 7, 10:5, 12:24 and 34 [cf. I 5:54 and 67], 13:7; cf. III 1:3, 5, 8, and 4:19, and Grimm, pp. 65–66). If so, our verse reflects the belief of Onias IV that, normally, Seleucids are impious; see above, p. 36.

However, one cannot exclude the possibilities that the expression means only "at the same time" (as at 7:1) or that even in the abridged history it is a meaningless piece of verbosity, as it is frequently in Polybius; see Jules-Albert de Foucault, *Recherches sur la langue et le style de Polybe* (Paris: "Les Belles Lettres," 1972), pp. 219–20.

the Place. The temple; the usage is contrary to the ideology of Onias IV. See pp. 36–37.

3. The pious writer is proud to report that King Seleucus paid all the expenses for the regular obligatory sacrifices at the temple. In so doing, Seleucus IV as king over the Jews probably continued practices of the kings of Israel and Judaea (see Ezek 45:17 and Roland de Vaux, *Ancient Israel* [New York: McGraw-Hill, 1961], p. 141) and of Persian kings (Ezra 6:9–10, 7:20–23) and of Antiochus III (J. *AJ* xii 3.3.140); see Bickerman, *Studies*, II, 72–81, and cf. J. *AJ* xi 1.3.16 and II 9:16. The texts on the kings of Persia and Antiochus III can be pressed to mean that the kings endowed a fund for sacrifice only on their personal behalf, but the most natural interpretation of Ezra 7:20–23 is that the king paid for the regular obligatory cult. In the time of Nehemiah the Jews themselves resolved to shoulder the expenses of the regular temple cult (Neh 10:33–34), perhaps because the king had ceased to do so, perhaps out of a desire to have the cult financed solely by the nation. A rabbinic text implies that the Pharisaic sages insisted the nation as a whole should defray the sacrificial expenses whereas the Boethusians (or Sadducees) held that the burden should be borne by generous individuals, and the rabbinic text says that the Pharisaic view prevailed (TB *Menahot* 65a; *Schol. Megillat*

Ta'anit 1 Nisan). Josephus agrees that in his time the expenses were borne by the nation (*AJ* iii 9.1.224, 10.1.237; *Ap.* ii 6.77). We can only guess when the Pharisaic view came to prevail; one might suggest the reign of John Hyrcanus (see J. *AJ* xiii 10.5.288–89) or that of Salina Alexandra (ibid., 16.2.408–9).

The writer tells of the generosity of Seleucus IV in order to contrast Onias III with his enemies: whereas Onias' piety induced the king himself to make huge contributions to the temple, wicked Simon instigated a royal attempt to violate the deposits there (vss. 5–11). The usurper Jason increased the royal taxes upon the Jews (4:7–9) and wicked Menelaus further increased the taxes (4:24), robbed the temple to bribe royal officials (4:32–34, 39–46), and served as the guide of Antiochus IV when he sacked the temple (5:15). The mention of Seleucus' contributions is not for the purpose of telling how the funds divulged to the king by Simon (vs. 6) came to be in the temple treasury. The royal government would not have tried to recover such contributions; see NOTE on vs. 6.

"Asia" was commonly used as an unofficial name for the Seleucid empire (Bickerman, *Institutions*, p. 5).

4. Jews and Christians were glad to put the wicked on view for condemnation. Simon was wicked, and his impious brother Menelaus was a usurper who purchased appointment to the high priesthood from wicked Antiochus IV. If the brothers had been of non-priestly descent, Jews and Christians would not be likely to conceal the fact. On the other hand, Jews and Christians on seeing the Greek word *phylê* would jump to the conclusion that it meant "tribe," as in the twelve tribes of Israel. But *phylê* also means "clan," even in biblical Greek (I Reigns 9:21, 10:21); see also Fritz Gschnitzer, "Phylarchos 5," PW, suppl. XI (1968), 1070–71. Hence, it is easy to pick the correct reading here. All Greek witnesses to the text and La^V and Sy have "Benjamin" as Simon's "tribe," La^L has *Balcea*, La^{BDM} and Arm (text) have *Balgei*, La^X has *Bargea*, and La^P has *Balgeus;* all reflect the name of the priestly clan Balga (Masoretic spelling: "Bilgah") mentioned at Neh 12:5, 18, and I Chron 24:14. Here, as often, the Latin and Armenian preserve the original reading.

In later times Jews held the clan of Bilgah in ignominy for impious acts of its members during the reign of Antiochus IV; see *M. Sukkah* 8:8, To. *Sukkah* 4:28, and Saul Lieberman, *Tosefta Ki-fshuṭah*, Part IV (*Mo'ed*) (New York: Jewish Theological Seminary of America, 5722=1962), pp. 908–10.

On the probable position of Simon and his family at this time in the clan politics of Jerusalem, see NOTE on 4:8.

We can only guess at the nature of Simon's dispute with Onias.

who held the post. The Greek *kathestamenos* means that he had been appointed or elected to his office. It was not his by heredity. See Bickerman, *Studies*, II, 161.

chief administrator of the temple. Whatever the Greek title *prostatês* means, it surely was that of a high office. Indeed, Simon's brother Menelaus became high priest. Simon himself, then, must have been a priest of high rank. The Greek noun *prostatês* ("chief," "guardian") and the related verbs (*prostatein, proistasthai*) are vague terms with many uses, civil, military, and religious; see Friedrich Preisigke, *Wörterbuch der griechischen Papyrusurkunden* (Berlin: Selbstverlag der Erben, 1925–31), III, 150, 218, 383. An inscription from

Delphi of 163/2 B.C.E. in the Delphic dialect mentions "the *prostatas* [=*pro-statês*] of the temple"; see Georges Daux, *Delphes au IIe et au Ier siècle* (Paris: É. de Boccard, 1936), pp. 431–33. At Dan LXX Bel 8 we hear of the "chief administrators of the temple," who are responsible for the food donated to the god Bel; there the perfect participle of a related verb is used (*prohestêkotes*). A priest in Egypt, presenting a petition in about 164 B.C.E., uses the present participle of the same verb to call himself "the chief adminis-trator" (*tou prostantos*) of a temple (*The Tebtunis Papyri*, vol. III, Part I, ed. by Arthur S. Hunt, J. Gilbart Smyly et al. [London: Humphrey Milford, 1933], no. 781, line 2). In translations from the Hebrew Bible the noun renders the vague *śar* ("officer"; I Chron 27:31, 29:6; II Chron 8:10). In the context dealing with the temple at II Chron 24:11 the noun renders the king's "supervisory bureaucracy" (*p^equddāh*) as well as the "supervisor" (*pāqīd*) ap-pointed by the high priest. On these derivatives of the root *pqd* see S. Yeivin, "*pqydwt*," Enc. Bib., VI (1971), 551–52 (in Hebrew).

At I 14:47 the verb *prostatein* is used of the prerogative of the high priest Simon to preside over all aspects of religious and civil life. Similarly, in the Greek manuscripts of Sir 45:24 the verb *prostatein* (or the related noun) is used of the prerogatives of Phineas and his descendants as high priests to be *chiefs over the temple* and over the people. At Num 25:12 only the priesthood is mentioned as the hereditary prerogative of the line of Phineas. Ben Sira probably drew on I Chron 9:20. There Phineas is said to have been in charge of the temple gatekeepers, with the (equally vague) title *nāgīd*, surely as the successor of his father Eleazar, whose headship over the princes of the Levites is called "the supervision [*p^equddat*] of those who kept guard over the sanctu-ary" (Num 3:32); see AB vol. 12, p. 70. We hear of high-ranking priests bear-ing the title "*nāgīd* of the house of God" (Neh 11:11; I Chron 9:11; II Chron 35:8), including the high priest himself (II Chron 31:10, 13; 35:8 with II Kings 23:4); the person bearing the title at II Chron 28:7 was probably a priest, too. Thus, both Greek *prostates* and Hebrew *nāgīd* were titles shared by the high priest with other high-ranking priests; see J. Liver, "*ngyd*," Enc. Bib., V (1968), 754–55 (in Hebrew).

In Josephus and in the New Testament the only high-ranking priest whose title contains the words "of the temple" is the *stratêgos* ("commander") of the temple. *Stratêgos*, too, is a vague term covering many civil, military, and even religious functions; see Hermann Bengtson, *Die Strategie in der hellenistischen Zeit* (3 vols.; München: Beck, 1937–52). The competence of the *stratêgos* of the temple, like that of Phineas and Eleazar, included both the command of the temple police (J. *BJ* vi 5.3.294; Acts 4:1, 5:24, 26) and influence over the priests who offered the daily sacrifices (J. *BJ* ii 17.2.409).

In rabbinic literature, the second-ranking priest receives the title "*s^egān* of the priests" (never "*s^egān* of the temple"). See Adolf Büchler, *The Priests and Their Cult* (Jerusalem: Mossad Harav Kook, 1966), pp. 78–88 (in Hebrew). Indeed, in the Targum "second-ranking priest" (*kōhēn mišneh*) is rendered "*s^egān* of the priests." Of Akkadian origin, *s^egān* ("appointee") is a synonym of *pāqīd* (which it renders in the Targum to Jer 29:26), *prostatês*, and *stra-têgos*; see R. A. Henshaw, "The office of *šaknu* in Neo-Assyrian Times," *Jour-nal of the American Oriental Society* 87 (1967), 517–25, and 88 (1968),

461–83, and T. L. Fenton, *"Skn,"* Enc. Bib., V (1968), 1045–46 (in Hebrew). The rabbinic word *mmwnh* ("appointee") is similar. Büchler presented persuasive arguments for identifying the *stratêgos* of the temple with the *s*ᵉ*gān* of the priests (*The Priests and Their Cult*, pp. 85–88 [in Hebrew]); cf. Schürer (New English version), II, 277–78.

Thus it becomes probable that Simon here was the second-ranking priest and would have been called *s*ᵉ*gān* by the rabbis. There is a possible confirmation of this suggestion in the confused traditions of the origin of the Oniad schism at TB *Menaḥot* 109b and TP *Yoma* 6:3(end), p. 43c–d. There the schism is said to have arisen from envy between Onias (Ḥonyā or Nᵉḥunyōn) and Simeon, sons of the high priest Simeon the Just. Josephus, too, reports that the high priests Onias and Jason and Onias-Menelaus were all sons of the high priest Simon II (*AJ* xii 5.1.237–38). Josephus here reflects anti-Oniad propaganda, but if the propaganda was believable, we may take it as probable that the name of the father of Simon and Menelaus of the clan of Bilgah was "Simon." The rabbinic traditions may have arisen from the same propaganda. In the rabbinic traditions, the jealous brother undermines the position of his high priestly sibling by dressing him in women's garments. The *s*ᵉ*gān* had the function of dressing the high priest in his vestments (*Sifra Ṣav* to Lev 8:7, sec. 1, par. 6, p. 41a Weiss).

In support of his theory that the funds mentioned in vs. 6 were from the king's own contributions to the temple cult, Bickerman (*Studies*, II, 161–62) equated the functions of the *prostatês* at the temple in Jerusalem with those of the *epistatês* in temples of Ptolemaic Egypt who was appointed by the king to control the expenditures of a sanctuary. However, there is no evidence for the equation, and the theory is unnecessary to explain the story of Heliodorus.

office of market controller. Gr.: *agoranomia.* We have no further information on this office at Jerusalem, though we can judge its great importance from the quarrel reported here; cf. *Leviticus Rabbah* 1:8. The office of *agoranomos* as supervisor of just weights and measures is frequently mentioned in rabbinic literature; see Samuel Krauss, *Griechische und lateinische Lehnwörter im Talmud, Midrasch und Targum,* Teil II (Berlin: Calvary, 1899), pp. 11–12. In Greek cities an *agoranomos* supervised and policed the market; he inspected merchandise for quality, controlled the licensing of merchants to sell their goods in the city marketplace (*agora*), saw to the legal validity of transactions and to the documents recording them, and might also have had religious duties. See Anneliese Mannzmann, *"Agoranomoi,"* Der kleine Pauly, I (1964), 142; Arnold H. M. Jones, *The Greek City* (Oxford: Clarendon Press, 1940), pp. 215–17, 230, 240. In Ptolemaic Egypt an *agoranomos* was a registrar of documents; see A. Bouché-Leclercq, *Histoire des Lagides* (Paris, 1903–7; reprinted, Bruxelles: Culture et Civilisation, 1963), IV, 134–35, and H. I. Bell, "The *agoranomeion to kai mnêmeion,"* Archiv für Papyrusforschung 6 (1920), 104–7.

5–8. The events reported here may reflect the privileged position of Jerusalem and Judaea; see AB vol. 41, NOTE on 1:4, *nations.* Simon here goes to the provincial governor, but the governor does not feel competent to act by himself, and the king entrusts the matter to the chief minister! However, both Greeks and non-Greeks normally hesitated to offend the gods by infringing on the sanctity of a temple, and the magnitude of the reported treasures required that a trusted official carry out the task.

5. *Apollonius son of Tharseas.* Such is the reading of VLa^{LV}, confirmed by La^{BDM} (*filium Tharsei*) and La^X (*Tarse;* La^X frequently omits *h* after *t* and writes *e* for *ae*). Though rare, "Tharseas" is attested as a Greek name (Wilhelm Pape and G. Benseler, *Wörterbuch der griechischen Eigennamen* [3d ed.; reprinted, Graz: Akademische Druck-und Verlaganstalt, 1959], I, 481; Markwart Michler, "Tharseas," PW, suppl. XI [1968], 1259–60). "Thraseas" (variant spelling: *Thrasaias*) was much more common as a name and is the reading of many witnesses to the text. One can understand how scribes would turn the rare name into the common one, especially when both names have the same meaning ("bold"). It is unnecessary to assume that the Apollonius here was identical to Apollonius son of Menestheus at 4:4 and 21 (cf. Abel, p. 318). Indeed, Jason of Cyrene seems to have sensed that his readers would be surprised at the sequence of persons named "Apollonius" in the important office of governor, so he added the words "at that time," which otherwise would be superfluous. Only a short time later, the governor of Coele-Syria and Phoenicia was Apollonius son of Menestheus. Nor need Apollonius here be identified with Ptolemaios son of Thraseas, who held the same post under Antiochus III (OGIS 230; cf. Bengtson, *Strategie,* II, 161–63).

The early medieval Christian traveler Theodosius, probably following the Jewish folk tradition at J. *AJ* i 6.1.127, took the word *Thars-* here to mean "of Tarsus," the great city of Cilicia from which the apostle Paul came (*De situ Terrae sanctae* 32, in *Itinera hierosolymitana saeculi IIII–VIII,* ed. by Paul Geyer ["Corpus scriptorum ecclesiasticorum Latinorum," vol. 38; Prague and Vienna: Tempsky; Leipzig: Freytag, 1898], p. 150). Abel accepted Theodosius' reading. However, all witnesses to the text have the word in the genitive case. To mean "of Tarsus" here it would have to be an adjective in the accusative. Moreover, both Jason of Cyrene and his probable source, Onias IV, were Hellenized Jews who knew how to spell "Tarsus" (see 4:30) and had no reason to change the spelling to agree with a folk tradition. No other evidence connects the Apollonius at 4:4 and 21 with Tarsus.

governor. Gr. *stratêgos;* see Bickerman, *Institutions,* p. 198.

Coele-Syria and Phoenicia. This was the huge province which included Judaea and all Seleucid territory between the Euphrates and the Mediterranean except for the *Seleukis,* the privileged area of Greek cities in northern Syria. See AB vol. 41, NOTE on 7:8.

6. *divulged the information.* The Greek word *prosangellein* is used of denouncing misconduct; cf. Bickerman, *Studies,* II, 162, n. 23.

treasury at Jerusalem. The rest of our chapter makes it clear that the treasury is the temple treasury. Cf. I 14:49. The first syllable of the Greek word *gazophylakion* is derived from the same Persian root as is the rabbinic Hebrew word for the temple treasurer (*gzbr*).

their total. Gr. *to plêthos tôn diaphorôn.* Though *diaphorôn* can mean "difference," or "balance," the first part of our verse and the rest of the story show that Simon was speaking not of balances but of solid cash on deposit, so that *diaphorôn* here is a synonym of the word "money" (*chrêmatôn*) earlier in our verse, a meaning it has at 1:35 and often in Hellenistic Greek, though scribes and the Latin translators were puzzled (cf. Bickerman, *Studies,* II, 163–65).

These funds . . . confiscate. The Greek of our passage is difficult. The language appears to be technical, but instructive parallels are few, and the textual variants show that the scribes, too, were puzzled. Nevertheless, the general outline of the verse is clear. The author loathes the factious Simon (cf. vs. 10) but does not wish to portray the Seleucid government at this point as absolutely unscrupulous. Seleucus IV and his officials, taught perhaps by the fate of Antiochus III, will not stoop to robbing funds consecrated for use in offering sacrifices. According to Jewish law such funds were inviolable; see M. Haran, *"Khnh,"* Enc. Bib., IV (1962), 43–44 (in Hebrew). According to rabbinic sources, the donor to the sacrificial funds lost all power to recover his gift from the very moment of his declaration that he was giving and even from the very moment of his mental decision; see TB *Qiddushin* 28b and "Heqdēš," Talmudic Encyclopedia, X (1961), 353–55 (in Hebrew). Greek law, too, held such funds to be inviolable and irrecoverable, though only from the moment that there had been an act of consecration or formal receipt, such as the temple clerk's entry of the acquisition in the temple account book. See *Syll.*[3] 672, lines 9–21, and see E. Pottier, "Dedicatio," *Dictionnaire des antiquités grecques et romaines,* ed. by Ch. Daremberg and Edm. Saglio, II 1 (1892), 41–42, and "Consecratio," ibid., I 2 (n.d.), 1448; Th. Homolle, "Donarium," ibid., II 1, 367b; Lieberman, *Hellenism,* pp. 147–52; Georges Daux, *Delphes au IIe et au Ier siècle* (Paris: É. de Boccard, 1936), p. 693.

Any money supplied by Seleucus IV for the sacrificial cult must have been formally received by the temple and was thus irrecoverable; it cannot have been included in the money reported by Simon. To take temple property was the crime of sacrilege (*hierosylia*). Nowhere in our chapter does the Greek root occur, though Jason of Cyrene used it to condemn the depredations of Lysimachus and Menelaus (4:39 and 42, 13:6) and Antiochus IV (9:2). Indeed, the point belabored in the story of the miracle (vss. 10–12, 15, 22) is God's protection of *private deposits* in His temple, not His protection of sacred funds or His exclusion of pagans from holy soil (cf. Bickerman, *Studies,* II, 160–72). The author of IV 4:3–6 also understood that Simon revealed the existence of private deposits. See also NOTES on vss. 10–14. Although a Greek could consecrate money to a god for safekeeping in his temple and still treat the money as an ordinary deposit (Th. Homolle, DAGR, II 1, 367a), that procedure was not open to a Jew: if a Jew consecrated his money, he gave it irrevocably to the temple.

had . . . offerings to. I translate here the difficult technical vocabulary, *prosenenkein . . . pros,* found only in A. All other witnesses to the text have the simple reading *prosēkein . . . pros,* which would make our passage mean "did not belong to."

In translations from the Hebrew Bible the verb and preposition found in A regularly render *hqryb 'l* "bring near to," "offer as a sacrifice to, at, or upon" (Lev 1:1 and 15, 2:8, 9:9; Num 5:25). This use of the expression exists also in non-Jewish Greek (Aristotle *Fragment* 101). The verb also means "pay" (Polybius xv. 8. 7; J. *AJ* xvii 11.4.319). Simon could well have so expressed himself in order to say that the funds were not God's sacred property (Greek: *hiera;* Hebrew: *heqdēš*).

Bickerman (*Studies,* II, 164–65) tried to interpret our passage to say that the money of the royal contributions had not been added to the sacrificial account (as it should have been). His interpretation is improbable. Under Greek law the money *might* then have been recoverable by the king, but surely the king would also have been able to prosecute the temple officials, including the high priest, for misconduct. Our story then would have contained indignant protests against Simon's false accusations (cf. 4:1–2).

There is no evidence that Jewish law ever permitted the priests to make free use of the surplus balance of the money given to pay for sacrifices. The assertion that in the Herodian temple the clergy made such use of the surplus balance (Bickerman, *Studies,* II, 165–66) rests on a misreading of a passage in Louis Finkelstein, *Akiba: Scholar, Saint, and Martyr* (New York: Covici-Friede, 1936), p. 283; see *M. Sheqalim* 4:3.

Prosenenkein is an active infinitive in indirect discourse here, and the subject is not expressed. I have taken the subject to be the vague "they" (the depositors) and have rendered the expression by the passive voice.

fall . . . confiscate. Greek: *hypo tên tou basileôs exousian pesein tauta.* The word *pesein* itself, which I have translated "fall," might mean "be confiscated," but I think, following Bickerman (*Studies,* II, 166, n. 53), that here we have an idiom *piptein hypo,* meaning "come under the provisions or classification of." Cf. 7:36, and see also Polybius ii. 14. 7, and Mayser, II², 514.

Exousia is the Greek word for all powers which the king has by virtue of his position as king (see W. Foerster, "*exousia,*" *Theological Dictionary of the New Testament,* ed. by Gerhard Kittel [Grand Rapids, Mich.: Eerdmans, 1964], II, 562–63). In the context here it can mean "the king's right to confiscate." See also NOTE on vss. 10–14. The word "all" (*hapanta*) is attested by VLaLXV.

7. *In conversation.* The Greek would fit either a chance conversation or an appointment made specially for the purpose.

disclosures. The Greek word (*mênythentôn*) usually refers to the denunciation of something illegal. See NOTE on vss. 10–14.

Heliodorus . . . minister. Heliodorus had been brought up from childhood with Seleucus IV and is reported to have brought about his death in 175 (Hans Volkmann, "Heliodorus I," Der kleine Pauly, II [1967], 995; see NOTE on 4:7). On the office of chief minister, see Bickerman, *Institutions,* p. 197.

The name "Heliodorus" ("gift of the sun") was very common in Syria, reflecting the popularity of sun worship there (Louis Robert, "Sur des inscriptions de Délos," in *Études déliennes* [Bulletin de correspondance hellénique, supplément I; Paris: É. de Boccard, 1973], p. 443).

8. One might have thought that the Jews' habit of obedience to the king (see NOTE on 1:7, *Jason . . . Kingdom*) would have made such subterfuges unnecessary. Heliodorus, however, must have been aware that some Jews would view his mission as an affront to their God. Hotheads might try to obstruct him. If his arrival was a surprise, even the prayers of the nonviolent majority would have less time to be effective, and none of the depositors could withdraw his funds.

9. Far from bringing any accusation against the high priest, Heliodorus asks him directly about the reported money.

the high priest and the city. Such is the reading of VL' 55 311 La (La^V is ambiguous) Sy Arm, and all witnesses agree in the similar passage at 4:22; however, A here has "the high priest of the city." Although Jason of Cyrene as a Jewish Greek might treat Onias as the high priest of the city-state of Jerusalem, the reading of A is corrupt already in having "high priest" in the nominative case after a preposition, and the omission of *kai* ("and") is probably another mistake.

10–14. The author has already presented the Seleucid government as reasonably scrupulous (see NOTES on vss. 3 and 6), and certainly he believes in the honesty of Onias III. If Onias III is quoted as saying that the money in question consisted of deposits, he must be telling the truth. Violation of a deposit was a very serious matter in Greek law (G. Humbert, "Depositum," DAGR, II 1 [1892], 103–4). Even more serious was violation of deposits in a temple (Th. Homolle, "Donarium," ibid., col. 367a; Ed. Cuq, "Sacrilegium," ibid., IV 2 [n.d.], 981). Both Jews and Greeks held that deposits in the Jewish temple were normally inviolable!

The key to understanding the story is probably the mention of Hyrcanus the Tobiad. Simon and his faction and the Seleucid government could have viewed Hyrcanus as a rebel whose goods were forfeit (Bickerman, *Institutions*, p. 12), whereas Onias and the mass of Jews who supported him may have viewed Hyrcanus as no rebel but as an independent ruler; see NOTE on vs. 11. Jerusalem and the temple had not received the privilege of being a place of asylum where the person and goods even of a rebel could have been protected (cf. 4:33). The course followed by the king and his agents shows that the case of Hyrcanus was ambiguous: Seleucus IV made no attempt to wage war against Hyrcanus (J. *AJ* xii 4.11.234), and we do not hear that Onias III was charged with giving aid to a rebel by accepting his deposits; but still the government, hard pressed for money, jumped at the opportunity to confiscate Hyrcanus' wealth. Meanwhile, Jews who saw that Seleucus did not wage war on Hyrcanus could view the attempt to confiscate Hyrcanus' deposits in the temple as an affront against their God. The widows and orphans in vs. 10, too, may have been widows and orphans of men (followers of Hyrcanus?) whom the royal government viewed as rebels.

10. Jewish widows at this time could own their dowries and the property bequeathed to them by their husbands. See further Bickerman, *Studies,* II, 169–70.

11. The reference at AB vol. 41, p. 309, to a NOTE here is a misprint. The NOTE is the one on 5:11, *treating . . . war.*

The Greek *tou Tôbiou* would normally be translated "son of Tobias," but the Hyrcanus of our verse is surely identical to the striking personality mentioned in J. *AJ* xii 4.6–11.186–236, Hyrcanus son of Joseph son of Tobias. Modern scholars call the members of Hyrcanus' powerful family "the Tobiads," but Josephus is the only source who names them as a group, and he, too, calls them only "the descendants of Tobias" (*hoi paides tou Tôbiou* or *hoi Tôbia hyieis*) even though Joseph was the father of the members in the narrative (*AJ* xii 5.1.238–39; *BJ* i 1.1.31). On Josephus' stories and on the Tobiad family in the third and second centuries B.C.E. see my article, "The Tales of the Tobiads," in *Studies Smith,* Part III, pp. 85–123. A brief sketch will suffice here.

Hyrcanus' father, Joseph, made a fortune as a tax farmer for the Ptolemies in Palestine and Syria in the last quarter of the third century B.C.E. Hyrcanus, born between 226 and 223, was the youngest of eight sons. A precocious and clever lad, he roused the envy of his brothers. In 210, Hyrcanus won the favor of Ptolemy IV by his wit and by extravagant gifts to the king and queen and thus estranged even his father. His brothers he inflamed to the point that they tried to kill him. After killing two of his brothers, Hyrcanus escaped to the family stronghold in Transjordan at the site now called 'Arāq el-Emīr. There he became a tax collector for the Ptolemaic government.

The Ptolemaic government, however, soon lost its hold on Syria and Palestine when Antiochus III conquered the area (202–197). The high priest Simon and the Tobiads except for Hyrcanus transferred their loyalties to the victor, but Hyrcanus continued to look to the Ptolemies and maintained himself as a practically independent ruler in Transjordan. Antiochus III, at the peak of his power, probably felt Hyrcanus could be safely ignored. The crippling terms of the Peace of Apameia in 188, which followed the disastrous defeat of the Seleucid empire at the hands of Rome, left Antiochus III and Seleucus IV in no position to risk their resources in challenging Hyrcanus. They may well have refrained from declaring him to be an enemy of the realm, even though he controlled territory claimed by the kingdom. Hyrcanus, for his part, made no move against territory actually controlled by the Seleucid empire.

As a sort of robber baron preying on the neighboring Arabs, Hyrcanus probably could not trust even his own subordinates and therefore would need a safe place to deposit his loot. Onias III was Hyrcanus' second cousin. The prudent high priest was always loyal to the Seleucids, but saw no wrong in accepting Hyrcanus' deposits. In doing so, however, he showed himself to be an enemy of Hyrcanus' brothers. Josephus lets us know that Menelaus, the later usurper of the high priesthood (II 4:23–25), was an ally of Hyrcanus' brothers (*AJ* xii 5.1.239). The remark at II 4:23, that Menelaus was the brother of Onias' enemy Simon, surely is intended to associate wicked Menelaus with his wicked sibling. Here we gain a picture of clan politics among the Jews, with Onias III and Hyrcanus standing on one side, and Simon, Menelaus, and the Tobiads standing on the other.

Hyrcanus eventually committed suicide, believing it was hopeless to resist the strong Antiochus IV. His despair probably followed Antiochus' conquest of most of Ptolemaic Egypt in 169.

Jason of Cyrene and the abridger are intent on showing the power of God and the sanctity of the temple of Jerusalem. They could easily have omitted Hyrcanus' name. The original author, whoever he was, would not have mentioned the name to an audience who knew nothing of Hyrcanus. Yet an audience who knew of Hyrcanus would perceive how the high priest weakened his own case by identifying one of the depositors as a man who could be viewed as a rebel against the kingdom! Only Onias IV, son of Onias III and admirer of Hyrcanus, had reason to show how God protected the deposits of Hyrcanus in answer to the prayers of Onias III. Thus our passage must be derived from the work of Onias IV.

The sums declared by Onias are far from incalculable but also not insignificant. Assuming that the ratio of silver to gold was one to ten (F. M. Heichelheim, "Money," OCD[2], p. 698), the total on deposit amounted to 2,400 talents of silver. The annual installments of the heavy indemnity imposed by the Romans in 188 upon the Seleucid empire were only of 1,000 talents of silver (Polybius xxi. 42. 19 Paton [43. 19 Buettner-Wobst]).

12. Ancient depositors chose to put their money in temples for safety, for the deposits there did not bear interest (Bickerman, *Studies,* II, 168–69). The inviolability Onias and the author claim here for the temple depends on its holiness, not on any privilege conceded to it by the king. On the expression "the place," see second NOTE on vs. 2. Here I leave the word uncapitalized, for there would be no point in alluding to Deut 12:5, etc., when speaking to a pagan.

14. I do not understand why Heliodorus "set a day" and did not proceed to carry out his inspection on the day of his arrival when none of the surprised depositors could have had time to smuggle out his money.

The treasury must have been in a part of the temple mount open to pagans, for the narrator never brings up the issue that Heliodorus' mere entry into the temple treasury would violate the law. Contrast III 1:10 – 2:23, and also IV 4:11, where the author knows the location of the treasuries in the temple of Herod. See Moses Hadas, *The Third and Fourth Books of Maccabees* (New York: Harper, 1953), pp. 95–96, 164–65. Even in the Herodian temple the treasuries may have been accessible to pagans, for J. *BJ* v 5.2.200 is obscure in giving their location. See George A. Smith, *Jerusalem: The Topography, Economics, and History* (London: Hodder and Stoughton, 1907–8), II, 510, and Israel S. Horowitz, *Jerusalem* (Jerusalem: Rubin Mass, 1964), pp. 366–67 (in Hebrew).

The inspection must have had to do with the nature of the deposits, not with the inviolable sacrificial fund. No honest subject of the king could have objected to an inspection of the sacrificial funds. Nothing tells us how the sacrificial funds were kept in this period. They may have been kept in specially marked vessels (see Samuel Krauss, *Talmudische Archäologie* [Leipzig: Fock, 1910–12], II, 415–16) or heaped up on the floor as is implied at *M. Sheqalim* 3:2–4 (describing the practice in the decades which preceded the destruction of the temple). The deposits of Hyrcanus and his accomplices, however, would have been kept in containers bearing their names and would have been immediately vulnerable to seizure; cf. Tobit 1:14, 5:3, 9:5.

14–23. *Great . . . decree.* A fine example of the sensational style of writing cultivated by Jason of Cyrene and deplored by Polybius (ii. 56). See above, pp. 20–21. The pattern of mass supplication may be derived from Joel 2:15–17 and was imitated at III 1:16 – 2:20 (see introductory NOTE on this chapter).

15. The officiating priests naturally wore their vestments. The point here is that even the priests who were not officiating on that day put on their vestments to pray. Clearly, the garments were believed to have special efficacy; cf. III 1:16 and J. *AJ* xi 8.4.327, 5.331. The vestments are described at J. *AJ* iii 7.1–7.151–78.

The laws of deposits are at Exod 22:6–14.

16. The changed countenance of the high priest is a motif used by Onias IV to contrast pious Onias III with contemptible Onias II. See Appendix XI.

17. *immersed.* See NOTE on vs. 27.

18. *the Place.* See second NOTE on vs. 2.

19. Women in mourning wore robes of goat's hair ("sackcloth") so draped as to expose the breasts and made fast ("girt") about the waist. See Abel, p. 322, and the woman holding the dead child in the picture at the left edge of the lowest band of painting on the west wall of the synagogue of Dura-Europos (published in Erwin R. Goodenough, *Jewish Symbols in the Greco-Roman Period,* vol. 11 [New York: Pantheon, 1964], plate VIII and fig. 335).

One might judge from our verse that Jewish women ordinarily were not to be found in the streets, but see Sir 9:7 in its context. The writer's wording implies that not all maidens were kept in seclusion, though he approves of the practice, like Ben Sira (Sir 7:24, 42:10–12). The writer knows how to construct a rhetorical climax. If maidens peering out through windows appear last, the "gateways" (*pylônas;* see first NOTE on 1:8) here must be those of the houses, not those of the city or the temple, and similarly the "parapets" (*teichê*) must be those of the balconies or rooftops, and some of the Latin translators understood; cf. III 1:18. The writer's opinions are close to those of Philo on the restrictions to be observed by Jewish females (*De specialibus legibus* ii. 31. 169–71, *In Flaccum* 11.89).

24–39. Moffatt (*Apocrypha and Pseudepigrapha of the Old Testament,* ed. by R. H. Charles [Oxford: Clarendon Press, 1913], I, 135) perceived the probable reason for the overloaded character and inconsistencies in the description of the punishment of Heliodorus: Jason of Cyrene found two accounts and, like many ancient pagan and Jewish writers, rejected neither but wove both into one narrative (Bickerman, *Studies,* II, 188; Herodotus in viii 37–39 also rejected none of the traditions, but he presented them separately, refraining from weaving them together). Bickerman carried out the fundamental analysis of our passage (*Studies,* II, 172–90), though one must make many corrections in the details of his treatment.

Although the verb *ôphthê* ("was seen") in vs. 25 can refer either to physical objects or to dreams (e.g., at Acts 2:3), the helpless terror of Heliodorus' attendants in vs. 24 shows that they, too, saw the horse and rider. Those supernatural beings should have been sufficient to stop Heliodorus. Yet in vs. 26 two more young men appear "to him" (i.e., to Heliodorus). Indeed, Heliodorus' fall is described in vs. 27 by the adverb "suddenly" or "unexpectedly" (*aphnô*), inappropriate if the spectators had been able to see the approach of the horse and rider. Heliodorus' attendants are practically paralyzed, yet in vs. 27 they have the courage and strength to proceed to pick him up and carry him out in a litter (Greek verb: *epheron,* in the imperfect tense). For the sake of more elegant English, I have translated the pluperfect Greek verb in vs. 29, *erripto,* as "lay prostrate," but one should note the literal meaning, for it implies that Heliodorus still was cast down prostrate, as if his attendants had not picked him up. Vss. 24–25 and 29 are thus incompatible with vss. 26–28. The scribe responsible for La^{-V} may have perceived the incompatibility, for he omitted (deliberately?) the words I have translated by the sentence, "Charging . . . forehoofs."

The incompatibility exists despite the fact that the writter was an artist who, far from cutting and pasting passages from his sources, restyled what they gave him and worked it into a unified narrative, omitting duplications; these considerations dispose of the objections of Doran (*Temple Propaganda*, p. 19, second par., and pp. 20–21).

Ancient believers in divine intervention in human affairs enjoyed two types of stories. In one, the god and his worshipers are the focus of attention; the god's power destroys the adversary or overwhelms him, and the faithful and even outsiders praise the mighty deity, and there is no further interest in the adversary. Such are the stories in Exod 1 – 15:21 and II Chron 32:1–23, and there were similar stories among the Greeks (see Nilsson, II, 105–6, 225–28; *Inscriptiones Graecae, Editio minor*, vol. IV, Part I, no. 128, lines 55–77). Greeks took delight in stories of corporeal manifestations of armed superhuman beings (Bickerman, *Studies*, II, 176–77), though as time went on they tended more and more to describe divine intervention rather in terms of the power of the god over natural forces (Nilsson, II, 226–27). Jewish stories in this genre do not differ significantly from pagan. If Israelites could not see their God bearing arms (except metaphorically), they could see His supernatural agents (Josh 5:13; II Kings 6:17), and the forces of nature, too, are the LORD's agents (Ps 104:4). In the other type of miracle tale, the victim or beneficiary of the god's wondrous act goes on to admit the power of the god and usually also to proclaim it widely. Such stories were often presented in the first person, as in Dan 4 and in many Greek texts (see Nilsson, II, 228; Bickerman, *Studies*, II, 186–87), but they could also appear in the third person (e.g., *The Oxyrhynchus Papyri*, vol. XI [London: Egypt Exploration Fund, 1915], no. 1382), especially when incorporated into a historical narrative, as at II Kings 5. Although native Greeks seem not to have told stories in which a victim of divine intervention thereafter had the duty of proclaiming the might of the god, such stories were common in Greek-speaking Asia (Bickerman, *Studies*, II, 186–87).

Let us now examine our two incompatible sets of verses. In vss. 24–25 and 29 we have a horse and rider, visible to all, who overwhelm Heliodorus and leave his attendants powerless. Vs. 29 is linked in Greek to vs. 30 by the Greek paired particles *men* and *de*, and the rhetorical antithesis between the two verses is well constructed: in vs. 29 Heliodorus lies hopeless and helpless, and in vs. 30 the joyous faithful give thanks for the miracle. We have here in vss. 24–25 and 29–30 a story of the first type, which we shall call "Version A."

In vss. 26–28 beings visible only to Heliodorus flog him, but his attendants are able to help him. They remove him from the place guarded by his invisible assailants. In vs. 31 we hear of more efforts by Heliodorus' comrades, which could not have been made by the demoralized attendants in vs. 24. The next verses give the sequel to these efforts and hence belong with vs. 31. In vss. 34–36 Heliodorus becomes a proclaimer to everyone of the greatness of God. Thus, in vss. 26–28 and 31–36 we have a story of the second type, which we shall call "Version B."

Version A probably comes from the Common Source; Version B is derived from the *Memoirs* of Onias IV. See introductory NOTE to this chapter.

Vss. 37–39 are strange. They can be attached only to Version B, but other stories of this type do not go into detail on where the victim carried out his task of proclaiming (Bickerman, *Studies*, II, 187, 190). Moreover, though Version B belongs to Onias IV, vss. 38–39 assert that the temple of Jerusalem is the Chosen Place. Onias IV was satisfied to let Heliodorus serve as the witness to how God acted on behalf of Onias III. Other pious Jews, however, knew that Heliodorus did not proceed on his own initiative but only as the agent of Seleucus. Agents of royal wickedness can be destroyed, as were the troops and commanders of Ahaziah at II Kings 1:9–12, but if they survive, they should return to the king to teach him his lesson, as do the last commander and his troops at II Kings 1:13–16. Hence, we may guess that a pious Jew, probably Jason of Cyrene himself, felt a lack and added vss. 37–39 to Version B.

24. *Master of the spirits and of every power.* "Master" translates Gr. *dynastês*. "God of the spirits" occurs in the Hebrew Bible (Num 16:22, 27:16), but "Master of the spirits" does not. A similar expression occurs at 14:46. The difference between "Master [*dynastês*] of the spirits" and "Lord [*kyrios*] of the spirits" may be only a matter of a translator's preference in rendering a Hebrew or Aramaic expression. "Lord of the spirits" occurs in two inscriptions contemporary with Jason of Cyrene, of Jewish prayers for vengeance, found on the Greek island of Rheneia, and it occurs also in Greek liturgies and magical texts; see Adolf Deissmann, *Light from the Ancient East* (New York: George H. Doran, 1927), pp. 413–22. "Lord of the spirits" is also common in the "Similitudes" or "Parables" of Enoch (Enoch 37–71; e.g., at 38:2, 4, 6), and the Greek word for "Lord" was probably *kyrios*. I hope to show elsewhere that the Similitudes probably were written not long after the death of Judas Maccabaeus by a member of a sect different from the sect of the author of Enoch 85–90. The author of the Common Source of First and Second Maccabees may have belonged to the same sect as the author of the Similitudes (see also AB vol. 41, p. 94, n. 17). Finally, "Lord of the spirits" occurs in an Iranian text which may go back to the time of Alexander the Great; see E. W. West, *Pahlavi Texts*, Part I (Vol. V of *Sacred Books of the East*, ed. by F. Max Müller; Oxford: Clarendon Press, 1880), p. 192, and Samuel K. Eddy, *The King Is Dead* (Lincoln: University of Nebraska Press, 1961), pp. 15–19, 26–32(top), 343–49.

The scribes of V and L found the divine epithet "Master of the spirits" so unfamiliar that in V "the spirits" (*tôn pneumatôn*) has been changed to "all the patriarchs" (*tôn pantôn paterôn*), and in L "spirits" has been changed to "patriarchs" and the more familiar "Lord" has been inserted, to make "Lord of the patriarchs and Master of every power." Indeed, "Master" (*dynastês*) is only rarely used of God in Greek translations from the Hebrew (Gen 49:24 and Sir 46:5, 6, 16). The scribes could make their alterations all the more easily if the words before them were abbreviated, "spirits" as *pnatôn* and "patriarchs" as *prôn*.

"Power" (*exousia*) usually means the inherent ability of God, but here it is used parallel to "spirits" and with the word "master," so it probably means a concrete supernatural being; see Foerster, in TDNT, II (1964), 564–65, 571–73. The same use of the word may exist at Enoch 41:9, 61:10.

miraculously intervened. Lit. "performed a great manifest intervention" (*epiphaneian megalên epoiêsen*); see NOTE on 2:21.

25–26. Interest in the personal appearance and clothing of supernatural beings is common to both pagans and Jews (*Inscriptiones Graecae, Editio minor*, vol. IV, Part I, no. 128, lines 63–64; Dionysius of Halicarnassus vi 13 and Plutarch *Aemilius Paulus* 25.1–2; Pliny *Epistulae* vii 27; Ezek 9:3 and 11, 10:2 and 6–7; Dan 12:6–7; Test Levi 8:21).

The narrative portions of the Hebrew Bible do not tell stories of manifest interventions against the enemies of Israel by such figures. Our writer here, rather, drew on Greek patterns such as those of Dionysius of Halicarnassus vi 13, although, as a Jew, he did not call the intervening figures gods (Doran, *Temple Propaganda*, pp. 99–100, 102–3).

25. Though Jeremiah predicts that a righteous Judah will have horses and chariotry (17:24–25, 22:3–4), there are many biblical texts strongly opposing Israelite use of or reliance on them (Deut 17:16; Josh 11:6; II Sam 8:14; Mic 5:9; Isa 30:15 – 31:3, etc.; see also NOTE on 10:24–38). This very tendency, however, must have led Israelites to see their horses and chariotry, if needed, as coming from God, whether in the person of prophets (II Kings 2:12, 13:14) or of apparitions (II Kings 2:11, 6:17, 7:6; Hab 3:8; Zech 1:8–11, 6:1–8; cf. Zech 10:3). Under the influence of the equestrian character of the Persian, Parthian, and Macedonian monarchies, the Near Eastern subject peoples followed the natural tendency of portraying their gods like kings and turned all the more to equestrian models; see Bickerman, *Studies*, II, 176, n. 109. Both the author of the Common Source and Jason of Cyrene had lived under Macedonian dynasties and could be expected to mount God's angel, if not God Himself, on a horse. Cf. 11:8 and IV 4:10 and *Bereshit Rabbah* (=*Genesis Rabbah*) 75:10.

One motif here is surely borrowed from the Greeks and Macedonians, as Bickerman demonstrated in great detail (*Studies*, II, 178–80). In equestrian stunts a horse can rear and strike with his forehoofs, but not in nature or in war. But Greek myths and Greek art teem with representations of gods and heroes mounted on horses who do so.

26. Although the two angels are invisible to all but Heliodorus, they give him a real whipping. Bickerman (*Studies*, II, 180–82) has collected parallels for this motif in ancient miracle stories. The whipping serves to punish Heliodorus for his criminal attempt, in accordance with both Greek and Jewish practice (ibid., pp. 182–83).

Since vs. 29 is incompatible with vs. 26, the occurrence of the root *riptein* in both "lay . . . upon" here and "lie prostrate" there is coincidental.

27. *immersed in deep darkness.* The use of the same verb here as in vs. 17 is probably deliberate. In both places the verb (lit. "pour around," "drench") is metaphorical. Since in Version B the supernatural actors are visible only to Heliodorus, the deep darkness here is metaphorical, meaning that Heliodorus lost consciousness.

28. *as one . . . him.* Manuscripts of the class q have "arms" (*tois hoplois*). In A′ it has been corrupted to *tois cholois* ("biles," "rages") and in 46–52 to

tois ochlois ("mobs") and in 55 to *tois holois* (the passage would then mean "as one who had become altogether helpless"). VL' 311 La Sy omit the words and change *auton* to *heautô(i)* (the passage would then mean "as one who had become powerless to help himself"). Hanhart rightly adopted the reading of q as best. In Greek, "bodyguard" is "spear bearers" (*doryphoroi*). Hence, in q the two parts of the verse are in vivid contrast: Heliodorus enters presumptuously with his impressive armed bodyguard but is carried out, helpless, by his attendants when arms prove to be of no avail. Scribes who failed to see the sharp contrast omitted or altered the words *tois hoplois* because they thought them pointless: surely Heliodorus was absolutely helpless, beyond the aid not only of arms but of any human device.

learned. The same verb is used in Greek tragedy of mortals who had been punished by a god (Sophocles *Antigone* 960).

30. "Had glorified" and "had been full" are expressed by present participles in Greek, which ordinarily would not be translated by a pluperfect. However, the first participle reflects the Hebrew construction with a participle after "praise" or "bless"; cf. Pss 72:18, 144:1; J. Heinemann, *Prayer in the Period of the Tanna'im and the Amora'im* (Jerusalem: Magnes Press, 1964), pp. 57–66 (in Hebrew, with English summary, p. iv). The second participle is idiomatic Greek, probably stressing that the fear and trepidation had been continual; see Kühner-Gerth, *Grammatik*, I, 200.

Does "had glorified his Place" echo Isa 60:7? If so, Jason or his source hints that the thwarting of Heliodorus, in the context of the provision of the temple expenses by Seleucus IV (vs. 3), is a partial fulfillment of Isa 60.

31. *Highest.* Only here does this name for God (*Hypsistos*) appear in Second Maccabees. Though also used by Jews (Deut 32:8; II Sam 22:14; III 6:2, etc.), it seems to have been an official designation used by pagans for the God of Israel (I Esdras 2:2; Dan 4:2 [Aramaic Dan 3:32]; OGIS 96; document *apud* J. *AJ* xvi 6.2.163; Acts 16:17).

On the other hand, pagans frequently used *hypsistos* as an epithet of their own deities. See Colin Roberts, Theodore C. Skeat, and Arthur Darby Nock, "The Guild of Zeus Hypsistos," *Harvard Theological Review* 29 (1936), 55–72, and A. Thomas Kraabel, "*Hypsistos* and the Synagogue at Sardis," *Greek, Roman, and Byzantine Studies* 10 (1969), 87–93.

32–35. As befits a work of Onias IV, Version B here tells of the patriotism of Onias III. The king's agent had been physically beaten, though witnesses saw no assailant. Jews and pagans might believe in the miraculous power of God (see Bickerman, *Studies*, II, 183), but Seleucus could be as skeptical of the God of Jerusalem as Daniel was of Bel in the apocryphal story (AB vol. 44); see Bickerman, *Studies*, II, 189, nn. 185–86.

The high priest offered an expiatory sacrifice for Heliodorus. In the Hebrew Bible sin and guilt offerings are brought only by the individual or corporate sinner, though Jason of Cyrene knows of sin offerings on behalf of the dead (12:43–45; see NOTE on 12:42–45). We do not know what system of Jewish law Onias followed. According to the rabbinic law a non-Jew could not bring a sin or guilt offering but he could bring a burnt offering (*M. Sheqalim* 1:5), and Onias or Heliodorus' friends could bring a burnt offering on Heliodorus' behalf (cf. Job 1:5). Such a burnt offering could secure atonement (Lev 1:4;

the requirement of laying hands upon the animal did not apply to a non-Jew; see "Gōy," Talmudic Encyclopedia, V [1953], 301–2, 305 [in Hebrew]), and Schürer, II, 357–62.

33. Again, Heliodorus is the only one said to have seen the two young men.

34. The vanishing of supernatural apparitions is a common motif (Judg 6:21; Tobit 12:21; Oxyrhynchus Papyri, vol. XI, no. 1381, lines 124–45; Pausanias i. 32. 5).

35. In addition to burnt offerings, some rabbinic authorities held that pagans could bring thank offerings (TB Menaḥot 73b). Heliodorus also vowed to give very great offerings in the future; see Schürer, II, 362–63.

The writer here makes an artistic contrast with vss. 8–9. There Heliodorus, the powerful agent of the king on a mission of confiscation, is warmly greeted (apodechtheis) on his arrival by Onias; here the chastened Heliodorus, after making great donations, greets (apodexamenos) Onias and departs.

37–39. The king does not abandon his project until Heliodorus demonstrates its impossibility. Kings get rid of troublesome persons by sending them on missions sure to prove fatal both in Greek myth (e.g., in the story of Bellerophon) and in biblical narrative (II Sam 11:14–27).

39. "Watches over" (epoptês esti) may echo "the LORD watches over mankind" at Greek Zech 9:1 and God's utterance "For now I see [heôraka] with my own eyes" after His promise to prevent exactors of money from coming against the Jews (Zech 9:8). Similarly, "those who come" may echo "one who marches to and fro" (m'br wmšb) at Zech 9:8. On the thwarting of Heliodorus as a fulfillment of Zech 9:8, see introductory NOTE to this chapter.

40. The verse closes the unit on Heliodorus but contains the Greek particle men to let the reader know that there will be more to come.

V. THE ATROCIOUS SINS OF THE HELLENIZING USURPERS
(4:1–50)

4 1 We have told how Simon acted as an informer against the money and against his own country. This same Simon spread slanders about Onias, declaring that Onias it was who had incited Heliodorus and had been the author of the evil affair. 2 He had the audacity to call the benefactor of the city and protector of his countrymen and zealous defender of the laws a "plotter against the commonwealth." 3 The hostility grew so extreme that murders were perpetrated by one of Simon's trusted henchmen.

4 Perceiving how dangerous was Simon's feud and how Apollonius son of Menestheus, the governor of Coele-Syria and Phoenicia, was involved in making Simon's wickedness still worse, Onias journeyed to the king. 5 His purpose was not to bring charges against his fellow Jews but to look to the collective and individual interests of all the people. 6 Indeed, he saw that without provident intervention by the king the commonwealth could never more have peace and Simon would never desist from his madness.

7 When Seleucus passed away and Antiochus, called Epiphanes, succeeded to the throne, Jason, Onias' brother, usurped the high priesthood. 8 He did so by presenting a petition in which he offered the king 360 talents, plus 80 talents of other revenue. 9 In addition, he promised to pay 150 talents if he should be granted by virtue of his office the power to establish a gymnasium and an ephebic organization and to draw up the list of the Antiochenes in Jerusalem. 10 The king consented.

On taking office, Jason immediately brought his fellow Jews over to the Greek style of life. 11 He cast away the humane royal concessions gained for the Jews by John, the father of the ambassador Eupolemus, who negotiated the treaty of friendship and alliance with the Romans. Overthrowing the civic institutions of the Torah, Jason brought in new usages which were contrary to the law. 12 Indeed, he took pleasure in founding a gymnasium beneath the very citadel and in making the education of the noblest adolescent boys consist of submission to the broad-brimmed Greek hat. 13 The enormous wickedness of the impious Jason—no true high priest he!—brought it about that the aping of Greek manners reached a peak and the adoption of gentile ways a height, 14 such that the priests were no longer eager to perform their duties at the altar but made light of the temple and neglected the sacrifices, in their haste after the gong sounded calling them to participate in the illicit entertainment in the wrestling yard. 15 Setting at nought their hereditary distinctions, they put the highest value on Greek honors. 16 For that very reason, grievous troubles came upon them: the Greeks, whose way of life they admired and whom they wished to ape in every way, became their enemies and the executers of their punishment. 17 It is no light matter to be impious toward the laws of God. That, however, will be seen from the events which followed.

18 When the quinquennial games were being celebrated at Tyre in the presence of the king, 19 the abominable Jason sent a delegation representing the Antiochenes from Jerusalem bearing three hundred drachmas to pay for the sacrifice to Herakles. The bearers themselves, however, decided not to use the money for a sacrifice, since that was not proper, but to donate it to be spent for another purpose. 20 Jason, in sending the delegation, had intended that the money be contributed for the sacrifice to Herakles, but because of the bearers it was contributed for the fitting out of triremes.

21 Through the mission to Egypt of Apollonius son of Menestheus to attend the *Protoklisia* of King Philometor, Antiochus learned that Philometor was now hostile to his kingdom. Accordingly, he took measures for his own safety. Thus it was that he came to Joppe and then went to Jerusalem. 22 He was sumptuously greeted by Jason and the Jerusalemites, and he was brought into the city with a torchlight parade and shouts of applause. Thereafter in the same manner he and his army marched off to Phoenicia.

23 Three years had passed when Jason sent Menelaus, brother of the aforementioned Simon, as bearer of the money to the king and as his agent for executing royal decisions on pressing matters. 24 On being introduced to the king, Menelaus magnified his own importance by giving the impression that he was a man of authority, and by adding three hundred talents of silver to Jason's bid, he gained for himself the high priesthood. 25 He came home holding the royal decrees but with no qualifications for the high priesthood, possessing only the temper of a cruel tyrant and the passions of a savage beast.

26 Thus Jason, who had usurped his brother's office, saw his own usurped by another and was forced to flee to the Ammanitis.

27 Menelaus took over the office but failed completely to make the promised regular payments to the king. 28 Hence, Sostratos, the commander of the citadel, whose duty it was to collect the money, repeatedly demanded payment. As a result, both men were summoned by the king. 29 Menelaus left as substitute high priest his brother Lysimachus, and Sostratos as his deputy left Krates, the commander of the Cypriot mercenaries.

30 At the very time of this agitation there were uprisings in the cities of Tarsus and Mallos because they had been given as a gift to Antiochis, the king's concubine. 31 The king, in great haste, came to put down the revolt. He left as his deputy Andronikos, a man of high prestige. 32 Menelaus believed that here was a favorable opportunity. He purloined some of the gold vessels of the temple and made a present of them to Andronikos. In fact, he had sold other vessels to buyers in Tyre and the neighboring cities. 33 Onias, fully informed of Menelaus' acts, withdrew to a place of asylum at Daphne by Antioch and denounced him. 34 Thereupon, Menelaus took Andronikos aside privately and begged him to do away with Onias. Brazen in treachery, Andronikos went to Onias, accepted his right hand, and gave him his own in oath. Though Onias held him in suspicion, Andronikos induced him to come out of his place of asylum and then, with no respect for justice, immediately did away with him.

35 As a result, not only Jews but many from other nationalities were scandalized and outraged over the wicked murder of the man. 36 On the king's return from the regions of Cilicia, the Jews of the city, supported in their indignation by the Greeks, presented a petition to the effect that Onias had been killed without justification. 37 Deeply perturbed and touched with pity, Antiochus shed tears over the upright character and altogether orderly life of the departed. 38 Passionately incensed, he forthwith stripped Andronikos of his purple and tore off his clothes and after parading him around the entire city brought him to the spot where he had committed the sacrilege against Onias. There he removed the murderer from the world, and thus the LORD repaid him with the punishment he deserved.

39 Meanwhile, back in the city many sacred articles had been stolen by Lysimachus with the connivance of Menelaus. When reports of the matter spread to the countryside, the people massed against Lysimachus. By that time many gold vessels had already been sent abroad. 40 Confronted by the rising of the populace and their surge of

indignation, Lysimachus armed some three thousand men and wickedly took the offensive. In command was a certain Auranos, a man advanced equally in age and in madness. 41 When the people saw Lysimachus' attack, some snatched up stones, others heavy pieces of wood, and still others the dust and ashes that lay at hand. Wildly they hurled them at Lysimachus' men. 42 In this manner they wounded many of them, shot others down, and routed the whole force. They did away with the temple robber himself at the treasury.

43 These events became the basis for a suit against Menelaus. 44 When the king came down to Tyre, three men sent by the Council of Elders argued the case in his presence. 45 Menelaus had all but lost the contest when he promised considerable sums of money to Ptolemy son of Dorymenes to have him win the king over. 46 Thereupon, Ptolemy took the king out to a courtyard for a breath of air and induced him to change his mind. 47 As a result, the king acquitted Menelaus, the man to blame for the entire evil affair, and condemned to death the poor men who would have been released as innocent even if they had pleaded their case before Scythians. 48 Quickly the unjust penalty was inflicted on the men who had been the spokesmen for city and country villages and the sacred vessels. 49 In consequence, even Tyrians were indignant and gave them a magnificent funeral. 50 Menelaus, however, retained his office, thanks to the greed of those in power, and devoted himself to wickedness, having proved himself to be a plotter against his fellow Jews.

NOTES

4:1-38. For vss. 1-6 we may assume that Jason of Cyrene could have drawn on both Onias IV and the Common Source. The narrative in vss. 4-6 takes pains to excuse Onias III for seeking the aid of the Seleucid king; the effort to excuse suggests the hand of anti-Seleucid Onias IV. One might think that Onias IV would have been eager to expose how his father was unjustly deprived of the high priesthood. But the usurper was none other than his own uncle Jason, a legitimate member of the Oniad line, a man who sided with the interests of the Ptolemaic dynasty, of which Onias IV was a loyal supporter. See II 4:7; J. *AJ* xii 5.1.238-40, 3.246-47, *BJ* i 1.1.32; and my article in *Studies Smith*, Part III, pp. 91, 108-9. Moreover, Jason the Oniad was responsible for the peaceful Hellenization of Jerusalem (vss. 8-20), a fact Onias IV wished to conceal, as is indicated by the material Josephus drew from his *Memoirs* (*AJ* xii 5.1.239-41; *Studies Smith*, Part III, pp. 121-22). Indeed, the account condemning Jason the Oniad for the "heinous sins which brought on the persecution" (vss. 7–20) and the parallel passages at I 1:11–15, 41–43, and 64 must therefore be ascribed to the Common Source.

One might also think that Onias IV would have been eager to tell how Onias III in Antioch heroically opposed, at the cost of his own life, the temple robberies of the next usurper, Menelaus (vss. 32–34). But Onias IV seems to have faced a dilemma: how could he account for his father's presence as deposed high priest in Antioch without casting too much discredit on his uncle Jason? Josephus' narrative may reflect how Onias IV dealt with the dilemma, for Josephus writes (AJ xii 5.1.237) that the high priest Onias III died about the same time as Hyrcanus the Tobiad committed suicide (see NOTE on 3:11) and that Onias III was succeeded by Jason. This might suggest that Josephus' source, the Memoirs of Onias IV, passed in silence over Jason's usurpation and Hellenization and gave an obscure account of the end of the high priesthood of Onias III. Nevertheless, it seems difficult to believe that Onias IV was satisfied to say nothing of his father's heroic death. Perhaps, then, he found some way to account for his father's deposition without bringing too much discredit upon his uncle. If so, we can imagine that Josephus in his bald account of the death of Onias III at AJ xii 5.1.237 has rejected the narrative of the Memoirs. Propagandists for the Hasmonaean dynasty, including Josephus, were glad to exclude any possibility that the Oniad line had been meritorious. Such propagandists, interpreting the list of Jewish high priests, might have taken the end of the high priesthood of Onias III and the subsequent accession of Jason to imply that Onias III died in office (cf. AJ xx 10.2–3.234–35). Those propagandists would regard such evidence as sufficient for them to dismiss as fiction any report by Onias IV glorifying his father's death.

Anti-Seleucid Onias IV probably told nothing of how Antiochus IV punished the murderer of Onias III (vss. 35–38). The author of the Common Source revered Onias III enough to have given a complete account of the events in our passage.

1–6. Simon spread propaganda against Onias. Did he mean to embroil Onias with his fellow Jews or with the royal government? Though La^BMP and Sy and modern scholars (e.g., Abel, p. 329; Bickerman, Studies, II, 189) have chosen the second alternative, the meaning of the author's words and the course of his narrative prove that the truth lies with the first, as indicated by La^V and probably also by La^L and La^X. Crucial is the verb episeseikôs in vs. 1, which I have rendered "who had incited." Those who chose the second alternative were impressed by the fact that it is derived from the same Greek root as "struck" (eneseise) in 3:25. However, the verb here has "Heliodorus" in the accusative as a direct object. Elsewhere, if this verb means "intimidate," the person intimidated is in the dative. Where it takes a person in the accusative in classical and biblical Greek (Euripides Orestes 255; Judg 1:14; I Sam 26:19; II Sam 24:1; I Chron 21:1; and Aquila and Theodotion to Jer 43[Greek Jer 50]:3), it means "incite." Thus the occurrence of the same Greek root in 3:25 is probably a coincidence.

Also ambiguous at first sight is ta pragmata ("the commonwealth") in vss. 2 and 6, for at 3:38 pragmata certainly means "kingdom." The ambiguity of the expression ta pragmata even in the official domestic correspondence of an empire is illustrated by the way in which Hellenistic kings in their letters qualify the term with "our" (C. Bradford Welles, *Royal Correspondence in the Hellenistic Period* [Yale University Press, 1934], no. 12, lines 11–12, and no. 22, line 8, etc.). Far from fearing punishment at the hands of the king, Onias takes refuge in an appeal to him. The appeal was all too easily interpreted as an act against Onias' fellow Jews, so that the author takes pains to exclude that interpretation. Surely, then, Onias saw the king as his defender and his own misguided people as the threat. Onias' aim was to bring "peace to the commonwealth" by stopping Simon (vs. 6). Simon could indeed create a serious disturbance in tiny Judaea. To suggest that he was a menace to the tranquility of the Seleucid kingdom would have been grotesque.

Jason of Cyrene appears to have deliberately used similar terminology at 14:5–10 to describe the actions of the impious high priest Alcimus, and we must examine that passage. Jason ascribes to Alcimus the same "madness" he ascribes to Simon here, but otherwise Alcimus becomes a wicked counterpart of Onias. Like Onias, Alcimus seeks the king's "provident intervention" in order to suppress a turbulent opposition. In contrast to Onias' opponents, however, Judas and his followers in 14:6 have a history of dangerous rebellion against the kingdom, and Alcimus makes the most of the fact. In contrast to vs. 5 here, we learn at 14:8 from Alcimus' own lips that he is nobly seeking the king's interests and those of his fellow Jews in appealing against Judas and his followers. Alcimus there is answering the king's question on the mood and conditions among the Jews and speaks chiefly of *local* concerns. Hence, when he uses the same expression in 14:10, "As long as Judas survives, it is impossible for *the commonwealth to have peace*," the vague word "commonwealth" can well include both the kingdom and the community of Judaea. The antithesis in vs. 2 is also more pointed if the object of Onias' alleged plotting is not the pagan kingdom but the Jewish commonwealth.

The author at 13:3, as at 14:5–10, surely intended the reader to contrast patriotic Onias III with a selfish and wicked successor.

Some scholars have suggested that Onias III, with his brother Jason, was active in a pro-Ptolemaic party within the Seleucid empire, which also included Heliodorus; see Stern, *Zion* 25 (1960), 5–6 (in Hebrew). If so, some of Simon's accusations could have been true. But there is no evidence for connecting Onias III with either the Ptolemaic empire or with Heliodorus. Far from going to Egypt or to Hyrcanus' stronghold in the Ammanitis, Onias goes to Antioch to seek the support of Seleucus IV and even when deposed by Antiochus IV remains at Antioch (cf. Jason's behavior in vs. 26).

1. *author of the evil affair.* Lit. "builder of the evils," an expression found in Greek tragedy (Euripides *Fragment* 1059, line 7).

2. In a well-ordered commonwealth of the Hellenistic world, a "benefactor" (*euergetês*) and "protector" (*kêdemôn*) would be honored by having his name put on a public monument accompanied by those two laudatory epithets (OGIS 752). Pious Jews would not consider a man praiseworthy unless they could add the epithet "zealous defender of the laws" (cf. I 2:26–27, 50, 58). Far from receiving the honor he deserved, in the commonwealth disordered by Simon, Onias was calumniated as a plotter against the existing institutions of the community!

3. *trusted henchmen*. The Greek word (*dokimasmenôn*) is derived from the verb *dokimazein*, a term from Greek politics which means "to scrutinize for fitness to hold office and approve." The murderer was Simon's picked man.

4. *Apollonius son of Menestheus*. There is no reason to identify this Apollonius with the ones at 3:5 and 5:24; see NOTES ad loca. Polybius (xxxi. 13. 2–3) tells of an Apollonius who stood high in favor in the reign of Seleucus IV and had three sons, Apollonius, Meleagros, and Menestheus. Since Greeks frequently named a son after his grandfather, it is possible (but not certain) that Polybius' Apollonius is identical with the one here. Polybius reports (ibid.) that Apollonius withdrew to Miletus "when Antiochus succeeded to the throne," and that his three sons supported the cause of Demetrius, the surviving son of Seleucus IV. If Polybius is correct, and if by succession to the throne he means Antiochus' seizure of power in 175, our Apollonius, governing for Antiochus IV, could not be identical to Polybius'. A large influential family could have several members named Apollonius and Menestheus, with one branch supporting the line of Seleucus and the other accepting Antiochus IV. However, Polybius at xxxi. 13. 3 by Antiochus' "succession" might mean his seizure of undisputed power in 170 when he had the little coregent King Antiochus, son of Seleucus IV, put to death (Mørkholm, pp. 41–50, except where corrected by my remarks here). If so, the motive determining the position of Apollonius and his sons would seem to have been loyalty to Seleucus' line. As long as Antiochus IV could pose as the guardian of little King Antiochus, the family supported him. Thereafter they withdrew from the Seleucid empire and backed the cause of the surviving member of the line.

Our Apollonius also served Antiochus IV as an ambassador (vs. 21), and thus may well be the same as Apollonius, the prestigious ambassador who in 173 at Rome induced the Romans to renew for Antiochus IV the relations of friendship and alliance which had existed with his father (Livy xlii. 6. 6–12).

On Apollonius' title, see the last two NOTES on 3:5.

5. The Jewish-Greek author again takes pains to describe Onias in the stereotyped terms used in Greek politics to evoke favor for a man and hostility toward his opponents. Cf. Demosthenes *Oration* 18. 136, 277–79 and *Epistle* 2. 9–11.

Also not surprising in a Jewish-Greek is the use by Jason of Cyrene of *politês* ("citizen") for "fellow national" and in particular for "fellow Jew" (4:5, 50, 5:6, 8, 14:8, 15:30; cf. Greek Gen 23:11). Only in the non-Jewish document at 9:19 does *politês* have a different meaning. On the reading at the end of 5:23, see NOTE on 5:23–24, *disposed . . . slaves*.

6. Onias' thoughts here echo the Hellenistic philosophy of the function of kings as near-divine guarantors of law and order; see Erwin R. Goodenough, "The Political Philosophy of Hellenistic Kingship," *Yale Classical Studies* (1928), I, 55–102. "Provident intervention" here is the same Greek noun as is used for "divine providence" (*pronoia*). A verb from the same root expresses the same idea at 14.9.

The further course of the struggle between Onias III and Simon is unknown. Simon disappears from the sources. The author does not say Onias returned to Jerusalem. He may have found the political situation there too dangerous even before his brother usurped the high priesthood. He is at Antioch in vs. 33, and we may guess that he remained there throughout.

7–50. The author here does not portray the Seleucid kings as wicked. Benevolent at their best, they are no worse than other Hellenistic kings: they patronize Greek culture and can be deceived by corrupt subordinates. The purpose of Jason of Cyrene in so portraying Antiochus IV is to show that he was a typical Hellenistic king until sin in Judaea led God to employ him as the "rod of His anger." See also NOTE on 14:18–28. The author contrasts Onias III with Jason and Menelaus. See NOTE on 3:3.

Josephus rejected the narrative of Jason of Cyrene wherever it conflicted with his prejudices; see Appendix XI and AB vol. 41, pp. 56–60. For example, he could not believe that even a wicked high priest could have "Hellenized" Jerusalem without provoking violent resistance, and he held that Onias-Menelaus was a brother of Onias III and Jason (see NOTE on vs. 23, *Menelaus . . . Simon*). Hence, he rejected the account in 4:7 – 5:7 and read I 1:11–15 and the work of Onias IV in the light of his own prejudices to produce the strange narrative at *AJ* xii 5.1.239–41, which begins as follows:

(239) Jesus changed his name to "Jason," whereas Onias was called "Menelaus." When Jesus, the former high priest, gathered his faction and rose against Menelaus, who was appointed after him, the people were divided between the two of them. The Tobiads took the side of Menelaus and the majority of the nation supported Jason. (240) Hard pressed by him, Menelaus and the Tobiads withdrew and went to Antiochus. They told him they wished to abandon their ancestral laws and the way of life shaped by them in order to follow the king's laws and adopt the Greek way of life.

The next section (241) in Josephus is an obvious paraphrase of I 1:13–15. Indeed, the words in the passage I have translated, from "and went" to the end of section 240, are also a paraphrase of I 1:11–13. In First Maccabees the names and background of the Jews who presented the petition to Antiochus IV are not given. Josephus supplies the lack, in sections 239 and 240, drawing on the work by Onias IV to contradict the narrative here. For a detailed argument, see my article in *Studies Smith*, Part III, esp. pp. 121–22.

Josephus' inaccurate account at *BJ* i 1.1.31–32 was written from memory, when Josephus had no copies of his sources; see AB vol. 41, pp. 60–61.

7–38. From the information given in our passage and from other clues it may be possible to give a fairly precise chronology for the events. On the ambiguities to be faced in interpreting ancient chronological data containing cardinal or ordinal numbers, see Appendix VII. These ambiguities should be sharply reduced here.

In vs. 23 we hear of a tax payment coming "three years later." Moneylenders and borrowers and tax gatherers and taxpayers had to be accurate. Intervals for interest payment were reckoned accurately, not approximately. In the ancient world, where the economy was overwhelmingly based on agriculture, tribute could be collected only on the annual agricultural produce. This remained true even though tribute in the Seleucid empire consisted of a fixed sum, not of a percentage of the crops (Bickerman, *Institutions*, 106–11). In a text dealing with payment of tribute, "three years" can hardly mean anything but three periods for which taxes were paid. Indeed, Hebrew lease documents of 133 c.e. identify full years with years of taxation (*šnym šlmwt šny mksh*). See P. Benoit, J. T. Milik, and R. de Vaux, *Les grottes de Muraba'ât*, DJD, II (1961), Document 24E, lines 9–10, and Document 24F, lines 11–12.

There are instructive biblical parallels. Consider Greek Gen 14:4: "Twelve years they had served Chedorlaomer, and in the thirteenth year they rebelled." "Twelve" is a cardinal number; "served" means "paid tribute and other dues to" (cf. II Kings 17:3–4, 18:7); "thirteenth" is an ordinal number, and "in the thirteenth year" means "after the payment of the taxes of the twelfth year." Cf. Exod 21:2; Deut 15:12.

But are these texts parallel to our passage? Perhaps the three years of vs. 23 measure the interval of time since the last narrated event, Antiochus' visit to Jerusalem (vss. 21–22)! Let us examine the narrative in our passage, giving dates for the events where dates are available. Jason the Oniad became high priest (vss. 7–8) by offering to bring in higher tribute from Judaea after the death of Seleucus IV. Seleucus IV died on 10 Ululu (=Elul), 137 Sel. Bab.=September 3, 175 B.C.E. (Sachs and Wiseman, *Iraq* 16 [1954], 204, 208), just before the beginning of 138 Sel. Mac. Jason surely could not have made his expensive offers until the succession was sure. Antiochus probably became secure in power between October 23 and November 20, 175 B.C.E.; see Mørkholm, pp. 42–44. Jason's offer and elevation to the priesthood, then, must have come late in 175 or in 174 B.C.E.

Next we hear of Jason's "Hellenistic reform" (vss. 10–17), of his atrocious attempt to "pay for an idolatrous sacrifice" (vss. 18–20), and of Antiochus' defensive maneuvers against hostile Ptolemaic Egypt and his visit to Jerusalem (vss. 21–22). Despite the numerous events in vss. 10–22, the "three years" in vs. 23 are probably measured from Jason's appointment, for the tribute is referred to simply as "the money," as if vss. 7–8 were being resumed. On the possible dates for the quinquennial games at Tyre, see NOTE on vs. 18. On the *Protoklisia* of Ptolemy VI, see NOTE on vs. 21. Jason's first payment of taxes thus came in 174, and his third came in 172, whereupon Menelaus usurped the high priesthood (vss. 23–24).

Our fixation of the year of Menelaus' accession can be confirmed from other evidence. Menelaus, as high priest, had at least one tax payment fall due before the death of Onias III (vss. 23–34), and Onias was killed shortly after the post-sabbatical year began in autumn, 170 B.C.E. (see NOTE on vs. 34). According to the largely reliable list of high priests in Josephus, Menelaus' term as high priest lasted ten years (i.e., at least nine years plus a fraction); see AB vol. 41, Appendix VI. Menelaus was deposed in the course of the expedition of Antiochus V and Lysias (II 13:3–8; J. *AJ* xii 9.7.383–85), and the expedition lasted from ca. June, 163, to January or March, 162 (see AB vol. 41, pp. 315, 325). Hence, our date for Menelaus' accession is again confirmed.

We can also be fairly sure of the season at which the taxes fell due and Menelaus became high priest. The official Macedonian Seleucid year began near the autumnal equinox, at about the same time as the final harvest came in. Probably this was the time for paying taxes. Cf. the fiscal importance of the beginning of the Macedonian year in Ptolemaic Egypt (*Papyrus Revenue Laws*, ed. by Jean Bingen [*Sammelbuch Griechischer Urkunden aus Ägypten*,

Beiheft 1; Göttingen: Hubert, 1952], col. 34), and see Philo *De specialibus legibus* i. 142–44 and iv. 212–13.

In Ptolemaic Egypt, with its huge produce and long distances, the payment and collection of the taxes might stretch over a long period, with postponements making it difficult to determine what was the legal and what was the actual date of payment. Judaea under Jason and Menelaus was a compact country of limited productivity. Moreover, Jason of Cyrene here may draw on Onias IV, who showed great interest in how Jews loyally and punctually pay tribute (cf. J. *AJ* xii 4.1.158). Even though Onias was probably reticent about his uncle Jason and might even praise failure to pay tribute to the hated Seleucids, if the usurper Jason had been guilty of delays in paying the promised tribute, Onias might have spared him as little as Menelaus is spared at vss. 27–28. Hence, we may assume that Jason paid tribute punctually at the beginning of the Macedonian Seleucid year in the autumns of 174, 173, and 172 B.C.E.

7–20. In briefer form the content of our verses appears at I 1:11–15, 64. Both narratives condemn following the ways of the gentiles and focus on the gymnasium. The abridged history states, and First Maccabees implies, that the Hellenizing reforms carried out by Jason the Oniad and his followers roused the wrath of God and thus brought upon the Jews the sack of Jerusalem by Antiochus IV, the expedition of the Mysarch, and the persecution. It is conceivable that two so different authors could independently arrive at the same conclusions concerning the cause of the punishment of the Jews and the importance of the gymnasium. But all other early sources (the book of Jubilees, Enoch, the Testament of Moses, Daniel, and Ep. 0 and Ep. 1) disagree with those conclusions! See my article in *Jewish and Christian Self-Definition*, II, 80–81, and NOTE on 1:7–8 and NOTE on 1:7, *Jason . . . Kingdom*. Hence, the agreement of Jason of Cyrene here with the Hasmonaean propagandist suggests that both authors drew on the Common Source.

7–17. The content is summarized at IV 4:15–21.

7. The sources on Seleucus' death are troublesome for the historian. Appian (*Syriakê* 45) says that Seleucus perished through a plot of Heliodorus. The Babylonian list of Seleucid kings (Sachs and Wiseman, *Iraq* 16 [1954], 204, 208) where it is intelligible says only that Seleucus died on 6 Ululu, 137 Sel. Bab. (September 3, 175 B.C.E.), but it contains two untranslatable signs which might confirm Appian's account. Dan 11:20 probably means that Seleucus fell to a plot. The other witness from the second century B.C.E., OGIS 248, line 10, agrees with our passage in saying only that Seleucus "passed away"! OGIS 248 is an official proclamation of the Athenians, who were friends to Antiochus IV, thanking the royal family of Pergamum for helping Antiochus take power upon the death of his brother; see Maurice Holleaux, "Un prétendu décret d'Antioche sur l'Oronte," in his *Études d'épigraphie et d'histoire grecques*, vol. II (Paris: É. de Boccard, 1938), pp. 127–47. If Appian should be correct, our passage and OGIS 248 would reflect an official version of Seleucus' death published by the regime of Antiochus IV for whatever reason. For example, we do not know what happened to Heliodorus. If Antiochus failed to punish his brother's murderer, he might well have preferred to conceal the fact that

Seleucus was murdered. On the other hand, Seleucus may have died without foul play, and Appian's report may reflect only unsubstantiated public suspicions. Cf. M. Stern, "The Death of Onias III," *Zion* 25 (1960), 4 (in Hebrew).

Jason does not regard Seleucus IV as a persecutor. The king sent Heliodorus to confiscate the deposits at the temple only because he had received false information from Simon, and when Onias needed support against Simon and his faction, he turned to Seleucus. Seleucus' death prevented Onias from getting justice and thus was to be regretted. In no way could the author view the king's death as retribution. Perhaps for that reason he chose to record Seleucus' death using oı.ly the euphemism "passed away." The idiom arose in connection with heroes, who were worshiped after their deaths and could not be said to have died but rather "passed" or "changed" to another existence. Alexander and the Hellenistic kings were treated, upon their deaths, as heroes and gods (see, e.g., 11:23). By Jason's time, however, the euphemism was a mere synonym for "die" (Welles, *Royal Correspondence*, p. 348).

Josephus (*AJ* xii 5.1.237) has Jason succeeding to the high priesthood upon the (apparently) peaceful death of Onias III. Why did Josephus reject the account here if it was available to him? The best guess is that here, too, he was following his pro-Hasmonaean tendency to minimize the importance of the Oniad high priests. See Appendix XI; AB vol. 41, pp. 57–59; and my article in *Studies Smith*, Part III, pp. 85, 117–23. As told in 4:30–38 and in the work of Onias IV, the death of Onias III could be the event referred to at Dan 9:26. If so, Onias III was important enough for a true prophet to mention him as an "anointed one." Josephus probably had a propagandistic source which avoided the identification of Onias III with the "anointed one," and naturally he preferred it to our narrative here, which he despised. See NOTE on vs. 23, *Menelaus . . . Simon*.

Jason's Hebrew name was Jesus (J. *AJ* xii 5.1.237–38).

8. On the position of Onias III in the clan politics in Judaea, see NOTE on 3:11. As a supplanter of his brother Onias, Jason the Oniad need not have shared Onias' political position. Jason used Menelaus, brother of Onias' enemy Simon, as his own agent (vs. 23), and Menelaus, on becoming high priest, received the backing of the Tobiad clan (J. *AJ* xii 5.1.239). Hence, at the outset, Jason may have had the backing of the Tobiads of Judaea, the enemies of Hyrcanus. However, when Menelaus supplanted him as high priest, Jason betook himself to the Transjordanian stronghold of Hyrcanus (vss. 23–26), and Hyrcanus was probably still alive (see NOTE on 3:11). Jason struck at Jerusalem on hearing a false report that Antiochus was dead (5:5). On restoring order in Jerusalem, Antiochus is said to have slain many of the pro-Ptolemaic faction (J. *BJ* i 1.1.32), presumably supporters of Jason. If so, at that point Jason, like Hyrcanus, was pro-Ptolemaic. Jason then emerges as a man who could make alliances with either of the two factions of the Tobiad clan, all of whom were his cousins (J. *AJ* xii 4.2.160; Onias there is Onias II, grandfather of Jason). Jason pleased Antiochus because he was a "Hellenizer," eager to become an Antiochene. Menelaus pleased Antiochus still more. Hence, he, too, must have been a "Hellenizer," and so must the Tobiads of Judaea, who appear to have backed first Jason and then Menelaus. Onias IV, indeed, branded the Tobiads

of Judaea as Hellenizers; see my article in *Studies Smith*, Part III, pp. 91, 105–6, 121–22.

360 . . . revenue. The Greek here is probably elliptical and means "360 talents of regular revenue and 80 talents of other revenue"; cf. *Syll.*³ 1101, lines 13–14.

The regular revenue was surely the tribute (*phoros*), a fixed sum collected from the agricultural produce of Judaea (Bickerman, *Institutions*, pp. 106–11). Hitherto the tribute of tiny Judaea appears to have reached the already heavy figure of 300 talents (Sulpicius Severus *Chronica* ii. 17. 5 and cf. 21. 4; Bickerman, *Institutions*, pp. 107–8). See NOTE on 3:11(end). What the additional revenue was we can only guess; see Bickerman, *Institutions*, pp. 111–20.

To later generations inflation made the figures here seem too small. For "three hundred" here *L* reads "six hundred," and at IV 4:17 Jason is said to have offered an annual payment of 3,660 talents; see NOTE on 4:19.

9–15. Jason the Oniad here wishes to bring Jews of Jerusalem, under his own leadership, into Antiochus' scheme for an "Antiochene republic" in imitation of the Roman republic. As "Antiochenes," citizens of the republic, they would gain great privileges and would associate with other privileged citizens from all over the Seleucid empire. Though Antiochus imitated Rome, the institutions, language, and culture of his republic were to be Greek. Jason must have been very wealthy. He was ready to pay the vast sum of 150 talents for the privileges and power which would go to the founder of the citizen community. He would draw up the original list of adult citizens and would found the gymnasium and ephebic organization, the educational system through which privileged adolescents would enter the ranks of the citizens. Jason was a moderate Hellenizer. He had no intention of turning all of Jerusalem into such a privileged community, for many Jewish rigorists wanted no contact with Greek patterns. Just as Italians with Roman citizenship might live outside Rome in Italian communities, so Jews with Antiochene citizenship would continue to live at Jerusalem. For details, see AB vol. 41, pp. 110–22.

Jason might hold that the Torah permitted association with Greeks and adoption of Greek institutions, provided no idolatry was involved, for the Torah forbade literally only association with the natives of the Promised Land and adoption of their institutions and those of the Egyptians (Exod 23:32–33, 34:11–16; Lev 18:3; Deut 7:1–5). Far from being native to the Promised Land, Greeks came from a distant country, so that Jason and his followers could point to Josh 9:3–27 as evidence that scripture permitted association with them. Jewish rigorists, however, noted that the Torah, in forbidding association with the natives of the Promised Land, also called them "the inhabitants of the land" (Exod 34:12 and 15). By the time of Jason the Oniad, Greek settlers and their descendants had long since become inhabitants of the Promised Land, though few if any may have resided in the small area which at that time constituted Judaea proper. The rigorist propaganda of the book of Jubilees (written between autumn, 169, and spring, 167 B.C.E.) told Jews to shun all gentiles, including Greeks. See Introduction, Part V, section 1.

Some rigorist interpretations prevailed at Jerusalem from the time of Nehemiah and had been confirmed by royal decrees; see AB vol. 41, NOTE on 1:11–15, with the qualifications in my article in *Jewish and Christian Self-*

Definition, II, 73–81. Therefore, although the high priest was then the supreme authority on Jewish law (see Hecataeus of Abdera *apud* Diodorus xl. 3. 4–6, and cf. Jubilees 31:15), he had to get royal permission to associate with Greeks and establish Greek-style institutions.

Jason's case was hardly unique. Later, in the non-Greek city of Komana in Cappadocia, we learn of a high priest who also was head of the gymnasial organization; see Bickerman, *Gott,* p. 63.

9. *by virtue of his office.* Through his *exousia,* his authority as high priest. See NOTE on 3:6, *fall . . . confiscate.*

a gymnasium and an ephebic organization. See AB vol. 41, NOTES on 1:14–15. In the Hellenistic age a gymnasium and an ephebic system were essential ingredients of any civilized Greek community (Strabo v. 4. 7, C246; Pausanias x. 4. 1). Ephebes were males who had reached puberty. First at Athens and then throughout the Hellenistic world a system of civic and military training grew up to fit ephebes for their obligations as citizens. The training was not only physical but also moral and literary and took place in the gymnasium. To accommodate the nonathletic functions, additional chambers were built into the gymnasia. Passing through the ephebic education conferred great privileges; it could be a requirement for full rights as a member of a Greek community, and it was intended to be so in the Antiochene republic. At Athens the institution persisted for the aristocracy when it was no longer supported by the city, and the ephebic education became the prerequisite for membership in the aristocracy rather than for citizenship. Although at Athens the ephebic education began at eighteen, elsewhere the education for ephebes seems to have been the education of boys at the average age of puberty, fourteen or fifteen (Martin P. Nilsson, *Die hellenistische Schule* [München: Beck, 1955], pp. 34–42).

For a detailed account in English of these institutions, see Henri I. Marrou, *A History of Education in Antiquity* (New York: New American Library, 1964), pp. 147–86 (but not on points where Marrou disagrees with the views of Nilsson summarized in the preceding paragraph), 256–60. See also Nilsson, *Die hellenistische Schule,* and Jean Delorme, *Gymnasion* (Paris: É. de Boccard, 1960).

10–17. From no source do we hear of the abolition of Jason's Hellenistic practices or of the destruction of the gymnasium. Can it be that the "wicked" high priest Menelaus or the Antiochene community of Jerusalem themselves put an end to the institutions which seemed so clearly to have provoked God's wrath?

10. Similar language is used in the letter of Antiochus V at 11:24 to refer to these steps taken under Antiochus IV. The author here does not say all Jews went over to the Greek patterns and says nothing of the use of force. His truthful account is confirmed by I 1:11–15.

11. Hellenistic kings frequently granted special privileges to subject communities, and these were called "humane concessions" (*philanthrôpa*); see Bickerman, *Institutions,* pp. 135–40, and Welles, *Royal Correspondence,* p. 373, and no. 15, line 9; no. 22, line 17; no. 64, line 13, etc.

Evidently John gained the concessions from Antiochus III recorded at J. *AJ* xii 3.3–4.138–46, in which Antiochus confirmed rigorist interpretations of Jewish law. See Bickerman, *Studies*, II, 44–104. On Eupolemus, see AB vol. 41, NOTE on 8:17–18. On the treaty with the Romans, see I 8 and the NOTES on it in AB vol. 41. The writer shows special interest both in the family of John and in the Romans. In securing the concessions from Antiochus III, John acted as ambassador, probably on behalf of the Oniad high priest Simon II; see NOTE on 1:7, *Jason . . . Kingdom.* Pro-Ptolemaic Onias IV could not approve of John's mission, but the author of the Common Source could, and we would thus learn that either the author of the Common Source or Jason of Cyrene was friendly to the family of John.

The treaty with the Romans came during Judas' career as military commander, after the victory over Nicanor (I 7:43 – 8:32; II 15:25–36; see AB vol. 41, pp. 341–42, 346), the last event narrated in the abridged history. Hence we learn that Jason of Cyrene knew of later events than those at 15:25–36 and that his unabridged narrative probably included some. See also NOTE on 15:37.

civic institutions. Jewish Greeks, including Philo and Josephus, had no trouble using the Greek word *politeia* ("constitution," "republic," "citizenship," or "civic institution") for the law of the Torah. See Harry A. Wolfson, *Philo* (4th printing; Cambridge, Mass.: Harvard University Press, 1968), II, 322–426, and cf. AB vol. 41, NOTES on 8:1–16, 8:1, and 8:15.

12. A gymnasium in a Hellenistic Greek city occupied a prominent site, often near the civic center or a temple; see Delorme, *Gymnasion*, pp. 441–58. In accordance with that pattern, the citadel here (*akropolis*) is either the temple mount or the citadel hill (*Akra*) which lay just to the north; see AB vol. 41, NOTE on 1:33–40, and Louis Robert, review of *Griechische Mauerbauinschriften*, by Franz Georg Maier, *Gnomon* 42 (1970), 595–96.

The holiness of the temple made it a special case, but Jews of the Greek-speaking diaspora had no such horror of having gymnasia near their synagogues. The synagogue of Delos in the second century B.C.E. probably lay near the gymnasium (Delorme, *Gymnasion*, fig. 14), and the huge synagogue of Sardis in the late second century C.E. was built as a part of the gymnasium complex (Andrew R. Seager, "The Building History of the Sardis Synagogue," *American Journal of Archaeology* 76 [1972], 425–35).

The scribe of V missed the pun (*hypotassôn hypo petason* ["subduing under the broad-brimmed Greek hat"]) and omitted *hypotassôn*, believing it to be a scribal error. Another fact strongly suggests the correctness of our text: there seems to be a parody here of Ps 47(Greek Ps 46):4. Whereas in the Psalm, God subjects the nations to Israel, here Jason subjects Israelite youth to Greek ways. I have taken the verb *êgagen* to mean "he educated," as often in Greek (*Greek-English Lexicon*, s.v. *agô*, A, II, 5); the related noun *agôgê* ("educational curriculum," "way of life") occurs in vs. 16. (My translation also turns the verse into idiomatic English.) Perhaps I have been oversubtle. The most usual meaning of *êgagen*, especially in a context involving ephebes, is "he led in procession"; see *Syll.*³, vol. 4, p. 188. Then the translation would be "He took pleasure in subjecting the noblest adolescent boys to the wearing of the broad-brimmed Greek hat and in leading them in procession." The processions were part of the ritual of ephebic training, so that the difference between the two renderings is small.

Greek ephebes took their physical education naked, but to protect their heads from the sun and weather they wore the broad-brimmed *petasos,* which became their characteristic "uniform" (Hesychius, s.v.; E. Schuppe, "Petasos," PW, XIX¹ [1937], 1120). To speak of non-Jewish ephebes exercising while wearing the *petasos* would imply that they were naked. Has the author here made a reticent hint that the Jewish ephebes were naked? Reticence is out of character for him. Surely he intended to denounce loudly any departure from ancestral custom. We can thus infer that the Jewish ephebes at Jerusalem exercised while wearing the *petasos* but at least covered their loins (cf. Thucydides i 6). At Jubilees 3:31 we read, "It is prescribed on the heavenly tables as touching all those who know the judgment of the law, that they should cover their shame and should not uncover themselves as the gentiles uncover themselves." The book of Jubilees was written between autumn, 169, and spring, 167 B.C.E. (see Introduction, Part V, section 1). In view of our inference here that the ephebes at Jerusalem did not exercise naked, Jubilees 3:31 at most is a warning against the possibility that they might do so. See my article in *Jewish and Christian Self-Definition,* II, 77–78. Furthermore, we read at I 1:14–15 that the Hellenizers built a gymnasium in Jerusalem and underwent operations to disguise their circumcision. Does not this imply that the Antiochenes and ephebes in Jerusalem exercised naked? Certainly Josephus drew that inference (*AJ* xii 5.1.241), as did I at AB vol. 41, p. 200. Our text here, I believe, should be decisive against that conclusion. At AB vol. 41, p. 200, I demonstrated that but few could have undergone the operation to disguise circumcision. We may suppose that those few had in mind participation in Greek games outside Judaea.

13. *aping of Greek manners.* So I translate the Greek word *Hellênismos.* The word was used earlier to mean "use of a pure Greek style or idiom" (see the *Greek-English Lexicon,* s.v., II), but this is the earliest known occurrence of the word in the extended sense of "Greek culture," as in the modern term "Hellenism."

Greeks never forgot the history of the Persian wars of the sixth and fifth centuries B.C.E., in which one who deserted the cause of the Greeks to collaborate with their enemies was said to "Medize," since the Persian empire in the time of King Cyrus (who conquered the Greeks of Asia) was still called the "kingdom of the Medes." See M. A. Dandamaev, *Persien unter den ersten Achämeniden* ("Beiträge zur Iranistik," herausgegeben von Georges Redard, Band VIII; Wiesbaden: Dr. Ludwig Reichert Verlag, 1976), pp. 94–95, and the unpublished dissertation of David Graf, *Medism: Greek Collaboration with Achaemenid Persia* (University of Michigan, 1979). The implied antonyms of "Medize" and "Medism" were "Hellenize" and "Hellenism," which would mean "be loyal to the Greek cause." Here our writer, a literate Greek Jew, again reverses Greek habits of expression: just as he used "barbarian" to mean *"Greek-*speaking gentiles" (see NOTE on 2:21), so here he employs *Hellênismos* as a discreditable term, with the connotation "desertion of the Jewish cause." Note also his use of *Ioudaïsmos* ("Judaism") at 2:21.

14–15. The duties of the officiating priests consisted almost entirely of the preparation, slaughter, and offering of sacrifices and the eating of portions from them. There were far too many priests for the duties, so that the priests took turns in performing them. Pious zeal could make a priest so eager for such duty that he might take to violence against a rival, so that a procedure had to be devised for assigning duties by lot. See Schürer (New English version), II, 245–46, 292–308; *M. Yoma* 2:2, To. *Yoma* 1:12, and TB *Yoma* 23a. Jason's father, Simon the Just, is said to have held that the existence of the world depended on the sacrificial service of the temple (*M. Abot* 1:2). On the posts to which a priest could aspire, see Schürer (New English version), II, 275–308. Now the priests might wish to excel in gymnastics and also in the politics of the organization around the gymnasium; see Marrou, *Education in Antiquity*, pp. 158–59, and Nilsson, *Die hellenistische Schule*, pp. 53–59.

The "summons of the gong" might be translated "summons of the discus," but there is no reason why the discus should be singled out here. The daily activity of the gymnasium began with a visible or audible signal, here with the sound of a gong. Cf. Cicero *De oratore* ii. 5. 21, and see Adolf Wilhelm, *Neue Beiträge zur griechischen Inschriftenkunde, Fünfter Teil* ("AWW: Sitzungsberichte," 214. Band, 4. Abhandlung [1932]), pp. 44–47, and Louis Robert, *Études anatoliennes* (Paris: É. de Boccard, 1937), pp. 290–91.

I have translated by "entertainment" the Greek word *chorêgias*, which might mean "the duties of providing for the expenses." In Greek communities a person who donated his time and his money for the activities of the gymnasium received high honor (Marrou, *Education in Antiquity*, p. 163), but there could be only a limited number of wealthy donors, and the author complains of mass defection by the priests. Rather, *chorêgia* here means "entertainment," in the sense of "the use of the facilities provided by the gymnasial organization with the help of the donations of its benefactors." These facilities would include both permanent equipment and consumables, such as oil for anointing the body. See Wilhelm, *Neue Beiträge*, pp. 45–46, and Robert, *Études anatoliennes*, pp. 290–91.

As Doran suggests (*Temple Propaganda*, pp. 44–45, n. 91), our writer is probably engaging in his usual wordplay. The word I have translated "duties" (*leitourgia*) in Greek means "public service performed at one's own expense." It is a broad term, which includes *chorêgia* as one of its species. I still would think that *chorêgia* here should be taken in the passive sense, to mean the use of the facilities rather than the provision of them: instead of doing their public duty of attending to the holy service of the altar, the priests rush to partake of the illicit bounty provided at the gymnasium.

The "wrestling yard" (*palaistra*), the central part of a Greek gymnasium, was a courtyard surrounded by colonnades, in which most of the exercises and sporting events took place, except for those of the running track. On occasion the word may have been used as a synonym for "gymnasium." See Marrou, *Education in Antiquity*, pp. 180–83, and Delorme, *Gymnasion*, pp. 260–71.

16–17. Jason of Cyrene agrees with the author of I 1:11–15, 64: the Hellenizers' sin of following Greek practices, especially the pursuits of the gymnasium, incurred as punishment the sack of Jerusalem, the expedition of the Mysarch, and the persecution. At Test Moses 5, too, the provocative sins are ascribed to the Hellenizers, but nothing is said to connect the sins with *Greek* practices or with the gymnasium. There were other Jewish explanations of the disasters in Ep. 1 (see NOTE on 1:7, *Jason . . . Kingdom*) and in the books of Daniel, Enoch, and Jubilees (see my article in *Jewish and Christian Self-Definition*, II, 80–81).

18–20. "Quinquennial" games occur every four years; in the Greek word *pentaetêrikos*, the "inclusive" method of counting is used (see Appendix VII). We learn from vs. 19 that the games were dedicated to Herakles-Melqart, the great god of Tyre (see Will Richter, "Melqart," *Der kleine Pauly*, III [1969], 1184). However, our information is insufficient to fix the time of the four-year cycle of the games and the season at which they took place. We know that Alexander, at the end of his seven-month siege of Tyre, found trapped in the city a festive delegation from Carthage which had come there for an ancient rite of Melqart (Arrian *Anabasis* ii. 24. 5; Curtius iv. 2. 10; J. *AJ* xi 8.4.325). Since the siege ended, on the Athenian calendar, in the first month after the summer solstice (Arrian *Anabasis* ii. 24. 6; Bickerman, *Chronology*, p. 20), it began in December or January. But Curtius calls the occasion of the coming of the delegation from Carthage an *annual* rite. There is no reason to assume that the four-year cycle, common among the Greeks, existed at Tyre before the coming of Alexander, or that the proud Tyrians established a cycle of games to commemorate either the disastrous siege of 332 or the games to Herakles at Tyre presented in the spring of 331 by Alexander, the conqueror and destroyer (Arrian *Anabasis* iii. 6. 1). Greek games presented by the Tyrians themselves probably were a natural development arising from the progressive Hellenization of the refounded city; cf. Bickerman, "Sur une inscription grecque de Sidon," *Mélanges syriens offerts à M. René Dussaud* vol. 1 (Paris: Geuthner, 1939), pp. 91–99, and Eissfeldt, "Tyros," PW, VIIA² (1943), 1896.

Nor is there any reason why the institution of the games must have coincided with the beginning of the old Tyrian era in 275/4 B.C.E. (see Eissfeldt, PW, VIIA², 1896) or with an even fourth year thereafter. We learn from J. *Ap.* i 18.119 that the Tyrian festival of the Awakening of Melqart (*tou Herakleous egersis*) fell in the Tyrian month Peritios (February–March? see Bickerman, *Chronology*, pp. 50–51), but even if we could be sure when Peritios fell, nothing guarantees that the games coincided with the Awakening of Melqart. There were probably other festivals to Melqart in the Tyrian calendar; see Isidore Lévy, "Cultes et rites syriens dans le Talmud," *Revue des études juives* 43 (1901), 195–97. Nor is there any reason to assume that the second visit of Antiochus IV to Tyre (vs. 44) must have been for the next occurrence of the games. He had other reasons to come to Phoenicia (cf. vs. 22). Hence, despite the efforts of J. G. Bunge ("Theos Epiphanes," *Historia* 23 [1974], 63–66), in order to date the events of our verses we must first establish the dates of the other events in our chapter.

The Tyrians were not citizens of the Antiochene republic but received privileges analogous to those of the Latins in Roman Italy and thus held high prestige in the system established by Antiochus IV; see AB vol. 41, p. 118. The seamanship of the Tyrians and their strategic location surely had something to do with their prestige; the king may also have been pleased by their prowess in Greek gymnastics. The communities of Antiochenes and the king himself could think it important to attend the games at Tyre.

19. Greek games occurred on religious festivals, and the word for a member of a delegation to a celebration of games was the same as that for an envoy

sent for religious purposes (*theôros*). The "registration fee" or "admission fee" for participants in the games normally went to pay for sacrifices to the god in whose honor the games were celebrated. Jason the Oniad appears to have viewed the payment as a mere entrance fee, with no concern for how the hosts would spend the money. His own delegates were more strict about anything that could associate Jews with idol worship; cf. *M. 'Abodah zarah* 1:1. The Tyrians surely would not violate their own religious scruples, yet they were willing to accommodate the scruples of the Jewish Antiochenes and accept them as "secular" participants in the games sacred to Melqart. The fact by itself suggests that at this time participation in the games was widely viewed as a nonreligious activity and that Jason the Oniad had some justification for being unconcerned about the destination of the entrance fee, despite the indignant inference in vs. 20 as to his intentions. The author here wishes to parade the most heinous sins of Jason. If Jason or his associates had participated directly in idol worship, the author would have said so, loudly. Hence, we learn that the sweeping accusation at I 1:43, that the Jewish Hellenizers worshiped idols, is an exaggeration. Both our authors probably got their information from the Common Source, which Jason here reflects accurately, whereas the author of First Maccabees went beyond the evidence. If so, we have one more confirmation that I 1:41–43 tells of events before the persecution began and that its verbs are to be taken as pluperfects. See AB vol. 41, pp. 119–20, 221.

The 300 drachmas are of the right order of magnitude; cf. *Syll.*[3] 398, lines 44–45, and *Syll.*[3] 402, line 30 (400–500 drachmas for a sacrifice), and OGIS 319, line 20 (100 drachmas as *aparchê*). Cattle prices on the island of Delos at this time were between 70 and 120 drachmas per head (Fritz Heichelheim, *Wirtschaftliche Schwankungen der Zeit von Alexander bis Augustus* [Jena: Fischer, 1930], pp. 134–35), and a day's wage for an artisan or laborer was about one drachma (Michael Rostovtzeff, *The Social and Economic History of the Hellenistic World* [Oxford: Clarendon Press, 1953], III, 1600–1, n. 53). In Lucian's time (the early fourth century c.e.), wages and prices were at least twenty-five times as high (see Heichelheim, loc. cit., and Diocletian's edict on prices, translated in Naphtali Lewis and Meyer Reinhold, *Roman Civilization,* vol. 2 [New York: Columbia University Press, 1955], pp. 466–70). Hence, it is no surprise to find the figure 300 altered to 3300 in *L'* and Sy.

21–22. The Seleucid Chronicle probably told of the diplomatic and military maneuvers which brought Antiochus IV to the vicinity of Jerusalem. The details of his visit to Jerusalem, however, probably were recorded or remembered by a Jew, perhaps in a journal of the high priesthood of Jason the Oniad (see p. 47). Anti-Seleucid Onias IV probably reported nothing of Antiochus' visit. Jason of Cyrene and the author of the Common Source would have wished to display Antiochus IV as benevolent to the Jews until he became the rod of God's anger. Jason of Cyrene also had a special reason for telling of Antiochus' measures against the Ptolemies: thereby he could protect prophecies of Daniel from being challenged. By the time of Jason of Cyrene, believers, like Jerome later, were probably uncertain whether Dan 7:19–27, 8:9–14 and 23–24, 9:26–27, and 11:18–45 referred to events of the second century B.C.E. or to the period culminating in the End of Days. In order to mention the prophecies in the course of his narrative, Jason of Cyrene would have had to decide between the alternatives; hence, he refrains from mentioning them. On the other hand, skeptics were quick to point out that Dan 11:28–30 seems to imply that Antiochus IV in person came twice with hostile intent against Jerusalem, whereas historians, including Jason of Cyrene, knew of only one such attack. See NOTE on 5:1.

However, Jason of Cyrene found that hypocritical courtesies and hostile maneuvers between the Seleucid and Ptolemaic empires preceded a friendly visit of Antiochus to Jerusalem when Jason the Oniad was high priest. It was difficult but not impossible to interpret Dan 11:25–26 to refer to border skirmishes, and Dan 11:27 to refer to the hypocritical meeting by proxy of Antiochus IV and Ptolemy VI, Antiochus IV being represented by his ambassador. Then Dan 11:28 could be interpreted to refer to Antiochus' peaceful visit during the high priesthood of Jason; though Antiochus' behavior then was peaceful, it could still have been motivated by greed, if that was the meaning of the words in Dan 11:28, "his heart against the Sacred Covenant" (see AB vol. 41, last NOTE on 1:20). But Jason of Cyrene may have taken the Heb. *lbbw 'l* to mean "his heart shall be sympathetic to" (cf. *lbb 'l* at Josh 24:23; I Kings 8:58). To be doubly safe, Jason of Cyrene referred to Antiochus' defensive maneuvers in the vaguest of terms.

21. *Apollonius son of Menestheus.* See NOTE on vs. 4.

Protoklisia *of King Philometor.* King Philometor was the then very young Ptolemy VI. See Hans Volkmann, "Ptolemaios 24," PW, XXIII² (1959), 1702–4. He reigned from 180 to 145 B.C.E. *Prôtoklisia* is derived from the Greek roots "first" (*prôt-*) and "recline" or "couch" (*klin-*). It is the reading of q⁻²⁹ ⁷¹ ¹²⁰ ⁷³¹• 19 58 311, supported by La^BMP (*primas recubitiones, primos discubitus, primos accubitos*), and not opposed by La^LXV (*primatus*). A and *L'* read *Prôtoklêsia.* The second element, *-klêsia,* in the compound word would be derived from the Greek root "call" (*kale-*). Since *ê* and *i* were pronounced alike by the time of the scribe of A, either reading could easily be transformed into the other (see Abel, *Grammaire,* pp. 13–14, and note the use of *ê* for *i* in A at Gen 47:6, 11, and of *i* for *ê* at Tobit 16:9). No royal ceremony by either name is known from Ptolemaic Egypt or anywhere else. Polybius mentions (xxviii 12.8 – 13.4) a ceremony for Ptolemy VI called *Anaklêtêria* and explains that it was celebrated when Ptolemaic kings came of age and lets us know that the news that it had been celebrated reached Greece in the winter of 170/69 (see Mørkholm, p. 70, n. 24). By the time of the *Anaklêtêria,* then, Jason had long since ceased to be high priest, so that *prôtoklêsia* could not be a synonym for *anaklêtêria* even though both are derived from the same Greek root.

Prôtoklêsia would occur only here in extant Greek texts. *Prôtoklisia* here is neuter plural. The feminine singular word *prôtoklisia* occurs at Matt 23:6; Mark 12:39; and Luke 14:7 and 20:46, but there it means "the couch of honor at a banquet" (see Louis Robert, "Inscriptions d'Athènes et de la Grèce centrale," *Archaiologikê Ephêmeris* (1969), 13–14, and Walter Otto, *Zur Geschichte der Zeit des 6. Ptolemäers* [ABAW, new series, 11 (1934); München: Beck, 1934], pp. 16–18). Our context requires the name of a royal celebration, and the meaning of *prôtoklisia* in the New Testament would have to be considerably extended to fit here. Otto, indeed, argues for such an extension (ibid.), but if the scribes knew only the feminine singular word from the New Testament, they would be unlikely to substitute neuter plural *Prôtoklisia* for *Prôtoklêsia* here. On the other hand, if they knew the word *Anaklêtêria*, with the root *kale-* in mind, they might alter the unfamiliar *Prôtoklisia* to *Prôtoklêsia* (cf. Otto, ibid., p. 15, n. 3). *Prôtoklisia* here could easily mean the celebration of the first occasion on which the young king presided over a formal state banquet. It cannot refer, as "first marriage bed," to the marriage of Ptolemy VI to his sister Cleopatra II, which occurred before April 15, 175, long before Antiochus IV became king (Mørkholm, p. 68, n. 18).

J. G. Bunge ("Theos Epiphanes," *Historia* 23 [1974], 70–71) accepted the reading *Prôtoklêsia* and argued that as a compound of "first" and "calling" it meant the first anniversary of the assumption of the full set of the Egyptian cult names of the Pharaoh by Ptolemy VI, on the analogies of the word *prôtogenesia*, "first birthday," and of the *Sed* festivals of the Pharaohs, which marked the anniversaries of their accession. Bunge assumes that Ptolemy VI was crowned according to Egyptian rites and took a full set of Egyptian cult names in the spring of 175, around the time of his marriage to Cleopatra II. The assumed coronation, however, has left no trace in the documents, and the existing evidence does not favor Bunge's interpretation. Ptolemy VI did indeed add the epithets *theos* ("god") and *Philomêtôr* ("who loves his mother"), or their Egyptian equivalents, to his official titles in 176 after the death of his mother, Cleopatra I (Volkmann, PW, XXIII, 1703; P. W. Pestman, *Chronologie égyptienne d'après les textes démotiques* ["Papyrologica Lugduno-Batava," vol. 15; Leiden: Brill, 1967], p. 48), but the first anniversary of the assumption of those titles would fall in 175, too early for an event which occurred well into Jason's high priesthood.

Philometor was . . . kingdom. The Ptolemaic empire still resented the loss of Syria and Palestine to the Seleucids in 200 and was plotting to reconquer them. See AB vol. 41, NOTE on 1:16–19.

Joppe. Modern Jaffa (=Yafo); see Map 3.

22. The Jews of Jerusalem, probably both the Antiochenes and the non-Antiochenes, welcomed the king with exemplary loyalty. The words "thereafter in the same manner" (*eith' houtôs*) probably mean that the Jews showed the same enthusiasm in escorting the king out of Jerusalem. The words may also allude to Dan 11:28–29: this time Antiochus returned to his own land in this peaceful manner, not as reported at 5:17 and 21. The expression *eith' houtôs* occurs also at 15:13, where Onias III and Jeremiah appear in the same manner, praying; cf. also Wisdom 17:16.

Torchlight processions in the honor of kings were common in the Hellenistic monarchies. See Otto and Bengtson, pp. 154–55. Ephebes made torchlight processions in honor of their royal benefactors (Nilsson, *Die hellenistische Schule*, pp. 73–74). Ptolemy III as conqueror got a similar reception at Antioch in 246 (M. Holleaux, "Remarques sur le papyrus de Gourob," *Bulletin de correspondance hellénique* 30 [1906], 337–38).

The "shouts" (*boôn*) are the reading of all the important Greek witnesses, and are paralleled in the Gourob papyrus (Holleaux, ibid., p. 338, line 25). La^LX and 106 have "peltings" (*missilibus, bolôn*) and La^BM have "flowers" (*floribus*), both of which Abel rightly interpreted to mean "peltings of flowers," as at Herodian iv 18. 19.

23–50. On the possibility that Onias IV avoided recording how his righteous father came to be murdered through the intrigues of Menelaus, see NOTE on vss. 1–38. In any case, nothing prevented Onias IV from exposing the other crimes of the non-Oniad usurper, Menelaus. The author of the Common Source had no inhibitions about exposing all these matters. The seer at Dan 11:22–24 probably alludes to Menelaus' corrupt negotiations with the king and subsequent depredations. See AB vol. 41, Introduction, Part II, n. 28. If the correct interpretation of *bšlwh* at Dan 11:24 is "in time of peace," the seer, like Jason of Cyrene (3:1, 4:22), stressed how peaceful Jerusalem was before the wicked high priests brought civil strife and also incurred disastrous divine punishment. H. L. Ginsberg, however, has suggested to me that *bšlwh* reflects the Aramaic *šlw* ("deceit") and is to be translated "deceitfully."

23. See NOTE on vss. 7–38.

Menelaus . . . Simon. See NOTES on 3:4 and vs. 8. Josephus (*AJ* xii 5.1.238, 9.6.387, xx 10.3.235–36) says that Menelaus' Hebrew name was Onias and that Menelaus was son of the high priest Simon II and brother of Onias III and uncle of Onias IV. The information on the Hebrew name of Menelaus and on the name of his father as Simon may well be correct. The rest is probably pro-Hasmonaean anti-Oniad propaganda; see AB vol. 41, p. 59. Menelaus, like his brother Simon, belonged to the priestly clan of Bilgah (3:4) and cannot have been a son of the high priest Simon II, who belonged to the priestly clan of Yedayah. Josephus' assertion that Menelaus was the uncle of Onias IV is only a corollary. There is no reason to try to save it by saying that Menelaus was the brother of the wife of Onias III (cf. Stern, *Zion* 25 [1960], 12 [in Hebrew]).

Josephus read the abridged history (see Introduction, Part I, n. 80) and was well acquainted with the priestly clans. Only if he read in another source that Menelaus belonged to the Oniad line would he be likely to risk making the assertion here. The propaganda probably originated when Hasmonaeans were pressing their claims to the high priesthood, long before the time of Josephus.

agent . . . matters. The "royal decisions" here are called *hypomnêmatismous* ("memoranda") because the original document recording them was an entry in the royal journal (*hypomnêmata* or *ephêmeris*); the king made his pronouncement orally, and it was recorded by his secretary. See Welles, *Royal Correspondence,* pp. 283–84, and Bickerman, *Institutions,* pp. 194–95. The verb here for "to execute" such a decision is *telein;* at Welles, *Royal Correspondence,* no. 70, line 4, it is *syntelein.*

24. The Greek here (*DOXASAS AUTON*) is ambiguous. Did Menelaus magnify his own importance or the king's? Early scribes did not put in the breathing marks which could have made the Greek unambiguous, and later scribes and interpreters guessed. The Latin versions have Menelaus flattering the king, and the Syriac has him magnifying himself. I follow Abel in thinking that the context, "by giving the impression [that he was a man] of authority," is decisive for agreeing with the Syriac.

Menelaus' bid probably increased only the amount of regular tribute to 660 talents, a very heavy burden, which he was unable to impose on Judaea (vs.

27). On "authority" (*exousia*), cf. NOTES on 3:6, *fall . . . confiscate,* and on vs. 9, *by virtue of his office.*

25. *holding . . . decrees.* Surely the decrees (*entolas*) appointing him high priest and deposing Jason. The same word is used at 3:13 of the orders borne by Heliodorus, and the author may intend the reader to view Jason as a successor not of Onias III but of Heliodorus.

but . . . beast. The qualifications of the ideal priest are at Mal 2:4–7.

26. Jason of Cyrene believed in precise divine retribution, and even when the text in speaking of retribution does not mention God, it is likely that the author saw there the hand of God. We are not told whether the king banished Jason or whether local political pressures forced Jason's withdrawal from Judaea. The stronghold of Hyrcanus the Tobiad lay in the Ammanitis, and Hyrcanus was probably still alive. See NOTES on 1:7, *Jason . . . Kingdom,* and on 3:11.

27. *make . . . regular payments.* The Greek verb is *eutaktein,* commonly used in official documents of the Hellenistic monarchies.

28. The Greek word *diaphora* here probably means "money," as at 1:35 and 3:6. If so, it appears that Sostratos had the duty of collecting the regular payments. To prevent a Jewish subordinate from repeating his own exploit, Menelaus may have seen to it that henceforth the garrison commander should receive the tax money and send it on to the king. On the other hand, *diaphora* here might mean "arrears" (Bickerman, *Studies,* II, 163–64). The only body at Jerusalem which was available to act as police for the king was the garrison of the citadel. On the citadel see NOTE to vs. 12.

In any case, Menelaus was summoned by the king for failing to pay and Sostratos for failing to collect.

29. I have rendered Greek *diadochos* as "substitute" and "deputy," the person who acts for a person in his absence. Cf. vs. 31 and 14:26 and Polybius iii 87. 9.

Lysimachus figures prominently in vss. 39–42, but why did Jason of Cyrene mention Krates? Perhaps Krates, too, was a "persecutor" who came to a bad end, but the story has been lost through abridgment.

Cyprus was at this time under Ptolemaic rule, but mercenaries hired themselves out to the highest bidder. See Launey, *Recherches,* pp. 487–89, and cf. 12:2.

30–31. The uprisings in the Cilician cities of Tarsus and Mallos (see Map 2) are known only from here. Neither Jason of Cyrene nor his sources had any reason to invent this report, so we need not view it with skepticism. The cities were important enough so that their revolt demanded the king's personal attention. However, Antiochus may have yielded for the sake of peace in a strategic border province. We know from the coins of Tarsus that the king conferred upon it the privileges of an Antiochene city (see AB vol. 41, pp. 115–16), and an inscription shows that the privileges were still in force in 166 B.C.E. (Mørkholm, p. 60, n. 32).

The Seleucid kings ruled their realm by right of conquest and had the power to dispose at pleasure of subject communities by gift or sale. See Bickerman, *Institutions,* pp. 133–34. The citizens of the two cities probably found Antiochus' gift of them an affront to their pride. Their purses probably would not suffer if the revenues of the towns went to the woman instead of to the king, but the woman also acquired the king's power to intervene in the affairs of the cities, and the citizens could think the caprice of a woman to be more demeaning than the whims of Antiochus IV. Cf. Cicero *Against Verres II* 3.33, but see also the conjectures of C. Bradford Welles, "Hellenistic Tarsus," *Mélanges de l'Université Saint Joseph* 38 (offerts au Père René Mouterde, 1962), 49–52.

31–38. Our passage tells the story of the death of Onias III. Many scholars have questioned its veracity; see the discussion of Martin Hengel, *Judaism and Hellenism* (Philadelphia: Fortress Press, 1974), vol. 2, p. 183, n. 132, and p. 185, n. 142. M. Stern decisively refuted the challenges (*Zion* 25 [1960], 1–16 [in Hebrew, with very brief English summary, p. i]), but his article is inaccessible to many. Scholars have said that our passage contradicts the information on Onias III at *BJ* i 1.1.33, vii 10.2.423, and in rabbinic literature. But Josephus wrote from inaccurate memory in writing his *War* and later recognized and corrected his errors in his *Antiquities;* see AB vol. 41, pp. 59–61. The rabbinic legends probably reflect unhistorical propaganda; on them, see NOTE on 3:4, *chief . . . temple.* Far from confirming the accounts in Josephus' *War*, the commentary of Theodorus of Mopsuestia to Greek Ps 54 (Hebrew Ps 55) is itself derived from those accounts, as Stern conclusively demonstrated (*Zion* 25 [1960], 13–15).

It is strange that Jason of Cyrene allows the reader to infer that saintly Onias III took asylum in a pagan shrine (see NOTE on vs. 33), but the strangeness makes it most unlikely that he or anyone else fabricated a falsehood here.

Scholars have also raised objections based on pagan sources. Diodorus xxx 7.2 implies that a person named Andronikos, on behalf of Antiochus IV, did away with little Antiochus, the son of Seleucus IV, only to be executed in turn by Antiochus IV. The story also appears in John of Antioch, Fragment 58 (in *Fragmenta Historicorum Graecorum*, ed. by Carolus Müller [Paris: Firmin-Didot, 1878–85], vol. 4, p. 558), though Andronikos is not mentioned by name (on the death of little Antiochus, see Mørkholm, pp. 42–50). The Seleucid king list from Babylon (*Iraq* 16 [1954], 204, 208) lets us know that little Antiochus was put to death in the fifth month of 142 Sel. Bab. (July 31–August 28, 170 B.C.E.). From Dan 9:26 we learn that Onias III perished in the post-sabbatical year, 170/69 B.C.E; see NOTE on vs. 34. It is hard to avoid the conclusion that the gentile sources and our passage are speaking of the same Andronikos. Yet in the gentile sources he is executed for murdering little Antiochus and in the Jewish sources for murdering Onias III!

Jason of Cyrene wrote over three quarters of a century after the events. By that time Jews could have inferred, from the facts that Andronikos did away with Onias III and was executed by Antiochus IV, that the former was the reason for the latter. However, Onias IV may have written accurately about the death of his father. As Stern noted (*Zion* 25 [1960], 4–5), Antiochus IV may have been glad to have the pretext of the murder of Onias III in order to rid himself of Andronikos, though Andronikos was his own trusted agent. For thus he could hope to still the talk of his own complicity in the death of little Antiochus without having to mention little Antiochus at all. Meanwhile, persons hostile to Antiochus IV would remark that the king really executed his own embarrassing accomplice, and their view would have survived in our pagan sources. On the lack of hostility here of the Jewish writer to Antiochus IV, see NOTE on vss. 7–50.

Jason says that Menelaus induced Andronikos to do away with Onias. Yet Menelaus was able to conceal any guilt of his from the royal government, for the king, in punishing Andronikos, left Menelaus untouched. One would therefore like to know how Jason or his source learned that Menelaus was implicated. Was it a mere guess?

31. *deputy*. See NOTE on vs. 29.

32. Menelaus was doubly vicious. Not only did he stoop to temple robbery in a crisis—even before, he had done so. In return for Menelaus' bribes, Andronikos appears to have acquitted him of failing to pay the taxes, for we hear no more of the matter. One wonders, however, why Antiochus, after punishing Andronikos, did not pursue it again. How was Menelaus any more able to deliver the promised taxes? He himself is not further accused of selling temple vessels to raise money.

33. It was dangerous to denounce an accomplice of the person who was acting in place of the absent king. Virtuous Onias was not silenced by the danger but took the precaution of withdrawing to a place of asylum, where religion and law should have protected him from injury. Surely most if not all places of asylum at Daphne were pagan shrines. One might have thought that it was discreditable for a saintly high priest to resort to a pagan shrine, and that the abridger or Jason's source would have taken care to exclude the possibility that the shrine was pagan. Our passage shows no such concern, and perhaps Onias III and our writers saw nothing wrong in so preserving one's life, as long as no idolatry was involved. Cf. Herod's procedure at *BJ* i 14.2.277 and *AJ* xiv 14.2.374. If the place of asylum had been a synagogue, on the other hand, our writers probably would have mentioned the fact.

Daphne was about five miles from Antioch and had a famous temple of Apollo and Artemis, the precinct of which was a place of asylum (Strabo xvi. 2. 6, C 750).

34. Menelaus was in a difficult position: even if he should not be convicted, Antiochus might prefer to replace unreliable Menelaus with faithful Onias.

The seer at Dan 9:26 probably alludes to the murder of Onias III. I shall treat the verse in detail in my commentary on Daniel. According to Dan 9:24, Israel is to suffer for seventy weeks of years in order to expiate sin, and then will come the great vindication, in fulfillment of the words of the Prophets. According to Dan 9:25, the seventy weeks of years contain a period of seven and a period of sixty-two weeks of years before the final week. The final week is to end with the end of the sabbatical year, in autumn, 163; see AB vol. 41, pp. 42–43, as corrected above, Introduction, Part V, section 3.

Dan 9:26 describes events of the final week: "And after the sixty-two weeks, an anointed one will be cut off, though he will not possess, and the people of the prelate who will come after him will work destruction upon the city and the sanctuary. . . ." "Anointed one" here probably means "high priest"; see NOTE on 1:10b. The text of "though he will not possess" is probably defective. We may guess that what the anointed one did not possess was either guilt or his rightful office as high priest. Either description would fit Onias III. The "people of the prelate who will come after him" are said to do exactly what

Jason and his supporters did, according to 1:7–8 and 5:5–6, and the date of Jason's coup is securely fixed in autumn, 169 B.C.E.; see AB vol. 41, p. 207.

Thus we have a high priest being "cut off" at the beginning of a sabbatical week of years, not too long before Jason's coup of autumn, 169 B.C.E. Surely, then, the "anointed one" is Onias III, and his death is to be placed in 170/69 B.C.E., the first year of the sabbatical cycle.

I shall show elsewhere that Enoch 90:8 reflects events of the end of the third century B.C.E. For that reason alone, the verse cannot refer to the death of Onias III. Moreover, the text there has "The ravens flew upon those lambs and took one of those lambs, and dashed the sheep in pieces and devoured them." How can one fit into that picture the murder of Onias III as described here? The author who produced Enoch 90:8 could hardly have thought so highly of Onias III as to make his death a major atrocity perpetrated by the gentile enemies of Israel, for Onias III presided over the temple offerings, which that author viewed as unclean (Enoch 89:73).

Brazen in treachery. The Greek here, *peistheis epi dolôi* ("persuaded on treachery") has puzzled translators ancient and modern. *Peistheis* is the aorist passive participle of *peithein* ("persuade"). In biblical Greek, by far the most frequent form of *peithein* is the intransitive second perfect *pepoithenai,* which often occurs with the preposition *epi* governing a dative, with the meaning "trust in" or "be confident in" (7:40; Greek Isa 30:12, 15, 32; Job 6:20, etc.). I believe our expression here to be similar. If the aorist was not so used in ordinary speech, it may have been in the affected style used by Jason of Cyrene and the abridger. Abel, in his commentary (p. 342), suggests a similar rendering, though on an insecure basis; strangely, his translation does not agree with his commentary!

accepted . . . oath. I follow here the reading of A (*dexiastheis meth' horkôn dous dexian*), supported by La[P] (*et esset acceptus cum iure iurando data dextra*). The reading contains the rare word *dexiastheis.* The word obviously has something to do with the right hand (*dexia*). One who was unfamiliar with the word and its precise meaning could find the passage redundant and would then try to correct it. La[LXVBM] and *L* omit *dexiastheis,* but no one would have inserted the difficult word if it had not been in the original text. Jason of Cyrene was fond of rare words and of multiple use of a Greek root in a single verse. The misguided efforts of scribes to turn the unfamiliar word into a familiar expression (V 46–52 55 106 311 542) also strongly suggest that A preserves the original reading. Since *dexiastheis* occurs only here, one must guess at its meaning from the context and etymology. As a passive participle in the nominative case, it should refer to action upon Apollonius by Onias. La[P] seems to have rendered it correctly, and I have translated accordingly.

In the Hellenistic world a handclasp was not a perfunctory gesture but one supposed to reflect sincere friendship; see Hug, "Salutatio," PW, I[A] (1920), 2062–63. Handclasps also were used to solemnize sworn agreements between individuals not to harm one another; see G. Glotz, *"Jusjurandum (Horkos)—* Grèce," DAGR, III 1 (1899), 752a.

did away with. Gr. *parekleisen* ("shut up"), a euphemism for "kill." Cf. Polybius v 39.3 in conjunction with Plutarch *Agis and Cleomenes* 37.4.

35-37. Jason of Cyrene follows his tendency to cite instances of friendly relations between Jews and gentiles. See AB vol. 41, p. 34.

35. *were scandalized.* Gr. *edeinazon;* the word is wrongly defined in the *Greek-English Lexicon.* Literally it means "regard as *deinon* ["horrible"]." Cf. 13:25.

37. "Upright character" (*sôphrosynê*) and "orderly life" (*eutaxia*) are cardinal virtues for a citizen or subject of a Greek state. See Plato *Alcibiades I* 122c. Polybius describes Scipio in the same terms (xxxi 25.8). The Jewish-Greek author intelligently portrays Antiochus as admiring the pious Jew Onias for his virtues of the Greek type.

38. A purple robe was the uniform of members of the order of the Friends of the King (Bickerman, *Institutions,* p. 42; Meyer Reinhold, *History of Purple as a Status Symbol in Antiquity* ["Collection Latomus," vol. 116; Bruxelles: Latomus, 1970], pp. 34-35). By stripping off the purple, Antiochus stripped Andronikos of his rank as a Friend. By tearing off his other clothing (*chitônas* ["tunics"]), Antiochus probably stripped him naked in preparation for his execution; cf. *M. Sanhedrin* 6:3; John 19:23-24. The parade of the naked criminal through the streets to his place of execution was probably also standard practice. In a world without newspapers, it served as publicity to deter others from committing similar crimes.

removed . . . world. The word *apokosmein* has this sense only here, but the context demands that it mean Aristonikos was executed, and so the Latin and Syriac translators understood it, and etymology allows our translation.

thus . . . deserved. As seen by Jason of Cyrene, already here Antiochus IV serves as God's punishing instrument.

39-42. The author abstains from accusing Menelaus of thefts beyond those mentioned in vs. 32. Lysimachus was the thief, but with Menelaus' connivance. We are not told whether Menelaus was still in Antioch when the events of our chapter took place. If he returned to Jerusalem, he was again absent during the riots, for he could hardly have abstained from action. According to the tradition preserved in the *Mishnah,* a person guilty of stealing a vessel from the temple was an outlaw to be killed by any zealous person (*M. Sanhedrin* 9:6), precisely what happens here as a mob of indignant Jews gathers against Lysimachus and kills him despite his effort to arm a force of supporters to protect himself.

It is noteworthy that riots in Jerusalem broke out only against Lysimachus, not against Menelaus. Menelaus was appointed by Antiochus. To riot against him would be to rebel against the king, a sin no pious Jew would commit (see NOTE on 1:7, *Jason . . . Kingdom*). Against Menelaus, the only recourse was an appeal to the king (cf. vss. 33, 43-50).

39. The city here is Jerusalem. The presence of the phrase "in the city" suggests that the Greek adverb *exô* ("outside") here means "to the countryside," and I have so translated. Does the author mean to imply that most of the city Jews were Lysimachus' accomplices and that some of them purchased the stolen articles? Perhaps. See vs. 40.

sent abroad. Greek *dienênegmenôn.* My translation fits the etymology and is supported by La^{LV} (*exportatis*).

40. The Seleucids left to the subject communities the conduct of ordinary police affairs, but arms for 3,000 would be another matter. By what authority did Lysimachus acquire them and distribute them to his supporters? Perhaps this fact was included in the accusations later brought against Menelaus.

"Wickedly took the offensive" is a common Greek idiom (*cheirôn adikôn*, with *katarchesthai* or *katarchein* or *archein;* Polybius Fragment 99 Buettner-Wobst, ii. 45. 6, 56. 14, etc.). The author wishes to stress that Lysimachus was not merely trying to defend himself.

The rare name "Auranos" is preserved by A. La *L'* Sy Arm all have the common word or name "Tyrannos," whereas V has "Auranos Tyrannos." V thus supports A, and A is correct, for no scribe would turn a common word into a rare one.

Why does Jason single out Auranos for mention? As a "persecutor," Auranos probably fell in the course of the riot, but the abridged narrative does not say so. The name was borne in the Hasmonaean family, for "Auran(os)" is a variant of "Auaran" (the additional name of the Hasmonaean brother Eleazar) in the manuscripts of I̊ 2:5 and 6:43 and is the version of the name given by Josephus at *AJ* xii 6.1.266 and probably also at *AJ* xii 9.4.373 (it is the reading of manuscripts FAMWVE). Perhaps the anti-Hasmonaean writer here is suggesting that a kinsman of the Hasmonaeans was an ardent supporter of Lysimachus. Also, if old Auranos here, like the Hasmonaean brother, bore the name "Eleazar," Jason of Cyrene would seem to have presented the wicked old man as yet another evil Hasmonaean counterpart of the martyr Eleazar who is the hero of 6:18–31. The same Greek words (*probebêkôs tên hêlikian*) are used to describe each as "advanced in age," here and at 6:18. On the martyr Eleazar as a counterpart of Hasmonaean Mattathias, see NOTE on 6:18–31.

41–42. The unarmed mob had to improvise weapons from street rubbish, and yet routed 3,000 armed men. The temple robber, a Jewish Heliodorus, met retributive death right at the temple treasury. Jason of Cyrene intended the reader to see the miraculous hand of God in the events.

43–44. Menelaus could have been culpable for his own thefts (vs. 32), for conniving at those of Lysimachus (vs. 39), for illegal possession of arms (see NOTE on vs. 40), and for failing to prevent bloodshed in Jerusalem; cf. vs. 48. On the Council of Elders, see NOTE on 1:10b. Here we learn that the Council could act in opposition to the high priest; cf. Bickerman, *Institutions,* p. 165. From the Greek one cannot tell whether the delegates were members of the Council. Since they argued the case before Antiochus IV, they certainly spoke Greek, and they may well have been Antiochenes, like the scrupulous bearers of the admission money to the Tyrian games (vss. 19–20). The number three may have been a requirement of Seleucid law or of Jewish law (Deut 19:5).

From 5:1 we might infer that the king came to Tyre in order to prepare for his campaign against Ptolemaic Egypt, but the words "at about this time" in 5:1 are too vague for us to be sure.

45–46. *Ptolemy son of Dorymenes.* We meet him later (8:8; see also AB vol. 41, NOTE on 3:38, *Ptolemy son of Dorymenes*) as governor of Coele-Syria and Phoenicia, an office he may well have held already, since he was present at a trial in Phoenician Tyre. Here he sides with the Jewish faction of Menelaus against the spokesmen of the Jewish Council of Elders. There is no reason to regard him as a thoroughgoing hater of Jews.

47. Scythians were regarded as the cruelest of barbarians. Cf. III 7:5. As an absolute ruler, the king had the power to condemn any subject to death (see Bickerman, *Institutions*, p. 186), but he might have sentenced the "false accusers" in accordance with some law, perhaps even Jewish law (Deut 19:16–21).

48. See NOTE on vss. 43–44. "Villages" (*dêmôn*) here means Judaea outside Jerusalem, so I have rendered the word as "country villages."

49. See NOTE on vss. 35–37.

50. *devoted himself to.* The Gr. *epiphyomenos* is metaphorical, "attached himself to, as if it were a natural growth from him."

a plotter. The seer at Dan 11:23–24 alluded to Menelaus as a treacherous plotter, if the interpretation of that passage in the NOTE on 10:1–8 is correct.

VI. HOW JASON REBELLED AND ANTIOCHUS PUNISHED JERUSALEM
(5:1–27)

5 ¹ At about this time, Antiochus made preparations for his second departure against Egypt. ² Simultaneously throughout the city for almost forty days apparitions were sighted in the air: there were cavalry at a gallop, dressed in garments of cloth of gold, and troops of armed spearmen formed into regiments; ³ sabres were drawn; squadrons of cavalry formed for battle; there were charges and countercharges from both sides; shields were moved, spears were massed, missiles flew, gold trimmings flashed, and there was all manner of armor. ⁴ In consequence, everyone prayed that the supernatural manifestation might portend good.

⁵ On hearing a false report that Antiochus IV had passed away, Jason took at least a thousand men and perpetrated a surprise attack on the city. The defenders upon the walls were driven off, and finally, just as the city was falling, Menelaus took refuge in the citadel. ⁶ Meanwhile, Jason was mercilessly massacring his own fellow Jews without regard for the fact that victory over one's own flesh and blood is the greatest of defeats. Instead, he thought that he was winning triumphs over enemies, not over men of his own nation. ⁷ Far from recapturing his office, he gained infamy as the end result of his plot, and as a fugitive succeeded in slipping back through to the Ammanitis.

⁸ Finally he came to a miserable end: first he was imprisoned in the realm of Aretas the Arab dynast; then he fled his pursuers from country to country, loathed by all as a rebel against the laws and detested as the executioner of his fatherland and his fellow Jews, and found himself driven like driftwood into Egypt; ⁹ and lastly, the man who had banished many from their fatherland came to perish in banishment after he sailed to Lakedaimon in the hope of finding refuge there as a member of a kindred people. ¹⁰ The man who had cast out multitudes of dead to lie unburied ended up unmourned and received no funeral and no burial among the graves of his ancestors.

11 When the king received the news of the events, he concluded that Judaea was in revolt. Accordingly, he broke camp and set out from Egypt. With the fury of a wild beast he took the city, treating it as enemy territory captured in war. 12 He ordered the soldiers to slay mercilessly whomever they met and to butcher those who withdrew into their houses. 13 Young and old were put to death, women and children perished, and maidens and infants were butchered. 14 Eighty thousand were brought to ruin in the course of three days, of whom forty thousand fell by the sword and an equal number were sold as slaves. 15 Unsatisfied with these atrocities, Antiochus had the audacity to enter the holiest temple in the whole world, taking as his guide Menelaus, the man who had betrayed the laws and his country. 16 With polluted hands he seized the sacred vessels and swept up the gifts deposited by many other kings to magnify and glorify and honor the Place, and he handed them over to his unclean hands.

17 Allowing his vain imagination to soar, Antiochus failed to perceive that the LORD had neglected the Place only because He was for a moment angry at the sins of the inhabitants of the city. 18 As it happened, they had previously been implicated in many sins. But for that fact, Antiochus would have been whipped immediately, as soon as his guide had brought him in, and deterred from his rash project in the same manner as Heliodorus, the man sent by King Seleucus to inspect the treasury. 19 However, it was not for the sake of the Place that the LORD chose the nation; rather, He chose the Place for the sake of the nation. 20 Therefore, even the Place itself partook in the misfortunes of the nation but then shared in the victories which came later. The Place, which had been abandoned at the moment of the Almighty's wrath, was restored to full glory in the time of the great LORD's forgiveness.

21 Hence, Antiochus, after carrying off one thousand eight hundred talents from the temple, hastened back to Antioch, thinking in his arrogance that he had made the land navigable and the sea passable by foot, so high did his vain imagination soar. 22 He went so far as to leave officials in charge of maltreating our race: at Jerusalem, Philip, a Phrygian by birth, but by character more barbaric than the man who appointed him; 23 and at Mount Gerizim, Andronikos; and in addition, Menelaus, who was worse than the others inasmuch as he lorded it over his compatriots.

Disposed to hate the Jews, 24 he sent the Mysarch Apollonius with an army of twenty-two thousand, under orders to butcher all men who were of age and to sell the women and children as slaves. 25 On his arrival at Jerusalem, Apollonius pretended to have peaceful intentions. He waited until the sacred Sabbath day. Sure that the Jews were resting, he ordered his troops to fall into armed formation 26 and had them stab all who had gone out to see the spectacle. Then, dashing into the city with his soldiers, he laid a considerable multitude low. 27 Judas, also known as Maccabaeus, in a group of about ten, withdrew to the mountains, where he and his men eked out a living like beasts. There they stayed, eating herbs for food, in order to keep clear of defilement.

NOTES

5:1–23. The Seleucid Chronicle surely reported that Antiochus IV sacked Jerusalem after his Egyptian campaign of 169 B.C.E. But the accounts here and at I 1:20–24 contain material of purely Jewish interest which probably came from a Jewish source: that the king had Jews massacred (vss. 12–14, and see AB vol. 41, pp. 208–9), entered the temple (vs. 15; I 1:21) and carried off its sacred furnishings and treasures to his capital (vss. 16, 21; I 1:21–24). Nevertheless, one must grant that a pagan historian took note of the unusual circumstance, that pagan Antiochus IV entered the Jewish temple (Diodorus xxxiv–xxxv 1.3). Surely Jewish is the detailed inventory at I 1:21–22. Our authors both speak of the king's arrogance (vs. 21; I 1:21, 24). These factors, plus the parallels of content and arrangement, between vss. 15–16 and 21 here and I 1:21–24 are sufficient to justify the inference that our authors both drew from the Common Source. Neither could date the king's sack of Jerusalem except by connecting it with his campaign in Egypt. The Common Source must have indicated the chronology in the same manner.

The rank of the gentile officials mentioned in vss. 22–23 was probably too low for them to have been mentioned in the Seleucid Chronicle. Jason probably got the information on them from the Common Source, and the Hasmonaean propagandist omitted it, just as the name of Gorgias (10:14) does not stand at I 5:3 and those of the officials mentioned at II 12:2 (except Timotheus) are absent from I 5.

1. The author's mention of the "second" departure against Egypt, interpreted normally, would date the events of our passage in 168 B.C.E., yet the sack of Jerusalem referred to in vss. 11–21 is securely dated in 169 at I 1:20; see NOTE on I 1:20, *in the year 143*. The expression "second" here has caused trouble not only for writers of the history of the Jews but also for writers of the history of Antiochus' expeditions against Egypt; see Otto, *Zur Geschichte der Zeit des 6. Ptolemäers* (ABAW, new series, 11 [1934]; München: Beck, 1934), pp. 40–42 (especially the footnotes), and Abel, pp. 348–49.

Our verse has another perplexing peculiarity. Jason of Cyrene chose the unusual word *aphodos* ("departure") where one would expect *ephodos* ("expedition"). His wording was so strange that scribes altered it. Antiochus' operations in 169 and 168 were not mere "departures" but full-scale invasions, and thus scribes made *ephodos* to be the reading of most witnesses to the text. But A and La^{LXVM} (*profectio*) give the best of attestations for the more difficult reading.

The two perplexing aspects of our verse are probably connected. Again the author is trying to shield the prophecies of the book of Daniel from skepticism. See NOTE on 4:21–22. Here he faced the problem that Daniel reports two expeditions by the King of the North against Egypt, and a furious attack on Jerusalem seems to occur only after the second one (Dan 11:25–28, 29–30). But Antiochus' famous second expedition against Egypt, referred to at Dan 11:29–30, occurred in 168 B.C.E. Both the author of First Maccabees and Jason of Cyrene knew that Antiochus IV did not act against Jerusalem in that year. However, by using the ambiguous word *aphodos,* Jason of Cyrene could count the defensive operations narrated in 4:21 as the first "departure" or "expedition" against Egypt, so that the famous sack of Jerusalem, of 169 B.C.E., could be said to have occurred after the "second" departure against Egypt. The result was still unsatisfactory, since nothing occurred in 169 to correspond to the intervention of the Romans ("Kittim") mentioned in Dan 11:30. But by giving no dates, by using the vague expression "at about this time" and the vague word *aphodos,* and by speaking of the "departure" of 169 as the "second," Jason of Cyrene had done much to protect the veracity of Daniel. For a more complete treatment of the problems, see AB vol. 41, pp. 45–46, 49–52, and NOTES on 1:16–19, 20.

2–4. The "miraculous" apparitions are all explainable by mirages projected from Antiochus' army because of the presence of a strong atmospheric temperature inversion, in which cold denser air overlies warm lighter air. The phenomena called "looming" and "towering" would lead to images of the distant army being perceived as in the air and near, and the phenomenon of a "double superior mirage," the lower image inverted, the upper one erect, would account for the charges and countercharges; see William J. Humphreys, *Physics of Air* (2d ed. rev.; New York: McGraw-Hill, 1929), pp. 451–55, and cf. J. *BJ* vi 5.3.296–98, Pliny *Natural History* ii 58.148, Tacitus *Histories* v 13. The atmospheric conditions leading to mirages can recur over a period of many days, though forty days of recurrences may strain belief. If mirages had been seen five times within forty days, a report surviving down to Jason's time could easily have taken the form given in our verse. The Ptolemaic army was routed in the Sinai peninsula (see AB vol. 41, NOTE on 1:16–19), much too far away for any mirages to have been seen in the vicinity of Jerusalem, and the author himself says (vs. 1) that the apparitions were seen during the preparations, not during the conflict itself.

The Greek writer in vss. 2–3 strives for vividness by using a sequence of nouns rather than clauses.

The prophecy at Joel 3:3–8(Hebrew Joel 3:3 – 4:3) led Jews to expect that the apparitions portended great, terrible, and wonderful things.

2. Some witnesses to the text (*L'*$^{-381\ 534\ 542}$ La^{-VP}) failed to understand the use of *lonchas* for "troops of armed spearmen" (well attested in Sophocles and Euripides) and read *lochous* ("troops of infantry") instead.

The Greek verb *exoplizesthai* means "to make an *exoplisia*," "to fall into armed formation" (cf. vs. 25).

To describe the formation, the author uses the Greek adverb *speirêdon*, "in *speirai*," "in companies." A *speira* was a Macedonian tactical unit of perhaps 256 men (Michel Feyel, "Le règlement militaire trouvé à Amphipolis," *Revue archéologique*, 6ᵉ série, 6 [July–Sept., 1935], 46–47; Launey, *Recherches*, pp. 363–64). Polybius may have been the first to use *speira* to designate the Roman tactical unit, which in his time was the maniple (*manipulus*) of about 120 men (Polybius vi. 24. 5–8, 33. 8; Frank W. Walbank, *A Historical Commentary on Polybius*, vol. 2 [Oxford: Clarendon Press, 1967], p. 302; Henry M. D. Parker, *The Roman Legions* [reprinted with corrections; Cambridge: Heffer; New York: Barnes & Noble, 1958], p. 14). Jason of Cyrene may mean that the formations of the infantry in the apparitions were of the Roman type. Antiochus IV imitated Roman military procedures; see AB vol. 41, pp. 104–5. On why I translate *speirêdon* here by "into regiments" instead of by "in companies," see NOTE on 8:23, *division*.

3. I follow the reading of A and q, but the words "sabres were drawn" are probably misplaced and should come after "massed," as they do in *L'*⁻⁵⁴² La Sy Arm.

5–16. As soon as the "second departure" in vs. 1 is properly understood (see NOTE on vs. 1), the accounts at I 1:16–23 and here supplement one another and are probably true, though the statistics in vs. 14 may be inflated. Josephus' accounts of the same events in the *War* and the *Antiquities* are mostly to be rejected where they contradict those in First and Second Maccabees.

Josephus' strange account at *BJ* i 1.1.31, 33 is full of errors because Josephus, lacking copies of his sources, wrote it from inaccurate memory; see AB vol. 41, pp. 60–61, and my article in *Studies Smith*, Part III, p. 91. Josephus' strange account at *AJ* xii 5.1–2.239–42 turns the first establishment of Greek-style institutions at Jerusalem (which occurred in late 175 or in 174 B.C.E.) into a consequence of Jason's coup (which occurred in 169; see NOTE on vs. 1) and places the coup before Antiochus' campaigns against Egypt. Josephus was misled by his preconceptions into so reconstructing the evidence, much of which he drew from Onias IV. The absence of names and dates from the account at I 1:11–15 left him free to do so. See NOTE on II 4:7–50.

After writing *AJ* xii 5.1.241 Josephus was ready to begin paraphrasing First Maccabees. However, he, too, wished to protect the book of Daniel from the challenges hurled by the author of First Maccabees (see NOTE on vs. 1 and AB vol. 41, pp. 45–46). Hence, in *AJ* xii 5.2.242–44 he set the scene of Antiochus' campaigns in Egypt by giving a brief summary of them from a pagan source, probably Polybius, being careful to avoid any mention of a first or second expedition. In section 245 he tried to conceal his own errors in the *War* by pretending that his new account was the full version of what was merely summarized in the *War*. On his strangely modified paraphrase of I 1:20–64 at *AJ* xii 5.3–4.246–56, see AB vol. 41, Appendix V.

We can only guess at the cause which gave rise to the false rumor. The death of Antiochus IV would have left the Seleucid empire in a difficult position. His son, the future Antiochus V, was a small child (see Mørkholm, p. 48, n. 41), and Demetrius, the seventeen-year-old son of Seleucus IV, was a hostage in

Rome (Mørkholm, pp. 34–36). In the absolute Seleucid monarchy, the personality of the king was a vital factor. Even if Demetrius should be capable of ruling and should be able to leave Rome, there was sure to be a struggle between partisans of the line of Antiochus IV and those of the line of Seleucus IV. We cannot, however, be sure that material factors were enough to impel Jason to carry out his coup. He may have been a pious enough Jew to believe that God forbade rebellion against the king (see NOTE on 1:7, *Jason . . . Kingdom*). With the king dead and the succession clouded, however, one might say that there was no longer any king. Jason could feel free to rebel, and all the more so if he expected an imminent fulfillment of the prophecy at Dan 2:37–45. In my commentary on Daniel, I shall discuss the implications of Dan 2:37–45 in 169 B.C.E., that both the Seleucid and the Ptolemaic empires were soon to fall. The immediate objective of Jason's coup might not even have constituted rebellion against the Seleucid empire: he aimed at deposing Menelaus and at seizing the high priesthood *de facto* (vs. 7). If the king was indeed dead, Menelaus was no longer high priest and the office was vacant until a new king should appoint or confirm someone in it (see AB vol. 41, pp. 75–76, and cf. NOTE on II 14:3–4).

Jason probably gathered his men at 'Arāq el-Emīr, the stronghold of Hyrcanus the Tobiad (see NOTE on 3:11 and on 4:26). The small size of his force argues for the truth of the narrative. Onias IV may well have given good information on the forces available to his uncle Jason.

If Hyrcanus the Tobiad had participated in Jason's coup, one would have expected Josephus to mention the fact. Indeed, by this time Hyrcanus may have committed suicide. The Ptolemaic cause looked hopeless. He had behaved hitherto as an independent ruler, thus annoying the Seleucids, but now surely he would be crushed by the powerful Antiochus IV. Jason, up to the time of his coup, was no rebel against the king and could hope to survive, but thereafter he found it impossible to stay in Transjordan and fled to Egypt (vs. 8).

The author gives no indication that Jason had supporters within the city: he was resisted at the walls, had to capture the city by force, and then slaughtered his fellow Jews. Josephus, on the other hand, drawing on Onias IV, says that the majority of Jews supported Jason. Onias IV probably was interested in magnifying any evidence that would mitigate his uncle's role as the "cause of all the evil"; see NOTE on 1:7–8 and on 1:7, *Jason . . . Kingdom,* and my article in *Studies Smith,* Part III, pp. 91, 105–9, 121–22. Mere probability would indicate that Jason's relatively small force must have had help from within Jerusalem before it could capture the city, force Menelaus to flee to the citadel (cf. 4:39–40), and inflict heavy casualties upon the other Jews. On the other hand, two contemporary (or near contemporary) Jewish sources speak of Jason's men as foreign or as rebels against the main body of Jews (II 1:7 and Dan 9:26; see NOTE on 1:7, *Jason . . . Kingdom,* and AB vol. 41, pp. 49, 124). Hence, Onias IV exaggerated the support given to Jason. The narrative here makes no false assertions but passes in silence over the support for Jason which must have existed within Jerusalem.

We shall find this kind of reticence repeatedly in our passage. The author does not wish his reader to believe that Antiochus punished Jerusalem for valid political motives. Rather, God used Antiochus as the rod of His anger to punish

Jerusalem for tolerating the sins of the Hellenizers (vss. 17–18). Antiochus' conscious motives were a delusion imposed upon him by God. There is similar reticence in First Maccabees, and for the same reason (see AB vol. 41, NOTE on 1:20, *in the year 143*). On reading such reticent accounts, Josephus came to believe that Antiochus perpetrated an unprovoked attack upon an innocent city (*Ap.* ii 7.83–84, 8.90; cf. *AJ* xii 9.1.357–59).

Josephus (*BJ* i 1.1.31–32; cf. *AJ* xii 5.3.247) says that the coup at Jerusalem was perpetrated by a pro-Ptolemaic faction. His information is drawn from Onias IV and contains at least a measure of truth.

At the time of Jason's coup, the Ptolemaic government was in a desperate state, having lost everything to Antiochus except for Alexandria (see AB vol. 41, NOTE on 1:16–19). In rebelling upon hearing a rumor of Antiochus' death, Jason may have expected the imminent fulfillment of the prophecy at Dan 2:37–45. Nevertheless, if not Jason himself, surely many of his supporters must have looked toward their natural allies, the Ptolemaic empire. Judaea was a borderland. Rebels against the Seleucids in Judaea could hardly do otherwise than to look to the rival empire across the border. See my article in *Studies Smith,* Part III, p. 100.

The author's assertion that Menelaus took refuge in the citadel is compatible with Josephus' account at *AJ* xii 5.1.240, where Menelaus and the Tobiads, hard pressed by Jason, withdraw and go to seek Antiochus' aid. Again, Josephus probably drew on Onias IV. Menelaus and his backers later may have slipped out of the citadel. Or perhaps Josephus is inaccurate, and only a messenger slipped out of the citadel while Menelaus and his partisans remained under siege.

The author does not say that the slaughtered Jerusalemites had been resisting Jason and his supporters; his source may have been Ep. 1 (1:8). On the other hand, he also does not say that the dead were helpless unarmed noncombatants. His narrative, indeed, is very strange if it does not imply that Jewish resistance at Jerusalem blocked Jason's attempt to recapture the high priesthood and forced him to retreat back to Ammanitis. Antiochus' armed intervention at Jerusalem comes later (vss. 11–14), and Jason and his men are no longer present to face it. We last see Menelaus as a fugitive in the citadel. If Menelaus had succeeded in repelling Jason, Antiochus would have had no "rebellion" to suppress at Jerusalem. Thus, Jason's victims were Jewish opponents who ultimately gathered enough strength to drive him out and besiege his rival in the citadel. When Antiochus arrived at Jerusalem, he assumed that the Jews besieging Menelaus were rebels and punished them. Contemporary observers confirm this reconstruction of the events.

The seer at Jubilees 23:19–23 alludes to how the pious took to armed resistance against the wicked and to how Antiochus IV ("the sinners of the gentiles") sacked Jerusalem and punished the pious (see Introduction, Part V, section 1). The writer at Dan 7:21 and 25 calls Antiochus' victims the "saints" (*qaddīšīn*), and the seer at Dan 11:28 says that Antiochus' target was "the holy covenant."

Jews thwarted Jason's coup, yet Antiochus punished the thwarters as rebels! The seer at Dan 7:21 and 25 and Jason of Cyrene might write as if Antiochus turned to punish loyal subjects. Here again, we find Jason of Cyrene believing that God made Antiochus misjudge the situation in order to use the king as the rod of His anger against wayward Israel (4:15–17; 5:11, 17–20). As the seer of Daniel saw it, Antiochus' acts were part of a long series of divine visitations punishing the Jews for sins committed centuries before (see AB vol. 41, p. 43). We are not bound to accept the theological assumptions of Jason of Cyrene and the book of Daniel. If our inferences from the narrative here and from Jubilees 23:19–23 are correct, Antiochus IV had good reason to assume that the pious Jews were in rebellion against him. We can easily reconstruct a plausible picture of what happened. Victor Tcherikover was the first to suggest the outline (*Hellenistic Civilization and the Jews* [Philadelphia: Jewish Publication Society of America, 1959], pp. 187–88).

The introduction of Greek institutions by Jason the Oniad was almost entirely peaceful. Some Jews were glad to become Antiochenes, and most Jews at first must have abstained from attacking the Antiochenes and their institutions, for the king's own decrees had called them into being. Though the Torah required Israelites to wipe out the evil of idolatry from their midst (Deut 13:2–6, 17:2–7, etc.), it was not clear that the Antiochenes were idolaters. Hence, many Jews must have viewed attacking the Antiochenes as perilously close to rebellion against the king, an act forbidden by God (see NOTE on 1:7, *Jason . . . Kingdom*).

However, the Antiochenes were neither a blameless nor a harmonious community. Their origins lay in bribery and intrigue (4:7–9). The Hellenizers split into at least two factions around Jason and Menelaus. Jason could be accused of idolatry (4:18–20) and Menelaus of bribery (4:24, 45), temple robbery (4:32), suborned murder (4:33–34), and a share in the temple robbery and attempted mass murder perpetrated by his brother Lysimachus (4:39–42). Masses of Jews rose against Lysimachus (see NOTE on 4:39–42). The outrages perpetrated by Antiochenes must have led pious Jews to hate both factions. If news should come that the king was dead, leaving no competent heir, pious Jews were even more likely to act upon their theological and eschatological beliefs than Jason the Oniad was (see p. 249). At least, they would have felt free to attack the hated Antiochenes. Hence, pious Jews probably both drove off Jason's force and besieged Menelaus and his partisans in the citadel.

Menelaus held office by the decree of Antiochus IV and must have protested to the king that an attack of the pious on the king's appointee was an act of rebellion against the king. Tobiads and other Antiochenes probably argued similarly about the attacks of the pious on them. The king would have found the arguments reasonable after the events of 4:39–48. Pious Jews, on learning that Antiochus was alive, would be careful to avoid hostilities with the king but might keep Menelaus under siege in the citadel in hopes of convincing the king that the high priest was a criminal. Antiochus may have been surprised to find pious Jews opening the gates of Jerusalem to him (see AB vol. 41, NOTE on 1:20, *with a strong army*), but only a careful student of the intricacies of Jewish belief could have discerned the difference between rebellion and the pious Jews' conduct toward the Antiochenes and toward the high priest appointed by the king. Hence, the king assumed that the Jews' religious beliefs had turned them into rebels, and he proceeded to punish the city.

Was Jason's coup the sole or main reason for Antiochus' withdrawal from

Egypt in 169 B.C.E.? Polybius' account of the events survives only in fragments, so that we are reduced to inference and conjecture. We can, however, reject Jerome's report at *De Antichristo in Danielem* (=*Commentarii in Danielem*) iv to Dan 11:28b–30a. He says, citing "both Greek and Roman histories," that Antiochus was driven out by the Egyptians. One of his authorities may have been Porphyry, who wrote in the third century C.E. (FGH 260, F 50). Jerome's sources must have jumped to a wrong conclusion, since enough good evidence survives to let us know that in 169 Ptolemaic Egypt was much too weak to drive out Antiochus.

The Seleucid king had come near conquering all of the Ptolemaic kingdom. He held the person of King Ptolemy VI, and the diehards of the realm, rallying around Ptolemy's sister Cleopatra II and his younger brother (the future Ptolemy VIII), succeeded only in holding Alexandria. Antiochus posed as the defender of the interests of Ptolemy VI, and on withdrawing from Egypt in the autumn of 169 B.C.E. he left Ptolemy VI at Memphis as a sort of "vassal." Only after Antiochus' withdrawal did Ptolemy VI join forces with the regime in Alexandria, and even then the Ptolemaic regime was so incapable of coping with Seleucid power that it frantically sought help from Greece and Rome (Polybius xxviii 22–23, xxix 23–25; Livy xliv 19.6–14, 24.1–7, xlv 11.1–8; J. D. Ray, *The Archive of Ḥor* ["Excavations at North Saqqâra, Documentary Series," I; London: Egypt Exploration Society, 1976], pp. 124–26; Justin xxxiv 2.7–8; Mørkholm, pp. 86–91). Hence, the Egyptian regime did not drive out Antiochus.

There is no positive evidence for the assertion of J. D. Ray (*The Archive of Ḥor*, p. 129) that "The victorious Antiochus seems to have remained in Egypt throughout 169." Rather, there is good reason to suppose that Jason's coup forced Antiochus in 169 to postpone completing his conquest of Egypt, even though Jason had a force of barely one thousand, and Judaea lay inland, off Antiochus' land route back to his own capital. Antiochus, in conquered Egypt, had much to fear if he failed to suppress and punish a revolt in his own kingdom. He could not afford to leave the task to a subordinate. Rome, tied down by the Second Macedonian War, could not intervene militarily to stop Antiochus from conquering Egypt in 169 B.C.E., as she did as soon as the war was over in 168 (Polybius xxix. 27). But in 169 Rome was ready to exploit any opportunity for stopping the aggrandizement of Antiochus without the use of Roman arms. If the Romans should hear of a rebellion on Seleucid soil, they might be quick to send their hostage Demetrius to the spot as a rival pretender to the Seleucid throne. Later, in 165, Antiochus accepted the risk of going off on a distant campaign and leaving behind a subordinate to suppress a revolt in Judaea; see I 3:27–37 and the NOTES thereto in AB vol. 41. At that time, however, his campaign was no threat to Roman interests, and the Ptolemaic empire was weakened by the struggle between Ptolemy VI and his younger brother and by other troubles (Volkmann, PW, XXIII [1959], 1711). Even so, the Romans were to meddle with the Jews in his absence, early in 164 (11:34–38).

Porphyry interpreted Dan 11:44 to mean "While fighting against the Egyptians and passing through Libya and Ethiopia, he shall hear that wars have broken out against him from the north and east. Hence, he shall march back

and capture Arados despite the resistance of the citizens and devastate the entire province along the coast of Phoenicia" (*apud* Jerome, *Commentarii in
Danielem* iv, to Dan 11:44). There is good reason to think that Porphyry himself dated the events he associated with Dan 11:44 in or after the eleventh year
of the reign of Antiochus IV (ca. 165/4 B.C.E.); see Jerome, ibid., to Dan
11:40–41. Even so, Porphyry connects the devastation of Phoenicia with an
expedition against Egypt. One might suggest that he bears witness to revolts in
Phoenicia in 169 and that those revolts were the main cause of the withdrawal
of Antiochus IV from Egypt in that year.

Dan 11:44, however, is a prediction of the seer which was never fulfilled
(see AB vol. 41, p. 47). Jerome was right, in quoting Porphyry's interpretation, to describe it as a wild dream (*Porphyrius nescio quid de Antiocho
somniat*). The coinage of Arados and Phoenicia shows how highly privileged
they were throughout the reign of Antiochus IV; see Mørkholm, pp. 122–27,
and Jean-Paul Rey-Coquais, *Arados et sa pérée aux époques grecque, romaine
et Byzantine* ("Institut français d'archéologie de Beyrouth: Bibliothèque archéologique et historique," T. XCVII; Paris: Geuthner, 1974), pp. 159–60.
Anti-Christian Porphyry was too eager to say that the seer of Daniel merely
copied history. Porphyry tried to identify even unfulfilled prophecies with historical events. Nevertheless, Porphyry was from Tyre and had access to the
works of Polybius and other histories now lost. We may guess that Antiochus
IV at some time between 169 and 165 paraded his forces through Phoenicia in
order to intimidate any opposition but otherwise was careful to treat kindly
that strategic area. Porphyry found a source which reported the intimidating
parade, and he interpreted it in the light of Dan 11:44.

Hence, Jason's revolt probably was the sole immediate cause of Antiochus'
withdrawal from Egypt in 169 B.C.E. Antiochus thus was forced to leave his
"vassal," young Ptolemy VI, in control of conquered Egypt; see AB vol. 41,
NOTE on 1:16–19 and on 11:13. The young king soon made common cause
with the diehards in Alexandria. The reunited Ptolemaic regime was quick to
appeal for Roman help. See Mørkholm, pp. 88–93. Thus the stage was set for
the decisive Roman intervention in 168, which forever ended Antiochus' project of controlling Egypt and building an empire strong enough to oppose
Rome (see Mørkholm, pp. 93–96, and AB vol. 41, pp. 104–21). So fateful
was an abortive coup by some one thousand partly Hellenized Jews!

Our reconstruction of the course of events is contradicted by J. *Ap.* ii
7.83–84, where Josephus cites by name many pagan writers in support of his
assertion that Antiochus, solely out of greed for the temple treasures, attacked
the innocent Jews. Pagan writers probably drew up a list of the temples sacked
by Antiochus, including the temple at Jerusalem, and ascribed all the acts of
sacrilege to the king's avarice (cf. Polybius xxx. 26. 9, xxxi. 9, Granius
Licinianus xxviii, and J. *AJ* xii 9.1.358). Josephus then would have drawn his
mistaken inference from such testimony. His preconceptions led him to ignore
the causal connection between Jason's coup and Antiochus' sack of Jerusalem
in 169 B.C.E. (see J. *AJ* xii 5.1–3.239–47, and my article in *Studies Smith,* Part
III, pp. 122–23).

1:8 implies that Jason's men caused the burning of one of the temple gateways in the course of their coup. So, apparently, does Dan 9:26: "After the

sixty-two weeks an anointed one shall be cut off [Onias III] . . . and the army of the next prelate [Jason] shall inflict ruin upon the city and the sanctuary." Strangely, our writer in vss. 5–10 says nothing of the burning of the gateway, only to mention it at 8:33. It is hard to believe that the abridger would omit so important a fact as the burning of a part of the temple. Jason of Cyrene himself may have left it out.

Elsewhere I have reconstructed an original version of Test Moses 6:2–9 to read "There shall come upon them an insolent king. . . . He shall burn a part of their temple with fire"; see my article entitled "The Testament of Moses . . . ," in *Studies on the Testament of Moses,* pp. 45–46. The Testament of Moses is a source nearly contemporary with the events; see AB vol. 41, pp. 39–40. If my reconstruction is correct, the burning of the gate took place at the time of Antiochus' attacks in Jerusalem. We would have to assume that diehard supporters of Jason held out on the temple mount, and in the course of their attempts to fight off Antiochus a temple gateway was fired in such a way that Ep. 0, Ep. 1, and Dan 9:26 could blame the act on Jason's men, and the author of the Testament of Moses could blame it on Antiochus. To have mentioned any diehard supporters of Jason in Jerusalem would have impaired the thesis of Jason of Cyrene, that Antiochus acted solely as the rod of God's anger in punishing Jerusalem. In First Maccabees and Josephus the burning of the gateway is passed over in silence. The mention of the burning of the gateway before the shedding of innocent blood in 1:7–8 does not necessarily disprove this reconstruction. The senders of Ep. 0 may have mentioned Jason's sins in the order of their enormity: it was worst to "rebel against the Holy Land," for that was a violation of many commandments in Deuteronomy; next worst, to rebel against the Kingdom, a violation of the repeated teachings of the Prophets. See NOTE on 1:7, *Jason . . . Kingdom.* Next worst was to destroy part of the temple, in violation of Deut 12:2–5. The authors surely viewed murder as a dreadful sin, yet, if this reconstruction is correct, they viewed the other sins of Jason as still worse!

On the other hand, my reconstruction of the verses in the Testament of Moses may be wrong, and 1:7–8 may reflect the order of the events. We could then assume that Jason's men fired the temple gateway.

5. *attack on the city.* The Greek is *epi tēn polin . . . epithesin.* The noun *epithesis* means "attack" in such expressions (e.g., at Polybius v. 5. 4; cf. II 4:41, 14:15), but in translations from the Hebrew Bible it is used only for words meaning "conspiracy" or "treason" (*qešer:* II Chron 25:27; *mirmāh:* Aquila Gen 27:35, etc.; Symmachus Ps 54[Hebrew Ps 55]:12, etc.; Theodotion Prov 14:8); cf. Polybius xv. 29. 4. Indeed, the author himself in vs. 7 calls Jason's attempt a "plot" (*epiboulē*). Hence *epithesis* here might better be translated "coup."

6. *fellow Jews.* Gr. *politōn;* see NOTE on 4:5.

winning triumphs over. Lit. "setting up trophies of"; on "trophies" (*tropaia*), see AB vol. 41, NOTE on 13:29–30.

7. Our verse contains untranslatable wordplay. The word for "office" (*archē*) also means "beginning," and the word for "end result" (*telos*) also means "office."

In "succeeded in slipping . . . through," I have translated the reading of A and q (*parêlthen;* see the *Greek-English Lexicon* s.v. *parerchomai,* II, 1 and 2). There is strong witness (La *L* V) for the simpler reading *apêlthen* or *apêei,* which would mean "as a fugitive he went back to the Ammanitis." But the scribes of the simpler reading probably altered the reading of A and q because they failed to grasp its elegant irony: the defeated fugitive *succeeded* in slipping back through to his starting point.

8–9. In "Finally he came to a miserable end," I translate the reading of A′ Vl 55 311 La^{LXVBM}, supported by Sy. All these have *katastrophês* ("end"). Other witnesses, notably q, have the more difficult *anastrophês* ("faring," "way of life," "conduct"). The only natural way to construe the reading with *anastrophês* is to take "finally" (*peras*) as a noun in the accusative case, with the translation "He came to the termination of his bad conduct," or perhaps "He reached a peak of ill fortune." However, the verb "came to" (*etychen*) should take not the accusative but the genitive. The accusative begins to be found in nouns serving as the object of this verb in the first century c.e.

In this case I believe that the more difficult reading is to be ascribed to an oversubtle scribe who viewed Jason, the fugitive, as the antithesis of the steadfast Eleazar (6:18–31). Eleazar is said to have had the best possible *anastrophê* (6:23), and the scribe felt it appropriate to speak of Jason's bad *anastrophê* and trite to mention his bad end, especially since details of the bad end follow. On the oversubtlety of the scribe of q, see W. Kappler, *De memoria,* pp. 27–33.

Grimm (p. 100) argued for the more difficult reading. The easier reading certainly would speak of Jason's bad end. Details of Jason's bad end occupy the entire long independent clause which in Greek constitutes the rest of our passage ("first . . . banishment"). Usually in Greek, Grimm noted, a clause giving details would be introduced by the particle *gar* ("for," "that is to say"). But *gar* is often omitted by Greek authors (Kühner-Gerth, *Grammatik,* II, 344) and is at 11:10. Furthermore, "finally" (*peras oun*) at the head of a clause is a normal Greek combination (cf. Demosthenes *Oration* 56. 10), synonymous with *telos oun,* so that a Greek reader would hardly take *peras* as a noun.

The subsequent fate of Jason is rapidly described, mostly in participial phrases, suggesting that the abridger may have left only a skeleton summary. The name "Aretas" is well known from the line of the chiefs and kings of the Nabataean Arabs. The Nabataeans began as nomads in Transjordan and Arabia and vigorously maintained their independence against the Graeco-Macedonian kingdoms; see 12:10–12 and AB vol. 41, NOTES on 5:25 and 9:35, *his friends, the Nabataeans.* For a detailed account on the Nabataeans, do not use Nelson Glueck, *Deities and Dolphins: The Story of the Nabataeans* (New York: Farrar, Straus, and Giroux, 1965); see, rather, Schürer (New English version), I, 574–86, and J. Starcky, "Pétra et la Nabatène," *Dictionnaire de la Bible,* ed. by F. Vigouroux et al., suppl. VII (1961), 900–1017, and Avraham Negev, "The Nabateans and the Provincia Arabia," in *Aufstieg und Niedergang der römischen Welt, II: Principat,* ed. by Hildegard Temporini and Wolfgang Haase, Vol. VIII (Berlin and New York: Walter de Gruyter, 1977), pp. 521–640.

A dynast (*tyrannos*) was a local monarch with a measure of autonomy; see

AB vol. 41, NOTE on 1:4, *dynasts.* The failure of our writer to call Aretas "king" may indicate that Aretas is the earliest Nabataean chief known to us by name, if Nabataean chiefs, like those of the Jews, assumed the royal title only later as the Seleucid empire disintegrated. The only known evidence of possibly earlier Nabataean chiefs are (1) an Aramaic inscription dedicated to "Aretas, king [*mlk*] of the Nabataeans," in lettering variously assigned to the late third or to the second century B.C.E.; and (2) an enigmatic reference to "Rabilos, the king [*basileôs*] of the Arabs" at Stephanus Byzantius s.v. *Môthô.* See Negev, essay in *Aufstieg und Niedergang, II,* VIII, 529–30, 545–46; Starcky, article in *Dictionnaire de la Bible,* suppl. VII, 904, 905.

Though he had a measure of independence from Seleucid rule, Aretas might well have imprisoned the rebel Jason rather than face the might of Antiochus IV, and Jason could have escaped with or without Aretas' connivance. Compare the fate of Hannibal as a fugitive in Bithynia (Livy xxxix 51).

Ptolemaic Egypt was a natural refuge for Jason, a rebel against the Seleucid kingdom. He probably fled to Egypt before Antiochus invaded it in 168. See NOTE on vss. 9–10.

8. *imprisoned . . . dynast.* Where the Greek, supported by La Sy Arm, has *enkleistheis pros Aretan,* I have followed La[BMP] and construed the preposition *pros* as equivalent to Latin *apud,* French *chez,* and German *bei* ("with," "at the home of"). *Pros* frequently has just that meaning in the New Testament (Bauer, *Wörterbuch,* s.v. *pros,* 7, col. 1410; Blass-Debrunner-Rehkopf, *Grammatik,* section 239, 1) and may have it also at II 5:9 and 9:29. I have made my translation as vague as possible: "imprisoned in the realm of Aretas." A bolder guess would have been to assert that Aretas kept Jason under arrest in Aretas' own palace. If one did not so construe *pros,* there would be reason to accept an emendation suggested by Martin Luther, for otherwise *pros* makes odd Greek with *enkleistheis* ("imprisoned") but is normal with *enklêtheis* ("accused"). The emendation would make our passage mean "charges against him were laid before Aretas the Arab dynast."

fled . . . from country to country. Jason of Cyrene may be drawing on some poem, for "to country" is expressed by a bare accusative (*polin;* see Kühner-Gerth, *Grammatik,* I, 311–12) and the words scan as part of a dactylic hexameter (. . . ∪∪ | – ∪∪ | – – | – . . .), but cf. Herodotus iv 33.2, where *polin* is the subject of the infinitive *pempein.* Cf. also Sir 36:26–27 Rahlfs and Plato *Apology* 37d.

rebel against the laws. See NOTE on 1:7–8, on 1:7, *Jason . . . Kingdom,* and on 4:9–15.

found . . . like driftwood. So I translate *exebrasthê.* The same verb (*ekbrazein*) is used at 1:12, where I have translated it "cast away." It is used of bodies of water casting things on shore.

9–10. The author loves to show how divine providence brings precise retribution upon sinners. Cf. 8:33–36, 9:5–6 and 28, 13:6–8, and 14:32–33. See also NOTE on 4:38, *thus . . . deserved,* and NOTE on 4:41–42.

Jason probably fled Egypt for fear of Antiochus' invasion of spring, 168 (see Mørkholm, pp. 89–93). On Lakedaimon (=Sparta) as a city of kinsmen to the Jews, see AB vol. 41, pp. 446–52, 455–60.

Vs. 10 refers to the victims mentioned in vs. 6. Unlike the figures in the narrative of the Hebrew Bible, Jason neither "slept with his fathers" nor "was gathered unto his people."

11-27. In our passage as well as in 6:1 – 7:42, Antiochus is the rod of God's anger who goes beyond God's will in punishing Israel, just as Assyria once did (Isa 10:5-15). Like Assyria (Isa 10:16-27), Antiochus will be punished. As a Jewish Greek, the author also takes care to portray Antiochus as a bloodthirsty tyrant. Greeks believed that tyrannies were destined to fall. See AB vol. 41, NOTE on 3:29-30.

11-16. On the ravaging of Jerusalem and the sack of the temple and the reference to them at Dan 11:28, see AB vol. 41, NOTE on 1:20, *with a strong army*. On the possible references to the events in Test Moses 6, see my article in Nickelsburg, *Studies on the Testament of Moses*, pp. 45-48.

In our verses and in vs. 23 not an Oniad but Menelaus and a Seleucid king are the perpetrators of atrocities. Thus, here Jason of Cyrene could have drawn both on the Common Source and on the *Memoirs* of Onias IV.

11. The news probably came to the king through fugitives from the citadel. See NOTE on vss. 5-16.

treating . . . war. So I translate Gr. *dorialôton,* a legal and moral term. In the Hellenistic and Roman world, a conqueror had absolute power over the conquered, but it was considered illegal and immoral to massacre and despoil those who had surrendered without a fight. However, persons or cities captured through combat were completely at the mercy of the conqueror, as in vss. 12-16 (cf. Deut 20:10-15). Such a city was said to be "spear-won," *dorialôtos,* or captured "by force" (*kata kratos*), and not even its temples were exempt (Rostovtzeff, *Social and Economic History of the Hellenistic World,* pp. 200-2). Both Greek expressions are primarily legal and moral terms and should not be translated "by storm," since any kind of combat could place the defeated in the status of being "spear-won." See the decree *apud* Demosthenes *Oration* 18.181 (a forgery of the first half of the second century B.C.E.; see Piero Treves, "Les documents apocryphes du 'Pro corona,'" *Les études classiques* 9 [1940], 138-74). See also Polybius iii 35.4, ix 25.5, xxiii 10.6, xxiv 13.4; Appian *Bellum Civile* iv 52; III 1:5; Philo *In Flaccum* 60; and J. *BJ* i *Prooemium* 7.19 and 1.1.32.

At II 10:24 Timotheus does not plan to take Jerusalem or any other city by storm; he plans to take Judaea *dorialôton,* to reduce the country to the helpless state of a captive taken through combat.

The Latin here and at 10:24 uses the correct Latin equivalents *armis* (or *gladio*) *capere,* "take by arms" or "take by the sword." Another Latin equivalent is *manu capere.* See Sallust *Bellum Jugurthinum* 5.4 and Livy xxxvii 32.2.

See also Bickerman, "Remarques sur le droit des gens dans la Grèce classique," *Revue internationale des droits de l'antiquité* 4 (1950), p. 107, reprinted in German in *Zur griechische Staatskunde,* ed. by Fritz Gschnitzer (Darmstadt: Wissenschaftliche Buchgesellschaft, 1969), p. 482; and Pierre Ducrey, *Le traitement des prisonniers de guerre dans la Grèce antique* ("École française d'Athènes: travaux et mémoires," Fasc. XVII; Paris: É. de Boccard, 1968), pp. 21, 108-9, 112.

The author here expects the reader to understand, first, that Antiochus was wrong to believe Judaea was in revolt and also that the Jews of Jerusalem offered him no resistance, so that in treating the city as "spear-won," Antiochus was either an unreasoning instrument of God or a cruel monster. Josephus and the probable original version of I 1:20 made it explicit: the city was opened to the king without resistance. See AB vol. 41, NOTE on 1:20, *with a strong army.*

13. The variant found in A and *l*, which inserts "immature males and" (*anêbôn te kai*) before "women" probably arose from a dittography of the word which precedes (*anaireseis*).

14. At AB vol. 41, p. 209, I refer the reader to this NOTE for the reasons underlying the cruel sack. They are now in the NOTE on vss. 5–16.

Already around 300 B.C.E. Hecataeus of Abdera estimated the population of Jerusalem at 120,000 (*apud* J. *Ap.* i 22.197). It is likely that his estimate is too high even for 169 B.C.E., since Jerusalem still occupied only the eastern hill; see AB vol. 41, NOTE on 1:33–40, and see Map 1. Jews may have been afraid to have a real census (see II Sam 24:1–21 and I Chron 21:1–22), and Hecataeus' informant would then have given him only a traditional figure, and the figure for the casualties here may simply represent the author's belief that two thirds of the Jerusalemites were brought to ruin. Josephus seems to have found the estimate of the enslaved captives here too high, and in his reconstructed version of I 1:20–64 at *AJ* xii 5.4.251 he seems to have taken the number from here and reduced it to ten thousand; see AB vol. 41, Appendix V. Josephus was well acquainted with the size of Jerusalem, and his estimates should be more trustworthy than those of Jason of Cyrene.

The author of I 1:20–28 does not say that Antiochus took captives. The enslavement of prisoners was a commonplace of war and perhaps could be omitted when so dreadful an event as the sack of the temple was the focus of attention. Contemporary witnesses may have attested the taking of prisoners. On the possibility that the original text of Test Moses 6:8 did, see my article in Nickelsburg, *Studies on the Testament of Moses,* p. 47. There may be other attestations at Bar 1:9, 2:29, 3:7, 4:16, and 5:6; see my article in PAAJR 46–47 (1979–80), 179–99.

by the sword. On the Greek idiom here, *en cheirôn nomais* ("by action of hands," "in combat"), see A. Wilhelm, *"En cheirôn nomais* und *en cheirôn (cheiros) nomôi," Glotta* 24 (1936), 133–43.

15–21. Josephus (*Ap.* ii 7.83–84, 8.90) says that Antiochus sacked the temple from avarice and because of his need for money (cf. Justin xxxii 2.1; Sulpicius Severus ii 19.6; and see NOTE on vss. 5–16 and on II 8:10 and my article in *Studies Smith,* Part III, pp. 122–23). Rather, Antiochus' chief reason for the sack probably was to punish rebellion. Compared to the spoils of Egypt in Antiochus' hands (I 1:19; Dan 11:28; Polybius xxx 26.9), the considerable treasures of the temple (vs. 21 and I 1:21–24) were probably small, though welcome for supplying the king's extravagance.

15. Pagans were forbidden to enter the inner courts of the temple; see AB vol. 41, NOTE on 1:21, *entering the temple.* Nevertheless, the wicked high priest himself again betrayed the laws and conducted Antiochus into the innermost court! So unusual was Antiochus' penetration that a pagan historian recorded the fact (Poseidonius FGH 87, F 109=Diodorus xxxiv 1.3).

16. Good witnesses to the text differ widely in our verse, probably because

the author's intricate sentence proved beyond the comprehension of the scribes and translators. Their difficulties were compounded by confusing combinations of letters. I translate from the following reconstructed Greek text:

kai tais mierais chersi ta hiera skeuê lambanôn kai ta hyp' allôn basileôn pollôn anastathenta . . . tais bebêlois chersi syssyrôn epididou.

Scribes had no difficulty with the first eight words ("with polluted hands he seized the sacred vessels"). However, in ancient Greek manuscripts words were not divided, and the next six words ("and the [gifts] by many other kings") made a confusing combination which scribes came to believe could not be correct: *KAITAYPALLÔNBASILEÔNPOLLÔN. PALLÔN* and *POLLÔN* looked too much alike. Different scribes found different solutions. The scribe of q omitted *POLLÔN* ("many"). The scribe of A may have done the same at first, but then he erased what probably was *ALLÔN* and wrote *OPOLLÔN* in its place, in effect omitting "other." In *L* 311 La⁻ᴮ and Arm we find the work of a scribe who decided that *POLLÔN* was a mistake for *POLEÔN* ("cities"); he must have thought either that the author himself omitted "and" or that "and" had been omitted by a scribe. Thus, the gifts to the temple became "the gifts deposited by other kings and cities." Nowhere else do we hear that cities sent gifts to the temple. The scribe underlying Laᴮ appears to have seen a Greek text which still had no "and" between *BASILEÔN* and *POLLÔN* (or *POLEÔN*) and to have assumed that the latter word was miswritten for *POLEI*, to make the passage mean "the [gifts] to the city deposited by other kings." All these witnesses to the text except q thus attest the presence of both *ALLÔN* and *POL.ÔN,* and hence my reconstruction of the tenth to fourteenth words is on a solid basis. Variants in the middle of our verse are of little significance. Scribes substituted near synonyms which they may have thought were more appropriate.

The end of our verse, however, caused the great trouble. Indeed, the writer indulged in some rather subtle wordplay. The "polluted hands" belong to Menelaus, and the "unclean hands" to Antiochus. To make sure that the reader knew who was the subject in vs. 17, the writer was careful to specify "Antiochus." So construed, our verse becomes the sole justification in the abridged history of the claim in 13:8, that Menelaus "committed *many* sins around the altar," beyond the single one of guiding a pagan into the inner court. The scribe underlying *L'* 311 may have understood that the two pairs of hands were different, but the wordplay eluded most readers, who could see no reason for repeating "hands" with a synonymous adjective. Since the grammatical subject of vs. 15 was "Antiochus," they assumed that the subject of vs. 16 was, too, and that all the hands mentioned were those of Antiochus. Clearly the verb *epedidou* ("he handed them over") was in the original text. It is preserved by *L'* 311 Sy and Laᴾ, for the scribe of *L'* seems to have understood there were two pairs of hands. Furthermore, the readings of Laᴸ⁽ˣ⁾ⱽᴮᴹ can be shown to have been derived from *epedidou*. As soon as all hands mentioned belong to Antiochus, however, *epedidou* becomes nonsense.

Good sense could be restored by omitting *epedidou* and by attaching the rest of vs. 16 (where the Greek verbs are participles) to vs. 15. The resultant text of vs. 16, in A and q, could be translated "and the king seized the sacred vessels with his polluted hands and swept up in his unclean hands the gifts deposited by other kings to magnify and glorify and honor the Place." This text uselessly repeats "hands." In La^LBM we find the work of scribes who thought that the second occurrence of "hands" was a mistake, and that "swept up" was superfluous. The adjective "unclean" or "profane" (*bebêlois*), though feminine, was indistinguishable from the masculine or neuter. As for the apparently nonsensical verb *epedidou*, it could be a mistake for *apedidoto* (he sold). Thus the end of the verse would mean ". . . and the gifts deposited . . . and sold them to unclean persons [or "to profane places"]." The reading which underlay La^X was similar, but that manuscript has a gap where the word "he sold" once stood. At this point, however, the reference to the ultimate fate of the temple vessels is out of place. Antiochus took them with him to Antioch (vs. 21 and I 1:24). We learn elsewhere that he certainly did not sell all of them (J. *BJ* vii 3.2.44). The scribe underlying La^V preserved "swept up" as "handled with disrespect." Instead of *epedidou*, he read *apedidou* ("he rendered"), and he seems to have changed *bebêlois* to *bebêla* to produce "he handled with disrespect the gifts deposited . . . and rendered them unclean." But then the passage says only that Antiochus defiled the sacred objects; it does not say that he carried them off! Thus all readings different from that of *L* and La^P are awkward and derived from misreadings of it.

17. See NOTE on vss. 11–27 and AB vol. 41, NOTE on 1:21, *Arrogantly*.

soar. Cf. Isa 14:12.

neglected . . . angry. Cf. Isa 54:7–8.

18. See ch. 3. Heliodorus' mission was to confiscate, not merely to inspect (3:7, 13). But the scrupulous Heliodorus on hearing the protests of Onias III (3:10–12) proceeded first to inspect the deposits to see which were forfeit to the king. The writer here speaks of "inspection" in order to have his reader reason: if Heliodorus was punished for mere inspection, all the more, under normal circumstances, would Antiochus have been punished for unscrupulous looting.

19–20. Cf. II Chron 7:12–22; Jer 7:3–15; Zech 1:12–17, 2:14–16; and Dan 9:16–19. The partisans of the second temple as God's Chosen Place had to argue against the suggestion that the sack proved that God still rejected it.

20. *The Place . . . forgiveness*. Cf. Isa 54:7–13.

21. The total given here is a very large sum, though probably considerably smaller than the spoils of Egypt. It would include private deposits as well as the temple vessels and treasures; see NOTE on 3:12 and cf. I 1:21–24.

Antiochus may have had good reason to hasten back to Antioch in order to forestall any moves by partisans of the line of Seleucus IV. But the writer here stresses Antiochus' confidence; why does he mention Antiochus' haste? Perhaps he views it as a second fulfillment of Isaiah's prophecy of a "King of Assyria" who will "sweep as a flood on into Judah, overflow, and pass on."

thinking . . . soar. Cf. Isa 14:13–14, 37:24–25; Herodotus vii 22–24, 34–37; Aeschylus *Persians* 69–72, 744–51. Again Antiochus IV is treated as a latter-day king of Assyria, and now also as an analogue of the Persian King Xerxes, who dared to contend with the gods by bridging the Hellespont and digging a canal through Mount Athos. The punishment of the *theomachos*, the man who dares to contend with God, is a preoccupation of Greek as well as Jewish literature; see Wilhelm Nestle, *Griechische Studien* (Stuttgart: Hannsmann, 1948), pp. 228–30, 567–96, summarized in *Lactance: De la mort des persécuteurs,* ed. by J. Moreau (Sources chrétiennes, no. 39; Paris: Éditions du Cerf, 1954), pp. 60–64. The motif of Antiochus as *theomachos* will be prominent from here to the end of ch. 9. Jason does not leave the reader to infer for himself that Antiochus is a *theomachos.* He brands the king as being one by using the related verb *theomachein* at 7:19.

22. *He went so far as to.* So I translate the emphatic *kai.*

officials . . . race. Ironically the author writes as if the men's chief function and title was "official in charge of maltreatment." In fact, as we shall see, each man had a different function and title.

Philip. He probably received the post of commander of the garrison in the citadel (see 4:28). During the persecution his force could make forays into the countryside (6:11), but after the outbreak of the Hasmonaean revolt it was too small to engage the rebels. Other military units first undertook to suppress Judas Maccabaeus and his band, and upon their failure, Philip had to call for help from the provincial or imperial government (8:8).

Phrygian . . . him. Phrygia was in western Asia Minor. See Map 2. The Seleucids gave up the area by the treaty of Apameia in 188. See Introduction, p. 108, and AB vol. 41, NOTES on 8:7–8. We know little of Phrygia as a source of mercenary soldiers. See Launey, *Recherches,* pp. 481–83. Philip may have been a veteran from the reign of Antiochus III. His recruitment later by the Seleucid empire would have been a violation of the treaty; see AB vol. 41, NOTE on 6:29.

Phrygians had the reputation of being cowardly and slavish (Tertullian, *De anima* 20.3; Strabo i 2.30, C 36; Euripides *Orestes* 1369–79, *Alcestis* 675), but Philip here is said to be more barbaric than Antiochus IV! On the meaning of "barbaric," see NOTE on 2:21.

23. Mount Gerizim (*Argarizin*) was the sacred mountain of the Samaritans, near Shechem. The writer here includes the Samaritans in "our race" (vs. 22) and expresses no hostility to their holy place. Thus, Jason of Cyrene, the staunch partisan of the primacy of the temple of Jerusalem (vss. 15–20, 2:22, 3:12, etc.), here and at 6:2 concedes legitimacy to the Samaritan claims for Mount Gerizim, which, after all, had a basis in Deut 27:4–12. Jason may be copying the words of Onias IV, who held that the temple of Jerusalem had not yet resumed the status of God's Chosen Place. See above, pp. 13–17, 35–37.

We have no further information on Andronikos' position. Was he stationed at Mount Gerizim? Or was he the predecessor of Apollonius as military commander (see I 3:10) and "governor of the district [*meris*]" (*meridarchês*) of Samaria (see *AJ* xii 5.5.261)?

The Samaritans were later to protest that they had had no connection whatever with the unrest among the Jews (J. *AJ* xii 5.5.260–61). Some of them, however, may have been known to have sympathized with Jason the Oniad or with the Ptolemaic empire (see NOTE on vss. 5–16).

Menelaus remained high priest of the Jews. The word "compatriots" (*politais*) makes it impossible to infer from our passage that Menelaus also had authority over the Samaritans.

23–24. *Disposed . . . slaves.* I translate according to the readings of VL′–542 La^LXVP Sy Arm and Theodoretus. The subject of the verbs is Antiochus (explicitly so in $L'-$[542] Sy and Theodoretus); cf. I 1:29. The other readings are awkward. They arose from the perplexity of scribes who noticed that the subject of the verbs could be Menelaus. Some scribes accepted the possibility, for they read at 13:4 that Menelaus was demonstrably the "cause of all the evils" (cf. J. *AJ* xii 9.7.383) and found that after Antiochus' withdrawal from Egypt under Roman pressure "deserters of the Holy Covenant" had received a sympathetic hearing from the King of the North, who thereupon sent forces which inflicted desecration (Dan 11:30–31). Surely Menelaus was a deserter of the Holy Covenant. The scribes found that the expedition described in vss. 24–26 had desecrated the Sabbath and had brought defilement (vs. 27), which was surely a further desecration. They held that Greek *pempein* ("send"), like Latin *mittere,* could also mean "unleash" or "cause to be sent." Accordingly, they removed the ambiguity by inserting *politas* before the last word of vs. 23, so that there, too, "Jews" became "fellow Jews." Thus we get the version of La[BM], "Disposed to hate his fellow Jews, he had the Mysarch Apollonius sent . . ." Cf. Georgius Syncellus *Chronographia* in *Georgius Syncellus et Nicephorus Cp.,* ed. by Guil. Dindorfius (Bonn: Weber, 1829), I, 530, where the "abominable Menelaus" is said to have asked Antiochus to send Apollonius. I explain Apollonius' title, "Mysarch," below in the NOTE on vs. 24.

In my opinion, Dan 11:31 does not reflect the expedition of the Mysarch at all; rather, the seer intended Dan 11:39 to follow Dan 11:30. See AB vol. 41, pp. 45–46, as corrected here in Introduction, Part V, n. 34, and pp. 92–94. Dan 11:39, with its reference to the establishment of the garrison in the Akra (see Introduction, pp. 93–94, 106–7), certainly reflects the Mysarch's operations. Furthermore, Dan 11:22(end)–24 may assert that the garrison in the Akra was a long-standing plot of Menelaus'. The seer's obscure and now partly corrupt words could mean "And also a Jewish high priest through association with the king shall work treachery and thus rise to rule over Israel. In time of peace he shall come against the city and do what his ancestors had not done: he shall squander the property as spoil and plunder to the Greeks [?], and he shall meditate plots concerning fortifiers [read *m^{e}bass^{e}rīm*] until the appointed time" (on the first clauses, see AB vol. 41, p. 49, n. 28, but delete there the translation of the last clause as well as the last two lines of the note). So interpreted, Dan 11:22(end)–24 would provide evidence that a contemporary observer believed the establishment of the Akra was in some way the result of plotting by Menelaus. However, I do not think any ancient reader after the death of the seer interpreted Dan 11:22(end)–24 in this manner or perceived the original sequence of Dan 11:30 and 39.

Hence, the reading of La[BM] must have been derived by interpreting Dan 11:30–31. La[BM] are inferior witnesses which are never likely to preserve an original reading. Their text here cannot have been the original because it contradicts our writer's thesis: he holds that the cruel acts against the Jews were either divine punishment for sin or wanton deeds of arrogant Antiochus; they hit the Hellenizers, too (4:16–17), and were not done at the behest of the sinners. Thus, Jason of Cyrene must have had some other interpretation of Dan 11:30–31.

The scribes of A and q probably worked from a text in which *politas* had been inserted. They found it easy to believe that Menelaus hated his fellow

Jews, but they were Greeks and knew that where *pempein* means "cause to be sent," the middle voice, not the active, is used. Holding no military rank, the high priest could hardly have sent soldiers and given them orders (cf. 4:40). Nowhere does Jason of Cyrene accuse Menelaus of mass murder. Hence the scribes of A and q broke vs. 24 off from the end of vs. 23 by inserting the particle *de*. Their version, beginning from the middle of vs. 23, can be translated "as he lorded it over his fellow Jews and also was disposed to hate his fellow Jews. He [Antiochus] sent the Mysarch . . ." The version makes sense, but contains an awkward repetition.

By the phrase "disposed to hate the Jews," the writer expresses his belief that Antiochus was now following his passions, whereas previously there had been a case for viewing the king's actions against the Jews as punishment of them for rebellion against his rule.

24–27. The details here are very similar to those in the account at I 1:29–40 (see AB vol. 41, NOTES ad loc., to be corrected by the remarks here). In both passages, the Seleucid commander bears the title "Mysarch" (see AB vol. 41, pp. 211–12), is sent with an army, feigns peaceful intentions, perpetrates a surprise attack, massacres men, and takes women and children captive. Conceivably, two independent writers could so describe the Mysarch's expedition. But both authors also say that a result of the expedition was ritual defilement (vs. 27; I 1:37); what ritual defilement is not specified. It was common knowledge that corpses caused defilement. No one would have bothered to mention that fact. Hence, if both our histories contain the vague mention of defilement, we may infer that they both drew upon the Common Source.

The abridger may have omitted the looting and firing of the city (I 1:31, 32[end]). Jason himself omitted the building of the Akra (I 1:33; see below, pp. 264–65) and with it the associated breaching of the city walls (I 1:31) and perhaps also the taking of spoils (ibid.), since the spoils went into the Akra (I 1:35). The Hasmonaean propagandist, too, seems to have omitted matter. To mention the fact that the Mysarch took advantage of the Sabbath would raise the question: why did not Mattathias make his great enactment (I 2:41) earlier? Hence, in I 1:39, we have only a vague echo of what must have stood in the Common Source on the role of the Sabbath in the Mysarch's surprise attack.

I must correct an error in the translation of I 1:29 and the commentary thereto at AB vol. 41, p. 212. At the beginning of that verse, the Greek has *Meta dyo eté hêmerôn*, reflecting a Heb. *mikkēṣ šᵉnātayim yāmīm* (lit. "at the end of two years of days"). "Two years of days" is a Hebrew idiom for two *full* years, not merely for one year plus a fraction; see AB vol. 41, p. 268, and TB *Ketubot* 57b.

This correction of the translation of I 1:29 raises a problem. The sack of Jerusalem by Antiochus IV (vss. 11–21; I 1:20–24) must have occurred late in 143 Sel. Mac. (see AB vol. 41, pp. 203, 207). I shall show in my commentary on Dan 7:25 that the decrees of Antiochus IV requiring the Jews to observe the imposed cult (II 6:1–7; I 1:44–51) came in Nisan (early spring), 167 B.C.E., three and one half years before the beginning of the sabbatical year. The expedition of the Mysarch, accordingly, came somewhat earlier. Evidence in the apocryphal book of Baruch confirms this supposition and shows that the expedition came in February or March of 167; see my article in PAAJR 46–47 (1979–80), 180–96. Thus, the Hasmonaean propagandist is wrong in saying two *full* years elapsed.

What evidence did he have? And why did he add the word implying "full"? Did he do so merely to imitate Gen 41:1 (cf. II Sam 14:28; Jer 28:3, 11)? It is likely he had a more serious purpose. He could date the sack of Jerusalem by the king only by placing it in the aftermath of the campaign in Egypt which the Seleucid Chronicle dated for him in 143 Sel. The Hasmonaean propagandist surely knew from the Seleucid Chronicle that a Roman ultimatum drove Antiochus IV to withdraw from Egypt in 144 Sel. (see Mørkholm, pp. 88–96). The ultimatum and withdrawal are reflected in Dan 11:30. That verse, when compared with Dan 11:28, also seems to imply that Antiochus IV in person sacked Jerusalem twice, yet even Jason of Cyrene knew that he did so only once (vss. 11–26; see AB vol. 41, p. 45). The only easy way for a pious ancient reader to vindicate Dan 11:30 was to say that the apparent second sack by the king was the expedition of the Mysarch acting as the agent of Antiochus IV. (For my theory on what the seer meant at Dan 11:30, see AB vol. 41, pp. 212–13.) By placing the expedition two *full* years after the sack, at the earliest in 145 Sel., the Hasmonaean propagandist effectively excluded the easy interpretation. Jason of Cyrene proceeded similarly in II 14:1–4 (see NOTE ad loc.).

But where could he have found a source which he could interpret as giving an interval of two full years? Not in any local Jewish chronicle, for the sack of late summer or autumn, 169, occurred in 143 Sel. Bab., and the Mysarch's expedition of late winter or very early spring, 167, came in 144 Sel. Bab. The Seleucid Chronicle, with its Macedonian Seleucid dates, could have served: the sack by the king occurred in 143 Sel. Mac., and the Mysarch's expedition in 145 Sel. Mac. The language at I 1:29, indeed, dates a royal act, the sending of the Mysarch, not his arrival at Jerusalem (cf. I 9:3). The Seleucid Chronicle seems to have covered the king's acts year by year; see p. 41. In telling of 145 Sel. Mac., the Chronicle probably had something like "Observing that the Jews, two years after he sacked Jerusalem, were still turbulent, Antiochus Epiphanes sent Apollonius the Mysarch to punish them." "Two years," in a Greek work, might mean only one year plus an appreciable fraction; see Appendix VII. If the Hasmonaean propagandist had copied the mere "two years," his readers might have taken the interval as ending in 144 Sel. and still might have considered it possible that Dan 11:30 predicted the expedition of the Mysarch. To exclude that possibility, the Hasmonaean propagandist jumped to a conclusion and wrote "two full years." Jason of Cyrene, though he had a different interpretation of Dan 11:28 and 30 (see NOTE on II 5:1), omitted the interval, further to protect the veracity of Daniel.

Despite the writer's hint at the end of vs. 23, that the king in sending the Mysarch was merely following his passions, the cruel expedition was a punishment for further unrest among the Jews, especially for harassment of Antiochenes by the pious; see pp. 92–95. On Josephus' strange combination (*AJ* xii 5.3–4.246–56) of the Mysarch's expedition of 167 with the king's sack of 169 B.C.E., see AB vol. 41, pp. 558–68.

Conspicuous by its absence here from the account of the expedition of the

Mysarch is the establishment of the Akra and its garrison (I 1:33–38). The Akra was the newly strengthened citadel to the north of the temple; see AB vol. 41, pp. 213–19. So significant a violation of the sanctity and prestige of Jerusalem as the Akra can hardly have been omitted by the abridger, and the citadel and its garrison are mentioned at II 15:31 and 35. Again, the need to protect the prophecies of Daniel probably forced Jason of Cyrene to modify his narrative. In Daniel, the reference to the establishment of the Akra comes at 11:39, *after* the reference to the persecution (Dan 11:31–38); see AB vol. 41, pp. 45–46, 50. Jason of Cyrene waited until ch. 6 to tell of the persecution because he knew, like the author of I 1:29–64, that the persecution followed the expedition of the Mysarch. Thus, he had to imagine some later time for the founding of the community of the Akra. Jason of Cyrene may have had good reason to wish to date the founding much later. Reports probably circulated that pietists collaborated with the men of the Akra, when Judas put it under siege in 163, by supporting their appeal to Antiochus V to intervene; see AB vol. 41, p. 65. The abridged history (ch. 13) contains no reference to the siege of the Akra, as if Jason of Cyrene avoided the troublesome point. If he could find some way to assert that the community of the Akra was established at the *end* of the expedition of Antiochus V and Lysias, he could refute the embarrassing reports. Thus, he may have placed its establishment in 13:18–22, a passage now drastically abridged. More likely, however, he left the problem unsolved, for there is no hostility to Antiochus V at the end of ch. 13. Josephus had similar problems because of his belief in the veracity of Daniel. On his efforts to solve them, see AB vol. 41, NOTE on 1:33–40(end).

Thus, in the abridged history, the first mention of the Akra comes at 15:31 and 35, at a point so late that it poses no challenge to the veracity of Daniel.

From I 1:38–39 and II 11:25 we may infer that from this point on Jerusalem and the temple no longer belonged to the Jewish nation but were assigned to the community in the Akra. Nevertheless, until Kislev of 167 B.C.E. there was no interruption in the biblically prescribed rituals and observances at the temple (I 1:54, 59; II 10:5).

24. A Mysarch was a commander of mercenaries from Mysia in northwestern Asia Minor. At I 1:29 the title "Commander of Mysians" (*śar mūsīm* or *śar mīsīm*) is punningly distorted into "tax-gathering official" or "taskmaster" (*śar missīm*); see AB vol. 41, pp. 211–12. The distortion may go back to the time of the events and reflect disappointment in the expectations roused by the seeming fulfillment of Zech 9:8 against Heliodorus (see NOTE on ch. 3), for no divine apparitions stopped Antiochus IV or the Mysarch. Antiochus IV is known to have had a unit of 5,000 Mysians in his army (Polybius xxx 25.3). At this time Mysia was subject to the kingdom of Pergamum, an area still open to Seleucid recruiting. See AB vol. 41, NOTE on 6:29. On the numerous Mysians in Hellenistic armies, see Launey, *Recherches,* pp. 436–49.

The army of 22,000 is much too large for a punitive expedition against unarmed Jerusalem. See AB vol. 41, NOTE on 3:39.

25. Hellenistic armies had long since learned to take advantage of the Sabbath in fighting the Jews; see Agatharchides of Knidos *apud* J. *Ap.* i 22.2.209–11, and cf. 6:11 and I 2:29–38.

26. The unsuspecting Jews were attracted by the spectacle of the soldiers in

formation. From the fact that pious Jews did not hesitate to go outside the walls we learn that they may well have accepted the principle of the Sabbath limit ($t^e\hbar\bar{u}m$) of two thousand cubits from a city (M. 'Erubin 5:1–7; Schürer, II, 557), and that Apollonius' men encamped inside (or just outside) the Sabbath limit. Inscriptions may show the observance of Sabbath limits at Gazara (Gezer) in the late second or early first century B.C.E.; see Emil Schürer, The History of the Jewish People in the Age of Jesus Christ (New English version, rev. and ed. by Geza Vermes and Fergus Millar; Edinburgh: T. & T. Clark, 1973–), I, 191, n. 8, and B. Mazar, "Gezer," Enc. Bib., II (1954), 467 (in Hebrew). Like the martyrs later (6:11; I 2:36), the pious Jews did not even bar the city gates to Apollonius and his men.

27. The Mysarch's action was patently unjust, as seen by the Jews and by the writer here. Nevertheless, it could still be viewed as divine punishment for the sins of the Hellenizers and for tolerating them. In ch. 6, however, we shall learn how Antiochus arrogantly ordered the Jews to violate the Torah. At that point Antiochus could no longer be merely the rod of God's anger. Jason of Cyrene probably believed that a hero of Judas' stature would have either risen in revolt or suffered martyrdom as soon as the persecution began in Jerusalem. Yet Judas survived, and the Hasmonaean revolt began surprisingly late. Hence, probably reasoning a priori, Jason inferred that Judas, the "small help" of Dan 11:34, was no longer in Jerusalem when the persecution began.

The author of First Maccabees appears to have been better informed and less blinded by preconceptions. His readers might wonder why zealous Mattathias, who had been at least at times in Jerusalem, did nothing until the king's men came to his family's ancestral home at Modeïn, but the awkward facts are presented without hesitation at I 2:1–15. At first Mattathias, like all pious Jews (see NOTE on 1:7, Jason . . . Kingdom), believed God forbade resistance. Only when the king's men had cornered him in Modeïn did he rise in zeal. Like Jason of Cyrene, Josephus followed his preconceptions and was careful to assert that Mattathias, though a Jerusalemite, was not at the holy city but at Modeïn when the persecution began (AJ xii 6.1.265). The nine others here are presumably Judas' own family, including his father, Mattathias, whom Jason of Cyrene considered to be so wicked as to be unmentionable; see AB vol. 41, p. 79. The observations we have just made lead to the conclusion that if any of our writers has been driven by his preconceptions to abandon the awkward account of a reliable source, it is not the author of First Maccabees, who here may well reflect faithfully what was in the Common Source.

Jason of Cyrene removed Judas from Jerusalem but is inept in explaining why Judas left. The Greek is ambiguous. "Keeping clear of defilement" may be the purpose for staying in the wilderness or it may be the reason for eating herbs for food. The latter is nonsense, for herbs can become unclean and other foods can be ritually pure. Priests were required to keep clear of the uncleanness caused by corpses (Lev 21:1–3), but nowhere in the abridged history is there an admission that Judas was a priest, and the corpses of the massacred must have been quickly removed. Nevertheless, many pious Jews, even non-priests, strove to keep clear of uncleanness: certainly the Essenes and the Pharisees did so. Dan 11:31, as far as Jason of Cyrene knew, contained allusions to the expedition of the Mysarch (see AB vol. 41, pp. 50–51). The old Greek version at Dan 11:31 speaks of persons ("arms") who shall "arise" through the King of the North and "shall defile [*mianousi;* Heb. *whllw*] the sanctuary." Though Jason probably had a different reading for the noun "arms," which designates the persons who shall arise (see NOTE on 6:4–5), that reading, too, can be made to include the Mysarch. The Greek verb for "defile" at Dan LXX 11:31 is the one usually used to translate Heb. *tm'* ("render unclean"). It is hard to say what uncleanness Judas was avoiding, but the Mysarch could have brought something more permanent than the presence of corpses. Jason also may have drawn his inference from another pun which arose from Apollonius' title "Mysarch." *Mysós* in Greek means "Mysian," but *mýsos* means "uncleanness," and the Syriac renders "Mysarch" as "chief of all the unclean." According to the poem at I 1:37, the *men of the Akra* after the Mysarch's departure "defiled" (*emolynan*) the sanctuary.

The diet of herbs, then, probably has nothing to do with the avoidance of uncleanness. Rather, Jason here draws on the traditions that the Hasmonaeans fled to the wilderness; see 10:6 and AB vol. 41, NOTE on 2:28–38. Herbs were the only food available in the wilderness.

VII. THE IMPOSED CULT AND
THE PERSECUTION
(6:1–17)

6 ¹ Not long thereafter, the king sent Geron the Athenian to compel the Jews to depart from their ancestral laws and to cease living by the laws of God. ² He was also to defile both the temple in Jerusalem and the temple on Mount Gerizim and to proclaim the former to be the temple of Zeus Olympios and the latter (in accordance with the . . .ᵃ of the inhabitants of the place) to be the temple of Zeus Xenios. ³ The execution of the wicked project brought suffering and indignation to all. ⁴ The gentiles filled the temple with debauchery and revelry, as they lolled with prostitutes and had intercourse with women in the sacred courts and also brought forbidden things inside. ⁵ The altar was filled with prohibited offerings excluded by the laws. ⁶ No one was allowed to observe the Sabbath or to keep the traditional festivals or even to confess he was a Jew. ⁷ On the monthly birthday of the king Jews were cruelly compelled to partake of the meat of pagan sacrifices. When a festival of Dionysus was celebrated, they were forced to put on wreaths of ivy and march in the procession in honor of the god. ⁸ A decree was published in the neighboring Greek cities, on the proposal of the citizens of Ptolemais, that they proceed against the Jews in the same manner and compel them to partake of the meat of pagan sacrifices ⁹ and that they butcher those Jews who refused to go over to the Greek way of life.

It was clear that a time of trouble had come. ¹⁰ Two women were brought to trial for having circumcised their children. Their babies were hanged from their breasts, and the women were paraded publicly through the city and hurled down from the walls. ¹¹ Other Jews hastily assembled nearby in the caves to observe the Sabbath in secret. On being denounced to Philip they were all burned to death because they refrained from defending themselves, out of respect for the holiest of days.

¹² I beg the readers of my book not to be disheartened by the calam-

ᵃ See commentary.

ities but to bear in mind that chastisements come not in order to destroy our race but in order to teach it. 13 If the ungodly among us are not left long to themselves but speedily incur punishment, it is a sign of God's great goodness to us. 14 With the other nations the LORD waits patiently, staying their punishment until they reach the full measure of their sins. Quite otherwise is His decree for us, 15 in order that He should not have to punish us after we have come to the complete measure of our sins. 16 Consequently, God never lets His mercy depart from us. Rather, though He teaches us by calamity, He never deserts His people. 17 Let this be enough as a reminder to my readers. Now we must quickly return to our story.

NOTES

Ch. 6. Do our chapter and ch. 7 and the parallel passage, I 1:44–64, reflect the Common Source? One must take note not only of the similarities but of the differences.

Both here in vs. 1 and at I 1:44 the king sends an agent or agents to force Jews to abandon their own laws. In vs. 2 and at I 1:46 the temple is to be defiled. At vs. 3 and at I 1:53 we hear of the distress of loyal Israelites. In vs. 4 (see NOTE on vss. 4–5) and at I 1:54 we learn of idolatrous objects brought into the temple. In vs. 5 and at I 1:47(end) we hear of forbidden meat upon the sacrificial altar. In vs. 6 and at I 1:45(end) Jews are to be forced to violate Sabbaths and festivals. In vs. 7 and in I 1:58–59 we learn of the imposition of monthly participation in pagan observances (cf. I 1:51). In vss. 8–9 and in I 1:51(beginning) we learn that directives on the persecution of the Jews were also to be found in places outside Judaea (see NOTE on vss. 8–9).

There can be no doubt that vss. 10–11, 18, and I 1:60–63, 2:29–38 reflect the Common Source, and it is probable that the same source contained some of the material in vss. 18–31, in ch. 7, and in I 1:64; see NOTE on vss. 10–31.

We must return to consider the differences between vss. 1–9 and I 1:44–64. There is an obvious difference between I 1:44–64 and what we have here. There we get the common Hebrew scheme giving the details of a royal edict and then how it was implemented (see AB vol. 41, p. 224). Moreover, there the decrees are enforced in two stages: first, the king only appoints officials who intimidate pious Jews and embolden the "forsakers of the Torah" (I 1:51–53), but later he forcibly installs the Abomination of Desolation and compels Jews on pain of death to violate the Torah and observe the imposed cult (I 1:54–63). Here in the abridged history we read only of the final forcible implementation. There is thus no contradiction between the multiple messengers of I 1:44, who bore the copies of the king's edict, and the single Geron the Athenian here, who supervised the implementation (at AB vol. 41, p. 224, par. 2, I was wrong to include Geron the Athenian among the "officers to watch over all the people" in I 1:51). Josephus, too, tended to condense the somewhat redundant Hebrew scheme by narrating only how the king's decree was implemented (AB vol. 41, pp. 224, 567). The difference in narrative technique, therefore, leaves it possible that our authors here drew on the Common Source.

In I 1 there is no parallel for the debauchery and women mentioned in our vs. 4. The assertions in vs. 4 may come from an interpretation of Dan 11:31 and need not have stood in the Common Source; see NOTE on vss. 4–5.

On the absence of a parallel in our chapter to the cessation of offerings at I 1:45(beginning), see NOTE on vss. 4–5.

Jason knew of the illicit altars and shrines outside the temple mentioned at I 1:47 but not here; see II 10:2. The abridger may have omitted them here.

The prohibition of circumcision and of observance of laws on "uncleanness" at I 1:48 may be a mere inference from the stories in the Common Source reflected at I 1:60–63 and in the parallels here. On the other hand, if I 1:48 directly reflects the Common Source, Jason or the abridger could have found mention of the clauses of the royal decree superfluous when he could tell the vivid stories of their implementation at vss. 10–11, 18–31, and in ch. 7.

I 1:49 is essentially a repetition of I 1:44, and its content is covered by vss. 1 and 6 here. The case of I 1:50 is similar to that of I 1:48, already treated.

At I 1:52 we learn of large numbers of Jewish apostates who collaborated with the imperial authorities. The author of First Maccabees was glad to tell how the Hasmonaeans fought against such wicked persons. Jason or the abridger seems to have preferred to focus on the righteous martyrs at this point, leaving the presence of the wicked to be inferred from 8:6–7, 33, and 10:15 (cf. 2:21).

On the failure of the abridged history to mention the Abomination of Desolation (I 1:54, 59), see NOTE on vss. 4–5.

The case with I 1:55 is similar to that of I 1:47, already treated. There is no parallel here for the destruction of copies of the Torah and the slaying of those who possessed such copies or showed love for the Torah (I 1:56–57), but the points could be inferred from vs. 6 (end).

Accordingly, there is a strong case that both Jason and the Hasmonaean propagandist drew on the Common Source here.

1–7. By forcing the Jews to observe the imposed cult, Antiochus IV intended to punish and correct a turbulent subject-people. Antiochus portrayed the cult as a purification of the now corrupt Jewish religion. He was not imposing Greek patterns upon the Jews. See pp. 98–112 and AB vol. 41, pp. 125–59.

1. *Not long thereafter.* On the dates of the expedition of the Mysarch and of the issuance of Antiochus' decrees imposing religious changes upon the Jews, see NOTE on 5:24–27. No source gives us the interval between the expedition of the Mysarch and the implementation of those decrees (cf. I 1:29–44; Dan 7:25, 8:13, 24–25, 11:30–39). The events of vss. 1–7 reached their climax with the desecration of the temple on 15 Kislev, 167 B.C.E. We may guess that the Athenian of our verse arrived in Jerusalem at most a few weeks before.

Geron the Athenian. Gr. *GERONTA ATHĒNAION.* The words are ambiguous. In ancient Greek there were only capital letters. Proper nouns were not automatically distinguishable from common nouns. *GERŌN* (to use the nominative case of the word) is not only a rather uncommon man's name, it means "old man" and is also a title, "Elder." *ATHÊNAIOS* not only means "Athenian" but is a common name. It might be tempting to take *GERÔN* as a title, for at Ephesus and much later at Athens there was a body known as the sacred *gerousia* which supervised the conduct of religious festivals and the making of images; see James H. Oliver, *The Sacred Gerousia* (*Hesperia*, suppl. 6 [1941]), pp. 1–5, 28–29, 38. A member of a *gerousia* was naturally called a *gerôn*. In the Hellenistic age, the analogue of the Jewish Council of Elders (*gerousia*) at Athens was the Council of the Areopagus, which had jurisdiction over cults of foreign origin. See Daniel J. Geagan, *The Athenian Constitution after Sulla* (*Hesperia*, suppl. 12 [1967]), p. 50. A Jewish Greek might have given a member of the Council of the Areopagus the title *gerôn*. If, however, *GERÔN* here is a title, *ATHÊNAIOS* must mean "Athenian," for in the Hellenistic world such a title did not exist in a vacuum but always was attached to some political unit. And if *ATHÊNAIOS* means "Athenian," the author, contrary to his practice, has refrained from naming the person who committed the atrocity of imposing apostasy on Jews. Elsewhere he gives the names even of minor persecutors.

Furthermore, in the author's Greek, titles are preceded by the definite article (except in the predicate nominative and adjunct accusative constructions, "he became high priest" and "he appointed him high priest"). Nor can the article have been omitted because the "Elder" was only one of many members of a *gerousia*. In the author's Greek such titles are treated by using the genitive plural with the definite article, "[one] of the . . ." (see vs. 18, 8:9, 12:35, 14:37) or by coupling the title with *anêr* ("man"; see 8:9).

Thus *GERONTA ATHÊNAION* must mean either "the elderly Athenaeus" or "Geron the Athenian." As a parallel for "the elderly Athenaeus" one might cite the description of Auranos at 4:40: an elderly man should have known better than to embark on so rash a course. But the grammatical construction, with an adjective or appositive preceding a proper noun in the absence of the definite article, is unusual and is unparalleled in the abridged history. It is best to construe the words as "Geron the Athenian." Then the grammatical construction is completely regular in Greek, and Geron is attested as an Athenian name, though only in an inscription now lost, dated by the editors in the Roman period (*Inscriptiones Graecae, Editio minor*, II–III 5246), and is attested earlier elsewhere in Greece. See A. Wilhelm, *Akademie der Wissenschaften in Wien, Philosophisch-historische Klasse: Anzeiger* 74 (1937), 20–22.

One would indeed expect Antiochus to use an Athenian expert to supervise a cultic "reform" at Jerusalem. Antiochus IV enjoyed the hospitality of Athens during the time between his release from being a hostage at Rome (ca. 176) and his departure for the coup which brought about his accession as king in November, 175, and the Athenians sympathized with the coup (Appian *Syriakê* 45; OGIS 248, as interpreted by Maurice Holleaux, *Études d'épigraphie et d'histoire grecques*, vol. II [Paris: É. de Boccard, 1938], pp. 127–47; Mørkholm, pp. 40–42). Thereafter, Antiochus repeatedly showed his gratitude to Athens (Mørkholm, pp. 40, 58–60), and Jason of Cyrene appears to have been aware of the fact (see 9:15).

In the second century B.C.E. Athens held high prestige as a center of Greek culture and education; see M. P. Nilsson, *Die hellenistische Schule*, pp. 21–29. Antiochus in his religious policy, however, was not thinking to Hellenize Jerusalem but rather to purge the Jews of pernicious accretions on their once admirable religion; see NOTE on vss. 1–7. Athens was also the center for the ancient equivalents of anthropology and the comparative study of religion. When Ptolemy I wished to revitalize the cult of Serapis in Egypt, he, too, used an expert from Athens, Timotheus the "religious interpreter" (*exêgêtês*), a member of the Eumolpid clan which had the hereditary prerogative of presiding over the Eleusinian mysteries; see Tacitus *Histories* iv. 83; Plutarch *De Iside et Osiride* 28, pp. 361f–62a; Nilsson, *Geschichte der griechischen Religion*, II, 91, 156–58. According to the sources, Ptolemy also consulted the Egyptian expert Manetho.

Athenian experts could serve Antiochus' needs. Both Clearchus and Theophrastus had done their work at Athens and in their research had touched upon the Jews. On Clearchus, see Fritz Wehrli, *Die Schule des Aristoteles*, Heft III, fragment 6 (=J. *Ap.* i 22.176–82), and pp. 45, 47–49; Hans Lewy, "Aristotle and the Jewish Sage according to Clearchus of Soli," *Harvard Theological Review* 31 (1938), 205–35; and Y. Gutman, *The Beginnings of Jewish-Hellenistic Literature* (Jerusalem: Bialik Institute, 1958), pp. 91–102 (in Hebrew). On Theophrastus, see Porphyry *De abstinentia* ii 26; J. *Ap.* i 22.167, and Gutman, *Beginnings,* pp. 74–88. In the second century B.C.E. Athenian scholars could read the works of Clearchus and Theophrastus and go on to formulate fresh theories. Athenians could also observe the thriving Phoenician community which existed in Attica so as to use a comparative approach in studying the Jews (see Franz Poland, *Geschichte des griechischen Vereinswesens* [Leipzig: Teubner, 1909], pp. 81, 110, n. 2, 113, 313, 468). Thus, quite apart from his own attachment to Athens, Antiochus here had reason to use an Athenian expert.

On my error at AB vol. 41, p. 224, par. 2 (where I refer the reader to this NOTE), see Introduction, Part V, n. 70.

On the heterodox Jewish informants who may have helped in the formulation of the imposed cult, see pp. 105–12.

living by. The Greek verb is *politeuesthai* ("follow the civic institutions of"); see NOTE on 4:11, *civic institutions.*

2. Our writer mentions the temple at Jerusalem and the Samaritan temple on Mount Gerizim in the same breath, as if he regarded both as legitimate. See NOTE on 5:23. This surprising implication of our passage is in no way impaired by the obvious fact that the writer cannot have approved of the Samaritans' petition, also mentioned here. At 5:23 and 15:1–5 his attitude toward Samaritans is, if anything, sympathetic.

Only Jason reflects the views of the Jews who were indignant over the renaming of the temples. To other Jews, as to the Samaritans, the act may have been inconsequential, for *Zeus* in Greek was almost a common noun, "god," and *Olympios* could mean "heavenly," and *Xenios* only meant "protector of the rights of strangers." See AB vol. 41, p. 142. Pagans, including Greeks, regularly gave names from their own pantheons to foreign gods, and foreigners in speaking Greek would accept the use of Greek names for their own deities, without changing in any other way the nature of the god or his worship. See Appendix VIII, NOTE on J. *AJ* xii 5.5.259, *unnamed shrine.*

Jason may have taken *hammā'ōz* ("the fortress") at Dan 11:31 to be the Samaritan temple in the land of Ephraim; see Pss 60:9, 108:9.

Zeus Olympios. If the Jews were aware of the etymology of *Olympios* they would have good reason to reject *Zeus Olympios* as a Greek name for their God, even if they accepted the use of *Zeus* as a common noun ("god"). *Olympios* literally is "of Mount Olympus," and, by locating the god on a Greek mountain, identified him as distinct from the LORD, who dwells on Mount Zion. The same could not be said of the epithet *Xenios.*

The fact that the name of the great God of the Jews in the imposed cult was identical to that of the Zeus Olympios to whom Antiochus IV was especially devoted is probably a coincidence. On that Zeus, see Kent J. Rigsby, "Seleucid Notes," *Transactions of the American Philological Association* 110 (1980), 233–38.

(*in accordance . . . place*). All witnesses to the text of Second Maccabees have *etynchanon* at the point where I have left a gap in my translation. A literal rendering of the words in parentheses would be "as the inhabitants of the place happened to." A Greek writer could omit after *etynchanon* the participle, which would correspond to the English verb that would follow "to," leaving the reader to infer what it was from the context; see Kühner-Gerth, *Grammatik,* II, 67. If the reading *etynchanon* is correct, there are at least two possibilities. One might infer that the missing verb was "name," and in my idiomatic translation one should then fill the blank with "practice"; cf. La^BMP Sy. Or one might infer that the missing verb was "be" (see Kühner-Gerth, ibid.). Zeus Xenios was the protector of strangers and foreigners, and Jason surely believed II Kings 17:24–41 on the foreign origins of the Samaritans. Then one should fill the blank with "character"; cf. La^LXV. *Tynchanein* by itself can mean "obtain" and perhaps "obtain by request," but that meaning is unlikely here because the verb is in the imperfect tense. Cf. Robert Hanhart, "Zum Text des 2. und 3. Makkabäerbuches," *Nachrichten der Akademie der Wissenschaften in Göttingen, Philologisch-historische Klasse* (1961), pp. 458–59.

If Jason wrote *etynchanon,* however, he probably altered his source in order to sneer the more vigorously at the Samaritans. At *AJ* xii 5.5.257–64, Josephus presents an important text, the petition of the Samaritans to Antiochus IV in which they seek exemption from the persecution and ask that their temple be renamed. On that text and its relation to our verse, see Appendix VIII. In Greek, "to petition" is *entynchanein,* and scholars, including Niese and Abel, add the prefix *en-* to the verb here. Then the blank in my translation should be filled by "petition."

Jason and Josephus may have taken "those who wickedly violate the covenant" at Dan 11:32 to be the Samaritans.

Zeus Xenios. The variants for the epithet *Xenios* at J. *AJ* xii 5.5.261 and 263 in the Greek text and the Latin version are to be rejected. See Appendix VIII, NOTE on *AJ* xii 5.5.261, *We also . . . Zeus Xenios.*

Since *Olympios* is the Greek epithet for any of the gods in their aspect of living "on high," there is nothing surprising about the Greek name for the God of the Jews. Why, however, did the Samaritans choose *Xenios* ("protector of the rights of strangers") as the Greek epithet for their God? At first sight *Xenios* sounds less impressive than *Olympios,* though it is an extremely common epithet of Zeus (see Weinreich, "Xenios," in Roscher, VI [1924–37], 522–25).

It is likely that *Zeus Xenios* reflects a punning translation of *Garizin,* the name of the Samaritans' holy mountain. Jews and Samaritans surely knew of *Zēn,* the alternative form of the name of Zeus (see *Aristeas to Philocrates* 16; J. *AJ* xii 2.2.22; Aristobulus *apud* Eusebius *Praeparatio evangelica* xiii 12.7–8). The Hebrew equivalent for *xenos* ("stranger") was *gēr.* The theories of Jews in the Hellenistic age on proselytism led the Greek translators of the Hebrew Bible to render *gēr* in most places by *proselytos.* Nevertheless, at Job 31:32 *xenos* renders *gēr. Garizin* could thus be taken as "sojourning stranger protected by Zeus."

Central to the Samaritan religion is the holiness of Mount Gerizim. Apart from reflecting the name of the holy mountain, the epithet *Xenios* had other attractive aspects. It could be taken as a translation of an epithet of the God of Israel found in the Torah (Deut 10:18; cf. Ps 146:9). It could also be taken as reflecting the relationship of the Israelite to his God (Lev 25:23). An old Samaritan interpretation of Gen 14:18–20, preserved in Hellenistic Greek, tells how Abraham himself, as a stranger, received hospitality (*xenisthēnai*) at Mount Gerizim, the mountain of the Most High God (Pseudo-Eupolemus FGH 724, F1.5=Eusebius *Praeparatio evangelica* ix 17). Phoenicians, too, seem to have been glad to portray their relationship to their gods as that of sojourning stranger (*gēr*) to host, as is attested by names like *Gērysmôn* (*gr'šmn* ["*gēr* of Eshmun"]) and *gr'strt* ("*gēr* of Astarte"). See Javier Teixidor, "Bulletin d'épigraphie sémitique," *Syria* 45 (1968), 373, no. 73, and 47 (1970), 361, no. 20.

4–5. Our verses are the sole information in the abridged history on how the temple was desecrated by the imposed cult. Conspicuous by its absence both here and in Josephus is any mention of the Abomination of Desolation by name. The reason for the omissions is probably that Jason of Cyrene and Josephus did not feel safe in using the term. By their times it had many interpretations. Cf. AB vol. 41, Appendix V, n. 19.

On the other hand, our verses and *Schol. Megillat Ta'anit* 23 Marḥeshvan stand alone in asserting that the imposed cult involved prostitution. The heritage of the Torah and the Prophets, with their repeated condemnation of cultic prostitution, renders it impossible that hostile witnesses could pass over cultic prostitution in silence. Yet the contemporary witnesses (the Testament of Moses, Enoch 85–90, and Dan 7–12) say nothing of it, and the well-informed author of First Maccabees is also silent. We are thus forced to conclude that Jason of Cyrene and the author of the tradition in the *Scholia* to *Megillat Ta'anit* were mistaken. Correct accordingly AB vol. 41, pp. 156, 165. The lattice mentioned at AB vol. 41, p. 277, may have been a structure for the imposed cult, but it was not used for prostitution.

What could produce the belief that the imposed cult involved prostitution? The ease with which it could be fitted into the framework of Antiochus' decrees (see AB vol. 41, p. 156) is no answer, for otherwise our authors might have guessed that the imposed cult involved the use of statues or the sacrifice of human criminals, yet Jason of Cyrene and the *Scholia* make no such suggestion.

In fact, vs. 4 does not fit well into the framework of the imposed cult. In all other passages *Jews* are compelled to violate the Torah. In vs. 4, the violators are *gentiles*. Jason's favorite source was the prophecies of Daniel, and if we look at the account in Daniel of how the gentiles desecrated the temple, we shall indeed find the probable source for the reports concerning prostitution. Most translators render *zr'ym* at Dan 11:31 by "arms" or "forces," as if it was to be read *zᵉrō'īm* (so the Masoretic text, Dan LXX, and the Vulgate), but Theodotion read the word as *zᵉrā'īm* ("seeds"). Jason of Cyrene and the originator of the tradition in the *Scholia* seem to have read the word as *zārā'īm* or *zōrᵉ'īm* ("sowers of seed [in the sexual sense]"). Ancient readers could have found good reason to choose the sexual meaning. The usual plural of *zᵉrōa'* ("arm") is not *zᵉrō'īm* but *zᵉrō'ōt*, which is the sole form elsewhere in Daniel (10:6, 11:15, 22). A Jew who read in Dan 11:31 "Sowers of semen shall arise from him [sc. Antiochus IV] and desecrate the temple" would also know of how the Torah and the Prophets spoke of prostitution as desecration (Lev 19:29, 21:9; Amos 2:7–8; cf. Ezek 23:39[end]–49) and could easily go on to produce vs. 4 and the tradition in the *Scholia*.

Though the ancient reader could find justification for taking *zr'ym y'mdw* in Dan 11:31 as "sowers of seed shall arise," that meaning is excluded by the occurrence of the strange combination of the noun *zr'* and the verb *'md* ("stand," "arise") at Dan 11:15; there and at Dan 11:6 and 22 "arm" or "force" is the only acceptable meaning. At Dan 11:15 the noun appears with the normal plural suffix *-ōt*. The irregular plural suffix *-īm*, which it bears in Dan 11:31, is to be explained as a mechanical rendition of the Aramaic plural *dr'yn*, since the seer wrote the chapter in Aramaic and after his death a disciple turned his words into wretched Hebrew (see Ginsberg, *Studies in Daniel*, pp. 48, 41–61, and 81, n. 24, and AB vol. 41, p. 44).

I do not know why nothing is said here of the cessation or removal of the Continual Offering (*Tamid*). Cf. Dan 11:31 and I 1:45. Even our writer implies the fact at II 10:3. Perhaps the abridger omitted it, important though it was.

Vs. 4 speaks of the "forbidden things" brought into the temple by the gentiles. It is likely that the "forbidden things" are idolatrous objects, the three meteorites of the Abomination of Desolation (see AB vol. 41, pp. 142–56), as one would expect from Dan 11:31, "and shall put in the Abomination of Desolation." The Greek expression which I have translated "forbidden" is the same as the one at 4:19 which I translated "was not proper" (*mē kathēkein*). At 4:19 the expression is used of an idolatrous sacrifice, a fact suggesting that here, too, it is used of something idolatrous rather than of sacrificial offerings which were not kosher or were unclean (but note the use of *kathēkon* ["permitted"] in vs. 21). Indeed, the prohibited offerings are treated not in vs. 4 but in vs. 5, as is clear from the use of the Greek verb *diastellein* both in vs. 5 in the word "excluded" and at Lev 10:10 and 11:47, where in English it is rendered "distinguish." The word *athemitos* ("prohibited") is used at 7:1 of pork. Cf. I 1:47.

6. The prohibition of the observance of Sabbaths and festivals is easy to un-

derstand (cf. I 1:45), but what is the meaning of "no one was allowed to . . . confess he was a Jew"? There is no parallel in the contemporary apocalypses or in the accounts of First Maccabees and Josephus. Later the mere acknowledgment of the name "Christian" was to be a crime, but did Antiochus forbid Jews to call themselves Jews? Surely our studies have shown that in the imposed cult Antiochus was trying to force Jews to return to what he thought was the original "wholesome" Jewish pattern (see NOTE on vss. 1–7). The words may be hyperbole: Jews went on practicing Judaism in secret, but for a practicing Jew to admit he was Jewish was suicidal.

However, in speaking of "confessing that one is Jewish," Jason may be alluding to a ritual. Josephus (*AJ* iv 8.13.212) seems to call the recitation twice daily of the *Shema'* (Deut 6:4) or of some other such formula "bearing witness" (*martyrein*). See AB vol. 41, Introduction, Part VI, n. 171. Jason could have called the same ritual "confessing that one is Jewish."

7. Greeks did celebrate their birthdays monthly. See W. Schmidt, "*Genethlios hêmera*" PW, VII (1912), 1136. On the sacrifices and other observances in the Hellenistic monarchies on the monthly birthdays of the kings, see ibid., cols. 1138–39. To judge by I 1:58–59, the birthday of Antiochus IV was on the twenty-fifth.

The Greek verb *splanchnizein* and the related noun (vs. 21 and 7:42) *splanchnismos* refer to the eating of the *splanchna*, the parts of a sacrifice reserved to be eaten by the sacrificers at the beginning of their feast. Jews did not use the words in connection with their own peace offerings and were forbidden to eat the meat of pagan sacrifices (Exod 34:15). See also NOTE on vs. 21. Hence, I insert the word "pagan" in translating the verb and the noun.

Characteristic of festivals of Dionysus were processions of worshipers; see Jules Girard, "Dionysia," DAGR, II[1] (1892), 230–43, 246. Ivy leaves were much used in the worship of Dionysus. See III 2:29 and Grimm's note on our passage.

Dionysus in the imposed cult probably was the son of the LORD God of Israel and the Queen of Heaven. See AB vol. 41, pp. 152–56.

8–9. Antiochus IV had established an Antiochene republic, analogous to the Roman republic. The citizens of Ptolemais were now the Antiochenes of Ptolemais, citizens of the Antiochene republic. Represented in the legislative organ of the republic, they proposed a resolution to persecute the Jews living in all member states. The resolution was passed by vote and published in the member states, here called the "neighboring Greek cities." See AB vol. 41, pp. 111–21, 137–38. Ptolemais and the Akra were the only communities in or near Judaea known to have been members of the Antiochene republic; see AB vol. 41, Introduction, Part VI, n. 76, and pp. 123–24. Jason of Cyrene could call both "Greek cities."

It is doubtful, however, whether even Jason of Cyrene fully understood how Antiochus IV emulated Roman institutions. Jason does not use the technical vocabulary for proposing a resolution to voters, though it may have stood in his source. Instead he uses the vaguer verb *hypotithêmi*, which can be used of any proposal of a course of actions, to a private individual, to a king, or to voters (see Isocrates 1.12; Herodotus vii 237; Plato *Charmides* 155d, etc.). Still more puzzled were the scribes, who probably did not understand how a decree could be published in a Hellenistic absolute monarchy on the initiative of the citizens of Ptolemais. The Jews were not the business of the citizens of Ptolemais. Surely it was more natural for a courtier or a fellow king to advise a Seleucid king to issue a decree on the Jews! In Second Maccabees Antiochus IV has more than one courtier named Ptolemy (4:45–46, 8:8–9, 10:12–13), and King Ptolemy VI was reigning in Egypt. Hence, as might be expected, one finds in AVq the reading "on the proposal of Ptolemy." Surprisingly, however, the original version survives, difficult as it was for scribes to understand, in L'−542 (*Ptolemaiôn*). This contracted form for the genitive plural of *Ptolemaieus* ("citizen of Ptolemais"), instead of the uncontracted *Ptolemaieôn*, is quite normal for the atticizing tradition of L'; see Raphael Kühner, *Ausführliche Grammatik der griechischen Sprache*, Erster Teil: *Elementar und Formenlehre*, ed. by Friedrich Blass (3d ed.; Hannover: Hahn, 1890–1904), I, 447–48, and Hanhart, *Nachrichten der Akademie der Wissenschaften in Göttingen, Philologisch-historische Klasse* (1961), pp. 49–50, n. 6. Surprisingly, too, the original version was exactly reflected in La^V Arm Lucifer and is still recognizable in the contaminated version of La^LX (*suggerentibus Ptolomeis ptolemei artibus*) and has left its trace in the version of La^BDM. Ancient writers used both *Ptolema-* (as at 13:25) and *Ptolemai-* (as here) as the stem of the Greek word for "citizen of Ptolemais," and, if anything, the stem here is the better attested, at least for the genitive plural. See Preisigke, *Wörterbuch*, III, 324. Stephanus Byzantius s.v. *Ptolemais* gives the word only as *Ptolemaieus*, and the form with the iota is found in all manuscripts of *Aristeas to Philocrates* 117 and in good manuscripts of Josephus, especially P (see J. *BJ* i 13.1.249, *AJ* xiii 12.2.329, 3.332, and 13.1.350).

Can we be so positive that AVq reflect scribal alterations, not the original text? Hanhart (*Nachrichten* [1961], 49–50) was inclined to accept the reading with "Ptolemy," arguing scribes could think that a decree on the affairs of cities might be suggested to the king by citizens of one of them. Even if Hanhart's argument were acceptable, the reading of AVq must be rejected. The Greek word used here for decree is *psêphisma*, which normally means a resolution passed by vote; elsewhere in Second Maccabees *psêphisma* is used only with that meaning (10:8, 12:4, 15:36). The root meaning of the word is "to manipulate or count pebbles [*psêphoi*]," so that it is not surprising to find it used to render the "lot" (*pūr*) cast by Haman at Esther 3:7 and 9:24. The word can be used of decrees of groups of gods (presumably, those imagined to have been passed by vote); see Empedocles Fragment 115 (*apud* Plutarch *De exilio* 607c) and Aristophanes *Wasps* 378. At J. *AJ* xvii 2.4.43 a passive participle (*epsêphismenês*) of the related verb is used to say that the fall of Herod's dynasty has been decreed by the single God of the Pharisees; at *AJ* xiii 9.2.262 the passive participle *psêphisthenta* may be used to refer to decrees of Antiochus VII, but the variants in the witnesses to the text (FLV: *psêlaphêthenta*; Latin: *gesta*) suggest that the text is corrupt. At J. *AJ* xviii 3.4.69 *psêphisma* is used of the resolution of a single private person. However, wherever *psêphisma* is used in a metaphorical sense, the persons whose decision is so designated are specified. Here the *psêphisma* is not said to be of the king or of Geron the Athenian. The context mentions only the Greek cities and the citizens of Ptolemais, as one would expect if all were participating in a voting body. It is most unlikely that the scribes knew anything at all concerning the Antiochene republic, when even the king's contemporaries and the expert historian Polybius (xxvi 1, 1a) could not perceive the method in his "mad" passion for things Roman.

Privileges of the citizens of Ptolemais as Antiochenes are also reflected at 13:25–26.

The vote of the Antiochenes copied the king's decree, that the Jews observe the imposed cult on pain of death; cf. I 1:44–50. The fact of such an enactment by the Antiochene republic probably does not imply that Antiochus had otherwise denied himself the power to give such orders to Antiochene communities. Rather, Antiochus IV had aimed his decree at the rebellious Jews of Judaea and Jerusalem (I 1:44) but had circulated copies to all his kingdom (I 1:51) as indicating royal policy to be implemented against subversive Jews; see AB vol. 41, NOTE on 1:51. Ptolemais and the other communities of the Antiochene republic thereupon judged that their Jews were subversive. The hostility at Ptolemais toward Jews is attested at I 5:15.

The end of vs. 9 does not fit into the framework of the imposed cult: the imposed cult was not Greek. Did the cities of the Antiochene republic go beyond the king and impose Greek ways on their Jewish inhabitants? Hardly. We learn in vs. 8 that they voted to proceed against the Jews in the *same* manner as the king. Hence the words are probably a mistaken inference of Jason's from the document at 11:24 (see NOTE on 11:24–25) and J. *AJ* xii 5.5.263 (see Appendix VIII, NOTE).

9. *It was clear that a time of trouble had come.* Cf. I 1:64 and Test Moses 5:1. Jewish apocalyptic seers in 167 certainly believed the final Age of Wrath had come. Jason of Cyrene knew that it was not final and expresses himself more guardedly. Literally, the Greek says "One could see the trouble which had arisen."

10–31. Both here and in First Maccabees martyrs are classified according to the principles for which they give up their lives: circumcision (vs. 10 and I 1:60–61), the Sabbath (vs. 11 and I 2:29–38), and the dietary laws, including the prohibition on eating the meat of a pagan sacrifice (vss. 18–31 and 7:1–41; I 1:62–63). Not only the classifications but the incidents themselves, of the martyrs for circumcision and for the Sabbath, are obviously identical, surely because both authors drew upon the Common Source; see also NOTE on vs. 11. We may conclude that also the general statement at I 1:62–64 is an abridgment of stories in the Common Source which contained something like what we have here at 6:18 – 7:41; see pp. 285, 300, 316.

In view of the elaborate treatment in 6:18 – 7:41, it may seem strange that the martyrs for circumcision and the Sabbath are passed over so briefly in vss. 10–11. Indeed, more words are devoted to those martyrs in First Maccabees! Does the brevity here reflect only the activity of the abridger? To judge by 6:18 – 7:41, the abridger was reluctant to cut anything from a story of martyrdom. Thus, the brevity of vss. 10–11 may well go back to the unabridged work. Perhaps Jason, finding that his opponent had already stated the facts in First Maccabees, was content to be brief. Characteristically, however, he included details omitted in First Maccabees.

Why did the writer place his statement of theological principles (vss. 12–17) only after vss. 10–11? Vs. 12 suggests a simple answer: the purpose of the theological principles is to comfort the reader of so dismaying an account. After vss. 10–11 the reader has been sufficiently dismayed. There may be a reason for the position of vss. 12–17 before 6:18 – 7:42. The writer may have taken care to append his statement of principles to stories of martyrdom which had been accepted and preserved by both sides among the bitterly divided pious Jews. Having given the theory of God's merciful purpose in the persecution, he can go in II 6:18 – 7:42 to present at great length stories of martyrdom which teach lessons opposed to the Hasmonaeans and to their religious position.

10. See I 1:60–61 and NOTE thereto. Only here is the number of women specified as two. At I 1:61 the babies are hanged from their mothers' necks. Indeed, it is hard to see how they could have been hanged from the breasts. Here and at IV 4:25 the women are reported to have been hurled from the wall; the detail was probably preserved in the Common Source. Since the women were paraded through the *city* and hurled from the *city* walls, we learn from the account here that the executions occurred at Jerusalem.

Hurling from a height may have been a preferred method for executing women. In the third century B.C.E. the Seleucid queen Laodice so executed one of her ladies, Danaë (Phylarchos FGH 81, F 24=Athenaeus xiii 593).

On the parallels between the treatment of Jews who circumcised and the treatment of "effeminate" Epicurean philosophers, see AB vol. 41, Introduction, Part VI, nn. 143 and 153. The Cretan city of Lyktos is reported to have condemned Epicureanism as effeminate and to have provided by law that Epicureans who entered the city should be punished by being pushed off a precipice while dressed in women's clothing (Aelianus Fragment 39, p. 202 Hercher).

11. Jason, as one might expect, gives no hint that the Sabbath observers deliberately courted death because they interpreted prophecies to mean that by letting themselves be slaughtered they would provoke divine intervention. Cf. I 2:29–40, and see NOTES to I 2:28–40. In I 2:29–40 the incident is placed not at the outset of the persecution but after Mattathias' rebellious deed of zeal. The massacre of the Sabbath observers leads him and his comrades to proclaim that defensive warfare on the Sabbath is permitted. The Common Source probably presented the events much as we have them in I 2:24–41, with the mass martyrdom of the Sabbath observers coming after Mattathias' climactic act of zeal. Jason of Cyrene found it necessary to make omissions and to change the order of narration. He viewed Mattathias as wicked (see AB vol. 41, p. 79). For Jason, the climactic turning point came not with Mattathias' act of zeal but with the martyrdoms that were its counterpart, those of Eleazar and of the mother and her seven sons; see NOTE on vss. 18–31 and introductory NOTE on ch. 7. If Jason had told of the death of the Sabbath observers last, as at I 1:60 – 2:38 and as (probably) in the Common Source, he would have spoiled the literary effect of his intended climax. Even moving the story of the Sabbath observers to where it stands here was not sufficient, for at I 2:38, and probably in the Common Source, the number of those martyrs is given as one thousand, a figure which could eclipse the solitary martyrdom of Eleazar and the mere

eight of the mother and her sons. Hence, Jason does not specify the number of the martyred Sabbath observers.

Though at I 2:31–32 the troops who killed the Sabbath observers are said to have come from the Akra, Jason could not mention the Akra at this point; see NOTE on 5:24–27. He can, however, mention Philip, commander of the garrison in the Akra (5:22, 8:8), and thus he implies that the caves were in Judaea and probably not far from Jerusalem. Josephus (AJ xii 6.2.274–75) probably drew from here the information, absent from First Maccabees, that the Sabbath observers went to caves and died by fire.

Here, unlike I 2:34, there is no suggestion that the Sabbath observers perished also because they followed their interpretation of Exod 16:29 and refused to go out of the caves.

Here and at 12:38 and 15:4 Jason uses the Greek word *hebdomas* (which usually means "week") for "Sabbath"; cf. Lev 25:8 (where *šabbāt* means "sabbatical year"). Josephus frequently uses *hebdomas* for "Sabbath" (AJ xiii 8.1.234, xiv 4.2.63, etc.).

12 – 7:42. The comment referred to in AB vol. 41, p. 56, n. 10, and p. 57, n. 12, and p. 226 is in the NOTE on 6:18–31 and the NOTE on ch. 7 (the discussion of Josephus' treatment of the stories of martyrdom).

12–17. The abridger and very likely Jason of Cyrene, too, faced here, as they had to, the agonizing problem of the monotheist who sees the persecution of the righteous yet believes that God is just. Though author and abridger believed passionately in the inspiration of Daniel and perhaps in that of other apocalyptic seers (see AB vol. 41, Introduction, Part II), it was now clear that the persecution had not been the very last phase of the punishment for the sins committed in the kingdom of Judah half a millennium before. The obscure words of Dan 9:24 had to receive some other interpretation. In our writer's view, the persecution came as punishment for the heinous sins of the Hellenizers (4:16–17). With Israel, God is mercifully drastic: He promptly teaches Jews to cease from sinning, whereas temporary clemency would have allowed such dreadful sins to earn even more drastic punishment. Unlike the righteous Jews, the wicked and the gentiles come to suffer terrible punishment. The author may well have written with Ps 94:12–14 in mind. Cf. also Gen 15:13–16; Job 33:14–30, 36:8–15; Wisdom 12:22. The Amorite inhabitants of the Promised Land had been destroyed when their sins reached full measure. Jason provides his reader with the example of the dreadful end of Antiochus IV (7:16–17, 9:4–28), but the king was not a nation. As a Jewish Greek, the writer probably wishes his reader to compare the lot of the Jews, free and prosperous since the end of the persecutions, with that of Greece, Macedonia, and western Asia Minor. The Greeks there had been conquered by Rome in ruinous wars and were now the helpless victims of Roman exploitation (cf. I 8:9–11). God's contrasting procedures with Jews and gentiles are stated as present facts of history. Hence, it is unlikely that our writer had a Last Judgment in mind here.

In vss. 12–17 the writer explains how God in His mercy could allow righteous Jews to be persecuted at all. In ch. 7 we shall learn that, in addition, their suffering earns the mercy of God for the survivors, so that, led by Judas Maccabaeus, the survivors will defeat their wicked persecutors.

VIII. THE MARTYRDOM OF ELEAZAR
(6:18–31)

6 18 One of the leading sages was Eleazar, a very handsome man,
now of advanced age. Repeatedly they tried to force him to open his
mouth and eat pork. 19-20 He, however, preferred death with glory to
life with defilement. He spat, as one should when standing fast to
resist the temptation to let love of life bring him to taste what religion
forbids, and of his own free will he began to march to the whipping
drum. 21 The meat was part of a sacrifice, and to eat it was a violation of the Torah. The men appointed to compel him to do so had
known Eleazar for many years. They took him aside and in secret
urged him to fetch meat which he was permitted to eat, prepared by
himself, and pretend that he was eating the meat from the sacrifice as
ordered by the king, 22 for in so doing he would escape death and
would receive from them the kindness due an old friend. 23 Eleazar
came to a lofty resolution, one worthy of his years, worthy of the authority of old age, worthy of his conspicuous well-earned white hair,
and of his way of life, which had been exemplary from childhood.
More important, it was worthy of the sacred legislation established by
God. Eleazar showed himself consistent: he told them to send him off
to the netherworld without delay. 24-25 "Such pretense is unworthy
of my advanced age. My pretense for the sake of a brief transitory
span of life would cause many of the younger generation to think
that Eleazar at the age of ninety had gone over to the gentile way
of life, and so they, too, would go astray because of me, and I
would earn the defilement and besmirching of my old age. 26 Indeed,
even if I should be released for the present from punishment at the
hands of men, alive or dead I would not escape the hands of the Almighty. 27 Therefore, if I now bravely give up my life, I shall show
myself worthy of my old age, 28 as I leave to the young a noble example of how to go eagerly and nobly to die a beautiful death in the defense of our revered and sacred laws." Having spoken those words, he
went straight to the torture instrument.

29 What he had just said turned the men who shortly before had

shown him friendship into enemies, because they viewed it as perversity. 30 As he was about to expire under the lashing, he groaned forth, "The LORD, Who possesses sacred knowledge, perceives that, though able to escape death, in my body I submit to cruel torment under the lash, and that yet in my soul I am glad to suffer it, out of reverence for Him." 31 So he died, leaving his death as an example of nobility and as a precedent of valor to be remembered not only by the young but by the multitudes of his nation.

NOTES

6:18–31. The writer has indicated no change of scene. As "one of the leading sages" (vs. 18), Eleazar surely resided in Judaea, probably in Jerusalem. His tormentors, who had long known him (vss. 21–22), may well have been Jewish collaborationists, perhaps Antiochenes from Jerusalem. Hence, surely the writer believed that Jerusalem was the scene of Eleazar's martyrdom.

Earlier kings and governments with strong religious convictions had used force and capital punishment to impose their will on those who believed otherwise; see pp. 96–97. From almost all those persecutions, however, the literary remains describing the resistance and sufferings of the faithful are matter-of-fact statements like vss. 10 and 11. In particular, no literature survives from the reign of King Manasseh of Judah. Only from Nabonidus' persecution of the worshipers of Marduk do more elaborate texts and traces of texts survive, and it is possible that the patterns of the literature of the "Mardukist Martyrs" had something to do with the patterns we find here, as I hope to show in my book *When Chosen Peoples Fall to Foreign Domination*.

Our section and ch. 7 constitute the earliest surviving examples of elaborate stories of monotheists suffering martyrdom and are the direct source for the patterns that thereafter prevailed in Jewish and Christian literature: the cheerful acceptance by the martyr of terrible pain rather than commit an act viewed by pagans as trivial; the dialogue between the martyr and his persecutors and tormentors; the vivid description of the torments; the martyr's persistent faith to the death; the care to record both the anger and the admiration of the pagans as the tortures prove to be in vain; the presentation of the martyr as an example to be followed by the rest of the faithful. Heb 11:35–36 surely alludes to II 6:18 – 7:42. Absent from our section but present in ch. 7 and thereafter in Jewish (see IV 6:28–29) and especially in Christian tradition is the idea of the redemptive power of martyrdom: the martyr by his suffering wins the mercy of God for the survivors of his nation and for his own soul. An early elaboration of the patterns and ideas of II 6:18 – 7:42 survives in the Fourth Book of Maccabees. The author of Fourth Maccabees certainly had read II 6:18 – 7:42. The divergences in his narrative stem either from his own different rhetorical and philosophical purposes or from the fact that he wrote from memory. See NOTE on ch. 3 and NOTE on vss. 19–28. On Fourth Maccabees see Moses Hadas, *The Third and Fourth Books of Maccabees* (New York: Harper, 1953), pp. 91–243. On the influence of the patterns of II 6:18 – 7:42 on the later Jewish and Christian literature of martyrdom, see Hans-Werner Surkau, *Martyrien in jüdischer und frühchristlicher Zeit* (Göttingen: Vandenhoeck & Rupprecht, 1938); Grimm, pp. 133–34; W. H. C. Frend, *Martyrdom and Persecution in the Early Church* (Garden City, N.Y.: Doubleday, 1967), pp. 18–20, 34–37, 347, 414, 427–28; Ulrich Kellermann, *Auferstanden in den Himmel* (Stuttgarter Bibelstudien, 95; Stuttgart: Verlag Katholisches Bibelwerk, 1979), pp. 35–38; Gerson D. Cohen, "The Story of Hannah and Her Seven Sons in Hebrew Literature," in the *Mordecai M. Kaplan Jubilee Volume* (New York: Jewish Theological Seminary of America, 1953), Hebrew section, pp. 109–22.

Here and in ch. 7 the martyrs die rather than eat forbidden food. Thus they could all be classified together, and are treated together in Fourth Maccabees. They are all probably included in the summary reference at I 1:62–63. The abridger (and perhaps Jason of Cyrene, too) also treated the two stories as a unit; see 7:42. On the other hand, there are many signs that the stories were originally separate. Though we read in vs. 31 that Eleazar died as a heroic example to the young, indeed to his entire people, the young martyrs in ch. 7 never refer to him. Furthermore, the stories display contrasting religious beliefs. The story of the mother and sons is full of hints of the fulfillment of prophecy, whereas there are none in the story of Eleazar. In ch. 7 Antiochus IV is present and acts in response to the martyrs' defiance. Here he is absent. Conspicuous in ch. 7 are the belief in resurrection and the confidence in the redemptive power of martyrdom. There is no avowal of these beliefs here in vss. 18–31 (cf. IV 6:28–29, but see NOTE on vs. 30, *Who . . . knowledge*). We may thus infer that Jason of Cyrene has not changed the ideological content of the stories of Eleazar and the mother and her seven sons but rather has left them as he found them in his sources. Eleazar does not even give voice to the belief in the educative function of suffering taught in vss. 12–17. Rather, he is a pietist who will not violate the Torah and, unlike the Hasmonaeans, does not rebel against the king. Courageously he faces death and gives only the merest hints of the belief in resurrection or immortality (see NOTES on vss. 26 and 30). Jason is content to present him solely as an example of steadfastness.

Antiochus' decrees required the Jews both to sacrifice pigs to the deities of the imposed cult and to eat the meat of the sacrifices (I 1:47–48; see AB vol. 41, NOTES ad loc., and cf. IV 5:2). To pious Jews, sacrifices even to the LORD as represented in the imposed cult were idolatrous. Violation of the laws against idolatry for a Jew were far more serious than mere eating of pork. Yet both here (vs. 21) and in ch. 7 (vs. 42) the factor of idolatry is introduced awkwardly as an afterthought. Perhaps as originally told, the stories reflected the view that Jews must give up their lives rather than obey a royal order to violate any commandment in the Torah. On the other hand, the writer responsible for the present version may have held that the dietary laws might be violated under duress and that one need not give up one's life unless the royal order requires so grave a sin as idolatry.

Such a difference of opinion is attested later among Jews. The rabbis of the time of the Hadrianic persecution (ca. 132–38 C.E.) appear to have required martyrdom only when a Jew was commanded to violate the laws against murder, incest and adultery, or idolatry (TP *Sanhedrin* 3:5, p. 21b; TB *Sanhedrin* 74a), but later Rabbi Yoḥanan interpreted their decision as requiring a Jew to give up life rather than obey a royal order to violate any commandment (ibid., 74a[end]). If the original stress of the stories of Eleazar and of the mother and her seven sons has been changed from refusal to eat pork to refusal to eat the meat of an idolatrous sacrifice, who is responsible, Jason or the abridger? The change is small enough to allow us to ascribe it to either.

Thus far we could think it possible that the story of Eleazar could have been incorporated as is into First Maccabees! However, the pietist tradition drawn on here by Jason appears to have glorified Eleazar as hero in contrast to Mattathias, who was viewed as a teacher of wickedness.

Eleazar and Mattathias can be shown to be counterparts, with just the parallels and contrasts one would expect in the heroes of the Hasmonaean and anti-Hasmonaean parties of pious Jews (cf. Nickelsburg, *Resurrection*, p. 98). In this period, as in the time of the Talmudic sages, Jews, even those who were priests, did not presume to bear the illustrious names "Moses" and "Aaron." And the name of Aaron's son Eleazar appears to have been borne mostly by priests; see Menahem Stern, "The Relations between Judaea and Rome during the Rule of John Hyrcanus," *Zion* 26 (1961), 21, n. 119 (in Hebrew). Thus, Jason and his source (and their audiences) would know immediately that Eleazar was a priest. At IV 5:4 the author takes the trouble to say so.

Thus Jason's tradition and the author of First Maccabees each present the heroic act of an aged priest (at vss. 18–31 and I 2:1–28) between the details of the persecution and a pivotal last instance of group martyrdom. Each hero believes that the persecution renders life of no value (vs. 19 and I 2:13). Eleazar is helpless in the hands of the royal officials and perhaps still faithful to the principle that Jews do not rebel (see NOTE on 1:7, *Jason . . . Kingdom*); he refuses to violate the Torah by eating from a pagan sacrifice and marches straight to the torture instrument "as one should" and is killed. Mattathias in the presence of the royal officials, believing that the principle of obedience to the king no longer applies, rises in zeal and anger "as was fitting"; he refuses to tolerate violation of the Torah and slays a Jew about to offer a pagan sacrifice and also kills one of the king's men.

Each author takes care to describe the inducements for compliance offered to the hero and quotes the hero's obstinate reply. At the end of the parallel scenes, Eleazar dies as an example to be followed, and Mattathias calls all who are zealous for the Torah to follow after him.

Jason has no reservations concerning the righteousness of Judas' rebellion, so he probably no longer held to the pietist condemnation of Mattathias as a rebel against the legitimate king, but Mattathias, in contrast to Judas (8:26, 12:38–45), was still a wicked violator of the Sabbath and likely also a denier of the resurrection; see AB vol. 41, pp. 64–65, 79, 85.

The pivotal acts of martyrdom which in each book follow upon the act of the hero are also in fitting contrast: the fruitless death of the Sabbath observers impels the Hasmonaean party to establish the audacious principle that defensive warfare on the Sabbath is permitted, which proves to be an important ingredient for their ultimate victory. The deaths of the woman and her sons purchase God's mercy, through which Judas Maccabaeus wins his glorious victories.

It is unlikely that the story of Eleazar was written first and that the story of Mattathias was composed as a counterpart to it. Mattathias' deed was audacious and set a new precedent. Eleazar's martyrdom was brave but was based on old principles and during the persecution was not unique. Rather, those who disapproved of Mattathias presented Eleazar instead as the example to be followed in time of persecution: not Mattathias' zeal but the blood of the martyrs purchased God's mercy and brought victory for the Jews.

It is probable that the story of Eleazar as counterpart to Mattathias arose in Mattathias' lifetime or shortly after his death. Otherwise, a pious writer presenting a counterpart to Mattathias would have had to bring in heroic sons as well, yet Jason of Cyrene pointedly refrains from connecting the woman and her seven sons with Eleazar.

We shall try to show in the introductory NOTE on ch. 8 that the Common Source told of Mattathias' acts and gave him at least partial approval. If so, the story of Eleazar can hardly have stood in the Common Source.

Jason of Cyrene appears to have been a well-educated Greek. No educated Greek could miss the resemblance of Eleazar to Socrates. Though the wording of the story here bears no resemblance to Plato's, Jason may have written so as to accentuate the resemblance (except for the contrast between Eleazar's beauty and Socrates' ugliness). Both heroes were elderly and regarded their few remaining years as something easy to part with (vss. 18, 23–25, 27; Plato *Apology* 38c). Fear of death could not make either yield (vss. 22–29; Plato *Apology* 28b–d). The refusal to yield was in keeping with the earlier life of each, and yielding would have ill beseemed it (vs. 24; *Apology* 28d–30c, 34b–35b). Both reject "easier" alternatives (vss. 21–28; *Apology* 36b–38b, *Crito*). Both hold that it is better to go to the underworld maintaining obedience to the laws (vs. 23; *Crito* 54b–d). Both hold that though one may escape human punishment, one cannot escape divine punishment for wickedness (vs. 26; *Apology* 39a–b), and both trust in supernatural judges (vss. 26, 30; *Apology* 41a). Those who controlled their fates were offended by the speeches of each and condemned them to death (vs. 29; *Apology* 38c). Both die as superlative examples to posterity (vs. 31; *Phaedo* 118[end]). See also Hadas, *The Third and Fourth Books of Maccabees*, pp. 101, 116–17.

Both Jews and Greeks took pains to record the last words of a martyr (vs. 30; 7:6, 9, 11, 14, 16–19, 30–38; II Chron 24:22; Plato *Phaedo* 118).

Josephus probably alluded to the story of Eleazar in his brief reference to the martyrs at *AJ* xii 5.4.255–56, for his wording seems to echo our passage: *hypomenontes* (section 255) would echo *hypomenontas* ("standing fast") in vs. 20; *timōrias* (section 255) would echo *timōrian* ("punishment") in vs. 26; and *mastigoumenoi* (section 256) would echo *mastigoumenos* ("under the lashing") in vs. 30. Josephus does not paraphrase Mattathias' farewell address as given at I 2:49–68; rather, he presents an entirely different speech. Josephus may well have been drawing on vss. 30–31 when he has Mattathias say (*AJ* xii 6.3.281), ". . . Die for His laws, if need be, in the belief that when the deity sees you acting thus, He will not neglect you but will admire your valor." See also introductory NOTE on ch. 7.

18. At AB vol. 41, p. 359, I refer the reader to a NOTE here, but the discussion is now in the NOTE on vss. 18–31 (p. 284).

sages. The Greek has *grammateôn* ("scribes"); the use of this word for experts in the Torah is well known from Jewish literature and the New Testament.

very handsome . . . advanced age. Beauty and long life were gifts from God. The Jewish and Christian literature of martyrdom dwells on the martyrs' possession of such marks of divine favor (e.g., IV 6:2, 8:3–5, 9).

open his mouth and. This, the correct reading (*anachanôn*), was preserved by La^LXVP Arm and is still recognizable in A (*anachenôn*), but the rare word puzzled the scribes underlying VLa^BM Sy, who omitted it, and the scribes underlying L′ read *tynchanôn* ("who happened to be," "who was"), attaching the word to what precedes (". . . Eleazar, who was a very handsome man . . .").

eat pork. Forbidden by Lev 11:7 and Deut 14:8 (cf. Isa 65:4, 66:3, 17). See p. 109 and AB vol. 41, pp. 157–58.

19–28. Our verses are to be read as a straightforward narrative: Eleazar "began to march" (imperfect tense) to the torture instrument (vs. 19), was pulled aside by his old friends, but indignantly rejected their arguments, and "went again" (aorist) to the torture instrument. But for the sequence of tenses one might have taken vss. 21–27 as a flashback: "Before Eleazar marched to the torture instrument, his friends had taken him aside, but he indignantly rejected their arguments." The author of IV 5:1 – 6:30 had different rhetorical purposes and very likely wrote from a faulty memory of our passage: Eleazar does not march twice to the torture but is dragged, and the offer to let him escape through pretense comes while he is being beaten.

19–20. Vs. 20 is an incomplete sentence and grammatically belongs to vs. 19. In the Greek, "He spat" is a participial phrase (*proptysas de*) which follows "and of . . . to the whipping drum." The particle *de* probably indicates that *proptysas* is to be taken as parallel to the participial phrase at the beginning of vs. 19, which I have rendered "He . . . defilement." Both participles then refer to actions before the march to the whipping drum (see Kühner-Gerth, *Grammatik,* II, 274), and I have translated accordingly.

"He spat" in the Greek has no direct object, but the fact that Eleazar was resisting forcible feeding and the prefix *pro-* of *proptysas* both suggest that it would be better to translate "He spat it out."

19. *whipping drum.* Gr. *tympanon* can mean "stick" or "cudgel" as well as "drum." Here it appears to be a fixed object toward which one marches, a drum-shaped block on which Eleazar was tied and perhaps stretched; see K. Schneider, "Tympanum," PW, VIIA¹ (Erste Hälfte; 1943), 1753.

21. I have turned into complete sentences what the Greek expresses by adjectives and nouns. The word *splanchnismos* occurs in the first half of our verse. Its meaning, "eating of the meat of an idolatrous sacrifice," is a matter of inference (see NOTE on vs. 7). The end of our verse explicitly mentions meat from a sacrifice, removing any possible ambiguity.

23. I have translated the Gr. *asteion* as "lofty." The basic meaning of the

word is "urbane," "polished," or "refined," but it can also mean "noble" or "aristocratic," as at Philo *De vita contemplativa* 72.

The author probably was pleased by the heaping up of synonyms for old age which now looks awkward. Perhaps still more awkward in the Greek is the long parade of nouns in the genitive. In my translation I have taken them all as depending on *axion* ("worthy of"). One might reduce the awkwardness by making some or all of the nouns after "years" depend on the adverb *akolouthôs* ("consistent[ly]," "in keeping with"), but elsewhere the adverb is used only with the dative, not with the genitive.

As in vs. 18, Eleazar's long life is taken as a mark of divine favor and as a reward for his probity. I follow Grimm in rendering *tês tou gerôs hyperochês* as "the authority of old age" (cf. 15:13), rather than "his exceedingly old age" (cf. 13:6), which might seem repetitious after "his years" (*tês hêlikias*). Nevertheless, the passage is already so repetitious that the more redundant translation might be the more accurate.

The word "[well-]earned" (*epiktêtou*) is omitted in VLa‑BM, but it makes explicit here the idea of reward, and its presence turns the use of "earn" (*kataktêsomai*) in vs. 25 into an artistic piece of wordplay.

24–25. Rabbinic teaching later was to require martyrdom if one's own violation of the Law under duress, by being in public, would bring others to sin (TP *Sanhedrin* 3:5, p. 21b; TB *Sanhedrin* 74a). See also NOTE on vs. 23.

had gone . . . life. See NOTE on vss. 8–9, and cf. 4:10.

26. Eleazar expresses a belief that the soul survives and receives retribution after death, but he says nothing here of resurrection.

28. Eleazar's heroism is all the greater if he again marches voluntarily to the torture instrument (see NOTE on vss. 19–28). Hence, the reading of V 55 La Sy might be difficult to explain, for instead of "he went" (*êlthen*) it has "he was dragged" (*heilketo*). However, there is a clue in the fact Sy here for once differs from *L'*. Fourth Maccabees was translated early into Syriac, and at IV 6:1 Eleazar is indeed dragged to the torture instruments. The reading "he was dragged" is thus probably derived from IV 6:1. Since Fourth Maccabees was written between 20 and 54 C.E. (Bickerman, *Studies,* I, 275–81), the original Latin translation must have been written later.

30. *Who possesses sacred knowledge.* The author of First Maccabees loves to express himself through allusive imitations of biblical verses, especially where he wishes to hint to his reader that Hasmonaeans may have fulfilled a biblical prophecy. The abridged history, too, can hint that prophecies have been fulfilled. This fact makes the words here tantalizing, for in the Hebrew Bible and its Greek versions God is called a God of knowledge only at I Sam 2:3, in a context which could be taken as predicting the martyrdoms of the mother and her seven sons (vs. 5), the resurrection of the dead (vs. 6), and the defeat and destruction of the persecutors and the coming glory of God's anointed king (vs. 10). The extant Jewish literature written between the time of Nehemiah and the first century B.C.E. contains mentions of the "Son of Man" but never refers to the concept of a messianic king. See AB vol. 41, NOTE on 2:57, *for ages.* The hint here would break that absolute silence. Mattathias, on the point of death, uttered prophetic hints of Hasmonaean glory (I 2:49–68). Would it

not be appropriate for Eleazar, the anti-Hasmonaean counterpart of Mattathias, to utter on the point of death eschatological hints?

If there is allusive writing here, it originated with Jason of Cyrene, not with the abridger. Surely the abridger would have retained such sensational prophecies, if Jason had made them explicit, just as the abridger retains the speeches of the seven brothers in ch. 7. The words here become even more tantalizing because knowledge (*gnôsis*) is a concept with far-reaching connotations in the religions of the Hellenistic and Roman periods.

It is probably wrong, however, to see an allusion with far-reaching theological implications in our passage. The writer has spelled out none of the implications which an allusion to I Sam 2 might have carried. The author of Fourth Maccabees also noticed no such implications.

Any power of God could be called sacred (His arm: Isa 52:10; Ps 98:1; His word: Ps 105:42; His spirit: Isa 63:10–11), and the Hebrew Bible speaks repeatedly of God's knowledge of man's thoughts (Jer 11:20, 17:10; Pss 44:22, 94:11, etc.).

As George Nickelsburg informs me, Jews in the Hellenistic period frequently wrote of God's knowledge in contexts contemplating or praying for the vindication of the righteous or the punishment of the wicked. See Enoch 9:5–11, 84:3–6; Psalms of Solomon 14:5; 1QS 3:13 (which uses the language of I Sam 2:3!), and the texts collected at Nickelsburg, "Apocalyptic and Myth in I Enoch 6–11," JBL 96 (1977), 387, n. 16.

Eleazar's words therefore probably convey no more than his belief that God knows Eleazar is righteous and will punish his tormentors. The Greek text allows one other possibility. Though I have used the verb "know" in vs. 21, the Greek is expressed by means of the noun "knowledge" (*gnôsis*). Jason may have chosen his words to contrast the tormentors with God: the tormentors have profane superficial knowledge of Eleazar and regard his course as perverse; God's knowledge of the martyr is sacred, and God will regard Eleazar's course as glorious.

though . . . suffer it. Cf. Enoch 102:4–5.

31. *valor.* Jason, as a Jewish Greek, employs here *aretê*, the word widely used in Greek for "virtue," of which "valor" is one type. The Greek translators of the Hebrew Bible never use *aretê* in the moral sense.

multitudes. So I translate the Gr. *pleistois* (lit. "most"). The superlative does not imply that there was a minority for whom Eleazar's conduct was not exemplary and memorable, but rather that the Jewish multitude was very large. But cf. Esther 10:3.

IX. THE MARTYRDOM OF THE MOTHER AND HER SEVEN SONS
(7:1–42)

7 ¹ At that time seven brothers, too, with their mother were arrested, and the king tortured them with whips and thongs in an effort to force them to partake of pork contrary to the prohibitions of the Torah. ² One of them as spokesman for all said, "What do you expect to learn from questioning us? We are ready to die rather than violate the laws of our forefathers." ³ The king, enraged, ordered griddles and cauldrons to be heated red-hot. ⁴ As soon as they were red-hot, the king gave the order to cut out the tongue of the one who had acted as spokesman and scalp him and cut off his hands and feet while his brothers and his mother look on. ⁵ The body was now completely helpless, but the king ordered that he be brought, still breathing, to the fire and fried. As the odor of frying began to spread widely, the brothers and their mother exhorted one another to die nobly, saying, ⁶ "The LORD God looks on and truly is relenting concerning us, as Moses declared in the Song Which Confronts as a Witness: 'And He will relent concerning His servants.'"

⁷ When the first of the brothers had passed away in this manner, they brought the second to be wantonly tortured, and after ripping off his scalp by the hair, they asked him, "Will you eat before your body is torn limb from limb?" ⁸ He answered in the language of his forefathers, "No!" And so, he, too, in turn was tortured. ⁹ With his last breath he said, "You, you fiend, are making us depart from our present life, but the King of the universe will resurrect us, who die for the sake of His laws, to a new eternal life."

¹⁰ After him, the third was subjected to wanton torture. On demand, he promptly put forth his tongue and cheerfully held out his hands. ¹¹ His words were noble: "I received these from Heaven, and for the sake of His laws I hold them cheap. From Him I hope to receive them back." ¹² The king himself and his men were astonished at the spirit of the young man who set torments at naught.

¹³ When he, too, had passed away, they tormented the fourth with

similar tortures. 14 At the point of death, he said, "Better it is to pass away from among men while looking forward in hope to the fulfillment of God's promises that we will be resurrected by Him, for you shall have no resurrection unto life."

15 Forthwith they brought the fifth and began to torture him. 16 Gazing at the king, he said, "You wield power among men and work your will, but you are mortal. Think not that God has abandoned our people. 17 You wait and see His great might when He puts you and your seed to the torture!"

18 Thereafter they brought the sixth, and as he was about to die, he said, "Do not indulge in vain delusions! Through our own fault we are subjected to these sufferings, because we have sinned against our God. They pass belief! 19 You, however, think not to escape unpunished after having dared to contend with God!"

20 Most remarkable was the mother. She deserves to be held in glorious memory, for she looked on as her seven sons perished in the course of a single day and bore it bravely because of her hopes in the LORD. 21 Each one of them in turn she exhorted in the language of their forefathers. Filled with noble resolution, she took her womanly thoughts and fired them with a manly spirit, as she told them, 22 "I do not know how you came to be in my womb. It was not I who gave you spirit and life, nor did I determine the order of the composition of the elements of each of you. 23 Surely, then, the Creator of the universe, Who shaped man's coming into being and fathomed the fashioning of everything,[a] with mercy will restore spirit and life to you, inasmuch as you now hold your very selves cheap for the sake of His laws."

24 Antiochus sensed he was being treated with contempt. The reproachful voice roused his hostility. Nevertheless, there was still the youngest, and Antiochus not only addressed appeals to him again and again; he even made repeated promises on oath to make him rich and prosperous and admit him to the Order of the King's Friends and entrust important functions to him, provided he would depart from the ways of his forefathers.

25 When the youth paid him no heed, the king called upon the mother and urged her to give the lad the advice that would save his life. 26 In response to his insistent urgings, she consented to convince her son. 27 She bent over him, and with scorn for the cruel tyrant, she said in the language of her forefathers, "My son, have pity on me who carried you in my womb for nine months and nursed you for

---

a See commentary.

three years and reared you and brought you to your present age. 28 I ask you, my child, to look upon the heaven and the earth and to contemplate all therein. I ask you to understand that it was not after they existed that God fashioned them, and in the same manner the human race comes to be. 29 Do not fear this executioner, but be worthy of your brothers and accept death, so that in His mercy I may recover you along with your brothers."

30 She was still speaking the last of these words when the youth said, "What are you waiting for? I refuse to obey the king's command; I heed the command of the Torah given through Moses to our forefathers. 31 You, who have devised all evil against the Hebrews, shall surely not escape the hands of God. 32 As for us, we are suffering for our own sins. 33 If our living LORD has for a short time become angry with us in order to chastise and teach us, He will again become reconciled with His servants. 34 You, however, you impious wretch, most bloodstained of all men, do not soar with vain delusions as false hopes give you the insolence to lift your hand against the children of Heaven. 35 You have not yet escaped the judgment of Almighty God, Who watches over us. 36 My brothers, having borne pain for a short while, now have inherited eternal life under the terms of God's covenant, whereas you shall suffer through the judgment of God the just punishment for your arrogance. 37 I, following my brothers' example, give up my body and soul for the sake of the laws of our forefathers, praying to God that he speedily have mercy upon our nation. May you through being afflicted and scourged come to acknowledge that He alone is God. 38 With me and my brothers may the Almighty put an end to the rightful anger inflicted upon our entire people." 39 Enraged, the king, in his resentment over being mocked, treated him still worse than the others. 40 So he perished undefiled, having put his trust entirely in the LORD. 41 And last, after her sons, died the mother. 42 Let us end here the stories of compulsion by extreme torture to partake of the meat of pagan sacrifices.

NOTES

Ch. 7. See NOTE on 6:18–31. The history of the ideas and patterns underlying our chapter is highly complicated. Jason of Cyrene wrote of the events as part of Antiochus' persecution of the Jews, but he wrote scores of years after they occurred. Thus his narrative could reflect not only the events, ideas, and literary patterns of the 160's B.C.E., but those both of earlier and of later times.

On the evolution of the patterns and theological concepts here, see Nickelsburg, *Resurrection*, pp. 11–111. Let us consider first how the story of the
mother and her seven sons fits into the thought and actions of the 160's B.C.E.

Can such gruesome martyrdoms have occurred, even in Antiochus' persecution? They can. In persecuting the Jews, Antiochus thought he was punishing
rebellion. At the root of the rebellion Antiochus saw the Torah; thus, to obey
the Torah was an act of rebellion. Seleucid kings, surely drawing ultimately on
the patterns of the Assyrian empire, punished rebels with precisely such gruesome tortures (Polybius v 54.3–7, 10; viii 23; B. A. van Proosdij, "De morte
Achaei," *Hermes* 69 [1934], 348–50; Bickerman, *Institutions*, p. 208; AB vol.
41, pp. 128–29). Apocalypses written during the persecution confirm the report here of tortures (Dan 11:33, 35; Test Moses 8:2, 4–5).

The persecution confronted pious Jews with a hideous dilemma: whether
they obeyed or disobeyed the king they would suffer grievous punishment (see
end of NOTE on 1:7, *Jason . . . Kingdom*). In their predicament, the pious
desperately needed three things. They needed explanation: why had this visitation come upon them? They needed instruction: what should they do now?
They needed consolation, for the persecution inflicted upon them damage
which was irreversible in the course of nature, including maiming and death.
Among the pious, those who had claims to wisdom searched the Torah and the
Prophets for explanation, instruction, and consolation and taught their discoveries to their fellows. There was great variety in what the searchers discovered.

In abstract terms, the explanation craved by the pious was written throughout scripture: so dreadful a visitation must be punishment for sin. The original
author of the story of the mother and her seven sons in our chapter may have
been satisfied with the abstract answer, for the martyrs never specify the sin for
which they suffer. Jason of Cyrene, having already explained that the persecution was punishment for the sins of Hellenizers, could have incorporated the
speeches of the martyrs largely unaltered (but see NOTE on vs. 33).

The abstract answer, however, could not satisfy all. Many would ask, insistently, for an answer in concrete terms. The concrete answers were numerous.
The senders of Ep. 1 in part agreed with Antiochus: Jews had rebelled against
the king; in addition, Jews had offered sacrifices at a schismatic temple (NOTE
on 1:7, *Jason . . . Kingdom*). To our writer (4:10–17) the crucial sins were
the acts of the Hellenizers in associating too closely with Greeks and following
their practices. The author of First Maccabees agrees (1:11–15, 64). Much
the same view is probably found in Test Moses 5: the guilt shared with the
kings, the whoring after strange gods, the pollution of the temple, the unworthy priests, the bribery and injustice are all characteristic of the Antiochenes of
Jerusalem and their leaders, Jason and Menelaus. Most pious Jews, however,
surely noticed the disproportion: the sinful Hellenizers had not committed real
idolatry (see NOTE on 4:19), yet all Jews, even the pious, suffered frightful
persecution. To the authors of Dan 9 and Enoch 89:56–67, the sufferings of
the Jews under Antiochus IV were the last climactic stage of seventy periods of
punishment imposed by God for heinous sins committed before the destruction
of the first temple. If the authors of Dan 9 and Enoch 89 by skill or luck had

an accurate chronology, the sins occurred ca. 654 B.C.E., in the reign of Manasseh, archsinner among the kings of Judah.

There were other ways of accounting for the disproportion. Israelites before had received deadly punishment, double and more for their sins (cf. Isa 40:2). The book of Isaiah contains prophecies offering several solutions to the problem. The punishment may indeed have come for sin, but its magnitude may not have been God's intention, if God's punishing instrument had arrogantly and wickedly exceeded God's instructions (Isa 10:5–15), in going beyond the chastisement of sinful Israel to attempt her destruction (Isa 10:6–7; Greek Isa 14:20). This view was widely held. How could Antiochus IV be other than arrogant and wicked? Thus the martyrs here can assume the somewhat paradoxical position that they are suffering for their sins, but Antiochus is punishing them unjustly (vss. 16, 19, 27, 31, 34, 36).

All these answers to the question, what was the sin?, would seem to have left the pious with only bleak prospects in answering the question, what should they do? We have observed (NOTE on 1:7, *Jason . . . Kingdom*) the terrible dilemma of pious Jews who believed God commanded them to obey Torah and king, yet the king commanded them to violate the Torah on pain of death. Mattathias audaciously introduced the principle that God could not have commanded obedience to Antiochus. Mattathias' pious opponents disagreed and had to face the enormous difficulties. To justify even martyrdom as a solution required somewhat contorted logic: though they seemed to disobey the king's commands to violate the Torah, nevertheless they "obeyed" him by unresistingly accepting death, even death by torture. The pious knew many examples of Israelites who accepted the risk of death but were rescued by God (Dan 3 and 6; I Kings 19; II Kings 1, 18:9 – 19:35; II Chron 20:1–30, etc.). There were, however, a few examples of figures who accepted the risk of death and perished, but always with some promise that God would avenge or vindicate (Jer 26:12–15 with 26:20–23; I Kings 19:14–18; II Chron 24:20–22; Isa 52:13).

Such promises of vengeance or vindication were among the important consolations found by the pious searchers of scripture. Very large at this time loomed the book of Isaiah, regarded by all faithful Jews as the unitary work of one great prophet (see Sir 49:22–25). Isaiah spoke of the rod of God's anger, a king of Assyria or Babylon, who went beyond God's mandate and would be punished (10:5–15, 14:4–25; see NOTES on vss. 14, 17, and 34). Isaiah (52:13 – 53:12) spoke of God's suffering servant, disfigured, oppressed, and put to death, who would yet enjoy a glorious existence. Isaiah, indeed (25:8, 26:19), spoke of bodily resurrection of the dead. Writers during the persecution took the servant of Isa 52:13 – 53:12 to be either the nation Israel or the martyred pious leaders within Israel and went on to predict glorious posthumous vindication or resurrection, as we learn from Dan 12:2–3 and Test Moses 10. The author of Jubilees 23:16–31 drew similar conclusions from other texts in Isaiah (30:26, 54:13, 57:18–19, 65:20, 66:14). On the use of Isaiah by these authors, see Nickelsburg, *Resurrection*, pp. 17–33, 40–42, 58–84. Thus, the martyrs in our chapter are portrayed using the vocabulary and ideas of the book of Isaiah, as did the actual victims of the persecution.

The literary art is that of Jason and the abridger, but the original patterns have hardly been altered; cf. Nickelsburg, *Resurrection*, pp. 93–96, 102–8.

Human beings in torment seek another type of consolation: the hope that the torment will soon end, or, better yet, the hope that they can themselves do something to hasten the end. The standard procedure for hastening the end of a divine punishment was confession of sin, repentance, and renewed obedience to the Torah, but Antiochus' decrees punished with torture and death all acts of repentance and obedience to the Torah. If the pious were suffering the climactic phase of God's sentence for ancient sin, it would seem that their only course was to suffer and die until God's appointed time (cf. Isa 10:25, 26:20, 60:22); there were various attempts to fix its date in Dan 7–12 and Enoch 85–90; see AB vol. 41, pp. 40–44.

Other pious groups discovered hints in scripture of ways to hasten God's action. The Seekers of Justice and Vindication found theirs mostly in Isa 32 and 55–56: God would act on behalf of Sabbath observers in caves in the desert. See NOTE on 6:11 and AB vol. 41, NOTE on 2:28–38. They are not presented as deliberately seeking martyrdom: at worst they expected to observe the Sabbath in secret; at best God would come to their rescue. They did not expect to be denounced to the king's men and killed. First Maccabees reports that when the thousand Seekers of Justice and Vindication were about to be slaughtered they cried out, "Heaven and earth bear witness over us, that you condemn us unjustly." The reported cry is probably an allusion to Deut 30:19 and 31:28, verses which were taken as introductory to Deut 32. The poem in Deut 32 speaks of Israel as reduced to helplessness in the course of her punishment for sin (vss. 19–25). Nowhere does the poem speak of Israel's repentance. Rather, the God Who kills and makes alive, Who wounds and heals (vs. 39), upon seeing their complete helplessness (vs. 36b), even without Israel's repentance, will vindicate His people and will relent concerning His servants (vs. 36a). His invincible overwhelming vengeance (vss. 41–42) upon Israel's enemies will be "for the *blood of His servants*" (vs. 43). Here was a text promising vindication and vengeance for the blood of a people so helpless that the way to repentance was barred, a text which even hinted at resurrection of the dead and healing of the maimed.

We cannot tell whether the author of First Maccabees was correct in suggesting that the Seekers of Justice and Vindication looked to the fulfillment of Deut 32, but clearly there were other Jews who did. The author of Test Moses 9 suggests a way to rouse God to act based on Deut 32: a pious father, "Taxo," and his seven sons, still guiltless in the time of persecution (cf. Isa 53:9b) should fast for three days (an act of repentance on behalf of their sinful nation?) and then go out to a cave in the field, where they are sure to be killed, and God on seeing their *blood* will fulfill Deut 32 and other glorious prophecies of Israel's vindication. The Seekers of Justice and Vindication, men, women, and children, went to caves in the wilderness following their own interpretation of Isa 32:14–16. In the Testament of Moses it is not clear why the father and his sons should go to the cave in the field or why they will be killed if they do. Thus, the author of the Testament of Moses writes as if he and his audience knew of the Seekers' interpretation of Isa 32 and 55–56, and of its failure to be fulfilled, even though the Seekers numbered one thousand. To judge by the fact that the author of the Testament of Moses stresses the sinlessness of Taxo, his sons, and their ancestors, he must have held that the Seekers were unworthy to be called God's servants because of sinners among them. Only the guiltless could be "God's servants" (see Isa 53:9b) in the sense that for their sake God would relent (Deut 32:36), and only their blood would He avenge immediately (Deut 32:43). Taxo and his sons are deliberately to court and achieve martyrdom and thus induce God to act.

Although the original version of the Testament of Moses apparently made no allusion to Mattathias and his sons, it is possible that the work is written in opposition to Mattathias' policy of active armed resistance. Taxo is made to say that guiltlessness and the use of the promise of Deut 32 are "our strength," a statement which can be taken to be in opposition to Mattathias' teaching. In First Maccabees, indeed, the massacre of the Seekers of Justice and Vindication is placed after Mattathias' rebellion, and we have seen reason to date the Testament of Moses still later than the massacre.

The project in the Testament of Moses of rousing God's anger has a clear scriptural basis in Deut 32, but nowhere in the scripture was there anything to suggest to a writer during the persecution that a *father* and seven sons should seek martyrdom. Perhaps the author of the Testament of Moses wrote knowing of a pious man (himself?) with seven sons who was willing to carry out the project. Later we shall find reason to believe that Mattathias in addition to his five sons had two stepsons, and that propagandists probably tried to present the seven of them as heroes who gave their lives in fulfillment of prophecy. Could Taxo and his seven have been created as a counterpart to Mattathias and his seven? It is unlikely that they were. It is at least doubtful that stepsons then could have been reckoned as sons; when the Testament of Moses was written, Mattathias and his "seven" were all alive; and there is no evidence for any prophecy concerning a sinless *father* and seven sons earlier than the Testament of Moses. Rather, the concept of Mattathias and his seven as a fulfillment of prophecy arose in response to propaganda based on figures like Taxo.

Our chapter seems to represent later developments of the theories which the Seekers of Justice and the author of the Testament of Moses drew from Deuteronomy and Isaiah. If Taxo was a real person, he and his seven sons probably achieved martyrdom, but the fulfillment of the prophecies did not occur. Pious readers of the Testament of Moses could react in several ways to the failure of Taxo's project. Some might hold that Taxo and his family were not as guiltless as they claimed to be. Some might hold that Taxo's project had violated the commandment not to put the LORD to the test (Deut 6:16). Others might abandon the Testament of Moses as a forgery and false prophecy. Still others might consider the question of the authenticity of the work irrelevant: Deut 32 and Isa 52–53 were certainly authentic, yet a project based on "scientific" interpretation of them had failed. Perhaps success required the fulfillment of other preconditions in scripture. If a martyrdom of a father and seven sons was mentioned nowhere in scripture, that of a *mother* and seven sons was hinted at in highly suggestive contexts.

At Jer 14:19–22 there is a national prayer: Judah personified confesses her sins, repents, declares her faith in the Creator, and begs for His intervention to end her torment. As if in answer to the prayer comes God's stern reply in Jer

15:1–9: the sins of King Manasseh were so heinous that even Moses and Samuel would not have been able to intercede in the current era of punishment. In the list of horrors to be inflicted upon sinful Judah, the prophecy includes the following (vss. 8–9): "I have made her widows more numerous than the sand of the seas. I have brought against them, *upon young man along with mother* [*'l 'm bḥwr*], a destroyer at noon. . . . Forlorn is she who gave birth to seven; she has swooned away; her sun set while it was yet day; she has been put to shame and disappointed." The words *'l 'm bḥwr* might more easily be taken to mean "against the mother of a young man," but "against them" implies that the victims are plural, and we shall see (below, p. 300) how the wording of II 7 suggests that Jason or his source construed *'l 'm bḥwr* in accordance with my first translation; cf. Gen 32:12; Hos 10:14; Jer 14:19. Jer 15:9 could easily be interpreted to imply that there can be no reprieve for a generation suffering for sins like those of Manasseh until all of the horrors of Jer 15:2–9 have come to pass, including the death of a *widowed* mother with all seven of her sons. Lam 2:22 could have been used to support the inference. The mention of "widows" in Jer 15:8 would thus explain the absence of a father from the story in II 7. The seers of Dan 9 and Enoch 85–90 seem to have held that under the persecution Israel was in fact suffering the climactic stage of the punishment of the sins of idolatrous Manasseh. Other pious observers disagreed but could have held that the sins of the Hellenizers were like the sins of Manasseh. Taxo would then have failed because the martyrdom of a widowed mother with seven sons was required. This interpretation of Jer 14:19 – 15:9 could be confirmed and turned into a message of hope by combining it with Hannah's prophetic prayer (I Sam 2:2–11): she who had many children is forlorn (ibid., vs. 5), but God, Who kills and resurrects (vs. 6), will defeat the mighty enemy and punish the wicked, exalt the tormented righteous, and give strength to His own anointed king (cf. *Yosefon* 19).

Dan 7:27 and Enoch 90:38 show how the victims of the persecution looked forward to God's raising of a Jewish king to power over a great empire, a hope still unfulfilled in the days of Jason of Cyrene (but see *Yosefon* 19–20, where Judas Maccabaeus is regarded as "messiah" in the sense of the "priest anointed for war" [*mᵉšūaḥ milḥāmāh;* see Deut 20:2 and TB *Soṭah* 42a]). However, our chapter contains traces of the rest of the hopes that could have been based on the combination of Jer 14:19 – 15:9 with I Sam 2:2–11.

Jason of Cyrene believed that the martyrdoms reported in II 7 purchased God's mercy through fulfilling Deut 32:36 and gave victory to the Jewish forces led by Judas Maccabaeus (vss. 6, 37–38, 8:3–5, 27–28, 30). Cf. John Downing, "Jesus and Martyrdom," JTS, n.s., 14 (1963), 280–84. As presented in the narrative, the martyrs fulfill the prophecies and avoid the pitfalls which could have caused the failure of Taxo. They are a *mother* and seven sons. Nothing indicates they put God to the test by openly seeking martyrdom: somehow they came to be arrested. Strangely, our chapter contains no allusion to the blood mentioned in Deut 32:43; has one been lost through abridgment?

Already in ancient times readers were perplexed by the vagueness of II 7: what was the home of the mother and her sons, and where did they meet their deaths? The writer reports no change of scene between 6:10 and 7:42;

Judaea and Jerusalem seem clearly to be the scene for the deaths of the circumcising women, the Sabbath observers in the caves, and Eleazar. Jer 15:5–9 is addressed to Jerusalem, and only by contorted interpretation can events listed there be removed from Judaea (see especially Jer 15:7). The author of IV 18:5–6 unhesitatingly places the events of our chapter at Jerusalem, and some Christian writers follow him (Gregory of Nazianzus, *Oration* 15. 5, 7, 8, 11 [XXXV, 924–25, 932 Migne]; Georgius Cedrenus *Historiarum compendium*, vol. CXXI, p. 321 Migne).

On the other hand, the eight martyrs die in the presence of the king. If Antiochus had come again to Jerusalem after the sack of 169 B.C.E., surely the fact would have been reflected in a contemporary apocalypse or in First or Second Maccabees. Yet not even our chapter says Antiochus returned to Judaea, nor does it say that the mother and her sons were conveyed to Antioch, the king's capital. In Fourth Maccabees (4:22 – 5:4) and the work of Georgius Cedrenus and in the medieval Jewish *Yosefon* (chs. 18–19), the events are placed at or near Jerusalem, but only by regarding them as part of the immediate aftermath of the sack of 169 B.C.E. Even so, one can see traces of the writer's perplexity in both Fourth Maccabees and *Yosefon*. At IV 5:1 the king is said, vaguely, to have watched the martyrdoms while seated at "some lofty place" (where?). In ch. 18 of *Yosefon* the king "decides to return" (*hw'yl llkt ldrkw*) to his own country, and his commander Philip makes a circuit through all the land of Judah and Jerusalem. Yet Antiochus is said to be "still in Jerusalem." In ch. 19 of *Yosefon* the king "still had not gone far from Jerusalem" when the mother and her seven sons were brought to him. The author's insistence probably shows he was trying to solve a difficulty in his sources.

On the other hand, Jason of Cyrene seems to hint that the mother and her sons come, not from Judaea, but from a Greek-speaking city. Though they are able to speak the ancestral language, normally they speak Greek; when they choose to speak the ancestral language, the fact is so unusual that the author calls special attention to it (vss. 8, 21, 27; Yehoshua Gutman, "The Story of the Mother and Her Seven Sons in the *Agadah* and in I and II Maccabees," *Sepher Yoḥanan Levi*, ed. by M. Schwabe and J. Gutman [Jerusalem: Magnes Press, 5709=1949], p. 36). Though a Greek writer might call Aramaic "Hebrew," if he wrote of "the language of our forefathers," he probably meant Hebrew. See also NOTE on 12:37. Furthermore, in 6:1–7 Jason speaks of persecution in Jerusalem and Judaea, but at 6:8 he speaks of persecution in Greek cities. In 6:10–31 he gives examples from Jerusalem and Judaea. Should he not give examples from Greek cities before dropping the subject of martyrdom at 7:42?

In fact, Christian and Jewish traditions, from the fourth century C.E. on, do place the deaths of the mother and her sons at Antioch; see Mariano Cardinal Rampolla da Tindaro, "Martyre et sépulture des Macchabées," *Revue de l'art chrétien* 48 (1899), 290–305, 377–92, 457–65, esp. pp. 378–92; Bickerman, *Studies,* II, 192–209; and Margaret Schatkin, "The Maccabean Martyrs" *Vigiliae Christianae* 28 (1974), 98–108. (The rabbinic traditions of a "captivity at Antioch" cited by Schatkin, ibid., p. 99, concern the exile of the kingdom of Israel, not the persecution under Antiochus IV; see Ginzberg, *Legends,* VI, 408.)

If the source text for the idea of the martyrdom of a woman and her seven sons was Jer 15:5–9, a context implying that Jerusalem was the scene, how could our story contain so many hints that the events occurred in Antioch? The book of Jeremiah contains another story of the slaughter of children as a parent looks on: such was the lot of Zedekiah and his sons, captured by Nebuchadnezzar and brought to "Riblah in the land of Hamath" (Jer 52:9–11; II Kings 25:6–8). Jews identified Riblah with Antioch or with its suburb Daphne; see L. Heidet, "2. Rébla," *Dictionnaire de la Bible*, ed. by F. Vigouroux, V (1922), 997–98. Jeremiah had predicted (38:23) that Zedekiah's queens would be led off with him, so they could have been present at the slaughter of the children. In the Hebrew of Jer 15:8–9 the bereaved mother is in the singular and need not be identified with the widows of Jer 15:8a. Thus, the mother in Jer 15:8–9 could be identified with a queen of Zedekiah's, led off from Jerusalem into exile. Nowhere is the number of Zedekiah's sons specified. He could have had seven by one wife. Under this interpretation the punishment for a generation as sinful as Zedekiah's would include the slaughter of the sons at Riblah under the eyes of a parent. The Jews now had no king; hence, there was no counterpart for Zedekiah. But a mother could still suffer as Zedekiah's queen had.

If this interpretation of the text in Jeremiah underlies our story, it is most natural to regard the mother and her seven sons as Greek-speaking pious Jerusalemites who also know Hebrew. The combination is quite possible, especially for the Greek-Jewish writer Jason of Cyrene. On the other hand, we saw reason to believe that Jason intended to present in our chapter examples of Jewish martyrs from a Greek city, a possibility far more difficult to derive from biblical texts: it seems farfetched to reason that just as Zedekiah's queen received the status of exile and then was bereaved, so a Jewish woman living in exile in Antioch would be bereaved. Thus a story of the martyrdom of a family of Jews regularly residing at Antioch could hardly be presented as fulfillment of prophecy, though it could still be told as an example of heroism of Jews in the diaspora.

Jason of Cyrene and his abridger wrote to edify and to entertain. Other things being equal, they surely regarded ambiguity as an annoyance to the reader and as something to be avoided. Nevertheless, difficulties in Jason's sources did force ambiguity upon him; see pp. 63–68 and AB vol. 41, pp. 48–52. The silence here on the home of the martyrs and on the place of their martyrdom is thus probably deliberate: more than one story of a mother and her seven sons lay before Jason of Cyrene, and the settings varied. Jason may have been unable to decide which was correct and may have been unwilling to put a strain on the faith of his readers by presenting the strange coincidence of several such families of martyrs. If so, ambiguity of the narrative here is his method for avoiding the difficulties.

Our analysis has revealed three possible stories that could have lain before Jason when he wrote: story one, of a family from Antioch martyred at Antioch in the presence of the king; story two, of a family from Judaea or Jerusalem arrested and carried off to Antioch, there to be martyred in the presence of the king; and story three, of a family from Judaea or Jerusalem martyred in Judaea or Jerusalem. Since the generation which saw the persecution knew that Antiochus did not return to Judaea or Jerusalem after 169 B.C., story three, if created by members of that generation, could not have had the king present, and by itself could not have given rise to the story in our chapter. On the other hand, stories one and two have the martyrdoms unequivocally at Antioch, and by themselves could not have produced the ambiguity of our chapter.

The facts of the persecution so far as they are known to us would allow any of the three stories to have truly taken place. It is, however, hard to believe that all three did. Though certainty is unattainable, we can discuss the relative probability that our three stories are fact or fiction. The Jewish resisters ultimately prevailed, and many of the pious were unwilling to give the credit to the Hasmonaeans. Pious anti-Hasmonaeans must have searched both the scriptures and the facts of the persecution for the cause of God's sudden change from wrath to mercy upon Israel. If so, they could have reasoned that Jer 14:19–15:9 and I Sam 2:2–11 had somehow been fulfilled. Certainly whole families had been tortured to death during the persecution. Pious anti-Hasmonaeans could have had strong motives to produce story two and/or story three even if the particular event described here never happened.

Indeed, there are fairly strong clues suggesting that the story of the mother and her seven sons became an important element in anti-Hasmonaean propaganda: for a time, partisans of the Hasmonaean brothers appear to have tried to present them and their mother as the true "martyr family." All five of Mattathias' sons died by violence. We know nothing of the fate of Mattathias' wife or wives. Though Mattathias is reported to have had only five sons (John, Simon, Judas, Eleazar, and Jonathan), Jason of Cyrene takes pains to name two other brothers of Judas, Joseph (8:22) and "Esdras" or "Esdris" or "Esdrias" (8:23; cf. 12:36). The reading of the latter name, which varies in the witnesses to the text, makes no difference: all represent "Azariah" or short nicknames for it (but see NOTE on 12:36). We have no information on the deaths of Joseph and Azariah, but if they, too, were killed by enemies of the Jews, we would have another group of seven brothers who gave their lives, but in active combat.

By the time of the writing of First Maccabees, the Hasmonaeans wished to dissociate themselves from Joseph and Azariah, who disobeyed Judas' orders and suffered a disastrous defeat at the height of God's favor for Israel. The Hasmonaean propagandist explained that Joseph and Azariah "did not belong to that family of men to whom it had been granted to be the agents of Israel's deliverance" (I 5:54–62). The mere fact that they dared to disobey Judas' orders might suggest that Joseph and Azariah, too, had claims to be God's chosen agents. According to I 5:18, Joseph's father's name was Zechariah. Azariah's father's name is not given, but he, too, could have been the son of Zechariah. The accounts in First and Second Maccabees can both be true if the five Hasmonaean brothers were half brothers to Joseph and Azariah through their mother. We would then have an activist group of seven brothers united not through their father, but through their mother. Perhaps the mother, too, met a violent death.

If the story in II 7 at one stage was published in opposition to the claims of the partisans of the "activist seven," strange aspects of the story find easy explanations. The absence of a father, if the slaughter of Zedekiah's sons was the prototype, is puzzling, but if the brothers were counterparts of a set who were brothers only through their mother, the puzzle is solved. We can also explain the odd terminology in our chapter (noticed by Nickelsburg, *Resurrection*, p. 106): one would expect to hear of a mother with her seven sons; the sons should be in the prepositional phrase (cf. Gen 32:12; Hos 10:4; TB *Giṭṭin* 57b). Instead, we hear of seven brothers with their mother. The syntax probably was taken from Jer 15:8 (see above, pp. 295–96), but why does the writer use "brothers" rather than "sons"? In the biblical story of Joseph, the brotherhood relationship is vital, and we are not surprised to hear Jacob's sons referred to as "Joseph's brothers," but here the brotherhood relationship would not seem to be so important a factor. Again the puzzle is solved if the wording of the story reflects the fact that it was written in opposition to the claims of the partisans of the activist seven, who became famous as brothers.

The story of the activist seven brothers, all of whom gave their lives, could not exist before the murder of Simon early in 134 B.C.E. By the time First Maccabees was written, in the reign of Alexander Jannaeus, Hasmonaean propagandists, for whatever reason, took pains to dissociate the five Hasmonaean brothers from Joseph and Azariah; they no longer spoke of the activist seven. Story two or story three thus could have arisen at some time between the death of Simon and the reign of Jannaeus. Of the three, story two is the most likely to have been a propagandist's fabrication. Story three, too, could have been a propagandist's fabrication, but it has greater claims to reflect a historical event, particularly if it did not have Antiochus IV present, for the presence of the king is a stereotype in such tales (cf. Dan 3 and 5; Matt 10:18; Hans-Werner Surkau, *Martyrien in jüdischer und frühchristlicher Zeit* [Göttingen: Vandenhoeck & Ruprecht, 1938], p. 12; Nickelsburg, *Resurrection*, pp. 49–96). One can easily believe that large families suffered martyrdom in Judaea and Jerusalem, and a propagandist's fiction would have tended to include the pattern of the slaughter at Riblah of Zedekiah and his sons. Furthermore, to judge by I 1:62–63, story three may have stood in the Common Source. Still less likely to be a fabrication is story one, which is no obvious fulfillment of prophecy. If story one reflects fact, it is valuable evidence that the Jews of Antioch, too, suffered persecution.

Story one could well have been composed at Antioch. On the other hand, the vocabulary used is no clue that our chapter was composed there, as has been suggested (Solomon Zeitlin and Sidney Tedesche, *The Second Book of Maccabees* [New York: Harper, 1954], p. 21). It is true that apart from translations from the Hebrew, the word *Hebraios* for Jew occurs in the Greek Old Testament only at II 7:31, 11:13, 15:37, in Fourth Maccabees, and in Judith; and *Ioudaïsmos* for the Jewish religion occurs only at II 2:21, 8:1, 14:38, and IV 4:26. But IV 18:5 proves that the author of Fourth Maccabees believed that the martyrdoms occurred at Jerusalem, and the use by Philo, Josephus, and other authors of *Hebraios* and *Ioudaïsmos* demonstrates that there is no reason to connect the vocabulary with Antioch; see Walter Bauer, *Griechisch-deutsches Wörterbuch zu den Schriften des Neuen Testaments und der übrigen urchristlichen Literatur* (5th ed.; Berlin: Töpelmann, 1958), s.vv. (cols. 422 and 750).

Mattathias is said to have had seven sons in a Jewish legend quoted by Aḥa (Aḥai) of Shabḥa (680–752 C.E.); see *Sheeltot de Rab Ahai Gaon*, ed. by

Samuel K. Mirsky (Jerusalem: Sura, Yeshiva University, and Mosad Harav Kook, 1959–63), pp. 184–86. Probably the number there was derived from the seven in our chapter, not from an old tradition which counted the five Hasmonaean brothers plus Joseph and Azariah.

One other thread of tradition appears to have influenced Jason of Cyrene and perhaps the author of one or more of the stories which lay before him (Nickelsburg, *Resurrection,* pp. 106–8). At Bar 4:9–29 the city of Jerusalem personified utters a speech full of parallels to our chapter in language and content. Jerusalem calls herself a *widow* (Bar 4:12, 16) and says that God has *inflicted* (*epagein:* Bar 4:9, 10, 14, 15, 18, 27, 29; II 7:38) captivity upon all *her children,* whom *she had nursed* (Bar 4:11; II 7:27); the captivity is for their *sins* (Bar 4:12; II 7:18, 32); the captor is a nation from afar, ruthless, speaking a strange language, and shows no reverence for age and no pity for a child (Bar 4:15; the author of II 7 stresses the foreignness of the persecutor's language [vss. 8, 27] and in II 6:18 – 7:42 displays how both aged man and child fall victims). At Bar 4:17–29, Jerusalem apostrophizes her children; strikingly reminiscent of our chapter are the words of Bar 4:19–23 ". . . *Go,* my children, go . . . God . . . will deliver you from the tyrannical power, from the hand of enemies. I have put my *hope* in the Everlasting that you will be saved, and joy has come to me from the Holy One because of the *mercy* which will come to you speedily from your everlasting Savior. For I *sent you out* with sorrow and weeping, but God will *give you back to me* with joy and gladness forever" (italics mine). At II 7:20–23 and 29 the mother urges her sons to *go* away from her by accepting death. She does so through her *hopes* in God (vs. 20), that He will have *mercy* and will *give them back to her* (vss. 23, 29) (italics mine). At Bar 4:25 Jerusalem predicts the destruction of the enemy (cf. II 7:14, 17, 19, 36–37), and at 4:27 she insists to her children that God has not forgotten them (cf. II 7:6, 16, 31–35).

There is reason to believe that the book of Baruch was written in 163 B.C.E. as propaganda against Judas' siege of the Akra (see my article in PAAJR 46–47 [1979–80], 179–99), so that Jason or his sources could have drawn upon it. Nevertheless, the themes of sin, punishment, repentance, and vengeance upon the enemy which Bar 4 has in common with our chapter are conventional themes of Jewish piety. There is not a trace in Bar 4 of the influence of Jer 14:19 – 15:9; the entire passage draws on prophecies in Isaiah (see especially Isa 49:14–23, 54:1–13, 60:4–9, 66:9–12; "God will give back" at Bar 4:23 is probably derived from Isa 26:12). In Baruch, as in Isa 40–66, there is no hint that Jerusalem's captive children have been killed; indeed, in the entire book of Baruch the belief in the resurrection is conspicuous by its absence (see esp. Bar 2:17). Thus Bar 4 probably was not a decisive influence in shaping our chapter (cf. the later Jewish legend at *Pesiqta rabbati* 26[end], pp. 131b–32a Friedmann, summarized at Ginzberg, *Legends,* VI, 403, n. 43). The resemblance between the two female figures is coincidental. The verbal echoes, however, of Bar 4:21–23 in II 7:20–23 and 29 are probably not coincidental. The book of Baruch was cherished in some anti-Hasmonaean circles, and Jason could have drawn on its rhetoric. The book's failure to affirm faith in the resurrection was no more disturbing than the similar failure in most of the Hebrew Bible.

To judge by First Maccabees, our chief source for Hasmonaean propaganda, the activist Hasmonaeans viewed unresisting martyrdom with hostility and even contempt; see AB vol. 41, pp. 7, 73, 226. Since the martyr tales here were probably written as anti-Hasmonaean propaganda, the hostility is still less surprising. Hence, it is ironic that in Christian and Jewish popular lore the mother and seven brothers should have collectively received Judas Maccabaeus' additional name: they became the "Maccabees" (see pp. 3–4; John Malalas, *Chronographia* viii, vol. XCVII, col. 321 Migne; Schatkin, *Vigiliae Christianae* 28 [1974], 98–113). Even more ironic is the fact that their mother seems to have received the additional name borne by Mattathias Hashmonay, the archactivist; she became "Hashmonit" (see Julian Obermann, "The Sepulchre of the Maccabaean Martyrs," JBL 50 [1931], 253–60).

Already Josephus revered both the Hasmonaeans and the martyrs. His narrative in *AJ* xii bears clear signs that he read our chapter. Josephus at *AJ* xii 5.4.255–56 amplified the rather frigid account of the martyrs given at I 1:62–63. The content of Josephus' amplification certainly could have been derived from our chapter, and in his brief paragraphs occur words found here in the same sense: *patrios* ("ancestral," vss. 2, 24, 37), *aikizomenoi* (passive participle, "tortured," vs. 1, and with active meaning, vss. 13 and 15), and *basanous* ("tortures," vs. 8). The participle *empneontes* ("breathing") would echo the adjective *empnoun* in vs. 5. In addition *pikras basanous* ("cruel tortures") in Josephus may echo *pikras anankês* ("cruel compulsion") at 6:7.

The vocabulary in part was dictated by the subject matter, and all these words except the verb *empnein* occur frequently in Josephus. *Empnein*, however, recurs only at *BJ* v 11.2.458 and (of the wind) at *BJ* vii 8.5.317. If Josephus drew on biblical Greek vocabulary here, some of the words are rare or absent in the Greek Old Testament outside the books of Maccabees: *patrios* (II 6:1, 7:2, 8, 21, 24, 27, 37, 12:37, 15:29; eight instances in Fourth Maccabees; elsewhere only at Sir *Prologue* 8 and Isa 8:21); *aikizomenoi* (II 7:1, 13, 15, 8:28–30; III 5:42; IV 1:11, 6:16); *basanos* ("torture," I 9:50; II 7:8, 9:5; III 3:27; forty-one instances in Fourth Maccabees; elsewhere only at Sir 33:27 and Wisdom 19:4). On Josephus' probable borrowings from the story of Eleazar, see end of NOTE on 6:18–31.

The likelihood that Josephus drew the amplifications in *AJ* xii 5.4.255–56 from II 6:18 – 7:42 becomes a near certainty when we look at Josephus' revision (*AJ* xii 6.3.279–84) of Mattathias' farewell address (I 2:49–64). Josephus replaces the blatant propaganda for the Hasmonaean dynasty with the content of the words of the mother in our chapter! The vocabulary, too, contains echoes. In section 279 Josephus has Mattathias mention his own "resolution" (*phronêma*) as something to be maintained by posterity; cf. vss. 20–21. Section 280 echoes vss. 22–23, 27–28, 30, replacing the mother's functions by the father's: "The parent who begot you and raised you asks you to keep the ancestral laws." Section 281 echoes vss. 6, 23, and 29: "Keep God's laws even if you have to give up your lives, for God will see and restore to you your selves and your liberty." Josephus' dependence on vss. 23 and 29 is strongly suggested by the strange phraseology in section 281, which has puzzled translators and commentators, "restore to your your selves." The word "overlook," "hold cheap" (*hyperhoran*) occurs both in Josephus' section 281 and in vs. 23. Furthermore, in section 280, "the ancient constitution which is in danger of passing away" (*kindyneuousan oichesthai tên archaian politeian*) may be derived from II 2:22.

Inasmuch as the stories of Eleazar and of the mother and her seven sons are anti-Hasmonaean counterparts for the history of the deeds of Mattathias and his sons, it is not surprising that Josephus, despite his reverence for the martyrs of his people, only drew upon the stories and did not reproduce them (cf. I. Gafni, "On the Use of I Maccabees by Josephus Flavius," *Zion* 45 [1980], 91–92, n. 40 [in Hebrew]). On the use of our chapter by later Jewish and Christian authors, see NOTE on 6:18–31 and Abel, pp. 381–84.

Within the abridged history, the chief function of our chapter is to show how the courage of the martyrs won God's mercy and made possible the victories of Judas Maccabaeus (vss. 37–38, 8:3–5). Within the chapter itself, however, the theme of the courage of the martyrs itself is subordinated to the preaching of the ideas of retribution and resurrection—a sign that Jason of Cyrene found much of the material here already existing and worked it into the fabric of his history. See Kellermann, *Auferstanden*, pp. 38–40, 54–59.

There is a clear sequence of ideas in the successive speeches of the martyrs in our chapter. The first brother lays down the principle which all will obey: death is preferable to violating the Torah. The verb "exhorted" in the imperfect tense in vss. 5 and 21 shows that the exhortations which follow are to be taken as a constant "choral background" to the "tragedy" of the deaths by torture. We are thus to imagine the martyrs as fixing their attention upon the promise in Deut 32:36, that God will relent, and as being reminded by their mother, in the ancestral language, that the Creator will resurrect them, a promise surely derived here from Deut 32:39. Antiochus could understand neither the ancestral language nor the implications of the allusion to Deut 32:36. The martyrs, speaking Greek, must inform him of the messages in Deut 32. The poem there teaches that God is always mindful of Israel: Israel's disasters are divine punishment for sin, not signs that God has deserted His people (Deut 32:15–30); God will take vengeance on the enemy (Deut 32:35, 41–43), for whom there is no escape (Deut 32:39), and He will resurrect and restore the maimed martyrs (ibid.).

Accordingly, the second brother, after reiterating by his "No!" the principle laid down by the first, gives voice to his faith in resurrection (vs. 9). The third brother adds that in their resurrection the martyrs will have their mutilated and amputated members restored (vs. 11). The fourth reiterates the faith in resurrection and begins to allude to the imminent punishment of Antiochus: he will have no resurrection "unto life" (vs. 14; see NOTE ad loc.). The fifth begins to teach Antiochus that Israel has not been deserted by God, Who will take vengeance on him and his (vs. 17). It might seem paradoxical that suffering Israel has not been deserted by God, so the sixth brother explains that the suffering is for sin and goes on to tell Antiochus that God's vengeance is inescapable. All the ideas expressed hitherto are summed up in the final speeches of the mother and her youngest son (vss. 27–38): even women and little children hold fast to the teaching of the Torah. In the last words to be spoken by a member of the martyred family, the youngest utters a prayer (vss. 37–38) for the fulfillment now of Deut 32:36–43, for the martyrdoms should have accomplished all the preconditions.

In the author's portrait of the mother and her sons, the martyrs die bravely after uttering profound truths of theology and cosmology. In this, the author surely again draws upon the Greek narrative tradition of the depiction of the brave death of the philosopher, a tradition which goes back to Plato's dialogues on the trial and death of Socrates (cf. Kellermann, *Auferstanden*, pp. 46–50, 51–52).

Torture in antiquity was employed usually for two purposes: to get information and to punish serious offenses such as treason; see A. Ehrhardt, "Tormenta 2," PW, VIA² (1937), 1776–77. If the purpose was only to get information, the authorities might avoid inflicting irreparable damage on the victim. Accordingly, when the victims here find themselves only whipped, they assume that the king intends to question them (vs. 2). In fact, the king's intention in whipping them was probably not at all to elicit information, but to coerce them to obey. The irreparable tortures which the martyrs suffer upon their definite refusals would seem to be punishment for disobedience; at that stage the king is no longer coercing the martyr but making an example of him to others who might be inclined to commit the treason of disobedience. Thus it is strange that the second brother (and he alone), after being irreparably mutilated, is given the opportunity to change his mind (vs. 7).

1. The comments mentioned at AB vol. 41, p. 40, n. 9; pp. 56–57, n. 10; p. 138, n. 205; p. 239; and p. 304 are in the introductory NOTE on ch. 7. The comment mentioned at AB vol. 41, p. 220, has been eliminated as farfetched.

At that time. See NOTE on 3:2.

4. *scalp.* By the Scythian method (*periskythizein*), cutting all the way around at the level of the ears and removing the scalp by pulling and shaking (Herodotus iv. 64).

cut off his hands and feet. Gr. *akrotēriazein* literally means "to lop off the ends or extremities of." If the object of the verb is "the face," it means "to cut off the nose and ears." Vs. 5, speaking of complete helplessness, shows that the verb here refers to the amputation of hands and feet or even of arms and legs. The Assyrian kings so mutilated rebels; see van Proosdij, *Hermes* 69 (1934), 348–49.

5. Cf. Jer 29:22.

6. *The Lord God looks on.* Cf. Greek Zech 9:1 and Greek Job 34:23.

is relenting. Striking is the use of the present tense: even when confronted by such terrible tortures, the martyrs believe that the prediction at Deut 32:36 is being fulfilled.

the Song Which Confronts as a Witness. The title for Deut 32 is derived from Deut 31:21.

'And . . . servants.' Deut 32:36; the next words of the verse are "when he sees that they are helpless" (*kī yir'eh kī āzᵉlat yād*).

7. On *empaigmos* as "wanton torture," see Bauer, *Wörterbuch*, col. 507, s.vv. *empaigmonê, empaigmos, empaizô.*

ripping . . . hair. A still more painful scalping than that suffered by the first brother, whose scalp was cut around and then pulled off. The Greek preposition *syn* ("with," "by means of") is used freely in Second Maccabees as a synonym of *meta* with the genitive. Only here in Second Maccabees would *syn* be used as "by means of," but cf. *meta* at 6:16 and *syn* at IV 10:7, 13:26.

One might also translate our passage "ripping off the skin of his head along with the hair," but no matter how construed, that rendering is hard to fit into the context. Even if the youth was still alive, one could hardly demand of a man with a completely flayed head that he eat. If only the scalp was removed, why specify "along with the hair"?

On the strangeness of the procedure with the second brother, see end of NOTE on ch. 7.

8. *tortured.* I translate the reading of La$^{LX(BMP)}$ Sy Arm *L'*. The other witnesses to the text add the words *hôs ho prôtos* ("as the first had been"). A reading shared by *L* and La is likely to be correct (see AB vol. 41, p. 178), and the words make the narrative illogical: the first brother could not speak after his tongue was cut out, but the second brother makes a statement on the point of death (vs. 9). Probably, the writer thought that the word *hexês* ("in turn") was a sufficient indication of the nature of the tortures, but a scribe, failing to perceive the hint, thought a more explicit indication had fallen out and added the words "as the first had been."

9. Gr. *alastôr* ("fiend") means both "avenging spirit or deity" and "doer of monstrous and unforgivable deeds." Both meanings are appropriate for the "rod of God's anger" who criminally went beyond God's intentions. The martyr pointedly refrains from addressing Antiochus as "King"; see below, NOTE on "King of the universe."

making us depart. Cf. Tobit 3:6 (S), 3:13 (B A).

King of the universe. The phrase here is clearly intended to express an antithesis. Antiochus, the earthly king, is a mere "fiend," but God is "King of the universe." In Greek it may already have been a fixed formula of Jewish piety, though I know of no earlier datable occurrence. Certainly in Hebrew, as *melekh hā'ôlām*, it was to become a fixed formula of Jewish prayer. *Melekh 'ôlām* occurs at Ps 10:16 (and cf. Ps 145:13), but the context proves that *'ôlām* (Gr. *aiôn*) there means "eternity," as it probably does at Tobit 13:7, 11 (B A). It may be that Greek-speaking Jews were the first to call their God "King of the universe" in opposition to the earthly kings; somewhat later Hebrew-speaking Jews felt the need for a similar expression in their own language. In any case, by the first century C.E. *'ôlām* was being used with the meaning "universe," and by the third century C.E. Jewish authorities were insisting that Jewish prayers contain the expression "King of the universe." See Sasse, "kosmos," TDNT, III (1965), 881–83, and *"aiôn,"* ibid., I (1964), 203–4; TB *Berakot* 12a; Ismar Elbogen, *Der jüdische Gottesdienst,* p. 5; Schürer (New English version), II (1979), 531–33.

resurrect . . . life. A literal translation of the redundant Greek (*eis aiônion anabiôsin zôês hêmas anastêsei*) is very inelegant: "resurrect us to an eternal revivification of life." The redundancy is due to the writer's wish to reflect the language of Dan LXX 12:2 (*anastêsontai . . . eis zôên aiônion*), "will be resurrected to eternal life," and the content of the rest of that verse. The writer interpreted Dan LXX 12:2 to mean that there would be two kinds of resurrection: a permanent revivification of the righteous and an awakening of the wicked "for contumely and eternal dispersal" (*eis oneidismon . . . eis dias-*

poran . . .). By "eternal dispersal" he understood a dispersal of their elements, i.e., the annihilation of the wicked; see II 7:14(end), and cf. Epicurus *Epistle* 1.65. Jason and the translator of Dan LXX derived *dir'ōn* at Dan 12:2 from the Aramaic root *dry* ("scatter"; cf. Targum Onkelos to Exod 32:20). To specify unequivocally the kind of resurrection, Jason added here the word "revivification." There is no trace here or in vs. 36 of the idea that the martyr immediately after dying will be raised up to live in heaven (cf. Kellermann, *Auferstehung*, pp. 63–66, 67, 73, etc.).

11. *Heaven*. The context ("His laws") proves that the word here, as in First Maccabees, is an epithet for "God."

12. Our verse fits a common pattern in martyr tales; see above, pp. 282–83.

14. The hopes, as the allusive language shows, are based on Dan 12:2, which itself is based on Isa 26:14, 19, 66:24; see Nickelsburg, *Resurrection*, pp. 17–21.

Again, as in vs. 9, the writer is redundant because he draws on Dan LXX 12:2: Antiochus will have no resurrection unto life because he will awaken from death for eternal contumely and for annihilation; cf. also Greek Isa 14:20–21, which can be read as meaning that Antiochus and his children will have no resurrection unto life.

The author of Wisdom 3:3–4 ("their departure from among us . . . their hope is concentrated upon immorality") may well have drawn upon our verse.

16–19. Our verses are full of allusions to Dan 8:24–25. "You wield power" echoes "His power shall be great" (Dan 8:24). "Work your will" echoes "he shall work his will" (*w'śh krṣnw;* Dan 8:4, 11:36; cf. *w'śh* in Dan 8:24). "They [the mutilations] pass belief!" (*axia thaumasmou gegone*) echoes "he shall cause destruction past belief" (*wnpl'wt yšḥyt;* Dan 8:24). "Having dared to contend with God" echoes "he shall rise against the Prince of princes" (Dan 8:25). Accordingly, "but you are mortal" in vs. 16 may well allude to "but not through his own power" (*wl' bkḥw*) at Dan 8:24, and so may the implications in vss. 16 and 18 that God has not deserted Israel. The predictions of Antiochus' doom in vss. 17 and 19 would then allude to Dan 8:25.

17. Jason portrays the gruesome death of Antiochus IV at 9:5–28. His son, Antiochus V, was murdered (14:2; I 7:2–4). Jason may have believed that Alexander Balas was a son of Antiochus IV; Balas was murdered by beheading (I 11:17). Cf. Greek Isa 14:20–21, addressed to the king of Babylon or Assyria, ". . . You, too, shall not be clean, because you have ruined My land and killed My people; you shall not last forever, wicked seed. Prepare your children to be slaughtered for the sins of their [so read with B and with Aquila, Symmachus, and Theodotion] father, so that they may not rise again and inherit the earth. . . ." Antiochus was dead at the time of the murders of his heirs, but Jason must have believed that the king's soul survived to learn of them or would receive the information at the resurrection (see NOTE on vs. 9, *resurrect . . . life*).

18. *They pass belief!* These words look awkward in the Greek. In mss. A and V they lack the particle one would expect to connect them to the rest of the sentence; L' and Sy have the particle *dio* ("because"), and q has the particle *gar* ("because"). Not surprisingly, some texts omit the words (58 La^x Pass.Mac. W Cyprian). Nevertheless, the words probably belong in the text, as

one more allusion to Dan 8:24 (see NOTE on vss. 16–19). There are parallels for the lack of a connective particle in such cases; see Kühner-Gerth, *Grammatik*, II, 344.

Our words may also allude to Deut 28:59, "The LORD will make your afflictions pass belief."

19. See NOTE on 5:21, *thinking . . . soar.*

20. *deserves . . . memory.* The phrase may be a translation of the Heb. *zkwr ltwb* ("to be remembered for good"), used in honor of a meritorious person, especially Elijah (Hebrew Sir 45:1; *M. Baba meṣi'a* 4:12; TB *Baba Batra* 21a). Cf. Prov 10:7; Sir 46:11.

in the course of a single day. Cf. Esther 3:13; III 4:14.

21. It was womanly to think of herself as mother to her sons. In Greek the very word for courage is "manliness" (*andreia*).

22–29. Christian writers, from Origen (*Commentarius in Johannem* i 17.103, *De principiis* ii 1.5) on, took our passage (in particular vs. 28) as the first unequivocal statement in scripture of the doctrine of creation *ex nihilo*, that God created the universe from absolutely nothing, not from some preexistent raw matter. In fact, there is no unequivocal statement of the doctrine either in the Hebrew Bible or in the New Testament, and statements can be found even in rabbinic literature supporting the view of creation from preexistent matter. See David Winston, "The Book of Wisdom's Theory of Cosmogony," *History of Religions*, 11 (1971), 185–200, and the works cited therein, nn. 3–5, 21. Modern scholars have noted, because of the ambiguity of the Greek terms that even vs. 28 is not an unequivocal statement of the doctrine of creation *ex nihilo*. See Grimm, pp. 126–27; Winston, *History of Religions*, 11 (1971), 186–87, and nn. 4–5, 21; Georg Schmuttermayr, " 'Schöpfung aus dem Nichts' in 2 Makk 7, 28?" *BZ*, neue Folge, 17 (1973), 203–22; Gerhard May, *Schöpfung aus dem Nichts: Die Entstehung der Lehre von der Creatio ex nihilo* (Arbeiten zur Kirchengeschichte, 48; Berlin and New York: Walter de Gruyter, 1978), pp. 6–8.

The crucial phrase in vs. 28 is *ouk ex ontôn,* which I have translated "not after they existed." It might also be rendered "not from things which existed." *L* has *ex ouk ontôn,* which might be translated "from things which did not exist" or "from what did not exist." Greek usage allows the two readings to be either synonymous or distinct in meaning; see Schmuttermayr, *BZ*, neue Folge, 17 (1973), 217–27, and May, *Schöpfung*, p. 7, n. 27. Moreover, either reading could make the declaration in vs. 28 mean "Though no individual things existed, God created the world from undifferentiated raw matter." Socrates is quoted as having used the same phraseology as the reading of *L*, to say that parents cause their children to exist after not existing (*ek men ouk ontôn;* Xenophon, *Memorabilia* ii 2.3; cf. Philo *Legum allegoria* iii 10). Here, too, the phrase could mean "after they previously did not exist as heaven and earth, but only as raw matter." The Platonists used the very term *to mê on* ("the nonexistent") for "formless matter" (Aristotle *Physics* i 9.192a6–7; see May, *Schöpfung*, p. 17).

Even so, Jason may have thought that the reading *ouk ex ontôn* was an unequivocal statement of creation *ex nihilo.* It frequently happens in the language of philosophy, theology, and legal documents that ambiguities are perceived only after terms have been in use, and the perceived ambiguities then lead to reformulation. For an ancient reader, the reading of *L, ex ouk ontôn* ("from what did not exist") may well have been less ambiguous, and the Latin *ex nihilo* is unequivocally "from nothing"; cf. Schmuttermayr, BZ, neue Folge, 17 (1973), 228. An early assertion of the doctrine of creation *ex nihilo* thus could well have been phrased in terms that proved to be less than clear, so that the later scribes and translators then tried to improve upon it. Our passage contains multiple textual problems. Did Jason intend to state the doctrine of creation *ex nihilo,* and can the perplexing textual variants here be explained as efforts of later hands merely to clarify that intention? We shall see that the answer to the first question is probably no, but the interpretation of the Church Fathers has some foundation and is so old that one must give the case for it a full hearing.

The martyrs in our chapter and Razis at 14:46 state the doctrine of resurrection in its most extreme form: the martyrs will recover *these* members, *these* bodies which are being destroyed (cf. TB *Sanhedrin* 90a). Even unsophisticated unbelievers could think of objections: what if the matter of one of the bodies, after being eaten by worms, deposited in the soil, absorbed in a plant, and turned into food for human beings, should come to be part of another human body? The story here has the other martyrs inhaling and perhaps absorbing matter vaporized from the body of the first (vs. 5)! Such objections could be answered if God is omnipotent and can create *ex nihilo.* See Origen *De principiis* ii 1.1–3.3 and *Contra Celsum* 14 (adding later objections to the appeal to the omnipotence of the Creator); Saadia Gaon, *The Book of Beliefs and Opinions,* ed. and trans. by Samuel Rosenblatt (Yale Judaica Series, vol. I; New Haven: Yale University Press, 1948), pp. 410–14; Thomas Aquinas, *Summa contra gentiles* iv 80–81. Unbelievers with any smattering of Greek philosophy ridiculed both the doctrine of resurrection and that of creation *ex nihilo.*

I have found no ancient text explicitly indicating the reason why Jews and Christians came to insist upon the doctrine of creation *ex nihilo.* Nevertheless, it seems probable that they did so because of their ever-stronger adherence to the belief in bodily resurrection. If God had created only from preexistent matter, the believer would have no way of refuting the aforementioned objections to bodily resurrection. Cf. Winston, *History of Religions,* 11 (1971), 195–96. Those ancient Jewish writers who believed only in the immortality of the soul and not in the resurrection of the body had no need to believe in creation *ex nihilo,* nor did those Jews who held that the resurrected dead might be given, in whole or in part, some other body than the one they had had in life. Jason of Cyrene seems to have been an ardent believer in what we have called the most extreme form of resurrection. Although scholars have asserted that Jason and his Jewish contemporaries had not yet reached so high a level of philosophical acuity as to formulate the doctrine of creation *ex nihilo* (Schmuttermayr, BZ, neue Fogle, 17 [1973], 203–22; May, *Schöpfung,* pp. 1–25), I shall now show how Jason indeed could have been well enough versed in philosophy to have insisted upon creation *ex nihilo* as justification for the belief in resurrection. I hope to treat elsewhere the origins of the Jewish and Christian doctrines of creation *ex nihilo* and their connection with the belief in resurrection.

We have found elsewhere (NOTE on 6:18–31) reason to believe that Jason knew the works of Plato. The presence of technical philosophical terminology in our passage makes it most probable that Jason did know cosmological theories such as those taught by Plato and Aristotle and here could have expressed his disagreement in order to have a cosmological foundation for his belief in resurrection.

Jason has to argue not only against Greek skeptics. The book of Qohelet (Ecclesiastes) had wide circulation among Jews. Qohelet doubts that there is any human life after death (3:19–21; 9:2–6). Jason has the mother answer the skeptics in her two utterances. In vss. 22–23 she supplements the words of Qohelet with Greek philosophy to assert that God can revive the dead. Qohelet says (11:5), ". . . There is no one who knows the way the spirit comes to the bones in the womb of the pregnant woman; similarly you will not know the work(s) [Heb. *ma'ăśēh;* Gr. *poiêmata*] of God, as he fashions [Heb. *ya'ăśeh;* Gr. *poiêsei*] everything." Qohelet also says (8:17), "I looked at all the work(s) [*ma'ăśēh; poiêmata*] of God, for man cannot fathom [Heb. *mṣ';* Gr. *heurein*] the work which is fashioned [Heb. *na'ăśāh;* Gr. *pepoiêmenon*] under the sun; however much a man may toil in seeking, he will not fathom it, and even if a wise man should claim to know, he cannot fathom it." To a man of faith like Jason, man's ignorance should lead not to doubt but to affirmation of God's creative power! Thus, the mother says, paraphrasing Qohelet, "I do not know how you came to be in my womb." God, who fashioned her sons there, knows how He did so, for He created the universe and also the process of human reproduction. Consequently, He can fashion them again and resurrect them. Where she goes beyond Qohelet, her words become full of technical philosophic terminology. See NOTE on vss. 22–23. John Chrysostom (345–407 C.E.) seems to have been aware of how the mother sounded like a professional philosopher (*In sanctos Maccabaeos* 1.2, vol. L, cols. 620–21 Migne).

Having answered the doubts of Qohelet and having also shown her knowledge of philosophy in her first speech, the mother could have turned in her second speech (vss. 28–29) to enunciate the principle of creation *ex nihilo,* which can answer the stock philosophical arguments against bodily resurrection. In so arguing, she would have been opposing the insistent declarations of Greek intellectuals beginning with Parmenides, Democritus, and Empedocles in the fifth century B.C.E. (see *Die Fragmente der Vorsokratiker,* ed. by Hermann Diels [6th ed., rev. by Walther Kranz; Berlin: Weidmann, 1951–52], I, 234–36, 313; II, 84). The Greek philosophers insist that "Nothing can arise from what does not exist" with such emphasis that they must be opposing some other view. Aristotle, in the fourth century B.C.E., repeats the declaration, which we may call "the dogma of the philosophers," and adds that *nearly* all physical scientists (*tôn peri physeôs*) agree with it (*Metaphysics* xi 6.1062b). He does not name the exceptions. One may have been Xeniades of Corinth, of the fifth century B.C.E. (Sextus Empiricus *Adversus mathematicos* vii 53; Kurt von Fritz, "Xeniades 1," PW, IX^A2 [1967], 1438–39). In Jason's time, there may have been no Greek philosopher who believed in creation *ex nihilo* (but see G. C. Stead, review of *Schöpfung aus dem Nichts,* by Gerhard May, *Journal of Theological Studies* 30 [1979], 548). However, in the formulation of the Greek philosophical dogma "what does not exist" is always referred to in the singular, as *to mê on*. If Jason was directly confronting the dogma here, should he not have used the singular? Yet he uses the plural, "not from things which existed" (*ouk ex ontôn*). His wording seems ambiguous (see above, pp. 307–8) and perhaps even naïve (Schmuttermayr, BZ, neue Folge, 17 [1973], 203–28).

However, philosophical considerations could have dictated Jason's choice of words. He could have known of the use by some philosophers of the term *to mê on* for "formless matter" (see above, p. 307). Parmenides himself, in his poem where he gave the first statement of the philosophical dogma, also used the plural to say "This shall never be proved, that nonexistent [*mê eonta*] exist."

Aristotle's analysis demonstrated that the paradoxes of Parmenides' philosophy, which held that only one thing exists, arose because Parmenides confused *what exists* with *abstract being*. From the time of Aristotle, philosophers could distinguish the two by using the singular participle *to on* for "abstract being" and the plural participle *ta onta* for "the existent," "that which exists," "the things which exist." See Aristotle, *Metaphysics* iii 4.24–30.1001a4–35, xi 1.9–10.1059b22–32, xiv 2.5–16.1089a1–b24, and F. E. Peters, Greek *Philosophical Terms: A Historical Lexicon* (New York: New York University Press, 1967), pp. 141–42. Jason of Cyrene could have known of Aristotle's theories, and, in particular, of the passages in the *Metaphysics;* see Paul Moraux, *Der Aristotelismus bei den Griechen* (Berlin and New York: Walter de Gruyter, 1973), I, 3–31. Accordingly, Jason could have chosen to use the plural because the doctrine of creation *ex nihilo* does not discuss abstract being but denies that the world was created from something which existed previously. Although later readers appear to have found his formulation ambiguous, Jason could well have thought that he was avoiding ambiguity when he wrote "not from things which existed" (*ouk ex ontôn*) instead of "from what did not exist." Cf. Theophilus of Antioch *To Autolycus* ii 4, 10, 13.

However, all these considerations suggesting that Jason of Cyrene intended here to insist upon the doctrine of creation *ex nihilo* are of no avail against the arguments and wording he chose to use: they, indeed, exclude that interpretation. Both in vss. 22–23 and in vs. 28 the creation of the world and the growth of the embryo in the womb are placed on the same footing. Ancient intellectuals certainly knew that the matter for the growing embryo came from the mother. There is no record of any ancient belief that it grew *ex nihilo!* See Joseph Needham, *A History of Embryology* (New York: Abelard-Schuman, 1959), pp. 18–79. One might argue that vss. 22–23 say only that God in creating the universe also created man's reproductive capacity, but in vs. 28 God's creation of the universe is said to have been *in the same manner* as the human race now *comes to be* (present tense!).

It is true that there are variant readings in vs. 28. The present tense, "comes to be" (*ginetai*) is the reading of AVq. *L'* has the perfect tense (*gegenêtai*), so that the end of vs. 28 might be translated "and in the same manner the human race came to be." La^BMP have at the end of vs. 28 "and in the same manner He created the human race." La^LXV have at the end of vs. 28 only "and the human race." Then vs. 28 would say no more against creation *ex nihilo* than vss. 22–23.

In many cases a reading shared by L and La^{LXV} is superior to a reading of AVq, but here L and La do *not* agree. Lucian and the scribe underlying the text of La^{LXV} certainly are later than the development which saw Jews and Christians by the second century C.E. adhering to creation *ex nihilo*. If confronted by the embarrassing implications of the end of vs. 28, they would tend to emend the text. Indeed, they had probably already modified the words of the preceding clause, from *ouk ex onton* ("not after they existed" or "not from things which existed") of AVq, to *ex ouk ontôn* ("from the nonexistent") of L and to *ex nihilo* ("from nothing") of La^{LXV}. Can Greek Jews before the second century C.E., who disagreed with the doctrine of creation *ex nihilo*, have changed an original reading which agreed with L or La^{LXV}? It is most unlikely. The divergence of L from La^{LXV} would then be hard to explain. Moreover such Greek Jews probably would have held the doctrine of immortality rather than bodily resurrection and would have removed from our chapter the insistence on resurrection, as did the author of Fourth Maccabees.

What, then, is Jason doing in our passage? He is not troubled by the paradoxes urged later against the doctrine of bodily resurrection. We may guess that when he has the martyr predict that God will restore to him *"these* members," what he means is that God will create him again whole; Jason is not concerned whether the martyr's members will then be composed of the same matter as before. Jason argues against Jewish skeptics such as Qohelet and the Sadducees and against Greeks: resurrection only seems to be impossible. Human beings if they had not already seen the existence of the universe and human reproduction would declare them, too, to be impossible, for they can fathom neither. Yet the universe came into being after previously not existing, and so does every member of the human race. A dead human being has, indeed, ceased to exist, but he existed previously. Surely it is more conceivable that existence can be restored to what previously existed than that existence should be conferred on what did not exist! Therefore resurrection is *more conceivable* than the creation and than human reproduction!

Accordingly, I have translated *ouk ex ontôn* as "not after they existed." The peculiar word order arises from the fact that the mother wishes to persuade her son to accept temporary nonexistence: "Do not be afraid to cease to exist. You will live again, for it was not after existing that the world was created or that you yourself first came to be."

The Church Fathers and the scribes underlying L and La^{LXV} lived at a time when the doctrine of creation *ex nihilo* was thought to be fundamental to Christian faith. Searching the scriptures for support, they were glad to find in vs. 28 so philosophical a passage that seemed to lend itself to their purpose. Their aims blinded them to contrary implications. When they slightly altered the wording they believed they were only making things clearer for their readers, not falsifying the author's intentions.

22–23. Believers argued for resurrection by pointing to the mystery of the growth of the embryo in the womb; see TB *Sanhedrin* 92a.

The expression "spirit and life" (*to pneuma kai tên zôên*) is extremely strange and cannot be the result of the carelessness of the author or a scribe, for it occurs twice in our verses, and in reverse order (*tês zôês kai tou pneumatos*) it occurs at 14:46. An ancient Jew writing of the origin of human life, in a context which also mentions the creation, should use the language of Gen 2:7, "the breath [=spirit] *of* life," yet here we have "spirit [=breath] *and* life." It is not strange to find here "spirit" (Heb. *rūaḥ;* Gr. *pneuma*) instead of "breath" (Heb. *nešāmāh;* Gr. *pnoê*). In biblical Hebrew the two terms are synonymous (with Gen 2:7, cf. Gen 6:17 and 7:15, 22), and Jason again (see NOTE on vss. 22–29) probably reflects the language of the scriptural skeptic Qohelet (Eccles 12:7), who himself was paraphrasing Gen 2:7. But the substitution of "and" for "of" is unparalleled and requires explanation. At Greek Eccles 12:7 only the one term "spirit" is used, and there surely it means the "principle of life," that which makes the difference between a living and a dead body. A writer who did not know Gen 2:7 might have written here "spirit and [its result,] life" (cf. Grimm, p. 125), but the author knew Gen 2:7 and nevertheless departed from it.

Can "spirit" and "life" differ in that "spirit" is the higher manifestation, the rational soul, whereas "life" is mere animality or even vegetable existence? This seems the most probable solution, though admittedly the language of the Hebrew Bible and its Greek versions makes no such distinctions (Sjöberg, *"pneuma, pneumatikos* C," TDNT, VI [1968], 376–79). Furthermore, the terminology of pagan Greek philosophy would not lead one to expect a distinction between "spirit" (*pneuma*) and "life" (*zôê*). Aristotle and the Stoics do speak of higher and lower manifestations of "life" but also speak of correspondingly higher and lower manifestations of "spirit" (Kleinknecht, *"pneuma, pneumatikos* A," TDNT, VI [1968], 353–55), and even the Greek-Jewish book of Wisdom uses *pneuma* in a higher and a lower sense (Bieder, *"pneuma, pneumatikos* C," TDNT, VI [1968], 370–72). "Spirit" and "life" appear to be synonymous at Wisdom 15:11–12 and 16:13–14.

Philo in places uses *pneuma* in the same manner as the Stoics, but in other passages makes exactly the same distinction between *pneuma* and *zôê* as we have suggested here (see Bieder, TDNT, VI [1968], 372–73). At *Quod deterius potiori insidiari soleat* 23.83–84 Philo explains what Moses means by "spirit" (*pneuma*). We may summarize his explanation as follows: spirit is not air in motion but rather "a kind of impression stamped by the divine power"; Moses refers to it by the appropriate term "image," and thus indicates that God is the archetype of rational nature, whereas man in his highest form is a copy and likeness; man is a mixture of body and mind; our body partakes of "animal vitality" (*zôê*) but not of "intellect" (*nous*); man's thinking soul Moses calls "spirit" (*pneuma*).

Thus the philosophic tradition of Greek-speaking Jews did use the terms *zôê* and *pneuma* to distinguish the principle of animal vitality from the rational soul. In our passage we have an instance written about a century before Philo's philosophical career.

When she speaks of "determining the order of the composition of the elements" (*stoicheiôsin diarhythmizein*), the mother is using the technical language of a philosopher. The word *stoicheiôsis*, which I have translated "composition of the elements," etymologically means "the action or result of operating with *stoicheia.*" *Stoicheia* are, first, the letters of the alphabet. In philosophy, from Plato on, *stoicheia* are also the elements of which physical things are made (see the *Greek-English Lexicon* s.v. *stoicheion*, II, 1, 2). In Greek mathematics, *stoicheia* are the elements of proof. Our passage deals with the formation of the embryo in the womb and allows for *stoicheiôsis* only a meaning derived from the technical philosophical use of *stoicheion* as "physical element."

It was also the philosophers who spoke of the "proportioning" (*rhythmizein* or *diarhythmizein*) of the elements in the cosmos and in individual things, including the human body. See Aristotle, *De caelo* iii 8.306b, and cf. *Physics* vii 3.245b9–12. Philo, too, speaks of the proportioning of the elements, but without using the verb *rhythmizein;* see *Quis rerum divinarum heres* 30.152–53, where Philo says he cites the views of "expert physical scientists" (*hoi akribestata peri tôn tês physeôs*), and *De specialibus legibus* 16.208. Cf. also Wisdom 19:18.

23. The Greek of our verse is strange and so puzzled the scribes that in one place it is corrupt in all witnesses to the text and elsewhere it has suffered mistaken "emendations" in many witnesses. "Who shaped man's coming into being" (*ho plasas anthrôpou genesin*) is an unnatural expression, derived from Gen 2:7, 8, 15, where God is said to have "shaped" (Heb. *yṣr;* Gr. *plassein*) man, and from Greek Gen 5:1, "This is the book of the coming into being of mankind." Gen 5:1 introduces the account of how each human generation, male and female, gave rise to its successor. In our context the unnatural expression surely means "Who created and determined the form of the process of human reproduction." Lucian did not perceive the allusions to Genesis, and for good Greek altered *genesin* ("coming into being") to *genos* ("race").

The next phrase in all witnesses to the text has a repetition of *genesin,* which is so awkward in Greek that we can hardly believe that Jason or his stylish abridger intended to write it. We could translate the reading of AVqLa^LP by "and fathomed the coming into being of everything." Fortunately it is easy to explain how the awkward text arose and to correct it. We have established that Jason in our verse paraphrases Eccles 11:5 and 8:17. In those passages the word for the process of creation is not "coming into being" (*genesis*) but *poiêma* ("fashioning"). One of the commonest scribal errors, contamination, occurs when a scribe has two synonyms lying before him and after writing the first, instead of copying the second, writes the first again. Not only the source texts in Ecclesiastes suggest that contamination has occurred here. If the text of AVq at vs. 28 is correct (see NOTE ad loc.), that verse parallels ours. In vs. 28 "the human race" is said to "come into being" (*ginetai*) and God is said to have "fashioned" (*epoiêsen*) heaven and earth and all therein.

"Fathomed the fashioning" (*exheurôn poiêma*) is a strange expression, but the explanation is simple: Jason again is using the language of Eccles 8:17: man cannot "find out" or "fathom" (Heb. *mṣ';* Gr. *[ex]heurein*) what God has fashioned. Eccles 8:17 speaks of God's acts "under the sun," clearly after the creation. Though Greek Eccles 8:17 has *pepoiêmenon,* "what God has fashioned," presumably in the past, the Heb. *na'ăśāh* can mean the continuing present, as is suggested by Eccles 8:16. If so, our verse first speaks of God's original creation both of the cosmos and of man's reproductive capacity, then of His fashioning of things in the present (the secret of which He fathomed long ago) and, finally, of God's resurrection of the dead in the future.

Many readers failed to perceive the allusion to Eccles 8:17 and thought it pointless to say that God "fathomed" the fashioning of all. By a small alteration of *exeurôn* ("who fathomed") to *exereunôn* ("who seeks out") they produced a context which to them made sense: though man cannot watch the formation of the embryo in the uterus (vs. 22), God seeks out and observes the coming into being of all (La^LXP).

Lucian, too, failed to perceive the allusions to Ecclesiastes and wrote in our verse "who seeks out." He went still farther. On reading at the very end of our verse that God would resurrect the martyrs because they held themselves cheap for the sake of His laws, Lucian felt the verse should mention how God would know the intentions of the martyrs, so instead of "coming into being" (*genesin*) or "fashioning" (*poiêma*) he read "thought" (*phronêsin*). The scribe underlying La^BM appears to have proceeded similarly in reading "act" (*actum*).

with mercy. Cf. Greek Isa 54:7, which speaks of the period in which God seemed to have abandoned Israel as "a short time." The age of mercy is expected to be enduring. Jason may have viewed Isa 54:7 as echoing Isa 26:20. See next NOTE.

will restore. AVq have the Greek present tense, but it probably is the oracular present, to be translated as future (Kühner-Gerth, *Grammatik,* I, 138). Hence the Latin versions in giving the future tense may have had the same Greek text as AVq, and the change in L' to the Greek future tense was unnecessary. The wording may echo Greek Isa 26:12, "for You restored everything to us," which occurs in a context mentioning the annihilation of the wicked (vs. 11), the figurative pregnancy and labor pangs of the righteous (vss. 17–18), and the resurrection of the righteous dead (vs. 19).

24. In Greek the verse begins with two participial phrases, which I have translated by complete sentences. Since the two participial phrases are probably concessive, I have put a "nevertheless" before the remainder of the verse.

Scribes and translators who did not think of the possibility that the first two participles were concessive had trouble with the verse. Instead of the *hyphorômenos* (lit. "viewing with hostility") of AVq, L' and La have *hyperhorômenos* ("ignoring," "disdaining"), and the meaning of the elaborate paraphrase in Sy is similar.

On the Order of the King's Friends, see AB vol. 41, p. 232.

The king's officials made similar offers to old Mattathias and his sons. We have seen how Jason of Cyrene portrayed the martyrs as righteous counterparts of the sinful Hasmonaeans. Jason may have been pleased over the irony of having the king himself, not his officials, make the offers to a last surviving young child, not to an aged priest of high prestige and his vigorous sons. The boy will even be trusted with important functions!

27. As in vs. 22, the mother speaks as a mother, but Jason presents her as uttering a highly theatrical paradox: the boy is asked to have *pity* on his mother by allowing her to watch him, her last surviving son, be tortured to death.

The sequence of verbs, "carried . . . nursed . . . reared . . . brought," may be based on Lam 2:22. In the Masoretic Hebrew, that verse has only two verbs, *tippaḥtî wᵉribbîtî* ("dandled and raised"). The Greek renders the root *tpḥ* at Lam 2:20 by *thêlazein* ("suck at the breast"), though at Lam 2:22 it renders the root by *epekratêsa* ("possessed as my own"). Our verse could be an expansion on the Masoretic text itself. However, some Greek versions bear witness to a text with three verbs, *exethrepsa kai epekratêsa kai eplêthyna* ("reared and possessed as my own and made numerous," presumably from Heb. *giddaltī wᵉtippahtī wᵉribbītī*). All Greek versions mistranslate *ribbītī* ("raised") as "made numerous." Jason, however, could have understood a three-verb text of Lam 2:22 as meaning "reared and nursed and raised."

My translation follows the version of 71 107 347 La⁻ᴾ Pass.Mac. Sy Arm Cyprian Lucifer Augustine. Other witnesses to the text have yet another verb after "brought," *trophophorêsasan* ("nourished," "brought up"). As the text stands, the word is superfluous after "nursed" and "reared," both of which have the connotation "nourished." However, a scribe may have made a marginal note, explaining the rare word *trophophorêsasan* by the common word *ekthrepsasan* ("reared"), and, as often happens, the marginal note was absorbed into the text and the rare word, though preserved, was somehow displaced to an illogical position in the sentence. Even in paraphrasing Lam 2:22 Jason could have used the rare word, perhaps borrowing it from Greek Deut 1:31. Alternatively, however, a learned scribe who thought an allusion to Deut 1:31 would be striking may have made a marginal note containing the rare word, which then was absorbed into the text. If so, it becomes much easier to explain the illogical position of the rare word, and for that reason in my translation I have followed the witnesses which omit *trophophorêsasan*.

28. *to look . . . therein.* Jason may have been imitating Isa 40:26 and Exod 40:11.

29. Is there a reminiscence of Isa 51:13 in "Do not fear this executioner"? The Greek word for "executioner" is *dêmios* ("public one," i.e., "public slave"), for slaves owned by the state carried out executions. The mother uses the word to speak of the king!

In mentioning God's "mercy" (*eleos*), Jason is probably thinking of Greek Isa 54:8, 10, 56:1, 64:3, in all of which the word appears. The predicament of the helpless Jews matched the situation reflected in Isa 64:4–11.

30. *still . . . words.* I translate here the text of V and q⁻⁷¹ ¹⁰⁷ (*eti katalêgousês*), supported by A, which has the scribal blunder *eti katalgêgousês*. The verb *katalêgein* (lit. "leave off," "cease") occurs in the Greek Old Testament only here and at 9:5, and many scribes, surprised to find it, in both places thought it was an error for *katalegein* ("give a detailed speech"), a reading reflected here in 71 107 L La and at 9:5 in L Laᴮᴹ. Hanhart is probably wrong in following Kappler and changing *eti* ("still") to *arti* ("just"), the adverb which appears with *katalêgein* at 9:5. Kappler believed the scribes' perplexity came from the incompatibility of the adverb *eti* with a verb meaning "leave off" or "cease." My translation shows the two are compatible.

I refuse . . . forefathers. In so replying, the boy again becomes a counterpart of Mattathias. See I 2:18–22.

31–35. See vss. 16–19 and NOTES thereto.

31. *who have devised all evil.* Cf. Rom 1:30; Philo *In Flaccum* 4.20, 10.73.

33–38. Throughout our chapter, a dominating idea is the teaching of Deut 32:36: when God sees that His wayward people are utterly helpless, He will have mercy upon them and vindicate them. He will act when enough of their blood has been shed (cf. Deut 32:43; II 8:3–5). The mother and her sons do not *substitute* for the rest of suffering Israel. They are part of suffering Israel and hope that their deaths will mark the turning point prophesied by Moses, which is in any case sure to come. There is therefore nothing in our passage of the doctrine of vicarious atonement (cf. Kellermann, *Auferstanden,* pp. 12, 78); the idea is found at IV 1:11, 17:20–22.

33. Here the last martyred son, whose speech summarizes all the important lessons of our chapter, becomes also the spokesman for Jason's favorite explanation of Israel's suffering, the one enunciated at 6:12–16.

In speaking of God as "living," the boy's speech may echo David's at I Sam 17:26, 36. Like Goliath, Antiochus has shown disrespect to God. Or perhaps "living" is an allusion to Jer 10:10.

Here and in vs. 38, the boy alludes to the anger (*orgê*) of God, and the writer mentions it again at 8:5. If story three stood in the Common Source (see pp. 298–300), so may the reference to God's anger, and the author of I 1:64 may have taken it from there.

become reconciled with His servants may be an allusion to I Kings 8:34, 36; see NOTE on 1:5.

34. *soar . . . hopes.* An allusion to Isa 14:12–14. Antiochus IV is the latter-day king of Babylon and Assyria. Cf. 5:17, 21, and see NOTE on 5:21, *thinking . . . soar.* In this context I have translated *adêlois* (lit. "unclear," "uncertain") as "false."

give you the insolence . . . Heaven. The Greek has *phryattomenos* ("acting insolently"). The same Greek verb at Ps 2:1 translates *rāgᵉšū* ("rage"). Ps 2 contains a rebuke to presumptuous pagan kings. Was Jason alluding here to Ps 2?

lift your hand is omitted by *l* La⁻ᴾ Sy Arm Lucifer, but it is hard to see why a scribe would have added the phrase if it had not been there originally. The reading which omits the phrase might be translated "lead you to act insolently against the slaves of Heaven."

There is no way of carrying over into English the ambiguity of the Gr. *paidas,* which can mean both "slaves" and "children." Jason appears to have intended the word to carry both meanings simultaneously. For the meaning "children," compare the similar but unambiguous expressions at Greek Esther 8:12q and III 6:28, both written in or near our writer's times, and see also Enoch 101:1, Wisdom 2:13, 18, and Test Levi 4:2. The Jewish authors of the Hellenistic period drew on passages such as Deut 14:1; Isa 43:6, 63:16, 64:7, and Exod 4:22–23. If our verse alludes to Ps 2, Ps 2:7 and 12 also suggest that *paidas* here means "children." But our writer (cf. vs. 6) certainly alludes also to Deut 32:36, 43, and the unambiguous text of *L'* La Sy Arm Lucifer has "slaves." Forced in my translation to make a choice, I have rendered *paidas* as "children."

"Heaven" here, as frequently, is a synonym of "God."

35. God is still the *epoptês,* the One Who watches over the Jews, and He will punish their adversaries (cf. 3:39). *Epoptês* was widely used in pagan Greek as an epithet for a god (see the *Greek-English Lexicon,* s.v.).

36. *a short while* here echoes "a short time" in vs. 33. The syntax of the end of our verse has puzzled translators ancient and modern. They did not know how to construe the two words in the genitive case, *aenaou zôês,* and the verb

peptôkasi (lit. "they have fallen"). The scribes may have known their Greek better than the translators, since the Greek manuscripts have no variants affecting the points of difficulty. In fact, the genitive is the usual genitive with verbs of inheritance (Kühner-Gerth, *Grammatik,* I, 349–50), and *peptôkasi* means "they have fallen heir to" (cf. *Greek-English Lexicon* s.v. *piptô,* B, V, 1 and 3).

The covenant to which the boy refers is probably the one mentioned in Isa 55:2–3, ". . . Hearken diligently unto me, and you shall enjoy [lit. "eat"] what is good, and your soul shall delight in what is fat. Incline your ear and come to me. *Hearken, and your soul shall live, as I will make with you an everlasting covenant.* . . ." Cf. the commentaries of David Qimḥi and Abraham ibn Ezra to Isa 55:2–3.

The prediction that Antiochus will be punished reiterates vss. 17 and 19 and foreshadows ch. 9.

37–38. *have mercy upon* in the boy's prayer is probably a paraphrase of "relent" at Deut 32:36, the text on which the martyrs (vs. 6) placed their faith. The hope for the end of God's rage and the beginning of God's mercy foreshadows ch. 8, esp. 8:27. See above, p. 296. The prayer that Antiochus be afflicted and scourged probably looks to Deut 32:41, where God promises to "take vengeance" on His enemies and to "exact retribution" from His foes. The prayer that Antiochus thus will be forced to acknowledge that the Jews' God is the only deity foreshadows 9:12–17 (cf. 3:34, 36–39) and probably looks to Deut 32:39, "See, now, that I, I am He, and there is no God beside Me."

anger inflicted upon (*orgên* . . . *epi* . . . *epêgmenên*) may be an allusion to Greek Isa 26:21 (cf. Greek Isa 42:25). See also NOTE on vs. 33.

41. We are not even told whether the mother was killed or died from the strain of looking on. Has the abridger omitted the details? Or did Jason of Cyrene think that enough details had been given in vss. 3–5, 7, 10? The authors of Fourth Maccabees and *Yosefon* insisted on supplying detailed accounts of the mother's heroic death.

42. Cf. 3:40 and NOTE thereto.

Is our verse by the abridger? If so, Jason told more tales of martyrdom.

It is somewhat awkward to find the word *splanchnismous* ("compulsion to partake of the meat of pagan sacrifices") here, since the king is reported to have tried to force the seven brothers to eat only pork; nothing is said of the meat of pagan sacrifices. However, Jason may have assumed that the pork in ch. 7 came from pagan sacrifices, as did the meat mentioned at 6:7, 18–21. See also above, pp. 276, 283.

X. JUDAS' FIRST VICTORIES
(8:1–36)

8 ¹ Judas, also known as Maccabaeus, and his men stealthily slipped into the villages and enlisted the aid of their kinsmen and gained also the adherence of those who had remained faithful to Judaism. Thus they raised a force of about six thousand. ² They called upon the LORD to look upon His people, oppressed by all; to pity His temple, profaned by impious men; ³ to have mercy upon the city, which was being ruined and might soon be leveled to the ground; to hearken to the blood of the murdered, crying out to Him; ⁴ to be mindful of the wicked massacre of innocent babes and also to avenge the blasphemies perpetrated against His name.

⁵ Having gathered around him a band of partisans, Maccabaeus immediately became invincible over the gentiles, because the wrath of the LORD had turned to mercy. ⁶ Towns and villages Judas would take by surprise and burn. He would seize strategic points and rout considerable enemy forces. ⁷ He used especially the nights as cover for such raids. Reports of his bravery spread far and wide.

⁸ Philip observed how the man gradually made progress and then began to gain more and more through his victories. Accordingly, Philip wrote to Ptolemy, the governor of Coele-Syria and Phoenicia, to act in defense of the king's interests. ⁹ Ptolemy promptly appointed Nicanor son of Patroclus, a member of the Order of the King's Friends, First Class, and sent him in command of no less than twenty thousand gentiles of various stocks, with orders to destroy the entire people of Judaea. As co-commander with Nicanor, Ptolemy appointed Gorgias, a man who held the rank of general and had had experience in combat.

¹⁰ Nicanor resolved he would make up for the king, from the proceeds of selling the Jewish prisoners of war, the total of the tribute owed to the Romans, which amounted to two thousand talents. ¹¹ Immediately, he sent invitations to the coastal towns to come to an auc-

tion of Jewish slaves, promising to deliver ninety slaves for a talent. Little did he know that the Almighty's judgment would overtake him.

12 The news of Nicanor's march reached Judas. When he informed his men of the arrival of the army, 13 the cowards and those who lacked faith in the judgment of God ran away and removed themselves. 14 The rest sold what remained of their possessions, and together they prayed to the LORD, "Rescue us, for the impious Nicanor, before meeting us in battle, has sold us as slaves! 15 If not for our own sakes, act for the sake of Your covenants with our forefathers and for the sake of Your awesome and glorious name by which we are called."

16 Assembling his men, who numbered six thousand, Maccabaeus exhorted them, "Do not be terrified by the enemy, and do not fear the vast hordes of gentiles which are wickedly coming against us, but fight bravely. 17 Keep in mind the sight of the outrage they perpetrated upon the Holy Place in defiance of law and the wanton tortures they inflicted upon the city and also their abolition of our ancestral constitution. 18 They," he said, "put their trust in arms and in audacity. We, however, put our trust in God Almighty, Who can by a single nod overthrow not only those who are coming against us but even the entire universe." 19 He went on to tell them how God had come to our rescue in times of our forefathers: how He had done so in the time of Sennacherib, when one hundred eighty-five thousand perished; 20 and how He had done so at the battle fought against the Galatians in Babylonia: all the Jews, numbering eight thousand, had marched to meet the emergency in company with four thousand Macedonians, and when the Macedonians melted away, six thousand Jews destroyed one hundred twenty thousand through receiving the help of Heaven and took exceedingly vast quantities of spoils.

21 Through these stories he raised their spirits and made them ready to die in defense of their laws and their country. He then split his army into four units. 22 He appointed his brothers Simon, Joseph, and Jonathan as commanders of each regiment, assigning one thousand five hundred to each. 23 He also ordered his brother Ezra to read aloud the sacred book. After giving as the password "God's help," he took command of the first division himself and joined battle with Nicanor.

24 With the Almighty as their ally, they slaughtered over nine thousand of the enemy and left the greater part of Nicanor's army wounded and crippled, putting them all to flight. 25 They captured

the money of those who had come to purchase them as slaves. After pursuing the enemy for a considerable distance, they left off when the hour compelled them, 26 for it was the eve of the Sabbath. Accordingly, they did not prolong the pursuit. 27 Rather, they collected the arms of the enemy and stripped off the spoils and then turned to observe the Sabbath. They went to great lengths in blessing and thanking the LORD, Who had preserved them alive until this day, when drops of mercy had begun to fall upon them.

28 After the Sabbath, they allotted to the victims of torture and to the widows and to the orphans a share of the spoils and divided the rest among themselves. 29 With that done, the entire community turned in supplication to the merciful LORD, praying that He would be completely reconciled with His servants.

(*Vss. 30–32 are a parenthetical note clarifying Judas' policy after victories.*)

(30 Moreover, when they met the forces of Timotheus and Bacchides in battle, they slew over twenty thousand of them, captured towering fortresses, and gave the victims of torture, the orphans, and the widows and even the elderly, a share in the huge spoils equal to their own. 31 On that occasion they carefully collected the arms of the enemy and deposited them all at strategic points and brought the rest of the spoils to Jerusalem. 32 Of the two Timothei, they slew the phylarch, a most impious man who had done the Jews much harm.)

33 In the course of the victory celebration on their own soil they burned to death Kallisthenes and his followers, who had set fire to the sacred gateway. The men had taken refuge in a single hut, and thus they got the just recompense for their wickedness. 34 The heinous sinner Nicanor, who had brought one thousand dealers to sell them Jewish slaves, 35 through God's help was humilated by those whom he had regarded as beneath contempt. Putting off his splendid garments and dismissing his attendants, he fled cross-country like a runaway slave and was especially lucky to reach Antioch, considering that his army had been destroyed. 36 The man who had undertaken to raise the full amount of the tribute from the proceeds of selling the captivity of the people of Jerusalem now proclaimed that the Jews possessed a Champion and were invulnerable because they followed the laws which were His commandments.[a]

---

[a] In the abridged history, 10:1–8 stood immediately after 8:36 and was followed by 9:1–29, and then came 10:9 ff. See introductory NOTE on ch. 9.

NOTES

Ch. **8**. Except for the parenthetic note (vss. 30–32), the content of our chapter is parallel to that of I 3:1 – 4:26. The early stages of Judas' guerrilla warfare are narrated in almost exactly the same order, as if our two authors drew on the same source.

Judas' band grows and becomes invincible; they enforce the observance of the Torah in rural Judaea and smite Jewish sinners (vss. 1–6, "Judas . . . burn"; I 3:1–6, 8). They also defeat enemies who are not said to be Jews, and Judas' fame spreads (vss. 6–7, "He would seize . . . wide"; I 3:7, 9–26). The news reaches the higher levels of the royal government; as a result, the high officials Ptolemy, Nicanor, and Gorgias are involved in an expedition to destroy the Jews (vss. 8–9; I 3:27–40). Local slavers come, expecting to purchase Jewish prisoners of war (vss. 10–11; I 3:41).

The Jews learn of the expedition, pray, and observe the commandments of Deut 20:1–9 on preparation for war (vss. 12–15, 23; I 3:46–56). Judas exhorts his men to fight bravely (vss. 16–21[beginning]; I 3:58–60, 4:8–11). He appoints officers and deploys his army (vss. 21[end]–22; I 3:55, 4:12–13). The Jews go into battle and win (vss. 24–25[beginning]; I 4:14) but restrain their pursuit of the defeated foe (vs. 25[end]; I 4:16–18) and later take the spoils (vs. 27[beginning]; I 4:23) and turn in prayer to God (vs. 29; I 4:24). The enemy survivors report their defeat to the royal government (vss. 35–36; I 4:26).

On the other hand, there are differences between the account at I 3:1 – 4:25 and the one here. Some merely reflect differences in scale of narrative, perhaps as a result of the abridger's activity. See NOTE on vss. 5–7. Others probably reflect differences in the authors' literary interests. See NOTE on vss. 8–34 and NOTE on vss. 12–13.

Still other differences between our chapter and I 3:1 – 4:25 reflect the bitter differences of opinion between the two authors, each of whom would have been glad to discredit the other. See NOTES on vss. 8–34, 11–15, 16–23, and 28.

Not one of the differences between the two accounts invalidates the parallels which point to a common source. It is hard to see how such close parallels in two such different works could arise merely from the fact that the two narrate the same course of events. Even if they could so arise, there are more facts pointing to a common source.

In the absence of tape recorders and stenographers, ancient writers could hardly find good texts of what army commanders had said in exhorting their troops or in extemporizing prayers before battles. Nevertheless, for each prayer or speech in our chapter, one can find a parallel in the poems, prayers, and speeches of I 3:1 – 4:26; see NOTES on vss. 2–7, 11–15, 16, 18–19, and 27, *blessing . . . upon them.* We may infer that the author of the Common Source, too, was a literary artist who composed such pieces.

Furthermore, in some instances there are parallels not only of content but of phraseology, all the more surprising because Jason wrote in Greek, and his rival in Hebrew; see NOTE on vss. 2–7.

Conspicuously absent from the abridged history is any mention of Mattathias and his career, which are treated in I 2 immediately after the martyrdoms (I 1:60–64). We miss the old priest's act of zeal, the flight to the mountains, the legislation allowing defensive warfare on the Sabbath (a reaction to the mass slaughter of Sabbath observers), and the early guerrilla campaign. We have presented arguments to show how Jason of Cyrene deliberately omitted all mention of the "wicked" Mattathias (AB vol. 41, pp. 5–7, 79).

The seer of Enoch 90:6–9, too, passed over Mattathias in silence, though he recognized that Judas Maccabaeus, the "great horned ram" (see AB vol. 41, p. 41), arose from Jewish circles (sheep) distinct from the men of the seer's own sect (the seeing lambs). Though the Hasmonaean propagandist was later to insist (I 2:42) that the Asidaioi joined Mattathias, the seer (a contemporary of the events) has the men of his sect joining forces with the Hasmonaeans only after the rise of Judas Maccabaeus. Can we assert that the Common Source told of the events from Mattathias' act of zeal down through the early guerrilla campaign? We can. Mattathias' deeds belonged to the Age of Wonders. Even the author of Dan 11:34 appears to have expressed misgivings but also approval in calling Mattathias' enterprise a "small help," for Dan 10:1 – 12:3 was written before anything was known of the plans of Antiochus IV to march east in 165 B.C.E., and therefore probably before Judas' reputation became great; see AB vol. 41, p. 43. Later, the seer in Dan 12:7 refers unambiguously to Judas' force, and there he calls it the "hand of the Holy People," far more than a "small help"; see AB vol. 41, pp. 43, 48. The author of the Common Source was probably at least as favorably disposed to Mattathias as was the seer of Dan 11. See also NOTE on 6:11. Only sectarians like Jason needed to pass Mattathias over in silence. And even Jason (and perhaps earlier writers used by him) patterned the stories of Eleazar and the mother and her seven sons (6:18 – 7:41) as counterparts to Mattathias and his family (see NOTE on 6:18–31 and introductory NOTE to ch. 7).

The similarity of Mattathias' campaign as told in I 2:42–48 to that of Judas narrated here in vss. 1–6 and in I 3:1–8 does not show either that the campaign of Mattathias is an invention of the Hasmonaean propagandist to fill a blank in the old priest's career or that it was not reported in the Common Source (contrast Schunck, *Quellen,* pp. 58–62). In any case, tradition probably reported that Mattathias led a guerrilla campaign for one year (see below). Under the circumstances, what else would Mattathias have done during that time? And surely at first Judas followed his father's pattern of waging war!

In AB vol. 41, I did not scrutinize closely the traditions on Mattathias. I must therefore go on here to supply the lack. Other than the events from the deed of zeal through the guerrilla campaign, what facts did the Hasmonaean propagandist know about the old priest, and where, if not in the Common Source, did he get them?

At I 2:1–5 there is a genealogy of Mattathias and his sons. The names of the sons could have been derived from the narrative of the Common Source or from Hasmonaean family tradition. If the Common Source did not contain the names of Mattathias' father and of his priestly clan, the Hasmonaean propagandist could have derived them from family tradition and from the document at I 14:29. Mattathias' sometime connections with Jerusalem and his departure thence for Modeïn (I 2:1) had embarrassing potentialities but nevertheless are mentioned; clearly they stood in the author's source, which could well have been the Common Source. See NOTE on II 5:27.

The one other fact on Mattathias given in First Maccabees is the year date of his death, 146 Sel. (2:70). The Common Source may have given it, but hardly the high priestly journal of Menelaus or the records of the temple from the years of the persecution. Moreover, the formula of the date at I 2:70 suggests that it was drawn from no Jewish source: with the date at I 6:20, the one at I 2:70 is peculiar in First Maccabees because it uses the formula characteristic of the Seleucid Chronicle (year date alone) for an event of purely Jewish history (see Introduction, Part II, Section 3). The Hasmonaean propagandist derived the date at I 6:20 only by (incorrect) inference; see AB vol. 41, pp. 315–18. It is likely that he also only inferred the date of Mattathias' death. Hasmonaean family tradition may have said that Mattathias lived on as guerrilla chief for one year. The "year" (*ymym*) at Dan 11:33 could also have served as the clue or as confirmation (*ymym* there is usually translated "some days," but it is an idiom for "one year"; cf. Lev 25:29 in Hebrew and Greek). The Hasmonaean propagandist knew of one dated event which shortly preceded Mattathias' act of zeal: that of the desecration of the temple, on 15 Kislev, 145 Sel. (I 1:54). A career of one year for Mattathias would place his death in 146 Sel. Such seems to have been the author's inference. On I 2:49–69 as the author's own propagandistic composition, see pp. 30–31, esp. n. 12.

1. The resemblance to I 3:1–2 suggests a common source. An especially strong indication is the formal manner in which both name and nickname of Judas Maccabaeus are given, even though the reader has previously been introduced to both (I 2:4; II 5:27).

Our verse has characteristic differences from I 3:1–2. The author of First Maccabees admired Mattathias and Judas' brothers. Jason condemned Mattathias as wicked and disapproved of the brothers (see pp. 18–19 and AB vol. 41, p. 79). Hence, whereas there we read of "brothers," here we find "kinsmen," and whereas there we read of "the steadfast followers of his [i.e., Judas'] father," here we find "those who had remained faithful to Judaism."

The figure of six thousand here can be reconciled with the figure of three thousand at I 4:6 for Judas' combat force. Judas probably kept some troops in reserve. On the other hand, at II 8:13 we learn that part of Judas' force deserted, yet even so at II 8:16 we find Judas committing a force of six thousand at the battle against Nicanor. Thus we probably have another instance wherein Jason contradicts First Maccabees. Did he do so here on the basis of good evidence? He may have, especially if his original version had Judas' force as initially consisting of eight thousand and as reduced thereafter by desertion to six thousand. See below, NOTE on vs. 20.

Either author can be suspected of having arrived at his figure through a mere guess based on his own presuppositions. The core of the Hasmonaean army seems to have consisted of three thousand strongly loyal effectives (I 4:6, 7:40, 9:5). Other parties might, in response to events, join this nuclear force. The author of First Maccabees may have assumed that the victories over Nicanor and Gorgias were won solely by the nuclear force. Jason may have assumed that God's saving power would not have come to the aid of an unmixed Hasmonaean force, that other pious Jews must have constituted half of the victorious army.

2–7. Not only does the similarity of the content of our verses to that of I 3:3–9 strongly indicate a common source (as we argued above in the introductory NOTE to this chapter). The parallelism of the function of our verses to that of I 3:3–9 and the apparent echoes of phraseology point to the same conclusion.

The prayer in vss. 2–4 is the counterpart of the glorification of Judas in the poem at I 3:3–9. For the Hasmonaean propagandist, the strength of Judas' personality brought about the vital change for the better in the fortunes of Israel. For the writer here, the function of the prayer placed in the mouths of Judas and his men is to suggest that the blood of martyrs and the blasphemies of the enemy brought *God* to make Judas invincible. Both authors demonstrate how Judas participated in the vital change. The Common Source probably had a sober summary of the facts, as given above in the introductory NOTE to this chapter.

The prayer here may also be a deliberate contrast to the lament of Mattathias at I 2:7–13, where the old priest is ashamed how many Jews failed to resist but suffered the atrocities and gave up their lives. Jason trumpets his faith that God will be angry over the atrocities and will avenge the innocent dead.

The apparent verbal echoes suggesting a common source are the following:

The "band" (*systema*) of vs. 5 seems to echo the "band" (*athroisma*) at I 3:13. Because First Maccabees was written in Hebrew and the abridged history in Greek, it is harder to see how *systema* in vs. 5 could be an echo of the related Greek verb *synestēsato* ("he waged") at I 3:3. More obvious are the God's "wrath" (*orgē*) at vs. 5 and at I 3:8, "towns and villages" at vs. 6 and at I 3:8. The lion simile at I 3:4 may have been suggested by the nocturnal raids of II 8:7. The burning at vs. 6 may be a misreading of the "purging" mentioned at I 3:5 (see AB vol. 41, p. 244).

The poem at I 3:45 and the prayer at I 3:50–53 come before the battle against Nicanor, not before Judas' earliest victories, but vss. 2–4 here and I 3:45 and 50–53 are so similar as to suggest that they draw on a common source.

2. *oppressed.* I translate the reading of AqL (*kataponoumenon*). The verb *kataponein* ("oppress") is much less common in biblical Greek than *katapatein* ("trample"). Greeks appear to have used verbs from the two roots *ponein* and *patein* together as synonyms (Theophrastus, *Historia plantarum* viii 7.5). Hence, it is not surprising to find many witnesses to the text (*Vl* La^{-BM} Sy Arm) reading "trampled" and to find La^{BM} (*conculcatum et dolentem*, "trampled and tormented") reflecting both members of the synonymous pair.

In the poem at I 3:45 and in the prayer at I 3:50–53 the verb "trample" occurs, but with reference to the temple, not the people.

3–4. The plight of Jerusalem is mentioned at I 3:45, not in I 3:50–53.

I have added the words "of the murdered," though they are absent from the Greek and are superfluous for readers habituated to think of Gen 4:10.

Jason or his source surely must also have been thinking of the "blood of His servants" at Deut 32:43 and of the slaughtered victims and martyrs of chs. 6 and 7. On the significance of Deut 32:43 during the persecution, see above, pp. 294–95.

Jewish sin might be so heinous that even the shedding of Jewish blood on a vast scale would not suffice to rouse God. In that case, He still had promised to act on behalf of the Chosen People to preserve His own name from blasphemy (Ezek 20; Deut 32:27; cf. Ps 79:9). Antiochus IV committed blasphemy in his arrogance after the sack of Jerusalem (5:17, 21), repeating the sin of an earlier king of (As)syria (see II Kings 19:22–24; Isa 37:23–25). He also did so by presuming to set aside the Torah (cf. Dan 7:25, 11:36) and by forcing Jews to violate it, for violation of the Torah by Jews leads gentiles to speak of the ineffectiveness of God's commands and thus constitutes "blasphemy" (Ezek 36:16–27). It is also possible that Jason viewed the Greek name for the God of Israel as blasphemy (6:2).

The prayer of the warriors here seconds the prayer of the youngest son at 7:38, and later the warriors show their awareness of how the blood of martyrs contributed to victory (vs. 28).

5–7. Judas' earliest victories, listed in some detail in I 3:10–26, are here merely summarized. Cf. 2:21(end). Not found in First Maccabees at this stage is the remark in vs. 7 on how Judas used the cover of night. On the other hand, Jason omits the later use of the cover of night by Gorgias and Judas (I 4:1–6). Perhaps Jason moved the reference to the cover of night to vs. 7 because he reduced Gorgias to a mere name in his narrative in order to focus attention on Nicanor (see NOTE on vss. 8–35).

5. the wrath . . . mercy. The prayer in 7:38 begins to be fulfilled. See also NOTE on 7:33.

6. The towns and villages Judas struck were inhabited by sinners. In "rout considerable enemy forces" I translate the text of Aq. The complicated variants state that Judas killed large numbers of the enemy. In the abridged history there is an effort to stress how Judas slew the enemy; see NOTE on vss. 30–32. Scribes may have sensed the tendency. Hence, the description of Judas' campaigns with no reference to enemy dead is likely to be the original version, altered (except in Aq) by scribes.

7. spread. I translate diecheito, the reading of VqL La. A l 55 have diêcheito ("resounded").

8–35. Vss. 6–7 carry Judas' career through the victory over Seron, the point at which Judas' fame spreads far beyond the confines of Judaea (see I 3:13–26). The narrative of First Maccabees at that point has information not given here: Antiochus IV himself wished to suppress Judas; however, he found himself short of money and marched off in 147 Sel. with half the army to collect the taxes of the lightly held eastern regions of his empire, leaving his minister Lysias as viceroy in the west with the task of restoring order in Judaea (I 3:27–37).

There is a reason for the presence of the information in First Maccabees and for its absence here. The prophecies of Dan 7–12 failed to predict the king's departure. The author of First Maccabees held the prophecies to be a forgery and flaunted the fact of the expedition and was careful to date it in 147 Sel. As a believer in the prophecies, Jason of Cyrene had to omit mention of the expedition at this point. See AB vol. 41, pp. 46–47, 52.

On the other hand, where the author of First Maccabees erred, Jason delightedly corrected him. In fact, Antiochus' departure eastward probably had nothing to do with Judas' revolt. The king may well have been aware of the unrest in Judaea when he gave instructions to the chief minister Lysias, but the guerrilla warriors were still too small a concern to be a task for the viceroy himself. Yet in First Maccabees the viceroy sends out an expedition under three commanders, Nicanor, Gorgias, and Ptolemy son of Dorymenes (I 3:38); strangely, in the narrative of the campaign in I 3:40 – 4:25 Ptolemy son of Dorymenes is not further mentioned.

On these points, Jason gives a more credible account and rightly contradicts First Maccabees. The news of Judas' victories dismayed, not distant and mighty Antiochus, but Philip, the vulnerable commander of the garrison in the Akra. As a good subordinate, Philip, in turning for aid, went through the proper channels. He applied, not to the king, but to the provincial governor, Ptolemy son of Dorymenes (vs. 8). Not the viceroy but Ptolemy gave the order for the ensuing expedition of Nicanor and Gorgias, in which he himself did not serve as a commander. The Common Source regularly recorded the names of those who petitioned for expeditions against the pious as well as the names of those who sent and those who commanded the expeditions. Hence, Jason here probably drew on the Common Source.

The author of First Maccabees, on reading in his gentile source that the motive of Antiochus IV in marching east was to collect money, wrongly jumped to the conclusion that the cause of the king's pecuniary need was the guerrilla warfare of Judas! Even our author seems to have sensed the improbability of asserting that the Jewish resistance alone caused an appreciable drop in the royal revenues: he speaks in general terms of the "dissension and disorder which he had caused in his land by abrogating the laws which had been in force from the earliest times" (I 3:29; see AB vol. 41, NOTE on 3:29–30). But our author himself has excluded the possibility that gentiles could have contributed seriously to those disorders (I 1:42, 2:19). The author of First Maccabees went on to reason: if the Jewish guerrilla movement drove the king to march east, surely the king himself must have ordered the viceroy to see to the suppression of the rebels. Hence, our author "corrected" the account of the Common Source. He was faithful enough to it to preserve the name of Ptolemy son of Dorymenes even though that person plays no further role in his narrative.

Another contrast between the narrative in First Maccabees and the account here is surely a result of differences of literary technique. In I 3:38 – 4:25 the commander Gorgias has a role of his own. Here, he is a mere name in vs. 9. Jason organized his narrative in parallel sections around the Feast of Dedication and the Day of Nicanor and probably identified Nicanor here with Nicanor in II 14–15, since he uses the rare epithet *trisalitêrios* ("heinous sinner" or "thrice-accursed wretch") of both. Accordingly, Jason chose to focus attention on Nicanor, to the near exclusion of Gorgias.

Absent from the abridged history is the thorough knowledge of and intense interest in the geography of the Holy Land displayed in First Maccabees. The narrative here does not even mention that Ammaus (=Emmaus) was the site of the battle (I 4:3). See Map 4.

Having narrated Judas' minor early victories in vss. 6–7, Jason presents the victory over Nicanor as a resumption of God's miraculous interventions. The period of punishment is now over. Just as God in ch. 3 balked Heliodorus, who sought to gain for Seleucus IV money from the Jews, so here He balked Nicanor, who sought to gain for Antiochus IV money by selling Jews. Both Heliodorus and Nicanor finally have to acknowledge God's power to protect the Jews and their temple.

On the reflection, at Enoch 90:13–14, of the events in our passage, see AB vol. 41, n. 12, and below, NOTE on vss. 16–23.

8. On Philip, see 5:22 and NOTES thereto. On Ptolemy son of Dorymenes, see NOTE on 4:45–46. On Ptolemy's office and province, see NOTES on 3:5, *governor* and *Coele-Syria* and *Phoenicia*.

9. The author of First Maccabees followed a good source in stressing the high rank of the commanders sent against Judas (I 3:38), and Jason in vs. 9 gives the same stress. Both writers wanted the reader to understand that Judas and his men were already powerful enough to require the use of such high officers.

Nicanor son of Patroclus. "Nicanor" was a common name, and in the sources on our period it appears numerous times. We lack evidence to tell us whether any of those mentioned are one and the same person. See AB vol. 41, p. 259. Jason implies that this Nicanor and the one in 14:12 – 15:37 are the same person (see NOTE on vss. 8–35), but he may well be wrong.

Order . . . Class. On the gradations in the Order of the King's Friends, see Bickerman, *Institutions*, pp. 41–42. Nicanor belongs to the highest class of Friends.

twenty thousand. Is the figure exaggerated, like so many others given by ancient writers for the size of enemy forces? It is more reasonable than those at the parallel passage, I 3:39. See NOTE on vs. 24 and AB vol. 41, p. 259.

gentiles of various stocks. I translate the reading of AqL'−62 381, *pamphylôn ethnê*. Cf. I 3:39–41, where the Philistines are called *allophyloi* ("people of foreign stock"). For the construction *pamphylôn ethnê* ("gentiles [namely, people] of various stocks"), see Kühner-Gerth, *Grammatik*, I, 264. The word *pamphylos* ("of various stocks") is normally an adjective, though here the word is treated as a noun. As a noun, *Pamphylos* can mean "Pamphylian" (from Pamphylia in southwestern Asia Minor). Well-informed scribes, however, would not so construe the word, because the terms of the peace of Apameia (188 B.C.E.) forbade Seleucid recruiting in Pamphylia (see AB vol. 41, NOTE on 6:29), and in any case it was incredible that Pamphylians constituted so high a percentage of the Seleucid army (see Launey, *Recherches*, pp. 466–71). The somewhat unusual idiom here puzzled many of the scribes and translators, as can be seen from the variants in the Greek manuscripts and the Latin versions and from the omission of the words by the Syriac.

Gorgias. We lack evidence to prove that Gorgias here and at 10:14 and at 12:32–37 are one and the same. The description here of Gorgias favors the identification: such a man would be likely to share command of an important expedition and then to govern strategic areas. However, Gorgias' tactical blunders (I 4:1–22) contributed to the victory of Judas narrated here. Could Lysias have continued to trust him? Perhaps. On the other hand, it is very likely that Gorgias at 10:14 and at 12:32–37 are the same man; see NOTE on 10:14–15.

general. The Greek word is *stratêgos.* On its many meanings in the Seleucid empire, see Bengtson, *Strategie,* II, 1–193.

10. I have translated *diestêsato* as "resolved" though I know of no parallel in ancient Greek. Ordinarily the verb would mean "to separate" or "to be separated," "to be divided." Only one Greek scribe may show puzzlement (ms. 52 reads *synestêsato,* presumably "contrived"). I follow La^LXV (*constituit*), supported by La^P (*statuit*). La^BM have "promised" (*promisit, promittens*), and Sy has both "promised and resolved" (*'štwdy . . . w'qym*). "Promised" is a guess based on misconstruing *tôi basilei* as "to the king" rather than "for the king." The guess is surely wrong: the king was not present to receive a promise (I 3:27–39), and Jason has Nicanor dealing only with the governor Ptolemy, not with the king.

Antiochus IV went down in history as a king with a thirst for money. The reasons for his thirst were probably his ambitious projects and his extravagant if capricious generosity. See I 3:30; J. *AJ* xii 7.2.294, *Ap.* ii 7.83–84; Polybius xxix 24.13, xxx 25–26; Mørkholm, pp. 51–63; AB vol. 41, pp. 104–21, 310. Jason and the author of First Maccabees probably drew their information on this aspect of Antiochus IV from the Seleucid Chronicle.

By the first century B.C.E., however, ambition and extravagance apparently were considered insufficient to explain the greed of Antiochus IV. The author of I 3:29 jumped to the conclusion that the unrest caused by Antiochus' civic policies had drastically depleted the treasury; see AB vol. 41, pp. 251–52. Jason here implies that Antiochus IV had a grave need for money in order to pay the tribute imposed upon the Seleucid empire by the Romans. In so doing, Jason, too, probably jumps to an erroneous conclusion. Antiochus III, after his defeat in late 190 B.C.E., had been required to pay Rome 500 talents and 2,500 more upon ratification of the peace treaty by the Roman people (Polybius xxi 17.4–5; Livy xxxvii 45.14). Thereafter, by the terms of the peace of Apameia, he was to pay 12,000 talents in twelve equal yearly installments (Polybius xxi 45.21 Paton [46.21 Buettner-Wobst]; Livy xxxviii 38.13). The ensuing financial troubles of the Seleucid kings were well known: Antiochus III and perhaps Seleucus IV were thereby driven to attempt temple robbery; see ch. 3 and AB vol. 41, pp. 309, 352–53, and Mørkholm, pp. 31–34. However, Antiochus IV, in 173 B.C.E., probably paid in full the remaining amount of the indemnity to the Romans, with apologies for delay (Livy xlii 6.7; Mørkholm, pp. 64–65). By the terms of the peace of Apameia, the payments of the indemnity should have been complete by 177 or 176 B.C.E.

Jason could hardly be right even if we lacked Livy's testimony on Antiochus' payment in 173 B.C.E. If Jason knew the peace terms, our passage states that two installments still remained to be paid in 165 B.C.E., three years after Antiochus IV had shown himself so eager to comply with the Romans that he withdrew from Egypt. The rich spoils of Egypt, which he was allowed to keep (Polybius xxx 26.9, *apud* Athenaeus x 439), surely would have sufficed to cover any amount still owed to Rome.

Ninety slaves per talent means that each slave would sell for 66 2/3 drachmas. The scanty information in our possession confirms the implication here, that 66 2/3 drachmas for a slave, even as a wholesale price, was very low; see William L. Westermann, *The Slave Systems of Greek and Roman Antiquity* (Philadelphia: American Philosophical Society, 1955), pp. 36–37.

11–15. Again Jason's account diverges from that at I 3:40–54. At I 3:41 the slave dealers are not said to have been invited by Nicanor; they come spontaneously on hearing of the punitive expedition. In I 3:46–54, the author reports an assembly of repentant Israel at Mizpah under Judas and his brothers parallel to the assembly at Mizpah under Samuel, and the Jews follow procedures used by Hezekiah when faced by Sennacherib's ultimatum. In their prayers at I 3:47–53 Judas and his men strive to demonstrate in detail how helpless they are unless God aids them, but they are conspicuously silent about the martyrs. The parallels to procedure followed earlier by heroes in scripture probably served the purposes of Hasmonaean dynastic propaganda, as did the silence on martyrdom; see AB vol. 41, pp. 5–12, 77–78, 261–63. Accordingly, we are not surprised to find that anti-Hasmonaean Jason gave a different account. He says nothing of Mizpah, and in the narrative and in the quoted prayer he puts the stress upon the arrogance of Nicanor: even before fighting the battle, Nicanor has invited the slave dealers to buy up the captured Jews. Jason may be correct in saying that the slavers came at Nicanor's invitation, but in implying that Nicanor's procedure was unusual, Jason has written a piece of unconvincing rhetoric. In ancient times armies confident of victory would indeed come with fetters or slavers, expecting to have or sell the vanquished as slaves (see, e.g., Herodotus i 66; Pausanias viii 47.2).

The Common Source, too, probably had at this point a prayer of Judas and his men, one which mentioned at least the plot of the gentiles against the Jews as in vs. 14 and in I 3:52.

12–13. At I 3:55–56 the timid leave under *Judas' orders*, as Judas observes the requirements of Deut 20:8. On Jason's avoidance of portraying Judas as obeying Deut 20:1–9, see NOTE on vss. 16–23. Here, however, his main intention may have been to expose the cowards and those of little faith to condemnation: their own vices removed them from the battle.

14. Judas and his men were fugitive outlaws and could have had very little property left in their possession. That, too, they now sell. Jason takes the reason for granted and does not tell us why. Perhaps we are to think they believed that money was the safest way of preserving and transmitting a patrimony to their heirs. Jason points up the contrast: before the battle, the Jews sell in desperation while Nicanor "sells" in overconfidence.

15. Our verse is a traditional formula of Jewish prayer, based upon such verses as Lev 26:42–45; Deut 28:10; I Sam 12:22; Isa 43:7; Jer 14:7; Ezek 36:22; Dan 9:19, and II Chron 7:14. Cf. Sir 36:17. The formula is found in the prayer *Ābīnū malkēnū* (*Seder 'Abodat Yisra'el*, ed. by Baer, p. 393): "Our Father our King, act for Your sake if not for ours. . . . Our Father our

King, act for the sake of Your mighty and awesome name by which we are called." On the prayer, see Elbogen, *Der jüdische Gottesdienst,* pp. 147–48. In the Hebrew Bible the Jews are frequently called "the people of the LORD" (Num 11:29, etc.).

16–23. Omitted here is the story of how Gorgias attempted to take Judas by surprise and how Judas remarkably (miraculously, according to Enoch 90:14; see AB vol. 41, p. 41, n. 12) found out and himself took both Nicanor and Gorgias by surprise. One would like to know why either the abridger or the author passed over so edifying a miracle. The abridged history elsewhere contains matter apparently drawn from Enoch (see NOTE on ch. 15), so the sectarian nature of that prophecy does not explain the omission here. My guess is that Jason read Dan 11:45 – 12:1 as predicting that superhuman apparitions would come to the aid of the Jews only after the death of the King of the North; perhaps he also read Isa 30:15–36 as predicting that divine apparitions would come to their aid only after the idols of the Abomination of Desolation had been removed from the temple (see NOTE on 10:24–38). If so, he would not take Enoch 90:14 as evidence that, already before going into battle with Nicanor and Gorgias, Judas Maccabaeus had received the help of such an apparition.

The author of First Maccabees displays the priestly lineage of the Hasmonaeans (I 2:1) and takes pains to show (I 3:55–60, 4:8–11) that the Torah (Deut 20:1–9; Exod 18:21) not only taught Judas what tactics a priest leading the people in war should follow but also supplied him with the examples of how God's aid can bring victory. Jason, a pious Jew, pointedly refrains from the procedure of his opponent! Jason never says explicitly that Judas came from a priestly family, and here, unlike I 3:55–56, there is no remark that Judas' procedure followed the commandments of the Torah. Here Judas uses the example of God's victory over Sennacherib, from outside the Torah (II Kings 18:13 – 19:37; Isa 36–37), and he even cites an example altogether outside scripture. The four-division military formation of vs. 21 has no parallel in the Torah, and in scripture it has only the inauspicious parallel of Abimelech at Judg 9:34.

The author of First Maccabees takes such pains to display the obedience of the Hasmonaeans to the rulings of scripture because he wishes to demonstrate how the dynasty earned God's designation of them to be high priests and rulers. We are therefore not surprised that pious Jason, who surely believed that Judas obeyed the Torah, told the story differently. Jason's wish to deny the legitimacy of the Hasmonaean dynasty clearly was a factor here, as we learn from vss. 21–22, where the mention of the formation in four divisions, each commanded by a Hasmonaean brother, allows Jason to name the discredited Joseph as a brother of Judas, alongside the famous Simon and Jonathan. Perhaps there was a good source for the formation in four divisions, since Jason had two names, not one, to add to the Hasmonaean family and thus would have been glad to have five divisions instead of four. He is still able to bring in the discredited Ezra (=Azariah) as a brother by saying that Ezra performed the task of reading from the Torah before battle. Though the task is one for a priest (Deut 20:2–4), Jason nevertheless does not say that Ezra was a priest. See also p. 299 and AB vol. 41, pp. 79–80.

16. At AB vol. 41, p. 264, NOTE on I 4:6, I refer the reader to this NOTE, but the discussion of the number of Judas' men is now in the NOTE on vs. 1.

The similarity of our verse to I 3:58(first half) cannot be used to demonstrate the existence of our Common Source: both passages draw on Deut 20:1–3. See also NOTE on vs. 1.

17. Cf. I 3:58(second half)–59. Antiochus' desecration of the temple obviously violated the Torah, but by "in defiance of law" (anomôs) Jason may mean that the king violated the usages of civilized mankind. Pagans, too, considered it forbidden either to sack temples of peoples not in revolt or to violate the established rituals of any god (cf. Isocrates 7.30). By "ancestral constitution" Jason again means the Torah. For Greeks, abolition of a people's constitution was a heinous act (Demosthenes Oration 24.152; Plato Laws ix 864d; Xenophon Hellenica ii 3.38, etc.).

18–19. Cf. I 4:8–11, and see AB vol. 41, p. 264.

18. Cf. Ps 20:8.

20. Jason appears to have had an interest in presenting Judas as citing a nonscriptural example (see NOTE on vss. 16–23), but there is no reason to think he would fabricate a fiction here. His historical errors are mistakes and pieces of literary license acceptable in his time, not forgeries. There is nothing strange about the use of Jewish soldiers to defend the Seleucid empire (see my article in the Cambridge History of Judaism, vol. I, Part II, ch. 8, n. 5). Even if the story here deals not with regular soldiers but with men conscripted in an emergency, there is no doubt that the Jews constituted a significant portion of the population of Babylonia, and they may have been preferred over other ethnic stocks for their loyalty and martial qualities. See above, pp. 150–51; J. Ap. i 38.192, AJ xi 8.5.338; AB vol. 41, p. 486, vs. 24i, and p. 498; Schürer, III, 6–10; Launey, Recherches, pp. 582–83.

However, nowhere in our sources are Galatians as a nation said to have come near Babylonia. The Galatians were fierce Celtic tribes who invaded the Greek-speaking world in the first half of the third century B.C. A large body of them settled in central Asia Minor in that same century and long were a menace to the whole region. See Esther Hansen, The Attalids of Pergamon (2d ed.; "Cornell Studies in Classical Philology"; Ithaca and London: Cornell University Press, 1971), vol. 36, pp. 28–31. The Galatians ceased to be a major danger to their neighbors after a Roman expedition under Gnaeus Manlius Vulso pacified them in 189–188, though Eumenes II of Pergamum had to put down a Galatian uprising in 168–166. See Hansen, ibid., pp. 88–91, 120–26; Polybius xxi 40.1–2, and cf. I 8:2 and AB vol. 41, pp. 350–51.

Central Asia Minor is a long way from Babylonia. Can a Galatian force have penetrated so far, between the first half of the third century and Manlius Vulso's pacification, without leaving another trace in our sources? It is most unlikely. The Greek historian Polybius would have mentioned the fact if it had occurred in or after 220. Our sources on the mid-third century are extremely scanty, but so formidable were the Galatians that the Hellenistic kings boasted loudly of any victories they won against those fierce warriors (Hansen, Attalids, pp. 30–33, 123–24; Will, Histoire, I, 89–92, 124–25, 267). Nor can the battle fought by Antiochus I (281–261) against the Galatians, the place of which is not specified in the sources, be identified with the one here. According to the sources, it had to be much closer to the Ionian cities of western Asia Minor. See Bezalel Bar-Kochva, "On the Sources and Chronology of Antiochus I's Battle Against the Galatians," *Proceedings of the Cambridge Philological Society* 199 (1973), 1–6(second par.), 7(last par.)–8.

If a national force of Galatians cannot have invaded Babylonia, there is another possibility: the Galatians could have served some other power as mercenaries, and the local population and the power governing Babylonia could have had some reason to speak of the enemy not by his proper name but by the name of his mercenaries. The Galatians in fact were famous as mercenaries (Launey, *Recherches,* pp. 490–534). Seleucus II fought a bitter war against his younger brother, Antiochus Hierax, in which Galatians constituted the backbone of Hierax's force. Attalus I of Pergamum (241–197) in the inscriptions commemorating his victories mentioned one over "Galatians and Antiochus [Hierax]," then one over Galatians alone, and then one or two over Antiochus alone (OGIS 275, 276, 278, 279). One need not infer therefrom that Galatians ceased to serve Antiochus Hierax as mercenaries (cf. Will, *Histoire,* I, 267). Rather, in the battles mentioned in OGIS 275–276 the Galatians fought as members of their tribes, as allies of Antiochus Hierax. Later, the "national" troops of the Galatian tribes were not involved, but numerous Galatians still served Hierax as mercenaries (see Justin xxvii 2.10–12, 3.1–5).

Justin reports (xxvii 3.1 and 7) that Hierax was defeated by "Eumenes king of Bithynia" (an error for "Attalus I king of Pergamum"), who took over most of Asia Minor, but even thereafter Hierax pursued his war with Seleucus II, until the forces of Seleucus defeated him and forced him to flee to his father-in-law, the king of Cappadocia. The theater of this warfare can hardly have been Asia Minor if Attalus I held most of it and if Hierax ultimately fled to Cappadocia. Only isolated scraps survive to give us the information we need. From Pompeius Trogus *Prologue* to Book xxvii, we learn that it was in Mesopotamia that Hierax met defeat at the hands of his brother's army, but from Polyaenus *Stratêgêmata* iv 17 we learn that "Antiochus, the rebel against his brother Seleucus, fled *to* Mesopotamia and from there passed through the mountains of Armenia." Hellenistic writers could use "Mesopotamia" loosely to mean the entire land between the Tigris and Euphrates. But the provincial boundary lines usually led them to distinguish Mesopotamia from Babylonia. Mesopotamia lay northwest of Babylonia, extending from present-day Baghdad northwestward through the land between the Tigris and Euphrates, up to the mountains of Armenia, the range running east and west, from the neighborhood of Nisibis to the great bend of the Euphrates. See Map 2 and Arrian iii 7.3; Diodorus xviii 3.3; W. Röllig, "Mesopotamia," Der kleine Pauly, III (1969), 1237–38, and F. Schachermeyr, "Mesopotamien," PW, XV (1932), 1106–8. The summary prologue by Pompeius Trogus could well have used "Mesopotamia" loosely. Polyaenus wrote with precision. He has Hierax fleeing from his brother's armies *into* Mesopotamia and thence into Armenia; the direction is consistently northwestward. We may thus infer that Seleucus' forces defeated Hierax and his Galatian mercenaries in Babylonia, and that the battle described here figured in the events.

There would have been good reason for the regime of Seleucus II to speak of the rebel forces as "Galatians" and to avoid using the name of his brother Antiochus. The marauding Galatians were hated and dreaded throughout Asia (see above, p. 331, and Livy xxxviii 16.13; Justin xxvii 3.5). On the other hand, the Macedonian soldiers and settlers and even the native peoples seem to have displayed loyalty to the Seleucid dynasty. "Antiochus" was a dynastic name which had already been borne by two Seleucid kings (see Edwyn R. Bevan, *The House of Seleucus* [London: Edward Arnold, 1902], I, 53–54, 131, 142–43; Will, *Histoire*, I, 229; and cf. Justin xxxvi 1.3), and the first Antiochus had won distinction as victor over the Galatians. The need to call up Jewish troops would have been all the greater if Seleucus II at the time was indeed away campaigning in Iran with the bulk of the imperial army (see Will, *Histoire*, I, 278–81). Eusebius dates the battle against Hierax in which Attalus I won most of Asia Minor in 229/8 and Hierax's death as a fugitive in Thrace in 228/7 (*Chronicorum libri duo,* ed. by Alfred Schoene [Berlin: Weidmann, 1866–75], I, 254; Porphyry FGH 260, F 32.8; cf. Will, *Histoire*, I, 266–69).

Polyaenus (*Stratêgêmata* iv 17) reports that the fugitive Hierax in the mountains of Armenia first lost a battle to his brother's commanders and then treacherously ambushed *four thousand* troops of the victorious army. The prestige thus won by Hierax must have been brief, since we find him next as a fugitive in Cappadocia. The coincidence of the figure of four thousand for the ambushed troops in Polyaenus and for the Macedonian troops here is no reason to identify the treacherous ambush by the desperate Hierax in Armenia with the fearsome onslaught described here of Galatian mercenaries in Babylonia; correct accordingly Bar-Kochva, *Proceedings of the Cambridge Philological Association* 199 (1973), 6(third par.)–7(first par.).

The strange change in the number of the Jews facing the Galatians, from eight thousand to six thousand, is too well attested (AV 55 311 347 771 La^{LXV} Arm) to be dismissed as a scribal error. Rather, the "consistent" reading of other witnesses to the text is probably to be dismissed as a misguided scribal emendation. The simplest explanation would be that two thousand Jews, too, melted away in the same manner as all the Macedonians, so that only six thousand remained. The abridger or an early scribe may have omitted a clause saying so. Thus, Jason may have presented in the story of the battle against the Galatians an exact parallel to Judas' situation as described in vss. 13 and 16: six thousand Jews faced the enemy after the desertion of cowards from a larger force reduced the numbers of the army.

In view of the Galatians' reputation there is nothing incredible about the panic of the Macedonians. The word "Macedonian" may well be taken literally. We have no way of telling whether the Jews and Macedonians were regular troops or a hastily levied emergency force. If Seleucus II was indeed campaigning in Iran with the bulk of the imperial army, both contingents here probably consisted of emergency conscripts. Macedonians certainly constituted a large part of the Seleucid army (Bezalel Bar-Kochva, *The Seleucid Army* ["Cambridge Classical Studies"; Cambridge: Cambridge University Press, 1976], index s.v. Macedonians), and there were Macedonian settlers in Babylonia who could be levied in an emergency (J. *AJ* xiii 5.11.185; the great Graeco-Macedonian city of Seleuceia-on-the-Tigris lay in Babylonia). On the other hand "Macedonian" here may mean "troops levied by the Seleucid empire"; see Charles Edson, *"Imperium Macedonicum:* The Seleucid Empire and the Literary Evidence," *Classical Philology,* 53 (1958), 153–70, esp. p. 163.

I have given "melted away" as the translation of *aporoumenôn* by taking the root of the verb to be *rein* ("flow") rather than *aporein* ("be at a loss"); cf. Polybius v 26.11. Although one might have expected the derivative of *rein* to be spelled *aporroumenôn,* in Hellenistic Greek a single rho in such cases was common. See Blass-Debrunner-Rehkopf, *Grammatik,* p. 11, section 11.

In giving the number of the Galatians as 120,000, Jason or his source merely followed the tendency of all ancient writers to exaggerate the number of a defeated enemy. See NOTE on vs. 24. The total force of the Galatian tribes was only a fraction of the figure here (Livy xxxviii 16.2, 9). The number might have been taken from Judg 8:10.

took . . . spoils. I translate the reading *ôpheleian elabon hyper ti pamplêthê,* which underlay the Latin translations and is reflected by L'^{-381}. The Greek idiom *hyper ti* means "beyond measure," "exceedingly," and is found also at 15:11 and at Epistle of Barnabas 1:2. Many scribes and translators did not know the idiom, nor did they know that *ôpheleian* ("benefit") can also mean "spoils." La^{LX} have *beneficia acceperunt super multitudinem* ("they got benefits over the multitude"), which is nonsense, but still, *super* reflects *hyper,* and *multitudinem, pamplêthê.* In La^V, *pro his* reflects *hyper ti,* and *plurima, pamplêthê.* In La^B *paene* reflects *hyper ti* and *uniuersam multitudinem, pamplêthê;* the case is similar with *paene* and *omnem multitudinem* in La^M and with *paene* and *plurima* in La^P.

Most puzzled Greek scribes altered the text to read simply *ôpheleian pollên elabon* ("took much spoil"). The text of L'^{-381}, however, preserves both readings side by side, though only 64 and 236 preserve them completely free of corruptions (*ôpheleian pollên elabon hyper ti pamplêthê*).

22–23. Most witnesses to the text have difficult and surely corrupt readings. There is reason to believe that no witness preserves completely the original text. AVqLa^{-V} have "He appointed his brothers commanders of each force, Simon and Joseph and Jonathan, assigning one thousand five hundred to each, as well as Eleazar. After reading aloud the sacred book and after giving as the password 'God's help,' he took command of the first division himself. . . ." Eleazar enters awkwardly. Three brothers are already each in command of a force, Judas takes command of a force himself, yet there are altogether only four divisions (vs. 21). What is the function of Eleazar?

The names of Judas' brothers were famous from First Maccabees and Josephus' works, yet here an otherwise unknown "Joseph" appears, and in La and Arm we have "Ezra" instead of "Eleazar." "Joseph" and "Ezra" are probably the original readings here, since otherwise it would be hard to explain how they entered the text. See pp. 299–300.

My translation is based on a hypothetical original text which had somewhat careless syntax. From that original, it is easy to explain how all other readings arose. I have accepted the reading "Ezra" from La and Arm. The careless syntax can still be seen in L' and is presupposed by Sy and perhaps by La^V. The Greek participle *taxas* in vs. 22 can be translated both "he appointed" and "he ordered." The syntax is careless here, because the author used both meanings simultaneously, a condition called "zeugma." As "he appointed," *taxas* is followed by the names of the persons appointed (Simon, Joseph, and Jonathan) and the office (commanders) to which they are appointed. As "he commanded," *taxas* is followed by the name (in the accusative case) of the person receiving the command (Ezra) and the infinitive of the verb of the action commanded (*paranagnônai* ["read aloud"]). English usage requires that the beginning of vs. 23 have its subject and verb, "He commanded," but in Greek the participle *taxas* appears only once, in vs. 22. The infinitive *paranagnônai* is preserved in vs. 23 in *L* and is reflected in Sy, but it is far removed from the verb on which it depends, *taxas* in vs. 22. So much so that the connection between the two eluded the scribes underlying AVqLa⁻ᵛ, who took the apparently dangling infinitive and turned it into a nominative participle, *paranagnous:* Judas read the sacred book (as one might expect from I 3:55–56, 4:8–11, and Deut 20:2–9) and also gave the password and took command of the first division. Ezra, alias Eleazar, was left to dangle, presumably as an extra commander available to replace any of his brothers should one be incapacitated.

As reconstructed by me the text still contains clumsy but not impossible Greek. Vs. 22 would have been clearer had the writer written "He appointed each of his brothers . . . as a commander of a force"; see Kühner-Gerth, *Grammatik*, I, 286–88. The word "each" (*hekateras*) modifying "force" properly means only "each [of two]." It may be a slip of the pen, but Hellenistic writers could use the word loosely; see Mayser, II 2, 92–93.

23. *password "God's help."* Pagans and Christians used similar passwords (Xenophon *Anabasis* i 8:17; Appian *Bellum Civile* ii 76; Vegetius iii 3, etc.).

division. Judas surely did not assign to himself a smaller unit than those he had allotted to his brothers. The Greek word here is *speira*. The writer here would thus be using the word of a unit of at least 1,500 men. For us this may be a clue that he wrote no earlier than the end of the second century B.C.E. Until that time, so far as we know, a *speira* had far fewer than 1,500 men, even when the word was used to name the Roman tactical unit, which was then the maniple (see NOTE on 5:2). However, at the end of the second century B.C.E., through the reforms of Gaius Marius, the Roman tactical unit ceased to be the maniple and became the cohort, a "regiment" of 500 or 1,000 men, and *speira* became the Greek word for the Roman cohort. On the other hand, the *speira* of 1,500 here is considerably larger even than a Roman cohort of 1,000, so that the use of the word here is not a secure clue as to date. Is the use of *speira* here a hint that Judas imitated Roman tactics against a Macedonian phalanx?

24. God answered the prayers of vss. 14–15. The figure of 9,000 enemy dead here far exceeds the 3,000 at I 4:15, which should be correct. Nothing tells us how Jason arrived at his larger figure. Ancient authors of all nationalities tended to exaggerate the size of an enemy army; see Hans Delbrück, *Numbers in History* (London: University of London Press, 1913), esp. pp. 12–25, and AB vol. 41, p. 259.

25–26. Jason here sees, in Judas' refusal to press the pursuit of the defeated enemy, Judas' observance of the Sabbath. Since Jason makes no reference to Gorgias' force, he can do so. The account at I 4:16–18, that Judas restrained his men for fear of Gorgias' force, is more likely to be correct. Jason objected to the Hasmonaean ruling allowing defensive warfare on the Sabbath and makes every effort to prove that Judas made no concessions in rigorously observing the Sabbath. See 12:38–39, 15:1–3, and NOTES ad loca and AB vol. 41, pp. 5, 66, 75, 79, 85, 237. The Common Source *may* have recorded that the encounter with Nicanor occurred at dawn on a Friday and, without further comment, that Gorgias' force panicked and fled. The pious recorder of an Age of Wonders could have left it to his reader to infer that divine providence spared the Jews the need to defend themselves on the Sabbath. His brevity would have left the Hasmonaean propagandist free to omit all reference to the day of the week and would also have allowed Jason to draw the inference here.

27. By omitting reference to Gorgias' force, Jason's narrative (in contrast to I 4:17–23) can present the Jewish soldiers as proceeding directly to take the spoils.

blessing . . . upon them. In the parallel passage, I 4:24, Judas and his men are quoted as singing the hymns which were probably the Hasmonaean victory liturgy; see AB vol. 41, pp. 265–66, 286–87. The Common Source may have presented such words of praise to God, for the writer here, too, draws on the language of Jewish prayer and makes elegant allusions to biblical texts. The prayers of the victorious Jews follow the standard Hebrew formulas, "Blessed is the LORD who . . ." (*brwk yhwh 'šr . . . ;* cf. Exod 18:10; I Sam 25:39) and "Give thanks to the LORD, for . . ." (*hwdw lyhwh ky . . . ;* cf. Pss 106:1, 107:1; Jer 33:11). Our passage is the earliest attestation known to me of the Benediction of Thanksgiving. As now used by Jews it has three synonymous verbs, "Blessed are you O LORD our God, King of the universe, Who has kept us alive [*šeheḥĕyānū*] and preserved us [*wᵉkiyyᵉmānū*] and brought us to reach [*wᵉhiggi'ānū*] this time. Our passage has only the one Greek verb *diasôsanti*, which I have translated "who had preserved . . . alive." The earliest Hebrew texts of the Benediction of Thanksgiving have only one verb ("Blessed . . . who has brought us to reach this time"; *M. Berakot* 9:3 in the Kaufman manuscript and TP *Berakot* 9:3, p. 12d; To. *Berakot* 6 [7 in the Erfurt manuscript]:9, 10, and 6[7]:14 in the Erfurt manuscript and in the first edition). The version with three verbs is probably an effort to maintain the customs of three different groups, each of which used a different verb. If the original formulation had used the biblical verb *ḥḥyh* ("keep alive"; Josh 14:10), it is unlikely that the other formulations would have come to be. Formulas with two and three verbs are attested early in the Middle Ages (the Munich manuscript has all three verbs in the *Mishnah* at TB *Berakot* 54a; see also the printed editions of TB *Berakot* 59b and Rabbenu Asher to TB *Berakot* 54a, and TP *Berakot* 9:3, p. 14a).

"When drops of mercy had begun to fall upon them" is probably an allusion to II Sam 21:10 where the mother Rizpah stands watch over the bodies of *seven* "sons" (i.e., direct descendants) of Saul, two of whom were Saul's sons by her. They had been slain by David's orders in the hope of winning God's mercy to end a famine. She guards the bodies "from the *beginning* of the harvest until *drops of water fell* upon them from the sky." In the Greek version of the verse, at II Reigns 21:10, the italicized words are rendered by the same Greek words (*archê, staxai*) as appear here. Just as the deaths of the seven sons of Saul and the piety of the mother in David's time purchased mercy, so in Judas Maccabaeus' time did the deaths of the seven martyred brothers and their mother.

The metaphor of drops of mercy falling need not have been strange to a Greek of the first century B.C.E.; cf. Aeschylus *Agamemnon* 179–80 and Philodemus of Gadara at *Anthologia Palatina* v 13 (12).6. Nevertheless, readers who were unaware of the allusion to II Sam 21:10 found the expression strange. The verb *staxai* ("fall in drops," "be poured") is used rather of God's wrath against Jerusalem and Judah (Jer 42[Greek Jer 49]:18, 44[Greek Jer 51]:6; cf. II Chron 12:7). Even at Judg 5:4 and Ps 68:9 the reader would probably think of God's wrath against the enemy rather than of his mercy toward Israel. Accordingly, only the Latin versions and two manuscripts of the class q (243 731) preserve the reading *eleous staxantos* (lit. "mercy having fallen in drops"). Aq$^{-243\ 731}$ have *eleous taxantos*, a reading very difficult to construe in its context. It is perhaps in order to accommodate the reading *eleous taxantos* that in A and q the word "them" (*autous*) after "who had preserved . . . alive to reach" (*diasôsanti*) has been omitted, though it is present in *L'* 46–52 58 311 La Sy Arm and is supported by "us" in the Benediction of Thanksgiving. The scribes responsible for the text of A and q probably did not recognize the allusion to the benediction. By omitting "them," the accusative *archên* ("beginning") could be taken as the direct object of *diasôsanti*, and the genitive *eleous taxantos* could be taken as modifying *archên*. If so, one might translate the reading of A and q, ". . . and thanking the LORD Who had reserved for this day a beginning of Mercy's acting as their commander." It is unlikely that the scribe intended *taxantos* to be construed as a genitive absolute, with the translation ". . . and thanking the LORD Who had preserved them alive to reach this day and thus had ordained a beginning of mercy for them" (as suggested by Hanhart, *Nachrichten der Akademie der Wissenschaften in Göttingen, Philologisch-historische Klasse,* 1961, p. 33). Though Greek writers on occasion permitted themselves such loose syntax (Kühner-Gerth, *Grammatik,* II, 110–11; Blass-Debrunner-Rehkopf, *Grammatik,* section 423), there is no evidence that the writer of the abridged history did.

The scribe responsible for the text of *L'* found the syntax of the reading of A and q too contorted, and changed *taxantos* to the dative *taxanti*. The resultant text could be translated ". . . and thanking the LORD, their preserver down to this day, Who had commanded a beginning of mercy for them." Sy has, as usual, a free rendering of *L'* (". . . and thanking the LORD Who had wrought salvation for them on that day and had begun to act mercifully with them") and does not support A and q.

The stress here and in vs. 29, on the victory as incomplete and as a mere beginning, is in sharp contrast to I 4:24–25. If the Common Source put prayers in the mouths of the victors at this point, did those prayers agree with either I 4:24–25 or our vss. 27 and 29?

28. Jason, the believer in the efficacy of martyrdom, takes pains to show that Judas and his men also held that belief. The martyrs are counted as soldiers, to receive a share of the spoils. This would be a new practice, though it may well have been patterned on I Sam 30:24–25 and Num 31:26–27. The author of I 4:23–25 passes it over in silence, probably because of his hostility to the idea of unresisting martyrdom. See AB vol. 41, pp. 12, 33, 79.

I have translated the reading of V La⁻ᵛ Arm. The other witnesses to the text after "themselves" add "and their children." One might, indeed, argue that it is easier to explain how the words could have been accidentally omitted than it is to explain how they could have been mistakenly added. Nevertheless, I think that a scribe, after writing of the heirs of the martyrs, was not sufficiently attentive to what lay before him and let his mind drag his pen to add the absent parallel, the heirs of the living soldiers.

29. Only after showing proper gratitude to God and to the martyrs for what had already been accomplished could the victorious Jews turn to pray for what had not yet been achieved, a complete end to the persecutions which God had sent to punish sin. The king's proclamations against Judaism still stood, and the temple had not yet been purified. The prayer echoes the martyr's prediction at 7:33 and seeks its fulfillment. On the contrast with I 4:24–25, see NOTE on vs. 27, *blessing . . . upon them.*

30–32. In this "footnote," outside the chronological sequence of the narrative, Jason (or the abridger) seems to be countering objections. Perhaps Judas did not believe strongly in the efficacy of martyrdom; perhaps the action after the victory over Nicanor was a mere act of charity rather than a recognition that a martyr was as much a soldier as the men who went into combat! The writer insists, on the contrary, that Judas' policy consistently and repeatedly recognized the contribution of the martyrs to the victories.

An adherent of the Hasmonaean party might also have found fault with the portrayal of Judas as sparing the routed enemy for the sake of the Sabbath. For the Jews, the battle had begun as a defensive struggle. If not annihilated, the enemy force would surely return. Thus, to pursue them could still be viewed as an act of defensive warfare. Hasmonaean teaching permitted defensive warfare on the Sabbath, and scriptural teaching condemned sparing such an enemy (I Kings 20:29–42). Hence, the writer also insists that Judas later, when the Sabbath was not involved, had his army slaughter the enemy in exemplary fashion (vs. 30). Even on that occasion the enemy commander, like Nicanor, managed to escape, though through no fault of Judas' (see NOTE on vs. 30). Hence, Jason mentions in vs. 32 that after another later battle Judas' army, as was proper, slew Timotheus the phylarch (see NOTE on vs. 32).

Vs. 31 is surely part of the note and discusses the aftermath of the battle mentioned in vs. 30, not the aftermath of the battle in vs. 24, for the victors over Nicanor could not yet have brought the remainder of the spoils to Jerusalem, a city they recovered only later (10:1). It is easy to suggest the objections to which vs. 31 could have been a reply. The Jewish warriors were short of weapons (I 3:6); did Judas really let captured armor go to noncombatant invalids, widows, and orphans? The law and procedure in Num 31:12, 21–54 required bringing the spoils to "the camp" and giving first a share to the LORD before dividing them among the people. In the aftermath of the victory over Nicanor in our chapter there could be some doubt as to where "the camp" was. Was it Jerusalem, not yet in the hands of pious Jews? And how could God receive His share if the temple was not yet held by pious Jews? Jason himself may have failed to report how Judas dealt with these problems before he retook Jerusalem and the temple. In any case, our "footnote" reports that in later campaigns, at least, the captured arms were reserved for military purposes and sent to strategic points, and the rest of the spoils were taken to Jerusalem. In vss. 30 and 31 there does indeed seem to be an effort to parallel Num 31 so as to show that Judas conformed to the commandments there: we have slaughter of the enemy (as in Num 31:7–8), towering fortresses (Num 31:10, *ṭīrōtām;* the Hebrew noun at Greek Song of Sol 8:9 is rendered *epalxeis* ["battlements"]), spoils taken and brought to "the camp" (Num 31:12) and divided with shares going to warriors, noncombatants, and the sanctuary (Num 31:25–54).

Vss. 30–32 here could easily be attributed to the abridger: abridgment could have removed details which would have answered the objections which provoked the "footnote." It is possible, however, that Jason himself felt the ·need to deal immediately with the problems of Judas' conduct as described in vss. 25–29.

30. At AB vol. 41, p. 56, n. 10, I refer the reader to this NOTE for a hint that Josephus had read the abridged history. I have changed my mind. See instead NOTE on II 10:24, *Timotheus (the first . . . Jews).*

For a detailed argument showing that there were two persons named Timotheus in First and Second Maccabees, see AB vol. 41, pp. 296–97 (there, at p. 297, par. 2, line 1, for "33" read "32"). My argument there proceeds by using the information in the abridged history itself to make sense of an account which otherwise woud be extremely incoherent. Against the objections raised against my theory by Doran (*Temple Propaganda,* p. 59, n. 32), see the NOTES on the following passages: 8:30–32, 8:32, 9:3 (*and of Timotheus and his men*), and 10:24, *Timotheus (the first . . . Jews).*

The Hasmonaean propagandist at I 5:6, 11, etc., does not assert that the two Timothei are one and the same. He merely fails to assert they are distinct. Hence, the Common Source may have distinguished one from the other, a possibility which had not occurred to me when I wrote AB vol. 41, p. 297.

The Timotheus of our verse is Timotheus the Seleucid commander (*stratêgos*) mentioned in I 5:11–44 and in II 12:2, 10–26. Only in that campaign against a Timotheus are the Jews said to have taken spoils and plural fortresses. The writer here rounds off the figure of 25,000 dead given at 12:26. The Greek here (*tois peri Timotheon kai Bakchidên*) implies that Timotheus and Bacchides together faced the Jews. Bacchides may be mentioned here to indicate that the Timotheus in question was the one who had Bacchides on his staff. No Bacchides is mentioned in I 5:11–44 or in II 12:10–26. However, the author of I 5:11–14 perhaps saw no reason to mention the name even if it occurred in one of his sources. Jason may have found the name in his source, and the abridger may have omitted it from II 12:10–26, a passage which has lost much through abridgment. This Bacchides, if he survived the battle, might have been the same as the commander under Demetrius I, who gave Judas his final defeat (I 7:8–20, 9:1–18), but there is no evidence to decide the question.

Were all the elderly given a share along with the victims of torture and the widows and the orphans? Probably the elderly recipients were the parents of the slain martyrs and soldiers who had lost the sons who would have maintained them in their old age.

32. Although the writer sought to be unambiguous, the scribes found his

wording at the beginning of our verse so strange that they were impelled to alter it. The original reading was probably *ton phylarchên tôn Timotheôn* ("of the [two] Timothei, the phylarch . . ."). Even the best scribes probably did not expect to see the plural of the proper name Timotheus and changed the plural name to the accusative singular and inserted the preposition *peri* to yield *tôn peri Timotheon* as in Aq and as presupposed by La^P. The plural definite article (here, *tôn*) followed by *peri* is a grammatical pattern much used in the abridged history and in Hellenistic literature. The construction is annoyingly ambiguous. Literally, it could be translated here "those around Timotheus," but it could also mean only "Timotheus himself," and at Polybius v 1.7–9 is an example suggesting that here it could mean "the two Timothei"; see Jules-Albert de Foucault, *Recherches sur la langue et le style de Polybe,* pp. 113–15. Hence, the reading *ton phylarchên tôn peri Timotheon* might even be the original text. The scribes responsible for the text of VLa^{XV} 71–107 *l*$^{-93}$ 46–52 55 106 were unaware that there were two Timothei and took Timotheus here to be the same as Timotheus in vs. 30. By reading *ton peri* ("the one associated with") instead of *tôn peri,* they distinguished the phylarch from Timotheus. *L'* La^{LBM} Sy Arm insert the Greek equivalent of the English "to" before the noun *PHYLARCHÊS* and make vs. 32 a part of vs. 31, absurdly turning the phylarch (or the man Phylarches) into a Jew. Perhaps the scribes were led astray by their familiarity with the "tribes" (*phylai*) of Israel.

33. Like vs. 32, our verse reports the killing of enemies. Does it then continue the "footnote" of vss. 30–32 as I suggested at AB vol. 41, p. 297? One cannot exclude the possibility, but I now do not think so. If our verse were part of the footnote, the "victory celebration on their own soil" should be the one following the victory over Timotheus the phylarch. The victory over Timotheus did see Jews leaving the soil of Judaea (I 5:6–8; II 10:32–37), so that there would indeed be a point in writing of a celebration on the Jews' *own soil.* Nevertheless, the same was true of the victory over Nicanor and Gorgias (I 4:15–23; Ammaus was in Judaea, according to I 3:42). No other source suggests that apostate Jews, burners of the temple gates (see 1:8), would become vulnerable with the defeat of Timotheus. The presumably heterodox guides of Gorgias (I 4:2) could well have been trapped by Judas' men after the rout of the Seleucid army.

More than one source tells us of the burning of temple gates in this period. Unfortunately all the texts are obscure. In Ep. 0 we hear only of the burning of a singular gateway (*pylôn*), blamed upon Jason the Oniad and his followers. Here in our verse, the same word is used in the plural (*pylônas*), and Kallisthenes and his followers are blamed for the burning. At I 4:38 we hear of the burning of plural "gates" (*pylas*). See also NOTE on 5:5–16(end). Ps 74:6 may refer to the same incident; see AB vol. 41, pp. 332–34. Kallisthenes and his men were probably among the partisans of Jason mentioned in 1:7–8.

A monumental gateway (*pylôn*) could contain several gates, and the word *pylôn* may have been used loosely here to mean only "gate." However, the use in the sources of both singular and plural is probably not accidental. The texts have another peculiarity: they give disproportionate attention to the gateways or gates, when other parts of the temple structure surely suffered destruction or damage during the time of troubles (I 4:38; cf. II 10:3). Both peculiarities may have arisen because pious Jews connected the burning of the gate(s) with biblical prophecies.

According to Jer 17:27, the plural gates (Gr. *pylas*) in Jerusalem will be burned if the Jews do not observe the Sabbath; we hear, indeed, that apostates in the reign of Antiochus IV violated the Sabbath (I 1:43, 45, 52). One gate of the temple was also connected with eschatological hopes; see Ezek 44:1–2 and *M. Middot* 4:2. Perhaps this is the single gate mentioned in Ep. 0 and Ep. 1 (II 1:8). The destruction of that gate would call into question the fulfillment of Ezekiel's prophecy and would arouse grave apprehensions; the pious writers of the letters could pass over the destruction of the other gates in silence, whereas our two historians are interested in all damage to God's temple during the persecution and know that Ezekiel's prophecy is yet to be fulfilled.

their own soil. So I have translated the Gr. *têi patridi* (lit. "the fatherland"). If vs. 33 is not part of the "footnote," the word cannot mean Jerusalem, which Judas' men recovered only later (but see introductory NOTE on ch. 9).

Kallisthenes . . . gateways. I have translated the probable original Greek text, *TOUSEMPRÉSANTASTOUSIEROUSPYLÔNASTOUSPERIKALLI-STHENÊN* (in ancient Greek manuscripts there were only capital letters and words were not divided). On the plural definite article (here, *tous*) followed by *peri*, see NOTE on vs. 32. Scribes on seeing it could easily have jumped to the conclusion that *TOUSPER* was a mistaken repetition (dittography) of *TOUSIER* and thus could have omitted *tous peri*. Then, however, the singular noun "Kallisthenes" was in apposition with "who had set fire to the sacred gateways," expressed in Greek by an unambiguously plural participle. The scribes of A V La[L] did not venture to change the difficult text, but the scribes of q L l La[X] La[BM] Sy each dealt with the grammatical problem by making some alteration. The diversity of the attempted solutions shows that all are guesswork. My hypothetical original, present in no witness to the text, is more probable than the guesses of the ancient scribes because one can easily understand how it was turned by the scribes underlying AVLa[L] (the very best witnesses) into their reading.

Jason of Cyrene took every opportunity to show how the wicked suffer precise retribution: the burners of the gates were themselves burned to death. See NOTE on 5:9–10.

34–36. Nicanor may have escaped because Judas revered the Sabbath. Nevertheless, even his escape displayed precise divine retribution: the man who expected to sell the Jews as slaves was himself reduced to fleeing like a runaway slave. Jason may well have also believed that divine providence had reserved a later doom for Nicanor. He uses the same epithet *trisalitêrios* ("heinous sinner"; see next NOTE) both of Nicanor here and of Nicanor at 15:3, probably because he believed them to be identical. Like Heliodorus (3:36–39), Nicanor had undertaken to injure the Jews and in the end had to proclaim to the world the power of their divine Protector. On the parallels between Nicanor and Heliodorus, see end of NOTE on vss. 8–35.

34. *heinous sinner.* Gr. *trisalitêrios* ("thrice sinful"); *tris-* is frequently used as an intensifying prefix. Haman receives the same epithet in the king's letter at Greek Esther 8:12p.

35. *through God's help.* Jason probably means to suggest the efficacy of the password mentioned in vs. 23.

splendid garments. As a Friend of the king (vs. 9) Nicanor wore a purple broad-brimmed hat and a purple cloak. See Bickerman, *Institutions,* p. 42.

his army had been destroyed. Jason himself says there were survivors (vss. 24–26) but the army was too crippled to continue the campaign.

36. *captivity of the people of Jerusalem.* The words allude to Isa 52:2–3 and also probably to the larger context Isa 52:1–10. The words and their allusive connotation constitute an elegant synonym for the "Jews" mentioned in vs. 34, but they are misleading, for Judas did not yet hold Jerusalem (see 10:1, and cf. AB vol. 41, pp. 273–74).

On the expression "the people of Jerusalem" (*tôn en Hierosolymois*), see NOTE on 12:3–9.

XI. THE DEATH OF ANTIOCHUS IV
(9:1–29)

9 1 It so happened that about this time Antiochus had made an unseemly retreat from the regions of Persis. 2 He had marched into the place called "Persepolis" and had attempted to plunder its sacred treasures and subdue the town. When in response the townspeople rushed out to defend themselves by force of arms, the king could have been routed. Indeed, the result of the natives' sally was that Antiochus turned tail and withdrew ignominiously.

3 He was near Ecbatana when the news reached him of the fate of Nicanor (and of Timotheus and his men).ᵃ 4 In his furious rage he thought he would make the Jews pay for what he had suffered at the hands of those who had put him to flight. Accordingly, he ordered his charioteer to complete the journey without stopping. But the judgment from heaven was already upon him for being so arrogant as to say, "When I reach Jerusalem, I shall turn it into a mass grave of Jews." 5 But the all-seeing LORD, the God of Israel, smote him with a disease beyond remedy, one never seen before. Antiochus had just finished speaking when incurable pain seized his viscera and excruciating tortures his internal organs, 6 a punishment entirely fitting for the man who had inflicted many horrifying tortures upon the viscera of others. 7 He, however, far from abandoning his insolence, became still more arrogant as he breathed out against the Jews the fire of his rage and gave orders that the journey be further speeded up. At that moment he fell from his careening chariot. His body whizzed through the air and made a hard landing, and when he tumbled, all the members of his body were racked out of joint.

8 The man had gone in his boastfulness beyond what befits a human being, for he had been thinking of giving orders to the waves of the sea and had been planning to weigh the peaks of the mountains in a balance. This same person fell to the ground and was being carried in a litter as a demonstration to all of the manifest power of God. 9 Indeed, worms swarmed from the eyes of the impious man;

ᵃ See commentary.

and while he still lived, he suffered agonizing pain as his flesh rotted away. The stench of his decay was disgusting to his entire army. 10 Shortly before, the man had been thinking of touching the stars of heaven; now no one could stand to carry him, so unbearable was the stench.

11 At that point, in his shattered state, he began to put off much of his arrogance and to recognize that God's lash was inflicting upon him the agonies of unremitting torture. 12 His own stench, too, he found unbearable. Accordingly, he said, "Right it is to submit to God and for a mortal not to think to vie with a deity." 13 The bloodstained murderer made vows to the LORD, Who would no longer show him mercy. The wretch said, 14 "I shall proclaim Jerusalem a free city" (the same holy city toward which he had been hastening with the intention of razing it to the ground upon his arrival and turning it into a mass grave!). 15 "I shall give all Jews privileges equal to those enjoyed by Athenians" (the same Jews whom he had resolved to deny even the right of burial: he would have cast their bodies, with those of their little children, to be devoured by birds and beasts!). 16 "I shall embellish the holy temple with the finest votive gifts, and I shall make many-fold restitution for the sacred vessels, and I shall provide from my own revenues the sums required for the sacrifices" (the same temple which he had previously plundered!). 17 "Furthermore, I shall become a Jew and shall make a tour of the entire inhabited world, telling of the might of God."

18 All this, however, brought no relief for his torments. Indeed, God's righteous judgment had come upon him. Therefore, he abandoned all hope for himself and wrote to the Jews the letter quoted below, couched in a suppliant tone. Here is its text:

19 "To the good Jews, the citizens, warm greeting and wishes for health and welfare, Antiochus, king and praetor. 20 If you and your children are well and everything which belongs to you is as you would have it, I am most grateful to God. 21 I myself have been ill, but I remember you with affection.

"While returning from the regions of Persis I have fallen seriously ill. Therefore, I think it necessary to provide for the common safety of all. 22 I have not despaired of my own survival; on the contrary, I continue to have great hope for my recovery. 23 Rather, I note that my father, too, when he marched on expeditions to the inland regions, proclaimed who was his heir. 24 His aim was to see to it that if anything untoward should happen or any bad news should be reported, the people of the land, knowing who was the heir to the throne, would not be prey to disturbances. 25 In addition, I have in mind the neighboring rulers across the borders of our kingdom who are waiting upon opportunities and looking forward to what the future may bring. Consequently, I hereby proclaim my son Antiochus king, whom more than once I entrusted and commended to a great many of you as I was setting out for the inland satrapies. I have written him the letter copied below. 26 I ask you please to remember the benefactions you have received as a community and as individuals, and each of you please to continue to maintain the loyalty you now hold toward my son and me. 27 I am confident that he will have good relations with you: he will be gentle and humane and will keep to my own policy."

28 Thus the murderer and blasphemer ended his life, with a most miserable death in the mountains on foreign soil after suffering the most terrible agonies, equal to those he had inflicted on others. 29 Philip, who held the rank of Schoolfellow of the King, attempted to escort the corpse homeward. However, afraid of Antiochus' son, he managed to cross the border into Egypt and take refuge with Ptolemy Philometor.

NOTES

Ch. **9.** Several sources served our authors for the stories of the failure of Antiochus IV to plunder the pagan temple and of the king's death. The presence of a Macedonian Seleucid date at I 6:16 and the surprisingly favorable picture of the dying king at I 6:10 imply that the author of First Maccabees drew on the Seleucid Chronicle for I 6:1–17 (cf. Schunck, *Quellen*, pp. 40–42). Jason certainly drew upon the letter he quotes at II 9:19–27, and so might have his rival and even the author of the Jewish Common Source; see NOTE on vss. 1–3.

On the other hand, there is strong evidence that both our authors used the Common Source. See NOTES on vs. 2, *He had . . . the town;* on vs. 3, *news . . . Nicanor;* and on vss. 4–29 (the motif of retribution and repentance, p. 352). Other Jewish traditions, oral or written, underlie the fantastic account here of the king's death; see NOTE on vss. 4–29 and NOTES on vss. 7, 9, 10.

Jason took care to present the death of Antiochus IV as bearing out the predictions of Daniel, never as contradicting them; see pp. 66–69.

In the abridged history, 10:9 came immediately after 9:1–29. The proof lies in the words of 10:9. "Such were the circumstances of the death of Antiochus, called Epiphanes" makes sense only as a summation directly following upon 9:29, the end of the narrative of the king's death. It can hardly follow the story of the Feast of Purification. Cf. 3:40, 7:42, 13:26, 15:37. Grimm (p. 156) suggested that the writer himself inserted the story of the purification of the temple between 9:1–29 and 10:9 in order to have the first half of his book end with an event significant in the history of the temple, but if so, the writer would not have omitted to mention the temple in the summary at 10:9. Rather, he would have written, "Such were the circumstances of the death of Antiochus, called Epiphanes, and of the purification of the temple." Hence, 10:1–8 would seem to be out of place.

Doran (*Temple Propaganda*, pp. 61–62) argues that the wording of 9:28 and 10:1 proves that there has been no such displacement: the present order of 9:1 – 10:9, he holds, is the original order. Doran notes that the Greek particle *men* ("on the one hand") is found in 9:28, and the particle *de* ("on the other hand"), in 10:1. In Greek, if *men* occurs, *de* normally follows, and the phrase or clause containing *men* usually has some contrast with the one containing *de*. Though *de* is present also in 9:29, Doran finds no contrast in that verse to 9:28. Hence, that *de* for him is not correlated with the *men* in 9:28 but is (as often) a mere linking word. For Doran, the correlated contrast comes only with 10:1, and therefore 10:1 must always have stood near 9:28.

Doran's argument has no force. In 9:28 and 29 our writer may have been thinking of the contrast between the living wicked tyrant and his dead body. Furthermore, in the abridged history the coupled particles *men* and *de* are not used solely to point up contrasts. They can mark a mere succession of narrated facts, as at 11:5 and 12:18, or the transition from one set of events to another, as at 3:40 – 4:1 and 7:42 – 8:1. Here, too, one moves from the events before the king's death to the events after. Moreover, in the abridged history *men* appears several times without any corresponding *de* (4:11–12, 4:14, 5:11, 7:14). Doran seems to argue against this consideration by noting that *men* in 9:28 is immediately followed by *oun* ("thus"). He writes as if he believed that *men oun* in our writer's Greek was a special combination of particles (as it was among some earlier Greek authors), and he calls attention to the fact that *men oun* in the abridged history always is followed by a corresponding *de*. There is no way, however, to prove that *men* and *oun* here are linked in special combination. It is natural to assume, rather, that each has only its own separate force. *Men* in 9:28 may thus have no corresponding *de,* or it may be correlated with *de* in 9:29. Nothing requires us to link it with the remote *de* in 10:1. Hence, we may be sure that 10:1–8 are out of place.

To find where the abridger and Jason of Cyrene intended 10:1–8 to be, we must consider more than the historical facts. Jason of Cyrene made chronological mistakes, and could have been mistaken here. In First Maccabees, the report of the death of Antiochus IV comes at 6:1–16, after the report of the Days of Dedication (4:36–61) and after the account of the wars with hostile neighbors (5:1–68). Jason of Cyrene, however, was pleased to contradict First Maccabees whenever he could (see pp. 4–12, 17–23; Introduction, Part III, and AB vol. 41, pp. 12, 44–52, 78–89). In Ep. 2 the death of Antiochus IV is said to have preceded the days celebrating the purification of the temple, but the other details of the king's death in Ep. 2 obviously contradict the account here.

The wording of the abridged history leaves little doubt as to the original position of 10:1–8. The verses can hardly have stood later on in ch. 10. The writer of the abridged history announces first (10:9) that he has finished the story of the death of Antiochus IV, and second (10:10) that he now turns to give a brief account of the woes or wars of the reign of Antiochus V. The restoration of the temple cult is surely neither a woe nor a war. Indeed, two woes are listed immediately, each properly introduced by the Greek particle *gar* ("for," "in fact," "for example"): first, the appointment to power of Lysias and Protarchos, and second, the *failure* of the efforts of Ptolemy Makron to secure justice for the Jews, followed by his suicide. In all this there is no room for 10:1–8.

Throughout the rest of the narrative of the reign of Antiochus V the author first narrates an act of violence or aggression against the Jews and then tells how they responded, under Judas' leadership and with God's help. The failure and suicide of Ptolemy Makron were not in themselves acts of violence or aggression against the Jews, so that it is unlikely that 10:1–8 originally followed 10:13. In 10:14 we hear of the aggressions of the *stratêgos* Gorgias, and in 10:15 we learn that at the very same time the Idumaeans were harassing the Jews and giving refuge to *those cast out of Jerusalem*. Clearly, before that point Judas and the militant pietists had occupied Jerusalem, and 10:1 cannot have stood anywhere after 10:15. Accordingly, the writer of the abridged history believed that 10:1–8 fell in the lifetime of Antiochus IV.

In the story of the defeat of Nicanor, as far as 8:29 it is clear that Judas and his men have not yet recovered the temple and Jerusalem. The "footnote" 8:30–32 must follow directly on the passage containing the difficulties it solves; see NOTE on 8:30–32. Hence 10:1–8 cannot have followed 8:29. It is conceivable and even plausible that 10:1–8 preceded 8:33, in which case "their own soil" (*têi patridi*) could indeed mean Jerusalem, but then it is strange to have no reference to the most important fact of all, the recovery of the temple and the restoration of the cult, in the sentence which serves as a summary of the entire section (8:36). Hence, 10:1–8 originally stood after 8:36.

Other clues confirm our conclusion that 10:1–8 originally stood after 8:36. If the text is read in that order, the punishment of Antiochus IV as described in ch. 9 comes as a dramatic fulfillment of the prayer at 10:4, and the narrative presents an excellent series of contrasts. Judas and his men, led by their God, march victoriously to Jerusalem (10:1), in contrast to Nicanor, who flees ignominiously, without his men, to Antioch, where he must acknowledge the power of the Jews' Protector (8:34–36). Thereafter, Antiochus suffers an ignominious reverse and a gruesome death, his corpse is brought westward, and the loyal courtier Philip has to flee to Egypt, all in dramatic contrast to the victorious march of Judas and his men. In the order of verses as transmitted in the manuscripts, on the other hand, the Jews' victorious march is juxtaposed only to the king's death, not to Nicanor's defeat. See also NOTE on vs. 4.

Jason's words in 9:1 imply that the king's retreat and death were nearly simultaneous with the celebration of the Feast of Purification; see pp. 58–59. The author of Ep. 2 pretends to be writing from Jerusalem just before the Feast of Purification; he pretends to transmit the report of the death of Antiochus IV. Both the abridged history and I 6:7–16 contradict Ep. 2: no news of the death of Antiochus IV could have reached Jerusalem at the time of the Feast of

Purification. We have seen (p. 26) how Ep. 1 and Ep. 2 were prefixed to the abridged history so as to produce a text for ritual reading by Greek Jews on Ḥanukkah, analogous to the book of Esther for Purim. The chronological contradiction between Ep. 2 and the abridged history could be solved only by rejecting Ep. 2 or by rearranging the abridged history. The other factual contradictions were no problem: Judas and his contemporaries were thought to have written Ep. 2 when they possessed only inaccurate rumors about how the king died. Hence, the "Ḥanukkah scroll," Second Maccabees, presents a disarranged text of the abridged history.

The anomalous position of 10:9 in its present context was what allowed us to conclude that someone had tampered with the text. The person who rearranged the abridged history could have removed this clue by having 10:9 stand after 9:29. Why did he leave the clue? Was it because he did not dare to wipe out all evidence of the original order of the narrative (as has been suggested by Schunck, *Quellen*, p. 101)? Surely the tamperer was convinced of the authenticity of Ep. 2 and intended to leave no ambiguity! For him, the purification of the temple fell after the death of Antiochus IV and thus in the reign of Antiochus V. Rather, we may guess that the tamperer had a good appreciation of Greek style and knew that 10:9 was not to be separated from 10:10, linked as they are by sense and by the particles *men* and *de*.

1–3. Antiochus' ignominious defeat is presented in vivid contrast to the glorious march into Jerusalem of Judas and his men. Our verses are closely parallel to I 6:1, 3–5. See NOTES on vs. 1, *of Persis*, and vs. 2, *He had . . . the town*.

On the other hand, Jason contradicts First Maccabees: the festival of the purification of the temple and the king's death were not separated by several months but came close together in time; the king did not live to hear of the purification of the temple. The author of First Maccabees erred through his ignorance of the difference between the two Seleucid eras, whereas Jason probably followed his own (correct) understanding of the Common Source; see p. 58. Though the Common Source told of how the king received bad news from Judaea, we may assume that the account was sufficiently vague that the author of First Maccabees could jump to his conclusion. Jason's chronology of the expedition of Lysias also contradicted I 6:5–6; see pp. 58–59.

In quoting the letter in vss. 19–27, Jason has preserved a document which may have served as a source even for the Common Source. The abridged history says that Antiochus withdrew from the regions of Persis; the account in I 6:1 and 4 implies the same. On this point both those narratives and that of the Common Source could well have been drawn from the letter (vs. 21).

The king marched eastward in mid-165 B.C.E. The abridged history does not mention the event at its chronological place in 8:8. Daniel had utterly failed to predict the expedition, and the author of First Maccabees flaunts the fact at I 3:37. By omitting the event from its proper place, Jason could avoid reminding his audience of the embarrassing point. See AB vol. 41, pp. 47, 52, 251.

1. *unseemly*. I follow La^LXVP Sy in so rendering Gr. *akosmôs* (rather than as "in disorder"). The same translation would fit the occurrences of the word (or the related adjective) at Aeschylus *Persians* 470; Herodotus vii 220, and Homer *Iliad* ii 213.

of Persis. I follow here the reading *tôn kata tên Persida topôn*, of *L'* La^BM, supported by La^{LXV} Sy. AVqLa^P have "the regions around [*peri*] Persis." At I 6:1, 5, too, Antiochus is said to have been in Persis. "Persis" in Jason's time had more than one meaning. In the narrow sense, as "Persis proper," it meant the nuclear territories of the Persians, in southwestern Iran, the modern province of Fars. In an intermediate sense, it might include the neighboring areas of Elymais and Media, with their heavily Iranian populations. In the broadest sense, "Persis" meant the entire territory of the old Persian (Achaemenid) empire or of the Parthian kingdom. See AB vol. 41, pp. 252, 309-10, and cf. 1:19. Cicero (*De domo sua* 23.60) calls the Parthians "Persians," so perhaps pagans, too, might use "Persis" in the broad sense. The letter of Antiochus IV at vs. 21 appears to use "Persis" in an intermediate sense. Jason probably took the word in the narrow sense; see NOTE on vs. 2, *He had . . . the town*. Correct accordingly AB vol. 41, p. 252.

2. *He had . . . the town*. Only the abridged history connects the end of Antiochus IV with Persepolis. The testimony of I 6:1, II 1:13-15, and the non-Jewish sources suffices to show that the king was discomfited at the temple of Nanaia in Elymais. See AB vol. 41, p. 308, and add to the sources there J. *AJ* xii 9.1.354 and Jerome *Commentarii in Danielem* to Dan 11:36, 44-45, both of which follow Polybius. Persepolis is in Persis proper (see Map 2), not in Elymais. If Antiochus IV had turned tail at Persepolis, the storied capital of the old Persian empire, surely the Greek sources would have mentioned the fact. Hence, Jason's location of the king's discomfiture is most likely a mistake, though there may have been a temple at or near Persepolis in the time of Antiochus IV (see Erich F. Schmidt, *Persepolis* ["The University of Chicago: Oriental Institute Publications," vols. LXIII-LXX; Chicago: University of Chicago Press, 1953-70], I, 3, 55-57, 275, and III, 12, 44-49).

But how did Jason come to give Persepolis as the location? If Jason and First Maccabees drew here on a common source, and if I 6:1 reflects that source, we can see how Jason's account might have arisen from a misreading. Literally, the beginning of I 6:1 says the king heard that "there was in Elymais in Persis a city" (original Heb. *hyth b'lwm'ys bprs 'yr*). Even the author of First Maccabees appears to have been unfamiliar with the name Elymais; see AB vol. 41, p. 308. Manuscript variants at I 6:1 show that the Greek scribes, too, failed to recognize it. In the Greek Old Testament it occurs elsewhere only at Dan LXX 8:2 and Tobit 2:10; the related adjective *Elymaios* occurs at Judith 1:6. If the reader did not recognize "Elymais," he might skip the word and his eye might go on to read "in Persis city" (*bprs 'yr;* there is no indefinite article in Hebrew or Greek). In Old Persian, "Persepolis" and "Persis" were both *Pārsa* (J. Duchesne-Guillemin, " 'Persepolis' and 'Persis,' " *Der kleine Pauly*, IV [1972], 649, 653). Hence, an unwary reader might take *bprs 'yr* to mean Persepolis even though Hebrew grammar would normally require the definite article (*bprs h'yr*). If the reader took "Persis" in the narrow sense (see NOTE on vs. 1, *of Persis*), all the more would he jump to the conclusion that Persepolis was the city. Jason's own Greek may confirm our hypothesis of a misreading, if a manuscript of the class *l* preserves his original wording. The oldest Greek name for Persepolis was *Persai*. Ms. 93 has *Persai polin* ("Persai city"); ms. 19, also of the class *l*, has *Persaios polin* ("Persaios city"). See Jacob Wackernagel, *Kleine Schriften* (Göttingen: Vandenhoeck und Ruprecht, 1955), pp. 844-52.

Only here and at I 6:1 (and at Josephus' paraphrase of I 6:1 at *AJ* xii 9.1.354) is a city involved in Antiochus' attempt to sack the temple in "Persis." Cf. II 1:13. The reliable pagan historian Polybius says that Antiochus failed in his project because "the barbarians who lived around the [holy] place refused to yield" (xxxi 9; cf. Appian *Syriakê* 66; Porphyry FGH 260, F 55=Jerome *Commentarii in Danielem* iv to Dan 11:36, 44–45). The wording excludes the involvement of a city. Whose account is correct? Our meager evidence is equivocal but favors Polybius.

Strabo (xvi 1.18, C745) says that when, later, Mithradates I of Parthia sacked the temple of Artemis in Elymais he also took the large city of Seleuceia-on-the-Hedyphon, a city which earlier was called "Solokê"; on the city, see Honigmann, "Seleukeia 13," PW, IIA (1921), 2561. Strabo's story suggests that Seleuceia-Solokê was close enough to the temple of Artemis that an attack on one might be associated with an attack on the other. It is thus possible that I 6:1 and our verse are right against Polybius. But there is no reason why the events of Antiochus' campaign must resemble those of Mithradates'. The story in Strabo can even give reason to doubt the account of the Jewish historians. Mithradates' attack probably came between late 140, when he defeated and captured the Seleucid Demetrius II, and Mithradates' death in 138/7. See Neilson C. Debevoise, *A Political History of Parthia* (Chicago: University of Chicago Press, 1938), p. 24, and AB vol. 41, pp. 467–68. Thus the mention of a city here and at I 6:1 may reflect confusion of the facts surrounding Mithradates' attack with those surrounding Antiochus'. If the two Jewish historians share an error, the fact strongly suggests that they drew upon a common source. The Seleucid Chronicler, who had access to royal records, is unlikely to have made such a mistake. Thus we again would have strong evidence for the Jewish Common Source.

If the mention of the city is an error and already stood in the Common Source, I was wrong at AB vol. 41, p. 308, to ascribe it to a later scribe.

When . . . routed. Ancient translators and scribes were puzzled by the syntax. Good Greek grammar would require that the subject of "rushed out" (a genitive absolute) be different from the subject of the main verb of the sentence. In most witnesses to the text, the main verb is the intransitive *etrapêsan* ("they turned"). One might then take the verb to mean "Antiochus and his army were routed," but in the entire context Antiochus appears in the singular. His army is not mentioned, and our sentence would be redundant, since the very next sentence says the same. In defiance of good Greek grammar, La[BM] take the subject of *etrapêsan* to be the townspeople, as if the Greek meant "When in response the townspeople rushed out, they took to resistance by force of arms." My translation is based on the reading of *l*, dividing the letters as *an etrapê*. It is also based on taking *etrapêsan* of most witnesses as a mistake for *etrapê an*. The resultant text has good grammar and is not redundant. There is a further advantage: the text then agrees with Polybius xxxi 9 in implying that no battle took place; see AB vol. 41, p. 309.

3. *Ecbatana.* Ecbatana lies hundreds of miles northwest of Tabai in Paraitak-ênê (near Isfahan), where Antiochus died (see Map 2 and AB vol. 41, pp. 309–10). No other source mentions Ecbatana in connection with the king's death. How did Jason come to do so? We cannot be sure, but he or his source

may well have done so by interpreting the obscure word *'pdnw* in the prophecy of the death of the King of the North at Dan 11:45. Greek Jews did not recognize it as the Persian word for "pavilion." At Dan LXX 11:45 it is taken to mean "then." At Dan Th. 11:45 in the *Codex Vaticanus* (=B) the word is merely transliterated "He shall pitch his tent *ephadanô*," but even the transliterated word could be taken as a locative in Greek, "at Ephadan—" (I leave a dash for the last letter because Greek readers may have taken it as a case ending). Indeed, the readings of the passage in other witnesses to the text supply the preposition *en* ("in" or "at"). A has "at Phandan—"; *L* has "at Apadan—"; the Armenian has "at Ephadnon" or "at Ephadôn; and the pagan Porphyry writing in the third century read the passage as meaning "in the place Apedno" (FGH 260, F 56=Jerome *Commentarii in Danielem* to Dan 11:44–45). Even in Hebrew *'pdnw* could be taken as "at *'pdnw*." Dan 11:44–45 is a real attempt by the seer to predict a still-future event. The seer was mistaken; but from the time of the arrival of the news of the king's death, believers had to find some way of making sense of the erroneous prediction. Even official documents published at the time were vague about the sites of the king's last days (as at vs. 21). Believers might even reject a later report placing the king's death at Tabai in Paraitakênê if some other site could be made to fit Dan 11:45. In fact, "Ecbatana" could easily be viewed as a phonetic variant of "Ephadano," and an ancient observer might have thought it lay "between the seas" (Dan 11:45), namely, the Caspian and the Persian Gulf. If Jason knew something of the geography of the regions, he could confirm the identification of Ephadano with Ecbatana by reflecting that a road ran from Persepolis through Persis, Paraitakênê, and Media to Ecbatana and another ran from Ecbatana to Babylon. The king in retreat could indeed have followed that route (cf. I 6:4–5).

news . . . Nicanor. Nicanor's defeat occurred well before March, 164 B.C.E. (AB vol. 41, p. 164). Certainly news of it could have reached Antiochus IV long before the events of our chapter (see AB vol. 41, pp. 164–66). It is also doubtful whether the regime at Antioch would have considered it either urgent or prudent to inform the king of the setback in Judaea. Thus, it is unlikely that the king received bad news from Judaea just before his death, but the report occurs also at I 6:5–7 and serves the interests of pious Jewish belief; see AB vol. 41, p. 307. The story probably came from the Common Source.

(and of Timotheus and his men). The words appear in all witnesses to the text but are an error made by someone who took the "footnote" at 8:30–32 to be part of the chronologically ordered narrative. Jason dated the defeat of this Timotheus after the death of Antiochus (12:10–31). For a detailed discussion of the problem, see NOTE on 8:30–32 and NOTE on 8:30 and AB vol. 41, pp. 296–97.

The Greek of our passage itself suggests that "and of Timotheus and his men" is an interpolation based on 8:30. Jason and the abridger liked to write using parallelism (see e.g., 2:19–22, 25, 28, 5:2–3, 7:27, 8:2–3). If the words had been written by Jason, one would have expected Nicanor and Timotheus to be presented in parallel constructions. Nicanor, however, is mentioned by his name alone, though he was accompanied by an army. Timotheus enters through the ambiguous construction *tous peri Timotheon,* which I have translated "Timotheus and his men"; but it might also mean only Timotheus himself (see NOTE on 8:32). It is probably no coincidence that Timotheus is mentioned through the same Greek construction at 8:30.

4–29. Antiochus IV died in a remote corner of his empire, and the regime of Lysias probably did its utmost to suppress the authentic reports brought westward by Philip, whom Antiochus had appointed to replace Lysias; see NOTE on vs. 29. Eventually an official version was published and incorporated in the Seleucid Chronicle. It can be reconstructed from I 6:1–16 by subtracting the Jewish stories of the messenger bringing news of Judas' victories and of the king's repentance. See Introduction, Part II, n. 39. Before the publication of authentic reports, legends both pagan and Jewish were quick to spring up around the death of the eccentric royal temple robber. Polybius xxxi 9 cites the reports of "some" that Antiochus died insane, "possessed by demons" (*daimonêsas*). Jerome (*Commentarii in Danielem* to Dan 11:36) cites Polybius and Diodorus as authorities for the story that Antiochus was "driven mad by fearful hallucinations and then died of a disease" (*quibusdam phantasiis atque terroribus versum in amentiam, ad postremum morbo interiisse*). Appian (*Syriakê* 66) in his brief summary of the end of Antiochus' career says that "He plundered the temple of Elymaean Aphrodite and died of consumption." Another Jewish account is at 1:13–17. The account here is far more elaborate than that in I 6:8–16. Nevertheless, in both the king is first merely angry and distressed over the frustration of his designs; then the pain of his disease drives him to remorse and repentance for his sins against the Jews; finally he dies in agony "on foreign soil." In I 6:8–16 the king is punished for past sins and repents of them, whereas here the king is punished for his present intention to destroy Jerusalem and the Jews. The two narratives, however, are not in sharp contrast, for here, too, the exact retribution is for the king's past atrocities (vss. 6–9), and his repentance in vss. 12–17 certainly includes past deeds. The motif of retribution and repentance is not found in the letter in vss. 19–27 and probably is derived from the common Jewish source of First Maccabees and the abridged history. A believer in the veracity of Dan 11:44, perhaps Jason of Cyrene himself, added the motif of the king's present intentions; see NOTE on vs. 4.

From I 6:8–16 (cf. Jerome *Commentarii in Danielem* to Dan 11:44–45) one would infer that the king died of what would now be called a psychosomatic ailment. Jason's account, on the contrary, has the king suffer two kinds of purely physical punishment: a loathsome and painful disease and a fall from his speeding chariot. The disease in turn is divided into several distinct phases, including a painful attack on the viscera, the swarming of worms from the eyeballs, and the disintegration of the flesh in stinking putrefaction. Antiochus appears to have been killed more than once! Jason himself could have invented his account, impelled by the factors which we are about to list. I think, however, that he drew on earlier Jewish stories, some of them perhaps told very soon after the Jews heard Antiochus IV was dead. Three factors seem to have produced the story of the king's "multiple death" here.

First, there was the wish of Jewish storytellers to have Antiochus in his death agony suffer every torment he himself had inflicted on the martyrs (see vs. 28). Of the torments suffered by the martyrs, only the burning (6:11; 7:3, 5) is missing; the abridger or a careless scribe may have omitted a clause telling how the king was scorched by fever.

Second, the Jewish storytellers believed that Antiochus, the presumptuous King of the North who dared to vie with God, in dying must have fulfilled prophecies in Isa 14, Joel 2:20, Zech 14:12, and Dan 11:44–45. For details, see the NOTES to the individual passages; cf. Nickelsburg, *Resurrection,* pp. 79–80. Cf. also I 2:62–63 and NOTE thereto, though there the worms are surely those which eat the corpse after death.

Third, Jason or his source drew on the Greek traditions of divine retribution on mortals who dare to compete with gods, including death by gangrene and by worms (see NOTE on 5:21, *thinking . . . soar,* and NOTE on vs. 9).

The writer intended that the reader mark the parallels between the fate of Heliodorus and the death of Antiochus IV. Both are smitten upon moving to attack what God protects (3:24, 9:4); both are felled by the lash of divine powers and carried helpless in a litter, as an object lesson to all spectators of God's power (3:26–29; 9:8, 11). Heliodorus could have died, but for Onias' intervention (3:31–33); Antiochus was so wicked that no intervention could have availed (9:13, 18). Both bear witness thereafter to the power of God, Antiochus necessarily through a letter published after his death (3:36–39; 9:18–27).

In contrast to Antiochus IV, Herod I died where his subjects could see and know of his last disease. Thus, we may believe from *BJ* i 23.5.656–57 and *AJ* xvii 6.5.168–72 that Herod's final illness included fever, severe visceral pain, racking convulsions, gangrene, and a foul odor, that it did not yield to any remedy, and that it was viewed by contemporary observers as retribution for what Herod had inflicted on others. Nevertheless, Jason here appears to have set the fashion for reports of deaths of great persecutors and sinners in works by Jewish and Christian authors wherever the evidence (or lack of it) allowed pious writers to reuse the pattern. The factual details of Herod's death were quite close to the details given here. Josephus' accounts also contain the fictitious detail of having the wicked man devoured by spontaneously generated worms, as in our vs. 9 (see NOTE ad loc.). There is thus good reason to think that Josephus or his source drew on the pattern of our chapter. Did his copy of the abridged history contain the missing reference to Antiochus' fever?

Certainly the death in 311 C.E. of the Roman emperor Galerius as narrated by the Christian writer Lactantius (*De mortibus persecutorum* 33) is patterned on the account here and probably also on Josephus' accounts of the death of Herod; see the commentary of Moreau on Lactantius, pp. 383–87. Cf. the death of Judas Iscariot at Acts 1:18 and the death of Herod Agrippa I at Acts 12:23.

4. According to Dan 11:44, after hearing the dismaying news, the King of the North "will go forth in great rage [*thymôi*] to destroy and exterminate the Many [*pollous*]." Here the king is impelled by the same rage (*thymôi*) to wreak vengeance on the Jews by turning Jerusalem into a mass grave, literally "a receptacle for many men" (*polyandreion*). "Many" was an epithet for pious Jews; see AB vol. 41, p. 46, n. 20. Clearly Jason sought to portray the king's death as at least in part a fulfillment of Dan 11:44–45.

Our verse contains a confirmation of our view that 10:1–8 originally stood before 9:1–29. Antiochus' threat to turn Jerusalem into a mass grave has a far more effective setting if uttered against a city which the reader knows to have been newly restored rather than against Jerusalem in its ruined state before it was recovered by Judas and his men.

Rage and unremitting pursuit of victims characterize the doomed Assyrian or Babylonian tyrant at Hebrew Isa 14:6.

5–6. Jason shows his love of portraying how God makes the punishment fit the sin. See NOTE on 5:9–10. I know of no Greek precedent for disease of the viscera as retribution on a tyrant. Jason evidently draws upon a Jewish pattern. In II Chron 21 Jehoram of Judah is a murderous tyrant-king who led Jerusalem and Judah astray. God punishes Jehoram of Judah with precisely such a disease, there, too (vs. 18), said to be "beyond remedy." Jason's wording (*aniatôi plêgei*) is different from that at II Chron 21:18. Rather, it is identical to the words at Greek Isa 14:6 (where the RSV has "with unceasing blows"). There the words refer to what the tyrant inflicted upon his victims; here they refer to the retribution sent by God.

As justification of my translation of *aoratos* ("unseen") as "one never seen before," see Polybius iii 36.7. Antiochus' disease became extremely visible (vs. 9).

In the abridged history we are not told how Antiochus tortured his victims' viscera. The abridger may have omitted details in 7:8–19, 39. See IV 11:19.

For *xenizousais* ("astonishing") as "horrifying," cf. III 7:3.

7. *He, however . . . speeded up.* See NOTE on vs. 4.

At that . . . joint. The Jewish storytellers probably viewed the fall of the king from his chariot as a fulfillment of Isa 14:12. Though not identical to those in Isa 14:13–14, the king's arrogant aspirations to godlike feats at the beginning of vs. 8 are the same sort of thing (cf. Isa 40:12; Job 38:11; Ps 89:10). The storytellers surely saw here retribution for torment suffered by the martyrs on the rack (not explicitly recorded by the abridger in ch. 7, but cf. IV 9:17) and by the women who were executed by being hurled from a height (6:10).

After telling of the sacrileges committed by Antiochus IV, a pagan legend went on to say, "He died . . . at night. While his body was being transported to Antioch, it was swept away into a river when the beasts of burden suddenly panicked, and it disappeared" (Granius Licinianus xxviii, p. 6 Flemisch).

8. See NOTE on vs. 7, *At that . . . joint.* In reporting that bystanders saw how God's power brought the king low, the author may have had Isa 14:16 in mind.

9. Worms are mentioned in Isa 14:11 and 66:24, but those passages speak of worms in connection with a corpse in or on the ground, not of spontaneously generated worms as part of a disease. Sir 7:17 and Judith 16:17 are based upon Isa 66:24. Death by worms for cruel sinners is a motif found in Greek literature (Herodotus iv 205; Pausanias ix 7.2–4); Greek writers also knew of death by gangrene for tyrants and cruel sinners and for human beings so arrogant as to vie with a god (Herodotus iii 66; Diodorus xxi 16.4–5; Plutarch *De sera numinis vindicta* 2, pp. 548f–49a; cf. J. *Ap.* ii 13.143). Thomas W. Africa has called to my attention that it is likely Jason of Cyrene drew on Herodotus iv 205, the story of the gods' retribution upon Pheretime,

queen of *Cyrene:* her living body seethed forth worms. There was and is a disease (scabies, *phthiriasis*) consisting of infestation by mites, not worms, but it is not by itself fatal; see A. Keaveney and J. A. Madden, "Phthiriasis and Its Victims," *Symbolae Osloenses* 57 (1982), 87–99, and Africa, "Worms and the Death of Kings," *Classical Antiquity*, vol. 1, no. 1 (April 1982), 1–17. Since the ancients believed that putrefaction spontaneously generated worms, the putrefaction here and the eyes as the locus for the worms are probably derived from Zech 14:12. That verse predicted death by putrefaction for gentiles who marched in armies against Jerusalem, as Antiochus had done and was hastening to do again. Because Antiochus must voice his tardy repentance, his tongue does not rot, though one would expect it to from Zech 14:12. The painful disintegration of the king's flesh is retribution for tortures he inflicted (7:4, 7–8, 10).

Antiochus was the King of the North. Accordingly, storytellers certainly viewed the stench as a fulfillment of Joel 2:20 (the mention of the seas at Dan 11:45 is probably also derived from Joel 2:20). The stench is probably also intended to be viewed as retribution for the way the king raised the odor of frying human flesh (7:6).

Here and in vs. 10 the stench has one other function, that of reconciling a report in the Seleucid Chronicle with a prophecy of Daniel. The Seleucid Chronicle said that Antiochus IV died surrounded by his friends (I 6:10), yet Daniel (11:45) predicted that he would die with no one to help him.

In the Greek, the syntax of the last clause of our verse is strange, but the meaning seems clear.

10. The Jewish storytellers had Isa 14:12–19 in mind.

11–12. In writing of God's lash, did the author have Dan 8:25 in mind? The predictions of the martyrs (7:17, 19, 31, 35–36) are here fulfilled.

11. I have translated *to poly tês hyperêphanias* as "much of his arrogance." Did Jason think the king still retained some arrogance? Did Jason sense that the letter in vss. 19–27 was not so abject as one might think from vs. 18? Or should we rather follow La⁻ᴾ and translate, "his great arrogance"?

12. *Right . . . deity.* The king utters a version of a proverb repeatedly found in Greek drama. See Aeschylus, *Persians* 820; Sophocles, *Women of Trachis* 472–73; Antiphanes (writer of comedies in the fourth century B.C.E.), Fragment 289 in Theodorus Kock, *Comicorum atticorum fragmenta* (Lipsiae: Teubner, 1880–88), II, 127, and the anonymous line quoted at Aristotle, *Rhetoric*, ii 21, p. 1394b26.

13. The king's vows to the LORD are listed in vss. 14–17: he promises to perform them if cured of his disease. God's mercy is now for the Jews, and there is none for Antiochus, in fulfillment of 7:37.

14–17. In Greek, with its wealth of inflected forms, the passage is clear with its indirect quotations and without the use of parentheses. For clarity in English I have taken the liberty of using direct quotations and parentheses.

14. *a free city.* "Freedom" for a city was a vague term which was ordinarily made specific by the use of other words. Freedom in the fullest sense could mean complete liberty of internal government and complete exemption from taxation. See AB vol. 41, p. 514. Jason or his source here probably draws an inference from the words of the letter (vs. 19), "To the good Jews, the citizens." In idiomatic English it might be better to translate ". . . my citizens."

Kings in Greek did not so address their subjects; to do so would be to treat them as equals. If Antiochus treated Jews as his equals, surely he was setting them and their city free! But see NOTE on vs. 19, *To the good Jews, the citizens.*

turning it into. Lit. "building it as" in the sense of "using its building materials to make it into."

15. Athens lay outside the Seleucid empire, but her citizens may well have enjoyed great privileges when they came to the kingdom of Antiochus IV, though we have no direct evidence. Jason seems to know of the king's associations with and benefactions to Athens. After being released in 176 or 175 from being a hostage at Rome and before taking power as king, Antiochus IV resided for some months at Athens. Did the Athenians honor him by making him a citizen? No other source says so, but the narrator here appears to assume they did: his assertion that the king intended to give Jews rights equal to those of Athenians seems to be an inference from the address of the letter in vs. 19, "To the good Jews, the citizens," where the last two words can also be rendered, "my fellow citizens."

Jason assumes that to be treated like an Athenian is a privilege. In the second and early first centuries B.C.E., Athens was indeed a privileged free city in Roman-dominated Greece; see AB vol. 41, p. 447. However, no Greek could have written thus about the Athenians after the early 80's B.C.E. Sulla's Roman army inflicted a disastrous siege on Athens (87–86 B.C.E.) and thereafter severely punished the Athenians (William Scott Ferguson, *Hellenistic Athens* [London: Macmillan, 1911], pp. 447–59).

It was taken for granted that a citizen had the right to be buried in the territory of his city. Only those disfranchised, such as great criminals, were denied it. Cf. Gen 23:3–6, and see T. G. E. Powell, "Dead, Disposal of," OCD[2], p. 314. The denial of burial here follows strangely after the king's intention to turn or "build" Jerusalem into a "mass grave" (*polyandreion;* vss. 4 and 14); see NOTE on vs. 14, *turning it into.*

16. Antiochus promises to make restitution for his sack of the temple (5:16; I 1:21–24). He will return to the practice of Seleucus IV and pay for the expenses of the regular temple sacrifices (3:3); on the acceptability of such an offer, see NOTE on 3:3 and AB vol. 41, pp. 411–12. Did Jason infer the intention to make restitution from vss. 26–27?

17. The vow to become a Jew is probably inferred from the king's gratitude to "God" (in the singular) in the letter (vs. 20). On the mission of the cured sinner, to proclaim God's might to the human race, see 3:34, 36, and NOTE on 3:24–49; and cf. II Kings 5:1–18; Dan 4:31–34.

18. In the Greek, "righteous" (*dikaia*) has an emphatic position in the sentence: since it was God's righteous judgment, there could be no lightening of the king's punishment. The narrator believes that Dan 11:45 had been fulfilled and that the utterly helpless king was desperate. He regards vs. 22 as mere bravado, preferring to draw his inferences from the "suppliant tone" of vss. 19 and 26 and from the traces of Judaizing and repentance in vss. 20 and 21. The narrator, however, misread the letter. See the next NOTES.

The writer intended the reader to contrast Antiochus' "suppliant" last letter with the defiant words of the martyrs in ch. 7.

19–27. The letter here teems with problems. The opening formulas are unusual and seem to be full of stylistic blunders; see NOTES on vss. 19–21. Whatever the origin of the document, later hands have certainly tampered with it; see NOTE on vss. 20–21. We shall find that we can explain the seeming blunders in the form of the letter as no blunders at all or as the errors of later scribes. But the letter as a whole raises questions, too.

It purports to be from Antiochus IV to Jewish citizens of his Antiochene republic (see AB vol. 41, pp. 104–25). The only community of Jewish Antiochenes known to us was at Jerusalem. The governmental organs of the Antiochene republic were at Antioch. A letter with such an address can hardly have been published elsewhere than at Jerusalem or Antioch. From the address in vs. 19 we may infer that Antiochus habitually addressed proclamations to each community of Antiochenes individually. Very likely, he would draw up a master copy of a letter to all Antiochenes, leaving a blank for secretaries to fill in as they made out copies for each community, "To the _____, the citizens." Can Antiochus IV have written our letter on his deathbed?

At I 6:14–15, 55–56 (cf. II 9:29) we learn that Antiochus IV, in dying, made his courtier Philip the bearer and executor of his last commands. On the truth of that report, see NOTE on vs. 29. One might assume that only Philip could have brought our letter westward. Antiochus IV intended to depose Lysias or at least to subordinate him to Philip. However, by the time Philip neared Antioch, Lysias had had the helpless boy proclaimed full king and was firmly in control (I 6:17; II 10:11). Unable to enter Antioch, Philip had to flee to Egypt (vs. 29; see NOTE ad loc.). Our letter declares only that Antiochus V is the legitimate heir to the Seleucid throne and fails to mention either Philip or Lysias. It is true that we do not know what was in the "letter copied below" mentioned in vs. 25. However, it probably did not contain instructions to the small child Antiochus V to make Philip his guardian. Rather, if Antiochus IV wished to put Philip in power, would he not have written directly to his loyal Antiochene subjects on the topic? Thus Philip neither could nor would have published the letter preserved here.

Must we then regard the letter as a forgery? No. There is no reason to assume that only Philip could have brought the letter westward or (despite vs. 18) that Antiochus IV wrote it on the point of death. His final illness lasted many days (I 6:9), and he could have thought to take care for the succession to the throne in an earlier stage of his illness, long before he died and well before he decided to subordinate Lysias to Philip or to replace him altogether. A mounted courier could have rushed the letter westward immediately. It did not have to wait for Philip's slow march toward Antioch. We do not have the evidence to show that this is what happened, but we must admit, in the present state of our knowledge, that Antiochus IV might have sent such a letter. Correct accordingly AB vol. 41, p. 37.

Is there any way in which a forger might have produced our letter? One can indeed imagine a situation in which the regime of Lysias might have had it fabricated. Antiochus IV probably had reason to believe that Lysias would submit to Philip. Lysias, in defying the late king's orders, would have to fear the part of the royal army with Philip. Lysias also had to beware of the hostage in Rome, Demetrius son of Seleucus IV. To establish his own regime under the boy Antiochus V, Lysias had to appeal to the forces available in the part of the empire under his control. He could well have hoped to rally to his cause the communities of Antiochene citizens. We hear from Justin (xxxiv 3.6) that the *people* appointed Lysias guardian of the boy-king and that, when Lysias' regime lost the support of the people, it fell quickly to the bold enterprise of Demetrius I (Polybius xxxi 12.3–5; I 7:1–4; II 14:1–2; *AJ* xii 10.1.389–90; cf. Livy *Periocha* xlvi).

According to the theory and the formal institutional procedure of the Seleucid empire, however, the people did not appoint Lysias guardian. The little king himself appointed Lysias guardian and chief minister, as is indeed reported at 10:11; see Bickerman, *Institutions*, p. 21 (fourth par.). Philip might claim to bear the last commands of a dead king, but through the letter here Lysias could hold office through appointment by a living king, one raised to the throne while Antiochus IV still lived. Thus, Lysias' claim could have been legally superior to Philip's, and Lysias' regime could have forged our letter even though it says nothing of Lysias. Lysias and his supporters knew well the republican and Epicurean affectations of Antiochus IV (see NOTE on vs. 19) and could well have fabricated our document and sent a copy, individually addressed, to each community of Antiochene citizens.

Thus the letter may be a forgery, but it is most unlikely that a gentile hand later than the time of Lysias' regime fabricated it. The line of succession through Antiochus V died with him in autumn, 162 B.C.E. Scholars have held, rather, that Jewish hands forged a letter so full of "stylistic blunders." Indeed, the document contains many departures from the style followed elsewhere in Hellenistic royal letters. The departures do lend themselves to being interpreted to support the assertions in vss. 14–18. It is, however, well to be cautious. There may be other explanations for the departures. Antiochus IV was not a typical Hellenistic king but a highly exceptional one. Any Jewish forger had to believe that he could deceive his audience. Yet Jews and Greeks of Syria, Palestine, and Ptolemaic Egypt down through the time of Jason of Cyrene knew what royal letters looked like. If the departures from the usual royal style are blunders, a Jewish forger might have made some of them (cf. Bickerman, *Studies*, I, 116–27), but it is hard to believe he could have made them all.

In fact, the assertions of the narrator in vss. 14–18 can be shown to be based on misinterpretations of the quoted letter. Jason and his predecessors held it to be an abject document, written in desperation, tinged with Jewish piety, and addressed to pious Jews. Far from being so, it is a pagan document colored by Epicureanism, full of confidence for the future of the line of Antiochus IV; it is addressed to the same Antiochene citizen Jews whose sins, according to pious Jews, brought God to use Antiochus IV as the rod of His anger; finally, the letter may assume the pose of an ancient republican political campaigner, not that of a penitent sinner. See NOTES on vss. 19, 20–21, 26 (*I ask you please*), and 27. These considerations would explain all the seeming blunders, including one which is found throughout the entire letter: in this period Seleucid kings in their official correspondence usually spoke of themselves in the first person plural (see Welles, *Royal Correspondence*, pp. 10, 38), yet the document here displays only the first person singular.

Thus we are led to conclude that if the letter is a forgery it is not the forgery of a Jewish storyteller.

At Isa 14:21 the prophet foretells the slaughter of the heirs of the tyrant king. In quoting the king's letter, which ultimately failed to save the life of his little son, was Jason thinking of Isa 14:21? Cf. II 7:17.

Both in content and in arrangement, the letter is written in accordance with the rules laid down in Greek rhetoric for a father urging citizens to come to the aid of his son. Though the *Rhetorica ad Herennium* is in Latin and dates from the second decade of the first century B.C.E., from it we can learn the Greek practice around the time of Antiochus IV; see the introduction to Harry Caplan's edition and translation, [*Cicero*] *ad C. Herennium De ratione dicendi* (LCL; Harvard University Press, 1964), pp. vii–xxv. Other good sources for Greek rhetorical theory, from the fourth century B.C.E., are Aristotle's *Rhetoric* and Anaximenes' *Ars rhetorica,* which has come down to us as the *Rhetorica ad Alexandrum* ascribed to Aristotle.

The first task of a pleader is to win the attention of his audience (*Rhetorica ad Herennium* i 4.6–7; Anaximenes 29, p. 1436a). The civilities in vss. 19–21 (first half) are conventional (see NOTES thereto), but the writer has chosen the most effusive of such expressions, calculated to win the attention of the audience as well as their sympathy for their ailing king (see *Rhetorica ad Herennium* i 5.8). Thereupon, the king is made in vss. 21(second half)–25(first half) to base his case first on the citizens' *self-interest,* in this instance, on their need for *safety* from foreign and civil war (see Aristotle *Rhetoric* i 3.5, p. 1359b, and *Rhetorica ad Herennium* i 4.7, iii 2.3). In vss. 23–24 he argues also that his act, of designating his son as his successor, is *just,* for it is in accord with good precedents; see *Rhetorica ad Herennium* iii 3.4, and Anaximenes 7, pp. 1421b–1422a. In vs. 25 he reminds the citizens how he previously commended his son to them, as if even then they were his chief reliance (see Anaximenes 34, p. 1439b). Next, in vss. 26–27, the king is made to argue that the citizens will be doing what is *honorable* if they support his heir, for they will be paying a debt of gratitude to their benefactor's son, who is ready to give them further benefactions (see *Rhetorica ad Herennium* iii 3.4, and Anaximenes 34, p. 1439b). In vs. 26 the king curries more favor with the citizens by writing as if they were completely loyal (see *Rhetorica ad Herennium* i 4.7–5.8).

19. Our verse contains so many departures from the procedures followed in Hellenistic royal letters that scholars for that reason alone have declared the letter to be a forgery. In Greek letters, only in petitions to a superior does the name of the sender come last, after the name of the recipient(s) and the salutation. Among the surviving ancient documents there are petitions addressed to kings, but nowhere else do we have a petition from a king. See Exler, pp. 42–44, 71–72, and Ziemann, pp. 259–62.

Furthermore, the greeting formula in our verse is exceedingly strange. Other royal letters use only the simple *chairein* ("greeting"). Here we have the extravagant *polla chairein kai hygiainein kai eu prattein.*

Nowhere else do we find a Hellenistic king addressing the recipients with an adjective (here, "good"). In letters of Hellenistic kings to ethnic groups nowhere else do we find, beyond the name of the group, an additional title comparable to "citizens" here. Nowhere else do we find a king at the beginning of a letter giving himself an additional title (here, "praetor").

We have established that the letter here, whether authentic or forged, is a real Seleucid document. On the other hand, we shall find that in vss. 20–21 (see NOTE ad loc.) later hands have certainly deformed the original document to conform with Jewish or Christian belief as to what happened. Could not the same have happened here in vs. 19? We are faced with a difficult question of method: how can we restore the letter to its original form or at least to the form which lay before Jason of Cyrene? How can we interpret the difficult passages? If the letter had been found as a fragment on stone or papyrus and all the problematic passages in our verse had been illegible, the only justifiable assumption would have been that our letter was a normal document and that the illegible passages could be restored, if at all, only by assuming that formulas used in other normal documents stood there. Here, however, we have a document transmitted in a literary source, a document purporting to come from no ordinary king but from a highly eccentric one. If we assume that only ordinary formulas stood in it, we risk losing valuable evidence for the king's eccentric policies.

Fortunately, the Jewish author in several places misunderstood our verse. Here is a clue for determining what lay before Jason. Any words which he misunderstood obviously lay before him, and he could not have interpolated them himself. Furthermore, if words in a problematic passage contribute nothing toward substantiating Jason's assertions or even contradict them, those words, too, must have stood in the original. Thus we shall learn that "citizens" and "praetor" stood in the original document.

On the other hand, Jason could have said that the letter had a "suppliant tone" (vs. 18) merely on the basis of the polite formulas here and in vs. 26. Vs. 18 thus can be used to confirm that those formulas lay before Jason, but we cannot conclude therefrom that the strange word order here, with the king mentioned last, stood in the original document. That order could well be the work of someone who did not find that the letter otherwise had enough of a suppliant tone.

At least the use of the words "good" and "citizens" here and the polite formulas in vs. 26 led Jason to conclude that the desperate king was humbling himself and conferring privileges on his former victims. In the Greek world, where there was no regular procedure of naturalization, it was a great privilege to be a citizen. It is possible that the Jewish narrators recognized in "warm greeting and wishes for health" a formula traditional among Jews; see pp. 165–66.

Nevertheless, the inferences in vss. 14–18 are wrong. The king had not abdicated his power; he still is presented as "king and praetor," and those words must therefore be original.

The king has not conferred new privileges on the nation of the Jews. There were two procedures by which a Hellenistic king could confer a privilege by sending letters. By the first, the king would send a letter to the recipient, addressing him by his name and previous title, and in the body of the letter the king would confer the privilege. See Welles, *Royal Correspondence*, nos. 15, 25, 35, and I 10:18–19. By the second method, the king would send a letter to an official or foreign power saying that the beneficiary had received the privilege. This first letter constituted the act conferring the privilege. A second letter would then be sent to the beneficiary, addressing him by his new privileged title (if any), telling him that enclosed was a copy of the letter to the official, "in order that" the recipient should know. See Welles, *Royal Correspondence,* nos. 71–72, and I 11:30–37. Our document could record an act of conferring privileges on the Jews only if it could be viewed as the second letter in a grant in which the second procedure was used. Indeed, vs. 25 mentions the enclosure of a copy of a letter to the future Antiochus V, but the "in order that" clause does not occur in vs. 25. Hence, our document does not record an act of conferring privileges upon the Jews.

The letter, then, must be addressing Jews who are already citizens. A mass of evidence shows how Antiochus IV established an Antiochene republic and an Antiochene citizenship (AB vol. 41, pp. 105–25). The addressees are thus the Hellenizing Antiochene Jews, whose sin, according to Jason, brought God to inflict the persecution!

Our letter is the only evidence on how Antiochus IV addressed his citizens by word of mouth or in writing. As a document addressed in Greek to a citizen community, it still is extremely strange. All other such communications known to us address government organs and use the simplest greeting formula, e.g., "King Antiochus to the magistrates and the council and the people of Seleuceia in Pieria, the sacred and inviolable, greeting" (Welles, *Royal Correspondence,* no. 72, of 109 B.C.E.). In the Hellenistic world, the word "people," too, referred to a government organ, the citizens assembled in "town meeting." However, the Jewish Antiochenes could not be addressed as "the people of the Jews." They were also not a city-state but only a community of citizens of the Antiochene republic. We hear nowhere that they had a local council or a deliberative assembly of all local citizens. Any such local organs may have been abolished when Antiochus IV punished the turbulent Antiochenes of Jerusalem and reduced Jerusalem to the rank of a village. The Samaritans, too, had long had no recognized government organs (see pp. 534–36) and named none in the address formula at the head of their letter to Antiochus IV but spoke of themselves only as "the Sidonians in Shechem," and the king referred to them in the same manner (see p. 523). Hence, we may accept the unparalleled formula of address here, "to the Jews, the citizens."

The greeting formula and the word order, naming the king last, remain strange. Could they be the work of someone who altered the original? We have argued to show that Jason of Cyrene could not have done so (see pp. 55–70), but other hands could have been active, particularly those of later scribes. One can still argue that these strange aspects, too, stood in the original document.

The king was known for strange greeting behavior. "The king would doff his royal apparel and put on a toga (just as he had seen campaigners for office do at Rome), and he would accost ordinary people, *greeting* and embracing them one by one, on one occasion imploring them to give him their vote as aedile, and, on another, as tribune" (Diodorus xxix 32, derived from Polybius; cf. Polybius xxvi 1.5). We cannot tell whether the republican king used oddly humble greetings in other dealings with his Antiochenes, but it is clear he did so in political campaigns, again following Roman patterns, for Roman political candidates and their supporters assumed such humble poses. See Lily Ross Taylor, *Party Politics in the Age of Caesar* ("Sather Classical Lectures," vol. XXII; Berkeley and Los Angeles: University of California Press, 1949), pp. 67 and 209–10, n. 95.

The word order used by political campaigners in the time of the Roman republic is probably preserved in the many campaign posters of the 70's C.E. painted on the walls of buildings in Pompeii: in them the campaigner addresses the voters, humbly imploring them to vote for his candidate. First appear the candidate's name and the office for which he is running, both in the accusative case. Then comes the formula "I beg you to make" (*oro vos faciatis*). Last comes the campaigner's name in the nominative, either as subject of "I beg" (CIL IV 176) or as subject of its own verb which then follows: of *rogat* ("asks") in CIL IV 170; of *cupit* ("wishes") in CIL IV 174; of *facit* ("does") in CIL IV 175, etc.

Antiochus IV probably used similar humble formulas in seeking the votes of Antiochene citizens for himself or for candidates he supported. Election posters were not letters and contained no formulas of address and greeting. But campaigners surely wrote letters, too, and the letters may well have begun with formulas having the word order of a petition as here (contrast the electioneering letters of Julius Caesar, the dictator, at Suetonius *Julius* 41). Republican officials, including those at Rome, in opening formulas of their letters did name themselves with their republican titles, as Antiochus does here. Though I know of no parallel, the adjective "good" (*chrêstois*), too, may be electioneering rhetoric. In effect here Antiochus IV is campaigning on behalf of his son: he begs the citizens to accept the boy as king (vs. 26). Thus, the word order of our verse does not necessarily imply that the desperate king has turned in abject contrition to beg a boon of his citizens, the Jews.

Though used by Jews, the formula "greeting and wishes for health" was also used by pagans; see pp. 164–65. Where we have translated "greeting," "wishes for health" and "[wishes for] welfare," the Greek has the three infinitives *chairein, hygiainein,* and *eu prattein*. Among the surviving greeting formulas from ancient letters, no other has all three infinitives. Nevertheless, the philosopher Epicurus is known to have begun some of his letters using *chairein* (see Diogenes Laertius x 34, 83, 121a), others using *hygiainein* (Lucian *Pro lapsu inter salutandum* 6), and still others using *eu prattein* (Diogenes Laertius x 14). The philosopher Pythagoras is reported to have used *hygiainein* (Lucian *Pro lapsu* 5). *Eu prattein,* so far as we know, was not used as a greeting by ordinary persons before the last years B.C.E. (*Oxyrhynchus Papyri,* vol. IV, no. 822; Exler, p. 34). It was characteristic of Plato and his school; see Plato *Epistles;* Diogenes Laertius iii 61; Speusippus' letter, *Socraticorum Epistulae* 30; Demosthenes *Epistle* 5; and Otto Roller, *Das Formular der paulinischen Briefe* ("Beiträge zur Wissenschaft vom Alten und Neuen Testament," Vierte Folge, Heft 6; Stuttgart: Kohlhammer, 1933), p. 450, n. 269.

Thus, far from being Jewish, the greeting formula in our verse has the flavor of Greek philosophy. We learn elsewhere that Antiochus IV was a convert to Epicureanism (see AB vol. 41, p. 127). A courtier of his, Philonides, had a classified collection of the letters of Epicurus and published abridgments of them (Wilhelm Crönert, "Der Epikureer Philonides," *Sitzungsberichte der*

Königlich preussischen Akademie der Wissenschaften zu Berlin [1900], pp. 946, fragment 9; 947, fragment 14; 953, fragment 30, and 956). Thus, the letters of Epicurus were known to the king and to his subjects. Antiochus IV may have taken pleasure in parading his Epicurean sympathies to the Antiochene citizenry by using several of Epicurus' favorite greetings at once. A forger working for Lysias' regime could also have known the republican and Epicurean affectations of Antiochus IV and could have put them into the letter, believing that the Antiochene addressees would all the more readily think the late king had written it.

Finally, the long greeting formula here probably served no purpose whatever for Jewish readers. If it was not peculiarly Jewish, it also lent no peculiarly suppliant tone. The surviving ancient letters containing such lengthy greeting formulas do not lead one to conclude that the sender was usually in the position of a suppliant. We are thus entitled to assume that the long greeting formula stood in the original letter.

One peculiarity of the greeting formula, however, might be used to argue that the letter must have been forged long after Lysias was dead. *Chairein* ("greeting") appears here, not as a bare infinitive, but accompanied by the supplement *polla,* which I have translated "warm" (see NOTE on *warm greeting*). The infinitive *chairein* appears so supplemented in papyrus letters, but the earliest instance known to me is in an official letter of 118 B.C.E. (*The Tebtunis Papyri,* Part I, ed. by Bernard P. Grenfell, Arthur S. Hunt, and J. Gilbert Smyly [London: Henry Frowde, 1902], no. 12, line 15). However, the oral greeting *chaire polla* was in common use already in the fifth century B.C.E., the time of Aristophanes (*Acharnians* 832). Antiochus IV could have used *polla chairein* in writing an "electioneering message" even if other Greeks were not yet employing it in their letters. See Roller, p. 452.

the . . . Jews, the citizens. Cf. the procedure used in naming the communities of the Achaean league (of southern Greece) on the coins of the league. There, however, the general designation "Achaeans" comes first and is followed by the name of the particular community (e.g., "Corinthians"). See Percy Gardiner, *Peloponnesus* ("Catalogue of the Greek Coins in the British Museum"; Bologna: Forni, 1963), pp. 12–15.

warm greeting. For consistency with my previous practice in translating *chairein,* I so translate here. The Greek, however, is an infinitive expression, *polla chairein,* parallel to the infinitives I have translated "wishes for health and welfare." A more faithful translation would be "[wishes for] many joys."

welfare. Gr. *eu prattein.* Instead of *eu prattein,* V (supported by La^LVP) has *dieutychein,* which might be translated "[wishes for] continuous good fortune." L has both *dieutychein* and *eu prattein.* The infinitive *dieutychein* is found in a few papyrus letters from the middle of the first century B.C.E. (BGU, vol. VIII, no. 1770; Exler, p. 34; Roller, p. 452), always as part of a long elaborate greeting formula. Such use of *dieutychein,* too, may have originated among philosophers. See the treatment of *eutychia* ("good fortune") at Aristotle *Ethica Nicomachea* i 8.17.1099b6–8, vii 13.4.1153b21–24 (cf. ibid., i 7.15–16. 1098a16–20). Epicurus is said (Diogenes Laertius iii 61) to have used the somewhat similar *eu diagein,* "[wishes for] a well-spent life." Here a scribe may have been surprised to see *eu prattein,* which elsewhere always occurs alone, as part of an elaborate formula. If so, he may have substituted *dieutychein* for *eu prattein*.

praetor. The Greek has *stratêgos,* which usually means "general" or "governor." Why should an absolute Hellenistic king be given such a title? It might be hard to discover an answer. *Stratêgos,* however, is also the Greek translation of the Latin word *praetor*. In Rome, a praetor was a high, elected official. Polybius describes how Antiochus IV would run for republican office and hold it (xxvi 1.5–6), and I have argued in detail to demonstrate the full extent of the king's "Antiochene republic" (AB vol. 41, pp. 104–25). With that background, it becomes easy to understand how the word would appear here: addressing citizens of his republic, the king uses his republican title. Jason and the Hasmonaean propagandist did not understand the Antiochene republic. The word here had no meaning for Jason and must have been present already in his source.

20–21. Two factors are probably sufficient to explain the puzzling texts in the Greek manuscripts of our passage. First, there is the way in which the content of the letter contradicts the narrative. Scribes seem to have felt that a humbled, desperate man ready to become a Jew (vss. 11–18) should have expressed himself differently. Second, formulas of politeness passed out of style, and later scribes, unable to understand them, were driven to alter the text.

Greek letters down to the late second century B.C.E. commonly passed from the salutation to the *formula valetudinis*. The *formula valetudinis* consisted of the words "If you are well, I am delighted; I myself am well," or of variations on that theme. By 90 B.C.E., however, the *formula valetudinis* disappeared completely from Greek letters. Thereafter, ordinary Greek scribes might fail to recognize it. Even learned Greek scribes might find it strange in a royal letter, for the Hellenistic kings rarely if ever used it in writing to their subjects, though Antiochus III did so at least once (J. *AJ* xii 3.4.148), and so did Antiochus V (II 11:28). The formula survived longer in Latin letters, where it passed out of use in the first half of the first century C.E. See Ziemann, pp. 302–13; Exler, pp. 103–7; Bickerman, *Studies,* I, 119–20, 122–23; Welles, *Royal Correspondence,* nos. 56, 58, 59, 61 (by Eumenes II and Attalus II of Pergamum to an independent priest, treated as an equal), 71 (by a Seleucid king to a King Ptolemy), and 72 (by an Antiochus to the now-independent citizens of Seleuceia in Pieria). Fortunately Welles, *Royal Correspondence,* no. 71, survives to let us know that Seleucid kings in the second century B.C.E. might append to the *formula valetudinis,* after telling of their own health, the clause "and [or "but"] I remember you with affection," the same clause we have here.

Although many of the readings preserved in the old Latin versions are simply mistakes, the Latin very often reflects a text older than and superior to the Greek manuscripts, and such is clearly the case in vss. 20–21a.

La^{LV} present a text which almost perfectly reproduces a *formula valetudinis:* "If you and your children are well, and everything yours is as you would have it, we have the utmost gratitude. I am ill, but I remember you with affection."

The Latin translators and scribes did not insert a *formula valetudinis* into Epp. 1 and 2 or into three of the letters in ch. 11 or into the letters in First Maccabees. Hence, if here the Latin versions alone preserve the *formula vale-*

tudinis, the Latin writers must have seen it in the text and copied it, very likely because they recognized it; whereas the Greek scribes here and at 11:28 failed to understand it and made changes in the text. Even so, all Greek versions contain corrupt but recognizable fragments of a *formula valetudinis.*

The Latin versions themselves probably are somewhat imperfect reflections of the original text. Parallels from the third and second centuries B.C.E. can be found for all features of the Latin but one: elsewhere, if the writer uses the word "gratitude" (*charin*) he specifies that it is to a deity or deities. Gratitude to "the god" or "God," in the singular (*tôi theôi*), is attested even on a non-Jewish papyrus (*The Flinders Petrie Papyri,* ed. by John P. Mahaffy ["Royal Irish Academy, Cunningham Memoirs," vol. XI; Dublin, 1905], no. 53o, *theôi pleistê charis*). The garbled texts of L and *l,* which (as we shall see) contain recognizable corruptions of a *formula valetudinis,* have the words *tôi theôi,* as do many other minuscules. Hence, the original text probably had the words "to the god" after "gratitude." Jason of Cyrene, had he written English, would have made the letter say "to God," with a capital "G," rather than "to the god," but we have seen that the writer was not really presenting Antiochus as a near convert to Judaism, and in English he would have written "to the god." Unfortunately, in English it is impossible to preserve the ambiguity of *tôi theôi.* I cannot explain why the words *tôi theôi* were omitted from the Latin. It may have been an accident.

One other peculiarity of the *formula valetudinis* in the Latin versions may represent a misreading of the Greek original: the inconsistent use of the first person plural and the first person singular. Such inconsistencies, however, are attested in contemporary documents. See 11:28–29 (plural) and 32 (singular); Exler, p. 104; Mayser, II¹, 40–42. Nevertheless, a scribe may well have misread *ECHÔMEN* (*echô men* ["I have"]) as *echomen* ("we have"). If so, the original text of vss. 20–21a was *ei errôsthe kai ta tekna kai ta idia kata gnômên estin hymin, echô men tôi theôi tên megistên charin. kagô de asthenôs diekeimên,* as in our translation ("If . . . ill").

On the other hand, Greek scribes of the first century B.C.E. or later seem to have known nothing of the *formula valetudinis.* On finding it in vss. 20–21, they could wonder both why the king should put such verbiage into his letter and why the letter so lacked the humility and Jewish postures they expected after reading vss. 11–18. A puzzled Greek reader (let us call him "Mr. X") seems to have written into the margin the sort of words he thought the king should have used. He omitted the *ei* ("if") of the *formula valetudinis* and took *errôsthe* ("you are well") either as the imperative (also *errôsthe*) or as the infinitive (*errôsthai,* pronounced almost the same as *errôsthe*). The infinitive in the initial greetings of a Greek letter is equivalent to the imperative (see Gustav A. Gerhard, "Untersuchungen zur Geschichte des griechischen Briefes," *Philologus* 64 [1905], 27–58). If so, Mr. X meant to suggest that instead of our "If you . . . have it," the text should say "Be well, you yourselves and your children, and may everything yours be as you would have it." Thus the tardily repentant king could be seen to wish the Jews well (the greetings in vs. 19 were empty stereotypes). In his abbreviated note, Mr. X only turned *ei errôsthe* ("if you are well") into the imperative or the infinitive ("be well"). He did not spell out the change of "is" (*estin*) to "may . . . be" (*estô* or *einai*), and no later Greek scribe was able to fathom his intention: A has "will be" (*estai*), and all other Greek witnesses have "is." Hence, all Greek witnesses here have an incoherent sentence, "Be well . . . and everything yours is [or "will be"] as you would have it."

By changing the "if" clause into the king's heartfelt greeting to the Jews, Mr. X rendered incongruous the words which followed, "I have the utmost gratitude to the god." The wish which preceded was no occasion for gratitude, nor was the king's illness, mention of which followed. Mr. X might find fault with the incongruous clause also because "the god" could be a pagan expression. Far better it would be, Mr. X thought, if the desperate king had tried to conceal his desperation and attempted to impress his Jewish subjects with his new, pious hopes by stating that he now "had his hope in Heaven." Mr. X wrote out this suggestion in full, and all witnesses have it except 347 La Arm. In AVq, Mr. X's suggestion has completely displaced the king's expression of gratitude. In *L* and *l*, Mr. X's suggestion follows upon a slightly altered version of the expression of gratitude. Mr. X probably went too far here. Greeks did indeed speak of "hopes [for aid] in . . ." (*elpidas eis* . . .); see Thucydides iii 14.1. Pagan Greeks also called the gods "the ones from heaven" (Aeschylus *Prometheus Bound* 897). But "Heaven" as a substitute for a divine name or as the location from which a god sends help seems to be a Jewish usage, especially in Greek. See Traub, "*Ouranos*. A. Greek Usage," TDNT, V (1967), 498–501; von Rad, "*Ouranos*. B. Old Testament," ibid., pp. 506–7, 509; and Traub, "*Ouranos*. C. The Septuagint and Judaism," ibid., pp. 510, 512. Cf. also II 2:21, 3:34, 8:20, 15:8; J *AJ* viii 11.3.282 and xii 7.3.300. A Seleucid king writing from distant Persia might conceivably humble himself, but who there would teach him Jewish phraseology?

Mr. X had to harmonize his altered text not only with vs. 20 but also with vs. 21. Ignorant of the *formula valetudinis*, Mr. X found the mention of the king's ill health at the beginning of vs. 21 out of place in a context of clauses aimed at currying the Jews' favor. He also found it redundant, since it duplicated the report of the king's illness farther on in vs. 21. Surely, then, the awkward clause was a mistake, to be deleted! Mr. X removed it and thereby was able to turn his version of the king's pious hopes into a participial phrase depending on what was left of the beginning of vs. 21: "Having my hope in Heaven, I remember you with affection." For good Greek syntax he changed *de* ("but") to *te* (untranslatable in English).

Mr. X's work was not yet finished. He had no way of knowing that the letter was addressed to "Antiochene" Jews who had done their best to obey the king. Mr. X believed with Jason of Cyrene that the letter was addressed to the Jews of Judaea, including the pious. Even a repentant persecutor currying favor with his former victims could only enrage them by saying "I remember you with affection" (on vss. 26–27, see NOTE ad loc.). On the other hand, Jews had shown respect and loyalty to Antiochus IV before the persecution (4:22). Mr. X revised the clause to read "I remember your respect and your loyalty with affection."

Thus Mr. X's version of vss. 20–21, if written out in full, would have been "Be well, you yourselves and your children, and may everything yours be as you would have it. Having my hope in Heaven, I remember your respect and loyalty with affection." However, Mr. X wrote his suggestion as incomplete marginal notes. We have seen how later Greek scribes failed to comprehend his intentions: even in A and V, which come closest to giving Mr. X's revised text, the writer failed to change "is" to "may . . . be." Other later scribes faced another difficulty: the original reading in part or in full still lay before them. Thus, in q the "if" reappears, though no sense can be made of the result ("If you are well, you yourselves and your children, and everything yours is as you would have it, having my hope in Heaven, I remember . . ."). The scribes underlying L and l could still see the clauses "I have the utmost gratitude to God" and "I myself am ill."

The scribe of L tried to make sense of the jumble of clauses by changing "I have" (*echô men*) to "I pray" (*euchomai men*), so that vss. 20–21 could be translated "Be well, you yourselves . . . as you would have it. I pray to God for the greatest favor, having my hope in Heaven. I myself am ill. . . ." There are, indeed, ancient letters (even from the first century B.C.E.) which have a prayer in the greeting (see Bickerman, *Studies*, I, 121, n. 49; Exler, pp. 32–33; Roller, pp. 63–64, 463–64; Ziemann, pp. 308, 317–20). Here, however, the prayer is incongruous: it is for God's favor (upon the sender himself?) instead of for the health or welfare of the recipients.

The scribe of l changed *echô men* to *echoimi men;* the difficult result may mean ". . . May I have the utmost gratitude to God, having now my hope in Heaven. I myself am ill. . . ." Thus every word of the original we have reconstructed on the basis of the Latin is reflected in at least one Greek witness: "if," by q; "you are well . . . as you would wish," by all Greek witnesses; and "I have . . . to God. I myself am ill . . ." by L and l and some other minuscules. The incoherent and difficult Greek versions thus join the Latin in confirming our reconstructed text.

21. *I have been ill.* Other extant Greek letters show that the writer of a *formula valetudinis* could speak of his own illness and did not have to feign health for the sake of politeness (see Bickerman, *Studies*, I, 119, n. 41).

The past tense in the Greek of the verbs "have been" (*diekeimên*) and "remember" (*emnêmoneuon*) is the common epistolary usage, the sender writing the tense which would be appropriate from the point of view of the recipient at the moment of receipt (Mayser, II¹, 209–10).

returning. The letter uses a neutral word and does not present the king as confessing he had been repulsed; cf. Polybius ii 26.6, iii 14.2, iv 67.5.

22–25. *I have not . . . satrapies.* Our passage in Greek is a single sentence, explaining why and how the king is providing for the safety of all. One would expect such a Greek sentence to be introduced by the particle *gar,* but *gar* was frequently omitted, as here; see Mayser, II³, 179–83, and Kühner-Gerth, *Grammatik*, II, 344.

22. The verse is in character for a king who is dangerously ill but may yet recover; if by a forger, it adds an authentic touch: as long as there was life, there was hope.

23. Cuneiform documents show that Antiochus III designated his eldest son, Antiochus (older brother of Antiochus IV), as coregent and heir from 210/9 to 193/2 and his son Seleucus (the future Seleucus IV) as coregent and heir from 189 to 187; see Parker and Dubberstein, *Babylonian Chronology*, p. 22;

Bickerman, *Institutions*, pp. 21–22. Antiochus III was in Media when he so designated his eldest son, who was then only ten years old. Directly thereafter, Antiochus III set out on his spectacular campaigns (209–204), which took him through Iran to the borderlands of India. The future Seleucus IV was an adult at the time of the death of his older brother Antiochus in 193. At the beginning of 189 the Romans decisively defeated Antiochus III at the battle of Magnesia. From then until the ratification of the Peace of Apameia in spring, 188, Antiochus III had to remain close to his capital of Antioch in order to deal with the Romans and keep control of the nerve center of his kingdom. By October 11, 189, he had named Seleucus as his coregent and heir (Parker and Dubberstein, *Babylonian Chronology*, p. 22). The expedition of Antiochus III to secure the provinces he claimed in Iran could begin only after the conclusion of the Peace of Apameia. In the course of that expedition the king was killed while trying to plunder the temple of Bel in Elymais, on July 3 or 4, 187 (ibid.). Thus, it is not precisely true that Seleucus was named coregent just at the time his father marched eastward, though Antiochus III may have had the expedition in mind when he so appointed his son. For a detailed account of the events and the sources, see Will, *Histoire*, II, 46–59, 160, 167, 173, 177–202.

On "the inland regions" (*hoi anô topoi*) as meaning Mesopotamia and Iran, see AB vol. 41, NOTE on I 3:37, *inland*.

24–25. Euphemisms are employed in our verses to allude to the possibility of the king's death.

Decades of war followed when Alexander the Great died leaving no clear heir. Soldiers gathered around various aspirants to power, fighting in the hope of great rewards should their man win the kingship. Subjects of the kingdom suffered grievously in such wars.

Antiochus knew how great was the potential for internecine wars of succession within his kingdom. He himself had usurped the throne and eliminated his brother's son, little King Antiochus (see AB vol. 41, pp. 197–98). The little king's elder brother, the future Demetrius I, still survived as a hostage in Rome, and the line of Seleucus IV could still command some support in the realm (Polybius xxxi 2, 1–2, 12.2–5; AB vol. 41, p. 329).

In vs. 25 nothing is said of the possibility that Rome might back the claims of Demetrius or might at least release him. Neither Antiochus IV nor the regime of Lysias had any wish to provoke the Romans by making such mention of them. But it was well known how the nearby kingdom of Pergamum had aided Antiochus IV in his usurpation (AB vol. 41, p. 198).

The struggle between Ptolemy VI and his brother, the future Ptolemy VIII, for the throne preoccupied the energies of the Ptolemaic empire in late 164 and early 163 B.C.E.; see Will, *Histoire*, II, 302–3. Nevertheless, surely the Ptolemies still wished to recover their lost domains in Syria and Palestine and had good reason to seek to retaliate upon Antiochus IV for his aggression and attempt to meddle with the Ptolemaic succession (see AB vol. 41, pp. 202–3). Antiochus IV on his eastward march may have gained the submission of Artaxias, who claimed to be king of Armenia (Jerome *Commentarii in Danielem* on Dan 11:44–45; Will, *Histoire*, II, 296). If so, Artaxias, too, might welcome the disintegration of the Seleucid realm.

Antiochus IV himself surely was aware of these dangers. Partisans of Demetrius could dispute the right of the son of Antiochus IV to receive the throne by inheritance. To minimize the cogency of their claims, the letter presents Antiochus IV, while he still lived, as making his little son full king, not merely coregent. There is a report that Ptolemy I, while he still lived, thus made Ptolemy II full king (Justin xvi 2.7–9; Eusebius *Chronicorum libri,* ed. by Schoene, I, 162; cf. Cornelius Nepos xxi 3.4). Though the report is false (Hans Volkmann, "Ptolemaios 18," PW, XXIII² [1959], 1629), it shows that the procedure was known to the political theory of the Hellenistic kingdoms.

The word "king" (*basileus*) was, indeed, ambiguous as used in the Hellenistic monarchies. It could refer either to a full king or to a coregent. The powers of the coregent depended upon the will of the full king and on what he said when he publicly conferred the royal title. The full king might announce that the coregent was to have power over certain provinces (Plutarch *Demetrius* 28.8; Appian *Syriakê* 61; Plutarch *Antony* 54.4). Or the full king might only proclaim the coregent to be his heir and for the present grant him only the royal title and the right to wear the emblems of royalty (J. *AJ* xvi 4.6.133–35; *BJ* i 23.5.458–65). Because of the ambiguity of the word *basileus,* the full king, in every case of appointing a coregent with limited powers, took care, in the public speech validating his act, to specify what he meant. Since here Antiochus IV puts no such limitations on the power of his son, clearly the letter presents him as making the boy full king.

If Antiochus IV is the author of the letter at 11:27–33, our verses present no difficulty. But if Antiochus V is formally the author of that document, he could have been presented as the sender only if Antiochus IV had appointed him coregent over provinces in the western part of the empire before marching eastward in 165 B.C.E. (see NOTE on 11:16–21, NOTE on 11:27–33, NOTE on 11:34–38, and AB vol. 41, pp. 252–54). In that case, our verses would present something of a puzzle. Whether our letter was written at the command of Antiochus IV or is a forgery for the regime of Lysias, its author surely was aware of the coregency. Yet he would seem to ignore it. Though the verb "proclaim" in vs. 25 is in the perfect tense (*anadedeicha*), it must be translated here as a present. In the words from "I have not" in vs. 22 through "may bring" of vs. 25, Antiochus gives the thoughts which motivated him to make the proclamation mentioned in vs. 25. The thoughts, in turn, are presented as reactions to his illness. Consequently, the proclamation in vs. 25 must be later than the onset of the illness. Hence, the perfect tense of *anadedeicha* must be an epistolary perfect tense, signifying (from the point of view of the recipients) that the king at the time of sending the letter had carried through the act of making his son king (see Mayser, II¹, 183–84). Should not the writer have made Antiochus IV allude to the fact that he had earlier made his son coregent king?

Perhaps we can solve our puzzle by noting how the writer dealt with other difficulties. The verb "proclaim" here is the regular expression used for a king conferring a royal title on someone else, but literally it means "to display someone on high." Normally, to validate the act of conferring royal power, the one conferring it would place the recipient on a high platform and present him as king to a public mass meeting. See Bickerman, *Institutions,* pp. 23–24, and *"Anadeixis,"* AIPHOS 5 (1937), 117–24. Antiochus IV died far from his son, far from his capitals, and far from any important center of population. One thing he could do, though his son was absent: he could treat his assembled army as the public mass meeting and announce to them that he was making his son full king (cf. Appian *Syriakê* 61). The writer presents Antiochus as trying also to make up for the absence of his son from the proclamation ceremony. Though he could not now display his son on high to the mass meeting, he had displayed him to mass meetings of Antiochenes on several occasions shortly before his march eastward in 165.

Strangely, the writer uses two verbs to describe what Antiochus IV did with his son in the presence of those mass meetings of Antiochenes. The first of them, *parakatatithesthai* with the accusative and dative, means "deposit with," "entrust to," "put the fate of someone in the hands of" (see Tobit 10:13; Demosthenes *Epistle* 3.27; Aeschines 1.9). Antiochus, before marching, demonstrated his trust in his Antiochenes and appealed for their loyalty by calling upon them to help protect his little son (cf. Tacitus *Histories* iii 68; Demosthenes *Epistle* 3.27).

The second verb, *synistan,* from the literal meaning of "put in the presence of," gets to mean "introduce," "entrust," "commend," "recommend," "appoint to an office" (see Jeanne Robert and Louis Robert, "Bulletin epigraphique," *Revue des études grecques* 59–60 [1946–47], 354; Polybius xvi 9.1, xx 3.7; Greek Num 27:23). Since *parakatatithesthai* here clearly means "entrust," *synistan* should mean something else. I have rendered it by the ambiguous "commend," following the Latin translators. "Commend" in the context of vs. 25 may mean "commend, as coregent or heir, to" or "appoint as coregent or heir in the presence of." Plutarch *Demetrius* 28.4 may be an instructive parallel. In the narrative there, Demetrius has long been coregent king with his father, Antigonus (see ibid., 18.1). Antigonus, apprehensive before going into the battle of Ipsos, presented Demetrius to the army and "commended" (*synestêse,* third person singular of the first aorist tense of *synistan*) him to them as his successor. Plutarch had to specify the word "successor." Here, the letter has alluded to the concept of "full king," and the addressees knew what word ("coregent," "heir") was to be understood after the first person singular of the first aorist of *synistan.* Even if the writer did not thus express himself elliptically, the difficulty of his apparently ignoring the coregency can be solved. The letter is addressed to Antiochenes, and Antiochus IV at the time of his departure eastward may have given the little coregent no power over the Antiochene republic. Then "commend" could have one of its weaker senses, perhaps "introduce."

Some of the Latin translators (La^LXV) and the Syriac found the two verbs so synonymous that they rendered them by only one verb. The Latin uses the verb *commendo,* which was indeed regarded as equivalent to both Greek verbs; see *Thesaurus linguae Latinae* [Leipzig: B. G. Teubner, 1900–], vol. III [1906–12], col. 1840). The Syriac has *'g'lth* ("I entrusted him"). Hence, we should not assume that only one of the verbs lay before the ancient translators.

I have been unable to find an instance of *synistan* in a context of political campaigning, but it is worth noting that its Latin equivalent, *commendare,* was so used, with the meaning "recommend to the voters for political office"; see

Oxford Latin Dictionary (Oxford: Clarendon Press, 1968–), s.v. *commendo,* 4a. Then we would have another instance of the forger or Antiochus aping Roman electioneering behavior. But *commendare* is also used of Hellenistic kings commending their heirs to a mass meeting of their subjects (Pliny *Natural History* vii 53; Valerius Maximus ix 14 extern. 1).

Since Antiochus made only one expedition to the inland satrapies (Mørkholm, pp. 166–80), the adverb "more than once" (*pollakis*) must modify "entrusted and commended," not "setting out." The "inland satrapies" were Mesopotamia and Iran; see AB vol. 41, NOTE on 3:37.

26–27. Polybius and his contemporaries in the second century B.C.E. took it for granted that subjects of beneficent kings "not only preserve the royal office for the kings themselves, but also for their descendants, because they are convinced that those who are born to such kings and brought up by them will follow similar policies" (Polybius vi 7.2). Cf. Welles, *Royal Correspondence,* no. 14, lines 12–14, and no. 15, lines 30–34.

Mr. X could leave our verses untouched, even though he altered vss. 20–21 (see above, pp. 365–67), because he understood the writer to be referring to benefactions made after Antiochus' tardy repentance, shortly before his death.

26. *I ask you please.* The Greek, *parakalô kai axiô,* "I ask and request," is a very polite formula of request and probably helped Jason to jump to the conclusion that the letter was an abject and contrite petition. On *axiô,* see Welles, *Royal Correspondence,* p. 314. Kings are known to have used *parakalô* in letters containing requests to cities subject to them (ibid., nos. 14, line 12, and 15, line 30). The formula with both *parakalô* and *axiô* appears in *Syll.*³ 346, lines 32–33 (an Athenian *stratêgos* makes a request of two resident aliens, before 302/1 B.C.E.) and in *Syll.*³ 590, line 30 (ambassadors from Miletus are instructed to make a request at Kos, ca. 196 B.C.E.). The polite request here, with its two verbs, may also be a Greek equivalent for the Latin electioneering formulas *oro* ("I beg") and *rogat* ("asks"); see NOTE on vs. 19.

the benefactions . . . individuals. Antiochene citizens as individuals and in communities must have received liberal treatment from Antiochus IV; see AB vol. 41, pp. 115–21. Even the hostile witness at I 6:11 allows the king his claim to have been "kind and popular" in his realm (see AB vol. 41, p. 310).

27. The election posters at Pompeii say of the candidate that he is a "good man" (*vir bonus*).

28. Antiochus suffered both the torments of the martyrs and the privations of Judas and his men, who had to go to the mountains of Judaea and Samaria (5:27, 10:6; AB vol. 41, pp. 235–36). Jason intended that the reader notice the contrast between Judas and his men, celebrating in Jerusalem, and Antiochus, dying in the mountains, on foreign soil. The area around Tabai in Paraitakênê, where Antiochus IV died, is indeed mountainous (Strabo xv 3.12, C 732, and xvi 1.17, C 744), but it may still have been Seleucid soil (see AB vol. 41, p. 310). The parallel at I 6:13 shows that Jason and the author of First Maccabees drew on the Common Source.

For the date of the king's death, see the second par. of the NOTE on 1:10b – 2:18.

29. *Schoolfellow (syntrophos)* was an honorary title conferred by the king

on courtiers, who might or might not have grown up with him; see Bickerman, *Institutions*, pp. 42–43.

Attempted to escort is my rendering of the Greek verb, in the imperfect tense, *parekomizeto*, used to indicate that Philip did not succeed in his enterprise (Kühner-Gerth, *Grammatik*, I, 140–42). Compare the pagan legend quoted in NOTE on vs. 7, *At that . . . joint*.

Jason of Cyrene had no reason to insert the name of Ptolemy VI Philometor if all he wished to do was to say that Philip took refuge in Egypt (cf. 5:8). Hence, the reference to Philometor must have stood in his source. The source could well have been the work of Onias IV, faithful beneficiary of Philometor; see my article in *Studies Smith*, Part III, pp. 85–123. In October, 164 B.C.E., Ptolemy VI Philometor's younger brother drove him out of Egypt and seized the throne. Ptolemy VI recovered Egypt only in April or May, 163; see Alan E. Samuel, *Ptolemaic Chronology* (München: Beck, 1962), pp. 142–43. It is true that the younger Ptolemy (the future Ptolemy VIII Euergetes II) at the time also bore the name "Philometor," but any source available to Jason (whether Onias IV, Polybius, or someone else) probably used "Philometor" to refer only to Ptolemy VI and called Ptolemy VIII either "the younger Ptolemy" or "Ptolemy Euergetes."

We may thus conclude that Philip fled to Egypt no earlier than April, 163, long after the death of Antiochus IV in November or December, 164. The bearer of the king's body and last instructions should have made every effort to march quickly to Antioch. Military and political maneuvers, if not battles, between the supporters of Lysias and those of Philip, must have filled the interval between the king's death and Philip's flight to Egypt. If so, we can understand more easily why the Seleucid government did not intervene to stop the victorious campaigns of Judas and Simon in early 163 against the hostile neighbors of Judaea (I 5; cf. II 10:14–38, 12:2–37).

The account here differs sharply from that at I 6:14–15, 55–63. There, though Lysias had been the guardian of the future Antiochus V, Antiochus IV, in dying, appoints Philip to replace Lysias as guardian. Philip is, in effect, to be the executor of the late king's will. He succeeds somehow in returning westward and seizes Antioch while Lysias and Antiochus V are busy fighting in Judaea. Lysias and the little king patch up a peace with the Jews and, turning their full force against Philip, defeat him and recapture Antioch.

Here, in contrast, nothing is said of Philip's appointment as guardian. Philip acts only as the escort of the king's corpse homeward. In the abridged history Antiochus V, though he was a child, acts forcefully on the basis of his own will (see also 10:10–13, 11:15–33, 13:1–26). Philip here never reaches Antioch; he has some unspecified reason to fear Antiochus V (not Lysias!) and finds refuge with Ptolemy VI Philometor of Egypt. At 13:23 the author sharply distinguishes, from the executor of the will of Antiochus IV, the Philip who carried out a coup at Antioch while Lysias and Antiochus V were fighting in Judaea. The latter Philip is there said to have been "left at Antioch in charge of the government" by Lysias' own regime!

Where is the truth to be found in these rival accounts? Historians can easily confuse two persons bearing the same name if they are ignorant of evidence distinguishing them. The author of First Maccabees may well have known of the *Memoirs* of Onias IV, but, if so, he regarded them as unreliable for the period before the death of Judas and ignored what they had to say (see p. 37). If Jason followed another source to distinguish the two Philips, it may have been totally unknown to the Hasmonaean propagandist. We may conclude that Jason of Cyrene was almost certainly right against his rival in distinguishing two Philips, just as he was in distinguishing two Timothei (see NOTES on 8:30, 32). In both cases he may well have contradicted the narrative of his rival deliberately, in order to discredit it.

The narrative at I 6:55–56, indeed, contains a gross improbability, made all the worse by the mistaken chronology in First Maccabees placing the expedition of Antiochus V and Lysias in 150 Sel. (see AB vol. 41, pp. 315–19). Antiochus IV died in 148 Sel. What was Philip doing during the long interval? If he was idle, surely his supporters would desert him and declare for Lysias' regime. If he was not idle, how could the king and his chief minister have left Antioch and gone on a campaign against the Jews?

On the other hand, Jason based his narrative in our chapter on the letter here. With some fairly subtle thinking, we were able to reconcile the content of the letter with the dying king's appointment of Philip (p. 357). The subtleties could well have eluded Jason. If the letter is a forgery, it deceived Jason. Accordingly, Jason could only reject any report available to him of the appointment of Philip.

Did the king in fact risk disrupting the Seleucid realm by deposing Lysias and appointing Philip? Could not the report of Philip's appointment be false propaganda spread by Philip, as suggested by Erich Gruen ("Rome and the Seleucids in the Aftermath of Pydna," *Chiron,* VI [1976], 79–80)? Nothing in the evidence rules out such an action by Antiochus. I was wrong to assume (AB vol. 41, p. 310) that the appointment of Philip as guardian necessarily meant the deposition of Lysias from all his functions. Lysias' sphere was restricted to the western provinces, and Antiochus IV may have intended only to appoint Philip to be Lysias' superior, as minister in charge of the entire empire. On the other hand, Antiochus IV may have intended to depose Lysias completely. Lysias had failed to keep order in his provinces. Antiochus IV may have been mostly victorious in his expedition to the east (see Mørkholm, pp. 166–80). Lysias' troops may have been demoralized by their failures to defeat the Jews. Antiochus IV may have believed that Lysias was unlikely to defy Philip's authority, backed by a superior army. Lysias, in turn, may have frustrated the king's purposes by outbidding Philip for the support of the army and the people (cf. Justin xxxiv 3.5).

False propaganda for Philip's cause would consist of reports fabricated for an ephemeral losing cause. Would such reports be likely to survive down to the time of the author of First Maccabees? Rather, if any false propaganda survived from the period, it was that written for Lysias' temporarily victorious cause. The suffering Jewish Antiochenes, and later even pious Jews, found the king's last message flattering, whether it was real or forged. There was nothing flattering to Jews in the report of Philip's appointment. Nevertheless, that report survived, probably because too many in the army knew of the fact for Lysias to suppress it completely.

XII. THE FESTIVAL OF PURIFICATION
(10:1–8)

10 1 Maccabaeus and his men, with the LORD leading them, recovered the sanctuary and the city. 2 They destroyed the illicit altars which the foreigners had built around the marketplace and also the illicit shrines. 3 After purifying the temple, they made another altar. Using fire they got by igniting stones, for the first time in two years they offered sacrifices and incense and installed the lights and set out the showbread. 4 That done, they prostrated themselves and prayed to the LORD that they never again would come to suffer such disasters. Rather, if they should ever sin, let them be chastised by the LORD himself, with clemency, and not delivered over to the hands of blasphemous and barbarous gentiles. 5 On the very same date on which the temple was profaned by foreigners occurred the purification of the temple, on the twenty-fifth of the ninth month (that is, Kislev). 6 Joyfully they held an eight-day celebration, after the pattern of Tabernacles, remembering how a short time before they spent the festival of Tabernacles like wild beasts, in the mountains and in the caves. 7 Therefore, holding wreathed wands, and branches bearing ripe fruit, and palm fronds, they offered songs of praise to Him Who had victoriously brought about the purification of His Place. 8 By vote of the commonwealth they decreed a rule for the entire nation of the Jews to observe these days annually.

NOTES

10:1–8. On the original position of our passage in the abridged history, see introductory NOTE on ch. 9.

Before Judas and his men could recover Jerusalem, according to the account in I 3:45–46, 4:26–37, they had to resist the first expedition of Lysias. On why Jason of Cyrene moved the expedition to the reign of Antiochus V, see p. 57.

Combat in the first expedition of Lysias ended with the bloody battle of

Beth-Zur. Negotiations followed, in which the high priest Menelaus as well as pious rebels had roles. As a result, the Seleucid regime ended the persecution, and Lysias withdrew from Judaea, surely in the belief that Menelaus and Jews who now would again be loyal to the kingdom would be able to keep order. For details, see NOTES on ch. 11.

The terms by which the government ended the persecution did not turn control of the temple over to the pious. However, upon Lysias' withdrawal, no force was strong enough to prevent Judas and his men from taking Jerusalem. The garrison in the Akra might on occasion make a sally to harass the pious (I 4:41), but most of the time that outnumbered force did not leave the safety of their citadel. If any followers of the imposed cult remained in Jerusalem, they abandoned the temple for fear of attacks by pious Jews. Nevertheless, the pious rebels waited for months, until the beginning of the sabbatical year on their defective calendar (ca. July 25, 164 B.C.E.), and only then did they march in and purify the temple, which by that time bore the scars not only of years of conflict but of months of neglect. See AB vol. 41, pp. 273–81, 284.

One might guess that the delay came from purely political causes. The peace of Lysias did not give the temple back to the Jews. Lysias may well have intended to leave it in the hands of the followers of the imposed cult. The Jews weaned away from Judas' force by the amnesty may have feared to provoke the imperial government by violating the terms and seizing the temple. Judas had to rally public opinion for such a coup; perhaps he had to summon up courage to act himself, with the nuclear Hasmonaean force and without mass support. Meanwhile, the months of inaction could have elapsed. However, the long abandonment of the temple by apostates renders unlikely the guess that purely political causes produced the delay. Rather, pious Jews insisted on waiting for the prophesied miracles to occur, as argued in AB vol. 41, pp. 273–81. We would have to ask how believers reacted to the failure of the miracles to occur even if we did not have to explain why the Jews were slow to recover and restore the temple.

Conspicuous by its absence from our passage is any use of the Greek root *kain-* ("new"), found in the Greek words *anakainizein* ("renew," "restore") and *enkainizein* ("dedicate"). One may infer that for Jason of Cyrene, too, there could be no "dedication" of a temple altar unless miraculous fire came down from heaven; see NOTE on 1:18 and AB vol. 41, pp. 280–82. Even in vs. 3, Jason wrote not of a "new" altar but of "another" one. Cf. the use of "new," "dedicate," and "dedication" by the Hasmonaean propagandist in I 4:36, 47, 49, 53–54, 56, 59.

Normally, the Jewish temple was under the control of the high priest, and Menelaus in fact had negotiated for the amnesty which left the way open for the purification. The pious rebels surely loathed him and must have taken the unusual step of taking the temple out of the high priest's control; they may even have denied him access to it. See I 4:42, where Judas' chosen priests are meant to contrast with Menelaus.

Dan 11:24 probably contains an echo of these events. In my commentary on Dan, I shall argue that the "appointed time" mentioned in Dan 11:24 is the beginning of the sabbatical year, the time of the prophesied end of the persecution, and that Dan 11:22(end)–24 means "And also a Jewish high priest through association with the king shall work treachery and thus rise to rule over Israel. In time of peace he shall squander the property as spoil and plunder to the Greeks, and he shall meditate plots concerning fortifiers until the beginning of the sabbatical year." See NOTE on 5:23–24. Thus the seer of Daniel would appear to know that at the beginning of the sabbatical year Menelaus lost his power to plot against the pious. Admittedly, it is also possible that the predicted downfall of Menelaus in Dan 11:24 is a real prophecy, made before the fact. However, if it was, the pious surely took advantage of the prophecy to justify excluding Menelaus from his high priestly prerogatives. Menelaus may even have ceased to hold office *de jure,* if Antiochus V failed to confirm him as high priest after the death of Antiochus IV. More likely, Antiochus V did confirm Menelaus in his office, and Menelaus then held it at least until the middle of 163 B.C.E. See NOTE on 13:3–8 and AB vol. 41, pp. 75–76. In any case, Judas and his pious supporters, in late summer or early autumn, 164 B.C.E., must have refused to recognize Menelaus' authority and must have excluded him from the temple, so that in 163 B.C.E. (13:3) he asked the royal government to confirm him in high priestly power. Dan 11:24 thus would refer to Menelaus' exclusion from the temple by pious Jews, not to his deposition by the royal government; correct accordingly AB vol. 41, p. 167.

On the ritual of lighting lamps and on the rabbinic legend of the miracle of the oil which burned for eight days, see AB vol. 41, pp. 281–84. In the middle of the first century B.C.E. a somewhat similar miracle was reported at the temple of Zeus of Panamara in western Asia Minor: when the sanctuary came under attack, "The lamps of the god were discovered to have lit themselves and they continued to burn throughout the siege" (P. Roussel, "Le miracle de Zeus Panamaros," *Bulletin de correspondence hellénique* 55 [1931], 74, 84, and fold-out leaf of p. 85 [line 27]).

After I 4:36–59, his parallels to our verses, the Hasmonaean propagandist in I 4:60–61 added material absent from the abridged history telling how Judas fortified the temple mount and Beth-Zur. Jason of Cyrene may well have omitted the fortification of the temple mount. By so doing he could more easily avoid mentioning the destruction of those walls by Antiochus V (see NOTE on 13:24). I see no reason why Jason would have chosen to omit the fortification of Beth-Zur (cf. 13:19). Perhaps the abridger left it out. The content of I 4:60–61 thus probably stood in the Common Source.

1–2. Our verses contain both parallels to and contrasts with I 4:36–37. Both texts agree that Judas and his men recovered the temple, and thus they may have drawn on the Common Source. At I 4:36, however, the leadership is ascribed to Judas and his brothers; here, in contrast, the leadership is ascribed to God.

It is hard to understand why I 4:36–40, in contrast to our verses, concentrates completely on the temple mount and the temple and says nothing of the city of Jerusalem. The silence there is all the stranger because it follows eloquent and emotional depictions of the plight of Jerusalem and the presence there of idolatrous shrines (I 1:31, 38, 47, 55; 2:7, 3:45), and the author of First Maccabees nowhere else tells how Jerusalem (outside the temple) recovered from those outrages. Josephus seems instinctively to have felt the lack and to have been driven to interpret, wrongly, "Mount Zion" at I 4:37 to mean "Jerusalem" (*AJ* xii 7.6.316–17). See AB vol. 41, p. 287; and for clear evidence that Mount Zion in First Maccabees is the temple mount, cf. I 4:60 with I 6:7, and see I 6:51 with I 6:61–62.

Perhaps the explanation of the strange omission of Jerusalem in I 4:36–40 is that the author of First Maccabees refused to grant that Judas recovered and restored Jerusalem. The city was still unwalled (I 1:31), and the Akra still contained a hostile garrison (cf. II 15:37). For our author, if so, only Jonathan and Simon "recovered" Jerusalem (I 10:10–11, 13:49–51).

If our writers drew on the Common Source, what did it have? We can only guess. Perhaps it said, "Judas and his men recovered Jerusalem and the temple." If so, the author of First Maccabees omitted "Jerusalem" and added I 4:36; and Jason, probably in reaction to I 4:36, inserted "with the Lord leading them" (drawing on Isa 58:8?).

1. The demonstration referred to at AB vol. 41, p. 174, n. 27, is in the NOTE on vss. 1–8.

2. The construction of altars (*bomous*) and shrines (*temenê*) around the marketplace, outside the temple area, violated Deut 12:5–29, and hence they were illicit; see I 1:47, 54–55. In line 8 of my NOTE on I 1:54–55 at AB vol. 41, p. 225, I should have included a reference to Louis Robert, "Sur un décret d'Ilion et sur un papyrus concernant des cultes royaux," *Essays in Honor of C. Bradford Welles* (American Studies in Papyrology, vol. I; New Haven: American Society of Papyrologists, 1966), pp. 186–210. *Temenos* in Greek can mean a grove of trees sacred to a pagan god. That meaning is unlikely here and at I 1:47; see AB vol. 41, p. 222. Indeed, all the Latin versions here and at 11:3 and at I 1:47 have "shrines" (*templa* or *delubra*). The Greek verb *kathaireô* ("destroy," "tear down") in translations from the Hebrew Bible renders verbs of smashing or tearing down structures, and its presence also confirms our view, that *temenê* here and at I 1:47 means "illicit shrines" rather than "sacred groves."

3. Our verse contains striking parallels of content and wording to I 4:41–54, so as to indicate strongly the reality of the Common Source. The differences between the two accounts are all explainable by the prejudices of the two authors.

Here and at I 4:41 and 43 the temple is said to have been "purified." Here and at I 4:47 a new altar is said to have been built. On both points, cf. 1:8, and see NOTE ad loc., and on the use here of "another" rather than "new," see NOTE on vss. 1–8. Here and at I 4:40–51 the incense, the lamps, and the showbread are mentioned in that order (cf. II 1:8 and see NOTE on II 1:8, *We brought . . . showbread*). Here and at I 4:52–54 the renewed offering of the daily sacrifices is reported and an indication given of the duration of the period during which the sacrifices ceased.

At I 4:53 the sacrifices come *after* the other ritual acts; on the difference, see NOTE on II 1:8, *We brought . . . showbread*. Here we read how fire was obtained by igniting stones, a substitute for a miracle (see NOTE on *using . . . stones*); the author of First Maccabees preferred to pass over in silence the failure of miraculous fire to come down from heaven (see AB vol. 41, pp. 280–81). On the other hand, the writer here avoids mention of the "loathsome structure," the Abomination of Desolation (cf. I 4:43–46, and see NOTE on

II 6:4–5). The "two years" here are probably in deliberate contrast to the (correct) three years implied by I 1:54, 59, 4:52–54; see pp. 55–63.

purifying the temple. The imposed cult had rendered the temple unclean both through the practice of idolatry and through the introduction of persons and materials declared to be unclean by the Torah; see AB vol. 41, pp. 222, 482; Schürer (New English version), II, 83–84, 284–85, 475–78; "Purity and Impurity, Ritual," Enc. Jud., XIII (1971), 1405–12.

they made another altar. One would expect the writer to say why "another altar" was needed (cf. I 4:44–47 and see AB vol. 41, p. 285). Has the abridger omitted the reasons, in the belief that 6:5 was sufficient explanation?

Using . . . stones. The brevity of the accounts here and at I 4:53 probably conceals embarrassing religious problems. God should take note of the dedication of His altar by sending miraculous fire. If God does not do so, how can the pious light the altar fire without risking the fate of Nadab and Abihu (Lev 10:1–2)? See AB vol. 41, pp. 280–81, and NOTE on II 1:18 and NOTE on II 1:19–36.

The problem of how to light the fire did not exist later for the rabbis (see p. 173). The only Jewish source to face the problem, other than our verse, is Ep. 2, where the altar fire is said to have been ignited by sunlight shining upon petroleum (1:21–22). There is a Roman parallel: when the fire of Vesta went out, the Vestal virgins rekindled it by using a fire-by-friction drill apparatus made of the wood of fruit trees (Festus, in *Pauli excerpta ex libro Sexti Pompei Festi* s.v. *Ignis,* p. 94 Lindsay, p. 106 Mueller). One might then expect to have our passage mean that the fire was ignited by sparks struck from stones.

On the methods used by the ancients to kindle fires and on the terminology employed in Greek and Latin, see Alfred Jacob, "Igniaria," DAGR, III (1899), 371–72. The Greek expressions here seem to exclude the interpretation that sparks were struck from stones. Nowhere else does the transitive verb *pyroun* mean "strike sparks from." Rather, it means "set on fire" or "make red-hot." Moreover, if *pyrôsantes lithous* here did mean "striking sparks from stones," the next participial phrase, "and taking fire from them," would seem to be redundant. An ancient audience knew that fires were commonly ignited by striking sparks from stones.

Therefore I have chosen to render the meaning of the verb as literally as possible, though for good English I have altered the syntax. One might follow the Syriac and render the Greek participles "heating stones red-hot and taking fire from them," but the expression is again unnatural. Can one "take fire" from ordinary red-hot stones, which do not blaze? On the other hand, the mineral, coal, was widely known, at least from the early third century B.C.E. Theophrastus (*De lapidibus* 16) tells of how it can be ignited, using the same verb, *pyroun;* see also Lagercrantz, "Kohle", PW, XI (1922), 1044–45. The mineral can only have been a rarity in Judaea. Why did Jason suggest it was used to kindle firewood on the altar? The wonderful is strange to man, but normal for God. We may guess that fire from "stones" (coal), like fire from "viscous water" (petroleum; see 1:21) was enough of a wonder so that the pious might believe that God would not regard it as "strange." Cf. I Kings 18:38; Ezek 28:14, 16. Correct accordingly the paraphrase of our passage at AB vol. 41, p. 281, par. 2

offered . . . lights. The Greek uses only one verb, *anênenkan,* to express the three different actions of "offering" sacrifice, "burning" incense, and "installing" lamps into a candelabrum. The multiple use of the single verb was probably as unnatural in Greek as it would be in English, but all three actions could be expressed in Hebrew by the single verb *h'lw* (for sacrifices, cf. Gen 8:20, etc.; for incense, Exod 30:9; for lamps, Exod 40:25, Num 8:3). In Ep. 1 (1:8) the "kindling" of the lamps receives its own verb.

Both our passage and I 4:49–50 refer to the renewal of those incense offerings which accompanied the Continual Offering (*Tamid;* see NOTE on II 1:8, *We brought . . . showbread*), whereas II 1:8 says nothing about the offering of incense. We may infer that our two historians drew upon the Common Source here, not upon Ep. 0 or Ep. 1. Correct accordingly AB vol. 41, p. 35.

sacrifices. The vague word *thysias* here as at 1:8 refers to the offerings of the *Tamid.* Here, unlike 1:8, the word seems to include both the animal and the vegetable components; cf. S. Daniel, *Recherches,* pp. 203–14, 220–22.

showbread. See NOTE on 1:8, *We brought . . . showbread.*

4. The parallels of wording and content here to I 4:38–40 strongly indicate the existence of the Common Source. The religious gesture of prostration, expressed by the verb which literally means "fall" (Gr. *pesein;* Heb. *npl*), occurs in First Maccabees only in connection with the prayers connected with the purification and rededication of the temple (I 4:40, 55). In the abridged history it occurs in the same connection in our verse and only at one other place (II 10:26). Expressed by other verbs or by nouns, it occurs at II 3:15 (*riptein*), 21 (*proptôsis*), 13:12 (*proptôsis*). Even the sketched content of the prayer here is somewhat parallel to what we find at I 4:38–40: the religious acts at I 4:39–40 and the prayer here are in reaction to the atrocities perpetrated by the gentiles. The theological motif here, of the educative purpose of suffering such atrocities, is characteristic of the abridger and very likely of Jason (see II 6:12–17 and NOTE ad loc.). Thus, the writer here has probably added that motif to what lay before him.

The rest of the abridged history serves to demonstrate that the prayer in our verse was fulfilled.

For "prostrated," the Greek here has "having fallen on their *bellies,*" an expression otherwise unknown to me in Greek or Hebrew. In Egyptian texts the equivalent was common. See, e.g., "The Story of Si-nuhe," ANET², p. 21. Until 96 B.C.E., Jason's home city of Cyrene was ruled by the same Ptolemaic dynasty that ruled Egypt. Jason's education could have included exposure to Egyptian linguistic patterns.

5. Our verse is so similar in wording, style, structure, and content to I 4:52, 54 (". . . On the twenty-fifth day of the ninth month (that is, the month of Kislev) . . . at the very time of year and on the very day on which the gentiles had profaned the altar, it was dedicated . . .") as to argue for the existence of the Common Source. Noteworthy in both passages is the formal indication of the month, by ordinal number and by name. In First Maccabees such a double designation is found elsewhere only at 16:14, and in the abridged history only at II 15:36.

At AB vol. 41, p. 286, I was probably wrong to suggest that "and on the very day" at I 4:54 is an interpolation. Even "at the very time of year" (*kata ton kairon*) there means "on the anniversary of the day"; see my article in PAAJR 46–47 (1979–80), 181.

Here in our verse, where I have "ninth" (Gr. *enatou*), all Greek witnesses have "same" (*autou*), but La^{-P} and Sy have no word at all. In view of the existence of the stereotyped expression "In the xth month (that is, y)" (Esther 2:16, 3:7, 12, 8:9; I 4:52, etc.), it is probable that in an early copy the ordinal number "ninth" became blurred. Some scribes "restored" it by guessing from the other occurrence of "same" in the context, whereas the scribes reflected by La^{-P} and Sy omitted the illegible word.

6–7. The cross-reference at AB vol. 41, p. 56, n. 10, to a NOTE here should be deleted.

6. Our verse has so striking a parallel at I 4:56 ("They celebrated . . . for eight days, joyfully . . .") as to argue for the existence of the Common Source. There was good reason for Jason not to use the expression found at I 4:56, "the dedication of the altar"; see NOTE on vss. 1–8. There was also good reason for the author of First Maccabees to omit the connection of the Days of Dedication with the festival of Tabernacles. See AB vol. 41, pp. 273–82. There I show how the earliest attested name for the Days of Purification (=Days of Dedication) came to be "Days of Tabernacles in the month of Kislev," as in Ep. 1 (1:9). I also explain how the origin of that early name was embarrassing for the pious, so that the facts were quickly forgotten with the passing of Judas' generation.

Though the origin was forgotten, Ep. 1 and the strange name still had to be explained. Our verse, which attempts to do so, has its own linguistic obscurity. My translation follows La^{LXVP} in taking "the festival of Tabernacles" as the direct object of "spent" (*êsan nemomenoi*, a form of the verb *nemesthai*). However, to my knowledge, only the poet Pindar uses *nemesthai* in this manner and sense (see *Nemean Ode* 10.55–56), and our passage is pure prose!

The alternative, however, is worse: to take "the festival of Tabernacles" as an accusative of duration of time, "throughout the festival of Tabernacles," and *êsan nemomenoi* as "went about seeking their food" (La^{BM}Sy). Grimm cites 5:27 as confirmation for this version. But how can one speak of going about seeking food in *caves*? And if the point were the delicious food missed during the months of guerrilla warfare, why is there no mention of the delicacies enjoyed during the Days of Purification? Cf. Esther 9:17–22.

7. Jason's intention is to describe the rituals of the Days of Purification as imitating those of Tabernacles. The Greek words here certainly do not fit the practices of Jews today, and there is some difficulty even in fitting them to the biblical texts bearing on Tabernacles.

If a non-Greek ritual object had some resemblance to one used by Greeks, Greeks would naturally give the non-Greek object the same Greek name as their own. A *thyrsos* (translated here "wreathed wand") was a wand made from any kind of wood, wreathed in ivy and vine leaves, with a pine cone at the top; it was used in the worship of Dionysus (F. v. Lorenz, "Thyrsos," PW, VIA^1 [1936], 748). An *eiresiônê* was a branch of olive or laurel wound around with wool and hung with fruits, used in the worship of Apollo. Hence, the apparatus of palm, myrtle, and willow branches and *hādār* fruits, which Jews were commanded to take on the festival of Tabernacles (Lev 23:40), came to be called in Greek *thyrsos* (J. *AJ* xiii 13.5.372) or *eiresiône* (J. *AJ* iii 10.4.245); cf. Judith 15:12.

Here, however, the *thyrsos* is distinct from the palm branch. Nothing indicates that the *thyrsos* consists of myrtle and willow. Indeed, Plutarch reports that Jews on Tabernacles practice both a rite of carrying a *thyrsos* and one of carrying tree branches (*Quaestiones conviviales* iv 6.2., p. 671e). Jason of Cyrene and other Hellenized Jews may well have imported the *thyrsos* into their observance of Tabernacles, adding it to the traditional apparatus. For other evidence of the ways in which Jews and Greeks viewed the festival of Tabernacles as being close to or identical with pagan rites, see Deissmann, *Light from the Ancient East* (New York: George H. Doran, 1927), pp. 115–16, and Saul Lieberman, "On Persecution of the Jewish Religion," in *Salo Wittmayer Baron Jubilee Volume on the Occasion of His Eightieth Birthday,* ed. by Saul Lieberman (Jerusalem: American Academy for Jewish Research; New York: distributed by Columbia University Press, 1974), Hebrew Section, p. 217.

The text speaks strangely of *kladous hôraious,* which I have translated "branches bearing ripe fruit." The adjective *hôraios* translates the Hebrew *hādār* at Lev 23:40 and in Greek frequently means "pertaining to the fruits of the season." Josephus and rabbinic sources both identify the *hādār* fruit with the citron (*AJ* iii 10.4.245 with Athenaeus iii 83d–f; TB *Sukkah* 35a), but Lev 23:40 says nothing about the fruits being attached to branches. Nevertheless, Josephus at *AJ* xiii 13.5.372 says that on Tabernacles Jews hold "*thyrsoi* taken from palms and citron trees," so perhaps Josephus and Jason both attest the carrying of *branches* bearing citrons. There is no trace of such a practice in rabbinic texts.

"Offered songs of praise" (*hymnous anepheron*) is the reading of Vq and some minuscules. As a strange but intelligible expression, it probably is the one used by Jason. Hellenistic Greek poets did use the verb *anapherein* to mean "utter" (*Greek-English Lexicon* s.v. *anapherô,* I, 3). Early scribes omitted the strange expression (La^LXV) or changed it to the commonplace "they gave thanks" (*eucharistoun* or *eucharistountes;* so AL').

Inasmuch as the first half of our verse connects the Feast of Purification with Tabernacles, it could have no parallel in First Maccabees even though Jason probably derived it from the Common Source. See NOTE on vs. 6. The rest of our verse, however, has strong parallels in wording and content at I 4:54–55, ". . . to the sound of singing . . . and thanks to Heaven Who had brought them victory." The Greek verb *euodoun* occurs both here ("had victoriously brought about") and at I 4:55 ("had brought victory"). It represents Heb. *hṣlyḥ*. The verb occurs elsewhere in First Maccabees at 3:6, 14:36, and 16:2; in the abridged history it recurs only at II 10:23. This evidence argues for the existence of the Common Source.

8. Evidence for the existence of the Common Source can be found in the closeness of our verse to I 4:59, "Judas and his brothers and the entire assembly of Israel decreed that the days of the dedication of the altar should be observed at their time of year annually for eight days." Typically, the writer here avoids the word "dedication" (see NOTE on vss. 1–8) and fails to speak of the prestige of Judas' brothers, whereas the author of First Maccabees uses

the word and takes care to include the brothers (see AB vol. 41, pp. 74, 79–80).

On the rituals and liturgy of Ḥanukkah, see AB vol. 41, pp. 18–19, n. 33, 281–84, 286–87. On the decree and how it was passed, see AB vol. 41, pp. 287, 501–4, 507, 509 (on the assumption that the procedure here was similar to that which produced the decree at I 14:27–47).

The pattern of annually commemorating the dedication of a temple or altar is unknown among the Greeks. On Jewish festivals to commemorate miracles, see AB vol. 41, p. 283. *Megillat Ta'anit* singles out 1–8 Nisan for observance as the days on which "the *Tamid* was established." Their observance may reflect a corresponding interpretation of Exod 40:2, 16, 29; Lev 8:1–9:24. If so, those days would commemorate the institution of the *Tamid* by Moses and Aaron and would be something of a parallel to what we have here. *Megillat Ta'anit* 4 Elul lists that day as commemorating the dedication of the wall of Jerusalem. Syrians are known to have celebrated the anniversary of the dedication (*ḥnkt'*) of a temple; see Robert Comte Du Mesnil du Buisson, *Les Tessères et les monnaies de Palmyre* (Paris: É. de Boccard, 1962), pp. 571–72.

By vote . . . rule. It is difficult to make sense of the text of the Greek manuscripts, *edogmatisan de meta koinou prostagmatos kai psêphismatos* "By a rule and a vote of the commonwealth, they decreed"; for *meta* as "by" cf. 6:16. The words *prostagmatos kai* ("a rule and") look intrusive. They are absent from the parallel passage at 15:36. Nevertheless, *prostagma* is the word regularly used in the Greek Bible for a rule ordained by human beings, especially one setting up a commemorative observance (Gen 47:26; Judg 11:39; I Reigns 30:25; II Chron 35:25). The ancient versions here reflect the difficulty. The Syriac gives a simple paraphrase, "They concluded unanimously." La^BM similarly omit the difficult word. La^L, however, frequently reflects a text earlier than that of our Greek manuscripts, and here it has the absolutely unintelligible *Decrevimus de communi imperio decreto* ("We decided, from a rule vote of the commonwealth"), the word "and" after "rule" being omitted. One might guess from this evidence that *prostagmatos* crept into the text as an explanatory synonym of *psêphismatos* ("vote"); similar is the suggestion of de Bruyne (*Les anciennes traductions*, p. xx). However, the word does not explain anything here. To judge by the parallels from the Greek Bible, *prostagma* does belong somewhere in the text. Indeed, another peculiarity of the Greek suggests that the original had *prostagma*, in the accusative case, either before *meta* ("by") or after *psêphismatos*. Elsewhere, if the verb *dogmatizein* (here translated "decree") has no noun as direct object, the content of the decree is expressed by a clause or by a construction with an accusative subject and an infinitive predicate (cf. the document at J. *AJ* xiv 10.22.249 and Diodorus iv 83.7). Here the content of the decree is expressed by a dative noun and an infinitive verb, a fact suggesting that originally "rule" (*prostagma*) stood as the direct object of "they decreed." I have translated accordingly.

XIII. TROUBLES EARLY IN THE REIGN OF ANTIOCHUS V
(10:9–38)

10 9 Such was the end of Antiochus, called Epiphanes. 10 Now we shall relate the history of the reign of Antiochus Eupator, who was the son of the impious king, with a brief account of the chief woes brought by the wars. 11 Upon inheriting the kingdom, Eupator proclaimed a certain Lysias to be chief minister over the empire, and Protarchos to be governor of Coele-Syria and Phoenicia.

12 The reason for Protarchos' appointment was as follows. Ptolemy, surnamed Makron, took the initiative in keeping to a just policy toward the Jews, to compensate for the injustice they had suffered. Continually he tried to maintain peaceful relations with them. 13 The result, however, was that the King's Friends denounced him to Eupator. From every direction he heard himself called "traitor," because he had deserted his post in Cyprus, entrusted to him by King Philometor, and had gone over to the side of Antiochus Epiphanes. He did not . . . noble the authority. . . .[a] Accordingly, he took poison and put an end to his life.

14 Gorgias, on becoming governor of the territories, engaged mercenary troops, and from every direction he fed the flames of war against the Jews. 15 Simultaneously with him, the Idumaeans, who controlled strategic fortresses, harassed the Jews. Joining forces with the renegades from Jerusalem, they attempted to feed the flames of war.

16 Maccabaeus and his men offered up prayer, asking God to be their ally, and then they marched forth against the fortresses of the Idumaeans. 17 Attacking them boldly, they overran the terrain and drove back all the defenders who were fighting upon the walls. They slaughtered all in their path, killing at least twenty thousand. 18 As many as nine thousand took refuge in two very strong towers, which were completely provisioned for a siege. 19 Maccabaeus himself departed to take care of urgent matters elsewhere, leaving a detachment

---

[a] On the gaps, see NOTE on vs. 13.

sufficient for besieging the enemy, consisting of Simon and Joseph and Zacchaeus and his men. 20 Simon's force, however, in their greed for money, took a bribe of seventy thousand drachmas from some of the besieged and let them slip out. 21 Their deed was denounced to Maccabaeus, who assembled the leaders of the people and prosecuted the men for having sold their brothers for money by setting their enemies free to act against them. 22 He executed those who were guilty of treason and forthwith captured the two towers. 23 In combat he was completely successful, slaying over twenty thousand in the two fortresses.

24 Timotheus (the first of the two by that name to be defeated by the Jews), having assembled a huge force of mercenary troops and having mustered a large number of the horses . . . ,[b] marched, intending to conquer Judaea by force of arms. 25 As he approached, Maccabaeus and his men, in supplication to God, spread dust on their heads and girded their loins with sackcloth. 26 Prostrating themselves upon the platform opposite the altar, they prayed that He have mercy upon them and "be an enemy to their enemies and a foe to their foes," as the Torah states. 27 On finishing their prayer, they took up their arms and marched out a considerable distance from the city. As they drew near the enemy, they halted. 28 At the crack of dawn, the two sides charged. Besides their own valor, the Jews found their refuge in the LORD to be their guarantee of success and victory, whereas their enemies followed into battle the lead of their own fury. 29 When the battle grew hot, from heaven there appeared to the enemy five majestic men, riding horses with gold-studded bridles, who posted themselves at the head of the Jews. 30 They surrounded Maccabaeus and by shielding him with their armor kept him invulnerable. Meanwhile, they kept shooting arrows and thunderbolts at the enemy. As a result, blinded and thrown into confusion, they fled in all directions in complete disorder. 31 Twenty thousand five hundred were slaughtered, along with six hundred cavalrymen.

32 Timotheus himself fled to a fortress called Gazara,[c] a very strong citadel, where Chaireas was in command. 33 Maccabaeus and his men, in high spirits, besieged the fortress for four days. 34 The defenders within, trusting in the strength of their position, shouted unrestrained blasphemies and spat forth impious words. 35 As the fifth day began to break, twenty young men of Maccabaeus' force, stirred to fiery rage by the blasphemies, charged the wall with manly

b On the gap, see NOTE on vs. 24, *a huge force.*
c See commentary.

valor, and with the fury of wild beasts they cut down any in their path. 36 While the attentions of the defenders were thus distracted, others with equal boldness scaled the wall to attack those within, and they set fire to the towers. The fires they kindled burned the blasphemers alive. Meanwhile, the first force cut through the gates, let the rest of the army in, and captured the town. 37 Timotheus had hidden in a cistern, but they slew him and his brother Chaireas as well as Apollophanes. 38 Having accomplished these feats, they turned with hymns and songs of gratitude to bless the LORD for being very good to Israel and granting them victory.

NOTES

10:9-13. A probable source for our passage, as for I 6:17, was the Seleucid Chronicle. The account here probably copied from it the formal language reflecting Seleucid dynastic theory (the legal fiction that the child king appointed Lysias); see NOTE on vs. 11. The author of I 6:17 saw through the legal fiction and reported the reality.

9. This verse originally followed 9:29. See introductory NOTE on ch. 9.

10-38. Here and in ch. 12, Jason takes care to show that Judas and his men fought mostly against the forces of royal officials who acted on their own initiative to attack the Jews of Judaea. In contrast, in I 5 the author takes pains to state that Judas and his men were fighting wars against hostile neighboring peoples who attacked the Jews living among them. In First Maccabees, Seleucid officials do nothing against the Jews in Judaea between Lysias' withdrawal in 164 (I 4:35) and his expedition with the little king in mid-163 to relieve the Akra (I 6:20-31; cf. II 13:1-2). Even outside Judaea, in the narrative of I 5, the *stratêgos* Timotheus is the only imperial official to act against the Jews (see AB vol. 41, pp. 296-97), but at I 5:11, 34, and 37, Timotheus is named only as the leader of the native anti-Jewish force. By viewing the wars as being against hostile neighbors, the author of First Maccabees is able to hint that Judas and his men fulfilled prophecies and equaled the feats of earlier heroes of scripture (see AB vol. 41, pp. 294-96, 298-99, 301-2, 304-5; I could have said more there: in I 5 we read of victories over Ammon, Yazer [a city of Moab!], Edom, the eastern peoples, and the Philistines, and also of a partial ingathering of the Jewish diaspora, and all these facts could be viewed as a partial fulfillment of Isa 11:11-14).

It is probable that the account in First Maccabees is largely correct. The neighboring peoples were living on land which the Jews believed God had promised to His Chosen People. Those gentiles now feared that the resurgent Jews would try to dispossess them and were ready to take preventive action. Meanwhile, the central government had to cope with the threat of Philip (see NOTE on 9:29). As long as Ptolemy Makron was governor of Coele-Syria and

Phoenicia, Judas and his men may have had a free hand against the hostile gentiles (see NOTE on vss. 12–13). On the other hand, local Seleucid officials in the areas around Judaea may well have sympathized with the enemies of the Jews, so that Jason's account here is no fabrication. Nevertheless, there are some equivocations. The language in vss. 14–15 leaves it unclear whether the Idumaeans acted in concert with the Seleucid governor, Gorgias, or only simultaneously with him. Jason himself identifies Timotheus of vss. 24–37 as Timotheus the phylarch (8:32), and a phylarch was a native chief, not a Seleucid commander; see NOTE on 8:32 and AB vol. 41, pp. 296–97. At vs. 24, however, he may wish to give the impression that Timotheus, like Gorgias (cf. vs. 14), was a royal official. In so doing Jason excludes the possibility of interpreting Judas' victories here as fulfillments of prophecies of redeemed Israel's great victories over neighboring peoples. Jason himself (or his source) saw fulfillments of other prophecies in the victories of Judas described in vss. 10 and 12. Like the author of First Maccabees, he did not cite the prophets by name but, in telling the stories, made unmistakable allusions to their words.

Each author makes his own characteristic use of facts drawn from the Common Source; each chooses scriptural prophecies, of which those facts could be viewed as fulfillments. We have seen how the author of First Maccabees liked prophecies of victories over neighboring peoples. He also chose particularly prophecies which spoke of great heroes as the victors: the "saviors" of Obad 15–21, the "star" of Num 24:17–19, the "mighty men" of Zech 10:3–8, and perhaps even the "child" or "son" of Isa 8:23 – 9:6; see AB vol. 41, NOTES on 5:3, 4–5, 23, and 9–54. Though Isa 52:9–12 speaks only of the great acts of the LORD, the author of First Maccabees had Judas Maccabaeus perform God's task of gathering up the stragglers; see AB vol. 41, NOTE on 5:53–54. There are other possible allusions to prophecies in I 5: to Jer 31:6–12 in 5:23, to Isa 34 in 5:28, to Joel 1:6 and 2:7–10 in 5:30, to Joel 1:14 in 5:33, to Isa 25:1–8 and 35:10 in 5:53–54. In Jer 31:6–10, Isa 25:1–8, Isa 35, and Joel 1:14, there are references to Israel's humility or to prayers for suffering Israel. The author of First Maccabees, too, regarded arrogance as a sin and believed in the efficacy of prayer! But he was most interested in prophecies about mighty men of valor.

In contrast, Jason or his source dwelt upon prophecies of how God would rescue humble repentant Israel in response to prayer: Isa 30:15–36, Zech 9:9–16, and Joel 2:11–3(4 H.):21. See NOTE on vss. 24–38. Allusions to prophecy in ch. 12 are faint, if present at all, but the prophecies reflected in the narrative in ch. 11, of Lysias' first expedition, show the same pattern as those here: they stress Israel's humility and condemn reliance on military might. See introductory NOTE on ch. 11 and NOTES on the following passages: 11:8, 9, 10, 11–12; see also first par. of NOTE on 11:13–38.

Scholars have suggested that our section has suffered almost incredible dislocations. They were led to do so by the false hypothesis that Jason of Cyrene knew of only one enemy of the Jews named Timotheus. See, e.g., Christian Habicht, 2. Makkabäerbuch, Band I, Lieferung 3 of Jüdische Schriften aus hellenistisch-römischer Zeit, ed. by Werner Georg Kümmel (Gütersloh: Mohn, 1976), pp. 250–51. In fact, there were two Timothei; see NOTE on vs. 24, NOTE on 8:30, and AB vol. 41, pp. 296–97.

10. The cult epithet "Eupator" means "born to a noble sire." Antiochus V was probably only nine years old when he became full king. See AB vol. 41, p. 311.

the chief woes. Gr. *ta synechonta kaka.* For the expression, cf. "the chief goods" (*ta synechonta agatha*) in Philodemus *Peri theôn* (cited in the *Greek-English Lexicon,* s.v. *synechô,* I, 3).

11. In the abridged history Lysias appears first here, and the writer's wording takes note of the fact by calling him "a certain Lysias" (cf. 3:4, 6:18, 12:35, 14:3 and 37). In fact, however, Antiochus IV, before marching off in 165 B.C.E. on his eastward campaign, made Lysias guardian of the heir to the throne and appointed him chief minister in the western half of the Seleucid empire; furthermore, Lysias led an expedition against the Jewish rebels which ended early in 164 B.C.E., long before the purification of the temple (I 3:32-36, 4:26-35; AB vol. 41, pp. 268-69). Jason of Cyrene pays no attention to Lysias' position under Antiochus IV. As for the expedition which ended early in 164, Jason reports it in II 11 as an event which occurred well into the reign of Antiochus V. On Jason's strange chronology and how it came to be, see above, pp. 56-63.

The law of the Seleucid empire took no note of the fact that the king was a helpless child. Though Lysias held the real power, officially he owed his position to having been appointed by the little king. See Bickerman, *Institutions,* p. 21.

There can be no doubt that "Protarchos" (lit. "primal" or "first-ranking") here is the name of the new governor (*stratêgos*) of the province of Coele-Syria and Phoenicia. Scholars have followed La and Sy in construing the word as a common noun or adjective, as part of the title of a second office held by Lysias ("first-ranking governor of Coele-Syria and Phoenicia"). In that case, however, the clause containing the word would have been introduced in Greek by the particle *kai* ("and"); it would not have been set off, as it is, by the particle *de,* which in this context surely indicates the appointment of a different man. No other instance is known in the history of the Seleucid empire of one being simultaneously chief minister (*epi tôn pragmatôn*) and governor of Coele-Syria and Phoenicia; surely the governor was always a subordinate of the chief minister. The title *stratêgos prôtarchos* is known nowhere else, though a reading *prôtarchôn stratêgos* has been restored on an inscription from Andros (*Inscriptiones Graecae* XII [5] 724) from the reign of Antoninus Pius (137-161 C.E.).

Bacchides probably held the office of governor of Coele-Syria and Phoenicia under Demetrius I, so Protarchos is probably not the last person known to have held it; see AB vol. 41, pp. 330-31, and cf. Bengtson, *Strategie,* II, 165.

12-13. Our verses in Greek constitute a single sentence, introduced by the particle *gar,* which indicates that they explain what precedes, presumably the appointment of Protarchos. In English the particle *gar* must be expanded into "The reason for Protarchos' appointment was as follows." The governor of Coele-Syria and Phoenicia did deal with the affairs of Judaea (see 3:5-6, 4:4, 45, 8:8-9), as did Ptolemy Makron. Clearly, then, Protarchos replaced Ptolemy Makron.

The abridged history gives no indication that Ptolemy Makron was the same man as Ptolemy the son of Dorymenes, who is mentioned at 4:45 and at 8:9, though both held the office of governor of Coele-Syria and Phoenicia. Indeed the two men can hardly be identical, as Terence B. Mitford has shown in his thorough study of what is known of Makron ("Ptolemy Macron," *Studi in onore de Aristide Calderini e Roberto Paribeni* [Milano: Ceschina, 1957], pp. 163–87). As governor of Cyprus, Ptolemy Makron still showed exemplary loyalty to Ptolemy VI Philometor when that king became of age in the second half of 170 B.C.E. (Polybius xxvii 13, xxviii 12.8–13.4; see NOTE on II 4:21, *Protoklisia*). The incompetent ministers of Philometor, later in 170/69, disastrously bungled the war with Antiochus IV which they themselves had provoked (see AB vol. 41, pp. 202–3), and only that fact explains the treason of the governor of Cyprus. Cyprus did not fall to Antiochus IV until 168 B.C.E. (Livy xlv 11.9–11, 12.7; Polybius xxix 27.9–10). Ptolemy Makron probably long remained loyal to Philometor. We may guess that it was well into 168 B.C.E. when he deserted his post. On the other hand, 4:45–46 probably implies that Ptolemy son of Dorymenes was governing Coele-Syria and Phoenicia for Antiochus IV, at the latest from 169 B.C.E. (see NOTE on 4:34 and NOTE on 5:1). Thus in 169 Ptolemy Makron was probably working for Ptolemy VI at the same time as the son of Dorymenes was working for Antiochus IV. According to 8:9, Ptolemy son of Dorymenes gave orders to exterminate the Jews, and one might infer that he could not later have pursued the policies described here. However, even if 8:9 is not mere rhetoric, the son of Dorymenes at that point may only have been executing the orders of his king (see I 3:35, 39).

Judas and his men took and purified the temple without royal authorization (see NOTE on 10:1–8), held it against the garrison in the Akra (I 4:41), and fortified the temple mount. Thereafter, they fought wars against hostile neighbors, some of whom had the support of royal Seleucid personnel (vss. 14–37, 12:2–37; I 5). Some of the battles may have occurred while Antiochus IV was still alive, and many of them surely were over early in the reign of Antiochus V (see pp. 67–68 and AB vol. 41, p. 293). Yet the higher authorities of the Seleucid kingdom long failed to act against Judas and his force. Ptolemy Makron's conciliatory policy toward the Jews would go far to explain this strange fact, and it also becomes easy to understand why other officials of the kingdom viewed Makron's inaction as treason. The menace of Philip's force may also have been a factor in the failure to curb Judas and his men; see NOTE on 9:29.

Jason of Cyrene appears to have made a point of recording instances of gentile kindness to Jews (3:3, 4:35–38, 49, 12:30, 14:23–25).

13. *He did not . . . noble the authority. . . .* The gaps mark the irreparable corruption of the text. At least the verb after "not" has become unrecognizable. AVq*l* have words unknown elsewhere in Greek, of which no sense can be made (*eugennasias, eugennaisas, eugennasas*). Grimm guessed that the original reading was *eugenisas*, the participle of the verb "to ennoble." However, the adjective "noble" already occurs in the clause. It is hard to believe that even the abridger, with his peculiar style, would so have expressed himself. Even if he had, the resulting text would presumably mean "He had not reflected credit on the office [he had held from Ptolemy]," surely a superfluous statement after

what precedes. As a mere guess, I suggest that the writer was playing upon the meaning of the king's epithet, "Eupator" ("born of a noble sire"). The *EU* of the Greek manuscripts would reflect an original *TOUEUPATOROS* and the *ISAS* would reflect an original *NOMISAS*. The translation would then be "He did not consider noble the authority of Eupator." The regime was an ignoble one, under which there was no hope for Makron.

The use here of the negative *mê* with the participle should occasion no surprise; cf. 3:5, 9:12, 11:24, 14:43.

14–15. See NOTE on 8:9, *Gorgias*. Vs. 14 seems vague in identifying Gorgias only as "governor of the territories." "The territories" (*hoi topoi*) in the terminology of the Seleucid empire meant unprivileged areas of the kingdom (Bengtson, *Strategie*, II, 9–12). Judaea had been a privileged area, and Jews could have used the expression to refer to less-favored neighboring regions, including Idumaea (cf. AB vol. 41, p. 195). In vs. 15 the Idumaeans attack the Jews simultaneously with Gorgias, and perhaps the author means they did so in concert with him. At I 5:59 we find a Gorgias fighting, with his base at Jamnia. Only a little later, at I 5:65–68, we find the Hasmonaean army campaigning in greater Idumaea. The parallel narrative of the same campaign at 12:32–41 may imply that Jewish soldiers entered Jamnia (12:40) and says explicitly that the enemy was Gorgias, the governor of Idumaea (12:32; Josephus at *AJ* xii 8.6.351 is probably wrong in jumping to the conclusion that Gorgias' title was "*stratêgos* of Jamnia"). All these events occur in the brief reign of Antiochus V, and it seems safe to conclude that we have here a single Gorgias, governor of Idumaea and other areas around Judaea. On the status of Jamnia in this period, see NOTE on 12:3–9.

Seeking to use idiomatic English, I have rendered the writer's *polemotrophein* (lit. "nourish war") in these two verses and at 14:6 by "feed the flames of war." The verb occurs only in those three places and may have been coined by our writer.

15–23. Characteristically, Jason is vague on matters of geography and, unlike the author of I 5:3–5, does not differentiate the Idumaeans of the Akrabattene (north of Judaea) and the Baianites from the Idumaeans of greater Idumaea to the south (see AB vol. 41, pp. 294–95). The events narrated here are unquestionably the same as those of I 5:3–5: in both passages Judas and his men oppose Idumaeans, trap enemies in towers, and turn thereafter to oppose a commander Timotheus, and in that campaign appears a town the name of which contains the sounds "z" and "r" (vs. 32; I 5:8).

One should also take note of a verbal echo: "were beleaguering" (*periekathênto*) at I 5:3 corresponds to "harassed" (*egymnazon*) here. We may infer that both our authors drew on the Common Source, each according to his own purposes and convictions. The author of First Maccabees omitted the story discreditable to Simon, while Jason was glad to include it (vss. 19–22). The Hasmonaean propagandist placed the narrative in a context of Hasmonaean operations to rescue harassed Jews from enemies outside Judaea proper; hence, he omitted how the enemy had given refuge to fugitive Jewish apostates. Jason, on the contrary, included the matter, for he placed the fighting in a context of gentile aggressions against the Jews of Judaea.

15. On the relationship of our verse to I 5:3–4, see NOTE on vss. 15–23.

Elsewhere we hear of apostate Jews taking refuge southward, at Beth-Zur (I 10:14); presumably they might also go through Beth-Zur to greater Idumaea (see AB vol. 41, NOTE on 7:19). The writer here does not name the strategic fortresses. They cannot have included Beth-Zur, which was already in Jewish hands (I 4:61) and before had been unfortified (AB vol. 41, p. 269). Clearly they include the Baianite towers (I 5:5) mentioned here in vs. 18.

17. *the terrain*. The Greek is *tôn topôn*, the same expression I translated as "the territories" in vs. 14, but clearly the Jews had yet to conquer all the territory of Gorgias' province (see 12:32–37). *Tôn topôn* here must mean the terrain around the strategic fortresses.

twenty thousand. An exaggerated figure, typical of Jason and of ancient authors generally when they write of enemy forces. See NOTE on 8:24. The author of First Maccabees, who likes to give figures for enemy dead, gives none at the parallel passages, I 5:5, 7–8. Hence, Jason may have invented the twenty thousand here and at vss. 23 and 31 and at 8:30.

18. I 5:3–5 shows that the enemies who took refuge in the towers, the Baianites, were distinct from Gorgias and the Idumaeans mentioned here in vss. 14–17. The abridger is probably responsible for leaving the transition unmarked, so that the reader is left free to infer, wrongly, that those who took refuge in the towers were the survivors of the slaughter mentioned in vs. 17.

nine thousand. No figure is given at I 5:4–5. The Baianites were so obscure a tribe that their name is known only from I 5:4–5 and Josephus' paraphrase of it. They probably were not so numerous as our verse implies.

19–23. The Simon of the unsavory incident narrated here is surely Judas' brother, though the text here does not say so. Jason did not feel any need to identify the famous Simon, especially when he mentioned him in association with Judas Maccabaeus and Joseph (cf. I 5:17–18, 55–56). Simon survived, but Jason's purpose in telling of the sordid incident is probably to discredit Simon; see AB vol. 41, pp. 31, 79–80, and see NOTE on vs. 20.

What were the urgent matters which removed Maccabaeus from the siege? We know only of the threat from Timotheus and his force (vs. 24), which was indeed pressing, but so much so that Judas could hardly have returned to capture the besieged forts before repulsing Timotheus.

"Zacchaeus" may well be a shortened nickname for Zechariah; see AB vol. 41, p. 67, n. 23, and p. 80. Joseph son of Zechariah at I 5:18–19, 55–62 is an incompetent commander, disastrously insubordinate to Judas, and clearly not favored by God. Jason may take Zechariah here to be Joseph's father, or perhaps he made the mistake of turning Joseph's father into a brother. In any case, Jason associates Simon with these ill-favored men. On the possibility that Joseph and Azariah (mentioned at I 5:18–19, 55–62) were half brothers of the Hasmonaean five, see pp. 299–300.

20. The writer has named several others in the besieging force (vs. 19) but here takes pains to associate the traitors with Simon. We are not told how many took the bribe money, but even if ten were implicated, each share represented something like 7,000 days' pay for a soldier or laborer. See NOTE on 4:19.

21. One would like to know who the "leaders of the people" were, before whom Judas put the traitors on trial. Judas seems to have been unquestioned

commander of the nuclear Hasmonaean force (I 2:66), but by this time men from other parties were fighting in his army (I 2:42, 4:29, 5:18–20; see AB vol. 41, NOTE on 4:29). Were the "leaders" a purely military council or court? Or had the pious formed national governmental organs of their own? The Seleucid regime had probably ceased to recognize the Jewish Council of Elders (*Gerousia*) at the time of the Mysarch's expedition in 167 B.C.E.; see AB vol. 41, p. 212. But members of that body surely survived, and the Council itself may have had authority *de facto* over some Jews. The Seleucid regime again recognized the Council by March of 164 B.C.E., before the events narrated here (Jason's chronology is erroneous; see II 11:27 and pp. 56–63). Although the Council of Elders may well have supported acts of Judas later (in 161 B.C.E.), it was probably too closely identified with a policy of collaboration with the Seleucids (see 11:27–33, 12:1) for Judas to use it as the court for trying the traitors.

Clearly, Judas did not feel able to condemn the men to death on his own authority. We do not know on what principle of law it was decided that the men should receive capital punishment. On Judas' relationship to the national organs of the Jews, see 13:10–13; I 4:59, 6:19, 8:17–20, and AB vol. 41, pp. 287, 357–58.

22–23. Judas as commander could execute traitors condemned in court. His quick success in capturing the towers is meant to contrast with the incompetence and perhaps criminal laxity of Simon and the other officers left to press the siege. Again the figures of the slain are certainly exaggerated; see NOTE on 8:24. The twenty thousand of vs. 23 do not necessarily contradict the nine thousand of vs. 18, because the two towers may have been garrisoned before the fugitives came.

At I 5:5 Judas is said rather to have set fire to the towers so that the defenders were burned to death.

23. *he . . . successful.* The Greek translates a Hebrew idiom found at Gen 39:3 and 23; cf. Dan LXX 8:25 and I 3:6.

24–38. The account of the struggle against Timotheus here is distressingly vague. We are not told what post he held or from what point he marched upon Judaea. The story here is in sharp contrast with the information on struggles against a Timotheus in I 5. Here, a force on the proportions of the Seleucid imperial army invades Judaea, aiming at violent conquest. Timotheus' troops are foreign mercenaries and include formidable foreign cavalry. No other source reports such an invasion at this point. The author of Dan 11–12 by this time had ceased to reflect minutely current events and would resume doing so only later. But one would expect such an invasion to be reflected in Enoch 90:14–16 (see AB vol. 41, p. 41, n. 12). However, in Enoch 90:14 the seer probably alluded to Judas' defeat of Gorgias and Nicanor with the help of a miraculous disclosure of Gorgias' stratagem. In Enoch 90:15 he predicted that thereafter a miraculous manifestation of God would rout the enemy, but he probably was speaking of the expedition of Lysias narrated in II 11, not the expedition of Timotheus here; see introductory NOTE on ch. 11.

We are not surprised to find the author of First Maccabees omitting reference to the superhuman apparition; throughout his work he reports nothing of the kind. But he glorifies the achievements of Judas and yet says nothing of the miraculous defeat of Timotheus' invasion. How could he have omitted it? Against a Timotheus he reports only two expeditions to Transjordan: one to Ammonite soil to fight Ammonites (I 5:6–8) and another to what is now southern Syria to rescue beleaguered Jews and to fight anti-Jewish townspeople and a local army and Arab mercenaries (I 5:9–45). Nothing could have possessed the author of First Maccabees to turn the remarkable campaign here into either of the punitive expeditions! Furthermore, Jason's false chronology (see pp. 56–63) blinded him to the facts that Judas' force was now so formidable that only the royal army was large enough to risk invading Judaea, and that even Lysias and the royal army had negotiated a peace rather than continue the war against the Hasmonaeans and their sympathizers.

Jason's version of Timotheus' campaign, as an invasion of Judaea, is thus false. How did it come into being? It probably arose from two factors: first, pious Jews like Jason sought to see in Judas' career the fulfillment of some of the biblical prophecies; second, Jason (perhaps through ignorance of the geography of Judaea and neighboring lands) misread a crucial name.

Even in the context of the abridged history our passage with its fivefold apparition is strange. Pious observers, when they see apparitions, usually see what they expect to see. Pious narrators who fabricate tales of apparitions after the fact usually report what they would have expected to see. Our chapter reports events of a time after the death of Antiochus IV when the idols of the Abomination of Desolation had been thrown away and when repentant pious Israelite soldiers, though facing cavalry, put their trust in God, not in horses (cf. 10:27 with 10:24, 31), and habitually, as their first line of defense, turned to pray to God for mercy (8:2–4, 14–15, 10:16, 25–26). What did pious Jews expect to see at such a time? At least three older prophecies in the Bible seemed relevant: Isa 30:15–36; Zech 9:9–16; Joel 2:11–3(4 H.):21. We also have two apocalypses surviving from the time of Judas, Dan 11:45–12:3 and Enoch 90:13–18.

In Isa 30:15–16, God, through the prophet, complains that the people rely on earthly power, on horses, and do not call upon Him. Because of Israel's misplaced trust, God allows even five of the enemy to put His people to flight. However, let the Israelites call upon God for mercy (Isa 30:19) and heed His commandments and throw away their idols (Isa 30:22)! Then great blessings will come from God (Isa 30:23–27), and, most important, God will come in wrath to destroy Israel's gentile enemies, especially Assyria (Isa 30:27–31). Corresponding to the five of the enemy who put Israel to flight, the reader of Isa 30:27–28, especially in the Greek, could count five manifestations of God which would rout the enemy: the LORD's name, His wrath, the word of His lips, His anger, and His spirit.

We have noted repeatedly how Jews took the Seleucid empire to be the latter-day Assyrian empire (see AB vol. 41, p. 210, and above, NOTES on 5:21). Thus, at a time soon after the Days of Purification, the prerequisites demanded by God in Isa 30 had been fulfilled, and one might expect a fulfillment of the promises there.

Jews also looked for fulfillment of Zech 9:9–16, though the king promised in Zech 9:9 failed to come. Israel and her leaders are to be humble and to have no cavalry or chariotry or archers (Zech 9:9–11). The "blood of the covenant" (easily interpreted as the "blood of the martyrs") is to set the imprisoned people free (Zech 9:11). The enemy is named as *Iāwān* ("Greece" or "the Seleucid empire"; see AB vol. 41, p. 192). The LORD is to "appear above them" with "arrows like lightning" and will "shield" them. In the passage there are four occurrences of *YHWH* ("LORD") and one of *Ādōnāy* ("LORD"), so that again one can account for the five apparitions. Jews in antiquity did apply Zech 9:11-16 to the wars of Judas Maccabaeus. See Jerome, *Commentarii in Zachariam*, ad loc., vol. XXV, cols. 1486-88 Migne.

Joel (2:11-3[4 H.]:21) predicted that, when the hard-pressed Jews turned to God in repentance and prayer, God would provide them with food, remove the Northerner to perish in stinking decay between the seas, and destroy the nations who had marched against Judah and Jerusalem and had gathered in the Valley of Decision. In Joel 3(4 H.):16-21, there are, again, five occurrences of "LORD" in the description of the Day of the LORD. The pious identified the Northerner as Antiochus IV; see NOTE on 9:4-29. Repentance, prayer, and the death of Antiochus IV were accomplished facts. Surely the victory in the Valley of Decision must follow!

Daniel predicted that, after the death of the King of the North, there would be an unprecedented time of troubles, during which the great angelic protector Michael would arise to aid Israel, and pious Jews would escape the danger (Dan 11:45 – 12:1).

Jason, in our passage, for the first time mentions a divine apparition coming to the aid of the Jews. On Jason's failure to record the earlier manifestation suggested by Enoch 90:14, see NOTE on 8:16-23. Indeed, nothing in our passage indicates that Jason used Enoch. On the other hand, Jason makes unmistakable allusions to these prophecies of Isaiah, Zechariah, and Joel; see the NOTES to the individual verses. He or his source thus seems to have searched for an event fulfilling the prophecies of Isaiah, Zechariah, and Joel, an event which could also be called the "unprecedented time of trouble" of Dan 12:1, and he seems to have found it in the expedition of Timotheus.

In fact, the campaign here is the same as the one narrated at I 5:6-8. The events here, like the ones there, follow a campaign against Idumaeans (or Seirites; see AB vol. 41, pp. 294-95), which ends with the taking of fortresses. Both here and there, a Timotheus leads the numerous enemy, more than one battle is fought, and a strong city with the sounds "z" and "r" in its name is taken (Yazer at I 5:8, Gazara here). It is likely that the name is slightly corrupt in one source or the other. "Yazer" in Hebrew was written *y'zr*, and "Gazara" was written *gzr*. *Y'* in hands of this period, if written close together, could be misread as *g;* see Frank M. Cross, Jr., "The Development of the Jewish Scripts," in *The Bible and the Ancient Near East: Essays in Honor of William Foxwell Albright*, ed. by G. Ernest Wright (Garden City, N.Y.: Doubleday, 1961), p. 176, fig. 2, lines 1 and 2. In Greek, *Iazêr* could easily be misread as *Gazêr*, and *Gazêra* was an alternative form of the name of Gazara (as at II Reigns 5:25 and I 4:15). For whatever reason, Hebrew *Ya'zēr* was rendered in Greek as *Gazêr* at I Chron 6:66 (81 G.). Yazer lay west of Rabbath-Ammon (Philadelphia), present-day 'Amman. Its site has not been identified with certainty, but one possibility is Khirbet Jazir. The consonants of Arabic "Jazir" are equivalent to those of Hebrew *gzr*. See S. Loewenstamm,

"Ya'zēr," Enc. Bib., III (1958), 712. In any case, both in Greek and in Hebrew the name "Yazer" could be transformed into "Gazara," and "Gazara" could be transformed into "Yazer." Since Gazara was more famous than Yazer, readers and scribes were more likely to turn "Yazer" into "Gazara" than vice versa.

The reading "Gazara" here is probably not the mere error of a scribe. It is likely that theological considerations brought about the preservation of the name "Yazer" at I 5:8, and the deliberate or unconscious substitution for it of "Gazara" here.

In contrast to the menacing invasion described here, at I 5:1–2, 6–8 the campaign is one of Jews invading Ammonite soil. The Ammonites are accused of murdering Jews living in Ammonite territory, but nothing indicates that they had invaded Judaea or intended to do so. The account at I 5:6–8, with the mention of the Ammonites and the reading "Yazer," hints that the Hasmonaean achievements rival those of Jephthah and of Moses' men (cf. Judg 11:29, 32–33; Num 21:32; see AB vol. 41, pp. 295, 297) and fulfill prophecies of victories over Ammon and Moab, for Yazer was in Moab. The account in First Maccabees also pointedly contradicts Dan 11:40–43 (see pp. 64–66).

The account here, on the other hand, reports superhuman apparitions, hints at the fulfillment of prophecies uttered by Isaiah, Joel, and Zechariah, and allows no challenge to be raised against the veracity of Daniel. Judas' victory over Timotheus was a fact, but our authors write not fact but theological interpretation when they present that victory either as a latter-day manifestation of the same power as appeared in Jephthah or as a fulfillment of prophecies about superhuman apparitions. The theological purposes easily explain many of the divergences of the facts in the two accounts. Jephthah faced an army of Ammonites, not of foreign mercenaries, so that it did not suit the purposes of the author of First Maccabees to reproduce from the source the report of the mercenary infantry and cavalry found in vs. 24.

Not one of the prophecies of how God or his angels would help a newly restored Israel to defeat invaders spoke of a force from Transjordan. The texts spoke rather of Assyria (Isa 30:31) or Greeks (Zech 9:30) or the Northerner (Joel 2:20) or gentiles from all directions (Joel 3:11). Thus it would not suit the purpose of Jason of Cyrene to mention the land of Ammon as the origin of the force even if the information lay in his source.

If Jason saw in his source that Timotheus began in the land of Ammon and if Jason then misread "Yazer" as "Gazara," the story here could easily have come into being. To get from the land of Ammon to Gazara one had to march the width of Judaea.

The inferences we have just drawn concerning the accounts here and at I 5:6–8 suggest the following conclusion: the Common Source reported at least that Timotheus and his followers in the Ammonite territory were a menace to Jews in Transjordan and perhaps were also a threat to Judaea, and that Judas defeated them at Yazer. Each of our authors then recast the story in accordance with his own beliefs and misconceptions.

Gazara was an important strong point leading into Judaea. Its eventual fall to Simon was cause for great celebration (I 13:43–47, 14:34). It had served as a refuge for the fleeing troops of Nicanor (I 4:15). See AB vol. 41, p. 265. Even the source of I 5:6 had described the enemy force as large. What inference would a pious Jew draw on reading a story that Judas and his men, soon after the purification of the temple, fought a large gentile force which had originated in Ammonite territory, east of the Jordan, and drove it to flee to Gazara, to the west of Judaea? Surely he would infer that the Jews beat off an invasion which threatened to march through all Judaea.

In his prophecy of the LORD's victory over the nations, Joel (3[4 H.]:14) had said it would occur in the "Valley of Decision." The Hebrew roots *gzr* (the root of "Gazara") and *ḥrṣ* (the root of *ḥārūṣ* ["decision"]) both mean "cut," "decide," "decree." Gazara stands on a ridge in the low hills of the Shephelah. Relative to the mountains of Judaea, it or its neighborhood could be called a "valley." See Josh 16:10 with Josh 17:16–18. Moreover, Gazara is close to the valley of Ayyalon, the site of part of Joshua's decisive victory over the five Canaanite kings (Josh 10:12). The victory prophesied by Joel could not be identified with the victory over Lysias narrated in ch. 11 because its site, to the south of Jerusalem, was far from any "Valley of Decision" (11:5–11; on the relative altitude of the site, see AB vol. 41, p. 269, NOTE on I 4:29).

If Jason or his source was to take an event from the aftermath of the purification of the temple and present it as the fulfillment of the prophecies we have just studied, he could find that event only in the story of Timotheus, and then only by reading "Gazara" instead of "Yazer." If Jason was aware that in First Maccabees the name of the place was "Yazer," not "Gazara," he was all the more pleased, for he rejoiced in contradicting his rival.

Characteristically, Josephus reasserts his understanding of the version of First Maccabees and rejects the account here. He makes it clear there was only one Timotheus (*AJ* xii 8.1.329–30, 3–4.337–44), and when he calls Yazer "the city of the *Iazôroi*," he may do so so as to leave no possibility of misreading the name as "Gazara."

24. *Timotheus (the first . . . Jews)*. Great controversy has raged over the meaning of the puzzling accounts in the abridged history concerning a man or men named Timotheus. The controversy can now be resolved: there were two Timothei. See AB vol. 41, pp. 296–97, and NOTE on II 8:30. Part of the difficulty arose because earlier interpreters wrongly rendered our passage as "Timotheus, who had previously been defeated by the Jews." The reading of A has the unambiguous *prôton* ("first"), where the other witnesses have the equivocal *proteron* ("first of two," "previously"). On the use of the adverb *proteron* instead of the adjective *proteros,* see Kühner-Gerth, *Grammatik,* I, 275–76, and Mayser, II², 170, 174. If *proteron* is the original reading, the scribe underlying A may have perceived the ambiguity and may have altered the text to remove it. If *prôton* is the original reading, the other witnesses to the text may reflect the error of a scribe who failed to perceive that 8:30–32 was not part of the chronologically ordered narrative and that two Timothei were mentioned there (there, too, the Greek is ambiguous for the unwary). For such a scribe, a Timotheus had indeed "been defeated previously." In fact, when properly interpreted, the language of the abridged history distinguishes between two Timothei, both here and at 8:30–32.

Josephus believed there was only one Timotheus (see AB vol. 41, p. 59, n.

22, and p. 297). He may have read our passage the wrong way, as "Timotheus, who had previously been defeated by the Jews," and he may then have applied it, at *AJ* xii 8.3.339, to Judas' battle against the other Timotheus, the one reported at I 5:29–34.

having assembled . . . marched. Cf. Joel 3(4 H.):9–11. The verb "mustered" (*synathroizein*) in Second Maccabees recurs only at 11:2, but is the word used at Greek Joel 4:11. Thus Jason or his source probably viewed the events as fulfillments of Joel's prophecy.

a huge force of mercenary troops and . . . a large number of the horses . . . Where I leave a gap, the many variants show the perplexity of the witnesses to the text. AVqLa^P have "the horses which had been of Asia" (*tous tês Asias genomenous hippous*). *L* has "the noble cavalry of Asia" (*tous tês Asias gennaious hippeis*). La^LX have "the cavalry of the breed of Asia" (La^L: *equitatu generis Asiani;* La^X: *equitatu de genere Asie;* both presumably reflect a Greek original, *tous tês Asias genous hippeis*). La^BM have "horses of the breed of Asia." The reading of AVq seems least probable. The abridged history has not spoken before of "horses of Asia." "Asia" in the narrow sense is Asia Minor, lost to the Seleucid empire since 188. No war-horses from that period could have served Timotheus in 164 or 163! "Asia" in the broad sense was the Seleucid empire. The horses were still in the Seleucid empire! What sense does it make to say they "had been of Asia"? The reading of *L,* "the noble cavalry of Asia," makes sense if "Asia" is taken to mean the Seleucid empire, but, before accepting it, one has to ask, how could so easy a reading perplex the scribes into producing the variants? As often, the Latin versions seem to have come closest to preserving the original. In this case, the inferior witnesses La^BM seem to have the best reading, but the difference between their reading ("horses") and that of the best witnesses La^LX ("cavalry") is not very great and makes little difference to the general sense. Nevertheless, "breed" is a term appropriate to horses, rather than to cavalry. We know nothing of a special breed of war-horses called that "of Asia." But there was in ancient times a very famous breed of war-horses called the breed "of Nisaia" or "the Nisaians," after their home territory, the Nisaian plain of Media, and their native riders were called "Nisaian cavalrymen." See Rudolf Hanslik, *"Nisaion pedion,"* PW, XVII^1 (1936), 712–13, and Ernst Herzfeld, *The Persian Empire: Studies in Geography and Ethnography of the Ancient Near East* (Wiesbaden: Franz Steiner, 1968), pp. 5–9, 15–16, 25. Later scribes could fail to recognize the Greek words "of Nisaia" or "Nisaian." In the manuscripts which preserve Polybius xxx 25.6, *Nisaioi* has become *Pisaioi.* Scribes who had never heard of the Nisaian breed of horses could easily jump to the conclusion that *Nisaias* was miswritten for *Asias,* and *genous* for *gennaious* or *genomenous.* Hence, where I show a gap, the source which lay before Jason of Cyrene probably had "of the breed of Nisaia."

What was Jason's own reading? He, too, may have written "of the breed of Nisaia." On the other hand, the misreading of *Nisaias* as *Asias* would turn "horses of the breed of Nisaia" into "horses of the breed of Asia," and the "breed of Asia" could be taken as "the breed kept by the Seleucid kings." We have just seen that Timotheus was a native chieftain, not a Seleucid commander, but we have also observed (NOTE on vss. 10–38) how Jason had reason to give the impression that Timotheus was an official of the royal Seleucid government. Misreading *Nisaias* as *Asias* would thus serve Jason's purposes, and he himself may have originated the misreading. A Jew of Cyrene could well have been ignorant of the breed of Nisaia.

Our passage poses a further difficulty. Could the native chieftain Timotheus assemble a huge force of mercenary soldiers and have access to the Nisaian horses and cavalrymen which were prized by kings? (see Hanslik, PW, XVII, 712–13). We have reason to believe that the nearly independent dynasts of the Ammanitis, ruling from their stronghold of Philadelphia (now 'Amman), were rich and powerful enough to do so, for Timotheus may have been the ancestor or at least the predecessor of the rich and powerful Zenon and Theodorus, "tyrants" of Philadelphia (see J. *AJ* xiii 8.1.235, 13.3.356, 5.374, 15.3.393; *BJ* i 2.4.60, 4.2.86–87, 3.89, 8.104). In the confusion following the death of Antiochus IV, mercenary soldiers, including the riders of the Nisaian horses, may have hired themselves out to the highest bidders.

At I 5:6, too, the author takes the trouble to stress the magnitude of Timotheus' forces. The parallel suggests the existence of the Common Source.

by force of arms. The Greek has *dorialôton.* The legal and moral implications of the term meant that Timotheus intended to put Judaea completely at the mercy of his force. See NOTE on 5:11, *treating . . . war.*

25. Cf. Josh 7:6 and Dan 9:3.

26. The first part of our verse draws upon Joel 2:17.

The Greek translators of Joel had trouble with the words which in the Masoretic text are *bēyn hā'ūlām wᵉlammizbēaḥ* ("between the vestibule and the altar"). The old Greek version of Joel has "In the middle of the *krêpis* of the altar." Normally *krêpis* means "base" or "walled edge," and it is hard to see how Hebrew *'ūlām* ("vestibule," "porch," "hall") could give rise to such a translation. Our passage, too, has the noun *krêpis* but differs from the Greek Joel in describing it as being opposite the altar (*epi tên apenanti tou thysiasteriou krêpida*). Hence, the *krêpis* here cannot be the base or the edge of the altar, and I have translated the word as "platform." The scribes of the La⁻ᴾ seem to have found the words *epi tên* unintelligible. By omitting them, they made the beginning of our verse mean "Prostrating themselves opposite the rim of the altar. . . ." The altar did have a rim, but if the priests were not on it, it is difficult to see why it should be mentioned; one would expect, rather, "Prostrating themselves opposite the altar. . . ."

The words "have mercy" (*hileôs . . . genomenon*) and "foes" (*echthrois*) may reflect Solomon's prayer at III Reigns 8:37–39 that Israel, when hard pressed by her foe (*echthros*), may offer her entreaty through the temple, and God in response will be merciful (*hileôs*).

"be an enemy . . . ," as the Torah states. See Exod 23:22.

27. In keeping with his usual geographical vagueness, Jason lets us know only that the battle occurred at a considerable distance from Jerusalem.

they halted. In translating, I follow Laᵛ. The Greek has *eph' heautôn êsan*, lit. "they kept to themselves," which probably means "they did not yet engage the enemy in battle."

28. In the report of the confidence of the enemy, is there an allusion to Joel 3(4 H.):10(end) and 11(end)?

29. Cf. Zech 9:14. On the five equestrian apparitions, see NOTE on vss. 24–38 and NOTE on 3:25. For parallels in Jewish legends, see Ginzberg, *Legends,* IV, 87, and VI, 251, n. 38. On pagan Greek parallels, see introductory NOTE on ch. 3 and NOTE on 3:24–39. As Doran points out (*Temple Propaganda,* pp. 101–2), two features here are purely Greek: the protection of a favored hero in battle by supernatural figures (often found in the *Iliad*) and the use by such figures of thunderbolts (*keraunoi*) as weapons (cf. Herodotus viii 37). The author here, as in Version B of the story of Heliodorus, says only that the Jews' enemies saw the apparitions, leaving it open as to whether they were visible to the Jews, too, and he also makes it clear that the acts of the apparitions in any case had tangible results; see NOTE on 3:24–39 and NOTE on 3:26.

30–36. Our verses tell of a battle, a siege, and death of the enemy by fire. At Isa 30:27–33 the prophet predicts battles and death by fire of the LORD's Assyrian enemies.

30. The author does not venture to say that all the Jews were so protected. Only Maccabaeus was made invulnerable. A Greek scribe with a one-dimensional imagination was perplexed as to how five apparitions (an odd number) could place Maccabaeus "in the middle," as the Greek literally says (*meson labontes*); the scribe inserted the word *dyo* ("two") to make the beginning of our verse in AqLa^V mean "Two of them took Maccabaeus between them." The context hardly tolerates the insertion. What did the other three do? The original version, without *dyo,* is amply attested by VL La^{-V} Sy Arm. The apparition from heaven, to the eyes of the enemy, fits Zech 9:14, where it is said that the LORD will appear over the sons of Zion.

One might guess that the divine protection here was seen as a fulfillment of Isa 31:5. However, I think that Isa 31:4–5 was probably the source which led Jews to expect the apparition mentioned at 11:8.

The thunderbolts (*keraunoi*) here probably reflect Greek Isa 30:30, where it is said that God will "thunder" (*keraunôsei*). For the arrows, cf. Zech 9:14. The "blind confusion" (*tarachê*) of the enemy probably reflects Greek Isa 30:28, where it is said that God's purpose is to throw the gentiles into "confusion" (*taraxai*) with fruitless wandering.

31. *Twenty thousand.* See NOTE on vs. 17, *twenty thousand.* The added five hundred do nothing to lessen the suspicion that the figures are invented.

32. Jason certainly intended to write "Gazara," but the events took place at Yazer in Moab. See NOTE on vss. 24–38. Chaireas may well have been in command at Yazer. In vs. 37 we learn that Chaireas was Timotheus' brother.

Jason's mention of Gazara as the site distorts not only the story of the fall of Yazer. It falsifies the history of Gazara. Judas and Jonathan are not reported to have held Gazara. It served as a Seleucid strongpoint until Simon captured it in 143 or 142 B.C.E. (see AB vol. 41, pp. 265, 391, 437, 482–83, 505).

33–37. Now, even without the aid of supernatural apparitions, Judas and his men perform mighty deeds against enemies bearing Greek names. The author may well have seen a fulfillment of Zech 9:13.

34–36. The stories about blasphemers, here and at 12:14–15, may be derived from the Common Source, though they are absent from the parallel accounts at I 5:7–8, 34–35.

34. The author may have believed Gazara to be the Valley of Decision of Joel 3(4 H.):14; see NOTE on vss. 24–38. If so, he may have viewed the blasphemies as fulfillment of Joel 3(4 H.):14, which the Greek renders "Sounds resounded in the Valley of Judgment. . . ." The sounds could have been those of pagan blasphemy. Cf. Ps 83, especially vs. 2(3 H.) where the Hebrew root *hmy* ("be in tumult") is the same as that of *hmwnym* ("echoes" or "multitudes").

35. *stirred to fiery rage.* At Isa 30:27, it is the LORD's wrath which is kindled.

36. Josephus may allude to our verse in saying (*AJ* xii 8.1.129) that Yazer was burned. See AB vol. 41, NOTE on 5:8, *After . . . suburbs.* However, if so, he was able to see that Jason's "Gazara" was an error for "Yazer."

37. The author of First Maccabees did nothing to distinguish the Timotheus in I 5:6–8 from the one in I 5:11–44. Jason here corrects the apparent error of his rival. Cf. 8:32 and NOTES on 8:30–32. Nothing further is known of Apollophanes. Earlier references to him may have been omitted by the abridger.

38. At Isa 30:29 the prophet predicts, after the fiery rout of the gentiles in Isa 30:27–28, the joyful singing to God on the temple mount. Our verse tells us that the Jews sang, "Blessed is the LORD who is good to Israel and grants them victory." The verb "be good to" (*euergetein*) renders Hebrew *gml*, as at Ps 13:6, 57:3. "Grants them victory" may be derived from Hebrew *nōtēn tešū'āh* (Ps 144:10; cf. II Kings 5:1). See also NOTE on 3:30 and NOTE on 8:27, *blessing . . . upon them.*

XIV. THE FIRST EXPEDITION OF LYSIAS
AND THE END OF THE PERSECUTION
(11:1–38)

11 ¹ Only a short time thereafter, Lysias, guardian and Kinsman of the king and chief minister, very angry over the course of events, ² mustered about eighty thousand men and the entire cavalry and marched against the Jews, intending to turn their city into a Greek settlement, ³ to make their temple subject to tribute like the shrines of the other nations, and to turn the high priesthood into an office to be put up for sale annually. ⁴ Puffed up by his consciousness of having his tens of thousands of infantry and his thousands of cavalry and his eighty elephants, he took no thought whatever of the might of God. ⁵ He invaded Judaea and approached Beth-Zur, a strong point about five *schoinoi* from Jerusalem, and pressed it hard. ⁶ When Maccabaeus and his men learned that Lysias was besieging the fortifications, they and the populace, with wailing and tears, turned in supplication to the LORD, begging him to send a good angel to save Israel.

⁷ Maccabaeus himself was the first to snatch up his arms. He then exhorted the others to join him, brave the dangers, and come to the aid of their brothers. Fired with zeal, they all surged out together. ⁸ Then and there, as they stood near Jerusalem, a man on horseback appeared at their head, dressed in white, brandishing his golden weaponry. ⁹ Together they all blessed their merciful God, and their courage rose, so that they were ready to plunge their weapons not only into men but also into the most savage beasts and into walls of steel. ¹⁰ They advanced under arms, accompanied by their ally from heaven, for the LORD had granted them His mercy. ¹¹ Like lions, they dashed upon the enemy and laid low eleven thousand of them as well as one thousand six hundred cavalry and put the whole force to flight. ¹² Most of them were wounded and escaped by throwing away their arms. Lysias himself escaped by shameful flight.

¹³ Since he was no fool, he pondered the defeat he had suffered and realized that the Hebrews were invincible inasmuch as their mighty

God was fighting as their ally. Accordingly, he sent them a message 14 and urged them to make peace, on terms restoring to them all their rights, and . . .[a] that he would make the king, too, become friendly to them. 15 Maccabaeus, who had an eye for the advantageous, consented to all Lysias' proposals, for the king granted all the requests concerning the Jews which Maccabaeus submitted to Lysias in writing.

16 The content of the letters written to the Jews was as follows; first, one from Lysias:

Lysias to the community of the Jews, greeting. 17 John and Absalom, the spokesmen sent by you, submitted the document copied below and presented requests concerning its provisions. 18 I have indicated what points have to be brought also before the king. Those points which I myself could grant, I did. 19 If you continue to maintain your loyalty to the state, I shall try in the future, too, to act for your benefit. 20 I have ordered your spokesmen and mine to discuss the details with you. 21 Farewell. In the year 148, on the twenty-fourth of . . .

22 The content of the king's letter was as follows:

23 King Antiochus to his brother Lysias, greeting. Now that our father has passed away to the gods, we wish the subjects of our kingdom to be undisturbed in the pursuit of their own private affairs. 24 We have heard that the Jews do not accept our father's decree for a change-over to Greek ways but prefer their own pattern of life and ask that they be allowed to follow their own legal usages. 25 Since we choose that this nation, too, may be free from disturbance, we decree that their temple be restored to them and that they govern their lives in accordance with the customs in force in the time of their ancestors. 26 You will do well to transmit this to them and to give them assurances, in order that they, knowing our policy, may take heart and gladly devote themselves to their own private affairs.

27 The king's letter to the nation was as follows:

King Antiochus to the Council of Elders of the Jews and to the rest of the Jews, greeting. 28 If you are well, that would be as we wish. We ourselves are in good health. 29 Menelaus has informed us that you wish to go back to your homes and turn to your own private affairs. 30 For those who go home by the thirtieth of Xanthicus, there shall be the assurance of safety and amnesty.

31 The Jews are to be free to follow their own way of life and their own laws as in earlier times, and no one is in any way to molest them

---

[a] On the gap, see NOTE on vs. 14.

because of the previous misunderstandings. 32 I am also sending Menelaus with instructions to put your minds at ease. 33 Farewell. In the year 148, on the fifteenth of Xanthicus.

34 The Romans, too, sent them a letter, as follows:

Quintus Memmius and Titus Manius, ambassadors of the Romans, to the People of the Jews, greeting. 35 As for the concessions granted to you by Lysias the Kinsman of the king, we endorse them. 36 As regards the points he decided to refer to the king, send someone immediately after you have considered them, so that we may present our views as befits your interests, 37 for we are now on our way to Antioch. Accordingly, make haste to send representatives, so that we may know what your views are. 38 Be well. In the year 148, in . . .ᵇ

ᵇ On the gap, see NOTE on vs. 38, *In the year 148, in . . .*

NOTES

Ch. 11. Jason tells here of the first expedition of Lysias against the Jewish rebels as if it occurred in the reign of Antiochus V. In fact, it occurred in the reign of Antiochus IV. On Jason's mistaken inference, see Introduction, pp. 56–63, 67–68. Jason's beliefs and his interpretations of his sources led him to disagree with First Maccabees also in dating the war against Timotheus the phylarch in the reign of Antiochus V (I 5:6–8; II 10:24–38). He had to determine which of the two events preceded the other. The sources he trusted seem to have given him no clear answer to the question (see p. 68) so that he would have had to proceed by inference. He may well have reasoned as follows:

The time following the death of Antiochus IV was one in which Lysias had to consolidate his power in Antioch (10:11–13), and even after his rivals had been removed, Lysias would be unlikely to leave the capital unless for grave cause. According to Jason's account, Lysias had not even avenged the defeat of Nicanor and Gorgias. Judas' first victories after the Feast of Purification were not over Seleucid forces but over Idumaeans (II 10:15–23). Even if officials of the kingdom were involved, such local feuds by themselves could hardly have provoked the intervention of the chief minister. However, Judas thereafter won the victory over Timotheus and the large force which Jason may well have regarded as royal troops (see NOTE on 10:24, *a huge force . . .*). That victory could well have perturbed the chief minister of an insecure regime. Proceeding like a modern "critical" historian, Jason could thus have found the "true" sequence of events.

The author of First Maccabees, to my knowledge, shows no inclination to portray Judas' repulse of Lysias' first expedition as a fulfillment of prophecy. It is enough for him to present the event as a parallel to victories won by David and Jonathan (see AB vol. 41, p. 270). For Jason, however, or for his source, Judas' repulse of the expedition, like the victory in 10:24–37, occurred after the death of the great persecutor, in a time of fulfillment of prophecies. The narrator here tells how miraculous apparitions helped the Jews rout Lysias' expedition. He seems to view the events as fulfillment of Isa 31:1–9 and of Zech 9:8–10:6.

Although Jason or his source seems to have seen the events in 10:24–38, too, as fulfilling Zech 9:9–16 (see NOTE ad loc.), the aspects fulfilled here are different from the ones there, so the author could connect both events with the same verses in Zechariah. In vs. 3, Lysias comes as a tax collector. Though the Hebrew word *nōgēś* at Zech 9:8 and 10:4 has been translated otherwise, ancient readers did take it as "tax collector" (Aquila at Zech 10:4; cf. Greek Job 3:18, 39:7). With that meaning, Zech 9:8 and 10:4 present God as promising that He Himself will keep all foreign tax collectors away from Jerusalem. Lysias comes trusting in his cavalry (vs. 4); at Zech 10:5 (cf. Isa 31:1, 3), God promises the discomfiture of enemy cavalry. On the other hand, Isaiah (31:1–9) rebuked the Israelites of his time for putting their trust in cavalry and in Egypt instead of turning to God for aid: if Israel repents, God will defeat the Assyrian enemy. Judas and his men certainly sought no aid from Egypt and are not said to have had cavalry (see NOTE on 10:24–38). By now, Israel has repented of the sins which caused the persecution, and Judas and his men, before marching out to meet the enemy, pray to God for aid (vs. 6; cf. I 4:30–33). On the subsequent fulfillments of the prophecies, see the NOTES below to the individual passages.

If Jason or his source believed that the events thus fulfilled the prophecies, they must have conceded that Zech 9:9–10 remained unfulfilled. Neither Judas nor any of his family was in their view the promised king. On how Jason may have interpreted Zech 9:12, see NOTE on 15:14–17.

Surely Jason intended the reader to understand that the miraculous apparition thwarting a tax collector here was a repetition of the one in 3:25. See introductory NOTE on ch. 3.

The seer of Enoch 90 was a contemporary of the events. The chronology suggested by his utterances agrees with that in First Maccabees, though in other details the seer's views are close to Jason's. As narrated here, the expedition comes to an abrupt end when the Jews rout it with the help of the divine apparition and Lysias formally ends hostilities. According to I 3:38–4:35, Lysias' invasion was the first Seleucid campaign against the Jews after that of Nicanor and Gorgias. At Enoch 90:14, the seer probably alludes to the campaign of Nicanor and Gorgias (see AB vol. 41, p. 41, n. 12). At Enoch 90:15, the seer "predicts" that thereafter a miraculous manifestation of God will rout the enemy and make them cease and desist. (The Aramaic original of the mysterious "into the shadow" [Ethiopic mss. *g m*] or "into his shadow" [*qtu* and the late and secondary class of mss.] probably was *bṭlw* ["they ceased"]; cf. H. L. Ginsberg, *Studies in Koheleth* [New York: Jewish Theological Seminary of America, 5711=1950], p. 22.) The verse probably refers to Lysias' first expedition, for the end of that campaign saw not only the repulse of the Seleucid force by the Jews with the help of a divine apparition but also the granting to the Jews of a royal decree of amnesty, as well as the withdrawal of Lysias. The probability is enhanced by the fact that Enoch 90:16 seems to refer to Lysias' second expedition (and perhaps also to Judas' wars against neighboring peoples).

1. The parallels in our verse to passages in First Maccabees are good evidence for the existence of the Common Source. Cf. "Lysias . . . very angry over the course of events" (*Lysias . . . lian bareôs pherôn epi tois gegonosi*) here with I 4:26–27, "[The survivors] reported all that had happened. On hearing the news, Lysias was perturbed and disheartened" (. . . *apêngeilan panta ta symbebêkota. ho de akousas synechythê kai êthymei*). Lysias' titles need not have been given here; they are practically the same as at I 3:32.

Here for the first time Jason takes note of the fact that Antiochus V was a child who could rule only through a guardian. See NOTE on 10:11. On the basis of his false chronology, the writer believed that Lysias was reacting to the events narrated in 10:16–38. In fact, the expedition of Lysias was a response to the defeat of Nicanor and Gorgias (I 4:1–28).

On the title "Kinsman," see AB vol. 41, pp. 254, 422.

2–3. There is an indication of the existence of the Common Source in the fact that both here and at I 4:28 Lysias "musters" a large army for the purpose of imposing his will upon the Jews. The size of Lysias' force here is even more exaggerated than it is there. See NOTE on 8:24.

Did Lysias publish the intentions ascribed to him here? They are somewhat strange. Foreign settlers had already been imposed upon Jerusalem (I 1:38), though Jason omits the story (see NOTE on 5:24–27). The temple had enjoyed financial privileges earlier (see NOTE on 3:2–3), but recently it had suffered plunderings which were far worse than taxation (4:32, 39, 5:15–21). Menelaus had already bid for and purchased the high priesthood (4:24). Jason of Cyrene may have had no direct evidence of Lysias' intentions. Rather, he seems to ascribe to Lysias the aim of undoing the results of Judas' victory. The victory had seemed to fulfill Joel 4:17 and Zech 9:8 and 10:4: Greeks and tax gatherers had at least temporarily been prevented from entering Jerusalem, and Menelaus, the purchaser of the high priesthood, was being excluded from functioning as high priest, though he still may have held office *de jure* (see NOTE on 10:1–8). Thus Lysias' intentions are presented as if Lysias' first expedition came after the purification of the temple, in accordance with Jason's false chronology. If so, Jason did not draw upon the Common Source for the list of intentions but only upon his own inferences. The resemblance of the intentions ascribed here to Lysias to the instructions Lysias is said at I 3:36 to have received from Antiochus IV is probably coincidental.

Jason was well informed on practices in Hellenistic kingdoms, so he is probably right in asserting that pagan temples were ordinarily taxed. Nevertheless, we do not know what taxes were levied upon them in the Seleucid empire. See Rostovtzeff, *Social and Economic History of the Hellenistic World*, pp. 467, 506, 1440, n. 282; Bickerman, *Institutions*, pp. 114(last par.)–15; Claire Préaux, *L'Économie royale des Lagides* (Bruxelles: Fondation égyptologique Reine Élisabeth, 1939), pp. 428, 480–81.

The sale of priestly office was common in Hellenistic kingdoms. See Bickerman, *Institutions*, p. 115; Préaux, *L'Économie royale*, pp. 403–4; Martin P.

Nilsson, *Geschichte der griechischen Religion*, vol. I (3d ed.; München: Beck, 1967), p. 732.

4. Cf. 3:24, 28, 5:17–21. We learn also at I 3:34 that Lysias had elephants, though none are mentioned in the parallel narrative at I 4:28. (I 3:34 has been misprinted at AB vol. 41, p. 249; read "Antiochus handed over to him half of his forces and the elephants and gave him orders concerning all his designs.") On the elephants in the Seleucid army, see also AB vol. 41, pp. 320–21.

5–8. In conformity with his false chronology, Jason writes as if Judas and his army were in Jerusalem and set out from there. In fact, however, Judas and his men occupied Jerusalem only after repulsing Lysias; see Introduction, Part III, section 1.

5–6. The parallels to I 4:29–33 argue for the existence of the Common Source. I 4:29 corresponds exactly to vs. 5, except for having "They marched into Idumaea" instead of "He invaded Judaea." Jason may have found the mention of Idumaea absurd, failing to understand that the writer was giving the route Lysias followed into Judaea; if so, he altered it to make sense. Both at I 4:30–33 and in vs. 6, Maccabaeus and his men react to the magnitude of the enemy force by turning to pray. Each author formulates the prayer in accordance with his own beliefs and aims. The propagandist for the Hasmonaean dynasty uses the victories which made kingship legitimate in Israel. Jason stresses that the coming victories were to be won through an angel rather than by Hasmonaeans emulating David and Jonathan.

Jason is probably wrong in saying that Lysias *besieged* Beth-Zur. Cf. I 4:29, and see AB vol. 41, pp. 268–70.

Here, for once in the abridged history, we have a fairly accurate geographical notice, though even here, unlike I 4:29, there is no mention of the fact that Lysias reached Beth-Zur by way of Idumaea. Beth-Zur lies twenty-eight kilometers south of Jerusalem on the road to Hebron (though only fourteen kilometers as the crow flies). The *schoinos,* according to Hero *Geometrica* 23.20, 43, consisted of thirty or forty-eight stadia. Since the stadium was about one fifth of a kilometer, the distance here is approximately correct if Jason's *schoinos* consisted of thirty stadia. The *schoinos* was a Persian measure (Pliny, *Historia naturalis* vi 30.124; Callimachus, *Aetia* i 18, in Callimachus, *Fragments,* ed. by C. A. Trypanis [LCL, no. 421; Cambridge, Mass.: Harvard University Press, 1975], p. 7), much used in Egypt (*Greek-English Lexicon,* s.v.).

6. *send a good angel.* Cf. 15:23; Tobit 5:22, and Exod 23:20–23, 33:2. The word "good" appears perhaps because the angel mentioned at Exod 23:20–23 could also punish Israel.

7. *all . . . together.* Judas, in facing Lysias, had 10,000 men (I 4:29), far more than the hard-core Hasmonaean force of 3,000 (see NOTE on 8:1).

8. The single equestrian apparition, brandishing his weapons, may be derived from Zech 9:14 and 10:3. The superhuman Protector makes his appearance at or near Jerusalem, in accordance with Isa 31:4–5. Jason and his source probably regarded the angel as identical to the horseman in 3:25. They may well have believed that the angel was Michael (see Dan 12:1). We may infer that Jason drew upon the same work as contained Version A of the story of

Heliodorus, probably upon the Common Source; see pp. 39–40, introductory NOTE on ch. 3, and NOTE on 3:24–39.

9. Accompanied by their Protector, the Jews gain superhuman courage against the Greeks, in fulfillment of Zech 9:13–14.

It is possible that "They all blessed their merciful God" here and "Let all . . . sing hymns of praise to you" at I 4:33 reflect the Common Source.

10. The Jews' confidence comes from the LORD's mercy, as predicted at Zech 10:6.

11–12. The Jews rout their foes with great slaughter, and even the would-be tax collector flees, his cavalry of no avail. Was all this not a fulfillment of Zech 9:15, 10:4–5, and Isa 31:8–9?

The writer at I 4:34 also takes the trouble to mention both slaughter and rout of the enemy, an indication of the reality of the Common Source.

The figures for the enemy dead are probably exaggerated. The figure of 5,000 at I 4:34 may be correct. See NOTE on 8:24 and AB vol. 41, p. 270.

13–38. As a result of the victory, peace comes, allowing the LORD's flock to graze in safety (see also 12:1). One may see a fulfillment at Zech 9:16–17.

Jason's account here is based upon the false assumption that the letter in vss. 23–26 is nearly contemporary with the others; see Introduction, Part III, section 1. The mistakes go beyond matters of chronology. Jason jumped to the conclusion that Judas negotiated a peace. The pro-Hasmonaean propagandist at I 4:35 gives a sharply different account. There Lysias concludes only that the Jewish rebels are tough opponents, not that they are invincible, and he leaves to raise a larger force, intending to fight them again. Nothing is said of negotiations or of a formal peace. We may infer that the Hasmonaean propagandist found reason to pass over the negotiated peace in silence (see AB vol. 41, pp. 270–71). But Jason's own documents hardly bear out his assertion that Judas participated in the negotiations; Judas is not mentioned in the documents. The silence in First Maccabees on the negotiations and the absence of Judas' name from the documents strongly suggest that the Hasmonaeans had nothing to do with the negotiations and may well have opposed them. The terms of the amnesty in vss. 30–31 are hardly generous. They do not restore the temple to pious Jews. Indeed, the letter in vss. 27–33 shows that Menelaus, surely a person hated by the Hasmonaean party, sought and gained the amnesty of Xanthicus, 148 Sel. Mac. (164 B.C.E.).

In order to find when and how the negotiations took place, we must ignore Jason's mistaken grouping of the documents and his narrative, based as it is upon false inferences. We must draw our conclusions by studying the documents themselves and the scraps of evidence available elsewhere. Only thus can we hope to solve the uncertainties and ambiguities. They are numerous: are the documents authentic? What is the true meaning of each? Are the dates in vss. 21, 30, 33, and 38 correctly transmitted? What is the date of the letter in vss. 23–26? In vss. 18, 23, 27, and 36 we must ask in each case whether the king is Antiochus IV or his little son, as coregent or successor? Only after we have established the probable meaning and background of every document can we proceed (below, pp. 426–28) to reconstruct the probable course of events.

The parallels and contrasts of our passage to I 4:35 suggest the existence of the Common Source. At the beginning of each passage the writer reads Lysias' mind: the Seleucid chief minister "ponders the defeat he had suffered" (here in vs. 13, *pros heauton antiballôn to gegonos elattôma;* at I 4:35, *idôn tên genomenên tropên*) and concludes that now is not the time to fight the Jews.

At AB vol. 41, p. 98, I was wrong to infer from peculiarities in the text here that Jason found the letters in vss. 16–21, 27–33, and 34–38 embedded in a source and added to them the letter in vss. 23–26. At vs. 16 the writer does seem to say that the text of letters *to* the Jews (*tois Ioudaiois*) will follow and does not mention a letter to Lysias *about* the Jews; but the dative *tois Ioudaiois* can also mean "for the Jews," "in the Jews' interest" (Mayser, II², 270–72; Blass-Debrunner-Rehkopf, *Grammatik,* section 188). At vs. 22 the writer does say that a letter of the king will follow, and though one might expect a letter to the Jews, the king's letter to Lysias does indeed deal with the Jews. The words in vs. 27, "The king's letter to the nation," always told against my erroneous inference; they take note of the fact that a letter to Lysias has preceded. In vs. 34 there is a masculine plural pronoun ("The Romans, too, sent *them* a letter"), which one would expect after "the Jews" of vs. 16, whereas "the nation" (*to ethnos*) of vs. 27 is neuter; but such use of masculine plural pronouns to refer to neuter collectives is common in Greek (Blass-Debrunner-Rehkopf, *Grammatik,* section 134).

Decisive against my earlier theory are the following considerations. Pious Jews surely at first treasured all four letters. What well-informed Jewish writer (whether he was the author of the Common Source, the Legendary Source, or some other work) would have included the letters at vss. 16–21, 27–33, and 34–38 and excluded the more favorable document at vss. 23–26? And if Jason had found the letters embedded in a coherent narrative, how could he have used them to construct his elaborate false chronology? Rather, Jason must have found all four preserved, not in a narrative, but as documents, very likely in an archive at Jerusalem.

13. Cf. 3:39, 8:36.

14. The text of the Greek manuscripts in the second half of our verse is so corrupt as to be untranslatable: *kai dioti kai ton basilea peisein philon autois anankazein genesthai.* The general sense, however, is clear, and in my translation I have left a gap where *dioti* stands and have omitted the word *peisein,* steps I shall try to justify. The author clearly believes that Lysias offered Maccabaeus two inducements to make peace: his government would restore to the Jews all their rights (*dikaia;* cf. 13:23), and he would also make the king friendly to them. The first inducement could be inferred from vss. 17–18, 25, and 31; and the second from vss. 18–19, 26, 32.

Only one fact cannot be deduced from the quoted documents. The author here has Lysias claim he would "make," indeed "compel" (*anankazein*), the king to turn friendly to the Jews! The author knew what he was doing. He was aware that Antiochus V was a child in the power of his guardian (see 10:11 and 13:1–2). The Greek scribes, however, found the idea of a minister compelling a king improbable and inserted the future infinitive *peisein* ("persuade") in the margin as a suggested alternative. As often happens, the marginal suggestion *peisein* was taken into the text without displacing the original *anankazein.* Even so, the interpolation is still absent from La^{LXV} (cf. Sy). We have thus explained how *peisein* is a later interpolation.

Our verse contains one other difficulty, the word *dioti*. Ordinarily it means "because" or, after a verb of saying or thinking, "that" or "why." Here there is no verb of saying or thinking. Ordinarily *dioti* introduces a clause wherein the verb is in the indicative. Sometimes, in a long complicated sentence, especially one which contains indirect discourse, a Greek writer can turn the verb in a clause introduced by *dioti* or *hoti* into an infinitive (Abel, *Grammaire*, pp. 279–80; Polybius xxxi 12.4; at Diodorus iv 76.2, the infinitive *hyparchein* in mss. *C* and *F* occurs in a subordinate clause which depends on an infinitive result clause). Here, however, the sentence is neither long nor complicated. Nowhere else in the abridged history is there such a construction. Hence, it is probable that *dioti* is a corrupt reading. Perhaps the original text had *dia to*, words which could easily be followed by an infinitive (as at II 3:38, 4:30, 6:11, 8:36, 10:13, 15:17; cf. 2:11). If so, the blank in my translation could be filled by "with the added inducement."

15. The author praises Judas for clear-seeing statesmanship: Judas perceived that at this time Lysias could be expected to fulfill his promises. Jason followed his probably erroneous assumption, that John and Absalom represented Judas, and deduced, from "submitted" in vs. 17, that Judas submitted peace terms in writing for Lysias to consider. The royal letters in vss. 23–33 together do seem to concede everything that Jason thought the Jewish rebels were seeking.

16–21. This letter cannot be a forgery. The regime of Lysias and the royal line of Antiochus IV and V became extinct soon after, in autumn, 162 B.C.E. The later Seleucid kings never persecuted the Jewish religion and even issued decrees favoring the Jews. There was thus no need after 162 B.C.E. to fabricate a letter ending the persecution. Before 162 B.C.E. any such forgery would have deceived no one. One might argue that pious Jews did not wish Menelaus to have sole credit for ending the persecution (see vss. 29–32) and fabricated our letter. But then they would not have forged vague references to "the document copied below" (see vs. 17); rather, they would have made a specific list of terms at least as generous as those in vss. 30–31.

Lysias' letter gives no hint that he has just conducted a hard-fought campaign against bitter resistance. The letter thus conforms to Greek rhetorical teaching: to win the goodwill of the other side in negotiations, one should pretend that the other side is already friendly and close to agreement. See AB vol. 41, p. 405. Even the "document copied below" (mentioned in vs. 17) may have said little or nothing about the bitter conflict which preceded the negotiations.

The letter of the Roman ambassadors (vss. 34–38) takes note of the contents of our letter and, in vss. 35–36, echoes vs. 18. The two letters cast light one upon the other. In vs. 36 the Romans imply that they are on their way to Antioch to meet the king who was mentioned in vs. 18. Antiochus IV never returned to Antioch after his departure on his eastward campaign in 147 Sel. Mac. (late spring, 165 B.C.E.; see I 3:37, 6:1–16, and AB vol. 41, pp. 249–51). Our letter here is an official government document. Hence, its year date is 148 Sel. *Mac.*, a year throughout which Antiochus IV was alive. Before Antiochus IV marched eastward there was no occasion on which Lysias could have forwarded to him petitions from the Jews. Hence, if the letter in vss. 34–38 is authentic (see NOTE on vss. 34–38), the king in vss. 17–21 and 34–38 must be the little coregent. It required considerable ingenuity for us to establish the existence of the coregency (see AB vol. 41, pp. 252–54) and to explain how the letter at 9:19–27 was compatible with it (see NOTE on 9:24–25). Our efforts now prove to have been justified.

16. *The content . . . from Lysias.* Although the plural word *epistolai* frequently means "letter," here the plural has its literal meaning, as is shown by the particle *men* (in *para men Lysiou*) and by the consistent use of the singular elsewhere in the abridged history (vss. 22, 27, 34, and 9:18; on 14:13, see NOTE ad loc.).

I have translated the reading of VqL⁻⁵³⁴, which has *hai gegrammenai*. The reading of A, without the definite article *hai*, was accepted by Hanhart but is difficult. One would expect the definite article, as in vss. 22 and 27. Without the definite article, a Greek would have taken *gegrammenai* with *êsan* to form a pluperfect passive, "Letters had been written . . . ," which does not fit the context.

16–17. *Lysias . . . you.* Whoever the Jews were to whom Lysias addressed his letter, they were no longer members of a privileged *ethnos*. See AB vol. 41, pp. 194–95, 211–12. Lysias addresses them as the *plêthos* ("community," "mass," "multitude") of the Jews. *Plêthos* is a neutral word, connoting neither privileged status nor its absence. See Welles, *Royal Correspondence,* no. 15, line 8; no. 22, line 14, and no. 52, lines 33 and 40; *Syll.*³ 581, line 95; and 695, lines 11, 20, 42. Polybius uses *plêthos* of the Roman people (*populus,* not *plebs*) at vi 15.11, and the word is so used at I 8:15. At I 8:20 it is used of the Jewish nation at a time when it had probably recovered its status as an *ethnos;* see AB vol. 41, p. 365. However, multiple translations underlie the Greek of First Maccabees. Only here do we find *plêthos* used in the address formula of a letter; hence, it is likely that Lysias deliberately chose to use a neutral word. Similarly, Lysias does not recognize the Jewish delegates John and Absalom as "ambassadors" (*presbeutai*) but only as "spokesmen" or "men sent" (*pemphthentes*). His own messengers to the Jews are designated by the same neutral expression (vs. 20); cf. Welles, *Royal Correspondence,* no. 32, lines 3–4.

On the other hand, it is possible that the Jews seeking to negotiate with Lysias called themselves "the multitude" or "the many," for "many" (*rabbīm*) was an expression used for pious Jews (Dan 8:25, 11:14, 34, 39, 44, 12.2–3; Cross, *Ancient Library,* pp. 231–34; AB vol. 41, p. 46, n. 20).

At AB vol. 41, p. 271, I was wrong to follow Tcherikover (*Hellenistic Civilization,* p. 217) and state that John and Absalom, the Jewish spokesmen mentioned in vs. 10, "surely" belonged to the same group as Menelaus. My former assertion is unlikely to be true. John and Absalom bear Hebrew, not Greek, names. The royal letter in vss. 27–33 takes no note of them, and Lysias' letter takes no note of Menelaus. John and Absalom may well represent pious Jews who hitherto had made common cause with the Hasmonaeans but were now willing to make peace in return for an end to the persecution; see NOTE on vs. 7 and AB vol. 41, pp. 5–6. Those Jews must have been numerous (see NOTE on vs. 34, the *People of the Jews*). Indeed, they probably were strong enough to make peace against the opposition of the Hasmonaean party.

Nothing else tells us who John and Absalom were. "John" was an extremely common name. Though Judas Maccabaeus had a brother John (I 2:2, 9:35–38), nowhere is that John said to have served as an ambassador, and nowhere is he mentioned in Second Maccabees. On the other hand, "John" is attested as a name used in a family of Jewish ambassadors (II 4:11, I 8:17), and the known ambassadorial functions of the members of that family show no necessary connection with Judas Maccabaeus (see AB vol. 41, pp. 357–58). "Absalom" is much less common as a name, perhaps because it was borne by King David's ill-fated son. A later member of the Hasmonaean family was named "Absalom" (J. AJ xiv 4.4.71), and two army officers under Jonathan and Simon each are called "son of Absalom." At 1QpHab 5:9 the Qumran commentator condemns the "House of Absalom" for not heeding the reproof uttered by the Teacher of Righteousness and for failing to support him against the Man of the Lie. One may infer that the House of Absalom consisted of pious men who might have been expected to heed the Teacher of Righteousness and to oppose the Man of the Lie. The Man of the Lie may well have been a Hasmonaean (Mattathias?). Thus the two officers, sons of Absalom, may well have belonged to the House of Absalom, and so may the Absalom here. The House of Absalom then would seem to have been an influential pious family, strong enough to have a policy of its own, which on occasion cooperated with the Hasmonaeans. See also AB vol. 41, p. 443.

17–18. Following Jason's interpretation in vs. 15, I have construed *epidontes* as the aorist participle of *epididômi* and have translated it "submitted," the meaning it has in many papyri from our period. One might construe it as the aorist participle of *ephoraô* and translate it "examined." The verb is used of examining documents at Herodotus i 48.1 and in Egyptian papyri written under the Roman empire, but I know of no example in a papyrus from our period. Furthermore, one would then like to know what document was examined by John and Absalom. It could not have been the letter in vss. 27–33, for that was written on the fifteenth of Xanthicus and became known to the Jews on the twenty-eighth (see NOTE on vss. 27–33). Lysias had his meeting in Judaea with John and Absalom on or before the twenty-fourth of the renamed month (see NOTE on vs. 21). Thus the meeting could not have been the channel through which the letter in vss. 27–33 reached the Jews, even if the month named in vs. 24 was identical with Xanthicus. Any other royal letter granting rights to the Jews should have been preserved and quoted here, not omitted.

No such difficulties arise if *epidontes* is construed to mean "delivered." There would then be good reason why the "document copied below" has not been preserved. The Jewish petitioners knew their own desires and probably did not preserve the copy, but Lysias could have had good reason to send it to them. We can guess what the documentary procedure was: Lysias sent back to the Jews a copy of their own petition, which he had marked up, with marginal notes and perhaps also with insertions.

We have many examples of somewhat similar procedure in the Ptolemaic empire in dealing with written petitions. The king or the official writes his decision below, on the sheet bearing the petition, and the resultant document is called, as here, a *chrêmatismos*. See Paul M. Meyer, "Zum Rechts- und Urkundenwesen im ptolemäisch-römischen Ägypten," *Klio* 6 (1906), 424–25, and

Welles, *Royal Correspondence*, p. 375. Here Lysias puts a summary communication of his decisions *above* a copy of the petition.

The Jewish representatives submitted a written petition and also made oral requests (Bickerman, *Gott*, p. 179, cites the parallel at Polybius xxviii 19.4). Lysias' "indications" in reply were probably both written and oral.

The coregent's consent could only have been a matter of form, but Lysias may have had to convince other powerful ministers to support his recommendations (note the plural "guardians" of Antiochus V mentioned at Justin xxxiv 3.5, 9). For that reason, he could have used the pretext of having to consult the king.

"I did" is my translation of *synechôrêsa*, the reading of *l*−93 542 La^BMP. The context and the echo of our passage at vs. 35 render the reading certain, even though at our verse the normally best witnesses have *synechôrêsen*, which would make our passage mean "Those points which the king could grant, he did."

Similar expressions are used in a letter of a high official of Ptolemy I to the Greek city of Iasos in Asia Minor, "As regards the other points, we have granted them; as regards the contribution, it seemed best to me to bring the matter before the king" (Jeanne and Louis Robert, "Bulletin épigraphique," REG 84 [1971], 502).

19. Cf. Welles, *Royal Correspondence*, no. 31, lines 18–20. The allusion to the loyalty of the probably pious petitioners may not be mere rhetoric, especially if they represented pious Jews who now opposed the Hasmonaean party. Lysias had good reason to offer such pious Jews incentives for future compliance.

to act for your benefit. Lit. "to be a contributory cause [*paraitios*] of good." The expression is found elsewhere in documents of Hellenistic diplomacy; see Welles, ibid., p. 353.

20. Detailed oral explanations are to remove possible ambiguities from the words of the written document.

21. The year 148 Sel. Mac. ran from October 2, 165, through September 21, 164 B.C.E. The year number is unlikely to be corrupt or to have suffered tampering. In the first place, it is written out in words, not in figures. Moreover, information which we possess (but which was unavailable to Jason and to the ancient scribes) makes that year number contradict Jason's own chronological theory. See Introduction, pp. 60–62. The reading "in the one hundred forty-ninth year" at vs. 38 in La^B cannot be what Jason wrote, either here or there. Whatever were the dates written in the original documents, La^B can only be a witness to what Jason wrote, and Jason must have believed our letter preceded the other three documents in our chapter, since he presents all four as resulting from negotiations at the end of Lysias' first campaign, and he must have recognized from the contents of vss. 34–38 that the letter there followed soon after Lysias'.

The context here leaves no doubt that the name of a month also appears in our verse, but the readings of all witnesses to that name are strange. There is another instance of a strange month name in the preserved text of a Seleucid royal letter of the period in the message of Antiochus IV concerning the Samaritans of 146 Sel., quoted at J. *AJ* xii 5.5.258–64 (see Appendix VIII). The eccentric behavior of Antiochus IV could have extended to the renaming of months, and there lies the most probable explanation of the puzzling name. "Hyrkanios," the odd month name in Josephus, seems to be a geographical term (taken from the name of a region in Iran claimed or coveted by Antiochus IV?), but the readings here cannot be made to fit that pattern. Other attempts at a solution are complete failures, and even our effort to ascertain the correct reading will end in an admission of ignorance.

Like other ancient calendars based on lunar months, the Seleucid calendar was kept in step with the seasons of the solar year by "intercalating," by adding a thirteenth ("intercalary") month when necessary. We have no other evidence on what the name was that the Macedonians in the Seleucid empire gave to the intercalary month, but the name here can hardly be that. Macedonian Seleucid intercalations almost certainly coincided with those of the Babylonian calendar (Bickerman, *Institutions*, p. 205; Bickerman, *Chronology*, p. 25; Alan E. Samuel, *Greek and Roman Chronology*, pp. 139–42), and, thus, not 148 Sel. Mac. but 149 Sel. Mac. was intercalary (Parker and Dubberstein, p. 41). As far as we know, Greeks, like Babylonians, gave an intercalary month the name of the month preceding it, adding the adjective "second" (*deuteros*) or "later" (*hysteros*) or "intercalary" (*embolimos*); see Samuel, *Chronology*, pp. 58, 68, 74, 100, 114.

All witnesses to the text agree that the first three letters of the month name are *DIO*. In the Macedonian calendar used in the Seleucid empire, *Dios* (genitive, *Diou*) is the name of the first month. In our period, *Dios* came at the beginning of autumn; from the first decades of the first century C.E., it came in mid-autumn (Samuel, *Chronology*, pp. 140–41). Of all the witnesses to the text, only the Syriac has an equivalent (*Tešri 'ḥray*) of the Macedonian month *Dios*. The Syriac is never likely to be the sole preserver of the original reading. Moreover, to put the letter in the first month of autumn, 165, we would have to view it as having been written long before the amnesty offered in vs. 30 (see NOTE on vss. 27–33). One might believe that a pious faction approached the chief minister so early. But then, after his friendly reply, months passed with no effect. Would the pious faction have preserved the futile document? Rather, it seems that pious Jews were unable to present appeals to the Seleucid government during the period which saw the march eastward of Antiochus IV (May or June, 165; see AB vol. 41, p. 251), the campaign of Nicanor and Gorgias, and Lysias' own preparations (lengthy, according to I 4:28) and campaign.

Two other months of the Seleucid calendar began with *D*. Daisios was the second month after the Xanthicus of vss. 30 and 33. We shall find good reasons to exclude that possibility (see the concluding NOTE on vss. 16–38). The other month beginning with *D* was Dystros, the month which immediately preceded Xanthicus. The reading *Dystros* here would involve no difficulties whatever in fitting the documents of our chapter into a coherent scheme. However, the Greek scribes were familiar with the Macedonian calendar. If they did not take the "obvious" solutions for someone familiar with the calendar, of reading *Diou* or *Dystrou*, the words which lay before them must have been so clearly written that they felt they could not depart from them, and modern scholars have been unable to suggest how an ancient scribe could have substituted for simple *Diou* or *Dystrou* anything like the strange readings of our witnesses to the text.

Dios Korinthiou ("of Corinthian Zeus") is the reading of all Greek witnesses and of La^B. Corinthian Zeus is a deity mentioned several times in Greek literature (Pindar, *Nemean Odes* 7.105; Aristophanes *Frogs* 439; Plato *Euthydemus* 292e; see J. B. Bury, *The Nemean Odes of Pindar* [London: Macmillan, 1890], p. 144). Corinth does not appear in the list of Greek cities which received favors from Antiochus IV. Nothing else suggests that he would choose to honor a Corinthian deity by naming a month after him. Moreover, though Greek months could be named for gods, such names were then adjectival or derived noun forms, not the bare divine name. The Greek scribes surely knew that fact, too. The word which originally lay before them must have been totally unfamiliar as a month name, if they substituted for it the more familiar name of Corinthian Zeus.

The Latin versions frequently preserve readings earlier than and superior to those of the best Greek manuscripts. Here La^L has *dioscordi*, La^XV *dioscori die*, La^M *deoscolori die*, and La^P *dioscoridis*. Since La^XVM have the word *die* ("day") in an anomalous position, between the supposed month name and the word *mensis* ("month"), all the Latin versions would attest a Greek *Dioskoridou*. As we shall see, the month date in vs. 38 probably bears witness to the month date here. There a Greek witness, too, attests *Dioskoridou*. Dioskorides is a man's name in Greek, and we know of no Greek month name formed with the ending -*ides*, or, in this period, from a bare human name.

The name *Dioskouros* is given in a chronological table from the time of the Roman empire as that of the sixth month in the Cretan year, which began just after the autumnal equinox (see Samuel, *Chronology*, pp. 171–75), and perhaps the name is corrupt and should be read *Dioskourios* or *Dioskorios;* that would be a normal form for a month named for the twin deities, the Dioskouroi or Dioskoroi (cf. Dittenberger, "Dioskorios," PW, V [1905], 1085–86). However, a Byzantine Greek lexicon compiled in the twelfth century C.E. knows of *Dioskoros* as "the name of a month" (*Etymologicon magnum,* ed. by Thomas Gaisford [Amsterdam: Hakkert, 1967], s.v.). By the terms of the Peace of Apameia (188 B.C.E.) Antiochus IV was barred from recruiting soldiers from Crete, and nothing else suggests that Antiochus IV favored Crete or her institutions. But the Dioskouroi were widely worshiped in the Greek world and appear on the coins of Seleucid predecessors and successors of Antiochus IV (Bethe, "Dioskuren," PW, V [1905], 1098–1106). In the reign of Antiochus IV they appear on the municipal coins of the important city of Tripolis as the special symbol of the city (Mørkholm, p. 127). Antiochus IV could have renamed one of the Macedonian months as *Dioskorios*, perhaps to honor Tripolis. But if that was the original name here, there is still some difficulty in explaining the *d* in La^−B (and in V at vs. 38) and the "Corinthian Zeus" in all other Greek witnesses. Perhaps an early scribe, for whom *Dioskoriou* was unfamiliar, inadvertently added the *d* from the familiar human name Dioskorides. But would not later scribes, puzzled by a month named for an obviously obscure human being, have replaced it by the divine name "Dioskoroi" rather than by "Corinthian Zeus"? What name in Greek did Antiochus IV give the Roman Jupiter Capitolinus, to whom he built the temple at

Antioch (Livy xli 20.9)? Did he rename a month in honor of that god? We must admit that we cannot be sure what the original month name was.

Whatever the name was, Jason of Cyrene believed that the month preceded Xanthicus, for he held that the letter here, sent on the twenty-fourth, preceded the letter in vss. 27–33, which he dated on 15 Xanthicus.

23–26. The considerations urged on behalf of the letter of Lysias at the beginning of the NOTE on vss. 16–21 also argue for the authenticity of the letter here. Often a Hellenistic king, on making a decision affecting a group of his subjects, would put that decision into effect by writing a letter to an official, so instructing him, and by having a copy of that letter sent to the affected group. See Appendix VIII, Commentary, Introductory NOTE. In such copies the concluding greeting and the date, which stood at the end of the letter, were usually omitted (see Laqueur, *Historische Zeitschrift* 136 [1927], 233–34). Thus the absence of those formulas from our letter is exactly what one would expect, and there are no other departures in it from what is known of the style of the royal letters of the time.

On the other hand, one would expect a pious forger to fabricate a letter addressed to the Jews themselves and in it to mention Judas Maccabaeus or some other pious person.

At first glance, our letter, written to Lysias, looks like the king's expected reply on the points which the chief minister sent on for his decision (see vs. 18), and Jason of Cyrene jumped to that conclusion. He believed that the document here was written in 148 Sel. Mac., shortly after Lysias' letter, and held it to be simultaneous or nearly so with the one in vss. 27–33. He used vs. 23 as the cornerstone of his erroneous chronology (see Introduction, pp. 56–63). Jason's hypotheses result in a false date for the death of Antiochus IV. But subtle difficulties in our letter argue against Jason's chronology even apart from that fact. Our letter is unlikely to be the expected reply because it ignores the Jewish representatives John and Absalom and their petition and says nothing of Lysias' previous concessions or of the letter from Lysias implied in vs. 18. Our letter can hardly be simultaneous or nearly so with the one in vss. 27–33 because the concessions here go far beyond those there (see NOTE on vs. 23), which we know the Jews accepted (see NOTE on vss. 27–33). For the same reason our letter could hardly have been written earlier than the one in vss. 27–33 (cf. Motzo, *Saggi*, pp. 144–50).

Since we know Jason's chronology for our letter is wrong, we must now try to place the document in its true setting. The letter contains a good indication. The young king begins by mentioning that his father has died. He goes on to declare his own principles: in his reign internal tranquility is an important goal. To secure tranquility also among his Jewish subjects, he proceeds to reverse his father's policies. The natural time for such a statement is at or very shortly after the accession of Antiochus V as sole king. There are abundant examples of such announcements at the accessions of Hellenistic kings. See Habicht, *Harvard Studies in Classical Philology* 80 (1976), 16–17, and cf. Henry Fynes Clinton, *Fasti Hellenici* (Oxford: University Press, 1834), III, 373; A. Lefèvre, "Maccabées (Livres I et II des)," *Dictionnaire de la Bible,* ed. by F. Vigouroux, Supplément, vol. V (1957), col. 609, and Schürer (New English version), I, 164.

Such a declaration repudiating unsuccessful policies of Antiochus IV was all the more appropriate a step for the insecure regime of Lysias and Antiochus V, established against the will of the late king (see NOTE on 9:19–27 and NOTE on 9:29). There was also good reason for the regime to assume a benevolent, perhaps even friendly, tone to the Jews. Our letter in some respects resembles the sarcastic edict of 311 C.E. by the Roman emperor Galerius in which he granted toleration to the Christians (translated in Naphtali Lewis and Meyer Reinhold, *Roman Civilization*, II, 601–2). Just as Galerius posed as benevolent, seeking that "the Christians, too, may be of sound mind," so Antiochus V poses as seeking that "this nation, too, may be free from disturbance." Thus, under the circumstances, one should not view our letter as being overfriendly to the Jews.

Accordingly, the letter here would be dated late in 164 or early in 163 B.C.E. A date early in 163 is confirmed by the probable meaning of Dan 8:14, which declares that the holy will be vindicated (*wᵉniṣdaq qōdeš*) 2,300 mornings and evenings (i.e., 1,150 days) after the desecration of 25 Kislev. The 1,150 days bring us to February 8, 163 B.C.E. (see AB vol. 41, p. 43, but for "January 28" there, read "February 8"). What could be a better vindication than the arrival of the announcement of the death of the persecutor and the repudiation of his policies, both by his own son?

In early 163 B.C.E. the Jewish calendar may still have been dislocated (see AB vol. 41, pp. 274–80); the equivalent of February 8, 163 B.C.E., was 23 Shebaṭ on the intercalated calendar or 23 Nisan on the defective calendar. Neither date is listed in *Megillat Ta'anit*. Why did not pious Jews observe annually the date of the fulfillment of Dan 8:14? Answers are not hard to find. The persecution was long since over by the time of our letter. The Jews had purified the temple and reinstituted the offering of sacrifices. The date of the arrival of the letter was not the date of the tyrant's death. The seer of Daniel, whose false prophecies were in danger of being exposed, had to publish the computation in Dan 8:14 to keep up the faith of his followers in Daniel's prophetic power. Soon afterward, however, it was clear to believers that many of Daniel's prophecies, if true, could not refer to the times through which they had just passed but only to some time in the future. We can use Dan 8:14 to determine when the Jews received their copy of the letter here, but believers soon after February 8, 163 B.C.E., could not do so.

February 8, 163 B.C.E., is early enough in the reign of Antiochus V to fit our suppositions about the background of the letter. The insecure regime of Lysias may well have tried to conceal as long as possible the fact that Antiochus IV was dead and that Philip was marching westward. The first official confirmation at Jerusalem of the senior king's death may well have been the publication of our letter.

The amnesty of Xanthicus, 164 B.C.E., still left in force some of the policies of Antiochus IV which were intolerable to pious Jews (see NOTE on vss. 27–33). To have mentioned the earlier amnesty here as a precedent would have been a blunder for a regime which was courting support by claiming to make a fresh start.

On the other hand, Laqueur argued (*Historische Zeitschrift* 130 [1927], 238) for connecting the letter here with the peace of 162 B.C.E., which Lysias and Antiochus V negotiated with the pious rebels whom they had been besieging in the temple (I 6:51–63). Laqueur noted how similar the words ascribed to Lysias at I 6:58–59 are to vss. 24–26, and how the threat of Philip's rebellion at Antioch could have forced the change of policy upon the regime. The implication in vs. 23, however, that Antiochus IV died *recently* and our other arguments for a date in 163 B.C.E. far outweigh Laqueur's points. The similarities between vss. 24–26 and I 6:58–59 indeed suggest that the author of First Maccabees knew the letter here and jumped, wrongly, to the conclusion that it was to be connected with the peace of 162 B.C.E. He knew that the Jews celebrated annually the day of the withdrawal of Antiochus V from Jerusalem (*Megillat Ta'anit* 28 Shebaṭ), and expected that a document of the occasion had been preserved.

Our comments here dispose of all the arguments which Schunck (*Quellen*, pp. 103–5) brought to show our letter is a forgery. He was driven to do so because he wrongly refused to ascribe to Jason the error of believing that the document here was written at nearly the same time as those in vss. 16–21, 27–33, and 34–38 (see my Introduction, pp. 56–63).

23. *his brother Lysias.* This is the normal way for a king to address a courtier who held the rank of Kinsman (Bickerman, *Institutions*, p. 43; cf. AB vol. 41, p. 400).

we wish. The king is made in vss. 23–26 to give his own motives for what he is doing ("we wish," "we have heard," "we choose"). Hence, though good witnesses (A q 58), by reading *boulomenou*, ascribe the wish to the dead king (". . . passed away to the gods wishing the subjects of his kingdom to be undisturbed . . ."), I have accepted the reading of all other witnesses to the text. The reading of A q 58 may be a mistaken emendation by a scribe who remembered the intentions of Antiochus IV as expressed in 9:21–24.

passed away to the gods. Such expressions were used of the death of a royal person. Cf. OGIS 308, lines 2–4, and 339, line 16, and see NOTE on 4:7.

undisturbed . . . private affairs. They have no right to meddle in the affairs of the kingdom. Their rebellion must cease. The regime is generous but insists on its own prerogatives. Cf. Polybius ii 57.3–4, and Welles, *Royal Correspondence*, p. 168.

24–25. Our verses are contemporary documentary evidence on the causes of Jewish rebellion in the reigns of Antiochus IV and V. Any theory on the causes of the Hasmonaean revolt must include an acceptable interpretation of this passage.

I have shown (AB vol. 41, pp. 140–57) that the imposed cult was not Greek. By no stretch of the imagination, then, could Antiochus V have called the persecution of the Jews by Antiochus IV "our father's decree for a change-over to Greek ways." Moreover, the amnesty of Xanthicus, 164 B.C.E., ended the persecution. Writing early in 163 B.C.E., the regime of Antiochus V must be offering the Jews something different from an end to the persecution. Indeed, after the end of the persecution, the changeover to Greek ways is still in force!

These facts argue strongly for interpreting the "changeover to Greek ways" to mean "exemption from Jewish law for Jews who become Antiochene citizens" (see I 1:13; II 4:10–11). Such Jews were henceforth to be governed under Greek or royal law (cf. J. *AJ* xii 5.1.240), and even pious Jews were expected to conform to Greek practice by leaving the Antiochenes unmolested. See AB vol. 41, pp. 118–19, 136–37. The language used at I 1:13–14 and II 4:10 is close to that of our document and confirms our interpretation of it.

The Hasmonaean party and many other pious Jews inferred that the persecution had been punishment for tolerating the sinful practices of the Antiochenes of Jerusalem on the soil of Judaea, especially the gymnasium and close association with Greeks. See pp. 92–95, my article in *Jewish and Christian Self-Definition*, II, 78–87, and NOTE on II 4:9–15 and NOTE on II 4:16–17. Accordingly, militant pious Jews could no longer tolerate those practices in Judaea: if they did not "wipe out the evil from their midst," the wrath of God would come down upon them.

The amnesty in vss. 27–33 had only permitted pious Jews their own observances. It had not brought Antiochene Jews back under Jewish law. Now the Seleucid government perceived that the Jews would fight rather than allow the Hellenizing "apostates" to be exempt from Jewish law. Antiochus V therefore put all members of the Jewish nation (*ethnos*) back under the rule of the Torah. Jews of Judaea could now punish Hellenizing apostates. In addition, the regime removed another bone of contention: the king conceded to the pious Jews the right to hold the temple, which was already in their hands. Between spring, 167 B.C.E., and the king's decree here, royal law may have put the right to control the temple into the hands of the adherents of the imposed cult.

Does the literal meaning of our document leave all Hellenizing Jews in the Seleucid empire open to persecution by pious zealots? It applied only to the recognized *ethnos* of the Jews, governed by its own national organs in the officially defined area of Judaea. We may assume that, outside Judaea, Jewish Hellenizers and Antiochenes were safe. Even Jewish rigorists conceded that apostates could be unmolested if they resided outside the biblically defined borders of the Promised Land. Our sources indicate that such apostates long were to be found in the Akra and in Beth-Zur (I 6:18–23, 10:14, 13:51; see AB vol. 41, pp. 124, 315, 400, 442–43). The Seleucid regime could protect them in those places without violating the words of our document. It would claim that the places were not part of Judaea (see I 15:28).

24. *decree for a changeover.* The Greek noun *metathesis* and the related verb *metatithenai* as legal terms have the meaning of changing or abrogating a law and replacing it by another. See Thucydides v 18, 29; Xenophon *Memorabilia* iv 4.14; Pseudo-Plato *Minos* 316c, 317b, and cf. the use of the middle voice of the verb at II 7:24.

25. *they govern . . . ancestors.* The language is almost the same as that in the document at J. *AJ* xii 3.3.142, where Antiochus III declares the Torah to be the law of the land for the Jews of Judaea. Indeed, the clause here reinstates the grants of Antiochus III, which had been set aside by Antiochus IV when he granted the petitions of Jason the Oniad (4:11).

26. The regime grants amnesty to the entire mass of rebellious Jews, even before they cease resisting and go home. Cf. vs. 31.

The "assurances" are literally "right hands" (*dexias*). The expression is regularly used in connection with amnesties; cf. Polybius v 54.8. On the solemn obligation symbolized by a hand-clasp, see NOTE on 4:34, *accepted . . . oath.*

27–33. This document is authentic. Pious Jews would never have forged evidence giving Menelaus credit for ending the persecution. If Hellenizers had falsely given Menelaus the credit, pious Jews would never have preserved the document.

The letter is addressed directly to the Council of Elders and the rest of the Jews. Though royal letters transmitted only in copy might be undated, here the Jews received a dated original. The letter offers Jews amnesty if they cease fighting and go home by 30 Xanthicus, and the letter itself as we have it bears the date 15 Xanthicus. If the king sending the letter was the little coregent, surely he was no nearer Judaea than Antioch, over 500 kilometers away! If the king was Antiochus IV, he was much farther away, in the territories east of the Euphrates. Scholars have found it incredible, under such circumstances, that the letter set the deadline for amnesty only fifteen days after the writing of the letter; see Christian Habicht, "Royal Documents in Maccabees II," *Harvard Studies in Classical Philology* 80 (1976), 13.

Against the skepticism of these scholars stands the evidence of *Megillat Ta'anit* 28 Adar: on that date "the good news came to the Jews, that they did not have to depart from the Torah." Macedonian "Xanthicus" and Babylonian and Jewish "Adar" normally named one and the same month, that which preceded the month of the vernal equinox. As described in *Megillat Ta'anit,* 28 Adar can only be the date of the arrival of the letter in vss. 27–33. The date of the arrival of the letter in vss. 22–26 was not 28 Adar; see NOTE on vss. 23–26.

The language in *Megillat Ta'anit* is specific: the date celebrated thereafter was the anniversary of the *arrival* of the announcement of the amnesty: it arrived only two days before the deadline. A message sent from Antioch on the fifteenth of a month could easily reach Jerusalem by the twenty-eighth (see Reincke, "Nachrichtenwesen," PW, XVI² [1935], 1537–41). Judaea was a compact area. The news of the offer to end the persecution could spread quickly. The government had good reason to press for a quick decision and no reason to give the Jews a long time to deliberate.

The few known ancient parallels are somewhat helpful. At the beginning of 43 B.C.E. the troops of Mark Antony had the commander favored by the senate, Decimus Brutus, under siege in Mutina, between 450 and 500 kilometers from Rome, and were pressing him hard. Cicero, in a speech to the senate delivered on January 1, proposed offering Antony's men amnesty if they would abandon the siege by February 1 (*Fifth Philippic* 34). Cicero and the senate were in a much less favorable position to press for a quick decision than was the Seleucid regime in our case. Even so, despite the distance to Mutina, the deadline was to be set only one month away. On February 3, Cicero suggested another offer to Antony's troops, with March 15 as the deadline (*Eighth Philippic* 33).

In our case, it is likely that after the battle of Beth-Zur there already was a truce *de facto:* Lysias after suffering heavy losses was not eager to suffer more; the majority of the pious Jews, hoping for an end to the persecution, may well have abstained from provocative acts. Menelaus and his followers, caught between the royal army and the militant pietists, may have urged restraint on both sides, while Menelaus went to Antioch to lay his petition before the little coregent, i.e., before the ministers powerful in the regime. If most of the pious rebels were expectantly waiting for the royal reply, the king could indeed have sent to Judaea on the fifteenth of the month a letter announcing that the deadline for amnesty would be the thirtieth. Cf. Menahem Stern, *The Documents on the History of the Hasmonaean Revolt* (Tel-Aviv: Hakibbutz Hameuchad, 1965), p. 71 (in Hebrew).

Thus the dates in our letter are by no means incredible. Unless we emend the date in vs. 33 (and the burden of proof is on the emender), the king in vs. 27 can be only the little coregent. Though Menelaus could have traveled to the distant eastern regions to lay his petition before Antiochus IV, there could be no assurance that a message sent from so far away on the fifteenth would reach Judaea in time to announce the thirtieth as the deadline.

Christian Habicht, restating views held earlier, as he says, by Henry F. Clinton and Georg F. Unger, has argued that the combination of dates in our letter is incredible (the position we have just refuted), and that Antiochus IV must have written the letter much earlier in 148 Sel. Mac. (indeed, late in 165 B.C.E.) to pacify the Jews, and that only after pious Jews rejected the offer and went on fighting did Lysias embark on his expedition (Habicht, *Harvard Studies in Classical Philology* 80 [1976], 13-18, and *2. Makkabäerbuch*, pp. 180-83). But *Megillat Ta'anit* 28 Adar attests that pious Jews accepted the offer of amnesty! Habicht's view is improbable also because there would then be no reason why pious Jews should have preserved, down to Jason's time, the document of an amnesty they had rejected.

Habicht even suggests (*Harvard Studies in Classical Philology* 80 [1976], 14; *2. Makkabäerbuch*, pp. 181, 258) that the amnesty in vs. 30 was intended chiefly for the surviving participants in the coup perpetrated in 169 B.C.E. by Jason the Oniad! Were they so numerous as to be the key to peace in Judaea in 164 B.C.E.? Did they, supporters of the deposed founder of the Antiochene community at Jerusalem, seek the right to observe Jewish law and follow the Jewish way of life, as provided in vs. 31?

In fact, the document here bore fruit for pious Jews, though the Hasmonaean party seems to have wanted no part of it. Even the address of the letter was probably a concession, for it seems to grant again to the Jews' Council of Elders the recognition which had probably been revoked in 167 B.C.E. (see AB vol. 41, pp. 211-12). Moreover, the letter here did end the persecution and led to Lysias' withdrawal. On the other hand, it did not restore the temple to the control of pious Jews nor did it make the Torah again the law for all Jews in Judaea. Antiochene Jews were still free, by decree of Antiochus IV (4:9-15), to follow Greek ways even in Judaea, and the imposed cult might still be practiced in the temple. We lack evidence to tell whether that cult continued for a time after the amnesty provided here. See NOTE on 10:1-8.

One aspect of our letter is strange if Xanthicus came later than the month named in vs. 21. Lysias and the Jewish delegates John and Absalom are not mentioned. One can, however, imagine a situation in which the Seleucid regime would avoid mentioning them. John and Absalom probably represented pious Jews who had been in rebellion. Despite the neutral phraseology in the letter of vss. 17-21, by negotiating with John and Absalom, Lysias had conferred upon them and upon their faction a kind of recognition. Hitherto, the royal govern-

ment had probably treated the high priest and his delegates as the sole spokesmen of the Jewish community, except in matters involving strife between the
community and the high priest himself. In the latter case, the spokesmen for
the community probably had to be members of the Council of Elders. See
3:1–12, 32, 4:1–11, 23–29, 43–48, 5:15, 23. Though the Council of Elders
had probably lost all official standing, many of its members surely survived.
Probably not one of them was in Judas' force, for the Hasmonaean propagandist, who reports the adhesion of the pious group called "Asidaioi" (I
2:42–43; in AB vol. 41, I translated the name as "Pietists"), says nothing of
members of the Council of Elders (cf. AB vol. 41, p. 275). Menelaus may
have approached the regime at Antioch not only to beg for an amnesty but also
to protest, on behalf of the old national elite, against Lysias' recognition of the
rebel faction. Lysias was powerful, but other persons important in the regime
may have refused to endorse his recognition of the rebels. If the leaders at
Antioch did not already know, Menelaus could have informed them how dis-
parate were the elements fighting under Judas. The regime did not have to
grant recognition to rebels. By merely granting amnesty and the right to observe the Torah, the government might induce Judas himself to stop fighting;
at the very least, it could drain away much of his support, for many pious Jews
would then return to their belief that God himself forbade rebellion against the
king. Under such circumstances, the best procedure was the one we find
here: for the king to offer an amnesty through Menelaus and the Council of
Elders without mentioning Lysias and the rebel delegates.

Our letter presents the king as speaking of himself in the first person plural,
except in vs. 32. We have only one other surviving example of a letter from a
junior coregent, Welles, *Royal Correspondence,* no. 32. In it, Antiochus, eldest
son of Antiochus III, speaks of himself in the first person singular. Hence,
Marcello Zambelli argued that the king here could not be the little coregent
("La composizione del secondo libro dei Maccabei e la nuova cronologia di
Antioco IV Epifane," in *Miscellanea greca e romana* ["Studi pubblicati dall'Is-
tituto italiano per la storia antica," Fascicolo sedicesimo; Roma, 1965], pp.
228–29). The evidence is too scanty for drawing such an inference, and the
cases of the two coregents are not parallel. Antiochus III had already granted
the petition of the ambassadors, and the son Antiochus in his father's presence
seconded the grant. Here, Antiochus IV would have been absent, and the little
coregent would have been acting as the head of state in the western part of the
kingdom. On the occasional use of the first person singular by the head of
state, see Bickerman, *Studies,* II, 66.

Our letter should bear strong witness against the theories of Bickerman
(*Gott,* pp. 117–39) and Hengel (*Judaism and Hellenism,* I, 283–308), that
Menelaus and the elite who were members of the Council of Elders were
"deserters of the Holy Covenant" (Dan 11:29) who *planned* the persecution,
using the power of Antiochus IV to force their own views upon the pious Jews.
Rather, a royal document attests that Menelaus appealed for an end to the persecution, and that the Council of Elders presumably was pleased to learn that
the king granted the appeal! See also NOTE on vs. 32 and AB vol. 41, p. 159.

27. The regime around the little coregent recognizes the Council of Elders
but does not recognize the Jews as a privileged *ethnos* (see AB vol. 41, pp.

194–96). Cf. the titles given the Jews by the Roman ambassadors (in vs. 34) and by Antiochus V (in vs. 25), and also the titles in I 8:23–29, 10:25, 11:30 and 33, 12:6, 13:36, 14:20 and 28, 15:2 and 9. On the Council, see NOTE on II 1:10b.

28. On the *formula valetudinis* ("If you are well . . ."), see NOTE on 9:20–21. Of the witnesses to the text here, only La^XVP understood the formula.

29–30. Cf. vss. 23 and 26. Similar language is used on the Rosetta Stone of 196 B.C.E. to tell of the amnesty granted by the regime of Ptolemy V to Egyptian rebels who cease resisting and go home (OGIS 90, lines 19–20).

29. See NOTE on vs. 23.

30. *For those who go home . . . amnesty*. To receive amnesty, a Jew must first withdraw from the guerrilla resistance force. Cf. vs. 26.

the thirtieth of Xanthicus. The date is equivalent to March 27, 164 B.C.E.

The Macedonian regent Polyperchon in 319 B.C.E. set 30 Xanthicus as the deadline for the restoration of exiles and the restitution of their property throughout the Greek cities (Diodorus xviii 56.5). We do not know the month and day of Polyperchon's proclamation, but the case there is hardly parallel to the one here. The proclamation there affected the far-flung cities of the Greek world, and the restitution of the exiles' property involved complex legal problems, so that much more time would have had to be allowed.

assurance of safety. See NOTE on vs. 26.

amnesty. See NOTE on vs. 31.

31. The first clause of our verse ends the persecution. Jews are no longer obliged to follow the imposed cult. The official who drafted the letter switched constructions in our verse. After using the future indicative in vs. 30, he turned to the imperative infinitive with accusative subject in the first clause of our verse and went back to the future indicative in the second. The phenomena all have parallels in documents from Ptolemaic Egypt. See Mayser, II¹, 150–51, and II³, 201, and Welles, *Royal Correspondence*, p. lxxii. Many scribes failed to recognize the imperative infinitive here and took the infinitive as depending on *adeia* ("immunity," "amnesty," "liberty") in vs. 30 and omitted the particle *de*, which probably was present in the original and still stands in L′⁻⁵³⁴. The end of vs. 30 and the beginning of vs. 31 would then be translated "the assurance of safety and liberty to follow their own. . . ." If the infinitive is so construed, however, the subject "the Jews" becomes superfluous and extremely awkward in Greek, whether left in the accusative (as in most witnesses to the text) or changed to the dative (as in La^LXBM and in 64 and 370 of the class q and 534 of L and 62 of l). Fortunately, these difficulties have little effect on the meaning of the passage.

way of life. I have accepted the emendation of Adolf Wilhelm (*Akademie der Wissenschaften in Wien, Philosophisch-historische Klasse: Anzeiger* 64 [1937], 22–25), reading *diaitêmata* ("customs," "way of life") instead of the *dapanêmata* of most witnesses to the text. *Dapanêmata* in an official document could have only its normal meaning of "expenditures" (and was so understood by La^LXBMP), but that meaning does not fit the context. Probably for that reason the scribes underlying L′ 311 Sy omitted the word. *Dapanêmata* came also to mean "that on which money is expended," "supplies," and it has that meaning at Polybius ix 42.4. Eventually it came to be a synonym for "food"; cf. Hesychius s.v. *dapanê*, where that noun is defined by *trophê* ("food"). But the dietary laws were a part of the laws of the Jews. In a verse where laws are mentioned, why should food be singled out? On the other hand, many aspects of the Greek way of life were not expressly forbidden by Jewish law, but pious rigorists had viewed the adoption even of such Greek practices as sinful; see AB vol. 41, pp. 199–200, and my article in *Jewish and Christian Self-Definition*, II, 76–81. Thus, the king had good reason to say that the Jews will not be forced to change their way of life (*diaitêmata*) even if the changes can be reconciled with the letter of the Torah.

misunderstandings. A euphemism for the bitter years of rebellion against the kingdom. Errors committed in ignorance are forgivable. Cf. I 13:39.

32. Later, Lysias was to decide that Menelaus had to be sacrificed for the sake of peace in Judaea (13:4), but at this time the leaders in the Seleucid regime must have believed Menelaus could be used to put at ease the minds of persons who wished to observe the Torah and the Jewish way of life. Could even the most obtuse regime have so used Menelaus if he had been one of the instigators of the imposed cult? See end of NOTE on vss. 27–33.

34–38. If the letter here had been omitted, no one would have missed it. There is no sign that Roman influence modified the decree of amnesty. For the abridger and probably for Jason, the important diplomatic contact with the Romans was the treaty of 161 B.C.E. mentioned at II 4:11 (see AB vol. 41, pp. 346–47, 357–69). Jason did not put the document here to counter Hasmonaean propaganda that Hasmonaeans had won Rome's support for the Jews; rather, he gives the ambassador Eupolemus, not the Hasmonaeans, credit for the treaty, and he gives Hasmonaean Judas credit for the achievements here. After the treaty of the Romans was made in 161, no Jew had any motive to forge the document here. Between the date of our document in 148 Sel. Mac. (165/4 B.C.E.) and 161 B.C.E., any such forgery risked prompt exposure by Jews, Romans, and Seleucid officials who remembered recent events. Thus, there is a presumption in favor of the authenticity of our letter.

Scholars have argued that the letter is a forgery (Walther Kolbe, *Beiträge zur syrischen und jüdischen Geschichte* ["Beiträge zur Wissenschaft vom Alten Testament," ed. by Rudolf Kittel, n.s.; Stuttgart: Kohlhammer, 1926], X, 82–87; Mørkholm, pp. 163–64). They urge the following points:

(1) Though vss. 35–36 show that the letter here was written after Lysias' message in vss. 16–21 (see NOTE on vss. 16–21), the date in vs. 38 is (supposedly) earlier than that in vs. 21.

(2) The names of the Roman ambassadors in vs. 34 are corrupt.

(3) The implication of the letter, that the ambassadors would see the king at Antioch, is nonsense. Antiochus IV was somewhere east of the Euphrates.

(4) The narrative of I 8 implies that Judas Maccabaeus first negotiated with the Romans in 161 B.C.E. and not previously.

For answers to points (1) and (2), see NOTES on vss. 38 and 34. Point (3) loses its force if the ambassadors would see the little coregent at Antioch. Point (4) is weak for more than one reason. The author of First Maccabees, for motives of his own, passes over in silence the negotiations reported here, and Judas may well have had nothing to do with them; see NOTE on vss. 13–38.

Josephus may have been aware of the contents and date of our letter when he wrote (*BJ* i 1.4.38) that Judas made the alliance with Rome between the death of Mattathias and a later (!) invasion of Judaea by Antiochus IV. On the other hand, Josephus, writing from memory, may only have confused the order of events (see AB vol. 41, pp. 60–61).

34. *Quintus . . . Romans.* Male Roman citizens in this period bore at least two names, the *praenomen* (personal name) and the *nomen* (the name of the *gens*, the extended family). At least "Manius," the *nomen* of the second ambassador as presented in the best witnesses (A V La^L L'), is corrupt. Though "Manius" is attested as a *nomen* (Münzer, "Manius," PW, XIV [1930], 1147–48), it was borne in this period only by obscure people, at a time when any important official of Rome, including an ambassador, had to be a member of a family already distinguished or a man of distinction himself. "Manius" here could be a corruption of "Mallius," "Manilius," or "Manlius." Indeed, La^{XVM} read "Manilius." "Manilius" and "Manlius" are often miscopied in ancient sources, especially in Greek (Münzer, "Manilius," PW, XIV [1930], 1114–15, 1133, and "Manlius," ibid., 1149). "Titus" is attested as a *praenomen* among the Mallii, the Manilii, and the Manlii (Münzer, "Mallius 10," PW, XIV [1930], 911; T. R. S. Broughton, *The Magistrates of the Roman Republic* [New York: American Philological Association, 1951–52], II, 493, 584–87). In addition to the *praenomen* and *nomen*, manuscript V has what appears to be the second ambassador's third name (*cognomen*), *ERNIOS*. No such Roman name is known, but *ERNIOS* could be a corruption of the Roman name "Sergianus," which *may* be attested among the Manlii (see Münzer, "Manlius 63, 64," PW, XIV [1930], 1191, and Broughton, *Magistrates*, II, 586, and *Supplement to The Magistrates of the Roman Republic* [New York: American Philological Association, 1960], p. 39).

Polybius (xxxi 1.2–8) reports that the Romans received an embassy from King Eumenes II of Pergamum which defended that king against charges brought by King Prusias of Bithynia. After hearing the speeches, the senate appointed Gaius Sulpicius and Manius Sergius as ambassadors to go to the eastern Mediterranean, particularly to investigate the actions of Eumenes II and Antiochus IV, because the senate feared there was collusion between the two kings. There is no reason to suspect the reading in Polybius. "Manius" there is Sergius' *praenomen*. This combination of names does occur in the Roman governing class (Broughton, *Magistrates*, II, 617). Beginning with Niese, some scholars have therefore tried to read "Manius Sergius" as the name of the second ambassador here; see Benedictus Niese, "Kritik der beiden Makkabäerbücher," *Hermes* 35 (1900), 478, 485, and Bunge, p. 393.

Niese supported his position by chronological considerations. Polybius gives fear of collusion between Eumenes II and Antiochus IV as the reason why the Romans sent the two ambassadors. It could seem odd that the Romans would do so when Antiochus IV was away campaigning far to the east or even dead, and one might be tempted, therefore, to date the sending of the two ambassadors no later than 165. Niese and others, indeed, have done so (see, e.g., Bunge, p. 394, n. 84), and then Sergius could perhaps have dealt with the Jews in 148 Sel. Mac. However, to find the date of the embassy of Sulpicius and Sergius we must deduce it from the surviving fragments of Polybius, which do not give it explicitly. The interpretation which is now accepted of the fragments of Polybius puts the event in 164/3 B.C.E. (see Konrat Ziegler, "Polybios," PW, XXI² [1952], 1478–84, and Samuel Koperberg, *Polybii Historiarum Liber XXX quoad fieri potuit restitutus* [Diss. Amsterdam; Campis: J. H. Kok, 1919]).

We can give here a brief justification of the dating of the embassy of Sulpicius and Sergius to 164/3 B.C.E. The Byzantine extracts which preserve Polybius xxxi 1.6–8 and other fragments of Polybius' work faithfully follow the original order. In discussing the chronology here I shall consider only those passages which come from the Byzantine extracts. Polybius' principles of composition are known from those books of his work which survive complete. He divided the events of each Olympiad year into geographical categories, narrating first affairs of Italy (including the reception of embassies at Rome), then affairs of Greece, then affairs of the Hellenistic kingdoms. (On the Olympiad reckoning, see AB vol. 41, p. 542.)

At xxx 18, Polybius reports the visit at Rome of King Prusias of Bithynia, an event of the second half of 167 B.C.E., as is clear from the fact that Livy tells of it at the very end of his account of the events of that year (xlv 44.4–21). Polybius turns at xxx 23 to events of Greece, so that, if he returns at xxx 28 to tell of embassies in Italy, at least one year has passed. From that point on, the excerpts must deal with events of 166/5 or later. In xxx 29 the excerpts treat affairs of Greece. Hence, xxx 30, which returns to affairs of Italy, must refer to events of 165/4 or later. Events of Greece occupy xxx 32, so that xxxi 1, which returns to embassies at Rome, must refer to events of 164/3 or later. In fact, it treats events of 164/3, since xxxi 2 treats the aftermath of the arrival at Rome of the news of the death of Antiochus IV.

Thus the embassy from Eumenes II of Pergamum mentioned in Polybius xxxi 1.2–5 cannot have received a hearing before the second half of 164 B.C.E. and probably was not heard before early 163 (see AB vol. 41, p. 358). Later yet came the embassy of Sulpicius and Sergius, strange though it may seem that the Romans still did not know Antiochus IV was dead (see NOTE on vss. 23–26). The letter here was written in the first half of 164 B.C.E. (see concluding NOTE to our chapter), and thus the embassy of Sulpicius and Sergius was too late to have anything to do with it.

Niese's emendation is ill-founded anyway. Niese and those who follow him cannot give a good explanation of how the extra *praenomen* "Titus" got into the text or why "Sergius'" colleague should be Quintus Memmius and not Gaius Sulpicius. There is no reason to assume that the surviving sources give us a complete list of all Roman ambassadors to the Hellenistic empires in the 160's B.C.E. The *ERNIOS* of V does not have to be a corruption of "Sergius." It could easily represent "Sergianus," as suggested above, or some other name. It is best to conclude that our passage is the sole surviving evidence for the embassy of Quintus Memmius and Titus Manlius(?) Sergianus(?). Indeed, nothing further is known of either man.

So to grant recognition to rebels against a recognized government was a hostile act. Roman ambassadors in this period, confident in the overwhelming might of Rome, repeatedly acted to undermine the position of Hellenistic kings. See Polybius iii 4.3 and xxxi 6 and 10.

the People of the Jews. The Romans address the Jews, indeed, only the rebels represented by John and Absalom, as a "People" (*dêmos*), thus recognizing them as at least a semiautonomous group. See AB vol. 41, p. 368. We may infer that John and Absalom represented a substantial fraction of the Jews.

Manuscript V and the inferior witnesses La^BM for *dêmos* here read *plêthos*. But *plêthos* is the word used in vs. 16. If *plêthos* had occurred here, too, no scribe would have changed it to *dêmos*. Hence, the reading *dêmos* must represent the original.

35–36. Cf. vs. 18, and see NOTE on vss. 16–21.

At vs. 1, Lysias is also called "guardian of the king" and "chief minister" (*epi tôn pragmatôn*). The Roman ambassadors, however, give Lysias as title only his rank among courtiers. "Kinsmen" were not necessarily blood relations; they were high courtiers who ranked above mere Friends of the King; see Bickerman, *Institutions,* pp. 42–44. Even official Seleucid documents took no note of the fact that Lysias was the guardian of the child king; see NOTE on 10:11. As for *epi tôn pragmatôn*, it was a vague term, with many meanings, ranging from "chief minister" (vs. 1, 3:7; Polybius v 35.7) through "foreign affairs official" (Polybius v 34.4) to mere provincial officials (III 7:1; Welles, *Royal Correspondence,* no. 31, line 26). The title may also have been only of domestic significance. Thus, we can understand how the Roman ambassadors did not use it.

36–37. "After you have considered them" is my translation of the best reading in vs. 36, *episkepsamenoi* (A q La *L*). V has *episkepsomenon*, with which the passage in vs. 36 might mean "send someone to discuss them [with us]," but vs. 37 makes it clear that the Roman ambassadors wish, not to discuss matters with the Jews, but rather to receive from them information.

38. *Be well.* This (*hygiainete*) is an unusual closing formula for a Greek letter (see Exler, pp. 69–70) and may well represent the Latin *valete*. It is unlikely a forger would have thought of this touch (Habicht, *Harvard Studies in Classical Philology* 80 [1976], 12, n. 24).

In the year 148, in . . . Romans certainly did not date by the Seleucid era or by Macedonian months or by the eccentrically named months favored by Antiochus IV (Bickerman, *Chronology,* pp. 43–46, 69). Thus, if our letter bears a Seleucid year date, it must be because the Jews who preserved it filed it under that date, doing so perhaps immediately or perhaps later by inference from the year date of Lysias' letter in vss. 16–21. The year date could hardly have been added by Jason or by the abridger, for if one of them had added a date here, he surely would have done so also in vs. 26. La^B, alone of all witnesses, gives the year as 149. The reading is to be rejected; see NOTE on vs. 21.

On the other hand, the month dates given by the various witnesses to our verse probably were added by later scribes. Had the month date been added to the letter when the preservers filed it, the name of the month would have been uniform in the witnesses, except for recognizable corruptions. But two different names appear in the witnesses to the text, as if two different scribes had guessed at the missing name. It would seem that to such scribes a letter without a date (such as the one in vss. 22–26) was tolerable, but if there was a year date, they felt the lack of month and day. The scribe responsible for the Greek manuscripts and La^V and Sy probably took the month name, Xanthicus, from vss. 30 and 33. Conscious of the close connection between the letter here and the one in vss. 16–21, the scribe responsible for La and Arm seems to have taken the month name from vs. 21 (here, La^V has *dioscordi;* La^{XMP}, *dioscoridis;* La^B, *die scuridis*). The Greek manuscript V has both *XANTHIKOU* and *DIOSKORIDOU*.

The scribe responsible for La^{-VP} and Arm was content to stop there, without adding the day numeral. The other witnesses all seem to have copied the day numeral from vs. 33. There was no logical difficulty in giving the letter here the same date as the one in vss. 27–33. The Romans' efforts could indeed have come too late to be of real help to the Jews. Evidence of Roman sympathy was still important enough to preserve. We must be content to say that the Roman letter was written shortly after the one in vss. 16–21.

CONCLUSIONS ON THE CHRONOLOGY AND MEANING OF THE LETTERS IN 11:16–38

There would now seem to be little difficulty in interpreting and dating the letter in vss. 23–26; see the NOTE thereto. With the other letters, however, a measure of uncertainty enters because we cannot be sure when the month named in vs. 21 fell. Where the evidence is so fragmentary, one can never be sure he has considered all possibilities. Nevertheless, we must now try to examine the possibilities and eliminate all but one. A valuable piece of external evidence is the information at *Megillat Ta'anit* 28 Adar that on 28 Adar the good news came to the Jews that they would not be required to violate the Torah, i.e., that the persecution had come to an end. Another consideration valuable for our purposes is the fact that the Jews had to have reason to preserve our documents. Evidence of mere sympathy on the part of the Roman superpower was worth preserving, but if either the letter in vss. 16–21 or the one in vss. 27–33 reflected only diplomatic gestures which had no real effect it would not have been preserved.

We must also take note of the contrast between the letters of Lysias and the Roman ambassadors on the one hand and the royal letter in vss. 27–33 on the other. The royal letter recognizes Menelaus and the Council of Elders; the other Jews are mentioned but are given no corporate status. Lysias and the Roman ambassadors ignore Menelaus and the Council of Elders and recognize what is probably a faction of pious rebels as the *plêthos* ("community") or *dêmos* ("People") of the Jews. It is hard to avoid the conclusion that here we have evidence of divisions of opinion, not only among the Jews, but also within the Seleucid regime.

The short time between the date in vs. 33 and the deadline specified in vs. 30 strongly suggests the existence of a *de facto* truce in which the pious Jews expectantly awaited the king's word. The evidence of *Megillat Ta'anit* 28 Adar strengthens the inference from vss. 30 and 33 (see NOTE on vss. 27–33). There is no evidence at present to prevent us from seeing the source of the Jews' expectations in the letter of Lysias in vss. 16–21. Both sides would wish to settle the issue as soon as possible. The message from Antioch reached Jerusalem in the thirteen days from 15 Xanthicus to 28 Adar (=Xanthicus).

If the renamed month was Dystros, the one which immediately preceded Xanthicus, a message sent from Lysias' camp in Judaea on the twenty-fourth could easily have reached Antioch in time for discussions of prominent ministers to produce, by the fifteenth of Xanthicus, the royal reply in vss. 27–33.

We may guess that Lysias forwarded the requests of the pious rebels, and perhaps they themselves sent a delegation to Antioch. The Roman ambassadors could have been in time, or could have been too late, to help the Jews' cause. At the same time, however, Menelaus and the old elite, annoyed at the recognition granted to rebels by Lysias, would have gone on a rival embassy and would have won from the regime recognition, an end to the persecution, and a tacit repudiation of Lysias' contacts with the rebels. If our guesses are correct, in vss. 27–33 we have the letter to that effect which went out in the name of the little coregent.

Nevertheless, the renamed month may not have been Dystros. It is unlikely, however, that it was much earlier than Dystros. Our reconstruction of the events would not be changed appreciably if the renamed month was the next earlier, Peritios. Our reasoning rejecting Dios as the renamed month (in NOTE on vs. 21) would seem to eliminate any month earlier than Peritios.

We must now consider the possibility that the renamed month was later than Dystros. "Dioskouros" or "Dioskourios" or "Dioskoros" or "Dioskorios" in the Cretan calendar was the name of the month just before the vernal equinox (see NOTE on vs. 21). Xanthicus, too, was the month just before the vernal equinox, and the variants in vs. 38 could easily be taken as implying that the renamed month was identical with Xanthicus. Then, however, the letter in vss. 16–21 would have been written on the twenty-fourth, after the letter in vss. 27–33 but before its arrival in Jerusalem on the twenty-eighth. One can imagine Menelaus and the old elite, caught between Lysias' army and Judas' rebel force, as pressing their petition at Antioch in the lull which followed as both sides tried to recover from the bloody battle of Beth-Zur. But then the negotiations between Lysias and John and Absalom would have had no effect in securing the amnesty. It is difficult to believe that Lysias' letter would then have been preserved. Hence, the renamed month is unlikely to have been Xanthicus.

The renamed month may have been later than Xanthicus. Pious Jews could have been unsatisfied with the rather ungenerous terms in vs. 30 and with the regime's decision to recognize Menelaus as the sole spokesman for the Jews. They could have been quick to declare their objections and to deliver their petition for modifications. Thus one might imagine that the renamed month was Artemisios (the month of the vernal equinox) or the next month, Daisios. Several considerations render this hypothesis unlikely. If it were so, the concessions granted by Lysias (in his annotations to the document copied below mentioned in vs. 16) went beyond the concessions in the name of the coregent, and one would have expected pious Jews to have preserved the document copied below. If the rebels had not yet approached Lysias, why did Menelaus apply to the distant coregent instead of to Lysias himself? If the pious majority was unwilling to accept an amnesty granted through Menelaus, why did they preserve the letter in vss. 27–33 and celebrate annually the date of its arrival?

Thus the most probable identification of the renamed month is Dystros, and the most probable reconstruction of the events is the one which we have built around that identification.

The regime would then have trusted Menelaus' insistence that most of the pious would accept the amnesty, and that he and the old elite would thereafter be able to control Judaea. If the letter in vss. 27–33 reflects the power of ministers who disagreed with Lysias, the chief minister was all the more pleased to be free from having to fight the Jews; upon withdrawal from Judaea, he could resume control over affairs at Antioch.

Welcome as the amnesty and Lysias' withdrawal were to pious Jews, the events presented difficult theological problems. What were Jews to do now? Many of them believed that the end of the persecution would be accompanied by the miraculous events of God's ultimate victory. There was a period of inaction, as the pious waited for the miracles. But Menelaus and his followers were unable to maintain control of Judaea. Judas and his men were not content to observe the amnesty. They did not "go home" (i.e., lay down their arms and return to peaceful pursuits). Eventually they induced the pious majority to join them in occupying and purifying the deserted temple and in dedicating a new altar. See AB vol. 41, pp. 273–82.

At this point the Jews' victory was miraculous enough to rouse the apprehensions of neighboring peoples who so feared fulfillment of the prophecies of Jewish imperial glory that they perpetrated on the Jews living among them the atrocities which led to the wars described in I 5 and in II 10 and 12. The account in First Maccabees is largely correct: Judas' force hardly touched the royal Seleucid army, except for intimidating the garrison of the Akra (I 4:41). In these months Judas may even have avoided combat with the royal army. The insubordinate commanders Joseph and Azariah, not the Hasmonaeans, fought the Seleucid commander Gorgias (I 5:56–59). Even so, the Jews' military exploits under Hasmonaean leadership were further undermining the authority of the insecure regime. Indeed, upon the death of Antiochus IV, Lysias had maintained himself in power through the helpless Antiochus V, against the declared will of the late king. In such a situation, the regime could welcome peace in Judaea. See NOTE on 9:29, NOTE on 10:1–8, and NOTE on 10:10–38. There was little difficulty in conceding to the Jews what they had already won, so the regime drew up the letter in vss. 23–26, which the Jews received on February 8, 163 B.C.E. The influence of Ptolemy Makron may have had something to do with that decision (see NOTE on 10:12–13).

Such seems to have been the background which produced the four letters in our chapter.

XV. LOCAL WARS
(12:1–45)

12 ¹ As soon as this pact had been concluded, Lysias marched back to the king, while the Jews devoted their energies to farming. ² However, the local commanders, Timotheus and Apollonius son of Gennaios, as well as Hieronymos and Demophon and also Nicanor the Cypriarch, gave them no chance to enjoy tranquility and live in peace. ³ The Joppites perpetrated an atrociously wicked act: pretending to have no hostile intentions, they provided boats and invited the Jews living among them—men, women, and children—to go on board. ⁴ Indeed, the invitation was made pursuant to a vote passed by the people of the city, and the Jews accepted it, wishing to live in peace and harboring no suspicions. But as soon as they went out to sea, the Joppites sent everyone to the bottom, drowning at least two hundred.

⁵ When Judas received the news of the cruel outrage perpetrated on his fellow Jews, he summoned his men and ⁶ prayed to God, the just Judge. Then he marched against the murderers of his brother Jews. In a night attack, he set fire to the port and burned the boats and massacred those who had taken refuge there. ⁷ Since the town was shut up tight behind its walls, Judas withdrew, intending to return and extirpate the entire Joppite citizenry.

⁸ On learning that the people in Jamnia also wished to perpetrate the same kind of outrage upon the Jews who dwelt among them, ⁹ Judas fell upon the Jamnites, too, by night and set fire to the port and the ships, so that the glare of the flames was visible as far as Jerusalem, two hundred forty stadia away.

¹⁰ . . . From there they had marched nine stadia on their way against Timotheus, when at least five thousand Arab infantry and five hundred cavalry attacked him. ¹¹ A hard-fought battle ensued. Judas and his men won, through the help of God. On being defeated, the nomads begged Judas to make peace with them, promising to give cattle and to help him and his men in other ways. ¹² Judas believed that the Arabs in fact would be useful in many ways and consented to

be at peace with them. After receiving handclasps of peace, the Arabs went home to their tents.

13 . . . Judas also attacked a walled town called Kaspin, which was strongly fortified and inhabited by gentiles of very mixed stock. 14 The people in the town, confident in the strength of their walls and in their store of provisions, treated Judas and his men with exceedingly uncivilized disrespect, reviling them and also blaspheming and uttering impious words. 15 Judas and his men prayed to the great Master of the universe Who overthrew Jericho in the time of Joshua without battering rams or siege engines. Then they charged the wall with the fury of wild beasts. 16 Having captured the town through God's will, they massacred innumerable victims, so that the adjacent lake, which was two stadia wide, appeared to have been filled from a spring of blood.

17 From there they marched seven hundred fifty stadia to reach the palisaded camp and the Jews called "Tubiakenoi." 18 On their arrival, they did not find Timotheus, the regional commander, for he had withdrawn then from the region on failing to take his objective; nevertheless, he had left in one place a very strong garrison. 19 Dositheos and Sosipatros, two of the commanders serving under Maccabaeus, marched off and wiped out the men Timotheus had left behind in the stronghold, more than ten thousand in number.

20 Maccabaeus, having drawn up his army in regimental formations, put them in command of the regiments. Thereupon he set out against Timotheus, who had with him one hundred twenty thousand infantry and two thousand five hundred cavalry. 21 On learning that Judas was on the march, Timotheus took the precaution of sending off the women and children and baggage to the fortress called "the Karnion," for it was difficult to besiege or attack because all routes of access went through narrow passes. 22 Nevertheless, at the sight of Judas' first regiment, fear and panic struck the enemy as a result of the manifest intervention against them of the One Who sees all. They rushed headlong to flee in every direction, so that many were injured by their own comrades and run through by the points of their swords. 23 Judas pressed the pursuit with great vigor and massacred the wretches, destroying about thirty thousand men.

24 Timotheus himself fell into the hands of Dositheos and Sosipatros and begged, very cunningly, that they release him unharmed, on the ground that he was holding prisoner the parents and brothers of many of the Jews, whose lives would be worth nothing. 25 After he used all manner of means to get them to believe his promise that he

would restore the prisoners unhurt, they released him in order to save their brothers.

26 Judas then marched against the Karnion and the shrine of Atargatis and slew twenty-five thousand persons. 27 After routing and destroying these, he turned to attack the strong town of Ephron, where Lysias had a residence. Stalwart young men posted before the walls put up a stout resistance. Inside the town were large stores of artillery and missiles. 28 Judas and his men prayed to the Master Whose might shatters the strength of the enemy. Then they captured the city and slew at least twenty-five thousand of the inhabitants.

29 On withdrawing from there, they marched against Scythopolis, a city six hundred stadia from Jerusalem. 30 However, the Jews residing there bore solemn witness to the Scythopolitans' goodwill toward them and to the kindness they had shown them in times of trouble. 31 Accordingly, Judas and his men thanked the Scythopolitans, urging them to continue in the future to be friendly to our people. They arrived at Jerusalem just before the time of the Feast of Weeks.

32 After the festival called "Pentecost," they set out to attack Gorgias, the governor of Idumaea. 33 He marched out with three thousand infantry and four hundred cavalry. 34 When they joined battle, a few of the Jews fell. 35 However, Dositheos, one of the Tubiakenoi, a strong cavalryman, kept pursuing Gorgias, caught him by the cloak, and began to drag him by brute force, intending to take the abominable wretch prisoner, but one of the Thracian horsemen charged Dositheos and cut off his arm at the shoulder, so that Gorgias escaped to Marisa. . . .

36 Ezri and his men fought on for a very long time and were on the point of exhaustion. Thereupon Judas prayed to the LORD to manifest himself as their ally and their leader in battle. 37 Taking up as a battle cry hymns in the language of his forefathers, he fell upon Gorgias and his men, took them by surprise, and routed them.

38 After reassembling the army, Judas came to the town of Odollam. The Seventh Day was almost upon them, so they purified themselves according to the established custom and observed the Sabbath there. 39 On the next day, at the time when work became permissible, Judas and his men went to recover the bodies of the fallen in order to lay them to rest with their kin in their ancestral tombs. 40 They found under the tunics of every one of those who had fallen objects which had been consecrated to the idols of Jamnia, forbidden to Jews by the Torah. It was clear to all that for this very reason the men had fallen. 41 They all blessed the judgment of the LORD, the righteous Judge

Who exposes what has been concealed. 42 Then they turned in supplication, praying that the sin which had been committed might be entirely blotted out. Noble Judas exhorted the people to keep themselves free from sin, inasmuch as they had seen with their own eyes what had happened to the fallen as a result of their sin. 43 He took up a collection from every man, for a total of two thousand silver drachmas, and sent the money to Jerusalem to be used to bring a sin offering—a deed altogether fitting and proper, for he had their resurrection in mind. 44 Indeed, if he did not expect the fallen to be resurrected, it would have been superfluous and foolish to pray for the dead. 45 Moreover, he perceived that a most glorious recompense is laid up for those who pass away in a state of piety—a holy and pious thought! Therefore he had rites of atonement performed for the dead, to absolve them from their sin.

NOTES

Ch. 12. Our chapter has many sharp contrasts with I 5. Many of the differences can be ascribed to special pleading on either side or both. See NOTES on the following passages: vss. 2, 3–9, 10–31, 29–31, 36, 40–41, 42–45, and esp. 10:10–38.

1–9. Our passage has no parallels in First Maccabees, but may well have been derived from the Common Source. It is easy to imagine why the Hasmonaean propagandist would omit vs. 2 (see NOTE ad loc.) and vss. 3–9 (see NOTE ad loc.). The Seleucid Chronicle probably did not give details about local commanders near Judaea.

1. Both sides at first fulfilled the terms of the "pact" (11:29–31). Jason believed that 11:25, too, had been fulfilled, since for him the passage occurred in a document of the peace of 148 Sel. Mac. (164 B.C.E.).

2. The Greek term *stratêgos* has a wide spectrum of meanings. Militarily, it ranges from "commander of an independent tactical unit [even a small one]" to "general." It can also mean "provincial governor." Here, the expression "local" lets us know that the persons are commanders or governors of lesser rank. See Bickerman, *Institutions*, pp. 64–66, and Bengtson, *Strategie*, II, 170–74, to be corrected by AB vol. 41, p. 246.

The writer leaves open the question whether the local commanders harassed the Jews with or without the consent of the central government. In an age without rapid communication, local officials could go far in violating policies laid down at the capital city.

In I 5 the author insists that the Jews fought against neighboring peoples known from biblical histories and prophecies. Here the writer gives a list of names that are all Greek, as if to argue, on the contrary, that the wars were against local Graeco-Macedonian officials. On the real nature of the struggles, see NOTE on 10:10–38.

The Timotheus here was the Seleucid commander in what is now northern Transjordan and southern Syria. This Timotheus is different from Timotheus the phylarch in the Ammonite territory. See NOTES on 8:30, 32, and on 10:24, *Timotheus*.

The author adds the name of Apollonius' father here and thus differentiates him from the other men of that name mentioned in Second Maccabees. "Gennaios" (lit. "noble") is attested as a name in various parts of Greece. It was the name of a leading citizen of Antioch in the mid-third century B.C.E. (Jerome *Commentarii in Danielem* iii, to Dan 11:6). Similarly, the writer identifies Nicanor as the Cypriarch to distinguish him from the other Nicanors mentioned in his book. A Cypriarch was a commander of Cypriot mercenaries; see NOTE on 5:24 and cf. 4:29. At this time, Cyprus was part of the Ptolemaic empire (Polybius xxix 26.9–10). We have no further information on the four remaining local commanders.

3–9. Here Jason makes no effort to ascribe the atrocities to local commanders of units of the royal army. He is content to say they are the acts of hostile neighboring peoples. There are two reasons why he could depart from the general tendency we spoke of in the NOTE on vs. 2. First, the author of First Maccabees omitted the incidents at Joppe and Jamnia, very likely because Judas was unable to save the Jews of either town. (The Hasmonaean propagandist may have included the atrocities there in his thinking when he wrote the general statement at I 5:1–2.) Second, Jason regarded both towns as Greek cities. Had the author of First Maccabees mentioned the events, he probably would have called the Joppites and Jamnites "Philistines" or "Canaanites" (cf. I 3:24, 41, 4:15, 22, and see AB vol. 41, NOTE on 4:26). In the official Greek usage of the Ptolemaic empire, only citizens of city-states received designations such as "Joppite" and "Jamnite." Members of communities which did not have the privileged status of a *polis* received only designations such as "the people in X" (*hoi en X;* 1:10b; cf. 14:37). See Bickerman, *Studies,* I, 239–40, although his remarks there on the unprivileged status of Jerusalem are questionable; Jerusalem clearly has a different status from the rest of Judaea already in Ep. 1 (1:1).

In any case, our passage is not in a legal document, and writers of history were not bound by the terminology of documents, as is clear from our writer's mention of the Jamnites in vs. 8 as "the people in Jamnia."

We have other evidence of the status of Joppe and Jamnia as Greek cities (Tcherikover, *Hellenistic Civilization,* pp. 93–94; Avi-Yonah, *The Holy Land,* p. 39). Both were important towns with harbors. See Map 7. On the other hand, there is no evidence to support Avi-Yonah's suggestion that Jamnia was the capital of the province of Azotus. J. *AJ* xii 7.4.308 is good evidence that Jamnia and Azotus were two separate political units, as shown on Map 5.

The writer's choice of words shows that the Jews only resided at Joppe and Jamnia and were not citizens of either town.

3–4. The Joppites would seem to have voted publicly to invite the Jews who lived among them to go on a pleasure cruise.

5. *summoned.* So I translate Greek *parangeilas,* following La and Sy. One might also render it as "passed the news on to."

6. *the just Judge.* Cf. Jer 11:20 in its context and Ps 7:12.

those who had taken refuge there. The Joppites who had been caught outside the walls when the city gates were closed fled to the port.

7. If Judas intended to return and destroy Joppe, he never accomplished the deed. See I 10:75–76, 12:33–34, 13:11.

9. Jason gives the approximate distance to Jerusalem from Jamnia correctly (about thirty miles or forty-eight kilometers).

10–31. Before our verses, the abridger has made an awkward cut, or perhaps the error of an early scribe has caused the omission of essential material. The narrative of the events at Jamnia seems to be complete in vs. 9, but in vs. 10 Judas and his men are on the march against Timotheus. Since II 10:24–38 corresponds to I 5:6–8, here one would expect to have a report of the campaign against a Timotheus which is narrated at I 5:9–54. Indeed, so close are the parallels between the two accounts that we can be sure both cover the same campaign.

However, in using I 5:9–24 to fill out what is missing here from the abridged history, one must be extremely cautious. There are very strong contradictions between vss. 10–19 here and I 5:9–36. In First Maccabees, the Jews of Gilead and Galilee send urgent messages to the Hasmonaean force, begging for help against the murderous designs of their gentile neighbors. The senders of the letter from Gilead report that they are in an endangered fortress and that the unit of Jewish mercenary soldiers called "Tubias' troop" (see AB vol. 41, pp. 298–99) has almost been wiped out. Judas divides the Hasmonaean force, sending Simon to Galilee; Maccabaeus himself goes to Gilead, leaving Joseph and Azariah to hold the home base in Judea. The story of Simon's campaign is straightforward (I 5:21–23): he wins victories over the enemies in the north and evacuates the Jews of Galilee and of (probably) Narbatta to Judaea (see AB vol. 41, p. 300).

The narrative of Judas' campaign in I 5:24–54 is far more complicated; there are especially strange features in I 5:24–36. One would expect Judas' force to march directly to the rescue of the Jews (including the remnants of Tubias' troop) who had begged for help. But instead, Judas, after a three-day march through the wilderness, happens upon Nabataean Arabs who inform him that Jews have barricaded themselves within the fortified towns of Gilead and are in danger of being massacred. The Nabataeans name the towns of Bosora, Bosor-in-Alema, Kaspho, Maked, and Karnain. That information makes Judas turn away from his previous course to attack Bosora (I 5:28), which probably was the easternmost of the named towns and was a night's march from the endangered Jewish fortress (I 5:29).

Because no one has yet fully perceived the difficulties and textual corruptions in I 5:26–27 we must pause here to treat them. My translation of I 5:26–27 and my NOTE on I 5:27 are wrong and must be corrected by the discussion here. In both verses, allmost all witnesses to the text have, not "had barricaded themselves" (*eisi syneilêmenoi*), but "were being held captive" (*eisi syneilêmmenoi*). If those Jews were indeed being held captive, Judas' subsequent course is foolish. According to I 5:9–12, 17, the original goal of Judas' campaign was to rescue menaced Jews who hold their own fortress, persons still defending themselves and capable of being rescued. But if Jews were being held captive in the fortified towns, Judas could hardly save them by attacking. Rather, the enemy could be expected to use the captives as hostages. Indeed, the Hasmonaean propagandist does not report that Judas saved the Jews of Bosora; he tells only how Judas destroyed Bosora and slaughtered its male inhabitants. Surely Judas should have gone first to save those Jews who could be saved! The adroit Hasmonaean propagandist could hardly have presented his hero as making so stupid an ordering of priorities.

Indeed, ancient and medieval scribes seem to have perceived the difficulty. A scribe who corrected ms. S altered *syneilêmmenoi* in both verses to *syn(e)il-êgmenoi*, which is surely a mere misspelling of *syneilegmenoi;* ms. 311 in vs. 27 has *syneilegmenoi*, and ms. 534 has the synonymous *synêgmenoi*. With those readings, our passage would mean that Jews "had gathered" within the towns to protect themselves (cf. Hebrew Esther 8:11, 9:2, and Hebrew and Greek Esther 9:15, 16, 18), presumably in fortified buildings and neighborhoods, since their enemies, too, lived inside the town walls, as is clear from Judas' subsequent treatment of the towns (I 5:28, 36, 44). Judas' priorities would then make sense: the Jews of Bosora were not yet helpless hostages.

Nevertheless, the attractive readings of the scribes are only conjectures, and a better solution is available. Much rarer than the Greek verb *lambanein* ("seize," "take captive") is the verb *eilein* ("shut in," "press"). The perfect middle participle of *eilein* and its compounds (*-eilêmenoi*) differs only on one letter from that of *lambanein* (*-eilêmmenoi*) and the variant readings of manuscripts show how often the forms of the latter verb were substituted for those of the former by unwary scribes, as can be seen from critical editions of Greek I Chron 9:20, J. *AJ* xiv 16.2.470, and *BJ* iv 4.6.293, and from my NOTE on II 15:19. The original reading at I 5:26–27 was *syneilêmenoi*.

We can thus be sure that Jews barricaded themselves in fortified buildings or neighborhoods within the walled towns of Gilead, where they were menaced by the gentile inhabitants. As presented in I 5:25–34, Judas' ordering of priorities becomes defensible but still is open to question. The Jews who had summoned him held their own fortress and were surrounded by open country (see I 5:30–34). The mere arrival of the Hasmonaean force would bring them effective help. To rescue the endangered Jews in the towns would require Judas and his men somehow to penetrate the town walls. Moreover, the towns were scattered. How could Judas hope to penetrate walls and rescue all those Jews in time? Indeed, the narrative lets us infer that Judas made a necessary compromise: before going to rescue the Jews who had summoned him, he attacked only one town, Bosora, and thereafter, by a forced night march, he did rescue the embattled Jewish fortress in the nick of time. The Hasmonaean propagandist goes on to tell how next Judas dealt with Maapha (?—on the name, see AB vol. 41, p. 302) as he had with Bosora, though Maapha is not listed as a place where Jews had barricaded themselves (see NOTE on vss. 18–19)! Thereafter, Judas went on to capture the remaining fortified towns in the list, but neither with Bosora nor with the other towns does the Hasmonaean propagandist say that Judas saved the beleaguered Jews, a claim he should have made loudly if the facts had allowed him to. We may assume from the nature of the case that Judas was able to save only a fraction of the Jews in the towns. Thus, the Hasmonaean propagandist still presents Judas as taking a course which could be challenged. In particular, the Jews who sent the letter summoning him need not have approved of his ordering of priorities.

The Hasmonaean propagandist's presentation of Judas' campaign becomes still more vulnerable when we compare it with the one here. Jason, hostile to Simon, could be expected to omit entirely Simon's victorious campaign. Abridgment or defective transmission of the text has removed any account of the origins and opening stages of Judas' march to northern Transjordan (Gilead). We hear only that his main objective was the aggressor Timotheus (vs. 10; cf. vs. 2). Whereas at I 5:24 Judas marches three days before meeting the Nabataean Arabs, here in vs. 10 his force meets the Arabs after marching only nine stadia (a bit over a mile) from a point the name of which is lost. Clearly, Jason's account reported some incident, at least a stop in Judas' march, where none is reported in I 5.

In contrast to I 5:25, we learn here in vss. 10–12 that the Arabs at first fought Judas' force and only after being defeated agreed to cooperate. Again some material has been lost by abridgment or defective transmission (see NOTE on vs. 13). In vss. 13–16 we find Judas capturing Kaspin (=Kaspho; see AB vol. 41, p. 301) and slaughtering its inhabitants. Nothing is said of beleaguered Jews; the crime of the people of Kaspin is their blasphemous behavior. In contrast to I 5:29–36, here Judas marches to the fortified camp of the Tubians (=Tubiakenoi; see NOTE on vs. 17) only after capturing Kaspin. The march is a *three-day* journey, and when he arrives, the Tubians are no longer in danger! Timotheus, on failing to capture their stronghold, had withdrawn, leaving behind a strong garrison in an unnamed fort. Two commanders with Greek names, Dositheos and Sosipatros (clearly not Hasmonaeans), serving under Judas, lead a force which wipes out that garrison.

On the (Nabataean) Arabs, the account in vss. 10–12 is probably correct against that in I 5:25 (see AB vol. 41, p. 301). If so, Judas' conduct in turning off to attack Bosora becomes stranger still: he did so on the dubious testimony of recently defeated enemies!

The differences of our two histories on the Tubians are significant. First Maccabees is so strongly focused on the Hasmonaeans that other Jews and Jewish groups are named only in order to serve Hasmonaean ends: either to discredit those named, if they were opponents of the Hasmonaeans, or else to show that they, too, supported Mattathias or his descendants. Why, then, are the Tubians mentioned at I 5:13?

That force of experienced Jewish mercenary soldiers, located in Transjordan, probably continued to hold the anti-Seleucid, pro-Ptolemaic views of their chief Hyrcanus even after Hyrcanus' suicide in about 169 B.C.E.; see AB vol. 41, pp. 298–99, and my article in *Studies Smith*, Part III, pp. 89–93, 99–101. Onias IV would therefore have been interested in them, and they in him (see p. 36). Hasmonaean propaganda would strive to minimize the importance of both the Tubians and the Oniads. Tubians are minimized in I 5:13 and (implicitly) in the dramatic rhetoric of I 5:29–34: the Tubians could not protect the Transjordanian Jews or even themselves; they had been almost entirely wiped out when Judas' force came in the nick of time to save the survivors. The account here, in contrast, reveals that the Tubians were able to save themselves and balk the efforts of Timotheus to take their stronghold. In the abridged history we are not told how and when Dositheos and Sosipatros joined Judas. The unabridged work may have said they were Tubians, even if the Dositheos of vs. 19 is different from the one in vs. 35 (see NOTE on vs. 35). In any case, vs. 35 shows that Tubians joined Judas' force.

Since the Hasmonaean propagandist does not suppress the awkward tactical compromise which Judas accepted, we need not suspect him of inventing the dangerous predicament of the Tubians and the other Jews in the fortress. Indeed, there is partial confirmation here, in the implication of vs. 17, that Timotheus had tried, though unsuccessfully, to take the stronghold. The Hasmonaean propagandist has only exaggerated the defenders' helplessness at the price of making Judas' decision to turn off to Bosora all the more questionable. Propaganda favoring the Tubians, in turn, must have tried to minimize the Hasmonaean contribution and may have criticized Judas' judgment.

Since their predicament was real, the survivors from the Jewish stronghold, including the Tubians, can well have censured Judas for not coming directly to their aid. With each delay, his course would become the more subject to censure. It was to the interests of Hasmonaean propaganda to make the delay as short as possible, as is done in I 5:28–29. Anti-Hasmonaean interests would be served if the delay could be presented as longer and as having been something other than a matter of life and death. The gap before vs. 13 could well have contained an account of the attack on Bosora, indeed making the delay longer; and the failure to mention beleaguered Jews in vss. 13–16 leaves the punishment of blasphemy as the only motive for the battle at Kaspin.

Jason and the abridger admired Judas and would not themselves have collected evidence which could be used to question his judgment, but Jason sought to contradict First Maccabees and used as a source the *Memoirs* of Onias IV, who was favorably interested in the Tubians. The omissions and the use of pro-Tubian propaganda make vss. 10–19 here to be very poor evidence for reconstructing the Common Source. Also unsatisfactory for the purpose is the account in I 5:9–36, for its tendentious nature renders it unlikely that it closely reflects the Common Source. I believe we can reconstruct neither the Common Source for vss. 10–25 and I 5:9–36 nor the true sequence of Judas' marches to Kaspin and the Tubians' stronghold.

Jason's unabridged account may have presented Joseph and Azariah (of I 5:18, 58–62) as half brothers of Judas; see NOTE on vss. 29–31, NOTE on 8:16–23, pp. 299–300, and AB vol. 41, p. 33.

The facts in I 5:9–13, 25–45 imply that there were large Jewish communities settled in regions south and southeast of Damascus. Kurt Galling argued that these populations had been there since the time of the kingdom of Israel ("Judäa, Galiläa und der Osten im Jahre 164/3 v. Chr.," *Palästinajahrbuch* 36 [1940], 72–75). A rabbinic tradition mentions areas in Transjordan which were settled by "Jews who returned from Babylonia," but it is probably a late theoretical reconstruction, not a historical source on the period from the sixth to the second century B.C.E.; see Y. Sussmann, "The 'Boundaries of Eretz-Israel,'" *Tarbiz* 45 (5736=1975–76), 213–55 (in Hebrew, with English summary, pp. ii–iii). We must admit our ignorance concerning the earlier history of these Jewish communities.

In contrast to I 5, here nothing is said of the Jewish populations in Gilead and Galilee which the forces of Judas and Simon rescued and evacuated to Judaea. Judas' expeditions in our chapter only punish aggressors. The Jewish army rescues no one. Other things being equal, surely Jason and the abridger would have been glad to portray Judas as rescuing Jews. Two related reasons probably led Jason to abstain from doing so: first, the evacuations gave the Hasmonaeans the opportunity of portraying themselves as fulfilling "messianic" prophecies (see AB vol. 41, NOTE on 5:53–54); second, the past existence of the Jewish settlements in Gilead (and Galilee) and the fact that they had been evacuated under duress could be used to justify the efforts of the later Hasmonaeans to conquer the regions (see pp. 18–19).

On the other hand, as we have seen, the Hasmonaean propagandist's own account leaves us to infer that at best Judas' force saved only a fraction of the Jews in the fortified towns. Those evacuated from Gilead probably consisted mostly of the defenders of the fortress and of Jews who managed to survive in the countryside.

The other differences between vss. 20–31 and the parallel account at I 5:37–54 are such that both narratives could be derived from the Common Source; see NOTE on vss. 20–25 and NOTE on vss. 26–31.

10. The abridger or an early scribe has left us with an ungrammatical text. Later scribes and translators tried to improve upon it. The best witnesses (A V q La^X) leave little doubt that the abridger's own Greek had *apospasantes stadious ennea, poioumenôn tên poreian epi ton Timotheon, prosebalon Arabes autôi* (lit. "Having marched from there nine stadia, as they were making their way against Timotheus, Arabs attacked him"). According to the rules of Greek grammar, the subject of "having marched" (a nominative participle) must be "Arabs," and the subject of "were making" (a genitive absolute participle) must be different from "Arabs." Surely Judas and his men were "making their way" against Timotheus. Both the nominative and genitive participles, then, must refer to the Jewish force. Also unnatural is the use of the dative singular "him" where one would expect a dative plural "them" (i.e., Judas and his men). Polished Greek would have had both participles in the dative case. Mixed constructions similar to those in the best witnesses here do occur in papyri but are hardly to be expected in a polished literary work (see Mayser, II^3, 66–70). It looks as if the abridger combined material from three separate sentences without being careful to readjust the numbers and cases of the words involved.

Other ancient witnesses to the text coped with the difficulties by making both participles refer to Judas (La^M), or to Judas and his men, by putting both into the genitive (L^{-93}) or by paraphrasing them (La Sy); some witnesses omit the difficult "him" (La^{LX}) or read "them" (L'). Mss. 46 and 52 even put both participles into the nominative case so that they refer to the Arabs. Arabs did fight on Timotheus' side (I 5:39), but their movements and previous stops would not have interested the Jewish writer.

11. *make peace.* Lit. "give them a right hand." Cf. vs. 12, and see NOTE on 11:26.

cattle. The nomads were herdsmen whose principal wealth was in livestock.

in other ways. This translation of *en tois loipois* fits "in many ways" in vs. 12; one might, however, render the phrase here as "in the future."

12. The writer stresses Judas' foresight. We know nothing of further aid to him from the Nabataeans. His brother Jonathan made use of them (I 9:35). On the significance of a handclasp, see NOTE on 4:34, *accepted . . . oath.*

13. The word "also" here suggests that Kaspin was not the first town to be attacked on the campaign. Hence, I have indicated an omission of material before our verse, whether by abridgment or by an accident of text transmission.

One can only guess at the location of Kaspin. At the point given that name on Map 6 (now called "Khisfīn"), there is a swamp which in ancient times could have been the lake mentioned in vs. 16. See AB vol. 41, pp. 300–1, and Abel, p. 436.

Literally, our verse begins "He also attacked a strong town" (*Epebale de kai epi tina polin ochyran*). In A and q, between "town" (*polin*) and "strong" (*ochyran*), appears the mysterious word *gephyroun*. The word resembles the Greek noun *gephyra* ("bridge," "dam," or "causeway") and verb *gephyroun* ("to bridge," "to dam," "to build a causeway"), but in this context either one would be ungrammatical and would make no sense. A bridge, dam, or causeway is not a means of strengthening the fortifications of a city. The word is probably a misplaced alternative spelling of "Ephron" in vs. 27. In the Semitic language of its natives, the town's name began with the letter *'ayin,* which sometimes is treated in Greek as silent and sometimes is represented by *g.* Indeed, Ephron is called "Gephron" at Polybius v 70.12. The *y* probably crept in because the resultant spelling resembled the Greek word *gephyra.* The description of Ephron in vs. 27 is almost identical to the description of Kaspin here. An early scribe, who intended to insert into the margin at vs. 27 the alternative spelling, mistook vs. 13 for vs. 27 and wrote the word into the margin here, and the scribes underlying A and q copied the word from the margin into the text.

Both among Greeks and among Jews there was the tendency to prize ethnic purity and to despise people of mixed stock (Isocrates 4.24; Num 11:4; Neh 13:3; Philo *In Flaccum* 1.4, *Legatio ad Gaium* 18.120). The tendency would explain the insistence on the mixed nature of the population here and in the variant to vs. 27; cf. 8:9.

14–15. Cf. 10:34–36, and see NOTE ad loc.

15. See Josh 6:1–21.

17. Only La^LP have preserved the original letters of the name borne by the group of Jews, and even La^L miswrites it as *tubianeci* (supported by La^X, *dudianeci*). La^L is, indeed, outstanding for preserving correct readings where other witnesses went astray. It is hard to see how the reading of La^LXP could have arisen from the readings of the other witnesses. Scribes had trouble again at the second occurrence of the name, in vs. 35. See NOTE thereto.

The Tubiakenoi were the survivors of a military unit commanded by members of the Tobiad (or Tubiad) family. See NOTE on 3:11, NOTE on 4:26, NOTE on 5:5–16; AB vol. 41, pp. 298–99, and my article in *Studies Smith,* Part III, esp. pp. 91–93. The Tobiad chieftains and their troops and territory were so famous that the adjective *Toubiakos* ("Tubian") must have been coined to refer to them, and the territory around the Tobiad fort probably came to be called the *Toubiakênê* and its inhabitants *Toubiakênoi*, or, as I spell it in English, "Tubiakenoi." With the death of Hyrcanus the Tobiad, Antiochus IV probably took control of the Tobiad fortress at 'Arāq el-Emīr and reset-tled the soldiers somewhere in northern Transjordan or southern Syria, at or near the place called "Dathema" (I 5:9–11, 29). See Map 6. Jason of Cyrene appears to have known of the fortified settlement at 'Arāq el-Emīr, which he calls the "palisaded camp" and locates some 750 stadia from Kaspin. See Map 6. He never suspected that the Tubians had been transferred elsewhere. In his eagerness to contradict First Maccabees, Jason did not balk at the ab-surdity of having Judas march a three-days journey south from Kaspin to 'Arāq el-Emīr and another three-days journey back to Karnion. If the Tubians had been at 'Arāq el-Emīr, Judas would have come to their aid and joined forces with them before, in the campaign against Timotheus of Ammon (I 5:6–8; II 10:24–37) or at an earlier stage of the campaign here.

One can be quite sure that *charaka* here is a Greek common noun ("palisaded camp"), not a place name in a Semitic language, although there is a place called "Kerak" in the region. Some Semitic town names had long-established Greek equivalents, such as *Tyros* for "Tyre" and *Hierosolyma* for "Jerusalem," and the abridged history uses them. Most Semitic place names, however, had no Greek equivalent. In the abridged history, such place names ending in consonants are treated as indeclinable, so no *a* would have been added if the Semitic name was "Charak"; Semitic place names ending in vowels are declined in the first or second declension, so if the name was "Charaka," the Greek would have *Charakan* or perhaps *Charakaon* (cf. *Des-saou* at 14:16). The presence of the masculine singular definite article *ton* excludes the possibility that *charaka* is a neuter plural place name. Finally, in the Greek of the abridged history, the definite article is not normally used with place names (but see vss. 21 and 26).

18–19. The Greek of vs. 18 was difficult for ancient scribes and translators, as is indicated by the many variants, but the reading preserved by A and q[−107 370] is intelligible and is likely to be correct. One must only recognize that *epi tôn topôn* is Timotheus' title, "local commander." One might expect to find the definite article before that title in the Greek, but the article is similarly omitted before Lysias' title, *epi tôn pragmatôn* ("chief minister"), at 11:1.

At the end of vs. 18 I have translated the Greek text as it stands (*ochyran*), but in view of "stronghold" in vs. 19 one would expect *ochyrôi*, with the trans-lation "a garrison at a very strong point." Such is the version of La[BM], and the versions of La[LXV] could reflect either reading.

Jason may have had positive evidence from pro-Tubian Onias IV (see NOTE on vss. 10–31) that Timotheus was not present (correct accordingly AB vol. 41, NOTE on 5:34). Indeed, the narrative at I 5:29–34 says only that Timotheus' army was present and says nothing about the commander himself, though the natural assumption from the narrative there and at I 5:37 is that he was on the scene. Here we are told that Timotheus had failed to take his objec-tive, surely the Jews' fortress, and had left behind a garrison in another strong-hold, which Judas' men proceeded to take. This account contradicts the one at

I 5:29–34. Both accounts are tendentious, as we explained in the NOTE on vss. 10–31.

The unnamed stronghold of Timotheus' garrison here is probably identical to the Maapha of I 5:35 (on the uncertainty of the reading there, see NOTE ad loc.). We can thus understand why Maapha does not appear in the list at I 5:26: no Jews had barricaded themselves there. As usual, the author of I 5:35 focuses sharply on the Hasmonaeans and gives credit only to Judas, the supreme commander, whereas the men who commanded in the combat at Maapha were probably the men named here.

"Dositheos" ("gift of God") is a purely Greek name, but of a type favored by Jews (J. *AJ* xiii 9.2.260, etc.; CPJ, I, 29, 281–82; M.-R. Savignac, "Mélanges," RB 38 [1929], 231–32, 236; Marcus Jastrow, *A Dictionary of the Targumim, the Talmud Babli and Yerushalmi, and the Midrashic Literature* [New York: G. P. Putnam's Sons, 1903], p. 287a). "Sosipatros," too, is purely Greek ("protector of his father") but is attested among Jews (J. *AJ* xiv 10.22.248; Rom 16:21). Judas' army thus contained Jews who bore Greek names.

20–25. Our passage parallels I 5:37–43. The details in both accounts probably come from the Common Source. The differences may be ascribed to the different aims of the two authors and to the abridger's desire for brevity. Jason or the abridger could have omitted the fact that Timotheus' new force consisted of local gentiles and mercenary Arabs (see NOTE on vs. 2), and the abridger could have omitted the name and description of the battle site (Raphon) and the tactics of the two commanders. At I 5:37–43 there is no parallel to vs. 21, but one can infer from I 5:43 that Karnain is the refuge for the enemy. The Hasmonaean propagandist was glad to pass over in silence the matter in vss. 24–25. The duped Jews were Judas' own men, perhaps Hasmonaeans. Even if they could be dissociated from Judas, there was no need to add to I 5:55–62.

20. The Greek is obscure and puzzled the Latin and Syriac translators. The pronoun "them" surely refers to Dositheos and Sosipatros (see vss. 19 and 24). On the unit called "regiment" (*speira*), see NOTE on 8:23, *division*. The data on how Judas subdivided his army here (under two commanders) and at I 5:33 (in three columns) refer to different stages of the campaign and need not be in conflict. As usual, the size of Timotheus' army is exaggerated. The witnesses to the text vary on the number of his cavalry. The figure here is that in V La Sy Arm. A has 3,700; q, 1,700; and *L*, 1,500.

See also NOTE on vs. 22.

21. According to I 5:43, Timotheus and his army fled to the town (*polis*) and pagan temple (*temenos*) at Karnain. In our period Karnain was certainly distinct from Ashtaroth, called Ashteroth-Karnaim at Gen 14:5; see Jubilees 29:10. With the help of Eusebius' *Onomastikon* and of traditions surviving among the Arabs, Ashtaroth can be located at Tell 'Aštara, and Karnain, nearby, at Šeikh Sa'ad. See Map 6; Félix-Marie Abel, *Géographie de la Palestine* [Paris: Gabalda, 1933–38], II, 255, 413–14; Benjamin Mazar, "'Ašterot qarnayim," Enc. Bib., VI (1971), 406 (in Hebrew). Accordingly, correct AB vol. 41, NOTE on 5:43. In First Maccabees, it seems clear that the temple was in the town of Karnain.

Jason may well present a different topography. He called Karnion a *chôrion*, and *chôrion* can, indeed, mean "town" or "village." It is possible that "Karnion" here is simply a Greek form for "Karnain," but if so, it is a departure from Jason's usual treatment of Semitic names of obscure places (see NOTE on vs. 17). Only here is Karnain given a Greek name form. Jerome and Eusebius call it "Karnaia," presenting an Aramaic form (see Abel, *Géographie*, II, 413–14). The ending *-ion* suggests, rather, that "Karnion" is the name of a fort or holy place in the territory of Karnain; see Raphael Kühner and Friedrich Blass, *Ausführliche Grammatik der griechischen Sprache, Erster Teil: Elementar- und Formenlehre* (Hannover: Hahn, 1890–92), II, 276. In Hellenistic Greek, *chôrion* often means "fortress" or "fortress along with the neighboring population"; see Louis Robert, review of *Griechische Mauerbauinschriften*, by F. G. Maier, *Gnomon* 42 (1970), 588–89. Thus the fortress called "the Karnion" and the temple of Atargatis called in Greek "the Atergation" (vs. 26) could have been two separate places, presumably Šeikh Sa'ad and Tell 'Aštara (see NOTE on vs. 26). If so, Jason may be correct here against his rival. On the other hand, Jason himself may have meant that the Karnion and the temple of Atargatis were both at Karnain, in agreement with I 5:43–44.

Jason is wrong about the narrow passes. The hills of Šeikh Sa'ad and Tell 'Aštara are surrounded by flat country.

The Greek has "the other baggage" (*tên allên aposkeuên*) because a soldier's "baggage" (*aposkeuê*) could include his wife and children; see Holleaux, *Études*, III, 15–26.

22. We are not told in what form the enemy perceived the divine intervention. Perhaps the panic itself was the sole manifestation of it, in fulfillment of Lev 26:8. Jason believes that Judas had three columns, perhaps a total of 4,500 (cf. 8:22). Lev 26:8 predicts victories over enemy forces outnumbering Jews by from twentyfold to one hundredfold. The victory over Timotheus' force, which is said to have had a total of 122,500 men, is in the proper proportion. Did Jews also see in the event a partial fulfillment of Hag 2:22?

In calling God the "One Who sees all," Jason or his source probably alludes to God's having seen previous sins of Timotheus and his men against helpless Jewish populations. Such sins are detailed in I 5:10–13, 25–27. Though the abridger here has left only the brief note at vs. 2, our context implies that Timotheus and his men, in contrast to the innocent Scythopolitans (vs. 30), were guilty of atrocities like those of the Joppites and Jamnites (vss. 3–4, 8). According to Deut 32:36, God will act as judge on behalf of His people when He sees their helplessness. The battles described here occurred not far from Damascus. At Greek Zech 9:1, God is said to have a sacrifice in Damascus and to "see" human beings and all the tribes of Israel. The verb "see" both here and there is *ephoran*. Thus it is likely that the writer saw the victory over Timotheus as a fulfillment of Zech 9:1. Cf. NOTES on 7:6.

Our confidence in the veracity of First Maccabees is enhanced by the fact that there the relatively high number of 8,000 make up the Jewish force, and no figures are given for the enemy. Indeed, on these campaigns Judas and his men struck quickly and moved on. There was no time to count the enemy dead.

23. We have the usual exaggerated figure for the enemy dead.

24–25. There is no reason to doubt the story here. Jason does not condemn the two commanders for being deceived.

Did Timotheus' deceit consist in claiming to hold as prisoners the kin of the Jewish soldiers? Or did it consist rather in breaking his promise to restore the prisoners unhurt?

24. *whose . . . nothing*. The condition, "if Timotheus should be killed," is to be understood and was inserted in *L'* and La^V.

25. *brothers*. Perhaps "kin" is a better translation here, so as to include the parents mentioned in vs. 24.

26–31. The parallels between our verses and I 5:46–54 argue for the existence of the Common Source. The events and their order are identical. Both authors call Ephron a "strong town." The abridger may have omitted the story at I 5:46(end)–48. The mention of Beth-Shan (Scythopolis) serves no ulterior purpose at I 5:52; surely the author took it from his source. The audacious allusions and claims in I 5:53–54 are Hasmonaean propaganda; see AB vol. 41, p. 304.

26. See NOTE on vs. 21. There can be no doubt that *Atergation* here means "temple of Atargatis": cf. I 5:43–44. In translating I have used the word "shrine" rather than "temple" because our writer uses the Greek words for "temple" (*hieron, naos*) only of Israelite sanctuaries. See pp. 13–14. The Syrian fertility goddess Atargatis was widely worshiped in Syria and Palestine; see Francis R. Walton, "Atargatis," OCD², p. 136. There is a controversy as to whether she was identical with the Canaanite fertility goddess Astarte, the biblical Ashtoreth (Loewenstamm, "'*Aštōret*," Enc. Bib., VI [1971], 408–9 [in Hebrew]). To judge by the name, the town of Ashtaroth was, or contained, a place sacred to Ashtoreth. An Egyptian stele at Tell 'Aštara has a relief of a goddess whose head bears the horns of a cow, and Ashtoreth was so portrayed in Egypt, having been identified with the cow-horned goddess Ḥathor (Loewenstamm, ibid., col. 411; Abel, p. 439), and that fact may be the reason for the biblical name "Ashteroth-Karnaim" ("Ashtaroth of the two horns"). On the other hand, Mazar (Enc. Bib., VI, 406) suggests that the name means "Ashtaroth near Karnain."

A temple of Astarte could become a temple of Atargatis either through the identification of Astarte with Atargatis or through the replacement of Astarte by Atargatis.

Again the numbers of the slain are exaggerated.

27. According to I 5:46, the only feasible route for Judas and those with him went through Ephron (see Map 6), and the townspeople refused to let them pass through.

There is nothing incredible in the assertion that Lysias "had a residence" or perhaps "formerly resided" (*katôikei*) in Ephron. Kings and noble families could have provincial "country seats" (see Bickerman, *Institutions*, p. 33). Ancient readers, however, found it strange that the chief minister should ever have resided in a Transjordanian town, so that the unadulterated original reading is preserved only by La^{LM} and Arm, though it is still reflected by La^X, which has "Lisanias" instead of "Lysias." At first the puzzled scribes doubted only the remark about Lysias and wrote into the margin their own suggestion, that the original reading here was the commonplace slur on the enemy population as an ethnic mixture (*pamphyla en autêi plêthê;* cf. vs. 13 and 8:9). The marginal note was then taken into the text by a later scribe, though the result, *en hêi pamphyla en autêi plêthê* ("in which there was a population of varied origins in it") was bad Greek. In A and q the marginal note completely displaced the reference to Lysias. In the text of *L'*, Sy, and La^BP the marginal reading and the reference to Lysias appear side by side.

The interest in the physical condition and fighting spirit of the enemy is characteristic of Greek writers and is conspicuous by its absence from the biblical histories and First Maccabees. Unlike the Joppites, the people of Ephron did not cower behind their walls. Moreover, they were well provided with weapons. Ancient artillery consisted of catapults.

28. Ephron could have put up protracted resistance (see NOTE on vs. 27). That the site fell quickly could only have been a miracle, in answer to prayer.

Again the number of the slain is probably exaggerated.

One would expect "Whose might shatters the strength of the enemy" to be an allusion to scripture, but there are no really close parallels. See, however, Dan LXX 3:44; Dan Th. 3:44, and Ezek 32:12, and cf. I 4:30.

Most witnesses to the text have here *alkas* ("strengths," "strength"), whereas A and some minuscules have *olkas,* which should not be taken as *holkas* ("weights," "weight"), but rather as a phonetic spelling of *alkas;* the various manuscripts at Sir 29:13 exhibit the same pair of spellings. There was a tendency in Greek for *a* followed by *l* to become *o* (Abel, *Grammaire,* p. 8).

29–31. As usual, Jason, the Jewish Greek, takes pleasure in recording instances of amity between Jews and non-Jews, whereas the author of First Maccabees passes them over in silence. See AB vol. 41, p. 34. In citing Judas' kind behavior toward the friendly Scythopolitans, Jason may also intend to hold up to unfavorable contrast harsh treatment of that city by the conquering Hasmonaeans, John Hyrcanus and Alexander Jannaeus (see J. *AJ* xiii 10.3.280, 15.4.396, *BJ* i 2.7.66). On the other hand, at I 5:54 there is the assertion that not one man in Judas' force was killed during the campaign in Gilead, which involved pitched battles and stormings of fortified towns. Only a miracle could produce that result! The writer here is silent on the possibility. Jason estimates the distance by road from Scythopolis (Beth-Shan) to Jerusalem correctly, as some 75 miles, or 120 kilometers.

"Feast of Weeks" is the literal translation of the Hebrew name for Pentecost (Exod 34:22; Deut 16:10, etc.). The mention of Judas' interruption of his campaigns to celebrate Pentecost may well be an effort to show that he followed Pharisaic practice. On the Sadducean and Essene interpretations, Pentecost would always fall on a Sunday (see Shemaryahu Talmon, "The Calendar Reckoning of the Sect from the Judaean Desert," *Scripta Hierosolymitana* 4 [1958], 174, 185–86). Judas would have had to interrupt his campaigns for the Sabbath which preceded a Sunday Pentecost (cf. 8:26–28 and 12:38). In that case there would be no special interruption for Pentecost. Moreover, the obligatory pilgrimage to Jerusalem for Pentecost, on the Sadducean and Essene interpretations, would require arrival in the holy city before the Sabbath. By not mentioning the Sabbath here, Jason may thus be hinting that Judas followed Pharisaic practice. On the unintercalated Jewish calendar of 163 B.C.E., the Pharisaic Pentecost (6 Sivan) fell on Wednesday, April 21. If the Jews had been observing a fully intercalated calendar, that Pentecost would have fallen on Saturday, June 19, and there would have been no special interruption of Judas' campaigning in order to celebrate the holiday. Our reasoning here involves unproved assumptions but still would confirm our hypothesis that Judas and his followers in 163 B.C.E. used an unintercalated calendar (AB vol. 41, pp. 273–80).

The Common Source probably reported how Joseph and Azariah suffered a disastrous defeat while Judas and Simon were rescuing beleaguered Jews (I 5:55–62). The story was useful for Hasmonaean propaganda (see AB vol. 41, pp. 74, 304). Anti-Hasmonaean Jason and the abridger could well omit it. Even if Joseph and Azariah might somehow be connected with the Hasmonaean dynasty, a mere defeat could well be passed over, inasmuch as a story of their treasonable conduct was available (see NOTE on II 10:19–23).

At I 5:63–64 we have pure Hasmonaean propaganda, contrasting Judas and his brothers with the unfortunate Joseph and Azariah.

32–45. Characteristically, for Jason the enemy is the Seleucid governor Gorgias, not the Idumaeans. On Gorgias, see NOTE on 8:9 and NOTE on 10:14–15. The campaign here is the same as the one in I 5:65–68, and both authors probably used the Common Source. See Map 7 and AB vol. 41, p. 305. The brave but unsuccessful efforts of Dositheos and Ezri and the deaths in vs. 34 are what the Hasmonaean propagandist scornfully sums up in I 5:67. Both Jason and the author of First Maccabees had to explain how so many Jews could have fallen in a campaign if Judas Maccabaeus was in command and enjoying the very peak of divine favor.

At I 5:68 this campaign of Judas ends with a raid on the territory of Azotus and on the pagan altars and idols therein. Here there is no mention of the raid. Has the abridger omitted it? Or did Jason omit it as discreditable? No source reports that Azotus had committed atrocities against the Jews, and Jason of Cyrene, a Greek, may therefore have disapproved of attacks such as are mentioned at I 5:68, 10:83–85, 11:4.

33–34. The abridger left the antecedents of "he" and "they" obscure, as is indicated by the ambiguous reading of A (and of La^BP) and by the many variants in the other witnesses. Did Judas have the force of 3,000 infantry and 400 cavalry, or did Gorgias? The presence of cavalry is not a decisive clue for making "Gorgias" the antecedent (see NOTE on 3:25), since there were cavalrymen in Judas' force, too (vs. 35). If Jason gave the enemy such modest numbers, he would appear for once to have derived his figures from a reliable source. Judas is said to have had 8,000 men for his campaign in Gilead (I 5:20). Would he have had so much smaller a force for the one here?

Even the good witnesses to the text had no better evidence than we for eliminating the ambiguity. La^LXV V L' Sy seem to be unambiguous in taking "he" as Gorgias and "they" as Gorgias' men. On the other hand, q makes the verb of vs. 33 plural, so as to fit "Judas and his men," and in vs. 34 consistently reads "joined battle against him" (La^M is similar). My guess is that La^LXV V L' Sy are correct here.

34. *a few . . . fell*. See vss. 36–45, and cf. I 5:67.

35. *Dositheos . . . Tubiakenoi*. By identifying him in this manner the writer surely means to distinguish him from the Dositheos in vss. 19 and 24. Ancient

scribes found confusing the succession of short syllables beginning with *t* in the Greek of "one of the Tubiakenoi" (*TISTÔNTOUBIAKÊNÔN*), the more so as in ancient manuscripts words were not divided, and *tou* was the genitive singular of the definite article. Already in vs. 17 most scribes had trouble reading the name of the Tubiakenoi (see NOTE thereto). Here, only La^P and Arm preserve all the letters of the name. La^{LX} took *tou* as the definite article and "corrected" it to the genitive plural (*de biacenis*). Their version is supported by La^B (*diacenorum*) and La^M (*bizacinorum*). La^{LXBM} all have nonsense, but still hint at the correctness of La^P and Arm. *L* and *l,* here as in vs. 17, turn the name into "Tubianoi" or "Tobianoi." The scribes responsible for A and q also took *tou* as the genitive singular of the definite article. For them, it had to be followed by a genitive singular noun. From the genitive plural ending *-ôn* they somehow managed to read the genitive singular ending *-oros* (like the genitive singular of the common name "Nicanor"). The misreading could have been facilitated by the practice of scribes to curve both vertical strokes of *nu* so that they were concave outward. Sigma was concave to the right, like our "C." Thus the scribe produced the otherwise unknown name "Bakenor," which also appears in La^V (*de bachenoris*). The reading of A and q and La^V would mean "Dositheos, one of Bakenor's group." The abridger could, indeed, have omitted passages which told who Bakenor and his group were, and thus one might be tempted to accept the unique name as the original reading. But our presentation of the cumulative evidence of the variants here and at vs. 17 should be decisive against doing so.

cavalryman. Biblical texts disapprove of the maintenance of cavalry by Jewish governments (see NOTE on 3:25), but the Tubiakenoi had been Jewish mercenaries in the service of the gentile Ptolemies and Seleucids. The biblical disapproval thus had not applied to them. Should they not now use their fighting talents against the enemies of the Chosen People?

cloak. Gr. *chlamys*. Regularly worn by cavalrymen, it was a cape fastened at the neck by a safety pin. It consisted of a piece of cloth, rectangular except at its lower end, where it curved into two "wings," somewhat like the tails of a formal coat. See E. Saglio, "Chlamyde," DAGR, I^2 (1908), 1115.

Thracian horsemen. As Seleucid governor of Idumaea, Gorgias had troops of the royal army, in which Thracian mercenaries and their descendants were prominent, especially as cavalry (see Polybius xxx 25.5; Launey, *Recherches*, pp. 373–74, 384, 393–94).

escaped to Marisa. At this time Marisa was one of the two principal cities of Idumaea (see Map 7 and Avi-Yonah, *The Holy Land*, p. 37; Abel, *Géographie*, pp. 239, 379). At I 5:66, Judas is said to have passed through Marisa. He is not, however, said to have captured the fortified town, so that the author there probably means only that the Jewish force passed through the rural territory of Marisa. Hence, the information there is compatible with the assertion that Gorgias escaped to Marisa.

36–40. At AB vol. 41, p. 305, I refer the reader to a NOTE here, but the discussion now stands in the NOTE on vss. 40–41.

36. Ezri is not identified, as if Jason had introduced him before. It is likely that Ezri was in command of the unit which suffered losses (mentioned in vs. 34) and that the abridger took insufficient thought for his readers and omitted

the fact there. The scribes accordingly had trouble with our verse, as one can see from the many variants. Our reading of the name stands on the sound testimony of A V La^{XV} *l* Sy, which could not have arisen from the "Gorgias" of q and *L* and has too much authority to be overruled in favor of the reading of La^{LBMP} (on which see below).

Can Ezri here be the same as Ezra at 8:23? Then there would be no need to identify him here. Both names are short forms for "Azariah," the name of the discredited commander (I 5:56–62) whom Jason seems to have insistently portrayed as a brother of Judas Maccabaeus (see NOTE on II 8:16–23). The incident here should be identical to the incident narrated at I 5:67, another piece of blatant Hasmonaean propaganda. If the author of First Maccabees had known that the discredited Azariah was again involved, surely he would have mentioned his name. This fact is a fairly strong indication that, to the author of the Common Source, Ezri was distinct from Ezra (=Azariah), so that he used the two different name forms deliberately. Nevertheless, despite the difference in nomenclature, Jason may have taken Azariah and Ezri to be identical (see also NOTE on vss. 40–41) and may have identified both with the Hasmonaean brother Eleazar! See AB vol. 41, pp. 79–80. Jason himself in his text appears to have copied the names as they were in the Common Source, but the scribe underlying La^{LBMP} probably represents Jason's understanding accurately in reading "Esdria" (="Azariah"). Did that scribe guess on the basis of I 5:18 and 56? Or did Jason himself, undecided what name to write, put "Ezri" in his text and "Ezria" in the margin? In any case, he probably viewed Ezri as a Hasmonaean and was pleased to tell how Ezri could not win without Judas' aid. Judas' success comes partly as a result of his never failing to invoke God's help.

37. Pious Judas takes even his battle cries from the holy words of the Psalms. Since the writer finds it necessary to call attention to Judas' use of Hebrew, he implies that Maccabaeus and his men usually spoke another language (Aramaic). Cf. 15:29.

38–39. Again Jason stresses Judas' strict observance of the Sabbath. See NOTE on 8:25–26. Odollam (biblical Adullam) lies some 7.5 miles, or 12 kilometers, northeast of Marisa. Though Edomites (=Idumaeans) encroached on much of southern Judaea, Adullam remained in the hands of Jews (Neh 11:30).

Judas and his men did not merely bathe; they ritually purified themselves (*hagnisthentes*). The writer could not have had in mind Num 31:19–24, where the process of purification takes seven days. Rabbinic law makes such purification obligatory only upon one who will enter the inner court of the temple; see Rashi on Num 5:2 and 31:19, 24. The purification here seems to be connected with the Sabbath, and nothing is said of the Sabbath at Num 31:19–24. Indeed, the writer calls the practice an "established custom," not a "law." Rabbinic law suggests he was right in his choice of words. In rabbinic sources there is no law requiring ritual purity on the Sabbath (by full immersion in a ritual bath). There is only the citation, with implied approval, of the practice of Rabbi Judah ben Rabbi Il'ay, of the mere washing of face and hands in warm water before the Sabbath (TB *Shabbat* 25b). Nevertheless, Hasidic Jews today zealously observe the "custom" of ritual immersion before the Sabbath (Raphael Posner, "Ablution," Enc. Jud., II [1971], 83).

The Essenes of Qumran required soldiers to purify themselves on the morning after a battle (1QM 14:2). If the battle fell on Friday, did they require that the purification be carried out before the Sabbath?

39. *at the time . . . permissible.* My translation of the obscure *kath' hon chronon to tês chreias egegonei* is a mere guess based on the context. Of the many meanings of *chreia,* relevant here may be "need," "military or naval service," "combat," "military engagement," "business," "employment," "function," and "use." Here the construction *to tês chreias* makes the word even vaguer. Philo's use of *chreia* in connection with the Sabbath at *De specialibus legibus* ii 7.65–66 might support my guess. La^{LXV} and Sy omit the difficult phrase. La^{BM} paraphrase it "in accordance with necessity," omitting the words *hon chronon.* La^P has "at the time at which it became necessary." Presumably the translators underlying La^{BMP} were thinking of the stench and danger of disease arising from the decomposition of the corpses. Perhaps those translators were correct, but I find it hard to believe that the writer would have expressed that idea by the obscure language found here.

40–41. Where the author at I 5:67 blames the men's death on their own rashness, Jason blames it on their sin of possessing idolatrous objects. Both authors are expressing theology, but facts in their sources surely underlie both accounts. We may discount the exaggeration that every one of the dead bore idolatrous objects, but enough did to impress pious observers ("all") who looked for the providential miracles which would signify the end of the age of God's wrath, especially for fulfillment of Jer 31:28–29 and Ezek 18. They may also have seen a partial fulfillment of Dan 12:1–2, in that the righteous in the time of troubles survived, and only the sinners perished. The consecrated objects (*hierômata*) are connected with the idols of Jamnia. There are two possibilities as to their nature.

First, Judas conducted a punitive raid against Jamnia, and the insubordinate commanders Joseph and Azariah also attacked the town, though they were beaten off with heavy losses. On either occasion, Jews may have plundered shrines outside the walls and concealed the loot under their tunics. Gold and silver ornaments were frequently dedicated to pagan gods and placed upon their statues, and gold and silver vessels were dedicated and placed in their temples. The Torah forbade Jews to possess such objects (Deut 7:25–26). La^L says that the objects were "from shrines" (*de sacrariis*). La^X calls them "metal plating" such as gold leaf (*laminas*). La^{VBMP} call them "votive gifts" (*donaria, dona*). Sy and *l* say the objects were of gold. Thus, all these witnesses support the first possibility.

Second is the suggestion of Isidore Lévy, *Recherches esséniennes et pythagoriciennes* ("Hautes études du monde gréco-romain," 1; Genève: Droz; Paris: Minard, 1965), pp. 65–71. Lévy argues as follows. On Greek inscriptions set up by Jamnites on the island of Delos, Herakles and Ḥoron are identified as "gods who possess Jamnia." "Herakles" is frequently used as the Greek equivalent of the name of a Phoenician (=Canaanite) Baal. Ḥoron and the Phoenician Herakles appear in ancient sources as protective deities. Jamnia lay in the territory once held by the Philistine city of Ekron, where Ba'al-zebul (called

"Ba'al-zebub" in the Hebrew Bible) was worshiped as a deity who protects and cures (II Kings 1:2–16). Accordingly, the consecrated objects are to be viewed as amulets to bring upon the bearer the protective power of the deities of Jamnia. Just as King Ahaziah died as a punishment for seeking the curative power of "Ba'al-zebub" (ibid.), so the Jewish soldiers perished for carrying pagan amulets.

Lévy's suggestion is improbable. For Judas and his men, as for Jason, greed was a much less serious sin than putting faith in false gods. No pious Jew would pray for the forgiveness of Ahaziah or of sinners like him. Achan's sin (Josh 7) was one of mere greed. He paid for it with his life, but he still received sympathetic treatment from Joshua (Josh 7:19). To my knowledge, there is no ancient context in which *hierôma* can be shown to mean "amulet." On the inscription from Crete which was once thought to mention *hierômata* in a list of medicines, see Margarita Guarducci, *Inscriptiones creticae*, vol. IV (Roma: Libreria dello stato, 1950), no. 145. At II Kings 1:2–16, Ba'al-zebub is presented, not as a god believed to have healing power, but as one believed to foretell the future. We are thus justified in following the first interpretation, supported as it is by ancient witnesses.

41. The usual Jewish formulas of thanksgiving blessed or praised God Himself; see NOTE on 3:30. Here, instead, God's judgment is blessed. The odd expression may well have arisen from our writer's contorted style, but cf. I Sam 25:33.

42–45. Jason has engaged in a complicated piece of logical gymnastics to prove that Judas believed in the resurrection of the dead. We can be quite certain that he misunderstood his source. The sin with which Judas and his men were so concerned was not the individual sin of the dead but rather the corporate guilt in which they had involved the still-living community. We still find this fact in vs. 42, unadulterated by Jason's theories.

Judas and his surviving force may have believed their case to be the one envisaged at Lev 4:13, taken literally. The rabbinic interpretation of that verse is different (see Rashi's commentary ad loc.). The *Sifra* to Lev 4:13 (p. 19a Weiss) considers and rejects the interpretation that "whole congregation" is to be taken literally. Judas and his men, however, lived long before the rabbis. Lev 4:13 is almost echoed in vss. 40–41: the community had unknowingly been tainted with the sin of idolatry through the secret misconduct of the soldiers, but the sin had now been exposed. If Judas and his men took Lev 4:13 to apply to their case, they found that Lev 4:14–21 required the community to bring a bull as a sin offering. Later, rabbinic law provided for a special collection from the community to pay for the bull (To. *Sheqalim* 2:6; TB *Menahot* 52a; see Lieberman, *Tosefta Ki-fshutah*, Part IV [*Mo'ed*], pp. 682–83), similar to Judas' procedure. Two thousand silver drachmas was far too much for a bull. According to rabbinic law, the extra money would be treated as a donation to the temple ("*Hattāt*," Ensiqlopediah talmudit, XIV [5713=1973], 485–86), and the law may have been the same in Judas' time. It is noteworthy that Jason himself, surely following his source, speaks in vs. 43 only of a singular sin offering. Had the sin requiring the sacrifice been the individual sin of the possessors of idolatrous objects, there would have been an offering for each sinner.

Nevertheless, Jason believes that the sin offering was brought to secure expiation for the dead! His view disagrees with rabbinic law. There, the principle holds that sacrifices do not secure expiation for the dead. The experience of death itself is their expiation. See TB *Zebaḥim* 9b and *"Ēyn kappārāh leמētīm,"* Talmudic Encyclopedia, I (5707=1946–47), 293b–294b. Again, neither Jason nor Judas and his men had to agree with rabbinic law, but we have found many indications that Jason misinterpreted his source. The words he took over from the source do not fit his opinion; indeed, the words hint that Judas and his men acted in literal fulfillment of Lev 4:13–21. Cf. Israel Lévi, "La commémoration des âmes dans le Judaïsme," REJ 29 (1894), 43–60, and Salomon Reinach, "De l'origine des prières pour les morts," REJ 41 (1900), 161–73.

Jason was driven to this kind of interpretation because he firmly believed in resurrection and had to justify his own approval of Judas, a member of a family notorious for rejecting the doctrine (see AB vol. 41, pp. 12, 85). If Jason had had direct evidence of Judas' acceptance of the doctrine, he surely would have quoted it. Judas did win the loyalty of many pious believers in resurrection (see NOTE on 8:1 and my study in CHJ, vol. 1, Part II, ch. 8), perhaps by avoiding any public expression of disbelief.

Our passage is an important source for Catholic and Eastern Orthodox doctrines. See J. H. Wright, "Dead, Prayers for the," New Catholic Encyclopedia, IV (1967), 672; J. F. X. Cevetello, "Purgatory," ibid., XI (1967), 1034; Abel, pp. 447–48; Abel and Jean Starcky, *Les livres des Maccabées* (Paris: Éditions du Cerf, 1961), pp. 21–23; Grimm, pp. 185–86; Kellermann, *Auferstanden*, pp. 11–13.

42. The effect of the sin of the greedy soldiers upon the community could have been as grievous as that of Achan's (Josh 7). Through prayer and through keeping themselves from sin, the survivors might be safe from further manifestations of the wrath of God.

43. The words *kat' andra logian* ("a collection from every man") in ancient manuscripts were written without punctuation and without word separation. They were misunderstood by some witnesses, as can be seen from the many textual variants. One puzzled reader wrote into the margin his suggestion, *kataskeuasmata* ("supplies"), which some later scribes took into the text. The original words are preserved in q and in V (which, however, has also moved the erroneous suggestion *kataskeuasmata* into the text). The meaning "collection" was understood by La and Sy. On the word "collection" (*logia* or, better, *logeia*), see Gustav Adolf Deissmann, *Bible Studies* (Edinburgh: T. & T. Clark, 1901), pp. 142–44, 219–20.

Judas' force had three columns (see NOTE on vss. 18–19, yet two thousand is not an exact multiple of three. That fact may be the reason La^{LXV} read here "twelve thousand," and L' Sy read "three thousand." Perhaps for the same reason, the scribes of La^{BMP}, who retained the reading "two thousand," chose to render *eis* as "approximately" rather than "for a total of." But there is no reason to insist that each man had to give a whole drachma or that each man gave the same sum.

44–45. I have translated the text of Hanhart, based on A V q. De Bruyne, however, may well be right in seeing in La^L traces of how an original text suffered interpolation. In La^L, our passage is a clause explaining vs. 43: *Quia eos qui prociderant resurgere sperabat* (*ex abundantia et vanum pro mortuis orare*), *considerans his qui cum pietate dormitionem ceperunt obtimam esse repositam gratiam* (*sancta et salubris cogitatio*), "Because he had hope that those who had fallen would be resurrected (it is superfluous and useless to pray for the dead), thinking that a most glorious recompense is laid up for those who take the sleep [of death] in a state of piety (a holy and salutary thought)." The first parenthesis, De Bruyne suggests, is an insertion by a skeptical reader (see also NOTE on vss. 42–45); and the second parenthesis, one by a believer in resurrection. The second parenthesis, however, is in character for Jason himself and is well enough expressed. If De Bruyne is right, the scribes responsible for A and q added the words *ei mê* ("If . . . did not") and left the words *an ên* ("would have been") unexpressed in Greek but were confident that the reader would supply them mentally; the scribes responsible for *L'* La^{VP} and Sy added not only *ei me* but also *an ên*. Thus the skeptic's note was brought into the sentence and made innocuous.

Charistêrion, to my knowledge, means "recompense" only here. Usually it means "sacrifice of thanksgiving."

Where my translation has "pass away," the literal meaning is "fall asleep."

XVI. THE EXPEDITION OF
ANTIOCHUS V AND LYSIAS
(13:1–26)

13 ¹ In the year 149 Judas and his men received the news that Antiochus Eupator had come in force against Judaea, ² along with Lysias, his guardian and chief minister. He had a Greek army recruited abroad, consisting of one hundred ten thousand infantry, five thousand three hundred cavalry, twenty-two elephants, and three hundred scythed chariots. ³ Menelaus, too, came before them for an audience and, thoroughly concealing his real motives, egged Antiochus on. His thought was not for the preservation of his country but for his own appointment to office. ⁴ However, the King of kings roused Antiochus' anger against the wretch. When Lysias argued to show that Menelaus was to blame for all the troubles, the king ordered that he be taken to Beroia and executed in the manner customary there. ⁵ Indeed, in Beroia there is a tower fifty cubits high, full of ashes, with a rotating device descending steeply from every direction into the ashes. ⁶ There the community joins in pushing to doom men guilty of temple robbery and perpetrators of other exceedingly heinous crimes. ⁷ Such was the death which befell the wicked Menelaus; he did not even reach the ground. His fate was altogether just. ⁸ He who had perpetrated many sins regarding the altar (the fire and ashes of which are holy) met his death in ashes.

⁹ The king's thoughts had roused him to barbarous fury as he came intending to show the Jews far worse treatment than they had received under his father. ¹⁰ On receiving this news, Judas issued orders to the people to pray to the LORD day and night that He come to their aid now, if ever, ¹¹ for they were on the point of losing their Torah and country and holy temple; and that He not let His people, who had just begun to revive, fall into the hands of blasphemous gentiles. ¹² All joined in doing so. For three days, weeping and fasting and prostrating themselves, they all unceasingly beseeched the merciful

LORD, and then Judas, after urging them to take heart, ordered them to stand by. 13 In a closed meeting with the elders, he recommended marching out and deciding the issue with the help of God, before the king's army invaded Judaea and seized control of the city. 14 Having entrusted the outcome to the Creator of the universe, Judas exhorted his men to fight nobly to the death for laws, temple, city, country, and national institutions. He pitched his camp near Modeïn. 15 After giving his men "God's victory" as the password, he picked the best of his young men and made a night attack on the king's quarters and killed two thousand of the men in the camp and stabbed the lead elephant to death along with the man in its howdah. 16 Finally, they filled the camp with terror and confusion and withdrew victorious. 17 Day was already dawning as he completed this feat through having the protecting help of the LORD.

18 The king, having tasted the boldness of the Jews, tried to invade their territory by devious routes. 19 He repeatedly attacked Beth-Zur, a strong fortress of the Jews, but again and again was repulsed, defeated, humiliated. 20 Judas kept sending in to the defenders the necessary supplies. 21 However, Rodokos, a soldier in the Jewish ranks, divulged their secrets to the enemy. He was tracked down and arrested and executed. 22 The king came off second best with the defenders of Beth-Zur, gave them the handclasp of peace, received the same from them, marched off. 23 He attacked Judas and his men, was worsted, received the news that Philip, who had been left in charge of the government at Antioch, had rebelled. Perturbed, Antiochus made overtures to the Jews, yielded, and swore to grant them all their rights, made peace, and brought a sacrifice. He showed honor to the temple and conceded privileges to the Place. 24 He granted an audience to Maccabaeus. He left behind Hegemonides as commander over the region from Ptolemais to the Gerrhenes. 25 He marched to Ptolemais. The citizens of Ptolemais were angry over the pact—indeed, they were indignant beyond measure. They wished to nullify its terms. 26 Lysias came forward on the speakers' platform, defended the terms as best he could, convinced and calmed his audience, won their support, marched back to Antioch. Such was the course of the king's expedition and return home.

NOTES

Ch. **13.** Our chapter contains many strange aspects. Let us begin by considering the following points:

(1) The vast expedition here of the Seleucid regime against the Jews was a drastic shift of policy, in violation of the agreements detailed in ch. 11. Jason and the abridger knew that Antiochus V was a young child who could not function as king without the help of a guardian (vs. 2; 11:1). And yet, the writer here ascribes the violent shift of policy to the unmotivated savage fury of the child king (vss. 1 and 9)! Perhaps the abridger omitted a better motivation for the shift, but more likely the account here is a good reflection of Jason's original.

(2) The actions of the regime contrast with the supposed savage fury of Antiochus V. The king and the chief minister rather seem to show great concern to conciliate the Jews: they have the hated Menelaus executed; they make peace with the defenders of Beth-Zur; and at the end of the campaign the king generously honors the temple, and the chief minister defends the peace agreements against the objections of the citizens of Ptolemais.

(3) The experienced commander Lysias knew that chariotry would be useless on the rugged terrain of Judaea (see Bar-Kochva, *The Seleucid Army,* pp. 83–84), yet the writer says (vs. 2) that the expeditionary force included three hundred scythed chariots.

In these three points the account here is strange in itself. It becomes stranger still when compared to the parallel sources.

Thus for the Seleucid regime's violent shift of policy, the account in I 6:18–28 gives, in contrast, excellent motivation: Judas and his followers had besieged the royal garrison in the Akra, the citadel north of the temple. As usual, the author of First Maccabees was pleased to contradict Daniel. In contrast to Dan 11:44–45, reports came from the *south* to infuriate the king!

Josephus' narrative at *BJ* i 1.4–5.40–41, probably written on the basis of his inaccurate recollection of I 6:18–33 (see AB vol. 41, pp. 60–61), displays interesting parallels and contrasts with the one here. There, too, as here, the siege of the Akra is unmentioned (deliberately? see AB vol. 41, ibid., and p. 219), but Josephus leaves the young king's fury well motivated by not reporting that the Seleucid regime had made peace with the Jews (*BJ* i 1.4.38–39).

The author at I 6:28 ascribes to the boy-king, not savage fury, but reasonable anger, so that there is no incongruity later when the hard-pressed regime shows leniency to the Jews (though not to their fortifications). The narrative of I 6:18–62 is thoroughly credible and coherent. The author describes, in the siege of the Akra and its aftermath, a campaign of his hero which failed and almost ended in disaster and did result in the humiliating destruction of the fortifications of the temple mount. Judas committed the bulk of his forces to the siege (I 6:19–20). He could use the rest of his army to block the difficult roads leading to Jerusalem from the coastal plain, but he could not afford to take the offensive against the large royal army while it still was in the coastal plain or the plateau. When the king's army circumvented the pitfalls of the difficult approaches to Jerusalem by marching through Idumaea and laying siege to the key Jewish fort of Beth-Zur, Judas made the difficult decision to raise the siege of the Akra and to confront the royal force at Beth-Zechariah, a short distance north of Beth-Zur. There, in a battle after sunrise, his brave army was defeated, and his brother Eleazar met a hero's death, stabbing the largest elephant from underneath. Judas and his men fell back upon the fortified temple, and only luck saved them from complete defeat. There is no reason to think that the author of First Maccabees or his sources invented a story so contrary to their purposes of glorifying the Hasmonaeans and of recording the providential acts of God. Indeed, we may assume that the author of First Maccabees was faithfully following his source. His account should be very close to that of the well-informed Common Source.

Coherent also is Josephus' paraphrase of I 6:18–62 at *AJ* xii 9.3–7.362–85. Whereas the author of First Maccabees will not mention Menelaus, Josephus at *AJ* xii 9.7.384–85 adds how Menelaus was executed at Beroia when Lysias persuaded the king that otherwise the Jews would not remain pacified. The gesture of executing Menelaus is indeed in character for a government anxious to end a provincial rebellion in order to hasten back to the capital and quell a revolt there.

The account here, as soon as we compare it to the others, invites suspicion. There were good reasons for Jason to keep silent at this point about the Akra (see NOTE on 5:24–27). Pietists and perhaps Jason himself believed that Jews were still subjected by God's will to Seleucid rule and that any siege of the Akra by Judas would therefore be a sinful act of rebellion, at best to be passed over in silence. The mere fact that Judas failed to take the Akra could be sufficient cause for Jason to omit the siege from his narrative. In Jason's account, Judas was not encumbered by the siege of the Akra. Had those been the true circumstances, Maccabaeus might have had a fairly large force free to challenge the numerically superior royal army at the edge of the hill country of Judaea. Even so, one could doubt that he would have dared to venture outside Judaea. Nevertheless, he is reported here to have done so in the vicinity of Modeïn, the first strategic point of Judaea near the roads leading from the heart of the Seleucid empire; see AB vol. 41, p. 231. But if Judas and his men had successfully made there an attack just before dawn on the royal tent as reported in vs. 15, surely the story would not have been forgotten, and the author of First Maccabees would not have passed over the heroic feat in silence. Stranger still, Jason, without mentioning Hasmonaean Eleazar, says that the largest elephant in the Seleucid force was slain near Modeïn. It would appear that Jason or his source has somehow distorted the battle of Beth-Zechariah, turning it from defeat to victory, moving it from Beth-Zechariah to Modeïn, and placing it before, not after, the Seleucid army laid siege to Beth-Zur, and before, not after, sunrise. In the aftermath, Jason presents as victors even the hopeless few who withstood a siege in the temple. How can such distortions have arisen?

There is some reason to believe that Jason was still following the Common

Source when he wrote vs. 1 and vs. 2, at least as far as "recruited abroad" (see NOTE on vs. 2, *He . . . recruited abroad*). If so, he deliberately omitted the report of the siege of the Akra. But Jason can hardly have produced the distortions in his subsequent narrative by deforming the Common Source. Nor is it likely that he simply invented the battle near Modeïn, though scholars have found other Greek historians, not only distorting reliable sources to make the account reflect more credit on the side they favored, but also inventing night attacks to liven up their narratives; see G. L. Barber, *The Historian Ephorus* (Cambridge: University Press, 1935), pp. 89–99, 141–42, and note especially how similar to our vss. 13–17 is the fictitious account of a night attack at Diodorus xi 9.3–10.4 (based on Ephorus). We have seen, however, Jason's laborious methods: elsewhere he misreads, misunderstands, and obscures difficulties, but he does not write lies.

Rather, we should assume that Jason found his strange sequence of events already reported in another source. In telling of the first expedition of Lysias and of the chronology of the Feast of Purification (II 10:1–8, 11:1–38), Jason found reason to desert the Common Source and follow his own inferences from the letters in ch. 11, whereas the parallel account in I 4:26–61 probably reflects the Common Source. Here, too, Jason could have deserted the Common Source while the author of First Maccabees followed it. In this case, he would have abandoned the Common Source to follow another which gave an account more to his liking. It is not difficult to suggest how such a distorted tradition could have grown up, especially in orally transmitted tales. Because of the nature of the case, our suggestions can only be speculation.

Characteristic of orally transmitted traditions is the existence of separate dramatic episodes which can be told in more than one order (let us call them "transposable episodes"). We have noted several transposable episodes in our chapter. All have been narrated in the sources in more than one place in the chronological sequence: the petition of Menelaus, the execution of Menelaus, the slaying of the elephant, and the siege of Beth-Zur. One can explain the changed placement of the execution of Menelaus without the hypothesis of an orally transmitted tradition (see NOTE on vss. 3–8). Even so, there may be yet other transposable episodes in our chapter. One is the feat wherein Judas, by an attack before sunrise on the enemy camp, prevents a hostile army from holding a base on the soil of Judaea (vss. 13–18). There is such a battle before sunrise in First Maccabees (4:6–22), but it is in a totally different context. See NOTE on vss. 13–18. Also possibly a transposable episode is the encampment at Modeïn; cf. I 16:4, and see NOTE on II 13:14.

What facts might have promoted the permutations of all these episodes in oral tradition?

The events which accompanied and followed the death of Antiochus IV flagrantly contradicted the predictions in Dan 11:40 – 12:13. Jason of Cyrene dealt with some of the resulting challenges to the veracity of Daniel by presenting the events of the reign of Antiochus V as having nothing to do with Daniel's prophecies: those prophecies would be fulfilled later (see pp. 67–69). Unlike Jason, however, some pious contemporaries of the events could have tried to fit them into the scheme of Daniel, and such efforts could have continued for decades, while the memory of the facts and their chronological order grew dimmer and dimmer.

Some events of 163–162 B.C.E. could indeed be made to fit the words of Dan 11:40–45. Antiochus V was a King of the North. He did come in wrath against the "Many" pious with cavalry and with a force that seemed like a flood. Antiochus V and his army naturally marched on Judaea from the north, from the heartland of the Seleucid empire. The roads ran through the coastal plain or the plateau. As soon as the king proceeded farther south than the northern border of Judaea, his royal tent, wherever he pitched it, could be said to be situated "between the seas and the glorious holy mountain" (i.e., between the Mediterranean, the Dead Sea, and the hills of Judaea or the temple mount; cf. Jerome *Commentarii in Danielem* on Dan 11:44–45). And after being deflected from his objective of fully subduing the Jews, Antiochus V soon did come, helpless, to his end. Other details in Dan 11:40–45 certainly did not fit the events, but probably the pious storytellers ascribed the discrepancies to God's inscrutable purposes and predicted ultimate complete fulfillment. Only a decade or two after the march of Antiochus V, nothing would prevent a pious storyteller from bringing the chariots of Dan 11:40 into his account of the child king's expedition, in the belief that he was telling the truth.

Pious storytellers might also unwittingly invent a battle of Modeïn. There appears to have been a tradition that Judas, as long as he enjoyed God's favor, prevented hostile armies from successfully encamping in Judaea; see NOTE on vss. 13–18. The northwesternmost strategic point within Judaea, the first point from which Judas could attack the camp of a royal army poised to invade Judaea, was Modeïn. The first possible royal campsites which could be said to fulfill Dan 11:45 would also be in the neighborhood of Modeïn, not of Beth-Zechariah; a straight line can be drawn on the map from the Mediterranean through Modeïn and Jerusalem to the Dead Sea, but one cannot be drawn from the Mediterranean through Jerusalem and Beth-Zur or Beth-Zechariah to the Dead Sea. Furthermore, Antiochus V had a large force, and yet he took the devious route by way of Beth-Zur. What deflected him from trying the direct route? Was it not a defeat suffered early in the campaign? Judas was known to have used successfully the cover of night (II 8:7). All these considerations could easily have given rise, after the lapse of at most one generation, to stories of a battle before dawn at Modeïn, and in oral tradition the story of the phantom battle could have attracted to itself details which belonged to other battles: the successful attack just before dawn, from the battle of Ammaus; the killing of the elephant, from the battle of Beth-Zechariah; and perhaps even the encampment at Modeïn, from the battle described in I 16:4–10.

We can also suggest how the defeats of the Jews disappeared from the account of the expedition of Antiochus V in Jason's source. Dan 11:45 predicted no further defeats for the Jews from the time when the King of the North encamped "between the seas" down to the king's death. The seer at Dan 12:12 predicted that the time of incredible troubles upon the Jews would have ended by August 12, 163 B.C.E., 1,335 days after the temple was desecrated on 25 Kislev (December 16), 167. Incompatible with the implications of Dan 11:45

was the defeat of Judas at Beth-Zechariah. Incompatible with the prediction at Dan 12:12 was the duration of the siege of the temple (I 6:51–61): Antiochus V did not withdraw before early 162 B.C.E. (see AB vol. 41, p. 325). Hence, the pious storytellers would tend to forget any defeats which came after the supposed battle of Modeïn or turn them into victories, the more so since the Jews' defeats were "moral victories." (The argument here supersedes the suggestions at AB vol. 41, p. 53; see also Introduction, Part III, n. 42.) When Jason wrote, he thus may have found the transposable episodes of our chapter being told and even being read as they are presented here. Jason may not be responsible for omitting to mention the siege of the Akra; it may have been omitted already by the storytellers.

Since the account in the Common Source was probably very close to that at I 6:18–63, the Common Source would have told of the siege of the Akra and perhaps also hinted that some pious Jews supported the hated garrison against Judas; it would have spoken openly of defeats suffered by the hero. Yet Jason seems to have believed that Judas enjoyed God's favor from his first victories (II 8) down through his triumph over Nicanor (II 14). Surely, then, Jason would have been glad to abandon the Common Source for a tradition which posed none of these difficulties. Let us call that tradition the "Legendary Source." If our reasoning is correct, Jason used the Legendary Source at least in writing vss. 9–18 and very likely also in vss. 22–23, where Jewish defeats have been turned into victories.

Josephus, as usual, in *AJ* xii 9.3–7.362–86 contradicts the account here wherever he can; see AB vol. 41, pp. 57–60, and NOTE on II 13:3–8.

1. The year 149 Sel. Mac. ran from September 22, 164, through October 9, 163 B.C.E. Other evidence supports the year date given here for the beginning of the expedition. See AB vol. 41, pp. 43–44, 315–19.

Jason probably displays the date in order to discredit the account in First Maccabees, where the siege, which precipitated the expedition described here, is given a date in 150 Sel., too late whether it is taken on the Babylonian or on the Macedonian form of the era (see AB vol. 41, p. 315).

How did Jason get the correct date? If it had been given in the Common Source or in the pagan history used in First Maccabees, the author of First Maccabees would never have made his mistake. At AB vol. 41, pp. 52–53, I suggest that Jason derived the date by interpreting Daniel. That suggestion is unlikely to be correct, for the following reason. The words of Daniel are notoriously flexible in the hands of interpreters. Jason did not wish to expose the prophecies of the seer to skepticism, especially when there was doubt as to the correct interpretation. He preferred ambiguous accounts which left it possible that the seer spoke the truth.

It is far more likely that Jason deduced the date in 149 Sel. Mac. from the mention of the sabbatical year in the Common Source and at I 6:49 and 53. The sabbatical year was indeed 149 Sel. Mac., and the expedition of Lysias and Antiochus V came in that part of the sabbatical year which also was 149 Sel. Bab. (AB vol. 41, pp. 315–18). Jason could discredit his rival by using the rival's own data!

On the other hand, Jason held that observance of the commandments brought the Jews victory, whereas the Common Source and First Maccabees admit that observance of the sabbatical year impeded the Jewish rebels. We can thus understand how Jason may have found it prudent to omit all reference to the sabbatical year. It is also possible that the abridger removed mention of the sabbatical year.

2. *Lysias . . . minister.* See NOTES on 10:11 and 11:1.

He . . . recruited abroad. Hanhart, following most Greek manuscripts (including A q L), reads *hekaston echonta dynamin* ("Each had a force"). Despite the good support in the manuscripts, the reading is impossible in the context. At the time of his accession, Antiochus V was probably only nine years old (AB vol. 41, p. 311). He could not have commanded a force independent of Lysias. Moreover, commands are divided for a purpose. Neither in First nor in Second Maccabees is it reported that in the campaign of Antiochus V and Lysias the Seleucid army split to operate in two directions. On the other hand, at I 6:29 the author notes that the Seleucid force had a large contingent of foreign mercenaries (cf. NOTE on 5:24). The reading of *l* is *ektos echonta dynamin* and is supported by La^LXBP. *Hoi ektos* is a common expression for "foreigners," especially in Polybius; see also Sir *Prologue* 5. However, it always appears with the definite article. Greek ms. 106, which at many other places preserves important old readings (see Kappler, *De memoria*, pp. 25–26) has a definite article before the corrupted word (*ton hekaston echonta dynamin*). The original text, in which words were not divided, probably had something like *PRAGMATÔNEKTÔNEKTOSECHONTA,* a puzzling configuration, which unwary scribes could easily have turned into any of the readings of the Greek manuscripts. I have taken that to have been the original reading and have translated accordingly.

Josephus' narrative at *AJ* xii 9.3.366, too, implies that the Seleucid expeditionary force had a large component of mercenaries recruited abroad (see Launey, *Recherches*, pp. 27–28).

There was nothing unusual in the employment of mercenaries by the Seleucid empire. Perhaps the Common Source found the fact worthy of notice here because of the possibility that the events fulfilled Zech 12:2–3. The strange "against Judaea" at I 6:48 may be an echo of Zech 12:2 rather than a translator's error; correct accordingly AB vol. 41, p. 322.

consisting . . . chariots. The figures here disagree with those at I 6:30, but both sets are exaggerated; see NOTE on 8:24. On the elephants in the Seleucid army, see AB vol. 41, pp. 320–21. On scythed chariots, see Bar-Kochva, *The Seleucid Army*, pp. 83–84.

3–8. Delete the second sentence of AB vol. 41, p. 174, n. 35, with its reference to this NOTE.

Josephus (*AJ* xii 9.8.383–85) puts the deposition and execution of Menelaus *after* the end of the campaign described in our chapter. If Jason had done the same, our verses would have come immediately after vs. 24. Josephus' narrative may be translated as follows:

". . . [Antiochus V] returned to Antioch, taking with him the high priest Onias, who was also called Menelaus. Indeed, Lysias advised the king to do away with Menelaus, if he wished the Jews to remain pacified and not cause him trouble. This man, he said, had been the original cause of the mischief, by persuading the king's father to force the Jews to desert the religion of their forefathers. Accordingly, the king sent Menelaus to Beroia in Syria and had him executed. Menelaus had been high priest for ten years and had been a wicked and impious man. For the sake of holding office, he had compelled his nation to violate their own laws. After Menelaus' death, Alcimus, also called 'Yakim,' became high priest."

Josephus does not tell of the strange means of execution and adds the length of Menelaus' tenure of the high priesthood, probably taking it from the list of high priests (see AB vol. 41, pp. 570–72). Unlike our writer in vs. 4 (see NOTE ad loc.), he presents Lysias as accusing Menelaus of instigating the persecution and the imposed cult. Despite these differences, the resemblance of the account in our verses to the one in Josephus is so strong that both must draw on the same source. Both accounts pretend to quote the verbal advice of Lysias, for which there was probably no documentary evidence. Both accounts exhibit tendencies known to have been characteristic of Onias IV. The surviving Oniad pretender must have written in indignant detail of how usurpers were raised to the high priesthood by wicked Seleucid kings. Onias IV also is known to have tried to blame non-Oniad Menelaus for the introduction of Hellenic practices into Jerusalem (including the gymnasium) and for the sack of the holy city in 169 B.C.E. Josephus, however, probably jumped to his own conclusion, first when he quoted Lysias, and farther on when he himself accused Menelaus of instigating the imposed cult. There is no evidence that Onias IV made that accusation. Although Josephus drew *AJ* xii 5.1.240–41 from Onias IV, he drew *AJ* xii 5.2–3.242–56 from other sources. See my article in *Studies Smith,* Part III, pp. 105–9, 121–22, and AB vol. 41, pp. 558–68.

Indeed, J. *AJ* xii 9.8.384–85 is incoherent. When Josephus says, "For the sake of holding office, he [Menelaus] had compelled his nation to violate their own laws," he contradicts the implications of his earlier quotation of Lysias, that Menelaus had to persuade an indifferent or reluctant king.

We ought, however, to consider the possibility that an official Seleucid source quoted Lysias' accusations against Menelaus. A royal decree deposing Menelaus as high priest could have cited them. If the Seleucid Chronicle treated the withdrawal of Antiochus V from Jerusalem in any detail, it might have quoted them. Even then, Lysias' words would have but slight value as evidence of Menelaus' responsibility for the imposed cult. Royal governments, when policies failed and had to be reversed, tended to save face by putting the blame on bad advisers, often falsely (cf. the effort of Ptolemy III at III 6:20–7:6, and Isaak Heinemann, "Wer veranlasste den Glaubenszwang der Makkabäerzeit?" *Monatsschrift für Geschichte und Wissenschaft des Judentums* 82 [1938], 153–54). But who would have preserved the royal decree deposing Menelaus down to the time of Josephus? The Seleucid Chronicle can hardly have been Josephus' source, for there is no other sign that he had read it.

Since we do not have the work of Onias IV or the Seleucid Chronicle or a copy of the decree deposing Menelaus, we must admit that one of those may have contained the charge that Menelaus instigated the imposed cult. But if so, Jason of Cyrene read the source and rightly rejected the assertion. Drawing on other sources, he knew that Jason the Oniad was to blame for Hellenizing Jerusalem and that Menelaus appealed for an end to the persecution (4:7–20,

11:29–32). Accordingly, the vaguer statement in vs. 4 would represent a correction by Jason of Cyrene of whatever source quoted Lysias' accusation. The ascription of the imposed cult to Menelaus thus comes from no good authority.

For the rest, we can confirm our hypothesis, that Josephus drew on Onias IV, by noting Josephus' subsequent narrative. After telling of Menelaus' death, Josephus (section 386) paraphrases I 6:63, on how Philip was defeated at Antioch, and goes on to tell how Onias IV, upon seeing the promotion of Alcimus, a non-Oniad, to the high priesthood, left for Ptolemaic Egypt and built his schismatic temple (sections 387–88). Josephus took sections 387–88 from the work of Onias IV. The paraphrase of I 6:63 interrupts the two sections taken from Onias IV because Josephus believed that such was the sequence of events: Onias IV left Judaea after Antiochus V and Lysias returned to Antioch. (Correct accordingly AB vol. 41, pp. 92–93, and p. 159, n. 337.) The whole argument there suffers from the improbability of my now-abandoned theories on the source *De Mortibus Persecutorum* (*DMP*). Furthermore, nothing indicates that Josephus ever saw the Common Source (alias *DMP*).

If Onias IV gave a detailed account of how and when non-Oniad usurpers gained and lost the high priesthood, and if he was the source both for our verses and for Josephus, how can it be that Josephus puts the deposition and execution of Menelaus at the end of the expedition, whereas here they appear at the beginning? The key to solving the problem may lie in Jason's efforts to leave it possible that prophecies in Daniel were true.

In Dan 9:26–27 there is first an allusion to the death of Onias III: it is to come at the beginning of the last of the seventy weeks of years; next there is an allusion to Jason the Oniad and his coup and its failure. See NOTE on 4:34. Next, the seer speaks of the dreadful wars which followed Jason's coup ("until the End there shall be war determined with desolations"). Thereupon, he tells how the time for "making strong the covenant" (*hagbēr bᵉrīt*) for the "Many" (pious Jews: see AB vol. 41, p. 46, n. 20) will occupy the entire final hebdomad, even though three and one half years of the period will see the cessation of Continual Offerings at the temple and the presence of the Abomination of Desolation upon the altar (see AB vol. 41, p. 147). One last event is mentioned in the predictions. It appears in the last clause of Dan 9:27, "until the decreed end is poured out on the desolator." Whether the "until" clause means that the desolator's end will come at the end of the three and one half years or at the end of the hebdomad, clearly the desolator will perish by the end of the week of years. I do not believe that the seer, by "desolator," meant Menelaus (I shall treat the matter in my commentary on Daniel), but Jason of Cyrene could easily jump to that conclusion. In a context which referred by epithet rather than by name to the two high priests, Onias III and Jason, the epithet "desolator" could well refer to the high priest Menelaus. For a Jew, the weeks of years mentioned in Dan 9 could hardly be anything but the seven-year cycles, each of which ended with a sabbatical year, and in my commentary on Daniel I shall present further arguments to establish that fact. Thus, Jason of Cyrene could have read Dan 9:26–27 as predicting that the death of Menelaus would come in or before the sabbatical year.

Accordingly, a believer like Jason of Cyrene would have been reluctant to say that Menelaus' death occurred after the sabbatical year (149 Sel. Mac.).

According to vs. 1, the campaign of Antiochus V began sometime within the sabbatical year, at the earliest in Tishri. Jason at least had to argue against persons who knew that the events of our chapter extended over more than five months and began after early spring of the sabbatical year, for that chronology could be deduced from the Common Source and from First Maccabees. The sabbatical year is mentioned at I 6:49, 53; the events are said to have come in the next Babylonian Seleucid year after the death of Antiochus IV; and two protracted sieges are described (I 6:31, 48–54). Even in the severely curtailed abridgment of Jason's own account, one of the protracted sieges still appears (vss. 19–22). Jews came to observe as a minor festival 28 Shebaṭ, the date of the withdrawal of Antiochus V from Jerusalem (*Megillat Ta'anit* 28 Shebaṭ). That date came not even five months after the beginning of the sabbatical and Macedonian Seleucid years. Thus in the space between the beginning of the sabbatical year and 28 Shebaṭ, there was hardly room for the events of our chapter. Jason could have felt compelled to conclude that the siege ended in 28 Shebaṭ, 162 B.C.E., in the post-sabbatical year, as in fact it did. Hence, to avoid the suggestion that the prophecy of Dan 9:26–27 was false, Jason may have moved the story of Menelaus' execution from its position in the work of Onias IV to where it stands in our chapter.

He still does not say explicitly that the death of Menelaus preceded the events of vss. 9–26. Indeed, the Seleucid regime may well have arrested Menelaus at the beginning of the expedition, knowing that his person was an irritant to Jews who might otherwise submit to Seleucid rule. And then the regime may well have kept the high priest alive until the end of the campaign in the belief that he and his supporters might still be useful. Then the account here would be compatible with the one given by Josephus and Onias IV. Josephus may have been unaware of the possible adverse implications for the veracity of Daniel. If so, he could follow the account of Onias IV without introducing the devious changes which Jason seems to have found necessary. Indeed, Josephus probably thought his own account contradicted the one here and felt his usual delight in contradicting the abridged history (see AB vol. 41, pp. 57–60).

The Common Source, too, may have named Menelaus as having been among the wicked Jews who urged Antiochus V to invade Judaea. It may also have reported his arrest and death, at what point we cannot tell. Jason seems to have ceased to follow the Common Source after vs. 2 (see introductory NOTE to this chapter).

My account here supersedes the argument at AB vol. 41, p. 53, which is far-fetched, if only because it depends on assuming Jason measured the three and one half years from the expedition of the Mysarch. See Introduction, Part III, n. 42.

3. When did Menelaus come before the king and Lysias? One might assume he came after the expedition had set out, but the Greek verb "came before" (*synemeixe*) is in the aorist tense and could also be translated by an English pluperfect. If Menelaus had come before them earlier, his mission could be Jason's version of the mission of the "men of the Akra" and the "wicked Israelites" in I 6:21–27, the mission which provoked the expedition.

Why does the writer say "Menelaus, *too*, came before them" (*synemeixe de*

. . . *kai Menelaos*)? Such a statement normally implies that others had come before the king. If that is the meaning here, the unabridged work of Jason must have contained an account of how appeals by the wicked induced Antiochus V to intervene in Judaea. If so, did the abridger remove the reference merely for the sake of brevity?

A new king could make his own appointment to the high priesthood (see AB vol. 41, pp. 75–76). Menelaus may already have received appointment from Antiochus V. If so, he was now seeking restoration to the high priestly prerogatives from which Judas Maccabaeus and his followers had excluded him. See NOTE on 10:1–8.

On the implied contrast here, between Menelaus and Onias III, see NOTE on 4:1–6.

4. *King of kings.* God. Cf. Enoch 9:4; Deut 10:17; Ps 136:3.

Menelaus . . . troubles. Menelaus' crimes had indeed provoked the first violence of the pious at Jerusalem (4:25–42). His usurpation of the high priesthood could even have been said to have caused Jason's coup and the disasters which followed upon it (4:23–24, 5:5–26). On the other hand, Menelaus could not have instigated the imposed cult. See pp. 100–3 and NOTE on vss. 3–8 and on vss. 5–8.

Beroia. Aleppo in Syria.

5–8. The Greek of vss. 5–6 is somewhat obscure and may be slightly corrupt. It is difficult to visualize how the rotating device worked. Where I have written "descending steeply," the Greek has only the adjective *apokrêmnon* ("sheer," "precipitous"); one would have expected a transitive participle ("driving down steeply"), as in La^{LXM}.

"The community joins in pushing" is my effort to render *hapantes prosôthousin*. One can imagine that an assembled crowd surrounded the culprit, who was placed just outside the tower; the crowd would then force him into the tower, so that all (*hapantes*) would have a share in the execution, as in the case of stoning. Niese and other scholars unable to make sense of *hapantes* have suggested reading *arantes prosôthousin* ("they take up and push"; Habicht, *2. Makkabäerbuch,* p. 267).

The method of execution is known to have been used by kings of the Persian empire (Herodotus ii 100; Ctesias *Persica,* FGH 688, F 15 [48, 51, 52]; Valerius Maximus ix 2, *Externa* 6; Ovid *Ibis* 315–16). What would be the immediate cause of the culprit's death? Grimm (ad loc.) suggests that the ashes were hot embers. Greek *spodos* can indeed have that meaning. The victim would then die by burning. But our passage and Valerius Maximus ix 2, *Externa* 6, suggest that the chamber of ashes stood ready over protracted periods. How could the embers have been kept hot? Therefore, it is likely that the victim sank into cold ashes and suffocated, as suggested by Walter W. How and J. Wells, *A Commentary on Herodotus* (Oxford: Clarendon Press, 1912), vol. 1, p. 217.

Menelaus was indeed a temple robber and perpetrator of heinous crimes (4:32–50). The writer takes pleasure in the thought that Menelaus, suspended in the ashes, was deprived of proper burial in the ground.

As usual, the writer stresses that God exacts precise retribution from the wicked. The abridged history gives no information about Menelaus' sins against the altar. Perhaps the abridger has omitted it. The regulations in the Torah on ritual purity and on sacrificial procedure contain many ambiguities. Jewish sects were bitterly divided over such matters. The sect which produced Enoch 89:73 found fault even with Menelaus' scrupulous Oniad predecessors. Menelaus' own sins against the altar are probably reflected at Test Moses 5:4, "For they will not follow God's truth; rather, some will defile the altar with . . . [there may be a gap in the text] offerings which they—who are not priests but slaves, sons of slaves—will put before the Lord." In the Testament of Moses these sins of the priests are sharply distinguished from the observances of the imposed cult: the sins are listed in ch. 5, and the imposed cult is described in ch. 8, as punishment. In Test Moses 8, Jews are said to participate in the imposed cult, but only under compulsion. Had Menelaus' sins against the altar included the instigation by him of the imposed cult, it is inconceivable that not only Jason of Cyrene and the abridger but also the author of the Testament of Moses (a contemporary of the events!) would have passed over the matter in silence.

On the sacredness of the altar fire, see Lev 6:6 and II 1:19–34 and NOTE on 10:3, *Using . . . stones*. On the sacredness even of the ashes, see Lev 4:12 and *Sifra* ad loc. (*pereq* 5, section 5, p. 18d Weiss), and Lev 6:3–4 and TB *Me-'ilah* 9a (bottom).

9. Surely the writer believes in the truth of his words here (cf. vss. 11 and 14). Nevertheless, there is no evidence the regime of Antiochus V intended to reinstitute the imposed cult or do anything more than put an end to Judas' siege of the Akra. But cf. I 6:59. The writer himself knew facts which contrasted with what he says here (see introductory NOTE to this chapter).

10–17. My argument (referred to at AB vol. 41, p. 231), to show how Jason came to tell of a battle at Modeïn when no battle took place there, is in the introductory NOTE to this chapter.

10–12. See p. 21, and NOTE on vs. 9.

13–17. Judas was soundly defeated by the army of Antiochus V and Lysias, as is recognized in I 6:47–54. Nevertheless, strong traditions later grew up which asserted that as long as Judas enjoyed the favor of God, he was able to keep hostile armies from maintaining themselves in camp on the soil of Judaea. The traditions had some basis in fact and in scriptural prophecy. See I 3:10–26 and (esp.) 42, 4:3–35. In the reign of Demetrius I, Nicanor, upon entering Judaea, may have had a skirmish with a force under Simon (see NOTE on 14:14–17), but thereafter he marched through Judaea as friend, not as foe (II 14:18–25; cf. I 7:27–29). By the time of the events narrated in our verses, the Jews of Galilee and Gilead had been evacuated to Judaea. Micah had promised (5:2–5) that at such a time Assyria would no longer be able to violate the borders of the Holy Land. On the Seleucid empire as the latter-day Assyria, see AB vol. 41, p. 210.

At I 3:10–26, 42, 4:3–35, the author of First Maccabees stresses how grave it was for a hostile army to encamp on the soil of Judaea, and he tells how Judas drove out the enemy by *a bold attack at dawn*. In II 8:9–36, his parallel to I 3:38–4:25, Jason of Cyrene says nothing of an attack at dawn and does not even mention that the battle occurred at Ammaus in Judaea. Even so, he seems to imply that battle did not take place on the soil of Judaea (II

8:33). Jason reports that Lysias invaded Judaea (11:5) and implies that Timotheus, too, did so (10:24–27) but says of neither that they pitched camp there. Only the treachery of Rodokos prevented Judas from foiling the besiegers of Beth-Zur (vss. 19–22). Thus Jason seems to be aware of a tradition that Judas kept hostile armies from successfully encamping in Judaea. But at the time of the victory reported in 8:9–36, for Jason the Age of Wrath had only partially ended: divine apparitions were not yet coming to the aid of Israel (see NOTE on 8:16–23). A pious narrator like Jason or his source would be pleased if he could put into the full Age of Mercy the theme of the dawn battle which kept the enemy from the Holy Land. Is that one reason why, in Jason's account, the episode of the battle before sunrise appears here in vss. 15–17, though the parallel account of the campaign of Antiochus V at I 6:33–46 clearly places the battle *after* sunrise?

Alexander Jannaeus must have suffered bitter criticism for his failures to keep hostile armies out of Judaea (J. *AJ* xiii 12.4–6.336–47, 13.5.372–14.2.383, 15.1–2.389–92). The writer here may intend to contrast Judas with Alexander Jannaeus.

13. Jason may have had good information on the Council of Elders, but he gives us only the briefest glimpse here of the role of that body in governing the Jews. Judas leaves the matter to the Elders' decision.

14. *Having entrusted the outcome.* So I translate the Greek idiom *epitropên didonai*, which regularly means "give power to decide."

for laws . . . institutions. These were not really at stake. See NOTE on vs. 9.

He pitched . . . Modeïn. Modeïn was the home town of the Hasmonaeans (I 2:1, 15–17, 28, 13:25), but Jason nowhere mentions that fact. In the introductory NOTE to this chapter we have considered how the fiction of a battle near Modeïn might have grown up. One would still like to know why both Jason and the author of I 16:4 take the trouble to record mere encampments at Modeïn. (Josephus' omission of the fact from his paraphrase, at *AJ* xii 7.3.226–27, is probably not significant; at that point Josephus is not paraphrasing First Maccabees but only repeating the erroneous account he wrote from faulty memory at *BJ* i 2.2.51–53. See AB vol. 41, p. 520.)

The locations of campsites are regularly reported in First Maccabees, but at I 16:4 we have not a real encampment but an ordinary spending of the night (in contrast, at I 11:6 an extraordinary spending of the night is recorded, one in the company of King Ptolemy VI). We may guess that our authors and their contemporaries saw something special about spending the night at Modeïn. Did they connect the literal meaning of the name ("those who make known") with a scriptural text (Jer 16:21; Hab 3:2; or Ps 76:2), so as to give the fact prophetic significance?

15. *After . . . password.* See NOTE on 8:23, *password "God's help."*

he picked . . . men. Against the enormous enemy force, Judas did not even use his entire army!

two thousand. At I 6:42 the number is only six hundred.

stabbed . . . howdah. The Greek is partly corrupt. "Stabbed" (*synekentêse*) is Grimm's emendation of the Greek manuscripts' *synethêke* ("put together," "constructed"), which makes no sense in the context. The emendation is supported by La[LXBMP], all of which have "slew"; Sy has "smashed and cast away."

My "man in its howdah" is based on the reading of AV, *tôi kat' oikian onti* ("the one in the building"). If the rendering looks forced, it would be easy to emend the Greek to *tôi kathizonti* ("its rider"; cf. Greek II Reigns 22:11), in accordance with La^X (*sessore*). Cf. I 6:43–46. Jason characteristically passes over in silence the heroic death of Judas' brother Eleazar; see AB vol. 41, p. 80.

17. Cf. Ps 46:6. Not perceiving the allusion to Ps 46, the scribe of V (and La^BM) found it more natural to attach the first clause of our verse to the end of vs. 16 ("withdrew victorious as day was already dawning").

18. Cf. I 6:47. According to the writer, the king no longer dared to take the direct invasion routes from the coastal plain into the hill country of Judaea; see AB vol. 41, p. 269. Since the king intended to invade Judaea (vs. 13), *katepeirase tous topous* here probably means "tried to invade their territory" (so La^M and probably Sy) rather than "tried to take the strong points" (so La^V and Grimm). Indeed, Beth-Zur is the only strong point mentioned.

19. On Beth-Zur, see AB vol. 41, pp. 269–70, 273. The heaping up of verbs, with no "and" in between, contributes to brevity and probably shows the hand of the abridger. The passage also displays other characteristics of his style: assonance and groups of three coordinated words, either with or (as here) without conjunctions in between (Richnow, *Sprache und Stil,* pp. 103–5; cf. 14:25).

According to I 6:31, the defenders of Beth-Zur withstood the siege for "many days." Our verse says much the same, though the rhetoric sounds more favorable to the Jews. Jason may have returned to draw on the Common Source at this point.

20. Even if hard pressed by the shortage of food in the sabbatical year (see I 6:49, 53), Judas would have done his utmost to supply strategic Beth-Zur.

21. The author of First Maccabees might have been glad to excuse Judas' defeats by blaming them on the treason of others, but the treachery of Rodokos is mentioned only here. Hence, the Common Source probably did not treat it. Rodokos' name is not Greek, Hebrew, or Aramaic, but Jews in this period also bore Iranian names, as do several of the elders who translated the Torah into Greek, as listed in Aristeas to Philocrates 49–50. In a letter of July 22, 1979, Professor Martin Schwartz of the University of California at Berkeley writes, "The name could be early West Middle Iranian (in this period it is difficult to distinguish Middle Persian from Middle Parthian). 'Rodokos' would be 'Mr. Rose,' 'Rosy.' The Iranian form would be **Wardak* or **Wurdak* or **Wṛdak,* adjectival (or diminutive) from the word for 'rose,' Old Iranian **wṛdă-*. The *-ok-* in the name would be for *-ak,* by way of the influence of *o* in the adjoining syllable(s). While we would expect **wṛd-* to be rendered by Greek *Ord-* (or the like), the form would be close enough to Greek *rhodon* ('rose') to be influenced by it."

executed. The Greek has a euphemism, *katekleisthê* ("was closed up"). See NOTE on 4:34, *did away with.*

22–26. Again, as in vs. 19, the heaped-up verbs, with no "and" in between, probably show the hand of the abridger; so do the heaped-up verbs connected by "and" (*kai*) in vs. 23. Again the passage exhibits characteristics of his style:

assonance and groups of three coordinated verbs (Richnow, *Sprache und Stil,* pp. 104–7).

22. **The writer turns defeat into victory.** The defenders of Beth-Zur fought in order to hold it against the king, not in order to receive the handclasp of peace. The writer does not even say that the defenders withdrew from Beth-Zur! Cf. I 6:49–50. Perhaps here, too, we may see the influence of the Legendary Source; see introductory NOTE to this chapter.

My "came off second best with" renders *edeuterologêsen,* an idiom taken from the language of the theater. A *deuterologos* is an actor who takes the second role in a play, inferior to the one who plays the main role. Hence, literally, *edeuterologêsen* means "he played the second role," just as *eprôtologêsen* means "he was the main actor." In English slang, one might render our verb by "was upstaged by" or "played second fiddle to."

23. Delete the reference to this NOTE at AB vol. 41, p. 56, n. 10. I have changed my mind.

The revolt of Philip and the king's oath and his peace agreement and perhaps his respectful visit to the temple are also found at I 6:55–62(beginning) and could have been derived from both the Common Source and the Seleucid Chronicle. On the other hand, the writer here gives no hint of the desperate plight of the Jews who were resisting the king and does not even say that they were besieged in the temple. Cf. I 6:52–54. Jason here may have been following the Legendary Source; see introductory NOTE to this chapter. On the possibility that Judas himself had withdrawn from the seemingly hopeless struggle, see AB vol. 41, pp. 322–23.

The writer here, unlike the author of I 6:55–56, sharply distinguishes the Philip here from the one who was present at the deathbed of Antiochus IV; see NOTE on 9:29. One may be sure that Jason contradicted the rival account deliberately and on the basis of good evidence; see AB vol. 41, p. 84. Jason's evidence may have been the Seleucid Chronicle, if read more carefully by him than by the Hasmonaean propagandist.

was worsted. The words conceal the desperate plight of the resisting Jews but in themselves are not necessarily false. The Seleucid army did fail in its attempt to take the temple by storm or to get the defenders to surrender quickly.

left in charge. The word (*apoleleimmenos*) occurs in an inscription from the Seleucid empire and may mean no more than "appointed"; see Jeanne and Louis Robert, "Bulletin épigraphique," REG 76 (1963), 180–81, and Baruch Lifshitz, "Sur le culte dynastique des Séleucides," RB 70 (1963), 78(last paragraph)–80. Nevertheless, the expression and related words seem always to be used when a king appoints men and departs (cf. 5:22–23). This may have been the case also in the inscription (see Robert, REG 76 [1963], 181; Lifshitz, RB 70 [1963], 80).

had rebelled. So La[VBM], supported by Sy. The Greek verb (*aponoeisthai*) literally means "lose all sense" or "be desperate." Its meaning here is confirmed through the use of the related noun *aponoia* to mean "rebellion" (Antigonus Nicaeanus *apud* Hephaestion Astrologus 2.18, cited by the *Greek-English Lexicon,* s.v. *aponoia*).

conceded privileges. Gr. *ephilanthrôpêse.* The verb is related to the noun *philanthrôpa* at 4:11, which I translated "humane concessions." Antiochus V indeed may have restored those privileges of the temple which were included in the reference at 4:11.

24–26. On the report that the king granted an audience to Maccabaeus, see below. What sources served Jason for the rest of our passage? Though the events do not directly involve the Jews, the author of the Common Source could well have regarded it as part of the Age of Wonders if a Seleucid chief minister defended a peace agreement with the Jews against the objections of the hostile citizens of Ptolemais. If Hegemonides later became involved with the Jews, all the more would that author have recorded what we have here. On the other hand, it would have been only natural for the Seleucid Chronicle to tell of the acts of the king and his chief minister.

24. The writer passes over in silence the king's "treacherous" destruction of the fortifications of the temple mount (cf. I 6:62) as well as the appointment about the same time of Alcimus to the high priesthood (cf. J. *AJ* xii 9.7.385; on Josephus' source, see NOTE on vss. 3–8). Both Jason and the storytellers who produced the Legendary Source would have found the episodes difficult to reconcile with their own beliefs. See introductory NOTE to this chapter.

He . . . Maccabaeus. There may indeed have been such an audience, recorded in the Common Source, but the author of First Maccabees seems to have taken care to give heroic Judas no role in the unfortunate events; see AB vol. 41, pp. 322–23. It is also possible that Jason or his source jumped to the conclusion.

Hegemonides. The name is very rare, but a monument at Dyme, in Greece, dedicated to Antiochus IV, to the queen Laodice, and to their son Antiochus, was set up by a certain Hagemonidas. "Hagemonidas" is a dialectical variant of "Hegemonides." The man of Dyme probably was a professional soldier identical to the commander here. See Christian Habicht, "Der Stratege Hegemonides," *Historia* 7 (1958), 376–78.

commander . . . Gerrhenes. The Gerrhenes have been wrongly identified by modern scholars, and far-reaching wrong conclusions have been drawn therefrom on the administrative history of the Seleucid empire. The reading "Gerrhenes" (*Gerrênôn*) may be taken as certain, supported as it is by V q^{-107} *L'*$^{-542}$ La. No scribe accustomed to writing biblical Greek would turn a familiar name into the one found only here in the Greek Bible. The *Gennêrôn* of A is unparalleled anywhere and is probably a mere slip of the pen.

Abel (p. 456) identifies the Gerrhenes as the people of the Gerrha in the Sinai peninsula, at the west end of Lake Sirbonis, east of Pelusium. See Map 3. However, he himself recognized that this Gerrha lay inside Ptolemaic territory, far outside the Seleucid borders. That Strabo writing later (xvi 33–34, C 760) put the borderlands of Phoenicia and Judaea by Lake Sirbonis proves nothing for Abel's theory, and even Strabo does not make the Gerrha in Sinai a border point.

Grimm (p. 191), followed by Habicht (*2. Makkabäerbuch*, p. 270), takes the Gerrhenes to be the people of Gerar, south of Gaza and west of Beersheba (the site has not been located with certainty). But Gerar in Greek is always *Gerara,* and wherever the place was, it lay inland and could have had no strategic significance for the Seleucid empire at this time. How, then, could its name serve as the boundary point for the province of a Seleucid commander?

Moreover, for this period, there is no other evidence that Gerar was inhabited or that in its vicinity there were people named for it. See Y. M. Grintz, "Gerar," Enc. Jud., VII (1972), 432.

Modern scholars have been led astray partly because they jumped to the conclusion that Hegemonides' province was similar to that given Simon the Hasmonaean at I 11:59 (see, e.g., Bengtson, *Strategie,* II, 176–81). I hope to argue elsewhere that Simon's province was the product of later developments and that in the reign of Antiochus V the Mediterranean coast of Palestine was still under the direct supervision of the *stratêgos* of Coele-Syria and Phoenicia.

Our context here supports a different interpretation. "Gerrha" was the native name of an important point in the narrowest part of the valley of Lebanon (Polybius v 46.1–3), east and slightly south of Beirut (see Map 8). Later it was called "Chalkis." See A. H. M. Jones, *The Cities of the Eastern Roman Provinces* (Oxford: Clarendon Press, 1937) pp. 234, 256, 453. This Gerrha was not a city in the Greek sense until sometime around the end of the second century B.C.E. (ibid., p. 256). Hence, Jason uses the precise Seleucid nomenclature: the area receives not the name of a city but that of the ethnic group living there.

Gerrha's importance at this time may well have lain in the fact that the area from Ptolemais northeastward to Gerrha included Galilee and other territory, in all of which the Jews had either holdings or claims (Num 34:7; Josh 19:24–39, 47; Judg 1:31 [Acco is Ptolemais]). Jews are known later to have been settled even in Chalkis-Gerrha (*Megillat Ta'anit* 17 Adar). Num 34:7 would have allowed Jews to aspire to land far to the north of Ptolemais and Gerrha, but at this time members of the Chosen People probably pressed no such extreme claims. Still, Jews had made no secret of the wide territories which God had promised would be theirs as soon as their term of punishment should reach its end. The inhabitants of the region of Ptolemais certainly felt menaced by the resurgent Jews (vss. 25–26; I 5:14–23, and AB vol. 41, p. 293). The campaign of Simon narrated in I 5:21–23 probably evacuated only the Jews of *western* Galilee, for Bacchides in his expedition of 160 B.C.E. found "many" to slaughter at Messaloth-in-Arbela (I 9:2). Though I described those slaughtered at Messaloth-in-Arbela as "innocent" (AB vol. 41, p. 372), the Seleucid army and the native gentiles living along the Ptolemais-Gerrha line may have viewed the remaining Jews of Galilee as a threat.

By withdrawing without compelling Judas and his men to lay down their arms, Antiochus V was at least leaving it possible for a Jewish force to try to restore to their old homes those evacuated by Simon and perhaps also leaving the way open for further Jewish expansion northward. Although Samaria lay between Judaea proper and Galilee, Judas and his men seem throughout to have moved freely through Samaria (I 5:21–23, 52–53; II 15:1–5; AB vol. 41, pp. 236, 294, 339, 386). Thus the appointment of Hegemonides may have had the purpose of checking the northward aspirations of the Jews and allaying the fears of the gentiles who lived along the Ptolemais-Gerrha line. If so, vss. 25–26 show that the citizens of Ptolemais still felt insecure. Indeed, the very location, so far north of Judaea proper, of Hegemonides' theater of operations indicated a retreat of Seleucid power, even if the provinces to the south and west of Judaea still were loyal to the regime and able to beat off Judas' men (I

5:55–68; II 10:14–15, and 12:32–37 [Judas suffered heavy losses in Idumaea and could hold no territory there]; I 6:31).

If Jason, too, so saw the appointment of Hegemonides as arising from the apprehensions of the Seleucid regime and of the gentiles to the north of Judaea, he had good reason to record the appointment as yet another testimony to the power of the Jews under Judas.

Georgius Syncellus (*Chronographia,* vol. I, p. 534 Dindorf) or his source seems to have understood our passage in the same way as I have, for he says that, after destroying the walls of Jerusalem (cf. I 6:62), Antiochus V gave Judas authority up to Ptolemais (*archein mechri Ptolemaïdos*).

25–26. Jews recorded the date of the departure of Antiochus V from Jerusalem (*Megillat Ta'anit* 28 Shebaṭ); it was equivalent to January 5, 162 B.C.E., if by the defective calendar, or to March 5, if by the fully intercalated calendar (see AB vol. 41, pp. 275–76, 325).

On the hostile attitude at Ptolemais toward pious Jews, see 6:8. On the fear at Ptolemais of the resurgent Jews, see NOTE on vs. 24, *commander . . . Gerrhenes.* On the status of Ptolemais in the Seleucid empire so as to be able to nullify the peace agreement, see NOTE on 6:8–9.

25. *terms.* The Greek word (*diastalseis*) occurs only here, but the related verb *diastellein* is used to mean "put under a separate heading in an agreement," "single out for special treatment in an agreement" (14:28; Preisigke, *Wörterbuch,* I, 361). The Latin translators guess at the meaning. La^L has "oath" (*iuramentum*); La^X, "treaty" (*fedus*); La^B, "agreements" (*pacta*).

26. We can see the hand of the abridger again, in the heaped-up verbs without conjunctions and in the final summary sentence.

We cannot tell whether Jason himself or the abridger omitted to mention that the king's army on returning to Antioch defeated Philip (I 6:63; J. *AJ* xii 9.7.386).

XVII. THE REIGN OF DEMETRIUS I: THE HIGH PRIEST ALCIMUS AND THE CAREER AND FALL OF THE GOVERNOR NICANOR
(14:1–15:36)

14 ¹ Three years later, Judas and his men received the news that Demetrius son of Seleucus had sailed into the harbor of Tripolis with a strong force and a fleet ² and had become master of the country and had done away with Antiochus and his guardian Lysias.

³ There was a certain Alcimus, who had previously been appointed high priest but had voluntarily defiled himself during the time of peace. Perceiving that there was no way for him to be secure or to have access henceforth to the holy altar, ⁴ he approached King Demetrius in about the year 151 and presented him with a gold crown and palm along with some of the customary gifts from the temple. On that day, Alcimus said nothing. ⁵ However, he found an opportune time for his mad designs when he was summoned by Demetrius to a meeting of the royal council and asked, "What are the present mood and aspirations of the Jews?" He replied, ⁶ "Among the Jews, those who are called 'Asidaioi,' under the leadership of Judas Maccabaeus, are feeding the flames of war and are in rebellion and refuse to allow your kingdom to become tranquil. ⁷ As a result, I have been deprived of the distinction of my forefathers (I mean, the high priesthood). I have come here now ⁸ for two reasons: first, because I have the king's interests truly at heart; and second, because I am seeking the welfare of my own countrymen. The folly of the persons I just mentioned has brought upon our entire nation no small misfortune. ⁹ Please take note of all this, Your Majesty, and take thought for our country, and bring your provident intervention to bear upon the land and upon our sorely beset nation with the ready kindness you show to all, ¹⁰ for as long as Judas survives, it is impossible for the commonwealth to have peace."

¹¹ When he had finished speaking, the rest of the Friends, who

were ill-disposed toward Judas, were very quick to egg Demetrius on. 12 He immediately appointed Nicanor, who had been commander of the elephant corps, and conferred upon him the title of governor of Judaea and dispatched him 13 with orders to do away with Judas, disperse his men, and restore Alcimus as high priest of the greatest temple.

14 The gentiles settled in Judaea, who had fled Judas, flocked to meet Nicanor, thinking that the Jews' defeats and disasters would be their own victories.

15 . . . When they[a] heard of the arrival of Nicanor and of the gentiles' hostile efforts, they strewed dust upon themselves and prayed to Him Who established His people forever, Who never fails to help His portion by manifesting His power. 16 When the commander gave the order, they immediately set out from there and met them at the village of Dessau. 17 Simon, Judas' brother, had already come to meet Nicanor and had suffered a slight setback because of the unexpected arrival of the opposition. 18 Nevertheless, upon hearing of the manly valor continually exhibited by Judas and his men and of their courage in their struggles for their country, Nicanor shrank from seeking a decision through bloodshed.

19 Accordingly, he sent Poseidonius and Theodotus and Mattathias to give and receive the handclasps of peace. 20 After the terms had been subjected to considerable scrutiny and the commander had consulted the rank and file and their opinion was clearly unanimous, they consented to make the treaty. 21 They fixed a day on which they were to reach agreement through closed discussions. From each side came a chariot, and they set up chairs. 22 Judas deployed ready men-at-arms at strategic points for fear of sudden treachery on the part of the enemy. Their conversation resulted in agreement.

23 Nicanor spent time at Jerusalem and conducted himself irreproachably. He dismissed the undisciplined mobs that had thronged around him. 24 Continually he kept Judas in his company. He was sincerely fond of the man. 25 He urged him to marry and beget children. He did marry; he experienced tranquility; he partook of life's blessings.

26 Alcimus, however, on perceiving their mutual goodwill, took a copy of the treaty they had made and came before Demetrius, saying that Nicanor had hostile designs against the state: indeed, he had appointed as his deputy Judas, the plotter against Demetrius' kingdom.

---

[a] I.e., Judas and his followers.

27 The king was infuriated and enraged by the slanders uttered by the archvillain. He wrote to Nicanor, saying that he was annoyed over the treaty and ordering him to make haste to send Maccabaeus in chains to Antioch.

28 When the news reached Nicanor, he was perplexed and troubled: should he revoke the terms of the treaty, though the man had done no wrong? 29 Since, however, he could not oppose the king, he sought an opportunity to carry out the order through trickery. 30 Maccabaeus noticed that Nicanor was behaving toward him with less cordiality and that he had turned rude in their usual meetings. Believing that the lack of cordiality could have no good cause, he assembled a good many of his men and went into hiding from Nicanor.

31 On realizing that he had been cleverly outsmarted by Judas, Nicanor went to the greatest and holiest of temples as the priests were offering the regular sacrifices and demanded that the man be handed over to him. 32 When the priests declared on oath that they did not know the whereabouts of the person he was seeking, 33 Nicanor stretched forth his right hand against the temple and swore, "If you do not hand Judas over to me, I shall raze to the ground this shrine of your God and tear down the altar, and I shall build in its place a fine temple to Dionysus." 34 Having finished speaking, he left. The priests stretched forth their hands toward heaven and prayed to the One Who has always been the champion of our people, saying, 35 "You, Lord of all, though You are in need of nothing, chose to have a temple of Your habitation in our midst. 36 Now, Holy One, Lord of all sanctification, preserve forever from defilement this newly purified house."

37 Razis, one of the elders of Jerusalem, was a patriot of excellent reputation, one who was called "father of the Jews" because of his love for his people, yet he was denounced to Nicanor. 38 Indeed, in the preceding time of war he had been brought to trial on a charge of practicing Judaism, and with the greatest zeal he had exposed himself, body and soul, to danger for the sake of Judaism. 39 Inasmuch as Nicanor wished to make a public demonstration of the hostility he felt toward the Jews, he sent more than five hundred soldiers to arrest him. 40 He believed that by arresting him and showing him disrespect he would deal a severe blow to the Jews.

41 The troops were about to capture the tower and were trying to force the outer door and were calling for fire to burn the doors. Since he was trapped, Razis fell upon his own sword, 42 nobly preferring to die rather than fall into the hands of men accursed and suffer vio-

lence which did not befit his nobility. 43 However, in his haste and anxiety, he aimed his blow badly, and as the troops poured through the entrances, he ran bravely up upon the wall and courageously hurled himself down upon the troops. 44 They quickly drew back and left a gap, so that he came down in the midst of the vacant space. 45 He was still breathing, and in the ardor of his passion, he stood up though his blood was gushing and his wounds were excruciating. Nevertheless, he dashed through the troops and stood upon a precipitous rock. 46 He was already almost completely drained of blood when he pulled out his intestines, and grasping them in both hands, he flung them at the troops and prayed to Him Who is master of life and of the spirit to restore them to him. Such was the manner of his death.

15 1 Nicanor, on learning that Judas and his men were in the region of Samaria, plotted to take advantage of the day of rest to attack them when he could do so in perfect safety. 2 However, the Jews who were being forced to accompany him said, "Do not perpetrate so savage and barbarous a massacre, but give due respect to the day which has been preeminently honored with sanctification by Him Who sees all." 3 The heinous sinner asked in reply, "Is He Who gave the command to keep the Sabbath day master in heaven?" 4 When they answered, "It is the living LORD Himself, the master in heaven, Who has given the order to observe the Seventh Day," 5 Nicanor said, "I, too, who give the command to take up arms and carry out the king's orders, am master, on earth!" Even so, he did not succeed in carrying out his cruel intention.

6 Nicanor, with the utmost boastfulness and arrogance, resolved to take up all the arms of Judas and his men and set them up as a monument of his putting them to rout. 7 Maccabaeus, however, never ceased to be confident, having every hope that he would get help from the LORD. 8 He exhorted his men not to be intimidated by the onset of the gentiles but to keep in mind the succor they had received before from Heaven, and so, to look forward now, too, to the victory the Almighty would give them. 9 By encouraging them with quotations from the Torah and the Prophets and by reminding them also of the struggles they had come through, he whetted their zeal. 10 He roused their anger and urged them on, as he held before them at the same time the broken faith of the gentiles and their violation of their oaths. 11 He armed each of his men not so much with the security

afforded by shields and spears as with the encouragement derived from the good words.

Furthermore, by telling them of a trustworthy dream, he roused their spirits beyond measure. 12 His vision was as follows: he saw Onias, the late high priest, a good man and true, of modest bearing and mild manner, whose utterances were always fitting, who from childhood had practiced every aspect of virtue. Onias stretched forth his hands to pray for the entire company of the Jews. 13 Thereafter, in the same posture, there appeared a man remarkable for his white hair and his dignity; he had a certain majesty about him, marvelous and magnificent. 14 On being asked, Onias replied, "This lover of his brethren, who offers many prayers for our people and for the holy city, is Jeremiah, the prophet of God." 15 Jeremiah stretched forth his hand to give Judas a golden sword, and as he gave it to him, he addressed him as follows: 16 "Take the holy sword as a gift from God, and with it shatter our enemies."

17 The altogether eloquent words of Judas had the power to stimulate the hearer to virtue and to fill the minds of the young with manly valor. Encouraged by them, his men resolved, not merely to march, but bravely to charge and with all manly valor close with the enemy and decide the issue, because the city and the sanctuary were at stake. 18 Indeed, their fear for wives and children and for brothers and kinsmen was of less concern to them; their greatest and foremost fear was for the hallowed temple. 19 Deep, too, was the anguish, which perturbed those shut up in the city, over the battle in the open country.

20 All now were awaiting the impending trial of strength. The enemy were about to engage; their army was drawn up for battle; the beasts were posted in an advantageous position; and the cavalry was positioned on the flanks. 21 On seeing the approach of the enemy masses, their military equipment in all its variety, and the ferocity of their beasts, Judas raised his hands toward heaven and called upon the LORD Who does wonders, knowing that not by strength in arms but according to His judgment does He grant victory to the worthy. 22 In his prayer he spoke as follows: "You, Master, sent Your angel in the time of Hezekiah, king of Judah, and he destroyed no fewer than one hundred eighty-five thousand from the camp of Sennacherib. 23 Now, too, LORD of the heavens, send a good angel before us to inspire fear and trembling. 24 Let those who have come blaspheming against Your holy people be terrified by the might of Your arm." With these words he ended his prayer.

25 Meanwhile, Nicanor and his men advanced to the sound of trumpets and pagan war hymns. 26 Judas and his men, uttering invocations and prayers, joined battle with the enemy. 27 As they fought with their hands, all the while praying to God in their hearts, they laid low no fewer than thirty-five thousand, rejoicing greatly in God's manifestation of His power. 28 Having brought the battle to an end, they were joyfully leaving the field when they recognized the fallen body of Nicanor in full armor. 29 There was shouting and tumult, and then they began to praise the LORD in the language of their forefathers. 30 The man who in every way had played the chief role, body and soul, in the struggle of his fellow Jews, the man who had throughout maintained his youthful love for members of his people, ordered that Nicanor's head and his arm up to his shoulder be cut off and brought to Jerusalem.

31 On his arrival there, he called together the members of his nation and had the priests stand before the altar. Then he summoned the men from the Akra 32 and showed them the head of the abominable Nicanor and the hand of the blasphemer, which he had boastfully stretched forth against the sacred house of the Almighty. 33 Cutting out the tongue of the impious Nicanor, he said he would feed it to the birds, bit by bit, and he ordered that the arm be hung opposite the temple as retribution for Nicanor's mad audacity. 34 All offered praises toward heaven, to the LORD Who had manifested Himself, saying, "Blessed is He Who has preserved His Place from defilement." 35 He had the severed head of Nicanor hung from the Akra as a clear and evident token for all of the LORD's succor. 36 By a unanimous vote of the people they decreed that they would by no means let that day pass unmarked, but that they would keep as a special day the thirteenth of the twelfth month, called Adar in Aramaic, the day before the Day of Mordechai.

NOTES

14:1 – 15:36. The parallel account is in I 7.

In our chapters the wicked priest Alcimus has the role played by Simon of the clan of Bilgah in 3:4–6; Nicanor in his mission, threats, and failure has the role played by Heliodorus in 3:7–30, but in his threats, failure, and death Nicanor also has the role played by Antiochus IV in 6:1 – 10:8.

14:1–4. The chronological information here is important for determining the methods used by Jason of Cyrene, but it is also perplexing because of our scanty precise data from other sources and because of the inherent ambiguities of the Greek expressions for measuring duration. What was the precise date of the accession of Demetrius I? From what point were the "three years" measured, and how were they counted?

The chronological evidence for the reign of Demetrius I is collected at Schürer (New English version), I, 129. For dating Demetrius' accession, there is still nothing better than the argument of Bickerman ("Makkabäerbücher," PW, XIV [1930], 783): Demetrius made his dramatic escape from Rome after the arrival there of the news that the Roman ambassador Gnaeus Octavius had been murdered while on a mission to the Seleucid empire (Polybius xxxi 2, 11–15; Appian Syriakê 46–47). The murder is dated firmly in 162 B.C.E. (Julius Obsequens 15). Demetrius escaped on board a regular sailing ship, that is, before the stormy season on the Mediterranean, which began November 3 (Vegetius iv 39). On the other hand, the author of First Maccabees derived his Seleucid dynastic dates from a well-informed pagan source, and he sets Demetrius' accession in 151 Sel. Mac., which began September 29, 162 B.C.E.

Of lesser importance is the fact that documents at Babylon were still being dated by the regnal years of Antiochus V on October 16, 162 B.C.E. (Schürer [New English version], I, 129), or even on January 11, 161 (see Otto Mørkholm, "A Greek Coin Hoard from Susiana," Acta Archaeologica 36 [1965], 136, n. 7). The Seleucid authorities at Babylon could have been slow to recognize Demetrius I as king. During the months which followed, the power in the eastern Seleucid provinces was Timarchus, the satrap of Media, a rebel against Demetrius. Timarchus' brother was Herakleides, an ardent partisan of the line of Antiochus IV (AB vol. 41, p. 398). Thus Demetrius' accession came between September 29 and November 30, 162 B.C.E.

Alcimus, who faced opposition among his own people (vs. 3), had to seek confirmation as soon as Antiochus V, the king who had appointed him, ceased to rule because the appointment of the high priest even under the current Jewish law was a royal prerogative (see AB vol. 41, pp. 75–76). If the date here, 151 Sel., is on a completely uncorrected local Jewish version of the Babylonian Seleucid era (see AB vol. 41, pp. 274–76, 342), Alcimus waited at least until January 26, 161, before approaching Demetrius. If the date is on a correct Babylonian calendar, Alcimus waited at least until March 25, 161. Even the shorter wait is unlikely. Hence, the date here must be on the Macedonian Seleucid era. See also NOTE on vs. 4, he . . . 151.

The most natural way to take "three years later" is as measuring the interval from the last event in ch. 13, or at least from the beginning of the long chain of events there, the expedition of Antiochus V. Unless there is some compelling reason, we should not look for other ways to understand the interval. At 4:23 and 10:3 the expression "x years later" (meta x-etê chronon) means "exactly or approximately x full years and at least x−1 full years plus a fraction" (see pp. 59–60 and NOTE on 4:7–38). Here, if Jason is correct and if the interval is measured from the events of ch. 13, the expression cannot mean that. Jason himself dated the beginning of the expedition of Antiochus V in 149 Sel. (13:1). Even if the expedition terminated in that same year, the interval between it and an event of early 151 Sel. Mac. could not be given as three full years or even as two years plus a fraction.

At AB vol. 41, p. 91, I assumed that *x-etês* in Greek always means "of at least x − 1 year-long periods plus a fraction." That assumption cannot be proved. In AB vol. 41, pp. 91–103, on the basis of that assumption, I went on to formulate farfetched hypotheses and departed from the natural way of understanding the three-year interval. There is a much simpler and better course: to assume that Jason, like other Greeks, could be inconsistent in his use of expressions of duration (see Appendix VII), and to see here, too, an instance of Jason's urge to contradict a rival's chronology. Jason contradicted the absolute chronology of First Maccabees by giving at 13:1 the correct 149 Sel. rather than the erroneous 150 Sel. of I 6:20 (see AB vol. 41, pp. 315–19). Here he would contradict also his rival's relative chronology. For Jason himself, the interval between 149 and 151 Sel. Mac. indeed fell within the three calendar years 149, 150, and 151 Sel. Mac. But the author of First Maccabees erroneously dated the expedition of Antiochus V not in 149 but well inside 150 Sel. (I 6:20–31). The interval between an event well inside 150 Sel. and an event at any time within 151 Sel. could not fall within three years; the end of that interval in no way could be said to be "three years later." Jason thus would seem to have chosen the expression which even on the most generous interpretation excluded the possibility that his rival's chronology was correct. The procedure of the Hasmonaean propagandist at I 1:29 was similar; see NOTE on 5:24–27.

One might suggest that Jason was aware of the ambiguities of Greek expressions of duration and that he even expected hostile readers to put ungenerous interpretations on his own words, so as to portray his "three years later" as inconsistent with the year dates in 13:1 and 14:4. One might then use those considerations to explain why, in vs. 4, Jason places the adverb "about" (*hôs*) before the year number 151, even though it was probably accurate and derived from a reliable source. However, such use of *hôs* would have been a sloppy way to deal with the problem when he could have removed the ambiguity by adding a few more specific words. Hence, the explanation of *hôs* in the NOTE on vs. 4 is better.

1–2. Except for naming Judas and his men as the recipients of the news, our verses strongly resemble I 7:1–4, a passage clearly taken from the Seleucid Chronicle; see Introduction, Part II, section 3. Hence, Jason here probably drew on that source, even though the Common Source, too, must have mentioned the change of kings.

1. *Demetrius son of Seleucus.* His father, Seleucus IV, had sent him to be a hostage in Rome. See AB vol. 41, p. 329.

Tripolis. The city gave its name to modern Tarablus in Lebanon. The ancient site is about three kilometers from the modern town. See Map 8 and AB vol. 41, p. 329.

with a strong force and a fleet. These words contradict not only the report at I 7:1, that Demetrius had only a "handful of men" (cf. J. *AJ* xii 10.1.389, "some mercenaries"), but also Polybius' firsthand account, according to which Demetrius took passage on an ordinary commercial ship and was accompanied by only sixteen persons (xxxi 12.11–13, 14.8–13). The Seleucid Chronicle was surely well informed on this matter, but the author of the Common Source may have jumped to conclusions about Demetrius' strong force on the basis of his quick success. If so, the Hasmonaean propagandist followed the Seleucid Chronicle, whereas our writer here followed the Common Source.

3-36. Striking are the contrasts between our verses and I 7:5-32, though both passages cover the same stretch of time. There are also strong similarities. Both here in vss. 3-4 and at I 7:5-6, Alcimus approaches Demetrius because he wants to hold the high priesthood, and vss. 12-13 here resemble I 7:26; we may conclude that both authors drew from the Common Source. Our vss. 5-11 also seem to be drawn from the Common Source; though they might be taken as paralleling I 7:6-9, more likely they parallel I 7:25, since in vs. 12 here as in I 7:26 we read of the appointment of Nicanor.

Indeed, conspicuously missing from the narrative here is anything to correspond with I 7:8-24. There we learn that when Alcimus first approached Demetrius I and successfully sought appointment to the high priesthood and military support against the Hasmonaean party, Demetrius sent a force under Bacchides to Judaea. The Hasmonaeans would have nothing to do with Alcimus and the force protecting him; on their probable reasons, see AB vol. 41, p. 324. On the other hand, the group called "Asidaioi" (vs. 6; I 2:42, 7:13) took the lead in accepting Alcimus and in trusting the expeditionary force. Vs. 6, I 2:42, and 7:13 are the sole contexts from which we can infer who the Asidaioi were. The name is hardly specific, being derived from the Hebrew or Aramaic ḥsyd ("pious"). I chose to render the term in English by "pietists" or "Pietists," capitalizing the word where I thought it referred to a particular sect. Etymologically, the procedure was convenient, but I now regret my choice because of the very specific connotations of the term in the history of Lutheranism. I now prefer to transliterate the Greek, leaving it as "Asidaioi." I do not Hebraize the word into "Hasidim," because the form as given in Greek suggests that in the time of our authors the name was not Hebrew but Aramaic. More than one sect among the Jews could have called themselves "the pious." At present I do not see how the Pharisees and the Essenes of Qumran could be divergent branches growing from the stock of the Asidaioi mentioned here (correct accordingly AB vol. 41, p. 6). The sharp differences between those two sects on the calendar and on other issues must go back much earlier.

From I 2:42 and its context we can infer that the Asidaioi were militant pious Jews. Before Mattathias' act of zeal, they, too, had believed God forbade Jews to rebel against the king, but they came to accept the Hasmonaean view that God demanded Jews fight against the imposed cult. The zealous young fighters of Jubilees 23:16, 19-20, and the "horned lambs" of Enoch 90:9-11 were just such militant pious Jews. The symbolism of Enoch 90 implies that the men of the author's sect for a time made common cause with the Hasmonaeans; see AB vol. 41, pp. 41-42, n. 12, as corrected above, Introduction, Part V, nn. 16, 34. Unlike the Asidaioi here, however, that sect, so far as we know, did not break with the Hasmonaeans over the acceptability of Alcimus as high priest (Enoch 90:19, as interpreted at AB vol. 41, p. 42, n. 12).

The problems of the history of the Asidaioi have pulled us away from our main topic, the absence of anything in the abridged history to correspond to I 7:8-24. Let us return to it. The narrative in I 7 tell us that though Asidaioi accepted Alcimus, nevertheless the high priest came to have sixty pious sages arrested and executed by the royal troops. In so doing, he alienated the pious, and Judas had great success in guerrilla warfare, punishing the "turncoat" Jews who had collaborated with Alcimus. The high priest appealed again to the king for support, and *at that point* the king commissioned Nicanor as governor of Judaea (I 7:26).

The propagandistic thrust of the language used in I 7:10–18 is unmistakable. The reader is to infer that the Asidaioi and the pious sages were fools to break with the Hasmonaeans and trust Alcimus and the Seleucid regime; see AB vol. 41, pp. 331–36. The course of events was embarrassing for admirers of the Asidaioi. Josephus, who admired them, counters the hostile propaganda of I 7:10–18 in his own way; see AB vol. 41, p. 336. The abridged history here passes over the matter in prudent silence (but see NOTE on vss. 6–7). Is the silence Jason's and deliberate? Or is it only the accidental result of abridgment? If I 7:8–25 had been omitted from I 7, no one would have missed the verses.

It is unlikely that the omission here is due to abridgment. If brevity was the goal, the sentence "On that day, Alcimus said nothing" should have been omitted from vs. 4. And the narrative here includes matter with a propagandistic thrust which the author of First Maccabees preferred to omit: Nicanor's maneuvers which brought defeat upon Simon and the subsequent negotiations and the peace during which Judas and his men themselves trusted Nicanor, the agent of the Seleucid regime (vss. 14–25). The taunts of the Hasmonaean propagandist receive the apt answer: if there was folly, the Hasmonaean party, too, was guilty of it. Both Jason and the abridger could easily have omitted our vss. 19–31, from "Accordingly" to "outsmarted by Judas," for example, by providing a transitional sentence after vs. 18: "Rather than fight Judas' armed band, though its numbers were limited, he preferred to seek his goal by intimidating the mass of pious Israelites and their priests." The Common Source probably told of the slaughtered Asidaioi and also of Simon's defeat and of both Judas' friendly and his hostile relations with Nicanor. All these were part of the wondrous events. The ultimate achievement of Jewish independence tended to discredit any collaboration with the Seleucid regime, even temporary. Thus Jason turns the Asidaioi into ringleaders of the opposition to Seleucid rule at the very outset of the reign of Demetrius I (vs. 6). Other things being equal, Jason would have been glad to omit vss. 19–31 by using the procedure we have sketched. But other things were not equal. Since Jason clearly includes vss. 19–31 to prove a point, just as clearly he must himself have omitted the expedition of Bacchides to prove a point.

Literary considerations may have reinforced Jason's decision to omit the expedition of Bacchides. The abridged history falls into two parts, each containing reports of martyrdom and each culminating in the death of a persecutor and in a victory saving the temple, which is to be commemorated ever after by festive observances (3:1 – 10:8, 10:9 – 15:36). In each there is a wondrous victory over a "heinous sinner" named "Nicanor." Though in the first wondrous victory Judas outwitted not only Nicanor but Gorgias (I 3:38 – 4:22), the narrative in the abridged history (II 8:9–36) has focused all attention on Nicanor, leaving Gorgias as a mere name in II 8:9. If Gorgias, whose activity was not embarrassing to Jason of Cyrene, could be left as a mere name in order to focus attention on Nicanor, surely Bacchides, whose expedition was embarrassing, could be omitted entirely and attention focused on Nicanor.

Literary considerations by themselves would not have been sufficient to eliminate the expedition of Bacchides. In the first part of the abridged history, the writer gives detailed reports of victories of Judas both before and after the victory over Nicanor, and even Gorgias' name survives in the narrative.

One can see how the Hasmonaean propagandist drew selectively on the Common Source. Even at I 7:27–29a, Judas is at first willing to negotiate with seemingly pacific Nicanor, as in vss. 18–21 here. At I 7:29b, as here in vs. 22, Judas has reason at that moment to be suspicious. But then the Hasmonaean propagandist jumps to Nicanor's later attempts to arrest Judas (I 7:30–31a, parallel to our vss. 30–31), with no indication that time had elapsed.

We are not surprised to find in vss. 31–36 and in I 7:33–38 that our two authors return to basic agreement; they join again in faithfully reflecting the Common Source.

3–4. Alcimus had been appointed high priest by Antiochus V to replace Menelaus (J. *AJ* xii 9.7.387). The hard-pressed Seleucid regime, eager for peace in Judaea, could have appointed only a pious Jew to the high priesthood. If Alcimus had been guilty of anything like apostasy before the reign of Demetrius I, the fact would have received loud condemnation in First Maccabees, yet in I 7 there is not even the accusation found here in vs. 3, that the would-be high priest had "voluntarily defiled himself." Indeed, Alcimus was no apostate, and even his enemies do not call him a Hellenizer. Though here and in First Maccabees he is mentioned only by his Greek name, Josephus knew the man also had a Hebrew name, "Yakim" or "Yoakim." See I 7:5–24 and AB vol. 41, pp. 332–36.

My clause "who had previously been appointed" translates a Greek perfect participle. As such, it might mean that Alcimus had previously been appointed high priest and had never been deposed. In view of vs. 7, however, Jason must have meant that at that time Alcimus had formerly been high priest and was so no longer. See Mayser, II¹, 176–83. In fact, a high priest held office only as long as the king wished, and a new king had the power to make his own appointment (see AB vol. 41, pp. 75–76). Even if Alcimus had been on good terms with all Jews, he would have had to seek confirmation promptly at the hands of Demetrius. High priests who had trouble with Jewish factions quickly sought the king's support, usually by bringing him rich gifts (II 4:5–6, 13:3; I 10:60–64, 11:24–27).

As presented in my translation, Alcimus' situation was difficult. Although there are problems in establishing and interpreting the text, we shall consider them later, in the NOTE on *during the time of peace*. Assuming my translation is correct, we must ask several questions. How had the high priest defiled himself? During which time of peace? Who threatened his security? Who or what barred him from access to the altar?

One might think that by "defiled" the writer means Alcimus had somehow made himself ritually unclean (*ṭāmē*). If Alcimus had deliberately entered the temple and served as priest while unclean, the Torah imposed upon him the penalty of "being cut off" (*hikkārēt,* called *kārēt* by the rabbis; see Lev 22:3 and Num 19:13, 20). We have no way of determining what that penalty meant to Jason of Cyrene (for rabbinic interpretation, see Israel M. Ta-Shma, "Karet," Enc. Jud., X [1972], 788–89). Under rabbinic law, Alcimus would have incurred "death at the hands of Heaven" or even lynching (*M. Sanhedrin* 9:6; To. *Keritot* 1:5; TB *Sanhedrin* 82b–83a). The writer here clearly views Alcimus' "defilement" as indelible. But there is no way in the Torah or in rabbinic law whereby a person can deliberately bring upon himself indelible uncleanness (cf. "Purity and Impurity, Ritual," Enc. Jud., XIII [1972], 1405–12).

The verb translated "defile" here (*molynein*) is relatively rare in the Greek Old Testament. It is never used to render *ṭm'*, the regular Hebrew root for "ritual uncleanness." Several times, however, it is used for the "stain" of bloodshed or of blood (Gen 37:31; Isa 59:3; Lam 4:14; IV 9:20; cf. I Esdras 8:83, where the Greek translator may have taken *niddāh* at Ezra 9:11 as a figurative use of the word meaning "menstrual blood"). Cf. also the use of verbs of defilement at Num 35:33–34. If Alcimus had been implicated in murder, he would have committed a capital crime, and pious Jews would then seek to have the death penalty inflicted upon him (Exod 21:12; Num 35:16–18, 29–31); he certainly would not have been safe in trying to enter the temple.

Pious Jews viewed deliberate idol worship, too, as a capital crime (Exod 22:19; Deut 13:7–18, 17:3–7), and they could have called it "defilement" (such language may be used at Jer 7:30, 32:34, and Isa 30:22; see also AB vol. 41, p. 482).

We have, however, already excluded the possibility that Alcimus had "defiled himself" by murder or idol worship, whether in the "times of peace" under Antiochus IV and V or in the "time of war" during the persecution; otherwise, the pious would never have accepted Alcimus, but we know that many pious Jews accepted him under Antiochus V and still did so at the beginning of the reign of Demetrius I (J. *AJ* xii 9.7.386, 10.1–3.389–400; I 7:5–7, 12–17; AB vol. 41, pp. 325, 330–32).

The Hasmonaean party condemned mere collaboration with the Seleucid regime in time of peace, but they did not call it "defilement" (I 7:5, 19; 9:23–24, etc.; see AB vol. 41, pp. 335, 337). The pious circles from whom Jason drew his information could not have said that Alcimus had defiled himself through mere collaboration with kings who were not persecutors. At AB vol. 41, p. 335, I was wrong to suggest that Jason viewed such collaboration as defilement.

It would thus appear that Jason's words here are false. Alcimus could in no way have defiled himself in time of peace down to his first audience with Demetrius. I am convinced that Jason never deliberately wrote outright lies. The falsehood here can be explained by Jason's religious position and perhaps also by rhetorical liberties of the sort taken by Greek writers of history.

Alcimus in fact was implicated in the arrest and execution of sixty pious sages, but *after* he had made his successful appeal to Demetrius I for confirmation in office (I 7:5–18; J. *AJ* xii 10.1–2.391–96). The victims and their followers had broken with Judas and the Hasmonaean party in order to accept Alcimus as high priest. The bitter fact was embarrassing to Jason, and he preferred to pass it over in silence; see NOTE on vss. 3–36.

On the other hand, Alcimus surely faced some prompt opposition as high priest during the reign of Antiochus V. The Hasmonaean party seems to have regarded Antiochus V as an illegitimate king with no power to appoint a high priest; see AB vol. 41, p. 325. Both the author of First Maccabees and our writer prefer not to report Alcimus' appointment by Antiochus V. In First Maccabees there is no hint of Alcimus' months in office under the boy-king, and the writer here does not tell of the fact in his narrative of the reign of Antiochus V but smuggles it in as an aside in vs. 3, in his narrative of the beginning of the reign of Demetrius I. Was the Common Source so reticent? Was there something in the events which could embarrass each of the *three* authors?

We can only guess. Alcimus was high priest by royal appointment, and pious Jews believed they had no power to depose him (see AB vol. 41, pp. 75–76). Judas' men had surely dispersed to their homes, to judge by I 6:54, 59, 61. The only armed force left in Jerusalem was the king's garrison in the Akra. A writer who held that it was righteous to oppose Alcimus would not like to dwell on the facts of such a period.

With the death of Antiochus V, however, Alcimus' appointment lapsed, and until he was reappointed by the new king, the Hasmonaeans and his other opponents felt free to regard him as no longer high priest and to exclude him from high priestly prerogatives. The period of such exclusion was brief. The compiler of the high priestly list used by Josephus took no note of it and recorded Alcimus as having had an uninterrupted term of four years (see AB vol. 41, pp. 569–72). This early period of violent opposition was long enough, however, so that both here and at I 7:5–7 we learn that Alcimus had trouble with Jewish opponents at the beginning of the reign of Demetrius. From I 7:6 and vs. 6 here we learn that Judas Maccabaeus was a leader in the opposition. To judge by I 7:5–6 the Common Source at least reported that Alcimus and his supporters were no longer secure in Judaea. Jason would need no more information than that to infer that Alcimus no longer had access to the temple either. If Jason then asked himself why Judas and his followers were so hostile to Alcimus, he could have jumped to the conclusion that Alcimus had "defiled" himself, for certainly the high priest later defiled himself by the slaughter of the sages.

It may well be that on the day of his first audience with Demetrius I, Alcimus contented himself with delivering the gifts he bore, and perhaps he also received immediate confirmation as high priest. Our vs. 4 would then be true. But, if so, Jason passed over in silence, as we have seen, important facts: that in the course of the same visit Alcimus received a second audience at which, backed by supporters from Judaea, he petitioned for the aid of the royal army to put down Judas and his followers, and that the king appointed Bacchides to lead an expedition for that purpose, the expedition in the course of which Alcimus was implicated in the slaughter of the sages.

3. *during the time of peace.* I have translated *epimixias,* the reading of L′ 58 311 La⁻ᴮᴹ Sy, by "of peace." There is room for controversy over both the text and its meaning. A V q have *amixias;* whatever *amixia* and *epimixia* may mean, they are antonyms. *Amixia* can mean "unwillingness to mix with foreigners," as at J. *AJ* xiii 8.3.245, 247—a trait exhibited by pious Jews (see AB vol. 41, pp. 134, 199–200, 293). *Epimixia* can mean the contrary, "willingness to mix with foreigners," such as characterized the "Antiochenes of Jerusalem"

(I 1:11, 15). Those meanings, however, are excluded here because of Jason's use of *amixia* in vs. 38. There the "time of *amixia*" clearly means "the time of persecution."

The solution lies elsewhere. In Greek literature, *epimixia* or *epimeixia* is commonly used to mean "state of peace," the consequences of the end of a state of war, so that human social and business contacts (the "mixture" implied by the literal meaning of the word) can proceed in safety. See Herodotus i 68 (there is *epimixia* when a Spartan can go to Tegea though Sparta and Tegea were usually at war); Thucydides v 35.2 (there is *epimixia* between Athens and Sparta as a result of the Peace of Nicias), 78.1; Xenophon *Hellenica* v 1.1 (*epimixia* directly opposed to *polemos* ["war"]). In papyri from the reign of Ptolemy VIII Euergetes II (145–116 B.C.E.) *amixia* often means "a state of war," of civil war and native Egyptian revolt. See Pierre Jouguet, "Les Lagides et les Indigènes Égyptiens," *Revue belge de philologie et d'histoire*, 2 (1923), 420, n. 1 (in the part printed on p. 421); Claire Préaux, "Esquisse d'une histoire des révolutions égyptiennes sous les Lagides," *Chronique d'Égypte* 11 (1936), 543.

The mere occurrence of *amixia* in vs. 38 should not be taken as an indication that the same word originally was found here. Our chapter, however, contains a pointed contrast between the wicked Alcimus here and the righteous Razis there. Consider the following antithesis, containing an unknown, *x:* Alcimus willingly defiled himself in time of *x;* Razis in time of *amixia* exposed himself, body and soul, to danger for the sake of Judaism. We have established that *amixia* means "state of war," here equivalent to "the persecution." Surely, then, the antithesis is most effective when *x* equals "peace," when the reading in vs. 3 is *epimixias*. Furthermore, as we have seen, if Alcimus had willingly defiled himself in the time of *amixia*, in the time of the persecution, he would never have been acceptable to the pious and would never have been appointed to the high priesthood by a Seleucid regime eager for peace in Judaea.

One still ought to explain how an original *epimixias* could have become *amixias* in most of our Greek manuscripts. Not even La^{-BM} and Sy understood *epimixias* to mean "of peace." They took the safe course of translating, etymologically and literally, "of mixture," and La and Sy were completely baffled by *amixias* in vs. 38. The Greek scribes, too, may have been unfamiliar with *epimixia* as used by Herodotus, Thucydides, and Xenophon, though the scribes show no puzzlement in vs. 38 over *amixias*. Moreover, the Greek scribes were Christians, and among Christians in the third and fourth centuries C.E. there was a burning issue of whether clergy who had committed idolatry or other grievous sins in time of persecution were still eligible to perform the rituals of the Church. See W. H. C. Frend, *Martyrdom and Persecution in the Early Church* (Garden City, N.Y.: Doubleday, 1967), pp. 309–14, 394–98, 409–14. Thus Christian scribes might well expect to see in vs. 3 *amixias* rather than *epimixias*, and their expectations would then have been confirmed by the presence of *amixias* in vs. 38.

Perceiving . . . secure. At I 7:25, Alcimus appeals to the king "knowing that he could not cope with them [i.e., Judas' force]." The language is close enough to indicate the existence of the Common Source.

4. *he . . . 151.* Demetrius I became king of the Seleucid empire early in 151

Sel. Mac. (above, NOTE on vss. 1–4). Alcimus would have had to seek prompt confirmation of his high priestly office at the hands of the new king. The date in our verse is probably exact. Why does Jason use the word "about" (*hôs*)?

The date here has only year, not month and day, the same dating pattern used in the Seleucid Chronicle. Here is a hint that Jason got the date from the Seleucid Chronicle. If so, it could only have been the date of Demetrius' accession. Jason appears to have allowed himself to give only dates of Jewish events; see above, pp. 22–23. He would give a date of an act of Alcimus, the high priest, but not one of a pagan king's accession. Jason may have been unable or unwilling to perform the task, difficult in the ancient world, of pinpointing Demetrius' accession more accurately within 151 Sel. Mac. If so, he could not be sure whether Alcimus' first approach to Demetrius fell in 151 or in 152 Sel. Mac. We may guess that was the reason why he added the word *hôs*.

a gold crown and palm. Simon the Hasmonaean sent a similar pair of gifts to Demetrius II (I 13:36–37). Subjects of the Seleucid empire would present their king with such a crown at the time of his accession (as is probably done here) or after a victory of his or on other suitable occasions. Such crowns were sometimes brought as voluntary gifts, but there were periods during which Seleucid kings viewed them as obligatory for their subjects. See Bickerman, *Institutions*, pp. 111–12.

customary gifts from the temple. I have rendered *thallôn* (lit. "branches") as "gifts." In documents from Egypt, the word *thallos* means "gift given to a landlord by one whose bid for a lease was accepted" (probably because such gifts at one time took the form of olive branches) or "gratuity additional to wages" (*Greek English Lexicon*, s.v.).

5. *meeting of the royal council.* The royal council (*synhedrion*) was not a cabinet or parliament with fixed membership but consisted of the king and any of his available Friends (see AB vol. 41, p. 232) whom he chose to have with him at the time. The king would seek their advice, but all decisions were his. See Bickerman, *Institutions*, pp. 188–90.

6–10. The speech ascribed to Alcimus here follows the rules of Greek rhetoric. The speaker wins the attention and goodwill of his hearer, the king, by answering the king's question at once, by then portraying himself and his supporters as victims in need of help, by claiming to have the king's interests at heart, by claiming to be patriotic, and by praising the king for his past benevolence and by telling him that he has the ability to save the situation (*Rhetorica ad Herennium* i 4–5.7–8; on that work, see NOTE on 9:19–27). Our writer's portrait of Alcimus implicitly contrasts him with Onias III; see 4:4–6 and NOTE on 4:1–6.

Alcimus' description here of Judas and the Asidaioi contrasts with our writer's constant effort to portray the pious Jews as orderly lovers of peace and their enemies as breakers of it; see p. 18.

There is a fairly strong indication that Josephus knew the abridged history in the fact that *AJ* xii 10.3.401 seems to be a paraphrase of the speech here rather than of the direct parallel, I 7:25, or of I 7:6–7 (which Josephus did paraphrase in *AJ* xii 10.1.391–92). One should also notice the possible echo in *AJ* xii 10.4.403 of the king's interest in and benevolence toward the Jews as mentioned here in vss. 5 and 9 (cf. Marcus, in *Josephus,* ed. by Thackeray et al., VII, 210, n. *a*).

6–7. On the extent to which "Alcimus' grievances" were true at the very beginning of the reign of Demetrius I, see NOTE on vss. 3–4. Here, however, we deal with the appeal of Alcimus which brought on the appointment of Nicanor as governor of Judaea; that appeal came later, though the writer here conceals the fact (see NOTE on vss. 3–36). By that time the slaughter of the sixty sages had led Asidaioi to make common cause with the Hasmonaeans in guerrilla warfare against Alcimus and his supporters, but only in the countryside (I 7:16–24). They did not yet dare to challenge Alcimus in Jerusalem. Neither *de facto* nor *de jure* could they deprive him of the high priesthood. Jason needed no source for Alcimus' speech here. Like almost all speeches in ancient works of history, it was the author's free composition. Jason mistakenly jumped to the conclusion that Alcimus had been deposed.

By omitting the expedition of Bacchides, Jason is able to present the Asidaioi as Judas' own party: they could not have been guilty of the folly ascribed to them in I 7:11–16, of breaking with Judas.

6. *feeding . . . war.* See NOTE on 10:14–15.

7. *distinction of my forefathers.* Although Alcimus was not a member of the Zadokite-Oniad line, which had long held the high priesthood (J. *AJ* xii 9.7.387), he could claim descent from the first high priest, Aaron (I 7:14), and perhaps even from Phineas, who received the high priesthood and became ancestor of all subsequent high priests (see AB vol. 41, pp. 6–8).

9. See NOTE on 4:6.

10. On the ambiguity of "commonwealth," see NOTE on 4:1–6.

11. *rest.* The word implies that Alcimus was a member of the Order of the King's Friends. He may well have been, like his Hasmonaean successors (I 10:20, 11:27, 57, 13:36, 14:38–39).

12. At AB vol. 41, p. 258, introductory NOTE on I 3:38–4:25, I refer the reader to this NOTE, but the discussion of how Jason concentrated on Nicanor is now in the NOTE on vss. 3–36.

We lack evidence to tell us whether this Nicanor is identical with persons by that name mentioned in connection with Antiochus IV and Demetrius I. See AB vol. 41, p. 259. The writer here says that Nicanor had been (*genomenos*) commander of the elephant corps (*elephantarchês*). The tense of *genomenos* implies that he held that office no longer. Indeed, the elephants had been an important component of the Seleucid army (see AB vol. 41, pp. 320–21; H. H. Scullard, *The Elephant in the Greek and Roman World* [Ithaca, N.Y.: Cornell University Press, 1974], pp. 77, 97–100, 120–23, 133–35, 138–45, 179–82, 185–88; Bar-Kochva, *The Seleucid Army,* Index s.v. "elephants"; Bickerman, *Institutions,* pp. 61–62), but in 162 B.C.E. a Roman embassy finally enforced the clause of the peace of Apameia which forbade the Seleucid empire to have the animals, and all the elephants were made useless by being hamstrung. See AB vol. 41, p. 329. The reports of Seleucid elephants at I 6:30–46 and II 13:2, 15 come from before the hamstringing. In sources other than the abridged history, no more Seleucid elephants are mentioned until Demetrius II takes over the African elephants of Ptolemy VI (J. *AJ* xiii 4.9.120; cf. I 11:18–19, 56). Thus Jason's apparent mention of elephants at 15:20–21 is probably a mistake. See Scullard, *Elephant,* pp. 188–89. The post of *elephantarchês* was a high office (Bar-Kochva, *The Seleucid Army,* p. 91; cf. Bickerman, *Institutions,* p. 61).

governor of Judaea. Only here in the sources on the Seleucid empire do we read that Judaea was treated as a separate province so as to have its own governor (*stratêgos*). Evidently, Nicanor's office was a temporary one, to deal with a single emergency. Hence, one might do better to translate the title *stratêgos tês Ioudaias* as "commander of operations in Judaea."

13. *orders.* My translation renders *entolas,* the reading of V L 55 La Arm (cf. 4:25, where the word is translated "decrees"). All other Greek manuscripts have *epistolas* ("letters," "written orders"), and Sy reflects a text which had both *entolas* and *epistolas. Entolas* is the more likely reading. It could easily have been corrupted into *epistolas* by contamination from the verb *exapesteile* at the end of vs. 12. Plural orders are easily understandable. Plural letters of commission born by Nicanor are less so, and though the plural *epistolas* is used to mean a single letter, nowhere else is it so used in the abridged history; see NOTE on 11:16, *The content . . . from Lysias.*

14–17. In my translation I have tried to reflect the ambiguity of the Greek. The verb *symmisgein* ("meet") in vs. 14 can mean either "have conversations with" (as at 13:3) or "join forces with" (as at Xenophon *Hellenica* i 3.7). The same verb in vs. 16 can mean either "join the conversations with" or "confront for battle," "join battle with" (as at 15:26). The verb *symballein* ("come to meet") in vs. 17 can mean either "have conversations with" (as at Acts 4:15) or "join battle with" (as at 8:23). Were those who came to Nicanor in vs. 14 armed soldiers or mere petitioners? Did Simon lose a skirmish at Dessau, or did he only lose out in diplomatic discussions? In the case of Simon's misadventure, ancient readers were aware of both alternatives. La^XVP and Sy have Simon joining battle with Nicanor. La^LBM have him conversing with the Seleucid commander, and the errors of the Greek scribes show that they did, too. Only La^−P and perhaps Sy preserve the correct reading, "arrival" (reflecting Gr. *aphixin*). The other significant witnesses all have *aphasian* ("speechlessness"). The Greek scribes seem to have misread "arrival" as "speechlessness" in the belief that Simon's failure came in the course of oral discussions. But the clause they wrote, if properly translated, can only mean "because of the unexpected speechlessness of the opposition"! If struck dumb, moreover, Simon would have suffered no slight or gradual setback.

In favor of interpreting the verbs to refer to conversations rather than combat, there is the possible implication of vs. 18 that Nicanor had not yet resorted to bloodshed. On the whole, however, it seems more likely that the verbs should all be taken in the warlike sense. The same verb and dative noun are used both at 8:23 and here in vs. 17: just as Judas successfully joined battle with Nicanor, so Simon unsuccessfully confronted him. Our writer would not have bothered to report the dismissal of the "mobs" in vs. 23 if they had not constituted a military threat. As for vs. 18, it need not imply that no bloody skirmishes had taken place, but only that any such clash had not been decisive.

14. The reading of the best Greek witnesses (A′ q), *hoi de epi tês Ioudaias pephygadeukotes ton Ioudan ethnê,* has an ungrammatical neuter plural, *ethnê*

("gentiles"), after a masculine participle ("who had fled"). In V L 55 58, the gender of the participle is corrected to the neuter. Habicht (p. 272) believes that "gentiles" is a mistaken marginal gloss which crept into the text, and that those who had fled Judas were Jews, Aicimus' supporters and apostates. If he is right, at the beginning of our verse we should render "Those in Judaea" instead of "The gentiles settled in Judaea." But the gentiles' efforts are mentioned also in vs. 15; it is less likely that a marginal gloss contaminated two verses. Indeed, all witnesses to the text have the word "gentiles" in both verses. Gentile settlers may well have come in as part of the punishment of the Jews by Antiochus IV (see I 1:34, 38; II 11:2; cf. J. *AJ* xii 4.1.159). For a demonstration that before Antiochus IV punished the Jews there were very few permanent gentile residents in Judaea proper, see my article in *Jewish and Christian Self-Definition*, II, 73–75.

By "settled in," I have translated the Greek preposition *epi* (cf. Abel, p. 460).

The verb *phygadeuein* is used to mean both "put to flight" (as at 9:4) and "flee" (as at 5:5, 10:15), but only here does it take a direct object when it has the meaning "flee."

15. The subject of the sentences changes abruptly to the Jews, after having been in vs. 14 those who flocked to Nicanor. The failure to identify the Jews with a noun rather than by the vague pronoun "they" is probably the fault of the abridger, who left out material providing the identification. Therefore I have placed ellipsis points at the beginning of our verse.

Who . . . forever. Cf. II Sam 7:24; Deut 28:9, 29:12–14.

His portion. Cf. Deut 32:9–11, and see NOTE on 1:26.

16. *When the commander . . . they . . . met.* The abridger seems to have been too abrupt here. "The commander" (*hēgoumenos*) here and in vs. 20 should be Judas, who may have been so called in his relationship to the Council of Elders (see NOTE on 13:13); his brothers are reported to have borne the title *hēgoumenos* of the nation (I 9:30, 13:8, 42, 14:35, 41). The word has not been used of Judas before in the abridged history, and the scribes reflected by A V q may have been misled by that fact to take "the commander" as someone other than Judas, for their text can be translated only as "When the commander [presumably Nicanor] gave the order, he [presumably Judas] set out from there and met . . ." Such language would be unnatural for expressing the fact that Judas was summoned to a parley. It is also unlikely that Jason at this point would portray Judas as obeying an order of Nicanor's. I have adopted in my translation what seems to be the correct reading, preserved by L' La^LXVP Sy.

from there. The abridger has not told us from where.

them. Nicanor and those who had come to meet him (vs. 14).

Dessau. The formation of the name is strange, and the first letter is uncertain. A and q have *Lessaou,* and V L'^−62 La^−B Sy Arm have *Dessaou.* Otto Plöger ("Die Feldzüge der Seleukiden gegen den Makkabäer Judas," ZDPV 74 [1958], 180) gives the name of the place as "Dessa," as if the *-ou* were the Greek genitive ending. But *-ou* is not regularly added as a genitive ending to Hebrew or Aramaic names ending in *-a*, and the Latin and Syriac translators took the *-ou* not as a Greek ending but as part of the name. There is no way in which we can pinpoint the location of Dessau. It lay within Judaea, probably near the border on one of the main roads from the coastal plain to Jerusalem. If it had been identical with Adasa, the location of Judas' great victory over Nicanor (I 7:40, 45) as suggested by Abel (p. 461), probably both Jason and the abridger would have named the site again in ch. 15.

17. See NOTE on vss. 14–17. The word "slight" (*bracheôs*) did not fit the preconceptions of some scribes who believed that Judas had come in the nick of time when Simon was losing an armed battle. Hence the variant "gradually" (*bradeôs*), intended to make our verse say "and was gradually losing" where I have rendered "and had suffered a slight setback." But one would then expect an imperfect tense, and our verse has the pluperfect!

Our verse shows moderation in telling of Simon's failure: it was "slight" or "'gradual" and at least partly excused by the sudden arrival of the opponents. On the other hand, Jason seems to have aimed at discrediting Simon (see AB vol. 41, pp. 80, 85, 88, 338). We might therefore attribute the moderation to the Common Source, here copied by Jason and passed over in silence by the author of First Maccabees.

18–28. Whereas in First Maccabees the enemies of the Jews are portrayed as wicked from the beginning, Jason likes to show how they turn wicked and are then punished by God. Just as Antiochus IV begins as morally neutral, becomes God's punishing instrument, turns willfully arrogant, and is punished, so Nicanor in our verses begins well in his relations with the Jews, then turns willfully arrogant in 14:29–15:26, and is punished in 15:27–35. Cf. Moreau, *Lactance,* I, 66–67.

18. *Nicanor shrank . . . bloodshed.* See NOTE on vss. 14–17.

19. At least one of Nicanor's delegates is a Jew with a Hebrew name, and even Theodotus bears a Greek name widely used by Jews. On "handclasps of peace," cf. 12:12, 13:22, and see NOTE on 4:34, *accepted . . . oath.*

20. Little is known of voting procedures among the ancient Jews; see AB vol. 41, pp. 502–3. "The commander" here means Judas; see NOTE on vs. 16, *When . . . met.*

21–25. Although in Greek main clauses are usually linked by connective particles, no particles link the clauses in our verses from "They fixed . . ." through "Nicanor spent time . . ." and from "Continually he kept . . ." through "he partook. . . ." We might again see the hand of the abridger, but perhaps Jason himself wanted to give his narrative a rapid character here.

21. *closed discussions.* Lit. "in private" (*kat' idian*). If Nicanor's delegation had included Alcimus or his supporters, and if Judas' had included Hasmonaean extremists, the two commanders would have had difficulty reaching agreement. Therefore, the commanders negotiated by themselves. The translation, "chariot" and "chairs," preserves the play on words in the Greek (*diphrax* and *diphrous*).

22. The writer records Judas' prudent distrust, though he passed in silence over causes which contributed to it (see I 7:11–25 and NOTE here on vss. 3–36). He probably copies the Common Source (cf. I 7:29–30).

23. On the mobs, see NOTE on vss. 14–17. Our verse completely contradicts the portrayal of Nicanor at I 7:26–30.

26–30. The author of First Maccabees passes in silence over the events of our verses. Since he never mentioned the episode of friendship between Judas and Nicanor, he could hardly find a motive for Alcimus' renewed appeal to the king.

26. *deputy*. See NOTE on 4:29.

28. *terms*. See NOTE on 13:25.

29–46. Our writer shows how Nicanor, *for reasons of his own*, turned into a persecutor and into a contender against God (*theomachos;* see NOTE on 5:21, *thinking . . . soar*) and incurred divine punishment. Such a portrayal is partly inconsistent with the character of our book. Nicanor, like Antiochus IV, turned into a doomed persecutor. In the case of Antiochus IV, our writer demonstrates forcefully that the sins of Jews brought God to turn the man into a persecutor, though the king's own arrogance led him to go too far (see esp. 4:13–17, 5:17–20, 7:18–19, 32–35). In the case of Nicanor, our writer mentions no Jewish sin. Unlike the martyrs of ch. 7, Razis confesses no national sin. I do not believe that the abridger has omitted a reference to such sin. Rather, Jason's own theological position left him unable to point to Jewish transgressions as the cause of the "persecution" of the Jews by Nicanor, though he surely would have done so if he could. A Jewish writer hostile to the pious groups who accepted Alcimus as high priest (see I 7:5, 22–24, 9:23–26, 29, 58–61) could have pointed to that acceptance as the sin.

29. Although the Greek is somewhat strange (see Habicht, *2. Makkabäerbuch,* pp. 274–75), the sense is clear.

31–36. See end of NOTE on vss. 3–36. In I 7:31–32, before Nicanor comes and utters his threat at the temple, Judas defeats him in battle at Chapharsalama. The abridger could have omitted the battle, or Jason himself could have found it awkward to mention the clash, since he holds that Judas successfully hid from Nicanor.

Where was the high priest Alcimus? What were his reactions to Nicanor's threatening oath?

33–34. The writer deliberately uses the same verb for Nicanor's act of stretching forth his hand in a threatening oath against the temple and for the priests' act of stretching forth their hands in prayer; see AB vol. 41, p. 343.

33. At I 7:35 Nicanor threatens only to burn the temple. Though Nicanor may indeed have made a threat to build a temple to Dionysus (in a reinstitution of the imposed cult?—cf. II 6:7), there is no evidence that Demetrius I took any interest in the worship of that god. The threat to build a temple to Dionysus may be Jason's own invention to heighten the drama.

My "fine" translates the Greek *epiphanes*. However, at 15:34 the LORD is called *epiphanês* ("Who had manifested Himself"). In view of the writer's love of reporting precise retribution, it is hard to believe that he did not intend rather to write here *epiphanei,* so as to have Nicanor swear to build a temple to Dionysus, who manifests himself.

35. *Lord . . . nothing*. The Greek can be construed in two ways. La^{-V} and Sy take "of all" (*tôn holôn*) with "Lord," as I have. The Hebrew Bible has "Lord of all the earth" (Josh 3:11, 13; Micah 4:13; Zech 4:14, 6:5; Ps 97:5) but not "Lord of all"; however, that expression and others like it are common in later Jewish literature in Hebrew, Aramaic, and Greek, from Ben Sira on; see Avi Hurwitz, *"Adon Hakkol," Tarbiz* 34 (5725=1964–65), 224–27 (in

Hebrew, with English summary on p. ii). If we so construe the words, the adjective "in need of nothing" (*aprosdeês*) stands without a qualifying genitive, as it does at *Aristeas to Philocrates* 211. Alternatively, *tôn holôn* can be taken with *aprosdeês* to mean "in need of nothing of all," i.e., "in need of nothing in the world." Cf. III 2:9, a passage which may well have been modeled on ours, and J. *AJ* viii 4.3.111. The thought goes back to I Kings 8:27; Isa 66:1–2, and Ps 50.

chose . . . midst. Our passage draws on Lev 26:11 and Deut 12:11, etc. Grammatical peculiarities seem to reflect our writer's peculiar attitude toward the second temple: it is, in a sense, the "Place which the LORD has chosen," but it is not yet the sole legitimate place for Israelite sacrifices. See pp. 13–17. Our writer is adept at handling the Greek language and knows well the meaning of the Greek tenses. In particular, he knows the difference between the Greek aorist and perfect tenses (Doran, *Temple Propaganda*, pp. 30–31). If he had had the priests say here, in the perfect tense, "You . . . have chosen [*êudokêkas*]," he would have implied that the act of choice was still valid in the present. But he had the priests speak in the aorist tense (*êudokêsas*), so as to assert only that God once chose the temple in the past, leaving open the question as to whether the act of choice was still valid in the present.

Another grammatical feature seems to have a similar effect: the word "temple" does not have the definite article. The priests thus do not assert that the sanctuary at Jerusalem has been chosen as *the* unique temple of the LORD. Contrast the use of the definite article at Tobit 1:4 and both Greek versions of Dan 3:53. Against this interpretation, one might object that the definite article was frequently omitted in the Greek translations of the Psalms, but the Psalms may exhibit that characteristic because they are poetry, whereas the prayer here is prose.

36. *Holy One.* Cf. Isa 40:25.

Lord of all sanctification. Again an expression of the form "Lord of all . . ."; see NOTE on vs. 35, *Lord . . . nothing.*

preserve . . . house. The writer will record in 15:34 the fulfillment of this prayer.

37–46. Our verses, in telling of the suicidal martyrdom of Razis, occupy in Part II of the abridged history (10:9–15:36) the place which 6:10–7:42, on the earlier martyrdoms, holds in Part I (3:1–10:8); see NOTE on vss. 3–36. However, the connection of the story of death here with the main narrative is much looser than there. If our verses had been omitted, no one would have missed them. Jason may have drawn the story from the Common Source; the Hasmonaean propagandist would naturally omit it, since it has nothing to do with Hasmonaeans. But Jason may have taken it from some other Jewish collection of traditions, perhaps the Legendary Source.

The martyr bears a name nowhere else attested for a Jew. The witnesses to the text contain many variants. "Razis" or mere variant spellings are exhibited by A V^c q La^M. La^V has "Razias"; La^X, "Radias." On the other hand, V has "Rachis"; L'^−62 and La^LP have "Raxis" or mere variant spellings and are supported by La^B ("Raxius") and Sy (*rgš*). One can only guess at the derivation of the name, whatever the correct reading may be. Like "Rodokos," it may be Iranian; see NOTE on 13:21. In a letter of July 22, 1979, Professor Martin

Schwartz writes, " 'Razis' can be compared with such Iranian proper names as Avestan *Frārāzi-*, as well as *Bagorazos* and *Phandarazos* (Bag-='god', and *phand-*='path'). Avestan *rāzan-*, *rāzah-* mean 'arrangement,' 'setting in order,' 'preparation.' 'Razis' would be a shortened nickname, made by cutting off the initial syllables of such a name."

I prefer to read "Razis" on the basis of the following speculation. The original author of our tale (the Common Source or another storyteller?), as in the case of the story of the woman and her seven sons (ch. 7), may well have told of Razis' suicide because he thought it fulfilled prophecy. Razis may have taken or even may have received his name as a symbol, just as the prophets Hosea and Isaiah gave their children symbolic names. Razis or the storyteller could have derived the name from the enigmatic word *rāzī* at Isa 24:16. It is possible to interpret Isa 24:16–18 as a prophecy of our Elder's leap to death: "Glory [in death] for a righteous man. . . . Razi is for Me [sc. the Lord], Razi is for Me. . . . Woe is me! . . . Treachery [sc. of Alcimus and Nicanor]! . . . He [Razi] who flees from the sound of terror shall fall into the pit." Isaiah goes on to predict (24:21 – 25:11) a great deliverance to follow this fall into the pit, in which there will be a resurrection of the dead (cf. our vs. 46), and the LORD will extend His hand to save the temple mount (Isa 25:10) as Nicanor extended his (II 14:33, 15:32) to threaten it.

37. *one of the elders of Jerusalem*. The use of this expression rather than an adjective "Jerusalemite" does not imply that Jerusalem held no privileges over the rest of Judaea. See NOTE on 12:3–9.

We cannot tell whether the description given Razis here means that he was a member of a national or local Council of Elders or that he was merely a respected old man.

yet . . . Nicanor. We are not told what charge was brought against Razis. Could he have known where Judas was?

38. We are not told how Razis escaped the fate of the martyrs of 6:10 – 7:42. See also NOTE on vs. 3, *during the time of peace*.

39–46. As told here, the story is hard to believe. Why should Nicanor wish to demonstrate his hostility to a population he was trying to pacify? Why should Razis so theatrically commit suicide? Nicanor may have remembered the united resistance of pious Jews to Antiochus IV. If so, he might have realized that in making the temple his hostage he was inducing the divided pious Jews to reunite against him. If there were real charges which could be brought against Razis, Nicanor, without provoking pious Jews to reunite, might arrest him, and then the popular Elder could be used as the hostage, to be tortured or killed if the Jews did not hand over Judas. Writers who focused their narrative on Nicanor's threat against the temple might still tell of Razis' suicide, but they would avoid telling how Razis was to be substituted for the temple as hostage.

If Razis knew where Judas was, he may have committed suicide to avoid being tortured to make him tell. If he did not know, he may have killed himself to prevent Nicanor from using him as a hostage to compel other Jews to hand over Judas or tell where he was. If Jason believed that Nicanor was about to reinstitute the imposed cult (see NOTE on vs. 33), perhaps he thought Razis' motive was to escape that. In any case he clearly admired Razis for his deed.

Among the Jews there were differing views on suicide, as is shown by the debate between Josephus and his men after the fall of Jotapata: they urge suicide, and he opposes it (J. *BJ* iii 8.4–7.355–91). Josephus' opposition to suicide in that instance could explain his failure to make any allusion to Razis' "martyrdom." See introductory NOTE on ch. 7, and cf. I. Gafni, *Zion* 45 (1980), 91–92, n. 40 (in Hebrew). Some rabbinic traditions strongly condemn suicide (*Semahot* 2:1–3, and notice the refusal of Rabbi Ḥanina ben Teradyon to hasten his death though he is being burned at the stake, TB '*Abodah zarah* 18a). But there are many instances where ancient Jewish writers praise those who took their lives under circumstances similar to those we have imagined for Razis. Josephus himself praises Phasael, who committed suicide rather than remain in the power of his mortal enemy Antigonus (*AJ* xiv 13.10.367–69, xv 2.1.13; *BJ* i 13.10.271–72). According to IV 17:1, the mother of the seven martyred sons committed suicide rather than let the king's men touch her body. The Sicarii at Masada killed themselves rather than fall into the hands of the Romans (J. *BJ* vii 8.6.320–9.1.401). Philo reports that Jews were ready to kill themselves and their families rather than see Caligula's proposed desecration of the temple (*Legatio ad Gaium* 32.234–35, 39.308). There are stories in rabbinic literature of righteous suicides who killed themselves rather than commit idolatry or sexual sin (TB *Giṭṭin* 57b; cf. the parallel at *Lamentations Rabbah* 1:50, where the narrator, unwilling to condone voluntary suicide, explains that the mother had become insane after watching the executions of her sons; cf. also *Qiddushin* 81b, and the strange legend of Yaqim quoted at AB vol. 41, p. 334). Rabbinic law requires one to give up his own life rather than commit idolatry, sexual sin, or murder (TB *Sanhedrin* 74a). A saintly Jew (like Razis), we are told, ought not to surrender a Jewish fugitive to the tyrannical government even in order to save a whole city (TP *Terumot* 8:10, p. 46b).

These principles allowing and even requiring suicide under certain conditions continued to be followed by Jews. The pious *Yōsēfōn* in the tenth century wrote his version of the suicide of Razis without disapproving of it (ch. 24), and whole Jewish communities committed suicide in medieval Europe rather than accept forced baptism. See Louis I. Rabinowitz and Haim H. Cohn, "Suicide," Enc. Jud., XV (1972), 489–91.

Members of the Donatist Christian sect in the fourth and fifth centuries C.E. became famous for the frequency of their suicides and took Razis as their example. In contrast, the Catholic Church took a very firm stance against direct suicide. Believing that our book was inspired, Catholics had to explain away our writer's approval of Razis; see Augustine *Contra Gaudentium* i 28.32–31.40 and *Epistula* 204, and T. C. Kane, "Suicide," New Catholic Encyclopedia, XII (1967), 781–83.

One would also like to know why it was necessary to send more than five hundred men to arrest Razis. Otherwise, would Jews have raised their hands to defend him? And how did Razis come to be in a fortified tower? Some or all of the obscurity may be the fault of the abridger.

40. The many variants to our verse display the perplexity of the scribes and translators. The Greek original was probably *edoxe gar ekeinon syllabōn kai alogēsas toutois energasasthai symphoran,* the text I have translated, except that for "to them" (*toutois*) I have substituted "to the Jews," for the sake of clarity. The ancient scribes and translators were confronted by a sentence con-

taining two third person pronouns, the first in the accusative singular, the second in the dative plural. Between the two pronouns were two participles (*syllabôn* and *alogêsas*), and after the second pronoun was an infinitive (*energasasthai*).

Scribes and translators appear not to have known the meaning of *alogêsas* (the verb means "have no regard for"). If they were unfamiliar with the verb, they would not know whether the second pronoun was to be taken with *alogêsas* or with *energasasthai*. At least one witness (534) was further confused by the occurrence of *alogistiai* ("folly") in vs. 8. We are therefore not surprised to find *alogêsas* absent from A V *l* q La^P Sy. La^V, too, probably reflects a text without *alogêsas* (*putabat enim si illum decepisset, se cladem maximam Iudaeis inlaturum* ["He thought if he could entrap him, he would deal a severe blow to the Jews"]). La^V, in turn, represents only a correction, on the basis of Greek manuscripts, of the earlier Latin tradition reflected in La^{LX}. In La^{LX} not only has there been failure to understand *alogêsas*. Through scribal incomprehension or carelessness, one of the third person pronouns has disappeared and the surviving pronoun has become a plural accusative. A plural pronoun could refer only to the Jews. In Sy, though two pronouns survive, both have become plural. The Syriac translator allows himself to write the nonsense that Nicanor thought of arresting "them [sc. the Jews]." The Latin translators were more thoughtful. Confronted with the plural pronoun, they were unwilling to write complete nonsense. Instead of rendering *syllabôn* by *comprehendere* ("arrest"), they used the verb *decipere* ("entrap," but also "deceive"). Thus, the use of *decipere* in La^{LXV} does not reflect *alogêsas*, though De Bruyne (*Anciennes traductions latines*, p. 9) thought so. Strangely, then, only L reflects a text which contained *alogêsas*, and even there the word has become ungrammatical through corruption. *Alogêsas* is not to be regarded as one of the interpolations characteristic of *L*. No one would have added the obscure word to the well-understood *syllabôn*. It is also possible, but, I think, less likely, that the Greek original had only *alogêsas* and that *syllabôn* is a marginal gloss which crept into the text.

41. The word I have translated "outer" (*aulaios*[=*auleios*]) with "door" (*thyra*) normally means "the outer door of a house," the one which leads from the yard into the entrance vestibule. The expression suggests that the tower was someone's fortified house. The abridger may be at fault for leaving our verse with both singular and plural doors. A double door could be treated as either singular or plural. Are the plural doors here the same as the singular door (so La^V and Sy)?

42. Cf. 6:23.

43. Again, one would like to know how Razis got from the "tower" to the "wall."

44. The writer probably means to convey the superhuman endurance of the dying Razis. Though he struck the hard ground, his fall being unbroken by the bodies of the soldiers, he still accomplished the acts recorded in vss. 45–46.

45. *stood . . . rock.* My "precipitous" translates the readings of A La^{LV} L Sy. With *aperrôgôs*, the reading of V q La^{XBMP}, our passage becomes "shattered, he stood upon a rock."

46. "master" here renders Gr. *despozonta;* cf. 3:24 and NOTE ad loc. For the thought here, cf. 7:11, 22–23, and see NOTE on 7:22–23.

Ch. 15. Jason or his source probably saw in the events of our chapter fulfillments of prophecies in Zech 9:8 – 10:8 and Enoch 85:59 – 90:42. See AB vol. 41, pp. 96–97 (through line 2). There are some more possible echoes of Zechariah; see NOTES on vss. 11, 19, 20 (*the cavalry . . . flanks*), 27.

1–5. Our verses have no parallel in I 7 but may be derived from the Common Source, if, indeed, Judas, unlike his father and brothers, abstained from defensive warfare on the Sabbath. The Hasmonaean propagandist would have omitted such material; see NOTE on vs. 1, *he . . . safety.*

1. *in the region of Samaria.* Gr. *en tois kata Samareian topois* probably means "in areas of the province of Samaria"; the prepositional phrase *kata Samareian* is equivalent to the genitive *tês Samareias.* Such, rather than "at points around the city of Samaria," is suggested by the parallel passages in the abridged history (3:8, 4:36, 9:1, 21). Indeed, the Hasmonaean force seems to have made much use of areas within Samaria. See I 5:21–23, 52–53, and AB vol. 41, pp. 236, 294, 339, 386. The Samaritans, despite their effort to disown their connection with the Jews, may have sympathized with Judas. Indeed, we find no evidence that they were hostile. Note the lack of hostility to Samaritans at 5:23 and the absence of condemnation of the Samaritan people at 6:2, and see AB vol. 41, pp. 245–46. The break between the Hasmonaeans and the Samaritans would then have come later (see AB vol. 41, p. 411). On the other hand, Jews, too, lived in the province of Samaria, and they may have been the ones who made the region hospitable to the Hasmonaean force. See AB vol. 41, pp. 410–11, 433, 439.

he . . . safety. Jason never speaks of Mattathias' decision to permit defensive warfare on the Sabbath (I 2:41); to him it was surely sinful (see II 8:26–28, 12:38–39). It is hard to believe that Judas completely avoided using the decision which was so vital for his father and his brothers, but stricter Sabbath observance on his part may account for some of his ability to rally the pious. See NOTE on 8:25–26.

2. *"give due respect to"* (*doxan apomerison*) is a strange expression in Greek, but it is a literal translation of the idiom *ḥālōq kābōd,* common in rabbinic Hebrew (To. *Berakot* 5:7; *Mekilta Pisḥa* 3, p. 23 Lauterbach, etc.). Since the idiom does not occur in biblical Hebrew, its occurrence here suggests that our writer knew Hebrew as a living language.

The end of our verse echoes Isa 58:13.

3. *heinous sinner.* Gr. *trisalitêrios.* See NOTE on 8:34. The use of the same word here as at 8:34 suggests that the writer believed that the Nicanor here was the same as the one there.

"Is He . . . in heaven?" The syntax of our passage is dictated by its word order and by the antithetic utterance of Nicanor in vs. 5 and was properly understood by the Latin and Syriac translators. Though A and q have the definite article before "master," it spoils the antithesis and must be omitted, as it is in V *L'* and even in 106, which usually agrees with A.

5. Our verse marks out Nicanor once again as an arrogant sinner worthy of death. If Judas indeed would not fight on the Sabbath, one would like to know

how Nicanor failed to carry out his intention. Has the abridger removed the story?

6–36. The similarities to I 7:39–49 speak for the existence of the Common Source, even though Jason has added rhetoric and omitted facts.

In vss. 22–24, as in I 7:41–42, Judas' prayer for victory alludes to God's thwarting of Sennacherib. In vss. 28–30, as in I 7:47, Nicanor's body is found after the battle, and his head and right hand (or arm) are cut off and brought to (or near) Jerusalem. In vs. 35 and in I 7:47, Nicanor's severed parts are hung in public. In vs. 34 and in I 7:48 there are festive observances, and in vs. 36 and in I 7:49 the Jews decree that the Day of Nicanor should be observed every year.

Neither here nor in I 7:39–49 is the year of the victory over Nicanor given. One may infer that it was absent also from the Common Source, especially since the lack seems to have caused the Hasmonaean propagandist some difficulty; see AB vol. 41, NOTES on 7:43 and 50.

6–11. Jason needed no source to write these verses. Ancient writers of history were free to use their imaginations to compose such passages.

6. *to take . . . rout.* A more literal translation of our passage would be "to set up a common trophy of Judas and his men." It would not, however, convey the meaning of the passage. There was an old custom among the Greeks to set up at the site of a victory in a land battle a *tropaion,* a single complete suit of armor, captured from the enemy, mounted on a cross so as to look like a man wearing armor. By our period such "trophies" were regarded as victory monuments and did not have to be at the site of the battle. By the second century B.C.E., moreover, trophies no longer necessarily consisted of a single complete suit of armor mounted on a cross. Imposing structures could be built and decorated with numerous pieces of armor. See I 13:29; AB vol. 41, pp. 474–75, and Friedrich Lammert, *"Tropaion,"* PW, XIIIA (1939), 669–72.

The Greek word "common" (*koinon*) is the antonym of "individual." We may guess that by a "common" trophy our writer meant, not one made from the armor of one individual soldier, but one made "wholesale," from the arms of Judas' entire company. The word is unlikely to mean "public" (as is suggested by La[BM]) or "on behalf of the commonwealth." Nicanor was working for an absolute monarch, not for a republic, and even if one supposes that he had the commonwealth of the Jews in mind, Greek word usage allows only Jews, not Nicanor, to set up a *koinon* monument of their commonwealth.

7–30. It is typical of our writer that he does not tell us either where the armies encamped or where the battle took place. Cf. I 7:39–45, where we learn that Nicanor encamped at Beth-Horon and Judas at Adasa, and it is implied that the battle occurred at or near Adasa; see Map 9 and AB vol. 41, p. 341.

Schürer suggested (New English version, I, 170, n. 29) that Adasa is "presumably identical with the Adasa in the vicinity of Gophna which was known to Eusebius (*Onomastikon,* ed. by Klostermann, p. 26); it therefore lay to the northeast of Beth-Horon." Against the location at Khirbet 'Adaseh, which we have adopted, Schürer urges that the identification involves rejecting the evidence of Josephus (*AJ* xii 10.5.408); Josephus says Adasa was thirty stadia from Beth-Horon. Khirbet 'Adaseh is about twice that distance. But the region of Gophna is still farther from Beth-Horon! It is best to assume, as I did at AB vol. 41, p. 341, that Josephus was mistaken and to accept the identification of Adasa with Khirbet 'Adaseh on the road to Beth-Horon from Jerusalem, for the narrative of I 7:39–46 fits well the idea that all action took place on and around that road.

7. Cf. Deut 20:1.

8. Our verse reads rather like Deut 20:3, but see NOTE on 8:16–23. The rest of Judas' speech (vss. 9–16), indeed, bears no resemblance to the speech of the priest in Deut 20:3–4, so that here, too, the writer may have taken care not to portray Judas as a priest.

9. Judas may have quoted promises of victory from the Torah and the Prophets. However, the mention next of the "struggles they had come through" suggests rather that he cited examples of Jewish victories against great odds both from ancient and from contemporary history. The Torah and the Prophets served him as ancient history, for the Prophets, by Jewish reckoning, include also the historical books from Joshua through II Kings.

10–17. Every feature in the speech ascribed to Judas in our verses seems designed to reply to theological objections which pious Jews could have raised against Judas and his men. Despite the victories of Judas, the greater miracles promised by God, which would signal the end of Israel's servitude to foreign rulers, had not yet come (see AB vol. 41, pp. 323–24). The Hasmonaean party was in rebellion against Demetrius I, a legitimate Seleucid who had not been a persecutor. They refused to accept as high priest Alcimus, the man legitimately appointed by the legitimate king. Jeremiah condemned the rebellion of King Zedekiah of Judah in violation of his oath to Nebuchadnezzar, the king placed in power over Judah by God (Jer 27:1–18, 28:14, 52:3); see NOTE on 1:7–8 and NOTE on 1:7, *Jason . . . Kingdom*. Judas and his men had sworn to obey the Seleucid king (14:19–22); were they not now as guilty of sin as were Zedekiah and his subjects?

Our verses make clear that not the Jews but their enemies were the ones who broke their oaths (vs. 10). Pious Jews could differ over the legitimacy of Alcimus. That high priest was appointed by the king, but he did not belong to the family which had held the high priesthood for many generations (J. *AJ* xii 9.7.387, xx 10.3.235). Believers in the sole legitimacy of the Zadokite-Oniad line, including its survivor, Onias IV, would hold Alcimus ineligible for the high priesthood. If so, Nicanor's mission to secure the high priesthood for Alcimus was against the will of God, and Jews would be free to oppose it. On the other hand, nothing suggests that Judas and his men were fighting to put in as high priest the "legitimate claimant," Onias IV, and his supporters might therefore suggest that Judas was not fighting for God's cause! Pious Jews could be divided over whom God wanted now to be His high priest. There could be no doubt, however, that the last high priest who was both righteous and clearly eligible for his office was Onias III, father of Onias IV. Onias III himself appears in a vision to endorse Judas' course, and after him, Jeremiah himself also endorses that course, giving decisive proof that Judas' act is not to be likened to Zedekiah's.

10. The writer probably has in mind Nicanor's failure to continue to honor his sworn peace agreement with Judas (14:19–22; cf. 14:28) rather than earlier gentile breaches of faith (5:25–26, 12:3–4).

11. The "encouragement" (*paraklêsin*) and the "trustworthy dream" here may be intended to contrast with the "dreams which speak lies" and "give vain encouragement" (*mataia parekaloun*) at Zech 10:2. The "good words" are probably the words of scripture; cf. I 12:9 and AB vol. 41, p. 453.

My "beyond measure" translates *hyper ti*, the reading of most Greek witnesses to the text, reflected but not understood by the Latin versions. On the rather uncommon idiom, see NOTE on 8:20, *took . . . spoils*. Only *L* and 311 and perhaps Sy have *hypar ti*, which must be taken in apposition to "dream," so that the end of our verse would become "by telling them of a trustworthy dream, a sort of waking vision, he roused their spirits." By themselves, *L* and 311 give poor attestation for a reading, and *hypar*, far from being employed to define more closely the word "dream," is usually used as its antithesis, "something seen by one's eyes while he is awake." It is, indeed, conceivable that our writer would enjoy so juxtaposing opposites, but I think that the evidence favors the other reading.

12–16. In the NOTE on vss. 10–17 we have considered the theological role played by the figure of Onias III here. Would a Jew writing generations after the death of Onias III have thought of bringing him into the story here? It seems more likely to me that Jason took the dream here from one or more of his sources. The author of the Common Source venerated the memory of the "anointed one" of Dan 9:26, the man through whose merit the honor of the temple had been miraculously preserved from Heliodorus (3:1–35). The author of the Common Source and, indeed, Judas himself could have spoken of the man of the miracle before the wondrous victory which preserved the temple from Nicanor. Still more, however, would it have been to the interest of Onias IV to press the claims of his family to divine favor. Onias IV left Judaea for Egypt when Demetrius I confirmed Alcimus in the high priesthood (J. *AJ* xii 9.7.387), but some partisans of the Zadokite-Oniad line probably stayed behind. When the Hasmonaeans not only refused to recognize Alcimus but also turned to resist Alcimus' Seleucid protectors, Onias IV probably approved, and his partisans may well have joined forces with Judas to fight against Nicanor. Thus the story of Judas' dream could have originated with Onias IV or his partisans (see AB vol. 41, p. 95, n. 22, but read "the Common Source's" instead of "*DMP*'s"). Indeed, suggestions from Onias IV or his partisans could have influenced Judas' mind on the eve of the battle, if Judas in fact reported such a dream. If so, the break between the Hasmonaeans and the party of Onias IV came after the battle with Nicanor, when it became clear that the Hasmonaeans would not fight to install an Oniad high priest.

Judas had only a dream or, at most, a waking vision (see NOTE on vs. 11) of Onias III and Jeremiah praying. The vision could be taken entirely as a symbol, that God approved of the course taken by Judas and his men (see NOTE on vss. 10–17). Catholics, however, have taken Judas' vision as a factual proof from scripture of the doctrine that the souls of dead saints may intercede for the living (P. J. Mahoney, "Intercession," New Catholic Encyclopedia, VII [1967], 567; P. Molinari, "Saints, Intercession of," ibid., XII [1967], 973). The belief is found at Philo *De praemiis et poenis* (*De exsecrationibus*) 166; cf. J. *AJ* i 13.3.231. On the "prayers of the dead" at Bar 3:4, see AB vol. 44, p. 290. The doctrine of intercession by the dead is foreign to ancient rabbinic texts; see Ginzberg, *Legends,* V, 419, and that fact may explain the omission of Judas' vision from *Yosefon* 24.

12. Part of the description of Onias III may be intended to reflect the description of the ideal priest at Mal 2:5–7. My "good [man] and true" translates *kalon kai agathon,* an expression used by Greek aristocrats to mean "the perfect Greek gentleman." In *Aristeas to Philocrates* it is used of the high priest Eleazar (section 3) and of the seventy-two translators (section 46).

13. *in the same posture.* See NOTE on 4:22.

14–30. Judas and his men may have been conscious of how their battle resembled Gideon's victory over Midian (Judg 7:20–25). In Judges, too, a sword is mentioned (7:20) and the defeated enemy leaders are beheaded (7:25). See AB vol. 41, p. 342, NOTE on 7:45–46.

14–17. Jeremiah's prophecies were much used in this period; see Dan 9:2, 24, and cf. II 2:1–8. He prophesied that the LORD's sword would fall on the wicked empire, Babylon (50:35–37). The Seleucid empire held Babylon and was viewed as the latter-day Babylon as well as the latter-day Assyria; see AB vol. 41, p. 210, and end of NOTE on II 9:4.

One of Jason's sources may have read Zech 9:12 as speaking of the return of Jeremiah, the "One who told of the Second [Jewish commonwealth]." See AB vol. 41, p. 96.

14–16. The sword is also mentioned at Enoch 90:19 and 34, verses written only shortly after the battle with Nicanor. Enoch 90:34 strongly suggests that a real sword was said to be the one handed to Judas in his vision. We cannot tell whether our writer believed the sword to be real, but there is no reason to think that he believed that Judas, having received it (whether real or symbolic), would henceforth be invincible, as suggested by Habicht, *2. Makkabäerbuch,* pp. 173–74, 278. To judge by Enoch 90:34, Judas gave up the sword to the temple after his victory over Nicanor.

The sword of victory handed by a god to his chosen commander or king is an Egyptian motif, used by the Ptolemies; see Otto and Bengtson, p. 151.

14. The author of so many bitter Jeremiads against the sinful subjects of Zedekiah is here called a "lover of his brethren." Passages such as Jer 2:1–3 would afford some foundation, but the intent of the writer is clearly to imply that, unlike the brethren in Jeremiah's lifetime, the brethren in Judas' time are righteous and worthy of Jeremiah's love. Jeremiah in his own time would have offered efficacious prayers for Judah and Jerusalem, but for the wickedness of his contemporaries (Jer 7:16–20, 11:14, 14:11–14, 37:3–10, 42:2–22). Now nothing impedes him from praying for the people and for the city.

15. For our writer, heavenly instruments are made of gold (3:25, 5:2).

16. *shatter our enemies.* The language may be taken from Exod 15:6.

17–21. See NOTE on vss. 6–11, and cf. 3:14–23.

17. *not merely . . . charge.* "Merely" is not expressed in the Greek, and in Greek idiom it is not really needed in such contexts. Nevertheless, the Greek scribe reflected in *L'* misunderstood the text and, taking *mê strateuesthai* to mean "not to march [at all]," felt forced to emend the text to *mê stratopedeuesthai* ("not to build a fortified camp").

Only here, to my knowledge, does the Greek verb *empheresthai* mean "charge," "take the offensive," but the etymology of the word ("carry oneself in") allows that meaning, and the word was so understood by La.

the city and the sanctuary. I translate the text reflected by La^L (*ciuitas et templum*) and found in two Greek manuscripts of small authority (46 52), *tên polin kai ta hagia.* The other Greek manuscripts have *tên polin kai ta hagia kai to hieron,* lit. "the city, the holy things, and the temple." But *ta hagia* ("the holy things") in First Maccabees regularly means "the temple," and it is so translated here by Sy. In Second Maccabees the expression occurs only here. Greek scribes did not understand it as "temple" but as "holy things other than the temple." Missing a reference in our verse to the temple, they added *kai to hieron* ("and the temple").

19. My "shut up in the city" translates the reading *kateilêmenois* reflected by La^BM (*conclusi*). A V q La^LXP have *kateilêmmenois* ("seized," "arrested," "held"), but nowhere else do we hear that Nicanor so treated the inhabitants of Jerusalem. *L* has *kataleleimmenois* ("left behind") and is followed as usual by Sy. The reading makes sense, but there is a similar set of variant readings at I 5:26–27, where I now think it best to read *syneilêmenoi eisi* ("had been driven to barricade themselves together"; see pp. 434–35). The parallel corruption at I 5:26–27 is one factor inducing me to read *kateilêmenois* here with La^BM, two very inferior witnesses. There are two other considerations in favor of the reading. It gives a very good antithesis with "the open country," and it puts into our verse a possible echo of the "prisoners of hope" at Zech 9:11–12 (see introductory Note to this chapter).

20. *about to engage.* I have emended the text. All witnesses reflect a text with a past (aorist) participle, and I have changed *symmeixantôn* to a future participle, *symmeixontôn.* The future participle is rare in Hellenistic Greek but was freely used by our writer. Greek scribes failed to recognize it or did not want to write it. Thus, at 4:23, the good witnesses have the future participle *telesonta* ("for executing"), but V 107 19 106 have the aorist participle *telesanta.* The case is similar with *anapsyxonta* at 4:46 ("for a breath of air"), where 71 120 534 *l* have the aorist participle *anapsyxanta.* If our verse had the aorist participle, it would mean that the enemy had already engaged, but the battle is not joined until vs. 26.

the beasts were posted. "Beasts" (*thêriôn*) here surely means "elephants," as very frequently in Polybius, but see Note on 14:12. I have translated *apokatastathentôn* as "were posted," in accordance with the context and La^LBMP, although to my knowledge the verb has that meaning only here.

the cavalry . . . flanks. Cavalry was usually so employed by Hellenistic armies. Though horses and elephants were of limited utility in rugged Judaea, Lysias used both (I 4:28, 6:30–38; II 11:2, 11, and 13:2). However, cavalry is not mentioned in the parallel account to ours, at I 7:39–46. Is the prophecy at Zech 10:5 the only reason cavalry is mentioned here? See introductory Note to this chapter.

21. "The Lord Who does wonders" is found at Pss 72:18, 86:10, 136:4. Does the end of our verse draw on Zech 4:6?

22–24. The parallel prayer of Judas at I 7:41–42 also asks for a repetition of the miraculous defeat of Sennacherib (II Kings 18:13 – 19:35; Isa 36–37). Both authors probably draw on the Common Source.

23. *good angel.* See NOTE on 11:6.

24. "By the might of Your arm" (*megethei brachionos sou*) is taken from Exod 15:16.

25–36. Our verses are so similar in content to I 7:43–49 that clearly both authors drew on the Common Source.

25–27. See AB vol. 41, pp. 341–43.

25. *pagan war hymns.* They were called *paianes* ("paeans") and were usually addressed to Apollo by soldiers going into battle.

27. Cf. Ps 149:6. Here and in vs. 34 we are told that God manifested Himself in the course of the battle. Yet no supernatural apparition is mentioned here, unlike 10:29–30 and 11:8–10. I do not think that Jason told of one and the abridger omitted the fact. Would the abridger omit a miracle? Rather, Judas' dream and the sword, if real, were already supernatural manifestations, and a reader of Zech 9:13–15, 10:3–6 could well take the mere victory of Judas' fired-up troops and even their rejoicing after it (cf. Zech 10:7) as manifestations of God's power. See introductory NOTE to this chapter.

As usual, the number of the enemy dead is exaggerated; see NOTE on 8:24. In First Maccabees, no figure is given.

28. *battle.* Greek *chreia* means "battle" also at Polybius i 84.7, and perhaps at II 8:20.

29. *the language of their forefathers.* See NOTE on 12:37.

30–35. At I 7:47 the author does not say that Nicanor's head and arm were brought into Jerusalem. Clearly he believes that the implications of Num 19:11–16, 21, and 31:19–24 forbid bringing those unclean objects into the holy city and, all the more, bringing them onto the temple mount. One might infer the same from J. *AJ* xii 3.4.146: if it is forbidden to bring into Jerusalem the flesh and pelts of unclean animals, should it not be forbidden to bring in parts of a human corpse?

Jason, however, clearly believes that Nicanor's severed parts were brought into Jerusalem, perhaps even into the court of women on the temple mount, and hung from the Akra, which adjoined the temple area (see AB vol. 41, p. 389). Indeed, a rabbinic text asserts that a corpse could be brought even into the court of women (To. *Kelim* 1:8[7]; see the commentary of Maimonides to *M. Kelim* 1:8 and the commentary of Samson of Sens to *M. Kelim* 1:7). We cannot tell which of our two authors is the one who correctly reports what Judas did with the severed parts of Nicanor. At AB vol. 41, p. 343, I implied that *M. Kelim* 1:4, 7, 8 would support the interpretation there, that the severed parts could not be brought into Jerusalem; however, the authority of *M. Kelim* 1:4, 7, 8 may well have agreed with To. *Kelim* 1:8(7).

At I Sam 17:54 David is reported to have brought the head of Goliath to Jerusalem, a fact I should have mentioned at AB vol. 41, p. 343, in my NOTE on 7:47, since that verse may echo I Sam 17:54.

30–33. The remarks referred to at AB vol. 41, p. 343, are in the NOTE to vss. 30–35.

30. *The man . . . fellow Jews.* The description fits the great horned ram of Enoch 90:9–19, 31. Indeed, Enoch 90:19 reports the victory over Nicanor; see AB vol. 41, pp. 41–42, n. 12.

31–32. No force was left to prevent Judas from marching into Jerusalem.

The garrison in the Akra, the citadel to the north of the temple, was safe behind its walls but was too hopelessly outnumbered to venture upon combat. Representatives of the garrison may have come out for a parley, or all of them may have come to see the head of Nicanor from atop the walls of the citadel. This is the first mention of the Akra in the abridged history. To have mentioned it earlier would have cast doubt on prophecies of Daniel and might have called attention to facts embarrassing to the pious groups favored by Jason of Cyrene. See NOTE on 5:24–27 and introductory NOTE on ch. 13.

32–33. Again our writer takes pleasure in recording the precise retribution inflicted by God upon a sinner. In vs. 33 there is a play on words as *epicheira*, which means both "arm" (as at Greek Jer 31[48 H.]:25) and "retribution," has both meanings simultaneously.

34. See NOTE on 3:30, and NOTE on vs. 27. The prayers of thanksgiving say nothing about the preservation of the temple from destruction. Clearly the writer regarded the threat of the defilement of the Holy Place by the erection of a temple to Dionysus as more serious than the threat of the destruction of God's temple (cf. 14:33, 36).

35. Since the king's garrison still held the Akra, we must assume that the head was affixed to the wall of the citadel.

36. On the voting procedure, see AB vol. 41, pp. 502–3.

The writer is aware that the name "Adar" is not originally Hebrew. In fact, it was taken into Hebrew and Aramaic from Babylonian.

Why does our writer call 14 Adar the "Day of Mordechai" instead of "Purim"? An Aramaic equivalent for Purim is used by Jews writing in Greek (Greek Esther 9:26, 28, 10:3[1] Rahlfs; J. *AJ* xi 6.13.295). Other Jewish sources name days of great Jewish victories after the vanquished enemy, not after the victorious leader, e.g., the Day of Midian (Isa 9:3) and even the day mentioned here, which is called the Day of Nicanor in *Megillat Ta'anit*. Indeed, our writer uses a purely Greek expression, which, rendered literally, would be the "Mordechaiic Day." Although such adjectives appear in Jewish works in Greek, they are never used there to name a day. See Hans Bardtke, "Der Mardochäustag," in *Tradition und Glaube, Festgabe für Karl Georg Kuhn zum 65. Geburtstag*, ed. by Gert Jeremias, et al. (Göttingen: Vandenhoeck & Ruprecht, 1971), pp. 97–101.

In all probability our writer chooses his words to stress the parallelism between Judas and Mordechai. By Mordechai's command, the Jews annihilated 75,510 of their enemies on 13 Adar and celebrated on 14 Adar (Esther 8:9–12, 9:12, 16), and the annual observance of 14 Adar was voted by the Jews on the proposal of Mordechai (Esther 9:20–28; see AB vol. 41, pp. 551–52). Just so, under Judas' command, the Jews destroyed 35,000 enemies, and the people decreed that the day of rejoicing should be observed annually. Neither in First Maccabees nor here are we told whether 13 Adar was the day of the battle or the day of celebration. The site of the battle, at or near Adasa, was close enough to Jerusalem that the fighting and the celebration could have occurred on the same day. Hence, it is probable that both in the case of Mordechai's triumph and in the case of Judas' the day of *rejoicing* was the one to be observed annually. Our writer, as a Hellenistic Greek stylist, was not bound by the practices of other Jews writing in Greek. Polybius freely uses such ad-

jectives and writes of "Antiochic times" and "Philippic times" (xxiv 11[13].3);
see J.-A. de Foucault, *Recherches sur la langue et le style de Polybe* (Paris:
"Les Belles Lettres," 1972), pp. 25–26. If so, the "Mordechaiic Day" was
probably not an unusual expression in Hellenistic Greek.

Had the abridger read the Greek book of Esther? If so, he took the epithet
"heinous sinner" (*trisalitêrios*), which he twice uses of a Nicanor (8:34,
15:3), from Greek Esther 8:12ᵖ Rahlfs, where it refers to Haman. We could
then be sure that the abridger worked after the Greek book of Esther was
brought to Egypt in 78/7 B.C.E; see AB vol. 41, pp. 551–57.

XVIII. THE ABRIDGER'S EPILOGUE
(15:37–39)

15 ³⁷ Such was the outcome of the affair of Nicanor. From that time on, the city has been held by the Hebrews. Therefore, I myself shall bring my account to a stop at this very point. ³⁸ If it is well and cleverly written, that was what I wished; if it is undistinguished and mediocre, that was all I could achieve. ³⁹ It is just as disagreeable to drink pure wine as it is to drink pure water. In the same manner that wine, once mixed with water, produces a delightful savor, so the apt mixture of styles delights the ears of the readers of a history. This shall be my final word.

NOTES

15:37. Our writer does not claim that an independent Jewish state held Jerusalem from that time on, but only that the city was in the possession of pious Jews rather than of apostates and foreigners (see I 1:38). Alcimus was to be high priest until May, 159, and was to hold power free from any interference by Judas from Judas' death in the spring of 160. If our writer was aware of that fact, he here concedes tacitly that Alcimus was a believing "Hebrew." Though Seleucid rule might again weigh heavy upon Jerusalem even in the reign of the mighty Hasmonaean prince John Hyrcanus (J. *AJ* xiii 8.2–3.236–47), the city and the temple remained uninterruptedly in the hands of believing Jews until Roman Pompey conquered them in 63 B.C.E. (J. *AJ* xiv 4.2–4.59–74). Thus we learn that the abridger must have written before Pompey captured Jerusalem and the temple.

The author of First Maccabees, though valuing highly Judas' victory over Nicanor, does not regard it as such a landmark in Jewish history. In his view, the Hasmonaean Jonathan took greater steps in freeing Jerusalem (I 10:6–11, 12:35–37) and Simon took the greatest ones of all in winning full freedom (I 13:39, 41) and in capturing the Akra (I 13:49–51).

Josephus resembles our writer somewhat in saying that *Judas* "liberated the nation and rescued them from slavery to the Macedonians" (*AJ* xii 11.2.434). But Josephus speaks of the *nation,* whereas our writer speaks of the *city.*

Our verse also allows us to infer that the abridger stopped before reaching the end of Jason's work. Otherwise, he would have written, "Since Jason brought his history to an end at this point, I, too, shall end my book here."

38. The abridger probably copied the end of a famous oration of Aeschines (3.260).

39. *once . . . savor.* I have translated the reading of A V q^{-71} ^{74} ^{130} La^{LX}, *hydati synkerastheis êdê kai epiterpê tên charin apotelei.* The particle *kai* may mean "also": mixture with water tempers the unpleasant strength of pure wine, but *also* produces a delightful savor. Or the particle may simply single out the "delightfulness" in this clause, just as a (correlative) *kai* in the next clause singles out the "delight" there. The scribes reflected by L' 71 74 130 La^{BMP} Sy appear to have read *kai* as "and." As such, it would have to link two grammatical units of equal rank, but a main verb (*apotelei*) follows and no main verb precedes. The scribes could make good sense of the passage by changing *êdê* ("once") to (h)*êdys* ("sweet") because "is" does not have to be expressed in Greek; accordingly, some of them made our passage read "mixed with water is sweet and produces a delightful savor." The result, however, spoils the balanced rhetoric: in the "so" clause, which ends our sentence, there is nothing to correspond with "is sweet." Other scribes made good sense by changing *êdê* to (h)*êdeian,* so that the "and" would link two adjectives, making our passage read "mixed with water produces a sweet and delightful savor," but again the rhetorical balance is spoiled: in the "so" clause there is nothing to correspond with "sweet."

Wines in the ancient Greek world were indeed so strong that they were usually drunk mixed with water (Charles Seltman, *Wine in the Ancient World* [London: Routledge and Kegan Paul, 1957], p. 91).

so . . . history. The abridger claims responsibility for the styles but says nothing about adding to the content of the narrative. From the expression "delights the ears of the readers" we learn again the well-known fact that the ancients read aloud.

MAPS

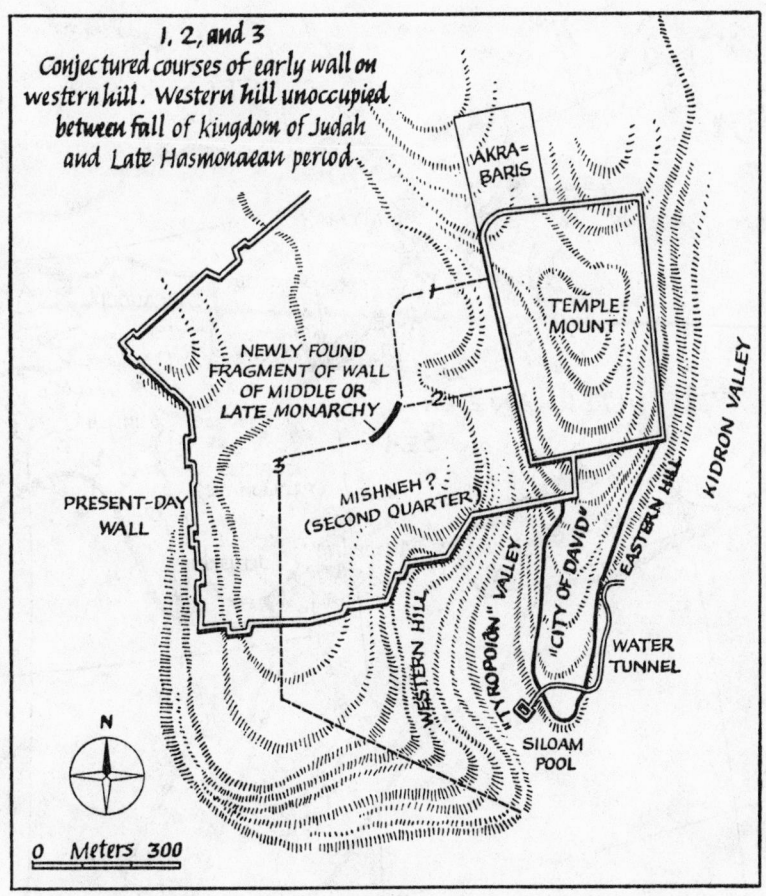

1. The walls of Jerusalem, the "City of David," and the eastern and western hills.

BLACK SEA

MYSIA

PHRYGIA

CAPPADOCIA

ARMENIA

PAMPHYLIA

CILICIA Mallos

Tarsus

MESOPOTAMIA

RIVER TIGRIS

MEDITERRANEAN

SEA

Antioch

CYPRUS
(PTOLEMAIC)

SELEU

RIVER EUPHRATES

Alexandria

Jerusalem

Seleuceia
Babylon

PTOLEMAIC

RIVER NILE

EMPIRE

RED
SEA

0   Miles   500

0   Km   1000

2. Areas important during the last campaigns of Antiochus IV, summer 165 to late autumn 164 B.C.E.

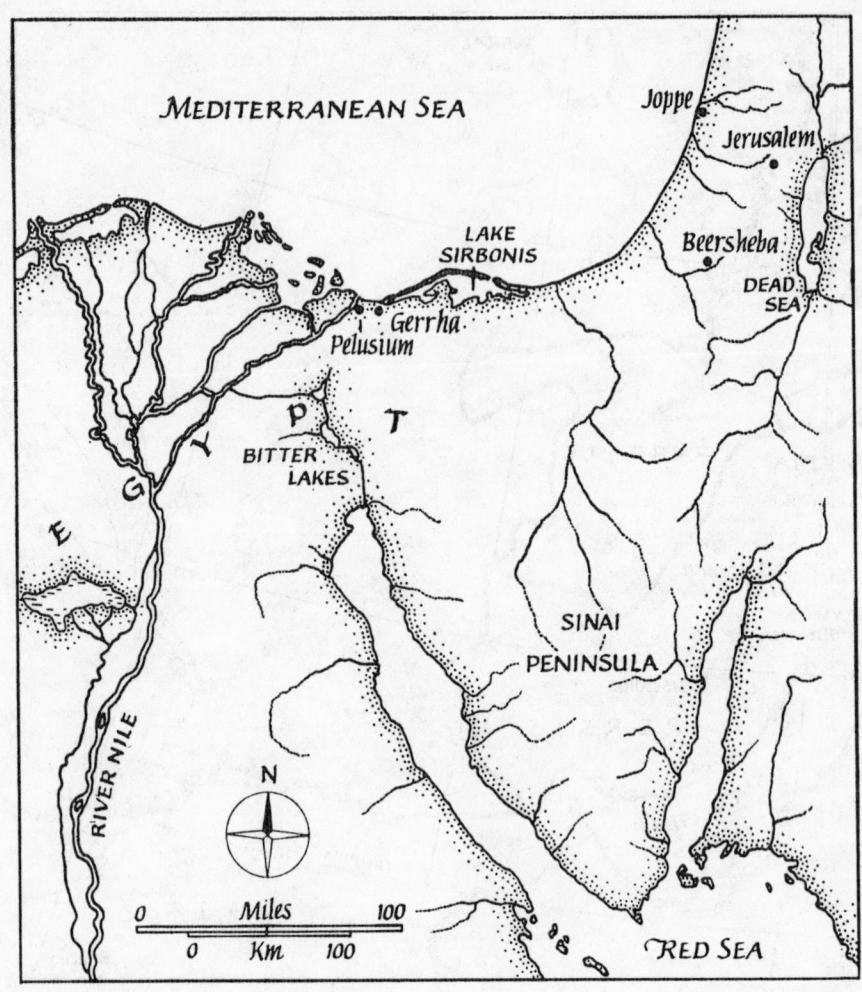

3. Southern Palestine and northeastern Egypt.

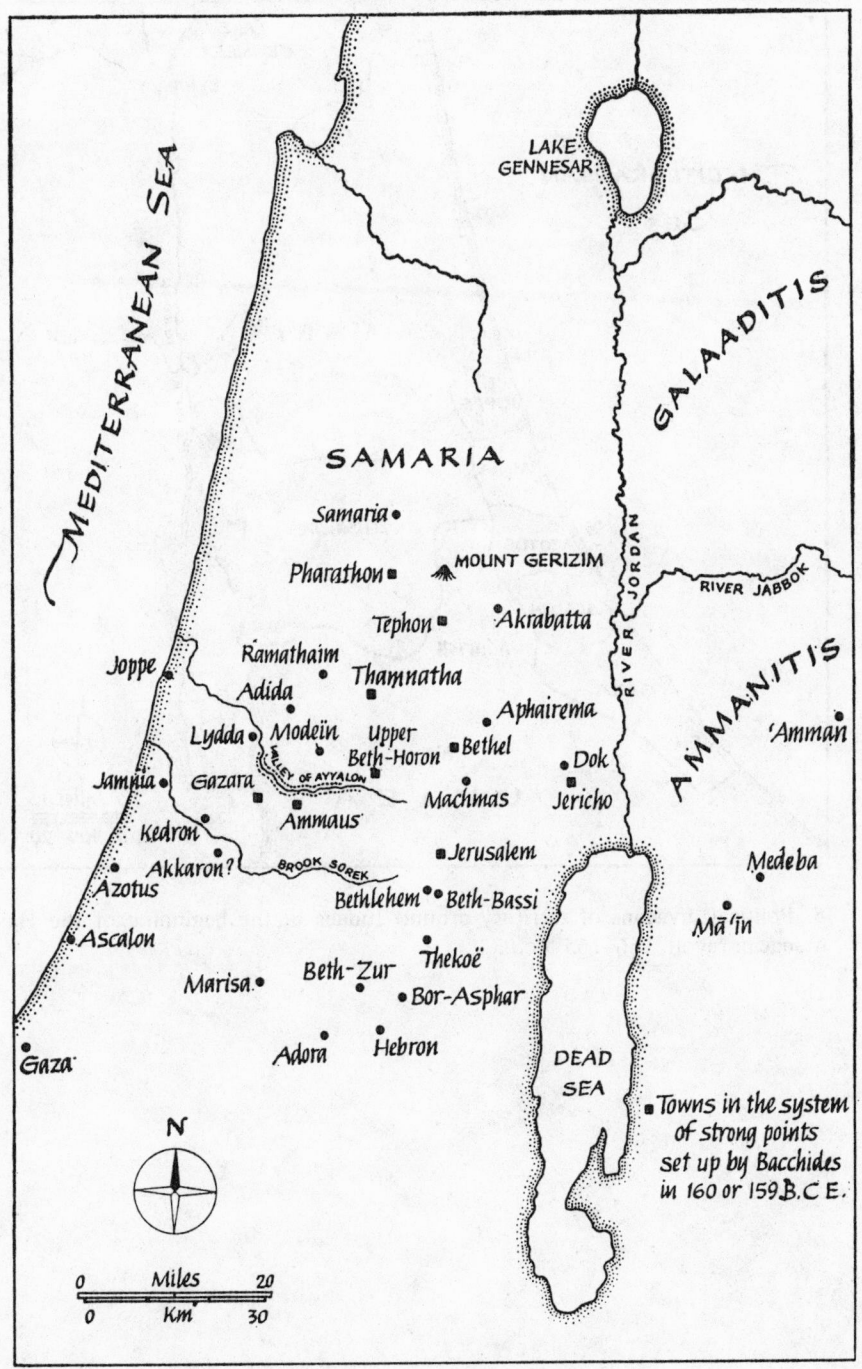

MEDITERRANEAN SEA

LAKE GENNESAR

GALAADITIS

SAMARIA

Samaria •

Pharathon ■ ▲ MOUNT GERIZIM

Tephon ■   • Akrabatta

RIVER JABBOK

Ramathaim •

Adida   Thamnatha ■

Joppe •

Lydda • Modeïn • Upper   • Aphairema

Jamnia • Gazara ■ Beth-Horon • Bethel

Kedron • Ammaus˙

Akkaron? • BROOK SOREK • Dok

Azotus • Machmas ■ Jericho

VALLEY OF AYYALON

RIVER JORDAN

AMMANITIS

'Amman •

Ascalon ◂

• Jerusalem

Bethlehem •• Beth-Bassi

Medeba •

Mā'in •

Marisa • Beth-Zur • Thekoë •

• Bor-Asphar

Adora • Hebron •

DEAD SEA

Gaza˙

N

■ Towns in the system
of strong points
set up by Bacchides
in 160 or 159 B.C.E.

0 ——— Miles ——— 20
0 ——— Km ——— 30

4. Important places in Judaea and her neighbors during the careers of Jonathan and Simon, 160–134 B.C.E.

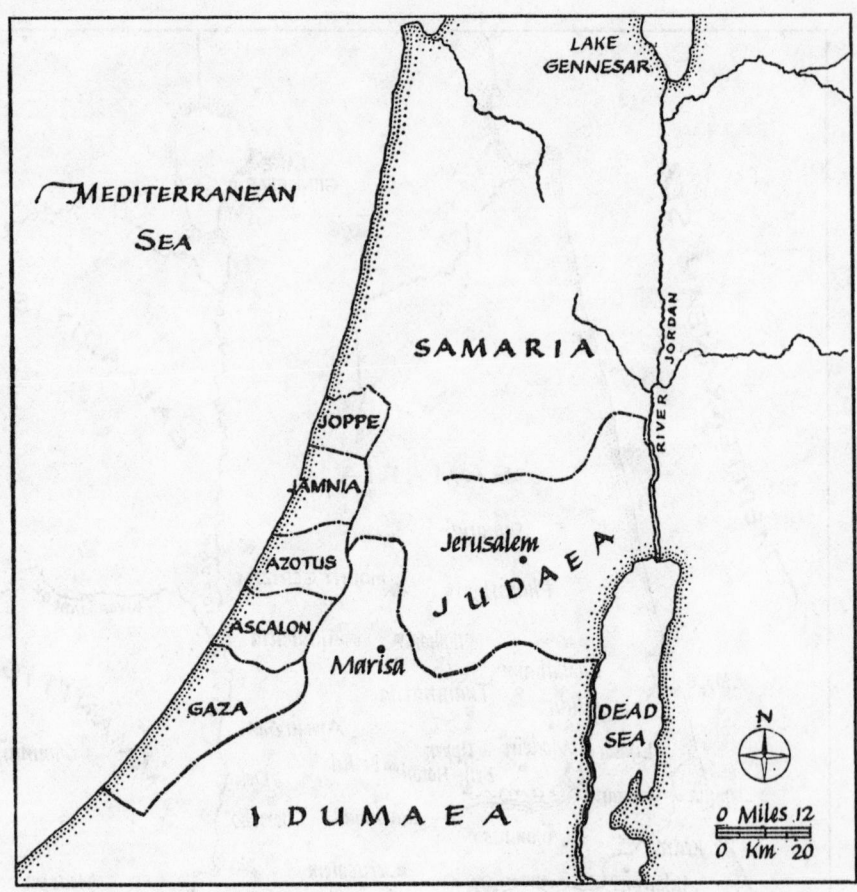

5. Political divisions of territory around Judaea at the beginning of the Hasmonaean revolt, 166–165 B.C.E.

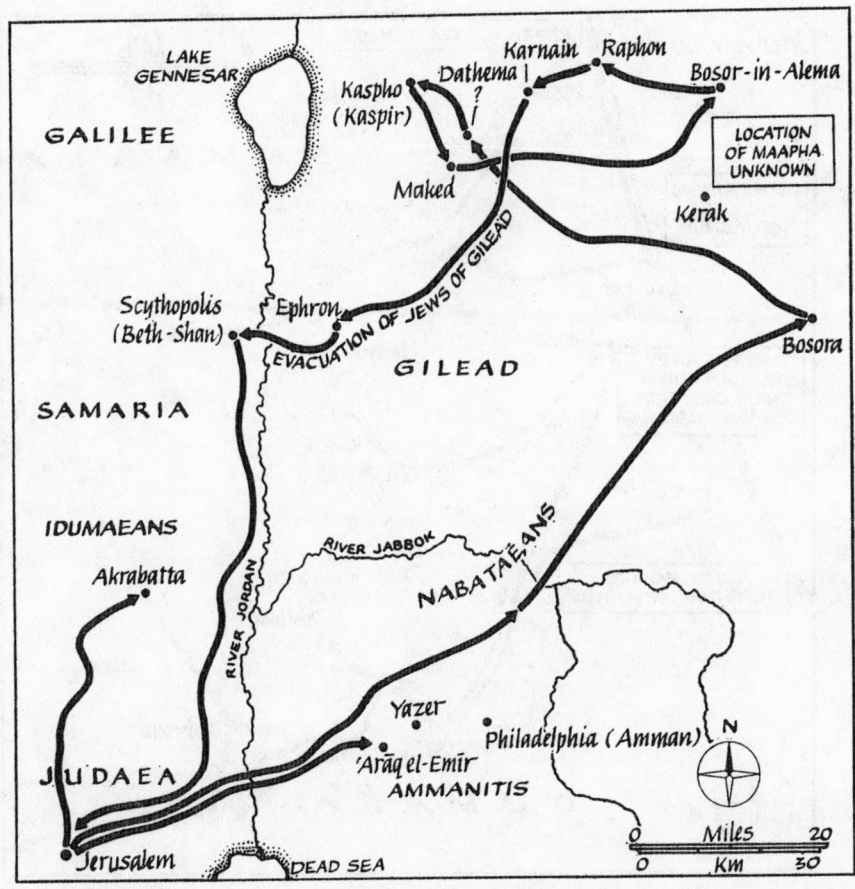

6. Judas' campaigns against Ammonites and Akrabattene (location of Baianites unknown); the campaign of Judas and Jonathan in Galilee, 163 B.C.E.

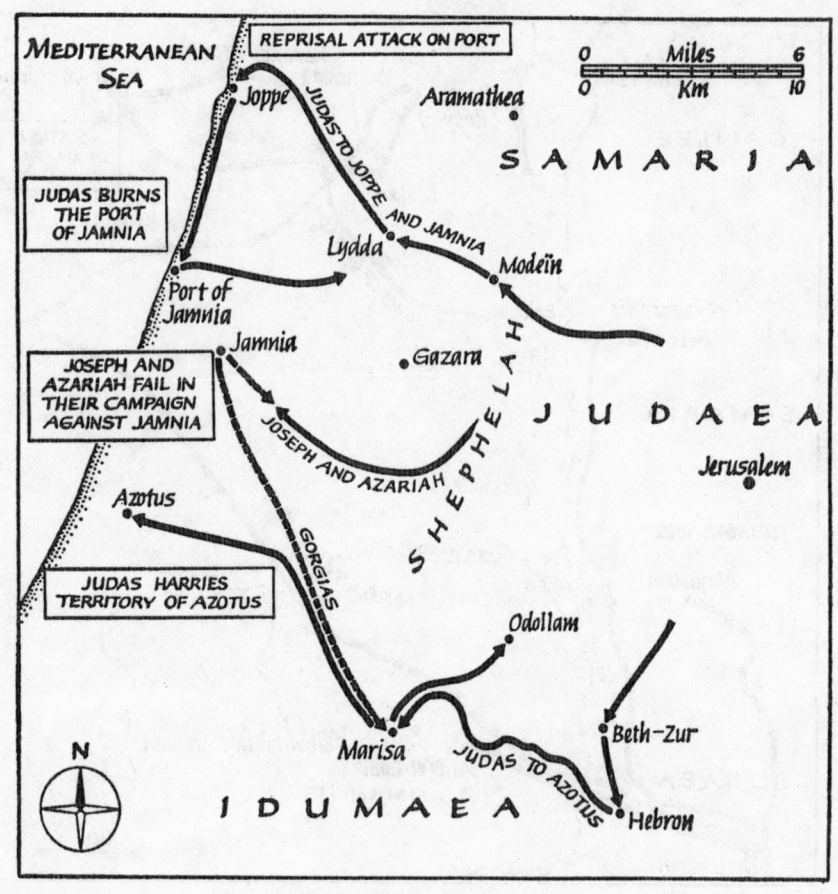

7. Judas in the costal plain and Idumaea, 163 B.C.E.

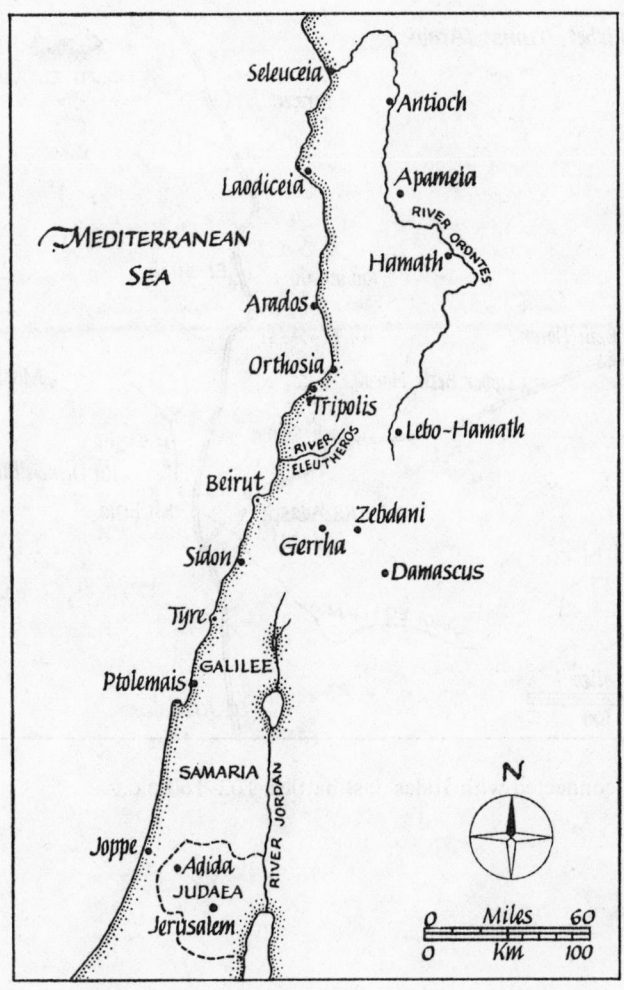

8. Judaea and the coast and interior of Coele-Syria and Phoenicia, ca. 162–143 B.C.E.

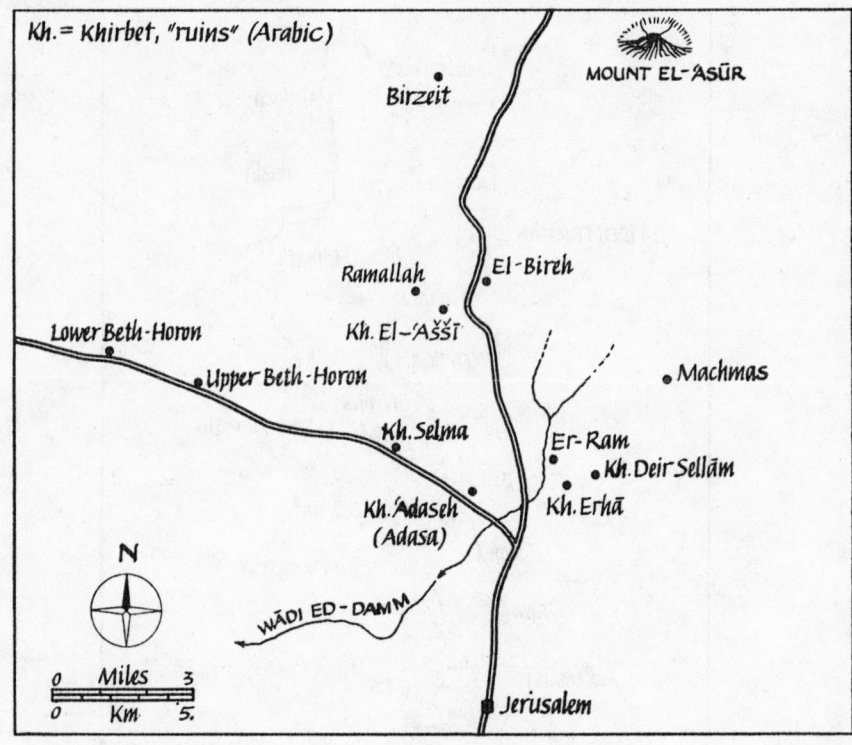

Kh. = Khirbet, "ruins" (Arabic)

MOUNT EL-ʿASŪR

Birzeit

Ramallah   El-Bireh

Kh. El-ʿAŠŠĪ

Lower Beth-Horon

Upper Beth-Horon   Machmas

Kh. Selma   Er-Ram
                              Kh. Deir Sellām

Kh. ʿAdaseh   Kh. Erhā
(Adasa)

N

WĀDI ED-DAMM

0   Miles   3
0   Km   5.

Jerusalem

9. Sites connected with Judas' last battles, 162–160 B.C.E.

APPENDICES

APPENDIX VII

HOW THE WRITERS IN FIRST AND SECOND MACCABEES COUNTED INTERVALS OF TIME

The terms used in ancient and modern languages for counting years are ambiguous. In ancient Greek, though *eniautos* unequivocally means "year-long period," its use in our texts is comparatively rare. The more common *etos* can mean either "calendar year" or "year-long period."[1] Moreover, there are many ways of employing such terms to represent intervals between two events. We may note the following: intervals may be represented (1) by actual length of elapsed time (December 31, 1967–June 1, 1969=1½ years);[2] or (2a) by number of year-long periods contained in the interval, appreciable fractions being counted as whole years (December 31, 1967–June 1, 1969=2 years);[3] or (2b) by the same procedure but with fractions being ignored (December 31, 1967–June 1, 1969=1 year); or (2c) by "inclusive counting" of year-long periods contained in the interval, any fraction, however small, being reckoned as a full year (games which occur June 20, 1965, and June 20, 1969, and so on, are "penteteric" or "quinquennial," because June 20, 1969, is the first day of the fifth year-long period);[4] or (3) by number of lapsed calendar years (December 31, 1967–June 1, 1969=2 years, 1967 and 1968 having lapsed); or (4) by number of calendar years of which any part fell within the interval (December 31, 1967–June 1, 1969=3 years);[5] or (5) by using an ordinal

---

[1] See AB vol. 41, p. 268; Bickerman, *Chronology,* pp. 63–64. Inasmuch as the Jews and the Seleucids in our period are known to have kept their calendars reasonably in step with the astronomical year, we need not consider the more extreme variability of the concept "calendar year" in antiquity; see Bickerman, ibid., pp. 63–70.

[2] See, e.g., Thucydides ii 65.6, iv 133.3, v 20, 25.3, and NOTE on II 4:7–38.

[3] See, e.g., Polybius iii 1.9 compared with i 1.5; Thucydides v 26.5 as interpreted in A. W. Gomme, A. Andrewes, and K. J. Dover, *A Historical Commentary on Thucydides,* Vol. IV (Oxford: Clarendon Press, 1970), pp. 13–14. The translation and NOTE to I 1:29 in AB vol. 41, however, are to be corrected by my remarks in the NOTE on II 5:24–27.

[4] Greek words formed by combining a cardinal number with *-etêris* or *-etêrikos* normally use "inclusive counting." On the normal practice and exceptions to it, see J. Beaujeu, "Grammaire, censure, et calendrier: quinto quoque anno," *Revue des études latines* 53 (1975), 354–56.

[5] This method was widely used by Greek authors, who frequently found in their sources events dated only by year with no further indication. See Thucydides v 20.2 and A. W. Gomme, *A Historical Commentary on Thucydides* (Oxford: Clarendon Press, 1945), I, 2–8. Athenians named each year by the archon who held office during it. Writers would reckon the ages of historical figures in Athens by counting the number of archons, beginning with the archon of the year of birth and ending with the archon of the year of death; see Felix Jacoby, *Apollodors Chronik* ("Philologische Untersuchungen," ed. by A. Kiessling and U. von Wilamowitz-Moellendorff,

number to describe the second event as having occurred in the nth of a series of consecutive year-long periods which began with the first event ("the event of June 1, 1970, occurred in the third year after the event of December 31, 1967"); or (6) by using an ordinal number to date the second event as having occurred in the nth of a series of consecutive calendar years ("the event of June 1, 1969, occurred in the third year after December 31, 1967"). All these methods can have been used both in ancient and in modern times. It is not always possible to determine even with a careful author which one he is using, especially when that author, like Polybius or Jason of Cyrene, is known to have drawn on more than one previous source.[6]

Formerly,[7] I was convinced that Greek adjectives of the form x-etês ("x-year") always give a measure of duration meaning "of at least x-1 year-long periods plus a fraction," as in method (2a).[8] That generalization is very difficult to prove, and I now believe it to be false. For many occurrences of the adjective form in ancient literature we have insufficient information to determine whether the generalization is true. I have found a possible counterexample in Josephus.[9] Etymologically, we should expect adjectives of the form x-etês to have all the ambiguities of the noun etos, from which they are derived. I now believe that at II 4:23 and 10:3 Jason of Cyrene wrote according to method (1) and meant by x-etês intervals of full years.[10] The occurrence of trietês at II 14:1, however, is best interpreted as an instance of method (4).[11]

---

sechzehntes Heft; Berlin: Weidmann, 1902), pp. 284–89, 316–28, 354–58, and cf. Joh. E. Kirchner, "Zur Datierung einiger athenischer Archonten," *Rheinisches Museum*, n.s., 53 (1893), 383, n. 1 (extending on to p. 384).

The discrepancy between J. *AJ* xv 9.6.341 (twelve years: *dodekaetei chronôi*) and xvi 5.1.136 (ten years) for the duration of the building of Caesarea might be solved by saying that in the former Josephus counts calendar years or regnal years of Herod, using method (4), whereas in the latter he counts elapsed time and ignores a fractional year, using method (2b); but cf. Walter Otto, "Herodes 14," PW, suppl. II (1913), 68–69, n.

[6] On multiple sources and inconsistencies of Polybius, see Bickerman, *Chronology*, p. 64; on Jason's, see Introduction, Part II, and NOTE on 4:1–4. For a probable inconsistency in Thucydides, who generally does not use method (2a), see n. 3. See also T. J. Cadoux, "The Athenian Archons from Kreon to Hypsichides," *Journal of Hellenic Studies* 68 (1948), 83–86, and Beaujeu, *Revue des études latines* 53 (1975), 330–60.

[7] AB vol. 41, p. 91.

[8] Cf. Beaujeu, *Revue des études latines* 53 (1975), 356.

[9] See n. 5.

[10] See NOTE on 4:7–38 and Introduction, pp. 59–60.

[11] See NOTE on 14:1–4.

APPENDIX VIII

THE PETITION OF THE SAMARITANS AND THE REPLY OF ANTIOCHUS IV AS PRESERVED BY JOSEPHUS AT *AJ* xii 5.5.258–64

A. *Translation*

(258) To King Antiochus Theos Epiphanes, a memorandum from the Sidonians in Shechem.

(259) Our ancestors, in response to drouths in the land,[a] followed an ancient religious tradition and adopted the practice of observing the day which the Jews call the Sabbath and also founded an unnamed shrine on the mountain called Garizein and offered there the appropriate sacrifices.

(260) Now that you have treated the Jews as befits their wickedness, the royal administrative officials, in the belief that common descent is the reason why we follow the same practices as they, hold us to be guilty under the same charges. But we are Sidonians in origin, as is clear from our civic records.

(261) Accordingly, we ask you, our benefactor and savior, to order Apollonius the *meridarchês* and Nicanor the royal agent to cease harassing us by holding us to be implicated under the charges brought against the Jews though we are foreign to the Jews both by descent and by our way of life. We also ask that our unnamed temple be called the temple of Zeus Xenios.[b] Thereby we shall be released from harassment and in security shall apply ourselves to our labors and increase your revenues.

(262) In response to those requests of the Samaritans, the king sent them the following reply:

King Antiochus to Nicanor. The Sidonians in Shechem have presented the attached memorandum.

(263) Their emissaries demonstrated to us in council with our friends that they are not implicated in the charges against the Jews but rather choose to live according to Greek ways. Accordingly, we absolve them of the accusations and order that their temple be called the temple of Zeus Xenios[c] as they ask.

(264) He sent the same to Apollonius the *meridarchês* in the year 146, on the eighteenth of the month. . . .

---

[a] The words "in the land" are probably a scribal interpolation. See commentary.
[b] See commentary.
[c] See commentary, NOTE on section 261, *We also . . . Zeus Xenios.*

B. *Commentary*

Introductory NOTE: Bickerman solved most of the problems of these documents and proved them authentic. His treatment of them ("Un document relatif à la persécution d'Antiochos IV Épiphane," RHR 115 [1937], 188–223=*Studies,* II, 105–35) is still fundamental and requires only a few corrections, despite the objections of Gedalyahu Alon (*Jews, Judaism and the Classical World,* translated from the Hebrew by Israel Abrahams [Jerusalem: Magnes, 1977], pp. 369–72) and Abraham Schalit ("Die Denkschrift der Samaritaner an König Antiochos Epiphanes zu Beginn der grossen Verfolgung der jüdischen Religion im Jahre 167 v. Chr.," *Annual of the Swedish Theological Institute* 8 [1972], 131–83).

Bickerman (*Studies,* II, 107–12) called attention to the practice whereby Hellenistic kings would let the letter sent to the official concerned serve as the document recording a royal decree. Thus the king did not make a direct reply to the Samaritans (though Josephus in par. 262 says he did). Rather, his subordinates gave them a copy of the letter sent to Nicanor. Indeed, we may guess Apollonius gave the Samaritans the text of the letter sent to him, and that text somehow reached Josephus.

In particular, Bickerman showed that Josephus' source was a letter of the king to Apollonius, dated on the eighteenth of some month in the year 146 Sel. Mac. In this letter Antiochus told Apollonius, "I have sent Nicanor the letter of which you have a copy below." The copy below consisted of par. 262 (second half) and 263 followed by a copy of the text of the memorandum of the Samaritans in pars. 258–61. Josephus could give a date neither for the Samaritan memorandum nor for the letter to Nicanor because the practice of the secretaries of the Hellenistic empires was to omit the dates in copies appended to other documents.

The full implementation of the persecution upon the Jews came in December, 167 B.C.E. The Samaritans were surely quick to appeal to Antiochus, and the date of the document in response to their appeal is precisely right, 146 Sel. Mac. (167/6 B.C.E.).

What situation underlies the Samaritan's petition? What were the "charges" under which the Jews were being punished (sections 260, 261, 263)? The documents here are crucial for Bickerman's interpretation of the persecution of the Jews by Antiochus IV (see Introduction, Part V, section 5).

As Bickerman reconstructs the situation (*Gott,* pp. 120–33), among the Jews of Judaea there was a "reform party," headed by the high priest, Menelaus. Members of this party had their own views of what the Jewish religion should be. At the request of that party, Antiochus IV in 167 B.C.E. issued a decree imposing their views upon those Jews who were politically subject to Menelaus, i.e., upon the Jews of Judaea alone. That decree was the "persecution." It forbade the observance of many of the commandments of the Torah, including the keeping of the Sabbath and the offering of the "perpetual" daily sacrifice (*Tamid*) at the temple. A considerable number of Jews refused to obey the decree imposing the "reform." Our documents, in speaking of the "wickedness" of the Jews and of the "charges" under which they are being punished, would refer to that disobedience to the reform decree.

One might think that Bickerman's own theory, that the reform decree was directed solely at the Jews of Judaea, was incompatible with the fact that the effects of the decree drove the Samaritans to address the petition here to the king. Good evidence shows that the Samaritans did not reside within the borders of Judaea and were not politically subject to Menelaus (I 10:38; see AB vol. 41, pp. 410–11, and Schürer [New English version], pp. 141–42). Bickerman gets around the difficulty by collecting evidence to show that administratively the Samaritans were in some (admittedly unknown) manner connected with Jerusalem: after Antiochus sacked Jerusalem in 169 B.C.E., he placed Philip in charge at Jerusalem *at the same time as* he put Andronikos in charge at the Samaritan holy place, Mount Gerizim (II 5:22–23); the first expeditionary force to march against Judas Maccabaeus came from *Samaria* (I 3:10).

Both pieces of evidence are far from proving Bickerman's conclusion. Before and even after the existence of modern communications, it was natural for a ruler to make appointments of regional officials when he passed through or near the region (cf. II 13:24); when Antiochus was in Jerusalem, it was natural for him to appoint officials in charge of Jerusalem and Mount Gerizim. The mere fact that he appointed two officials, with no coordinator over them, suggests rather that there was no administrative connection between the Samaritans and Jerusalem. The march of the expeditionary force from Samaria need not indicate any administrative connection. Rather, the garrison under Philip in the citadel of Jerusalem was too weak to cope with Judas, and the garrison at Samaria was the nearest larger Seleucid force. Furthermore, the expeditionary force probably consisted of gentiles and had nothing to do with the Samaritans; see AB vol. 41, pp. 245–46. Thus in the reign of Antiochus IV there is no evidence for any administrative connection between Jerusalem and Judaea on the one hand and the Samaritans or Samaria on the other. True, there were Jews in Samaria (I 11:34). But in the absence of Bickerman's alleged administrative connection, a royal decree imposing a reform upon the Jews of Judaea would hardly empower royal officials to impose that reform upon the Jews of Samaria, much less upon Samaritans (cf. *Gott*, pp. 123–24). Nevertheless, to show that there is no evidence for Bickerman's administrative connection is not yet to show that no such connection existed. Let us grant for the sake of argument that it did exist. We still can show that our documents are incompatible with Bickerman's theory.

In their petition, the Samaritans, far from concealing their Sabbath observance and the character of their sacrifices, confessed them openly (section 259). Bickerman supposes that the king's officials inferred from the assumed administrative connection and from the visible practices of the Samaritans that the Samaritans were Jews, subject to the reform decree and disobedient to it; therefore, they proceeded to punish the Samaritans. If so, one is indeed not surprised to find the Samaritans styling themselves "Sidonians in Shechem" and seeking to escape punishment by sending the petition here to the king, in which they insist that their religious observances are no proof they are Jews. Their plea, that they are not Jews, could indeed be an argument that the king's reform decree does not apply to them, as Bickerman proposes.

The language of the king's reply here excludes Bickerman's theory. Even in their petition, the Samaritans admit that they observe the Sabbath and perform the "appropriate" sacrifices, acts which (for Bickerman) constitute the substance of the charges against them and against pious Jews. Yet the king writes (section 263) that the Samaritans are not "implicated in the charges" and that he "absolves them of the accusations." If they confess to the charges, how can he deny they are implicated and say he "absolves" them? Under Bickerman's theory, if the king was to shield the Samaritans from punishment, he would rather have had either to declare expressly that Samaritans were not Jews or else to exempt them specifically from the reform decree. The king in his letter does neither. He gives the Samaritans the same name as they gave themselves, the "Sidonians in Shechem," but that is no declaration that they were not Jews. Calling themselves "Antiochenes from Jerusalem" certainly did not protect those Hellenized Jews of Jerusalem who remained loyal to the Torah (see II 4:7–20; AB vol. 41, pp. 158–59). Indeed, here the king abstains from committing himself on whether or not the Samaritans are Jews. Furthermore, we learn that the Samaritans, as proof they were innocent of the charges, used the fact that they "chose to live according to Greek ways." Since Hellenized Jews existed, living according to Greek ways was no proof that the Samaritans were not Jewish. The consideration could have been valid as an argument only if used to prove that the Samaritans were innocent of the charges brought against the Jews. Hence, the charges against the Jews must have in some way involved the Jews' refusal or failure to live according to Greek ways. Conformity to the imposed cult was in no way "living according to Greek ways" (see AB vol. 41, pp. 139–58). Bickerman himself demonstrated that imposed cult was not Greek (*Gott*, pp. 90–116).

There are further difficulties for Bickerman's interpretation. The petition of the Samaritans and the king's reply sharply contrast the Samaritans with the Jews. Even Hellenizing Jews are tainted with rebellion and are unlike the loyal Samaritans. The entire Jewish nation is being punished for crimes. If the persecution of the Jews had been suggested to Antiochus by loyal Hellenizing Jews as claimed by Bickerman, Antiochus would not have drawn this sharp contrast. Moreover, Bickerman himself rightly inferred, from clues in the Jewish sources, that most Jews lacked the will to become martyrs or guerrilla warriors and obeyed the king's decree on the imposed cult. Yet Bickerman must also hold that already in 146 Sel. Mac. (167/6 B.C.E.) Jewish disobedience was so widespread that it could constitute the "wickedness" of the Jews (section 260) and provoke imperial action against the entire community of the Jews on so large a scale that royal officials proceeded even against Samaritans! See also the arguments presented by Arnaldo Momigliano, *Alien Wisdom* (Cambridge: Cambridge University Press, 1975), pp. 108–9.

Accordingly, we must reject Bickerman's reconstruction. Disobedience to a reform decree is not the charge under which the Jews in our document are said to be undergoing punishment. Rather, in our theory, the decree imposing changes in religion is itself "treatment of the Jews as befits their wickedness," that is to say, punishment. The charges against the Jews stem from their turbulence ever since Antiochus IV issued his decree permitting a "changeover to Greek ways," allowing Jason the Oniad to organize the Antiochenes at Jerusalem and to establish a gymnasium (see NOTE on II 11:24–25). Pious Jews had taken to violence against the Antiochenes (see Introduction, Part V, section 3), and Antiochenes themselves, with Jason the Oniad as their leader, probably had interpreted apocalyptic prophecy as justification for rebellion (see NOTE on II 5:5–16). Both groups of Jews had thus departed from "Greek ways," whereas the Samaritans had not incurred such guilt. We do not hear of any "Antiochenes at Mount Gerizim," and perhaps the Samaritans were not faced with the choice of whether to tolerate such persons. On the other hand, since Israelites could be Antiochenes and still abstain from idolatry (see NOTE on II 4:19), we can imagine that Samaritan interpreters of the Torah, unlike Jewish zealots, found it possible to be tolerant (correct accordingly AB vol. 41, p. 137, which underestimates Samaritan fidelity to the Torah).

The king and the petitioners may also have been aware of a contrast which existed between the Jews and the Samaritans even before the reign of Antiochus IV: Jews, unlike Samaritans, won from their Hellenistic overlords the privilege of excluding pagan worship from their own territory of Judaea. As a result there were not even Greek villages in Judaea (see my article in *Jewish and Christian Self-Definition*, II, 73–75). In Samaria, on the other hand, there was at least one Greek city (Samaria), and perhaps there were others, such as Scythopolis (if Galilee was considered to be part of Samaria; see Abel, *Géographie*, II, 134).

From the content of the documents here and from I 1:44–51 and from our knowledge of the role of Torah and prophecies in the turbulence of the Jews, we can infer that Antiochus IV reacted to the continued unrest among them by issuing a decree addressed to the Jews of Judaea which can be reconstructed as follows: "Since you Jews have been guilty of wickedness and rebellion and have committed outrages against those who follow Greek ways and you claim that your criminal acts are obedience to your religion, I impose the following changes upon your religion [here followed what we have in I 1:44–50]." The king also sent letters out to officials throughout the kingdom containing a copy of the decree to the Jews and informing the officials that this was the policy to be used against turbulent Jews. Jews in most areas were not turbulent; hence, we hear nothing of persecution in most other areas of the empire (but see NOTE on II 6:8–9 and NOTE on II 7). See also AB vol. 41, p. 223.

The authorities in charge of the Samaritans were confronted with a difficult matter of judgment. The region of Samaria contained many Jews (I 11:34) and was to serve the archrebel Hasmonaeans as a main base (see AB vol. 41, pp. 236, 386). Indeed, nothing indicates that the Samaritans, beyond seeking their own safety, showed any hostility to the rebel Jews (see NOTE on II 15:1). Both Samaritans and Jews followed the Torah; Jews in Samaria were turbulent and, under the terms of the king's decree, deserved punishment. Should not the officials also punish Samaritans? Thus the background as reconstructed by us could have led to the petition we have here. And Antiochus IV could indeed recognize that the Samaritans had played no role in the turbulence of the Jews. To such charges the Samaritans do not confess in their petition, and thus the king can say he "absolves" them. They follow Greek ways at least insofar as they do not persecute Antiochenes and do not follow apocalyptic prophecy into rebellion. Though Jews might consider "Zeus Olympios" impious and outrageous as a name for their God, the Samaritans were able to reconcile the name "Zeus Xenios" with their obligations under the Torah (see NOTES on II 6:2, *Zeus Olympios* and *Zeus Xenios*, and AB vol. 41, p. 142). The Samaritans were delighted to exhibit the contrast as a confirmation of their innocence and their lack of connection with the Jews.

258. *King Antiochus Theos Epiphanes.* Although Antiochus IV seems to have been known abroad simply as King Antiochus Epiphanes, his official style within his kingdom was more elaborate. See AB vol. 41, NOTE on I 1:10. In a Greek inscription from Babylon dated in 147 Sel. (October 14, 166–October 1, 165, or April 8, 165–March 27, 164; see AB vol. 41, Introduction, Part VI, n. 72) the king is styled as here. It was believed that Antiochus IV was so styled on the coins he issued after his victories in Egypt in 169 down to his ostentatious celebration in 166 B.C.E., whereas thereafter he was styled "King Antiochus Theos Epiphanes Nikêphoros." See Edward T. Newell, "The Seleucid Mint of Antioch," *American Journal of Numismatics* 51 (1917–18), 22–32. Newell wrongly dated the ostentatious celebration in 167; see Mørkholm, p. 98, n. 37. Mørkholm, however, has argued that the coins with the epithet "Nikêphoros" were being issued already in 169/68 (*Studies in the Coinage of Antiochus IV of Syria* [Historisk-filosofiske Meddelelser udgivet af det Kongelige Danske Videnskabernes Selskab, Bind 40, no. 3 (1963)], pp. 34–37). It is possible but unlikely that the Samaritans and the author of the inscription from Babylon styled the king differently from the coins. Hence, Mørkholm's redating of the introduction of the epithet "Nikêphoros" is probably to be rejected, and the use in our document of the royal style which was changed in the summer of 166 strongly suggests that the document was written by a contemporary and is authentic. Cf. Bickerman, *Studies*, II, 112–17.

a memorandum. Petitions were often written in the form of a "memorandum" (*hypomnêma*); see Bickerman, "Beiträge zur antiken Urkundengeschichte, III," *Archiv für Papyrusforschung* 9 (1930), 164–82. In Ptolemaic Egypt the "memorandum" was not a form used in petitions to the king, but only to officials. In the third and second centuries B.C.E., however, the form was used in petitions to the king in the Antigonid kingdom of Macedonia (C. Bradford Welles, "New Texts from the Chancery of Philip V of Macedonia and the Problem of the 'Diagramma,'" *American Journal of Archaeology* 42 [1938], 246–49) and in the Seleucid empire (Jeanne and Louis Robert, "Bulletin épigraphique," REG 83 [1970], 471–72; Th. Fischer, "Zur Seleukideninschrift von Hefzibah," *Zeitschrift für Papyrologie und Epigraphik* 33 [1979], 132, lines 9, 11, 18, and 21).

In the Hellenistic kingdoms, a petition in the form of a memorandum began as here with the formula "To X, a memorandum by Y." Under the Roman empire, however, the word "memorandum" disappeared from the opening formula (Bickerman, *Studies*, II, 113).

the Sidonians in Shechem. See NOTE on par. 260, *in the belief . . . records.*

259. Antiochus believed that the Torah had made the Jews into a nation of rebels, and his purpose in the persecution was to purge the Jews' religion of those traits which to him seemed to have caused their rebellion. See Intro-

duction, Part V, section 5. In order to ask the king for exemption from the persecution, the Samaritans had to show that the charges against the Jews did not apply to them. Their case was indeed difficult. They, too, were devoted to the Torah. They, too, were conspicuous for observing the Sabbath. They, too, did not name their God when talking to Greeks. Their sacrificial cult was entirely in accordance with their interpretation of the Torah. Hence, they had to stretch the truth and explain away these embarrassing facts.

What they cannot hide, they admit: their Sabbath, their temple, and their sacrificial cult were copied from the Jews, but for a reason understandable to a Greek: the ancestors of the Samaritans, hard pressed by famine, adopted the practices, following the suggestion of an "old religious tradition" (see below). In the pagan world it was common to adopt new rites or even foreign rites when the ordinary rituals failed to put an end to calamity. Thus the worship of Kybele the Great Mother of Asia Minor is reported to have been adopted by the Athenians in order to rid them of a plague; see Martin P. Nilsson, *Geschichte der griechischen Religion* (3d ed.; München: Beck, 1967), I, 725–27. Later, in 205 B.C.E., the Romans, perhaps because they wished to have additional divine aid against Hannibal, also adopted the worship of Kybele, repugnant though her cult was to Roman mores; see Kurt Latte, *Römische Religionsgeschichte* (München: Beck, 1960), pp. 258–62. Cf. also II Kings 17:24–41. Bickerman (*Studies,* II, 124) and Schalit (*Annual of the Swedish Theological Institute* 8 [1970–71], 136, 144–45, 168, nn. 25–27, and 173, nn. 57–58) cite other examples from the Greek world.

One lucky circumstance aided the Samaritans in their plight: their foreign rulers long used "the Sidonians in Shechem" as the official designation for the Samaritans, though other Sidonians (i.e., Phoenicians or Canaanites) might well have disowned the Samaritans and called them "Israelites" or "Jews." See NOTE on paragraph 260, *in the belief . . . records.* The more the Samaritans could impress the king that they really were Sidonians and not Jews, the safer they would be.

A Phoenician myth told how two early human beings in Phoenicia, Genos and Genea, learned to worship the true Lord of Heaven: "When drouths occurred, they stretched forth their hands toward heaven in the direction of the sun. For they held it . . . to be a god, the sole Lord of Heaven, using the name 'Beelsamen,' i.e., 'Lord of Heaven' in Phoenician, 'Zeus' in Greek." The myth is preserved only by Eusebius, who took it from the *Phoenician History* written in Greek by Herennius Philo of Byblos (late first and early second century C.E.). Herennius Philo said he was translating the work of the Phoenician writer Sanchuniaton. He was probably telling the truth. Sanchuniaton's work could easily have been published well before the Samaritans wrote their petition; see Hans Gärtner, "Herennius Philon," *Der kleine Pauly,* II (1967), 1060, and W. Röllig, "Sanchuniaton," *Der kleine Pauly,* IV (1972), 1539. The myth could have been famous even without the work of Sanchuniaton. Samaritans and Greeks could have heard of it.

I believe that the myth was famous enough that the Samaritans borrowed its language ("drouths"), the better to pose as real Sidonians. But the Phoenician myth does nothing to connect the drouths with the Sabbath or even with a temple and sacrifices. Real Phoenicians could easily have exposed the falsity of the

Samaritans' claims if they had based their appeal upon Phoenician myth. Rather, having drawn the word "drouths" from Phoenician myth, the Samaritans stretched it to fit what they believed to be true: the story of how their Israelite ancestors went down to Egypt *because of famine in their own land of Canaan* (Gen 47:4) and (after the Exodus) *lacked water and food* in the desert and, as a result, came to accept first the Sabbath and then the rest of the Torah (Exod 15:22, 16:1–30, 19:1–8). The record of the Samaritans' claim was thus in the Torah itself, the same book that the Jews held holy! Artfully, by their choice of words, the Samaritans concealed the embarrassing fact.

Bickerman (*Studies*, II, 123–25) and Schalit (*Annual of the Swedish Theological Institute* 8 [1970–71], 136–49) interpret the petition as asserting that the Samaritan Sabbath had a pre-Mosaic origin, unconnected with the Torah. Their interpretations are farfetched. The words of the petition imply nothing of the sort, and the Samaritans could not risk asserting a falsehood that could be so easily exposed. Cf. Alon, *Jews*, p. 370.

Although the Greek word *deisidaimonia* early came to be used with the disparaging meaning "superstition," originally it meant "strong piety," the "fear of the gods," and was often used in favorable references to Jewish religion. See Peter J. Koets, Deisidaimonia: *A Contribution to the Knowledge of the Religious Terminology in Greek* (Diss., Utrecht; Purmerend: J. Muusses, 1929), pp. 1–41. Here the Samaritans use the expression "a certain *deisidaimonia*" ("religious belief" or "religious tradition") to refer to God's commands in Exod 16 and 19 or perhaps to the entire Torah.

The syntax of the sentence in Greek is artful. Only the Jewish Sabbath was absolutely distinctive, and only in connection with the Sabbath do the Samaritans explicitly admit any connection with the Jews. The abstinence from naming a god and the character of the sacrificial rites, the Samaritans and the Jews shared with neighboring peoples (see NOTES on *unnamed temple* and *appropriate sacrifices*). The Samaritans first speak of the Sabbath, mentioning its connection with the Jews, and then, in a separate participial phrase, speak of their temple as "unnamed" and of their sacrifices as "appropriate" (i.e., in conformity to the Torah). I have preserved the effect of the Greek syntax in idiomatic English by using the word "also."

drouths in the land. "The land" would normally mean "the land we now occupy," not "the desert." The famine which drove the ancestors of the Israelites to Egypt (Gen 47:4) could indeed be viewed as a remote cause of their Exodus and their subsequent acceptance of the Sabbath and the Torah. Thus the text of the petition as we have it makes sense. However, the immediate cause, the hunger in the *desert,* was much more obvious in the narrative of the Torah (Exod 16:1 – 19:8). The original text of the Samaritans' petition may not have referred to the remote cause at all and may have been based mainly on Exod 16, for the genitive phrase "in the land" (*tês chôras*) may be a later insertion by scribes surprised to find the words absent (cf. Gen 12:10, 26:1, 41:54; II Sam 24:13; I Kings 8:37; Ruth 1:1, etc.). Indeed, the genitive phrase is absent from the text of the epitome of Josephus (E), follows the noun it modifies in mss. P A M W, and precedes it in F L V and the old Latin translation, a fact strongly suggesting that it is a scribal insertion. Confirmation for the hypothesis that the phrase "in the land" is an interpolation can be found in the fact that it is absent from the myth told by Sanchuniaton (quoted above, p. 529).

The story of the Samaritans at II Kings 17:24–41 was famous. Josephus paraphrased it at *AJ* ix 14.3.288–91, and in speaking of the lions who plagued the settlers (II Kings 17:25–26), he used, as was proper, the Greek noun *loimos* ("plague"). Literate Greeks knew from Thucydides ii 54.2–3 that *limos* ("famine") was easily confused with *loimos* ("plague") in written and spoken Greek. Hence, it is not surprising that Greek scribes who knew Thucydides and II Kings and had already written *AJ* ix 14.3.288–91 thought that "drouths" (*auchmous*) could not be the correct reading here, though the word is unambiguous and is preserved in P A M W E. F, L, and the Latin read, predictably, *loimous,* and V has *limous!*

the day . . . Sabbath. A fine piece of ambiguous writing. An unwary reader might suppose that only the Jews, not the Samaritans, called the day the "Sabbath," but the words could also be interpreted as meaning the truth, that the Samaritans, too, kept the name.

founded . . . Garizein. On Mount Gerizim, see NOTE on II 5:23. The Samaritans here speak of their original national shrine. According to their traditions, it was founded in the time of Joshua. See Moses Gaster, *The Samaritans: Their History, Doctrines, and Literature* (London: British Academy, 1925), p. 8, and John MacDonald, *The Theology of the Samaritans* (Philadelphia: Westminster Press, 1964), p. 16.

Although in Samaritan tradition the shrine where Melchizedek was priest (Gen 14:18–20) also stood on Mount Gerizim, the Samaritans did *not* claim that their ancestors founded it. Hence, the interpretations of Bickerman (*Studies,* II, 125) and Schalit (*Annual of the Swedish Theological Institute* 8 [1970–71], 150–52) are to be rejected (cf. Alon, *Jews,* p. 370).

unnamed shrine. In this period there was a tendency among Phoenicians, Syrians, Jews, and Samaritans to avoid using the native proper names of their gods. Instead they would use circumlocutions like "Lord of the city X," "God of the nation Y," or "Lord of Heaven." The tendency was especially strong among the Phoenicians. Among Jews and Samaritans the avoidance was probably connected with their interpretation of the commandment not to "take the LORD's name in vain" (Exod 20:7; Deut 5:11), which made ordinary use of the divine name *YHWH* impossible: for most purposes it was ineffable, as Josephus (*AJ* ii 12.4.276) and Philo (*De vita Mosis* iii 11.114–15) state. There were many Greek translations from the Hebrew and many original works in Greek composed by Jews and Samaritans which circulated freely among those literate in Greek. Jews and Samaritans appear to have been careful not to use the name *YHWH* in any speech or writing to a pagan audience. Hence, it is absent from most manuscripts of Greek versions of the Bible and from all remains of Jewish and Samaritan Greek literature. Pagan writers like Livy (*apud* scholia to Lucan ii 531) and Lucan (ii 592) might believe that the God of the Jews had no name, though Dio Cassius (xxxvii 17.2) knew that His name was ineffable.

We lack evidence to explain the Phoenicians' and Syrians' avoidance of using the native names of their gods. We may guess, however, that they, too, came to regard the native proper names as ineffable.

Polytheistic peoples with no such tendency, including Greeks, found it difficult to understand the unnamed deities. Full acquaintance with and worship of a god required knowledge of his name (cf. Exod 3:13–15, 6:3). On the other hand, those polytheistic peoples were ready to adopt the worship of foreign gods, including the unnamed gods of Phoenicia and Syria. When they did so, they supplied the unnamed god with the name of one of their own gods. Gods of the seacoast might be called Poseidon and gods of the mountains might be called Zeus. Phoenicians and Syrians were themselves polytheists. For them only the native names were ineffable. As soon as they came to speak and worship in Greek, they, too, would use the Greek names for their own gods. The adoption of the Greek name and language did not otherwise change the nature of the god or the ritual by which he was worshiped.

Samaritans and Jews, on the other hand, were monotheists. Did Exod 23:13 forbid the use of the name of a Greek deity for their own god? Deut 12:3 and Hosea 3:18 made it clear that the use of Canaanite names for the LORD was forbidden, but the passages might be construed as leaving the question of Greek names open. Even the pious Greek translator of First Maccabees had no hesitation in calling God *Ouranos* ("Heaven"). The word is the name of a deity prominent in Greek myth. Thus we must not be surprised if Samaritans and even some Jews found unobjectionable the name "Zeus" for their god, especially since Greeks often used "Zeus" as a common noun ("god"). See par. 261 and *Aristeas to Philocrates* 16, J. *AJ* xii 2.2.22, and cf. Aristobulus *apud* Eusebius *Praeparatio evangelica* xiii 12.7.

For the evidence on the avoidance of the use of the native divine names among the Phoenicians, Syrians, Jews, and Samaritans, see Elias Bickerman, "Anonymous Gods," *Journal of the Warburg Institute* 1 (1937–38), 187–96, and *Studies*, II, 125–28. Bickerman's interpretation of the evidence differs from mine. He recognizes the possibility that gods may be left unnamed in practice because their names are believed to be ineffable (ibid., p. 191), but he holds that the four peoples treated their gods as completely nameless in the native language. To do so, he must dismiss the strong evidence for the survival of the use of the name *YHWH* among Hebrew- and Aramaic-speaking Jews. He holds (ibid., 195) that the evidence belongs to the sphere of magic, not religion. The distinction would not have been recognized by ancient Jews, and even if it had been, Bickerman's assertion is false, since the name was used throughout the Hellenistic period in religious ritual that had nothing to do with magic (Sir 50:20; J. *AJ* ii 12.4.275; Philo *De vita Mosis* iii 11.114; *M. Yoma* 3:8, *Soṭah* 7:6, *Tamid* 3:8 and 7:2; Schürer, II, 355). In Greek texts intended for the use of Jews alone, the divine name could be written out fully in Hebrew or in Greek letters. See Sidney Jellicoe, *The Septuagint and Modern Study* (Oxford: Clarendon Press, 1968), pp. 270–72. Bickerman also ignores the good evidence for the use of the name *YHWH* among Samaritans more freely than among Jews (TP *Sanhedrin* 7:8, p. 25b, and 10:1, p. 28b; James Alan Montgomery, *The Samaritans: the Earliest Jewish Sect* [Philadelphia: Winston, 1907], p. 213, and J. MacDonald, *The Theology of the Samaritans* [Philadelphia: Westminster Press, 1964], pp. 93–97), as Alon (*Jews*, pp. 370–71) was quick to protest. Even the pagan Diodorus (i 94.2) knew that

Moses said he had received his laws from the God named "Iao." See also
Hengel, *Judaism and Hellenism,* I, 260, and II, 171, n. 22.

Accordingly, we may suppose 'that the Samaritans here are again stretching
the truth in a manner credible to a pagan Greek audience. In Greek and to
Greek ears the God of the Samaritans and His temple had as yet borne no
proper name.

appropriate sacrifices. The offerings were in accordance with the Torah but
were not so very different from those of Syrians and Phoenicians. See Roland
de Vaux, *Ancient Israel* (New York, Toronto, and London: McGraw-Hill,
1961), pp. 438–41.

260. *Now . . . wickedness.* Our passage is a fundamental piece of evidence
as to why Antiochus instituted the persecution. He was punishing the Jews for
crimes against his kingdom: for violent attacks upon the "sinning" Jews who
had become the "Antiochene citizens of Jerusalem" and for open rebellion. See
Introduction, Part V, sections 3 and 5, and Bickerman, *Studies,* II, 133–35.

the royal administrative officials. The Greek (*hoi ta basilika dioikountes*)
covers any administrative official of the kingdom. It is analogous to "the administrative officials of the republic" (*hoi ta koina dioikountes*) in a Greek
city-state. Cf. *Papyrus Revenue Laws,* ed. by Jean Bingen (*Sammelbuch
griechischer Urkunden aus Ägypten,* Beiheft I; Göttingen: Hubert, 1952), col.
15; Welles, *Royal Correspondence,* no. 23, line 14, and no. 53 II A, line 3.

in the belief . . . records. The principle that an entire community could be
punished for crimes was unquestioned. The community might be a city, as
Demetrius II punished Antioch (Diodorus xxxiii 4.2–3), or a nation or ethnic
group, as the Romans punished the Epirotes after the Third Macedonian War
(Polybius xxx 15; Livy xlv 34.1–6). Antiochus in our instance decreed that
Jews were to be punished for their crimes. The militant pietists of Judaea were
clearly guilty of those crimes. Elsewhere, pious Jews may never have disturbed
public order, and there the royal officials may have assumed that they were not
to molest the Jews in their area unless they received specific orders from the
king. Samaria, however, bordered on Judaea, and within the province of
Samaria there surely were militant pious Jews, for the area was to serve Judas
Maccabaeus as a base (see AB vol. 41, NOTE on I 2:28), and the Seleucid
kings later conceded parts of it to Judaea (I 10:30, 38, 11:34). The turbulent
Jews of Judaea were obviously a nation. Ordinarily ethnic status was a matter
of birth and descent. Greeks who had long settled abroad were still identified
by the home city of their ancestor; see Dieter Nörr, "Origo," PW, suppl. X
(1965), 434–36. The Hellenistic monarchies continued the practice of the Persian empire, of identifying members of subject nations by personal name and
nation: "Mordecai the Jew," "Philip the Phrygian." Both Samaritans and Jews
claimed descent from Israel. Hence, the royal officials easily jumped to the conclusion that the Samaritans were included among the "Jewish criminals" of the
king's decree.

The Samaritans wisely abstain from impugning the motives of the king's
officials: in the course of loyally implementing the king's decree, the officials
have made a mistake; cf. Octave Navarre, *Essai sur la rhétorique grecque
avant Aristote* (Paris: Hachette, 1900), pp. 221–22. The Samaritans seek
safety in denying both kinship with the Jews and complicity in their crimes.

How could the Samaritans claim to be not of the same Israelite stock as the Jews but rather Sidonians of Shechem? Certainly the Samaritans did not come from the city of Sidon. "Sidonian," however, both in Hebrew and in Greek could be used for any Phoenician, and "Phoenician" was the Greek equivalent of "Canaanite"; see Bickerman, *Studies,* II, 118–19. The Samaritans were tenaciously loyal to the Torah, in which the Canaanites are condemned as abominable sinners. If the Samaritans ever came to be designated as the Sidonians (Canaanites) of Shechem, the name must have been imposed upon them by others. Indeed, the strange designation which the Samaritans here claim for their own was probably a result of the administrative practices of the Assyrian, Babylonian, and Persian empires, which the Hellenistic kingdoms at first took over without change. The descendants of the Israelites exiled upon the fall of the northern kingdom in the eighth century b.c.e. may long have been called "Israelites." Perhaps in an effort to diminish surviving nationalistic spirit among the Israelites who remained in the land, the Assyrians seem to have designated them only as "inhabitants of the province of Samaria" (*Šōmᵉrōnīm;* see II Kings 17:29), whereas the foreign settlers transferred to the province continued to bear their own ethnic designations (II Kings 17:30–31; Ezra 4:9–10). The later empires took over these practices. No ancient empire was to give its Israelite Samaritan subjects the satisfaction of addressing them by a national designation of their own; see Bickerman, *Studies,* II, 122–23. Ben Sira could say that they were "not a nation" (Sir 50:49). No empire declared that Samaria was to be resettled by Israelites. Hence, the official designation even of descendants of exiles who returned to Samaria was "inhabitant of Samaria," not "Israelite."

In contrast, the Babylonians seem to have made no effort to obliterate the national consciousness of the Jews after the fall of Jerusalem in 586. And Persian policy encouraged the resettlement of Jews in the territory which continued to be called "Judaea."

"Inhabitant of Samaria" in Greek was *Samareus* or *Samaritês,* from which we derive our "Samaritan." The Samaritans themselves eventually came to welcome the designation, interpreting it as *Šāmerīm,* "Keepers of the Torah" (Moses Gaster, *The Samaritans* [London: British Academy, 1925], p. 5; John MacDonald, *The Theology of the Samaritans* [Philadelphia: Westminster Press, 1964], pp. 18, 88, 272). However, from the time of the Assyrian empire the other stocks inhabiting the province of Samaria had a claim to be so designated. The Israelite Samaritans appear to have been the dominant aristocracy of the province when Alexander conquered the whole region in 333. When they confronted Alexander or his subordinates, their official designation probably had not changed. Josephus' report (*AJ* xi 8.6.344) that they already called themselves "Sidonians of Shechem" is anachronistic, for we now know that only later were the Samaritans forced to leave the city of Samaria and make their chief center Shechem. In 332 the Samaritans of Samaria rebelled and killed Alexander's governor. The rebellion was quelled, and Alexander or his subordinates established a military colony of Greeks and Macedonians in the city of Samaria. The survivors of the Israelite Samaritans established themselves at Shechem by Mount Gerizim, and that town was their center ever after. See Curtius iv 8.9; Georgius Syncellus *Chronographia* in *Georgius Syn-*

cellus et Nicephorus Cp., ed. by Guil. Dindorfius (Bonn: Weber, 1829), I, 496, and Eusebius *Chronicorum libri,* ed. by Alfred Schoene (Berlin: Weidmann, 1875), II, 118–19, both translated into English in Ralph Marcus, *Josephus,* vol. VI (LCL; Cambridge, Mass.: Harvard University Press, 1937), p. 524. See also Frank M. Cross, Jr., "The Discovery of the Samaria Papyri," BA 26 (1963), 110–21, and Cross's article "Papyri of the Fourth Century B.C. from Dāliyeh," in *New Directions in Biblical Archaeology,* ed. by David Noel Freedman and Jonas Greenfield (Garden City, N.Y.: Doubleday, 1969), pp. 45–69. The new settlers became the aristocracy of the province and used *Samaritês* as their own official ethnic designation (*Inscriptiones Graecae,* Editio minor, II–III 2943, 10219–21), though in common speech the name was still used of the Israelite Samaritans, as is clear from Josephus' employment of it.

Thereafter, what was the official ethnic designation of an Israelite Samaritan? In Ptolemaic Egypt and later in the Seleucid empire, it may have been "Jew"! See CPJ, pp. 4–5, and nos. 22, 28, and 128; I 11:34 and AB vol. 41, p. 433; and cf. J. *AJ* xii 1.1.7–10. The Hellenistic empires which ruled Palestine could choose freely any designation for the Samaritans. Already in the time of the Persian empire the officials of the foreign dynasty ruling the peoples of Syria and Palestine could be impatient with the minute ethnic distinctions between them, and members of the subject peoples themselves might not insist on being given their precise ethnic designations, as we learn from the Elephantine papyri, documents drawn up in Egypt under Persian rule. In those papyri, a person who in one document is called a Jew in another document can be called an Aramaean (=Syrian). Cf., e.g., *The Brooklyn Museum Aramaic Papyri,* ed. by Emil G. Kraeling (New Haven: Yale University Press, 1953), no. 5, line 2 (Jew of Yeb the fortress), with no. 2, line 2 (Aramaean of Syene), and similarly *Aramaic Papyri of the Fifth Century* B.C., ed. by Arthur Cowley (Oxford: Clarendon Press, 1923), no. 6, line 3, with no. 5, line 2; also Kraeling, *Aramaic Papyri,* no. 11, lines 1–2 (Jew of a unit which, according to no. 12, lines 2–3, was at Yeb), with Kraeling, no. 7, lines 1–2, and no. 12, lines 2–3 (Aramaean of Syene); and see Bezalel Porten, *Archives from Elephantine,* pp. 33–34.

How are we to explain the existence of two ways of designating Jews in documents drawn up under the official requirements of the Persian empire? Clearly the Persian authorities could use terms "Jew" and "Judaea." In a letter of April 8, 1980, Porten wrote that he is still "struggling" with the phenomenon, but he stands by his suggestion (*Archives from Elephantine,* pp. 16–17, 33–34) that if Jews were called Aramaeans it was because they used the Aramaic language. Indeed, they used Aramaic not only in their official documents, in which they were conforming to the linguistic requirements of the Persian government; they also used it on their private ostraca in notes and messages among themselves. In a letter of January 22, 1980, Jonas Greenfield wrote me, "I think that from the *Babylonian* point of view (perhaps already the Assyrian point of view, but I'm not sure) all westerners were 'Arameans' . . . and this usage continued on into the Persian period." As seen by Babylonians and Persians, both Jews and ethnic Aramaeans were westerners. In the same letter, Greenfield holds that Syene was the broader geographical area of which Yeb was a part. In any case, we find in official documents under the Persian empire Jews being referred to, not as Jews, but by a wider ethnic, linguistic, or geographical designation.

Greeks and Macedonians, too, could be impatient of fine distinctions. They could use "Syrian" of the Cappadocians of Asia Minor (Herodotus i 6.1) and of any of the peoples of Syria and Palestine (e.g., Scylax *Periplus* 104, in *Geographi Graeci minores,* ed. by Carolus Müllerus [Paris: Firmin Didot, 1855], I, 78). The Greek word "Syrian" is usually the equivalent of "Aramaean," and, in his letter, Greenfield suggested to me that this more inclusive use of "Syrian" in Greek is based on the more inclusive use of "Aramaean" by the Babylonian and Persian empires. On the other hand, the Greeks were well acquainted with the seafaring Phoenicians and easily distinguished them from the other "Syrians."

Though speakers of Greek soon recognized the ethnic separateness of the Jews, many of them continued to call Jews "Syrians" and their country "Syria" (see, e.g., Theophrastus *apud* Porphyry *De abstinentia* ii 26; Ovid *Ars amatoria* i 75, 415; Dio Cassius xxxvii, 15.1). When they did so they referred primarily to geography. Nevertheless, Jews under the Hellenistic empires spoke Aramaic and for ordinary purposes used the Aramaic alphabet in writing. For a Greek, Aramaic was the Syrian language (cf. J. *AJ* i 6.4.144). Language and alphabet probably were factors by which Greeks so readily distinguished the Jews from the Phoenicians and grouped them with the Syrians.

We do not know whether the Samaritans resisted the encroachment of Aramaic and held at all to Hebrew as their vernacular down to the time they received an ethnic designation from their Graeco-Macedonian rulers. It is certain, however, that they tenaciously resisted the substitution of the Aramaic alphabet for their old Hebrew letters, which they still use today. The Hebrew language and old Hebrew script for a Greek were indistinguishable from Phoenician. Hence, it is not surprising that a Graeco-Macedonian government would assign the Samaritans the name "Sidonians [="Phoenicians"] of Shechem." In Strabo's time Greeks were still observing "Phoenicians" among the natives of the interior of Judaea, which then included Samaria (xvi 2.34, C760). The designation may no longer have been the official one when the Samaritans sent their petition, for they had to inform Antiochus of it, but there were still plenty of documents in their archives upon which it appeared.

charges. Here and in sections 261 and 263 appears the Greek word *aitia,* and in section 263 appears the Greek word *enklêma.* Bickerman (RHR 115 [1937], 221–22) tried to draw a sharp distinction between the two, taking *enklêma* to mean "specific count of accusation brought against a defendant" and *aitia* to mean "prosecution," the "legal procedure used to obtain the punishment of the defendant." In fact in many contexts the two words are synonyms. Either can have either meaning.

For *enklêma* as "legal procedure to obtain punishment or redress," see Polybius vi 17.7, xx 6.1, xxv 3.1; OGIS 90, line 14, and 229, lines 43 and 54. For *aitia* as "count of accusation," see, e.g., *AJ* xi 6.12.275; Demosthenes 18.12; as "mere verbal accusation without proof" and as a synonym for "verbal abuse" (*loidoria*), it occurs at Demosthenes 22.21–22. For the interchangeability of *enklêma* and *aitia,* cf. our passage with J. *BJ* vii 11.3.450 and

OGIS 90, line 14; *BJ* i 24.6.487 with *AJ* xv 10.3.359; *AJ* vii 1.4.23 with *AJ* xvi 11.7.393; and *AJ* xviii 4.6.107 with *BJ* i 31.5.618. See also their use in a single passage as synonyms, at *AJ* vii 1.4.23, xi 4.9.117.

In most contexts, *aitia* and *enklêma* are best translated as "accusation," "charge," rather than by "prosecution" or by some other word implying judgment, trial, or sentence. In no case should either be translated as "imposition of punishment." In our context, "prosecution" is an unlikely translation for either word. Antiochus IV has already passed judgment upon the Jews: they are guilty as *charged* and are being punished (section 260). The word *aitia* in sections 260, 261, and 263 can hardly mean that the Samaritans are now being *prosecuted*. Rather, they are facing punishment because the king's officials believe that they, too, are Jews, guilty under the same *charges*.

Since the words are synonyms, I have felt free to render the plural of *aitia* as "charges" in sections 260 and 261 and as "accusations" in section 263, and to translate the plural of *enklêma* in section 263 as "charges."

261. *Accordingly . . . cease.* On the evolution of such formulas in papyri of petitions from Ptolemaic Egypt, see Paul Collomp, *Recherches sur la chancellerie et la diplomatique des Lagides* (Paris: "Les Belles Lettres," 1926), pp. 96–115.

Apollonius the meridarchês. He is probably the same as the Apollonius of I 3:10–12. A *meridarchês* had charge of a *meris*. Samaria in the Seleucid system was a *meris*, and, at least later, so was Judaea. See AB vol. 41, NOTE on I 10:65, and Menahem Stern, *The Documents on the History of the Hasmonaean Revolt* (Tel Aviv: Hakibbutz Hameuchad, 1965), pp. 63–64 (in Hebrew).

Nicanor the royal agent. Like "royal administrative official" in par. 260, "royal agent" is a very general term for an official. The synonymous expression *ho ta basilika pragmateuomenos* occurs at Ulrich Wilcken, *Urkunden der Ptolemäerzeit,* vol. I (Berlin: De Gruyter, 1927), no. 106, lines 4–5. In Greek city-states the term *ho ta koina prattôn* (Demosthenes *Epistle* 3.27) was an exact counterpart.

cease harassing. The Greek formula is used at I 10:63 and at J. *AJ* xii 3.4.153.

charges. See NOTE on par. 260, *Now . . . wickedness.*

foreign . . . by our way of life. Unlike the Jews, the Samaritans had not rebelled and had not molested Hellenizers in their territory. We do not know whether any Samaritans became citizens of the Antiochene republic. If any did, our text would be proof that Antiochene Samaritans and Jews did not worship Greek gods, for otherwise the Samaritans would have been bound by Exod 22:19 and Deut 17:2–5 to kill them. Correct accordingly AB vol. 41, pp. 136–37.

We also . . . Zeus Xenios. We may guess that the worshipers of a god could call his temple by any name they pleased. Here the Samaritans' request probably concerns the official name, to be used in the royal records and correspondence.

Greeks recognized many aspects of Zeus, and in worship always gave him an identifying epithet. The witnesses to the epithet here are in conflict: the manuscripts of II 6:2 have *Xenios* ("Protector of the Rights of Strangers"); the

Greek manuscripts of Josephus have *Hellênios* ("Hellenic"), and the Latin version of Josephus has *Cretaeus* ("Cretan").

Even so early a writer as the author of First Maccabees jumped to the false conclusion that Antiochus IV was propagating his own Greek religion; see AB vol. 41, p. 131. Crete is a Greek island. Hellenic Zeus and Cretan Zeus were well-known deities, distinct from the God of Israel; see Arthur B. Cook, *Zeus* (Cambridge: University Press, 1914–40), I, 149, and III, 164–65; Jessen, "Hellenios," PW, VIII (1913), 176; Hans Schwabl, "Zeus," PW, X^A (1972), 303, 326. Josephus presents the Samaritans as denying that their God is identical to the God of the Jews (*AJ* xii 5.5.257), and Antiochus' own response to the Samaritans' petition states that the petitioners convinced him that they lived "according to Greek ways" (section 263; see ad loc.). Hence, if the epithet "Hellenic" or "Cretan" had stood originally in the Samaritans' petition, no later scribe would ever have changed it to *Xenios*. On the other hand, the new Greek name for their God is the only thing in the Samaritans' petition which might show that they lived according to Greek ways. Ancient scribes could know that a Greek name for a god did not necessarily make him Greek, and *Xenios* in itself could mean "foreign," "non-Greek." Thus, puzzled scribes might well turn *Xenios* into an epithet that was more distinctively Greek.

On the other hand, the Samaritans in 167/6 B.C.E. had good reasons to give their own God the Greek name Zeus Xenios; see NOTE on II 6:2, *Zeus Xenios*. Accordingly, the Latin and Greek manuscripts of Josephus probably reflect the activity of at least two scribes who were puzzled by the epithet *Xenios,* jumped to the conclusion that it was wrong, and mistakenly corrected it, each in his own way (cf. Bickerman, RHR 115 [1937], 189, n. i). If Josephus himself wrote the epithet "Hellenic," it would be hard to explain why the Latin version has "Cretan," though Schalit (*Annual of the Swedish Theological Institute* 8 [1970–71], 172, n. 46) suggests that *Graeci* was misread as *Cretaei*(!). Hence, the alteration of the epithet probably came after Josephus.

Thereby . . . revenues. Petitioners would present to the king incentives for granting their request. The incentives tended to be stereotypes. See Collomp, *Recherches,* pp. 115–19. Nevertheless, revenue was a good incentive for the ambitious and extravagant Antiochus IV.

262. See above, introductory NOTE and NOTE on section 258, *a memorandum.* For *katachôrizein* as "attach," cf. Welles, *Royal Correspondence,* pp. 344–45.

263. *Their emissaries . . . ways.* As usual, emissaries of the Samaritans bore the petition to the king and expanded upon its content in response to the king's questions. It was usual for a Seleucid king to receive embassies and make decisions in council with high courtiers who belonged to the Order of the King's Friends. See Bickerman, *Institutions,* pp. 40–42, 46–50. Roman emperors in the time of Josephus in their rescripts made no such mention of consultation with courtiers (Bickerman, RHR 115 [1937], 197–98).

"According to Greek ways" does not appear in the Samaritan petition. The emissaries must have used the language to explain the words of section 261, "we are foreign to the Jews . . . by our way of life." Hence, the words need not mean that the Samaritans have become totally assimilated to Greeks, a meaning contradicted by Samaritan observance of the Torah and the Sabbath.

Rather, the Samaritans have not been guilty of the Jews' crimes of rebellion and of persecuting Antiochenes. In accordance with Greek ways they have remained loyal and have tolerated Antiochenes. See AB vol. 41, pp. 136–37.

order . . . ask. See NOTE on section 261, *We also . . . Zeus Xenios.*

264. He sent . . . meridarchês. See introductory NOTE and NOTE on section 261, *Apollonius.*

146. the manuscripts have "46," the figure for the hundreds having been omitted through a scribal error.

month. . . . The manuscripts name the month as *Hekatombaiôn Hyrkanios. Hyrkanios* is not otherwise known as the name of a month, though it may well be correct, for it is possible that the innovating Antiochus IV revised the calendar (cf. II 11:21). *Hekatombaiôn* is the name of the Athenian month which followed the summer solstice. As Bickerman suggests (RHR 115 [1937], 189, n. p) it is probably the gloss of a reader in order to explain the unfamiliar month name. Is the gloss correct? It is possible, though unlikely, that the king's response to the Samaritans' petition was issued as late as the end of June, 166.

APPENDIX IX

WHY IT IS UNLIKELY THAT EPISTLE 2 WAS COMPOSED BETWEEN 67 B.C.E. AND 73 C.E.

Although our analysis in the NOTE on 1:10b – 2:18 strongly suggests that Ep. 2 was fabricated as anti-Oniad propaganda, we must allow our opponents every opportunity to show that the document could have been produced between 64/3 B.C.E. and 70 C.E. Is it also possible that the forged letter is not propaganda? Ancient writers would produce letters of famous persons to sell to collectors; and without any intention to defraud, ancient literary artists would display their ingenuity by composing a letter on a historical theme. See Jonathan A. Goldstein, *The Letters of Demosthenes* (New York and London: Columbia University Press, 1968), pp. 31–33, 128. In our case, the writer could have chosen the theme "How would Judas Maccabaeus and his contemporaries have written to Aristobulus and the Jews of Egypt, calling upon them to observe the Days of Purification?"

By the 60's B.C.E., both First Maccabees and the abridged history had long since been published, and one might find it incredible that a forger or a writer of a historical fiction could have given a false report of the death of Antiochus IV. Nevertheless, the common man, and even intellectuals, in ancient times frequently believed popular legends which were contradicted by good, published historical sources. Tacitus' account of the Jews (*Histories* v 1–8) contains many such examples. The fantastic Ep. 2 even now stands as part of Second Maccabees! Hence, let us concede that a forger or a writer of a historical fiction might have written Ep. 2 after the publication of First and Second Maccabees.

However, the content of Ep. 2 guarantees that neither the forger for the collectors' market nor the writer of historical fiction could have fabricated such a document. The audience for either would expect to have the Jewish heroes of 164 B.C.E. dwell upon the famous historical events of the year, upon the persecution and upon their own wonderful victories, gained with the help of God, just as Mordechai and Esther in their communications told in detail of Haman's dreadful designs against the Jews and of how they were foiled (Esther 9:20–25). We have seen (above, p. 163) how Ep. 2 gives only small parts of three verses (1:11–12, 2:18) to such subjects, concentrating overwhelmingly on a demonstration that the second temple has been and is still the Place which the LORD has chosen. Hence, surely Ep. 2 was written as propaganda. There were Samaritans in Egypt who denied the holiness even of Solomon's temple. The arguments of Ep. 2 were absolutely useless against Samaritans, and we need not consider Samaritans further. As far as we know, the argument of Ep. 2, addressed to Egyptian Jews, could have been aimed only against the Oniads and their partisans and against their claims on behalf of the temple of Leontopolis. We have found (p. 162) reason to believe that the Oniads themselves in 102 conceded the superiority, though not the exclusive legitimacy, of the temple of Jerusalem. There is confirmation for our theory, that the claims on behalf of the Oniad temple were not a serious issue after 102 B.C.E.: neither in First Maccabees nor in the abridged history is the matter touched (but see Grimm, pp. 12–13). The abridged history even concedes some legitimacy to the Samaritan temple on Mount Gerizim (5:23, 6:2)!

Nevertheless, the confirmation of our theory from First Maccabees and the abridged history is an argument from silence, and the other evidence, too, is scanty enough for us to grant, at least for the sake of argument, that between 67 B.C.E. and the destruction of the temple of 70 C.E. there was still need to refute Oniad doubts that the temple of Jerusalem was the Place chosen by the LORD. But there are yet more ways to show that Ep. 2 can hardly have been fabricated after 67 B.C.E.

We have found hints in Ep. 2 that the author wrote it to give advice and consolation to the Jews of Egypt, who were then in distress. There is no evidence whatever that the Jews of Egypt were in distress between 67 and 30 B.C.E. On the contrary, Josephus' accounts in both the *War* and the *Antiquities* show that the Jews were on good terms with Ptolemy XII and his heirs, Ptolemies XIII and XIV and Cleopatra VII. When struggles broke out among the members of the dynasty, the Jews always managed to earn the gratitude of the winner. It is true that Cleopatra VII was usually hostile to Herod, but she was friendly to the Hasmonaeans and to other Jews. Since Cleopatra VII had a bad reputation when Josephus was writing, he would have gladly paraded any instances of her hostility to Jews, but all he could find was one obscure instance when she failed to provide Jews with grain in time of famine (*Ap.* ii 5.56–61). At *Ap.* ii 5.67, Josephus seems to ascribe hostile feelings toward the Jews to Cleopatra just before her death, but the text may well be corrupt; see Thackeray's n. 2 at *Josephus,* vol. I: *The Life, Against Apion* (LCL, 1956), p. 316. See also Hans Volkmann, "Ptolemaios 33–36," PW, XXIII^2 (1959), 1748–60, and *Cleopatra* (London: Elek Books, 1958), pp. 59–231; Schürer (New English version), I, 250–54, 296–301. Moreover, in Egypt under Roman rule we do not hear of trouble for the Jews until 38 C.E. However, the hints in Ep. 2 that the Jews of Egypt are in distress are vague enough to allow our opponents to regard this argument, too, as inconclusive.

Ep. 2 loudly proclaimed that the Jews of Judaea and Jerusalem have recovered the "heritage" and probably predicted confidently that the Jews would recover the "kingdom," the "priesthood," and the "sanctification" (2:17). We have explained the meaning of those terms (above, pp. 160–61, 187–88). Such claims were easy early in the reign of Alexander Jannaeus. Through four decades, with only brief interruptions, Judaea had been independent under Hasmonaean high priests who were also princes or kings (see CHJ. vol. I, Part II, ch. 8). Any present adversity might be temporary.

At the very beginning of the period for which *chairein kai hygiainein* may be said to be attested in papyri, the early and middle 60's B.C.E., a Jewish king still ruled Judaea, but the time of the bitter struggle between Hyrcanus and Aristobulus for the kingship and the high priesthood was hardly a propitious

time to preach to the Jews of Egypt on the superiority of the Hasmonaeans
and the temple of Jerusalem over the Oniads and over their schismatic temple.
The struggle between the brothers began in 67. The sanctity of Jerusalem did
not prevent the two factions from fighting there, and though a lull intervened
when Hyrcanus temporarily abdicated in favor of Aristobulus, their supporters
were still mutually hostile.

Egged on by the wily Antipater (the father of Herod), Hyrcanus won the
support of Aretas III, king of the Nabataeans, by offering to cede him territory. Aretas defeated Aristobulus' army, many of Aristobulus' troops went over
to Hyrcanus, and Aristobulus was besieged in the temple. The siege was still
going on in 65 B.C.E. Roman Pompey, with a powerful Roman army, was
making vast conquests in the eastern Mediterranean world. Pompey's assistant
commander (*proquaestor*), Scaurus, came to Damascus (Schürer [New English version], I, 236) and accepted a bribe from Aristobulus to side with him.
Scaurus ordered Aretas to withdraw, and Aristobulus was temporarily victorious. Nevertheless, when Pompey, in the spring of 63, came to Damascus, the
Jewish factions appealed to him. Roman interests were better served if Pompey
sided with the weak Hyrcanus, though at first the Roman tried to avoid conflict
with the more vigorous Aristobulus. Pompey soon was using his forces against
Aristobulus. He took Aristobulus prisoner and besieged Aristobulus' partisans
in the temple. Finally, with great slaughter, he captured the temple. See J. *AJ*
xiv 1.2.4–4.3.68.

Thus, from 67 to 63, even before Pompey's final conquest, there had been,
first, purely civil war and, then, increasing involvement of foreign troops in
Judaea and Jerusalem. It was no time to boast that God had restored the
"sanctification." The office of king over the Jews was being assigned not by
God but by Romans. It was no time to boast over the "restored kingdom."
Roman and Nabataean armies invaded the "heritage," and Hyrcanus ceded to
Aretas territory which had once belonged to the tribe of Reuben. It was no
time to boast over the "restored heritage."

The situation was still worse after Pompey's victory in 63. Jews perceived the
devastating lesson of the events: the Age of Wrath had not ended forever; God
was still punishing them by subjecting them to foreign empires (J. *AJ* xiv
4.4.74; *BJ* i 7.6.154). Pompey took away from Judaea large segments of the
"heritage," of the land promised by God in the Torah; he made pruned Judaea
pay annual tribute to Rome, and the figurehead Hasmonaean prince Hyrcanus
no longer bore the title "king."

The history of the period brought striking vindication to the claims of the
Oniads, that God favored them and had not yet made Jerusalem again his Chosen Place. God had wrought a miracle in response to the merit of Onias III to
prevent Heliodorus from violating the treasury of the temple of Jerusalem; but
in the absence of the Oniads, the Hasmonaean high priests had not been able
to prevent pagans from violating the temple. In 63 B.C.E. Pompey marched into
the Holy of Holies (J. *BJ* i 7.6.152; *AJ* xiv 4.4.71–72), and in 54 Crassus
plundered the wealth of the temple (*BJ* i 8.8.179; *AJ* xiv 7.1.105–9). Against
the strong arguments available for the Oniad case after 63 and 54 B.C.E., Ep. 2
would have been useless. The victory of Judas Maccabaeus and his men lay far
in the past. Events had proved it a temporary episode. And the author of Ep.

2, unlike the Oniads, could not even point to a real miracle to demonstrate that God had chosen the second temple.

We have seen that Ep. 2 has as its chief message the exclusive legitimacy of the temple of Jerusalem as against the claims of the Oniads. Less conspicuous is its advocacy of the claims of Hasmonaeans. If it can hardly have been published after 63 B.C.E. as pure anti-Oniad propaganda, can it have been published as a piece of primarily Hasmonaean propaganda? The prominence in Ep. 2 of the anti-Oniad theme, far above the pro-Hasmonaean theme, argues strongly against the hypothesis. Moreover, could any pro-Hasmonaean propagandist after 63 B.C.E. have been so ignorant of the account of the death of Antiochus IV in First Maccabees?

Nevertheless, let us further consider the possibility. Propaganda claiming that Hasmonaeans had restored the heritage, the priesthood, and the kingdom, and perhaps even the sanctification, again became conceivable around the time of Pentecost, in late spring, 40 B.C.E. At that time the last Hasmonaean ruler, Mattathias Antigonus, became king and high priest (J. *BJ* i 13.3.253; *AJ* xiv 13.4.337). He did so with the help of the troops of the Parthian empire. Antigonus' moment of prosperity was brief. Though he was still secure in power the following winter (J. *BJ* i 14.2.279; *AJ* xiv 14.3.377), by spring of 39 B.C.E. he had to contend with the resurgent forces of Herod (J. *AJ* xiv 14.3.377–79, 5.387, 15.1.394), and by later in the year Antigonus himself could no longer pose as an independent ruler, for he had to pay heavy tribute to the Roman commander Ventidius, who had driven the Parthians out of Syria (J *BJ* i 15.2.288–89; *AJ* xiv 14.6.392–93; Dio Cassius xlviii 41, 4–6). On the chronology, see Schürer (New English version), I, 281–82, n. 3, and H. Gundel, "P. Ventidius Bassus," PW, VIIIA[1] (1955), 807–10. Antigonus' victory in the summer of 38 was canceled by Herod so quickly that we need not consider it here (see J. *BJ* i 17.1–8.323–44; *AJ* xiv 15.10–13.448–64). Nothing indicates that Antigonus recovered for Judaea any part of Samaria or of the Greek cities which Pompey had freed. Nevertheless, during his brief prosperity, it is conceivable his propaganda could have contained the boasts of 2:17. "Persians" could have been said (1:13) to have undone the tyrannical foreign power, and there would have been some point in recording the benevolent interest of the "Persian" king (1:33–35). Jews called the Parthian empire "Persia" (I 14:2; AB vol. 41, pp. 193, 252, 324).

However, Antigonus put forth his claims against a legitimate Hasmonaean rival, the high priest and ethnarch Hyrcanus. Hence, Antigonus' case must have rested on his own forceful "Hasmonaean" policy as against Hyrcanus' subservience to Rome and to the family of Antipater and Herod. Thus propaganda for Antigonus surely would have contained the concentration on the Hasmonaean victories of Judas Maccabaeus which Ep. 2 so conspicuously lacks.

It is hard, moreover, to imagine any such propaganda being written in the first months of Antigonus' reign for an audience of Jews in Egypt. In 164 B.C.E. the Ptolemaic regime and the Jews of Egypt both had good reason to rejoice as Judas and his men defeated the Seleucid enemy. Similarly, in 103/2 the regime of Cleopatra III could join with the Egyptian Jews in hoping that the forces of Judaea under Alexander Jannaeus could withstand the onslaught of Ptolemy IX; at that time of adversity one might even have questioned the religious rectitude of the Oniads, favorites of the queen and mainstays of her power. In the late spring and summer of 40 B.C.E., however, the case was different. The Jews of Ptolemaic Egypt then had no reason to be disloyal to Cleopatra VII, and her kingdom was firmly united to the Roman enemies of the Parthian empire. Her lover was Mark Antony, who aspired to victory over Parthia and consistently backed Herod. Egyptian Jews themselves had no reason to be automatically sympathetic to Antigonus and the Hasmonaean branch descended from Aristobulus II. Antigonus was the creature of the Parthian enemy. Egyptian Jews who favored the Hasmonaeans might well choose the side of the branch headed by Hyrcanus, bitter enemies of Antigonus. Hyrcanus' branch had been supported by the Romans. Egyptian Jews might even prefer to back the house of Antipater and Herod against any Hasmonaean. See J. BJ i 8.7.175, 9.4.190–91; AJ xiv 6.2.99, 8.1.127–32. If the Oniads were important enough in 40/39 to have propaganda written against them, surely they, too, enjoyed a considerable following in Egypt. Partisans of Antigonus would probably seek to win as much support in Egypt as possible. It was hardly a time to attack the Oniads. It was no time to hint that the Parthian enemies of the queen and her lover were benevolent liberators.

The pressure of events tore Antony away from Cleopatra in late summer or early autumn of 40. In October at Brundisium, in Italy, he came to an agreement with his fellow triumvir Caesar Octavian in which he agreed to marry Octavian's sister Octavia. Reports of the marriage must have taken some time to reach Egypt during the season of storms on the Mediterranean, when few ships dared to sail. After Cleopatra received the news, she may have turned temporarily hostile to Antony and Rome. If so, after late autumn, 40, Egyptian Jews could have been receptive to a document like Ep. 2, but partisans of Antigonus could not have fabricated Ep. 2 after Herod's victories in the spring of 39 B.C.E. Thus, the unlikely possibility, that Ep. 2 is primarily propaganda by partisans of Antigonus, is possible only between October, 40, and spring, 39. And the remote possibility becomes still less likely when we consider the preservation of the letter. Antony left Octavia for Cleopatra in 37; and from then until the downfall of Antony and Cleopatra in 31, Egypt and the Antonian faction of the Roman republic were in close alliance. Though Jews of Egypt under Roman rule after Cleopatra's death expressed hostility to Cleopatra (see John J. Collins, The Sibylline Oracles of Egyptian Judaism [diss., Harvard; "Dissertation Series," no. 13; Missoula, Mont.: Society of Biblical Literature, 1972], pp. 57–64, 66–71), there is no reason to think they broke with her in her lifetime. If Ep. 2 had begun to circulate in Egypt in 40 or 39 and if the leaders of the Jewish community between 37 and 31 had any suspicion that it was pro-Parthian propaganda, the document probably would have been suppressed.

Once Herod was in power as sole king in 37, and especially after his great acquisitions of territory in 30, 23, and 20 (see Michael Avi-Yonah, The Holy Land [Grand Rapids, Mich.: Baker, 1966], pp. 86–93), anti-Oniads and pro-Herodians might speak of the restoration of the heritage and the kingdom, even though anti-Herodians might view Herod as the lackey of the Romans. But the character of Herod's appointees to the high priesthood was such that no propagandist writing against the pedigreed Oniads could have argued that the "priesthood" had been restored in Judaea; see J. *AJ* xx 10.5.247. Surely no propagandist for Herod, the destroyer of the Hasmonaean dynasty, would have chosen as his vehicle a letter of Judas Maccabaeus announcing Hasmonaean victories and calling Egyptian Jews to observe the festival which commemorated them! Herod was consistently pro-Roman and anti-Parthian. Propagandists for him could not have written II 1:13, 33–35.

Between Herod's death in 4 B.C.E. and the closing of the Oniad temple in 73 C.E. there was only one period in which a ruler of Judaea could claim to be a king with Hasmonaean descent—the reign of Agrippa I. Moreover, in Agrippa's time the Jews of Egypt were in distress (Schürer [New English version], I, 390–94). However, had the schismatic Oniad temple of Leontopolis been an issue worthy of propaganda during the reign of Agrippa, surely the fact would have been mentioned by Philo, a contemporary, and Josephus, a near contemporary, but neither author says anything of the kind. In the reign of Agrippa, and from then on, there is no trace anywhere of a Jewish challenge to the supremacy of the temple of Jerusalem (see Schürer, III, 147–48). Propaganda for Agrippa could indeed claim that the "heritage" and "kingdom" had been restored (J. *AJ* xix 5.1.274–75; *BJ* ii 11.5.215), but it had been restored by the Roman emperor Claudius rather than by God. It is more than doubtful whether Agrippa's partisans could say that his appointees to the high priesthood constituted a "restoration of the priesthood" equal to or superior to the appointment of an Oniad; see J. *AJ* xx 10.5.247; xix 6.2.297, 4.313–16, 8.1.342. And the "sanctification" of Judaea and the Jews under Agrippa surely was a precarious thing depending on the pleasure of the Romans (see J. *AJ* xviii 8.2–9.261–304; xix 6.3.300–11, 7.2.326, 8.1.388–42). There is also reason to think that Agrippa I was so popular among the Jews both of Judaea and of Egypt that to have written the devious Ep. 2 on his behalf would have been useless. See J. *AJ* xix 7.3.328–31 and F. H. Colson's n. *a* to his *Philo*, IX (LCL; Cambridge, Mass.: Harvard University Press, 1941), p. 318 (to *In Flaccum* 5.30).

Thereafter, until the great revolt of 66, the Jews no longer had a king, and Judaea was under direct Roman rule. As long as the Jewish rebels of 66 enjoyed success, they would write directly of their own achievements; they had no need to hide behind a forged letter of Judas Maccabaeus. Conspicuously absent during the revolt were claims of the restoration of the kingdom. The end of the revolt brought the destruction of the temple of Jerusalem and the closing of the temple of Leontopolis. Thus it is unlikely that Ep. 2 was written at any time during the period in which the greeting formula *chairein kai hygiainein* and its variants are attested in papyri.

APPENDIX X

WHY IT IS UNLIKELY THAT THE HASMONAEAN PROPAGANDIST DREW HIS ACCOUNTS OF SIMON AND JONATHAN FROM HIGH PRIESTLY JOURNALS

One would expect a history derived from dated high priestly journals to be full of Jewish dates and facts. But I 9:23 – 16:18 contains only six Jewish dates (9:54, 10:21, 13:41, 51, 14:26, 16:4). As we shall see, not one of them need come from a journal of Jonathan or Simon, nor is there any reason to think that the facts in the narratives were derived from such a source. Indeed, with Jonathan and Simon, we reach a period in which living memory could preserve large numbers of the facts recorded by the Hasmonaean propagandist.

Consider the chapters on Simon (I 13–16). Much consists of quoted documents (13:36–40, 14:20–23, 24c–24k [=15:16–24], 27–49, 15:2–9) or of material from the Seleucid Chronicle (13:31–32, 14:1–3, 15:10–14, 25, 37, 39 [end]). The material introducing the documents could have been inferred from the documents themselves, with the occasional help of the Seleucid Chronicle (13:34–35, 14:16–19, 24a [=14:24; Numenius' name may have been in living memory or may have been inferred from 14:22], 24b [=15:15], 25–26, 15:1). The Hasmonaean propagandist needed no source to describe the family monument at Modeïn (13:27–30); it was there for him to see. There, too, he could observe Jonathan's grave and deduce that the body had been recovered and reburied (13:25), of course with considerable ceremony (13:26). The information at 13:41–42 could have been inferred from the document at 14:27; the content of 13:33 from the document at 14:32–34. Except for the movable tower, the story of the taking of Gazara (13:43–48) could have been inferred from 14:34; except for the date and the promotion of John and his residence thereafter at Gazara, the story of the taking of the Akra (13:49–53) could have been inferred from 14:34, 36–37, and the month and day of the date were preserved by annual observance.

For his poem (14:4–15), the Hasmonaean propagandist needed no source beyond the document at I 14:27–49.

For what passages, then, might the Hasmonaean propagandist have needed further sources? Let us consider the possibilities:

13:1–24 tell how Simon rose to replace Jonathan, resisted Tryphon, and reluctantly delivered Jonathan's sons, and how Tryphon was balked by a snowstorm, killed Jonathan at Baskama, and withdrew. The details are striking enough and few enough to have been preserved in memory. Moreover, Tryphon claimed to be king, and Simon seriously imperiled the integrity of the empire; the events, therefore, could have appeared in the Seleucid Chronicle. Strange in 13:11 is the mention by name of a non-Hasmonaean hero. Could the reason be that Jonathan son of Absalom lived to be the Hasmonaean propagandist's informant?

The movable tower of I 13:43–44 could have been remembered, and so could the year number in 13:51. The year might also have been derived from the Seleucid Chronicle, because the Akra was a major issue for Antiochus VII (I 15:28, 16:18) and its fall could have been recorded there. The year number was the same in both Seleucid eras. The promotion of John and his residence at Gazara (13:53) could have been remembered or recorded in the chronicle of John's high priesthood (see I 16:24). Since the Jewish occupation of Gazara provoked the anger of Antiochus VII (15:28, 16:18), John's residence there could even have been mentioned in the Seleucid Chronicle.

From the point of view of the Seleucid empire, Antiochus VII was right to try to curb the dangerously powerful Simon if he could defeat the usurper Tryphon without the Jews' aid, as proved to be the case. The material in I 15:26–36 has only a few Jewish touches and might have been drawn from the Seleucid Chronicle. The Chronicle may even have recorded Simon's gold and silver drinking vessels, for no subject of the empire could use such without the king's permission (see I 11:58). The utensils and Simon's reply may have been reported there, for they were provocations. It would have been natural for the author of the Seleucid Chronicle to tell of the king's fury (vs. 36[end]). The next verse (37) reports Tryphon's escape and certainly was drawn from the Chronicle.

Immediately thereafter, 15:38 – 16:10 tell how Simon and John defeated Kendebaios. Again living memory could have preserved all, and again it is likely that we have been too conservative in assigning material to the Seleucid Chronicle. Antiochus VII may have been proud to see to the recording of how formidable was the Jewish menace, for he was to see the death of Simon and the defeat of John (J. AJ xiii 8.2–3.236–48). Jewish memory may have preserved the topographical information in 15:39–41 and the details on Simon and his sons in 16:1–10. Some of the information may have come from the chronicle of John's high priesthood.

Finally, the story of Simon's death and its aftermath (16:11–22) could have been remembered and certainly stood in the chronicle of John's high priesthood.

Thus there is no sign that our author drew on a journal of Simon's high priesthood.

If we proceed similarly with the sections on Jonathan (I 9:23 – 12:53), we find again that much is taken up with documents which lay before the author or with material derivable from them (10:15–21 [except for the date], 22–47, 11:28–37, 57–59 [vss. 58–59 are probably paraphrase of the document], 12:1–4 [probably based on the safe-conduct letters which the author mentions in vs. 4 but does not quote], 5–23). The Seleucid Chronicle was the source at least for 10:1–2, 48–58, 67–68, 11:1–3, 8–19, 38–40, and 54–56. Very likely, the Hasmonaean propagandist drew more from it. Jonathan was a great enough menace under Demetrius I that the high official Bacchides expended much time and effort to suppress him and finally made a truce with him. From the time Alexander Balas began to press his claim to rule over the Seleucid empire, Jonathan was an important factor in royal Seleucid affairs. Alexander

Balas would have been glad to record the victories won for him by his loyal subject Jonathan. Demetrius II and Tryphon might have been pleased to set down how the formidable Jewish leader rose and was exploited by them and cut down. Most of I 9:23 – 12:53 could therefore be a rewriting, from the Hasmonaean Jewish point of view, of material that stood in the Seleucid Chronicle. We may thus consider adding to the material drawn from the Chronicle 9:32, 43, 47–53, 57–72, 10:3–6, 69–89, 11:20–27, 41–53, 60–66, 12:24–34, and also 12:35–48 (the acts in vss. 35–38 could have been the provocation for Tryphon's measures in vss. 39–48).

Let us now examine the material which remains and is unlikely to have been included in the Seleucid Chronicle. Hasmonaean family members could have remembered and told how Jonathan took over after Judas' death (9:23–31) and especially how uncle John came to grief and was avenged (9:32–42). If the Seleucid Chronicle did not give all the details of 9:43–49, surely family members could tell how God allowed Hasmonaeans to prevail in defending themselves on the Sabbath against heavy odds, immediately after uncle John was avenged.

The wondrous end of the wicked high priest Alcimus (9:54–56) may have been in the Common Source, and it may have been recorded in a journal of his high priesthood; see Introduction, Part II, sections 5–6.

Jonathan's acts in 10:7–14 could have been remembered. The walls were there to be seen, and perhaps an inscription recorded Jonathan's connection with them.

The date in 10:21 could have been remembered; the year number may have been inferred with the help of a list of high priests and the lengths of their terms in office (see p. 46).

If the events associated with the royal wedding in Ptolemais (10:59–66) were not recorded in the Seleucid Chronicle, they could have been remembered. Onias IV, the loyal subject of Ptolemy VI, also may have touched upon the events in his *Memoirs* (see pp. 35–37). Onias IV could also have reported the content of 11:1–18.

The story in 11:67–74, of Jonathan's successful prayer, is unlikely to have stood in the Seleucid Chronicle. But, like 13:11, this passage is peculiar in mentioning non-Hasmonaean heroes. Again we may guess that one or both of the men mentioned survived to serve as informant to the Hasmonaean propagandist.

The content of 12:49–53 could have been remembered.

Thus there is no reason to assume that our authors drew on a journal of Jonathan's high priesthood.

APPENDIX XI

JOSEPHUS AND THE ABRIDGED HISTORY

Josephus can be shown to have read the abridged history.[1] As a proud descendant of the Hasmonaeans, Josephus was ready to attack both the abridged history and its source, the *Memoirs* of Onias IV. He may well have had both as his targets in writing *AJ* xii 4.1.156–3.1.167. There he appears to counter the claims of both concerning the virtue of Oniad priests. At II 3:1–2 the writer suggests that Onias III was a man whose piety and hatred for wickedness ensured the security of Jerusalem and induced King Seleucus to pay the expenses of the temple cult. At *AJ* xii 4.1.156 Josephus says that under Onias II the Jews of Judaea suffered much from the depredations of the Samaritans, and at *AJ* xii 158 he says that from pettiness and avarice Onias II failed to pay tax money to King Ptolemy. Royal emissaries frighten the people both at II 3:14–21 and at J. *AJ* xii 159, but whereas Jason of Cyrene at II 3:16–17 dwells on the change in the countenance of Onias III, Josephus says that because of his avarice Onias II was not at all discountenanced. Where Jason of Cyrene speaks of Onias III as the benefactor of the city and the protector of his fellow Jews (II 4:2) and praises him for his temperance (*sôphrosynê*, II 4:37), Josephus says Onias II took no thought for the safey of the members of his nation but was ready to endanger them rather than part with his money (*AJ* xii 4.2.161). Jason of Cyrene reports how divine intervention on behalf of Onias III thwarted the king's emissary (II 3:24–35), whereas Josephus reports that the human diplomacy of the wily Joseph mollified the ambassador and solved the crisis. Josephus probably found the contrast between Onias II and Onias III ready-made in the work of Onias IV, who would have wished to contrast his righteous kinsmen with the aberrant Onias II; to discredit the Oniads, Josephus omitted details on all Oniads of the third and early second centuries except Onias II.

THE JEWISH MONTHS

Month	*Normal Equivalent*
Nisan	March–April
Iyyar	April–May
Sivan	May–June
Tammuz	June–July
Ab	July–August
Elul	August–September

[1] See Introduction, Part I, n. 80.

Month	*Normal Equivalent*
Tishri	September–October
Marḥeshvan	October–November
Kislev	November–December
Ṭebet	December–January
Shebaṭ	January–February
Adar	February–March
Second Adar	
(in intercalary years)	

SELEUCID RULERS

Seleucus I	312–281
Antiochus I	281–261
Antiochus II	261–246
Seleucus II	246–225
Seleucus III	225–223
Antiochus III	223–187
Seleucus IV	187–175
Antiochus IV and	
Little Antiochus	175–170
Antiochus IV	170–164
Antiochus V	164–162
Demetrius I	162–150
Alexander Balas	150–145
Demetrius II	145–140/39
Antiochus VI	145–142
Tryphon (a usurper)	142–138
Antiochus VII	139/8–129

PTOLEMAIC RULERS

Ptolemy I	323–283
Ptolemy II	285–246
Ptolemy III	246–221
Ptolemy IV	221–204
Ptolemy V	204–180
Ptolemy VI	180–145
Ptolemy VII	145–144
Ptolemy VIII	145–116
Ptolemy IX	116–107/88–80
Ptolemy X	107–88
Ptolemy XI	80
Ptolemy XII	80–51
Ptolemy XIII and Cleopatra VII	51–48
Ptolemy XIV and Cleopatra VII	47–44
Cleopatra VII	44–30

INDICES

I. TOPICAL INDEX TO THE
INTRODUCTION, COMMENTARY, AND APPENDICES

II. INDEX OF PASSAGES FROM THE BIBLE, THE APOCRYPHA, AND THE PSEUDEPIGRAPHA

Excluded from this index are references to passages from I Maccabees that occur in their normal place in the summary (pp. 4–12) and the commentary and all references to I and II Maccabees in the tables (pp. 49–54, 113–23).